EASTERN CHEROKEE CENSUS
CHEROKEE, NORTH CAROLINA
1930-1939

CENSUS 1932-1933
WITH BIRTHS AND DEATHS 1930-1932
TAKEN BY AGENT R. L. SPALSBURY
VOLUME II

TRANSCRIBED BY
JEFF BOWEN

NATIVE STUDY
Gallipolis, Ohio
USA

Native Study LLC
Gallipolis, OH
www.nativestudy.com

Library of Congress Control Number: 2020913250

ISBN: 978-1-64968-005-1

Made in the United States of America.

This series is in memory and honor of
Joyce Welch Tranter,
her family, both past and present,
and the Cherokee people.

Whenever I drove toward the Cherokee Reservation it felt like I was going home. I wasn't born there. I don't have Cherokee blood in my veins. What I had was Joyce Welch Tranter in my life. She's someone who will never be replaced. That woman, when she prayed, God listened. She took us in her heart and never let go. Joyce has Alzheimer's now but knowing her she'd say, "I'm exactly where God wants me to be".

Joyce loved the Lord, her family, her church, and her people the Cherokee of Qualla Boundary. The hours spent with her made me understand the saying, "parting is such sweet sorrow." Because every moment was sweet and even with the sorrow of missing her she makes us remember the best parts of our lives even though she may not know our faces. Between Joyce, the joy of witnessing what they call the Blue Mist, and the Cherokee people, it makes you understand what being blessed is.

Jeff Bowen
2019

Not too long ago Joyce left to speak personally with the Lord from now on. We'll miss her but I know she is overjoyed. She doesn't have Alzheimer's anymore, that's a thing of the past.

We love you Joyce.
June, 2020

This series is for research, but these books are totally enshrouded by Joyce Welch Tranter's family history. The next few pages will show Guion Miller applications for two of her ancestors; one being William L. French, Joyce's great grandfather. This particular application shows him as being rejected but that's only because he was a Western Cherokee and his relatives were in Oklahoma during the removal. The next one will be a Supplemental Application for Minor Children that Wm. L's wife, Awee French, filled out for their children. Included in this application you will find the very first child mentioned, Maud French, (on Minor Children application Maud is spelled without an "e") age 13, born May 25th, 1894, who was Joyce's grandmother. Maud meant everything to Joyce. She was so fond of her grandmother that she made you feel like you knew her by the way she would talk about her. It's believed Joyce loved her family of the past as much as her family of the present, the reason she's in this genealogical book in spirit as well as physically.

The photographs presented in this book are personal pictures Joyce gave written permission to this transcriber to use in any book or books that he produced. Each photo will have individuals identified as able. There is a listing of Joyce's family along with her mother, in the 1937 Eastern Cherokee Census, North Carolina, that will be completed when this series is finished.

William L. French's Guion Miller Application
1906-1910

No. 8421

EASTERN CHEROKEES.

APPLICATION

OF

William L. French.

For share of money appropriated for the Eastern
Cherokee Indians by the Act of Congress approved
June 30, 1906, in accordance with the decrees of the
Court of Claims of May 18, 1905, and May 28, 1906.
6—624

INDIAN OFFICE
EASTERN CHEROKEES.
Rec JAN 2 1907
No.

BELVA A. LOCKWOOD,
Attorney and Solicitor,
619 F Street, NORTHWEST,
WASHINGTON, D. C.

Commissioner of Indian Affairs,
Washington, D. C.

SIR:

I hereby make application for such share as may be due me of the fund appropriated by the Act of Congress approved June 30, 1906, in accordance with the decrees of the Court of Claims of May 18, 1905, and May 28, 1906, in favor of the Eastern Cherokees. The evidence of identity is herewith subjoined.

1. State full name—

    English name: *William L. French*

    Indian name: *"Co-das-ki"*

2. Residence: *Brictown*

3. Town and post office: *do.* *Trough S.C.*

4. County: *Swain Co.*

5. State: *North Carolina*

6. Date and place of birth: *near Taleguah. Ind. Ter. Age 40 yrs.*

7. By what right do you claim to share? If you claim through more than one relative living in 1851, set forth each claim separately: *I claim in my own right. I am a full blood Cherokee. My father French French, or French Hawk a full blood and my mother Annie French, also a full blood.*

8. Are you married? *Yes.*

9. Name and age of wife or husband: *"Awee" French. age 30 years. a full blood Cherokee.*

10. Give names of your father and mother, and your mother's name before marriage:

    Father—English name: *French Hawk. - Hawk French*

    Indian name: *"Col-lun-see" Yar-lun-chi*

    Mother—English name: *Annie French*

    Indian name: *do.*

    Maiden name: *Annie Grease.*

11. Where were they born?

    Father: *North Carolina*

    Mother: *Georgia*

12. Where did they reside in 1851, if living at that time?

    Father: *near Taleguah. J.T.*

    Mother: *do.* *do.* *do.*

13. Date of death of your father and mother—

    Father: *died in 1874.* Mother: *died in 1873.*

14. Were they ever enrolled for annuities, land, or other benefits? If so, state when and where: *Yes. In Indian Territory in 1878.*

15. Name all your brothers and sisters, giving ages, and if not living, the date of death:

NAME	BORN	DIED
(1) *George French age 37, lives at Whittier N.C.*		
(2)		
(3)		
(4)		
(5)		
(6)		

16. State English and Indian names of your grandparents on both father's and mother's side, if possible:

FATHER'S SIDE. *Don't know.*   MOTHER'S SIDE. *Don't Know.*

17. Where were they born? *Don't know.*

18. Where did they reside in 1851, if living at that time? *Dead.*

19. Give names of all their children, and residence, if living; if not living, give dates of deaths:

(1) English name:
    Indian name:
    Residence:
(2) English name:
    Indian name:
    Residence:
(3) English name:
    Indian name:
    Residence:
(4) English name:
    Indian name:
    Residence:
(5) English name:
    Indian name:
    Residence:

20. Have you ever been enrolled for annuities, land, or other benefits? If so, state when and where. *near Talequah. Ind. Ter. On Roll in Cherokee nation 1863. I am now Secretary of the Council of the Eastern Band of Cherokee Indians.*

21. To expedite identification, claimants should give the full English and Indian names, if possible, of their paternal and maternal ancestors back to 1835: _____

Mother, Annie French and "Old Settler," and drew money as an Old Settler. My Father "French Wolf" was an Eastern Emigrant Cherokee.

REMARKS.

(Under this head the applicant may give any additional information that he believes will assist in proving his claims.)

I hereby appoint Belva A. Lockwood of Washington D.C. my true and lawful Attorney, for me, and in my name, place, and stead, and agree to allow her a commission of ten (10/0) per cent.

NOTE.—Answers should be brief but explicit; the words "Yes," "No," "Unknown," etc., may be used in cases where applicable. Read the questions carefully.

I solemnly swear that the foregoing statements made by me are true to the best of my knowledge and belief.

(Signature.) *William F. French*

Subscribed and sworn to before me this __26th__ day of __Dec__, 1906.

My commission expires

_____, 190   *De Witt S. Harris*
                              Notary Public

AFFIDAVIT.

(The foregoing affidavit must be sworn to by two or more witnesses who are well acquainted with the applicant.)

Personally appeared before me __John Sea__ and __Solomon Owl__, who, being duly sworn, on oath depose and say that they are well acquainted with __Wm F. French__, who makes the foregoing application and statements, and have known __him__ for __10__ years and __18__ years, respectively, and know __him__ to be the identical person __he__ represents __himself__ to be, and that the statements made by __him__ are true, to the best of their knowledge and belief, and they have no interest whatever in __this__ claim.

Witnesses to mark.   Signatures of witnesses.

_____   *Richard Ely*

_____   Solomon (X) Owl
                                              his mark

Subscribed and sworn to before me this __26th__ day of __Dec__, 1906.

My commission expires

_____, 190   *De Witt S. Harris*
                              Notary Public

NOTE.—Affidavits should be made, whenever practicable, before a notary public, clerk of the court, or before a person having a seal. If sworn to before an Indian agent or disbursing agent of the Indian service, it need not be executed before a notary, etc.

6—621

X

Awee S. French's Guion Miller
Supplemental Application for Minor Children
1906-1010

No. _1996_

EASTERN CHEROKEES.

SUPPLEMENTAL APPLICATION

OF

Awee S. French,

FOR MINOR CHILDREN

For share of money appropriated for the Eastern Cherokee Indians by the Act of Congress approved June 30, 1906, in accordance with the decrees of the Court of Claims of May 18, 1905, and May 28, 1906.

COURT OF
EASTERN CH...
JUN 17 ...

Supplemental Application for Minor Children

Special Commissioner of the Court of Claims,
   601 Ouray Building, Washington, D. C.

Sir:

   I hereby make application for such share as may be due my minor children of the fund appropriated by the Act of Congress approved June 30, 1906, in accordance with the decree of the Court of Claims of May 18, 1905, and May 28, 1906, in favor of the Eastern Cherokees, and I ask that this be made part of my original application No. *12496*

1. State your full name: *Awie S. French*
2. Residence and post office: *Bryson and Bryson*
3. County: *Swain*
4. State: *North Carolina*
5. Date and place of birth: *1878 Graham Co. N.C.*
6. Are you married? *Yes*
7. Name and age of wife or husband: *Wm G. French age 41 years*
8. To what tribe of Indians, if any, does he or she belong? *Cherokee Tribe West (Chickasaw)*
9. Names of all your children who were living on May 28, 1906:

	NAME.		AGE.	BORN.
(1)	*Maud*	*French*	*Fourteen*	*May 25 1894*
(2)	*Marous*	"	*Ten*	*Dec. 15 1897*
(3)	*Morgan*	"	*Eight*	*Dec 23 1899*
(4)	*Loggie*	"	*Six*	*March 23 1901*
(5)	*George B.*	"	*Three*	*May 21 1904*
(6)				

10. Were they ever enrolled for money, annuities, land, or other benefits? If so, state when and where, and with what tribe of Indians: *No*

REMARKS

(Under this head the applicant may give any additional facts which will assist in proving his claim.)

Grand father Soldier or Squirrel on roll of 1835+6
1848+1851 with Eastern Cherokee Indians
One child born since may 28 '76, Jonah French, born march 12 1912

   I solemnly swear that the foregoing statements made by me are true to the best of my knowledge and belief.

(Signature) *Awie S. French*

Subscribed and sworn to before me this *1st* day of *____* 1907.

W J Miller
Notary Public.

My Commission expires

aug 21 190 *8*

AFFIDAVIT

(The following affidavit must be sworn to by two or more witnesses who are well acquainted with the applicant.)

Personally appeared before me _Bird Partridge_ and
C. Y. Dunlap who, being duly sworn, on oath depose and say that they are well acquainted with _Avoe S. French_ who makes the foregoing application and statement, and have known _her_ for _20_ years and _13_ years, respectively, and know _her_ to be the identical person _she_ represents _herself_ to be, and that on May 28, 1906, _she_ had the children living as above set forth, and that the statements made by _her_ are true, and they have no interest whatever in _this_ claim.

Witnesses to Mark.   Signatures of Witnesses.

_____   _Bird Partridge_

_____   _C. Y. Dunlap_

Subscribed and sworn to before me this _14_ day of _June_, 1907.

N. J. Miller
Notary Public.

My commission expires _Aug 21_, 190_8_.

NOTE.—Affidavits should be made, whenever practicable, before a notary public or clerk of the court. If sworn to before an Indian agent or disbursing agent of the Indian service, it need not be executed before a notary, etc.

Photographs

Joyce with Maude - Making Pottery

Maude French Welch - At Her Pottery Stand

Photographs

Willie and Maude Welch on the Reservation during WWII

**Joyce and her cousin from National Geographic article
about the Eastern Cherokee.**

Photographs

Willie and Maude Welch with a few family members

Table of Contents

Introduction   xix

Census Instructions   xxiv

1932 Census   3

    Additions Made to 1932 Census   173

    Subtractions Made on 1932 Census   181

1933 Census   189

    Additions Made to 1933 Census   358

    Subtractions Made to 1933 Census   358

Births

    Unreported on 1931 Census   361

    April 1, 1930-March 31, 1931   362

    April 1, 1931-March 31, 1932   364

    April 1, 1931-March 31, 1932   366

Deaths

    Unreported on 1931 Census   371

    April 1, 1930-March 31, 1931   372

    April 1, 1931-March 31, 1932   373

    April 1, 1931-March 31, 1932   374

Limited Index   375

INTRODUCTION

These censuses were taken during the Great Depression Era (1929-1938), extending a few years before with births and deaths starting in 1924 to 1932. Also during this transcription in several places you'll find mention of a party here and there for instance where they were still on record in 1934 when they had passed in 1914.

While looking through these records you will find there are many different categories not just Census, Birth and Death records. You'll find at the end of different census, divisions of birth and death mentions, then afterward there will be an official birth roll and then an official death roll with a cause of death according to different yearly time spans. You'll additionally find record headings such as, Additions, Subtractions, Supplemental Rolls, Deduction Rolls, Deaths Unreported, Marriages, Supplemental Census, Live Births, Transfer or Adjustment Roll and Correction in Name Due to Marriage.

These volumes are meant to be used for family heritage only, even though a great deal of the records mention blood quantum. The reason is, not all agents that produced the censuses are equal in their math skills whether intended or not. As you browse through these pages, especially Volume I, it will be clearly understood. The value within these pages is the people and who they are or were to you today as your ancestors. As John R. Finger stated in his title, *Cherokee Americans*, "This inflation of the tribal roll made allotment much less attractive to reservation Cherokees and led to bitter disapproval of 'white' or 'five-dollar' Indians--the latter an allusion to fees collected by lawyers like Guion Miller for listing claimants of dubious Cherokee ancestry. What is curious is that enrollees tended to have either at least three-fourths or no more than one-fourth Cherokee blood. Relatively few were between those figures."[1]

The cover of this book was created from a photograph taken from the top of Clingman's Dome in the Smoky Mountains by the transcriber during October of 1998 and while in the company of the little girl on the front cover who was in her sixties at the time. The picture was taken where those same Cherokee hid from the army during the removal of 1838-1839 not wanting to be robbed of the right to live on their own land peacefully with their families. "By the end of June, most of the Cherokees had been rounded up for removal; some say about 1,000 managed to avoid capture (and eventual removal) by hiding in the almost inaccessible mountains. John R. Finger concluded:

Approximately eleven hundred North Carolina Cherokees avoided removal by hiding out in the mountains or taking advantage of a treaty provision allowing certain Indians to stay in their homes states if they wished to become citizens. Mostly full-bloods, they resided in several scattered settlements in the western part of the state--on land owned by friendly whites, on unsurveyed state lands, and, in a few cases, on their own property. Some seven hundred lived around Quallatown, near present-day

---

[1] Cherokee Americans, Finger; pg. 48, para. 3

Cherokee, with smaller concentrations along the Cheoah, Valley, and Hiwassee rivers."[2]

That little girl on the front cover is also within the pages of this series starting in the year 1936, titled: Roll Number 1., 1936 Roll. Supplemental Roll. Her picture was taken from a postcard her grandmother Maude used to sell with her handmade pottery. Joyce years ago gave all permissions in a hand signed letter to use her family pictures feeling honored to have them used on the covers of books created for people to find their ancestors. But in all honestly, it was this transcriber who was being honored with such understanding and giving.

This was also a time when the Cherokees in these censuses had family in Oklahoma watching people lose their homes and farms because the economy was rapidly falling apart. It wasn't just the stock market but mother nature was screaming out loud crushing the farmers and ranchers with record breaking heat for longer periods than ever, causing them to lose their crops during the worst droughts in this country in centuries. Oklahoma as well as other Midwestern states were completely devastated by huge dust storms wiping out everything. Unemployment wasn't leaving anyone unscathed. They couldn't pay their property taxes or the monthly payments. So they just waited for the bank to make them leave the ground they worked so hard to survive on. Thousands ended up living in shanties made up of anything they could fabricate from tin to cardboard while sitting in communities called, "Hoovervilles", trying to figure out where their next meal was coming from. Approaching 1930 hundreds of banks failed and even though fighting for nine more years to survive a battle in just being able to live through each day millions didn't realize they'd soon be facing World War II, 1941-1945.

Things weren't much better for the Eastern Cherokees of Qualla Boundary during these periods. Though the 1929 stock market crash had hit in October and people were jumping out of high rises because of their financial ruin. The 1930's was moving in fast. The depression was hitting like a tsunami while the average Cherokee wasn't affected by the storms surging all around them they were feeling their own pinch in just trying to feed their families. There was heavy unemployment with the lumber business in Western Carolina failing about the same time. Some Cherokees were reaching outside their homeland by looking for jobs further north or even joining the service while most just wanted to stay home. The lumber industry had fallen off because, "By the beginning of 1929, however, it was all over. The Ravensford and Smokemont mills had both closed, and employment for Indians elsewhere in the lumber industry was almost nonexistent. The band continued to log portions of the reservation--indeed, the average annual cut of tribal timber during the 1930s exceeded that of the previous decade--but this did not compensate for the decline of off-reservation employment. Furthermore, growing prospects for an Appalachian national park in North Carolina and Tennessee sounded the death knell for a revived lumber business in the immediate area. Like many of his predecessors, agent Ralph P. Stanion encouraged the Cherokees to reemphasize agriculture and stock raising, both

---

[2] The Cherokees, Thornton; pgs. 67-68, para's. 4 & 5

of which had declined during the days of wage labor."[3] With the National Park maybe becoming a reality, that meant roads and it was a time of interest in who the Cherokee were because so many had heard their family legends of having Cherokee blood. That meant the Cherokee culture and their skilled artisans would bring tourists to the reservation creating a new economy for the children of those that 100 years earlier had hidden in those very same mountains to save their families from a forced removal in the name of land.

Finger also points out the different Cherokee agents of the time. Throughout his study he mentions agents James Henderson, Ralph P. Stanion, L.W. Page, R.L. Spalsbury, and Harold W. Foght. Henderson surrounded with what was obviously a great deal of dissension. "In the midst of the enrollment controversy James Henderson was coming under fire from Indians and whites alike. Having held his position as superintendent for fourteen years, longer than anyone before or since, he could hardly hope to remain unscathed amid such turmoil and dispute. He had made enemies, and after an investigation he was forced to resign in the spring of 1928. R.L. Spalsbury briefly succeeded him and then, in quick order, Ralph P. Stanion, L.W. Page, and Spalsbury again."[4]

The Cherokee held strong though times were hard on the Boundary. It was in their blood to be strong. They were the children of those that had beaten the odds against an army that wanted to take their homes, culture and history. They held their ground strategically because they knew their ground. The people in these depression era censuses were a remnant of a band of survivors who refused to give into the world and lived to fight another day. These were individuals not following the persuasion of those who thought they knew better than them. "Perhaps the best example of cultural continuity on the reservation was the daily use of the Cherokee language in most households, though increasing numbers of Indians could also speak English."[5] Their key to outlasting those that have always wanted to diminish the Principal People, the Cherokee, was never forgetting who they were as their descendants are doing today in 2019.

Here is a little information about who the Cherokee are today. "The Qualla Boundary or The Qualla is territory held as a land trust for the federally recognized Eastern Band of Cherokee Indians, who reside in western North Carolina. The area is part of the Cherokees' historic territory. The land was not 'reserved' by the federal government; the tribe purchased the land in the 1870s and it was subsequently placed under federal protective trust. Individuals can buy, own, and sell the land, provided they are enrolled members of the Tribe of the Eastern Band of the Cherokee Indians.

"The main part of the Qualla Boundary lies in eastern Swain and northern Jackson counties (just south of Great Smoky Mountains National Park). A small portion of the main trust lands extends eastward into Haywood County. The trust lands include many smaller non-contiguous sections to the southwest in Marble, Hiawassee and Hanging Dog areas of Cherokee County, North Carolina, and the

---

[3] Cherokee Americans, Finger pg. 54, para. 2
[4] Cherokee Americans, Finger pgs, 48-49, para. 4
[5] Cherokee Americans, Finger pg, 60, para. 2

Snowbird community in Graham County, North Carolina. The total land area of these regions is 213.934 km² (82.6 sq mi), with a 2000 census resident population of 8,092 people."[6]

"The Eastern Band of Cherokee Indians (EBCI), (Cherokee: ᏣᎳᎩᏱ ᏓᏣᏓᏂᎸᎩ, *Tsalagiyi Detsadanilvgi*) is a federally recognized Native American tribe in the United States, who are descended from the small group of 800 Cherokee who remained in the Eastern United States after the Indian Removal Act moved the other 15,000 Cherokee to the west in the 19th century. They were required to assimilate and renounce tribal Cherokee citizenship.

The history of the Eastern Band closely follows that of the Qualla Boundary, a land trust made up of an area of their original territory. When they reorganized as a tribe, they had to buy back the land from the US government. The EBCI also own, hold, or maintain additional lands in the vicinity, and as far away as 100 miles (160 km) from the Qualla Boundary. The Eastern Band of Cherokee Indians are primarily the descendants of those persons listed on the Baker Rolls of Cherokee Indians. They gained federal recognition as a tribe in the 20th century. The Qualla Boundary is not a reservations per se because the land is owned by the Eastern Band of Cherokee Indians.

The Eastern Band of Cherokee Indians is one of three federally recognized Cherokee tribes, the others being the Cherokee Nation and the United Keetoowah Band of Cherokee Indians, both based in Oklahoma. Its headquarters is in the namesake town of Cherokee, North Carolina in the Qualla Boundary, south of the Great Smoky Mountains National Park. The Eastern Band members are primarily descended from about 800 Cherokee living along the remote Oconaluftee River who did not participate in the Trail of Tears to Indian Territory (now Oklahoma). Principal Chief Yonaguska, with the help of his adopted European-American son, William Holland Thomas, managed to avoid removal. The Eastern Band of Cherokee Indians have maintained many traditional tribal practices. Many prominent Cherokee historians are affiliated with, or are members of the Eastern Band.

Tsali (pronounced ['tsali]) opposed the removal. He remained in the traditional Cherokee lands with a small group who resisted the U.S. Army and tried to thwart the removal. Tsali was eventually captured. He was executed by the United States in exchange for the lives of the small band he protected. They were allowed to remain in the Cherokee homeland, with the condition that they give up Cherokee tribal citizenship and assimilate as US citizens.

Their descendants reorganized in the 20th century and gained federal recognition as a tribe known as the Eastern Band of Cherokee Indians (named in reference to the majority of the tribe who moved west to Indian Territory in 1839.) They bought back land in what is known as Qualla Boundary, part of their traditional territory that had been ceded to the US government by other Cherokee leaders prior to removal.

Their Museum of the Cherokee Indian exhibits an extensive collection of artifacts and items of historical and cultural interest, from the early Mississippian Period, of which there are remains in the area, to the Cherokee Culture brought by their migrants in the 16th and 17th centuries. They are an Iroquoian-speaking people related to those nations in the Iroquois Confederacy and other Iroquoian-speaking

---

[6] Wikipedia, Qualla Boundary

groups traditionally occupying territory around the Great Lakes. The Qualla Arts and Crafts Mutual, located near the museum, sells traditional crafts made by its members. Founded in 1946, the Qualla Arts and Crafts Mutual is country's oldest and foremost Native American crafts cooperative"[7]

Nobody says it better than John R. Finger who I have to thank for his continual contributions through his research and books during the 1990's otherwise there wouldn't have been such a complete study for this time period in the Cherokee's lives or this introduction for that matter. "Clearly the Eastern Cherokees were a people in transition, caught between old familiar ways and the mysteries and opportunities of modern America. More of their children attended school than before, but some parents and students were still skeptical about the benefits of education. And even after World War I, Cherokee pupils frequently appeared at school speaking only their native tongue. Most residents of places like Big Cove and Snowbird were still full-bloods who had little to do with the more acculturated tribal members. Factionalism, most apparent in arguments over enrollment and allotment, continued to plague them and presaged an even more bitter divisiveness to emerge in the 1930s."[8]

It is the hope that these pages will helps thousands in the future to find out who they are because of their past.

Jeff Bowen
NativeStudy.com

---

[7] Wikipedia, Eastern Band of Cherokee Indians
[8] Cherokee Americans, Finger pg, 73, para. 3

INSTRUCTIONS

(A) A separate roll is to be made of each reservation; also, of each *rancheria* or reserve, and a separate roll of Indians allotted on the public domain or homesteading. The roll is to be based on enrollment and not on residence.

(B) Persons are to be listed by families alphabetically; that is, not only by the first letter of the surname, but also by the second and subsequent letters, when the first letter or letters are the same. For example: Abalon, Abbott, Abeon, Abend, Abiet; Ball, Bell, Bill, Boll, Bull; Carley, Carmen, Carton, etc. Families having the same surname are also to be listed in this way, e. g.: Brown, *Anson*; Brown, *Bill*; Brown, *Charles*; Brown, *David*. In the case of English translations of Indian names, such as John *Flying-Elk*, Flying-Elk is the surname and is to be listed under F. In such cases the first word of the translated Indian name determines the alphabetical position. The best way to accomplish this will be to write the names of each family group on a separate card; then, arrange the cards alphabetically and type the names therefrom onto the census roll.

Members of a family are to be listed in the following order: Head, first; wife second; then children, whether sons or daughters, *in the order of their ages*; and lastly, all other relatives and persons living with the family who do not constitute another family group.

Annuity and per capita payment rolls are also to be prepared in the same manner.

(C) A family is composed of the following members:

    1. Both parents and their unmarried children, if any, living with them; all other relatives and persons living with the family who do not constitute another family group.

    2. Either parent and the unmarried children, if the other parent is dead; all other relatives and persons living with the family who do not constitute another family group.

    3. A single person over 21 years of age, not living with a relative.

(D) For each person the following information is to be furnished:

    1. NUMBER.—A number is to be assigned in serial order. Thus, the first person listed is to be numbered as "1," the second, as "2," and so on until the census is completed.

    2. NAME.—If there are both an Indian and an English name, the allotment or annuity roll name is to be given. First, the last or surname; then, the given name in full. Ditto marks are to be used under the surname of the head for the surnames of the other members of one family.

    3. SEX.—"M," for male; "F," for female.

    4. AGE AT LAST BIRTHDAY.—Age in completed years at last birthday is to be shown. For infants under 1 year, age in completed months, expressed as twelfths of a year. Thus, 3 months as $\frac{3}{12}$ yr.

    5. TRIBE.—Care is to be taken that tribe, not band or local name, is given. Thus, Ute tribe, not Pahvant, which is a band of Ute. Likewise, Hupa tribe, not Bear River, which is a local name for the members of the Hupa tribe living near Bear River.

    6. DEGREE OF BLOOD.—"F," for full blood; "¼+," for one-fourth or more Indian blood; "−¼," for less than one-fourth Indian blood.

    7. MARITAL STATUS.—"S," for a single or unmarried person; "M," for a married person; and "Wd," for widowed of either sex.

    8. RELATIONSHIP TO HEAD OF FAMILY.—The head, whether husband or father, widow or unmarried person of either sex, is to be designated as such. For the other members, the appropriate term which designates the particular relationship the person bears to the head is to be used.

    9. RESIDENCE.—

        (a) At *jurisdiction* where enrolled: Yes or no. The term jurisdiction includes all reservations and public domain allotments under the agency.

        (b) Or at another jurisdiction. The name of the jurisdiction is to be given.

        (c) Or elsewhere:

            1. Post office: Both the proper name of the post office and the class by which it is known (city, town, village, etc.) are to be given. Thus, Lewiston, city.

            2. County.

            3. State.

    10. WARD.—Yes or no. Wardship depends primarily upon the ownership of individual property held in trust or upon membership in a tribe living on a Federal reservation. See Circular 2145.

    11. ALLOTMENT, ANNUITY, AND IDENTIFICATION NUMBERS.—"Al," for allotment; "An," for annuity; and "Id," for identification, before the appropriate number or numbers. All numbers are to be shown.

(E) Rolls not prepared in strict conformity with the above instructions will be returned for correction.

U. S. GOVERNMENT PRINTING OFFICE: 1936   16—7979

Census of the Cherokee Tribe
Eastern Cherokee Agency, N.C.
As of April 1, 1932
Taken by R. L. Spalsbury, Superintendent.

Census of the **Eastern Cherokee** reservation of the **Cherokee, N.C.** jurisdiction, as of **April 1** , 19**32**, taken by **R. L. Spalsbury** , Superintendent.

Key: Number; Surname, Given; Sex; Date of Birth-Age at Last Birthday; Tribe; Degree of Blood; Marital Status; Relationship to Head of Family; Last C. Roll No.; At Jurisdiction Where Enrolled (Yes/No); (If no – Where); Ward (Yes/No); Allotment, Annuity and Identification Numbers (if given).

1;   Abernathy (Meroney Sallie Belle), Sallie Belle; F; 10/16/94-37; N.C. Cherokee; 1/16; M; Head; 1; Yes; Yes; Unallotted

2;   Abernathy, Miles Henry; M; 1/29/15-17; N.C. Cherokee; 1/32; S; Son; 2; Yes; Yes; Unallotted

3;   Abernathy, Tabitha Dell; F; 5/3/19-11; N.C. Cherokee; 1/32; S; Daughter; 3; Yes; Yes; Unallotted

4;   Abernathy, Fannie Bell; F; 8/12/23-8; N.C. Cherokee; 1/32; S; Daughter; 4; Yes; Yes; Unallotted

5;   Adams, Adeline; F; 7/10/83-47; N.C. Cherokee; 1/32; M; Head; 5; Yes; Yes; Unallotted

6;   Adams, Lionel; M; 2/6/08-24; N.C. Cherokee; 1/64; S; Son; 6; Yes; Yes; Unallotted

7;   Adams, Stephen; M; 6/25/14-17; N.C. Cherokee; 1/64; S; Son; 7; Yes; Yes; Unallotted

8;   Adams, Ever (Eva); F; 10/23/02-29; N.C. Cherokee; 1/32; M; Wife; 8; Yes; Yes; Unallotted

9;   Adams, Emma Lee; F; 3/12/24-8; N.C. Cherokee; 1/64; S; Daughter; 9; Yes; Yes; Unallotted

10;   Adams, Gudger; M; 9/16/01-30; N.C. Cherokee; 1/64; S; Head; 10; Yes; Yes; Unallotted

11;   Adams, John V.; M; 6/11/93-38; N.C. Cherokee; 1/32; M; Head; 11; Yes; Yes; Unallotted

12;   Adams, Trilba; F; 6/13/16-15; N.C. Cherokee; 1/64; S; Daughter; 12; Yes; Yes; Unallotted

13;   Adams, Stanley; M; 8/20/19-12; N.C. Cherokee; 1/64; S; Son; 13; Yes; Yes; Unallotted

14;   Adams, Juanita; F; 4/2/22-9; N.C. Cherokee; 1/64; S; Daughter; 14; Yes; Yes; Unallotted

15;   Adams, Lewis; M; 4/8/04-27; N.C. Cherokee; 1/64; S; Head; 15; Yes; Yes; Unallotted

16;   Adams, Monell; M; 10/15/04-28; N.C. Cherokee; 1/64; S; Head; 16; No; Culberson, Cherokee, N.C. Yes; Unallotted

17;   Adams, Parrie; M; 12/5/03-28; N.C. Cherokee; 1/64; S; Head; 17; Yes; Yes; Unallotted

18;   Adams, Rollins E.; M; 6/11/84-47; N.C. Cherokee; 1/32; M; Head; 18; Yes; Yes; Unallotted

Census of the **Eastern Cherokee** reservation of the **Cherokee, N.C.** jurisdiction, as of **April 1**, 19**32**, taken by **R. L. Spalsbury**, Superintendent.

Key: Number; Surname, Given; Sex; Date of Birth-Age at Last Birthday; Tribe; Degree of Blood; Marital Status; Relationship to Head of Family; Last C. Roll No.; At Jurisdiction Where Enrolled (Yes/No); (If no – Where); Ward (Yes/No); Allotment, Annuity and Identification Numbers (if given).

19;　Adams, Quincy; M; 3/14/07-25; N.C. Cherokee; 1/64; S; Son; 19; Yes; Yes; Unallotted

20;　Adams, Rollins Jr.; M; 6/11/10-21; N.C. Cherokee; 1/64; S; Son; 20; Yes; Yes; Unallotted

21;　Adams, Mattie; F; 2/15/12-20; N.C. Cherokee; 1/64; S; Daughter; 21; Yes; Yes; Unallotted

22;　Adams, Walter; M; 5/23/81-50; N.C. Cherokee; 1/32; M; Head; 22; Yes; Yes; Unallotted

23;　Adams, Frank; M; 3/16/06-26; N.C. Cherokee; 1/64; S; Son; 23; Yes; Yes; Unallotted

24;　Adams Belvia; F; 10/11/08-23; N.C. Cherokee; 1/64; S; Daughter; 24; Yes; Yes; Unallotted

25;　Adams, Marion; M; 12/8/11-20; N.C. Cherokee; 1/64; S; Son; 25; Yes; Yes; Unallotted

26;　Adams, Posey; M; 7/16/14-17; N.C. Cherokee; 1/64; S; Son; 26; Yes; Yes; Unallotted

27;　Adams, Mary; F; 5/10/16-15; N.C. Cherokee; 1/64; S; Daughter; 27; Yes; Yes; Unallotted

28;　Adams, Jesse; M; 10/5/19-12; N.C. Cherokee; 1/64; S; Son; 28; Yes; Yes; Unallotted

29;　Adams, Ruth; F; 8/6/21-11; N.C. Cherokee; 1/64; S; Daughter; 29; Yes; Yes; Unallotted

30;　Adams, Willard; M; 10/15/01-29; N.C. Cherokee; 1/64; M; Head; 30; Yes; Yes; Unallotted

31;　Adkins, Mary Sneed; F; 2/19/95-37; N.C. Cherokee; 1/8; M; Wife; 31; Yes; Yes; Unallotted

32;　Adkins, Mary L.; F; 5/28/24-7; N.C. Cherokee; 1/16; S; Daughter; 32; Yes; Yes; Unallotted

33;　Akin (Meroney, Margaret), Margaret A.; F; 7/16/99-32; N.C. Cherokee; 1/16; M; Head; 33; Yes; Yes; Unallotted

34;　Akin, Jack Barton; M; 1/11/22-10; N.C. Cherokee; 1/32; S; Son; 34; Yes; Yes; Unallotted

35;　Allen, John T.; M; 3/8/71-60; N.C. Cherokee; 4/4; M; Head; 35; Yes; Yes; Unallotted

36;　Allen, Eva; F; 12/16/81-50; N.C. Cherokee; 4/4; M; Wife; 36; Yes; Yes; Unallotted

37;　Allen (Murphy, Lillie B.), Lillie B.; F; 2/12/03-29; N.C. Cherokee; 1/8; M; Wife; 37; No; Violet, Cherokee, N.C.; Yes; Unallotted

4

Census of the **Eastern Cherokee** reservation of the **Cherokee, N.C.** jurisdiction, as of **April 1**, **1932,** taken by **R. L. Spalsbury**, Superintendent.

Key: Number; Surname, Given; Sex; Date of Birth-Age at Last Birthday; Tribe; Degree of Blood; Marital Status; Relationship to Head of Family; Last C. Roll No.; At Jurisdiction Where Enrolled (Yes/No); (If no – Where); Ward (Yes/No); Allotment, Annuity and Identification Numbers (if given).

38;   Allen, Guion; M; 11/26/22-9; N.C. Cherokee; 1/16; S; Son; 38; No; Violet, Cherokee, N.C.; Yes; Unallotted

39;   Allison, Maggie P.; F; 7/16/22-9; N.C. Cherokee; 1/64; S; Daughter; 39; Yes; Yes; Unallotted

40;   Allison (Lambert, Nannie I.), Nannie I.; F; 3/8/83-49; N.C. Cherokee; 1/16; M; Wife; 40; Yes; Yes; Unallotted
41;   Allison, Roy Robert; M; 2/13/04-28; N.C. Cherokee; 1/32; S; Son; 41; Yes; Yes; Unallotted
42;   Allison, Albert M.; M; 4/30/06-25; N.C. Cherokee; 1/32; S; Son; 42; Yes; Yes; Unallotted
43;   Allison, Felix W.; M; 2/6/12-20; N.C. Cherokee; 1/32; S; Son; 43; Yes; Yes; Unallotted
44;   Allison, Boyce J.; M; 8/12/14-17; N.C. Cherokee; 1/32; S; Son; 44; Yes; Yes; Unallotted
45;   Allison, Nora M.; F; 12/19/16-15; N.C. Cherokee; 1/32; S; Daughter; 45; Yes; Yes; Unallotted

46;   Anderson, Addie L.G. (Garland, Addie L.); F; 5/8/88-43; N.C. Cherokee; 1/16; M; Wife; 46; Yes; Yes; Unallotted
47;   Anderson, Gertie; F; 7/16/11-20; N.C. Cherokee; 1/32; S; Daughter; 47; Yes; Yes; Unallotted
48;   Anderson, Elbert; M; 4/23/14-17; N.C. Cherokee; 1/32; S; Son; 48; Yes; Yes; Unallotted
49;   Anderson, Marie; F; 3/6/17-15; N.C. Cherokee; 1/32; S; Daughter; 49; Yes; Yes; Unallotted
50;   Anderson, Emory; F; 9/28/21-10; N.C. Cherokee; 1/32; S; Daughter; 50; Yes; Yes; Unallotted

51;   Anderson (Raper, Dona), Dona; F; 3/20/89-43; N.C. Cherokee; 1/16; M; Wife; 46; No; Atlanta, Fulton, Ga.; Yes; Unallotted

52;   Anderson, Ella Mary; F; 3/14/10-22; N.C. Cherokee; 1/16; S; Head; 52; No; Culberson, Cherokee, N.C.; Yes; Unallotted
53;   Anderson, Wm. Burl; M; 12/3/12-19; N.C. Cherokee; 1/16; S; Brother; 53; No; Culberson, Cherokee, N.C.; Yes; Unallotted

54;   Anderson, Erma Za Payne; F; 3/7/07-25; N.C. Cherokee; 1/32; M; Wife; 54; No; Blue Ridge, Fannin, Ga.; Yes; Unallotted
55;   Anderson, James Olen; M; 5/5/24-7; N.C. Cherokee; 1/64; S; Son; 55; No; Blue Ridge, Fannin, Ga.; Yes; Unallotted
56;   Anderson, Lloyd; M; 6/21/17-14; N.C. Cherokee; 1/64; S; Son; 56; No; Culberson, Cherokee, N.C.; Yes; Unallotted

Census of the **Eastern Cherokee** reservation of the **Cherokee, N.C.** jurisdiction, as of **April 1** , 19**32,** taken by **R. L. Spalsbury** , Superintendent.

Key: Number; Surname, Given; Sex; Date of Birth-Age at Last Birthday; Tribe; Degree of Blood; Marital Status; Relationship to Head of Family; Last C. Roll No.; At Jurisdiction Where Enrolled (Yes/No); (If no – Where); Ward (Yes/No); Allotment, Annuity and Identification Numbers (if given).

57; Anderson, Earnest; M; 6/25/19-12; N.C. Cherokee; 1/64; S; Son; 57; No; Culberson, Cherokee, N.C.; Yes; Unallotted

58; Anderson, Evelyn; F; 7/25/21-10; N.C. Cherokee; 1/64; S; Daughter; 58; No; Culberson, Cherokee, N.C.; Yes; Unallotted

59; Anderson, (Raper, Pearl), Pearl Raper; F; 1/4/05-27; N.C. Cherokee; 1/16; M; Wife; 59; Yes; Yes; Unallotted

60; Arch, Codaskie; M; 6/2/99-32; N.C. Cherokee; F; S; Head; 60; Yes; Yes; Unallotted

61; Arch, Winnie; F; 3/6/07-25; N.C. Cherokee; 15/16; S; Sister; 61; Yes; Yes; Unallotted

62; Arch, Anna; F; 3/28/10-22; N.C. Cherokee; 15/16; S; Sister; 62; Yes; Yes; Unallotted

63; Arch, Johnson; M; 12/25/83-48; N.C. Cherokee; 3/4; M; Head; 63; Yes; Yes; Unallotted

64; Arch, Ella; F; 9/1/89-42; N.C. Cherokee; 1/2; M; Wife; 64; Yes; Yes; Unallotted

65; Arch, Cora; F; 9/2/07-25; N.C. Cherokee; 5/8; S; Daughter; 65; Yes; Yes; Unallotted

66; Arch, Horace; M; 5/16/09-22; N.C. Cherokee; 5/8; S; Son; 66; Yes; Yes; Unallotted

67; Arch, Elma Cleona; F; 2/28/11-21; N.C. Cherokee; 5/8; S; Daughter; 67; Yes; Yes; Unallotted

68; Arch, Bessie; F; 6/2/15-16; N.C. Cherokee; 5/8; S; Daughter; 68; Yes; Yes; Unallotted

69; Arch, Ethlyn; F; 12/31/19-12; N.C. Cherokee; 5/8; S; Daughter; 69; Yes; Yes; Unallotted

70; Arch, Johnson Jr.; M; 8/22/22-9; N.C. Cherokee; 5/8; S; Son; 70; Yes; Yes; Unallotted

71; Arch, Martha; F; 6/16/84-47; N.C. Cherokee; F; M; Head; 71; Yes; Yes; Unallotted

72; Arch, Jesse; M; 6/8/08-23; N.C. Cherokee; F; S; Son; 72; Yes; Yes; Unallotted

73; Arch, Jimme; M; 11/16/10-21; N.C. Cherokee; F; S; Son; 73; Yes; Yes; Unallotted

74; Arch, Eva Stella; F; 9/16/13-18; N.C. Cherokee; F; S; Daughter; 74; Yes; Yes; Unallotted

75; Arch, Joseph Lee; M; 11/12/20-11; N.C. Cherokee; F; S; Son; 75; Yes; Yes; Unallotted

76; Arch, Edna; F; 2/12/25-7; N.C. Cherokee; F; S; Daughter; 76; Yes; Yes; Unallotted

Census of the **Eastern Cherokee** reservation of the **Cherokee, N.C.** jurisdiction, as of **April 1** , **1932,** taken by **R. L. Spalsbury** , Superintendent.

Key: Number; Surname, Given; Sex; Date of Birth-Age at Last Birthday; Tribe; Degree of Blood; Marital Status; Relationship to Head of Family; Last C. Roll No.; At Jurisdiction Where Enrolled (Yes/No); (If no – Where); Ward (Yes/No); Allotment, Annuity and Identification Numbers (if given).

77;   Arch, Noah; M; 2/28/92-40; N.C. Cherokee; F; M; Head; 77; Yes; Yes; Unallotted

78;   Arch, Cinda S.; F; 5/3/00-31; N.C. Cherokee; F; M; Wife; 78; Yes; Yes; Unallotted

79;   Arch, Elizabeth B.; F; 9/15/19-12; N.C. Cherokee; F; S; Daughter; 79; Yes; Yes; Unallotted

80;   Arch, Elsie Jennie; F; 3/28/22-10; N.C. Cherokee; F; S; Daughter; 80; Yes; Yes; Unallotted

81;   Arch, Lulu Edith; F; 5/17/24-7; N.C. Cherokee; F; S; Daughter; 81; Yes; Yes; Unallotted

82;   Arch, Wm. Wayne; M; 2/28/30-2; N.C. Cherokee; F; S; Son; 82; Yes; Yes; Unallotted

83;   Arch, Olivan; F; 3/20/95-37; N.C. Cherokee; 3/4; M; Head; 83; Yes; Yes; Unallotted

84;   Arch, Pauline B.; F; 1/1/17-15; N.C. Cherokee; 3/8; S; Daughter; 84; Yes; Yes; Unallotted

85;   Arch, Nellie; F; 6/27/20-11; N.C. Cherokee; 5/8; S; Daughter; 85; Yes; Yes; Unallotted

86;   Armachain, Chewinih; F; 11/4/41-90; N.C. Cherokee; F; Wd; Head; 86; Yes; Yes; Unallotted

87;   Armachain, Davis; M; 1/4/51-80; N.C. Cherokee; F; Wd; Head; 87; Yes; Yes; Unallotted

88;   Armachain, Sevier; M; 1/22/04-28; N.C. Cherokee; F; S; Son; 88; Yes; Yes; Unallotted

89;   Armachain, Jesse; M; 1/28/96-37; N.C. Cherokee; F; M; Head; 89; Yes; Yes; Unallotted

90;   Armachain, Lucy Long; F; 1/16/99-34[sic]; N.C. Cherokee; 3/4; M; Wife; 90; Yes; Yes; Unallotted

91;   Armachain, Stella E.; F; 5/28/21-11; N.C. Cherokee; 7/8; S; Daughter; 91; Yes; Yes; Unallotted

92;   Armachain, Jesse James; M; 1/5/29-3; N.C. Cherokee; 7/8; S; Son; 92; Yes; Yes; Unallotted

93;   Armachain, Stacy; F; 3/6/31-1; N.C. Cherokee; 7/8; S; Daughter; --; Yes; Yes; Unallotted

94;   Armachain, Jonah; M; 8/6/95-36; N.C. Cherokee; F; M; Head; 93; Yes; Yes; Unallotted

95;   Armachain, Kiney Watty; F; 8/7/99-32; N.C. Cherokee; F; M; Wife; 94; Yes; Yes; Unallotted

Census of the **Eastern Cherokee** reservation of the **Cherokee, N.C.** jurisdiction, as of **April 1**, 1932, taken by **R. L. Spalsbury**, Superintendent.

Key: Number; Surname, Given; Sex; Date of Birth-Age at Last Birthday; Tribe; Degree of Blood; Marital Status; Relationship to Head of Family; Last C. Roll No.; At Jurisdiction Where Enrolled (Yes/No); (If no – Where); Ward (Yes/No); Allotment, Annuity and Identification Numbers (if given).

96; Armachain, Jim; M; 10/10/21-10; N.C. Cherokee; F; S; Son; 95; Yes; Yes; Unallotted

97; Armachain, DeHart; M; 5/22/23-8; N.C. Cherokee; F; S; Son; 96; Yes; Yes; Unallotted

98; Armachain, Lacy; M; 10/5/77-54; N.C. Cherokee; F; M; Head; 97; Yes; Yes; Unallotted

99; Armachain, Anna (Annie); F; 4/1/72-61; N.C. Cherokee; F; M; Wife; 98; Yes; Yes; Unallotted

100; Armachain, James; M; 6/21/10-21; N.C. Cherokee; F; S; Son; 99; Yes; Yes; Unallotted

101; Armachain, Louis; M; 6/12/99-32; N.C. Cherokee; F; M; Head; 100; Yes; Yes; Unallotted

102; Armachain, Dora; F; 2/18/99-33; N.C. Cherokee; 1/8; M; Wife; 101; Yes; Yes; Unallotted

103; Armachain, Emma; F; 4/30/19-12; N.C. Cherokee; 9/16; S; Daughter; 102; Yes; Yes; Unallotted

104; Armachain, Wm. Davis; M; 9/24/21-10; N.C. Cherokee; 9/16; S; Son; 103; Yes; Yes; Unallotted

105; Armachain, Calvin; M; 10/23/25-6; N.C. Cherokee; 9/16; S; Son; 104; Yes; Yes; Unallotted

106; Armachain, Wayne Lewis; M; 6/28/30-1; N.C. Cherokee; 9/16; S; Son; 105; Yes; Yes; Unallotted

107; Arneach, Jefferson; M; 4/7/74-57; N.C. Cherokee; F; M; Head; 106; Yes; Yes; Unallotted

108; Arneach, Sarah; F; 1/17/75-57; N.C. Cherokee; 7/8; M; Wife; 107; Yes; Yes; Unallotted

109; Arneach, Samuel; M; 12/26/08-23; N.C. Cherokee; 15/16; S; Son; 108; Yes; Yes; Unallotted

110; Arneach, John E.H.; M; 5/1/11-20; N.C. Cherokee; 15/16; S; Son; 109; Yes; Yes; Unallotted

111; Arneach, Stella P.; F; 2/23/13-19; N.C. Cherokee; 15/16; S; Daughter; 110; Yes; Yes; Unallotted

112; Arneach, Sylvester; M; 12/4/14-17; N.C. Cherokee; 15/16; S; Son; 111; Yes; Yes; Unallotted

113; Arneach, Francis N.; M; 11/7/17-14; N.C. Cherokee; 15/16; S; Son; 112; Yes; Yes; Unallotted

114; Ashe (Locust, Bessie), Bessie; F; 6/21/03-28; N.C. Cherokee; 1/4; M; Wife; 114; Yes; Yes; Unallotted

115; Ashe (Locust, Martha), Martha L.; F; 12/2/09-22; N.C. Cherokee; 1/4; M; Wife; 115; Yes; Yes; Unallotted

Census of the **Eastern Cherokee** reservation of the **Cherokee, N.C.** jurisdiction, as of **April 1** , 19**32,** taken by **R. L. Spalsbury** , Superintendent.

Key: Number; Surname, Given; Sex; Date of Birth-Age at Last Birthday; Tribe; Degree of Blood; Marital Status; Relationship to Head of Family; Last C. Roll No.; At Jurisdiction Where Enrolled (Yes/No); (If no – Where); Ward (Yes/No); Allotment, Annuity and Identification Numbers (if given).

116; Ashe, Joseph H.; M; 4/28/28-4; N.C. Cherokee; 1/8; S; Son; 116; Yes; Yes; Unallotted

117; Ashe, Margie L.; F; 10/14/30-1; N.C. Cherokee; 1/8; S; Daughter; ---; Yes; Yes; Unallotted

118; Austin, Vianey; F; 10/20/70-62; N.C. Cherokee; 1/16; M; Head; 117; No; Hiland[sic] Park, Hamilton, Tenn.; Yes; Unallotted

119; Austin, Howard; M; 7/5/11-22; N.C. Cherokee; 1/4-; S; Son; 118; No; Hiland Park, Hamilton, Tenn.; Yes; Unallotted

120; Austin, Jack; M; 8/10/00-32; N.C. Cherokee; 1/4-; S; Son; 119; No; Hiland Park, Hamilton, Tenn.; Yes; Unallotted

121; Austin, James; M; 5/11/90-42; N.C. Cherokee; 1/4-; S; Son; 120; No; Hiland Park, Hamilton, Tenn.; Yes; Unallotted

122; Austin, Lelia; F; 5/19/97-34; N.C. Cherokee; 1/4-; S; Daughter; 119; No; Hiland Park, Hamilton, Tenn.; Yes; Unallotted

123; Jones, Alice Austin; F; 7/16/03-28; N.C. Cherokee; 1/4-; SM; Daughter; 123; No; Hiland Park, Hamilton, Tenn.; Yes; Unallotted

124; Mullins, Maggie Austin; F; 5/11/95-37; N.C. Cherokee; 1/4-; S; Daughter; 121; No; Hiland Park, Hamilton, Tenn.; Yes; Unallotted

125; Axe, John D.; M; 12/16/62-69; N.C. Cherokee; F; M; Head; 124; Yes; Yes; Unallotted

126; Axe, Eva; F; 12/16/64-67; N.C. Cherokee; F; M; Wife; 125; Yes; Yes; Unallotted

127; Axe, Josiah Long; M; 6/16/64-67; N.C. Cherokee; F; M; Head; 126; Yes; Yes; Unallotted

128; Axe, Ella; F; 7/2/05-27; N.C. Cherokee; F; S; Daughter; 127; Yes; Yes; Unallotted

129; Axe, Dora; F; 2/21/13-19; N.C. Cherokee; F; S; Daughter; 128; Yes; Yes; Unallotted

130; Axe, Posey; M; 6/15/15-13; N.C. Cherokee; F; S; Son; 129; Yes; Yes; Unallotted

131; Axe, Lucindy; F; 4/29/22-9; N.C. Cherokee; F; S; Daughter; 130; Yes; Yes; Unallotted

132; Axe, Willie; M; 2/16/72-60; N.C. Cherokee; F; Wd; Head; 131; Yes; Yes; Unallotted

133; Baker (Webster, Bonnie F.), Bonnie Fair; F; 12/18/96-35; N.C. Cherokee; 1/16; M; Wife; 132; No; Wagoner, Wagoner, Okla.; Yes; Unallotted

134; Baker (Cole, Elizabeth), Elizabeth B.; F; 12/16/62-69; N.C. Cherokee; 1/8; M; Wife; 133; Yes; Yes; Unallotted

Census of the **Eastern Cherokee** reservation of the **Cherokee, N.C.** jurisdiction, as of **April 1** , **1932,** taken by **R. L. Spalsbury** , Superintendent.

Key: Number; Surname, Given; Sex; Date of Birth-Age at Last Birthday; Tribe; Degree of Blood; Marital Status; Relationship to Head of Family; Last C. Roll No.; At Jurisdiction Where Enrolled (Yes/No); (If no – Where); Ward (Yes/No); Allotment, Annuity and Identification Numbers (if given).

135;   Baker (Churchill, Ella McCoy), Ella McCoy; F; 1/13/78-54; N.C. Cherokee; 1/8; M; Wife; 134; Yes; Yes; Unallotted

136;   Baker, Mary R.; F; 4/24/05-26; N.C. Cherokee; 1/16; S; Daughter; 135; Yes; Yes; Unallotted

137;   Baker, Cora; F; 10/5/10-26[sic]; N.C. Cherokee; 1/16; S; Daughter; 136; Yes; Yes;   Unallotted

138;   Baker, Alice; F; 3/19/13-19; N.C. Cherokee; 1/16; S; Daughter; 137; Yes; Yes; Unallotted

139;   Baker, Thomas, Jr.; M; 2/23/16-16; N.C. Cherokee; 1/16; S; Son; 138; Yes; Yes; Unallotted

140;   Baker (Cole, Elmira), Elmire Cole; F; 1/1/72-60; N.C. Cherokee; 1/8; M; Wife; 139; No; Culberson, Cherokee, N.C.; Yes; Unallotted

141;   Baker, Ada; F; 3/13/10-22; N.C. Cherokee; 1/16; S; Daughter; 140; No; Culberson, Cherokee, N.C.; Yes; Unallotted

142;   Baker, Homer; M; 3/12/12-20; N.C. Cherokee; 1/16; S; Son; 141; No; Culberson, Cherokee, N.C.; Yes; Unallotted

143;   Baker, Luther; M; 3/13/95-37; N.C. Cherokee; 1/16; M; Head; 142; No; Culberson, Cherokee, N.C.; Yes; Unallotted

144;   Baker, Howard; M; 3/12/20-12; N.C. Cherokee; 1/32; S; Son; 143; No; Culberson, Cherokee, N.C.; Yes; Unallotted

145;   Baker, Lloyd; M; 9/1/23-8; N.C. Cherokee; 1/32; S; Son; 144; No; Culberson, Cherokee, N.C.; Yes; Unallotted

146;   Barnes (Payne, Grace Lee), Grace Lee; F; 9/22/03-28; N.C. Cherokee; 1/32; M; Wife; 145; No; Benham, Harlan, Ky.; Yes; Unallotted

147;   Barnett (Mashburn, Kate), Kate; F; 1/13/99-33; N.C. Cherokee; 1/64; M; Wife; 146; Yes; Yes; Unallotted

148;   Barnett, Clinton; M; 11/25/15-16; N.C. Cherokee; 1/128; S; Son; 147; Yes; Yes; Unallotted

149;   Barnett, Irene; F; 5/25/19-12; N.C. Cherokee; 1/128; S; Daughter; 148; Yes; Yes; Unallotted

150;   Barnett, Wilburn; M; 8/8/22-9; N.C. Cherokee; 1/128; S; Son; 149; Yes; Yes; Unallotted

151;   Barnett, Ruby; F; 12/1/18-13; N.C. Cherokee; 1/128; S; Niece; 150; Yes; Yes; Unallotted

152;   Bates (Raper, Dessie), Dessie; F; 11/9/05-26; N.C. Cherokee; 1/16; M; Wife; 151; Yes; Yes; Unallotted

153;   Batson (Crow, Henrietta), Henrietta C.; F; 9/15/86-45; N.C. Cherokee; 1/4; M; Wife; 152; Yes; Yes; Unallotted

Census of the **Eastern Cherokee** reservation of the **Cherokee, N.C.** jurisdiction, as of **April 1** , 19**32**, taken by **R. L. Spalsbury** , Superintendent.

Key: Number; Surname, Given; Sex; Date of Birth-Age at Last Birthday; Tribe; Degree of Blood; Marital Status; Relationship to Head of Family; Last C. Roll No.; At Jurisdiction Where Enrolled (Yes/No); (If no – Where); Ward (Yes/No); Allotment, Annuity and Identification Numbers (if given).

154; Battle, Adeline; F; 4/30/52-79; N.C. Cherokee; 1/16; M; Wife; 153; Yes; Yes; Unallotted

155; Battle, Bruce W.; M; 9/28/76-55; N.C. Cherokee; 1/32; M; Head; 154; Yes; Yes; Unallotted

156; Battle, Daisy L.; F; 5/23/09-22; N.C. Cherokee; 1/64; S; Daughter; 155; Yes; Yes; Unallotted

157; Battle, Addie Lee; F; 12/27/10-21; N.C. Cherokee; 1/64; S; Daughter; 156; Yes; Yes; Unallotted

158; Battle, Bruce W. Jr.; M; 5/19/13-18; N.C. Cherokee; 1/64; S; Son; 157; Yes; Yes; Unallotted

159; Battle, Joan; F; 11/25/20-11; N.C. Cherokee; 1/64; S; Daughter; 158; Yes; Yes; Unallotted

160; Battle, Wm. M.; M; 11/23/83-48; N.C. Cherokee; 1/32; S; Head; 159; Yes; Yes; Unallotted

161; Bauer, Fred; M; 12/27/96-35; N.C. Cherokee; 3/8; S; Head; 160; Yes; Yes; Unallotted

162; Beavers (Robinson, Fannie), Fannie R.; F; 4/23/94-37; N.C. Cherokee; 1/16; M; Wife; 161; Yes; Yes; Unallotted

163; Beavers, Cliffie; F; 10/5/13-18; N.C. Cherokee; 1/32; S; Daughter; 162; Yes; Yes; Unallotted

164; Beavers, Lexie; F; 2/3/16-16; N.C. Cherokee; 1/32; S; Daughter; 163; Yes; Yes; Unallotted

165; Beck, Eugene; M; 5/18/89-42; N.C. Cherokee; 1/8; M; Head; 164; Yes; Yes; Unallotted

166; Beck (Matthews, Gady), Gady M.; F; 11/27/07-24; N.C. Cherokee; 1/32; M; Wife; 165; Yes; Yes; Unallotted

167; Beck, Samuel; M; 4/11/90-40; N.C. Cherokee; 1/8; M; Head; 166; Yes; Yes; Unallotted

168; Beck, Sarah Sneed; F; 9/4/01-30; N.C. Cherokee; 1/16; M; Wife; 167; Yes; Yes; Unallotted

169; Beck, Samuel Foch; M; 5/18/18-13; N.C. Cherokee; 3/32; S; Son; 168; Yes; Yes; Unallotted

170; Beck, John Quentin; M; 8/11/20-11; N.C. Cherokee; 3/32; S; Son; 169; Yes; Yes; Unallotted

171; Beck, Wilma Lee; F; 1/19/23-9; N.C. Cherokee; 3/32; S; Daughter; 170; Yes; Yes; Unallotted

172; Beck, Paul Kevin; M; 5/29/29-2; N.C. Cherokee; 3/32; S; Son; 171; Yes; Yes; Unallotted

11

Census of the **Eastern Cherokee** reservation of the **Cherokee, N.C.** jurisdiction, as of **April 1** , 19**32,** taken by **R. L. Spalsbury** , Superintendent.

Key: Number; Surname, Given; Sex; Date of Birth-Age at Last Birthday; Tribe; Degree of Blood; Marital Status; Relationship to Head of Family; Last C. Roll No.; At Jurisdiction Where Enrolled (Yes/No); (If no – Where); Ward (Yes/No); Allotment, Annuity and Identification Numbers (if given).

173;   Ben, Cheick; M; 1/14/65-67; N.C. Cherokee; F; M; Head; 172; Yes; Yes; Unallotted

174;   Ben, Ollie; F; 7/18/84-47; N.C. Cherokee; F; M; Wife; 173; Yes; Yes; Unallotted

175;   Ben, Stan; M; 1/15/04-28; N.C. Cherokee; F; S; Son; 174; Yes; Yes; Unallotted

176;   Ben, Callie; F; 4/1/13-19; N.C. Cherokee; F; S; Daughter; 175; Yes; Yes; Unallotted

177;   Ben, Nannie; F; 4/18/15-16; N.C. Cherokee; F; S; Daughter; 176; Yes; Yes; Unallotted

178;   Ben, Louisa; F; 6/22/18-14; N.C. Cherokee; F; S; Daughter; 177; Yes; Yes; Unallotted

179;   Ben, Lucy; F; 7/12/21-10; N.C. Cherokee; F; S; Daughter; 178; Yes; Yes; Unallotted

180;   Biggers (Adams, Daisy), Daisy; F; 5/18/88-43; N.C. Cherokee; 1/32; M; Wife; 179; Yes; Yes; Unallotted

181;   Bigmeat, Isaiah; M; 12/16/78-53; N.C. Cherokee; F; M; Head; 180; Yes; Yes; Unallotted

182;   Bigmeat, Sarah; F; 8/20/80-51; N.C. Cherokee; F; M; Wife; 181; Yes; Yes; Unallotted

183;   Bigmeat, John; M; 12/7/12-18; N.C. Cherokee; F; S; Son; 182; Yes; Yes; Unallotted

184;   Bigmeat, Richard; M; 6/20/18-13; N.C. Cherokee; F; S; Son; 183; Yes; Yes; Unallotted

185;   Bigmeat, Nicodemus; M; 12/16/75-56; N.C. Cherokee; F; M; Head; 184; Yes; Yes; Unallotted

186;   Bigmeat, Robert; M; 2/16/92-40; N.C. Cherokee; 7/8; M; Head; 185; Yes; Yes; Unallotted

187;   Bigmeat, Carlotte L.; F; 6/12/87-44; N.C. Cherokee; 9/16; M; Wife; 186; Yes; Yes; Unallotted

188;   Bigmeat, Tinie C.; F; 7/16/13-18; N.C. Cherokee; 23/32; S; Daughter; 187; Yes; Yes; Unallotted

189;   Bigmeat, Ethel; F; 11/9/16-15; N.C. Cherokee; 23/32; S; Daughter; 188; Yes; Yes; Unallotted

190;   Bigmeat, Elizabeth; F; 6/21/19-12; N.C. Cherokee; 23/32; S; Daughter; 189; Yes; Yes; Unallotted

191;   Bigmeat, Mark Welch; M; 12/9/21-10; N.C. Cherokee; F; 23/32; Son; 190; Yes; Yes; Unallotted

192;   Bigmeat, Mabel; F; 1/15/25-7; N.C. Cherokee; 23/32; S; Daughter; 191; Yes; Yes; Unallotted

Census of the **Eastern Cherokee** reservation of the **Cherokee, N.C.** jurisdiction, as of **April 1** , **1932,** taken by **R. L. Spalsbury** , Superintendent.

Key: Number; Surname, Given; Sex; Date of Birth-Age at Last Birthday; Tribe; Degree of Blood; Marital Status; Relationship to Head of Family; Last C. Roll No.; At Jurisdiction Where Enrolled (Yes/No); (If no – Where); Ward (Yes/No); Allotment, Annuity and Identification Numbers (if given).

193; Bigmeat, Welch; M; 3/8/29-3; N.C. Cherokee; F; 23/32; Son; 192; Yes; Yes; Unallotted

194; Bigmeat, Yona; M; 12/16/77-54; N.C. Cherokee; F; S; Head; 193; Yes; Yes; Unallotted

195; Birchfield (Harden, Willie Pearl), Willie P.; F; 12/25/98-33; N.C. Cherokee; 1/64; M; Wife; 194; Yes; Yes; Unallotted

196; Birchfield, Odis; M; 9/25/20-11; N.C. Cherokee; 1/128; S; Son; 195; Yes; Yes; Unallotted

197; Birchfield, Willie Belle; F; 5/31/22-9; N.C. Cherokee; 1/128; S; Daughter; 196; Yes; Yes; Unallotted

198; Birchfield, Wanda; F; 2/7/24-8; N.C. Cherokee; 1/128; S; Daughter; 197; Yes; Yes; Unallotted

199; Bird, Annie Bradley; F; 6/15/02-29; N.C. Cherokee; 1/4; Wd; Head; 198; Yes; Yes; Unallotted

200; Bird, Eli; M; 4/7/92-39; N.C. Cherokee; F; M; Head; 199; Yes; Yes; Unallotted

201; Bird, Amanda Swayney; F; 1/12/01-32; N.C. Cherokee; 1/16; M; Wife; 200; Yes; Yes; Unallotted

202; Bird, Jerome J.; M; 10/8/21-10; N.C. Cherokee; 17/32; S; Son; 201; Yes; Yes; Unallotted

203; Bird, Bernardina L.; F; 7/30/23-8; N.C. Cherokee; 17/32; S; Daughter; 202; Yes; Yes; Unallotted

204; Bird, Carl Henry; M; 3/16/25-7; N.C. Cherokee; 17/32; S; Son; 203; Yes; Yes; Unallotted

205; Bird, Octa Iona; F; 5/30/26-5; N.C. Cherokee; 17/32; S; Daughter; 204; Yes; Yes; Unallotted

206; Bird, Going; M; 8/25/66-65; N.C. Cherokee; F; Wd; Head; 205; Yes; Yes; Unallotted

207; Bird, Solomon; M; 7/15/02-29; N.C. Cherokee; F; M; Head; 206; Yes; Yes; Unallotted

208; Bird, Minnie Rattler; F; 4/17/07-24; N.C. Cherokee; F; M; Wife; 207; Yes; Yes; Unallotted

209; Bird, Stephen; M; 4/27/55-76; N.C. Cherokee; F; Wd; Head; 208; Yes; Yes; Unallotted

210; Bird, Timpson; M; 12/18/85-46; N.C. Cherokee; F; M; Head; 209; Yes; Yes; Unallotted

Census of the **Eastern Cherokee** reservation of the **Cherokee, N.C.** jurisdiction, as of **April 1** , 19**32,** taken by **R. L. Spalsbury**   , Superintendent.

Key: Number; Surname, Given; Sex; Date of Birth-Age at Last Birthday; Tribe; Degree of Blood; Marital Status; Relationship to Head of Family; Last C. Roll No.; At Jurisdiction Where Enrolled (Yes/No); (If no – Where); Ward (Yes/No); Allotment, Annuity and Identification Numbers (if given).

211; Bird, Alkinney T.; F; 6/29/04-27; N.C. Cherokee; 7/8; M; Wife; 210; Yes; Yes; Unallotted

212; Bird, Annie; F; 11/27/19-12; N.C. Cherokee; 15/16; S; Daughter; 211; Yes; Yes; Unallotted

213; Bird, Lucinda; F; 9/20/21-10; N.C. Cherokee; 15/16; S; Daughter; 212; Yes; Yes; Unallotted

214; Bird, William; M; 5/17/24-7; N.C. Cherokee; 15/16; S; Son; 213; Yes;   Yes; Unallotted

215; Bishop, Lillie; F; 1870-62; N.C. Cherokee; 1/8; M; Head; 214; Yes; Yes; Unallotted

216; Bishop, Hattie Bell; F; 1912-20; N.C. Cherokee; 1/16; S; Daughter; 215; Yes; Yes; Unallotted

217; Blackfox, Charley; M; 1/13/81-51; N.C. Cherokee; 7/8; M; Head; 216; Yes; Yes; Unallotted

218; Blackfox, Nancy; F; 10/2/83-48; N.C. Cherokee; F; M; Wife; 217; Yes; Yes; Unallotted

219; Blackfox, Nancy; F; 3/1/12-20; N.C. Cherokee; 15/16; S; Daughter; 218; Yes; Yes; Unallotted

220; Blackfox, Ross; M; 5/2/15-16; N.C. Cherokee; 15/16; S; Son; 219; Yes; Yes; Unallotted

221; Blackfox, Joe; M; 1/17/21-11; N.C. Cherokee; 15/16; S; Son; 220; Yes; Yes; Unallotted

222; Blackfox, Dinah C.; F; 12/17/57-75; N.C. Cherokee; F; Wd; Head; 221; Yes; Yes; Unallotted

223; Blankenship, Arizona; F; 5/13/75-56; N.C. Cherokee; 1/8; M; Wife; 222; Yes; Yes; Unallotted

224; Blankenship, Lillian J.; F; 4/22/09-23; N.C. Cherokee; 1/16; S; Daughter; 223; Yes; Yes; Unallotted

225; Blankenship, Fred Turner; M; 1/18/11-21; N.C. Cherokee; 1/16; S; Son; 224; Yes; Yes; Unallotted

226; Blankenship, Helen K.; F; 11/8/12-19; N.C. Cherokee; 1/16; S; Daughter; 225; Yes; Yes; Unallotted

227; Blankenship, Leroy E.; M; 4/27/14-17; N.C. Cherokee; 1/16; S; Son; 226; Yes; Yes; Unallotted

228; Blythe, Arch; M; 7/19/77-54; N.C. Cherokee; 7/8; Wd; Head; 227; Yes; Yes; Unallotted

229; Blythe, Sampson; M; 6/3/03-28; N.C. Cherokee; 11/16; S; Son; 228; Yes; Yes; Unallotted

230; Blythe, Birdie B.; F; 5/21/10-21; N.C. Cherokee; 11/16; S; Daughter; 229; Yes; Yes; Unallotted

Census of the **Eastern Cherokee** reservation of the **Cherokee, N.C.** jurisdiction, as of **April 1** , 19**32,** taken by **R. L. Spalsbury** , Superintendent.

Key: Number; Surname, Given; Sex; Date of Birth-Age at Last Birthday; Tribe; Degree of Blood; Marital Status; Relationship to Head of Family; Last C. Roll No.; At Jurisdiction Where Enrolled (Yes/No); (If no – Where); Ward (Yes/No); Allotment, Annuity and Identification Numbers (if given).

231; Blythe, Francis M.; M; 2/13/13-19; N.C. Cherokee; 11/16; S; Son; 230; Yes; Yes; Unallotted

232; Blythe, Susannah; F; 2/11/16-16; N.C. Cherokee; 11/16; S; Daughter; 231; Yes; Yes; Unallotted

233; Blythe, Freddie; M; 8/21/18-13; N.C. Cherokee; 11/16; S; Son; 232; Yes; Yes; Unallotted

234; Blythe, Pauline T.; F; 3/3/22-10; N.C. Cherokee; 11/16; S; Daughter; 233; Yes; Yes; Unallotted

235; Blythe, David; M; 9/30/62-69; N.C. Cherokee; 5/8; M; Head; 234; Yes; Yes; Unallotted

236; Blythe, Nancy; F; 7/6/72-60; N.C. Cherokee; 7/8; M; Wife; 235; Yes; Yes; Unallotted

237; Blythe, Jarret; M; 5/30/86-45; N.C. Cherokee; 1/2; M; Head; 236; Yes; Yes; Unallotted

238; Blythe, Mary B.; F; 7/30/92-39; N.C. Cherokee; 1/8; M; Wife; 237; Yes; Yes; Unallotted

239; Blythe, Andy J.; M; 4/11/15-17; N.C. Cherokee; 5/16; S; Alone; 238; Yes; Yes; Unallotted

240; Blythe, Lloyd J.; M; 9/16/09-22; N.C. Cherokee; 5/16; M; Head; 239; Yes; Yes; Unallotted

241; Blythe, Rachel Bradley; F; 7/15/06-25; N.C. Cherokee; 1/4; M; Wife; 240; Yes; Yes; Unallotted

242; Blythe, Lloyd A.J.; M; 2/11/30-2; N.C. Cherokee; 1/2; S; Son; 241; Yes; Yes; Unallotted

243; Blythe, Alta Maine; F; 10/22/31-5/12; N.C. Cherokee; 1/2; S; Daughter; 242; Yes; Yes; Unallotted

244; Blythe, Rachel; F; 7/23/16-15; N.C. Cherokee; 5/16; S; Alone; 242; Yes; Yes; Unallotted

245; Blythe, Emma Katherine; F; 4/11/18-13; N.C. Cherokee; 5/16; S; Sister; 243; Yes; Yes; Unallotted

246; Blythe, Wm. Henry; M; 11/15/73-58; N.C. Cherokee; 5/8; S; Head; 244; Yes; Yes; Unallotted

247; Bowman (Timpson, Caldonia), Caldonia; F; 4/18/70-61; N.C. Cherokee; 3/16; M; Wife; 245; Yes; Yes; Unallotted

248; Bowman, Grace Rose; F; 3/31/99-33; N.C. Cherokee; 1/16; M; Wife; 246; Yes; Yes; Unallotted

Census of the **Eastern Cherokee** reservation of the **Cherokee, N.C.** jurisdiction, as of **April 1** , 19**32,** taken by **R. L. Spalsbury** , Superintendent.

Key: Number; Surname, Given; Sex; Date of Birth-Age at Last Birthday; Tribe; Degree of Blood; Marital Status; Relationship to Head of Family; Last C. Roll No.; At Jurisdiction Where Enrolled (Yes/No); (If no – Where); Ward (Yes/No); Allotment, Annuity and Identification Numbers (if given).

249; Bowman, Paul (Harold); M; 2/9/19-13; N.C. Cherokee; 1/32; S; Son; 247; Yes; Yes; Unallotted

250; Bowman, Catherine; F; 5/12/21-10; N.C. Cherokee; 1/32; S; Daughter; 248; Yes; Yes; Unallotted

251; Bowman, Nora Rose; F; 12/21/01-30; N.C. Cherokee; 1/16; M; Wife; 249; Yes; Yes; Unallotted

252; Brackett (Thompson, Iowa), Iowa; F; 10/4/94-37; N.C. Cherokee; 1/16; M; Wife; 250; Yes; Yes; Unallotted

253; Bradley, Eliza Jane; F; 5/5/72-59; N.C. Cherokee; 1/2; M; Wife; 251; Yes; Yes; Unallotted

254; Bradley, Lydia; F; 8/19/05-26; N.C. Cherokee; 1/4; S; Daughter; 252; Yes; Yes; Unallotted

255; Bradley, Seaborne; M; 10/25/07-24; N.C. Cherokee; 1/4; S; Son; 253; Yes; Yes; Unallotted

256; Bradley, Martha I.; F; 7/29/13-18; N.C. Cherokee; 1/4; S; Daughter; 254; Yes; Yes; Unallotted

257; Bradley (Lambert, Florence), Florence; F; 7/27/07-24; N.C. Cherokee; 1/16; M; Wife; 255; Yes; Yes; Unallotted

258; Bradley, Henry; M; 9/28/83-48; N.C. Cherokee; 13/16; M; Head; 256; Yes; Yes; Unallotted

259; Bradley, Nancy T.; F; 3/15/81-50; N.C. Cherokee; F; M; Wife; 257; Yes; Yes; Unallotted

260; Bradley, James; M; 1/20/06-26; N.C. Cherokee; 29/32; S; Son; 258; Yes; Yes; Unallotted

261; Bradley, Arnessa; F; 8/5/07-24; N.C. Cherokee; 29/32; S; Daughter; 259; Yes; Yes; Unallotted

262; Bradley, Dueese; M; 8/29/09-22; N.C. Cherokee; 29/32; S; Son; 260; Yes; Yes; Unallotted

263; Bradley, Shon; M; 6/5/11-20; N.C. Cherokee; 29/32; S; Son; 261; Yes; Yes; Unallotted

264; Bradley, George; M; 10/18/13-18; N.C. Cherokee; 29/32; S; Son; 262; Yes; Yes; Unallotted

265; Bradley, Ellen; F; 11/13/15-16; N.C. Cherokee; 29/32; S; Daughter; 263; Yes; Yes; Unallotted

266; Bradley, Reva; F; 3/9/18-14; N.C. Cherokee; 29/32; S; Daughter; 264; Yes; Yes; Unallotted

267; Bradley, Fred; M; 1/16/20-12; N.C. Cherokee; 29/32; S; Daughter[sic]; 265; Yes; Yes; Unallotted

268; Bradley, Rowena; F; 12/16/22-9; N.C. Cherokee; 29/32; S; Daughter; 266; Yes; Yes; Unallotted

Census of the **Eastern Cherokee** reservation of the **Cherokee, N.C.** jurisdiction, as of **April 1** , 19**32,** taken by **R. L. Spalsbury** , Superintendent.

Key: Number; Surname, Given; Sex; Date of Birth-Age at Last Birthday; Tribe; Degree of Blood; Marital Status; Relationship to Head of Family; Last C. Roll No.; At Jurisdiction Where Enrolled (Yes/No); (If no – Where); Ward (Yes/No); Allotment, Annuity and Identification Numbers (if given).

269;   Bradley, James Walter; M; 7/8/94-37; N.C. Cherokee; 1/4; M; Head; 267; Yes; Yes; Unallotted

270;   Bradley, Eva Calhoun; F; 1/16/98-34; N.C. Cherokee; F; M; Wife; 268; Yes; Yes; Unallotted

271;   Bradley, Helen; F; 7/4/22-9; N.C. Cherokee; 5/8; S; Daughter; 269; Yes; Yes; Unallotted

272;   Bradley, Juanita; F; 7/7/28-3; N.C. Cherokee; 5/8; S; Daughter; 270; Yes; Yes; Unallotted

273;   Bradley, Johnson; M; 5/18/80-51; N.C. Cherokee; 1/2; M; Head; 271; Yes; Yes; Unallotted

274;   Bradley, Ethel; F; 1/2/10-22; N.C. Cherokee; 1/4; S; Daughter; 272; Yes; Yes; Unallotted

275;   Bradley, Antoine R.; M; 12/16/11-20; N.C. Cherokee; 1/4; S; Son; 273; Yes; Yes; Unallotted

276;   Bradley, Margaret Lou; F; 9/28/13-18; N.C. Cherokee; 1/4; S; Daughter; 274; Yes; Yes; Unallotted

277;   Bradley, Ardis Elinor; F; 1/21/15-17; N.C. Cherokee; 1/4; S; Daughter; 275; Yes; Yes; Unallotted

278;   Bradley, Robert F.; M; 9/19/18-13; N.C. Cherokee; 1/4; S; Daughter[sic]; 276; Yes; Yes; Unallotted

279;   Bradley, Joseph; M; 5/28/82-49; N.C. Cherokee; 1/2; M; Head; 277; Yes; Yes; Unallotted

280;   Bradley, Johnson; M; 6/11/09-23; N.C. Cherokee; 1/4; S; Son; 278; Yes; Yes; Unallotted

281;   Bradley, Lucinda; F; 2/24/11-21; N.C. Cherokee; 1/4; S; Daughter; 279; Yes; Yes; Unallotted

282;   Bradley, Lewis; M; 4/11/13-18; N.C. Cherokee; 1/4; S; Daughter[sic]; 280; Yes; Yes; Unallotted

283;   Bradley, Betty; F; 1/15/15-17; N.C. Cherokee; 1/4; S; Daughter; 281; Yes; Yes; Unallotted

284;   Bradley, Raymond; M; 8/19/17-14; N.C. Cherokee; 1/4; S; Son; 282; Yes; Yes; Unallotted

285;   Bradley, Freeman; M; 8/9/20-11; N.C. Cherokee; 1/4; S; Son; 283; Yes; Yes; Unallotted

286;   Bradley, Judson; M; 8/11/02-29; N.C. Cherokee; 1/4; M; Head; 284; Yes; Yes; Unallotted

287;   Bradley (McCoy, Julia), Julia; F; 12/2/03-28; N.C. Cherokee; 1/16; M; Wife; 285; Yes; Yes; Unallotted

288;   Bradley, Wm. Lee; M; 11/11/21-10; N.C. Cherokee; 1/32; S; Son; 286; Yes; Yes; Unallotted

289;   Bradley, Olene G.; F; 5/22/23-8; N.C. Cherokee; 1/32; S; Daughter; 287; Yes; Yes; Unallotted

Census of the **Eastern Cherokee** reservation of the **Cherokee, N.C.** jurisdiction, as of **April 1**, 19**32**, taken by **R. L. Spalsbury**, Superintendent.

Key: Number; Surname, Given; Sex; Date of Birth-Age at Last Birthday; Tribe; Degree of Blood; Marital Status; Relationship to Head of Family; Last C. Roll No.; At Jurisdiction Where Enrolled (Yes/No); (If no – Where); Ward (Yes/No); Allotment, Annuity and Identification Numbers (if given).

290; Bradley (McCoy, Mary), Mary; F; 5/19/01-30; N.C. Cherokee; 1/16; M; Wife; 288; Yes; Yes; Unallotted

291; Bradley, John Winford; M; 10/14/21-11; N.C. Cherokee; 1/32; S; Son; 289; Yes; Yes; Unallotted

292; Bradley, Charles Coolidge; M; 2/2/24-8; N.C. Cherokee; 1/32; S; Daughter[sic]; 290; Yes; Yes; Unallotted

293; Bradley, Irene; F; 9/26/23-8; N.C. Cherokee; 1/4; S; Alone; 291; Yes; Yes; Unallotted

294; Bradley, Morgan; M; 2/15/26-6; N.C. Cherokee; 1/4; S; Brother; 292; Yes; Yes; Unallotted

295; Bradley, Nancy; F; 5/20/74-57; N.C. Cherokee; 1/2; M; Wife; 293; Yes; Yes; Unallotted

296; Bradley, Minda; F; 1/6/06-26; N.C. Cherokee; 1/4; S; Daughter; 294; Yes; Yes; Unallotted

297; Bradley, Etta L.; F; 6/22/12-19; N.C. Cherokee; 1/4; S; Daughter; 296; Yes; Yes; Unallotted

298; Bradley, Jerome; M; 4/16/14-17; N.C. Cherokee; 1/4; S; Son; 297; Yes; Yes; Unallotted

299; Bradley, Luvinia; F; 12/9/16-15; N.C. Cherokee; 1/4; S; Daughter; 298; Yes; Yes; Unallotted

300; Moles, Vera Bradley, Vera W.; F; 1/5/09-23; N.C. Cherokee; 1/4; M; Daughter (married); 299[sic]; Yes; Yes; Unallotted

301; Moles (Bradley), Racheal M.; F; 6/23/31-9/12; N.C. Cherokee; 1/8; S; Grand daughter; ---; Yes; Yes; Unallotted

302; Bradley, Nick; M; 4/13/95-36; N.C. Cherokee; 1/2; M; Head; 299; Yes; Yes; Unallotted

303; Bradley, John R.; M; 3/28/27-5; N.C. Cherokee; 1/4; S; Son; 300; Yes; Yes; Unallotted

304; Bradley, Jarret T.; M; 2/12/29-3; N.C. Cherokee; 1/4; S; Son; 301; Yes; Yes; Unallotted

305; Bradley (Lambert, Pearl), Pearl L.; F; 11/19/98-33; N.C. Cherokee; 1/32; M; Wife; 302; Yes; Yes; Unallotted

306; Bradley, Arizona; F; 10/17/19-12; N.C. Cherokee; 1/64; S; Daughter; 303; Yes; Yes; Unallotted

307; Bradley, Nannie C.; F; 8/23/21-10; N.C. Cherokee; 1/64; S; Daughter; 304; Yes; Yes; Unallotted

308; Bradley, Rachel; F; 7/15/06-26; N.C. Cherokee; 1/4; ~~M~~S; Head; 305; Yes; Yes; Unallotted

309; Bradley, Harold Calvin; M; 11/29/24-7; N.C. Cherokee; 1/16; S; Son; 306; Yes; Yes; Unallotted

Census of the **Eastern Cherokee** reservation of the **Cherokee, N.C.** jurisdiction, as of **April 1**, **1932**, taken by **R. L. Spalsbury**, Superintendent.

Key: Number; Surname, Given; Sex; Date of Birth-Age at Last Birthday; Tribe; Degree of Blood; Marital Status; Relationship to Head of Family; Last C. Roll No.; At Jurisdiction Where Enrolled (Yes/No); (If no – Where); Ward (Yes/No); Allotment, Annuity and Identification Numbers (if given).

310; Bradley, Freda Anna; F; 3/29/28-4; N.C. Cherokee; 7/16; S; Daughter; 307; Yes; Yes; Unallotted

311; Bradley, Roy; M; 6/14/04-27; N.C. Cherokee; 1/4; M; Head; 308; Yes; Yes; Unallotted

312; Bradley, Alice Crowe; F; 6/4/98-33; N.C. Cherokee; 13/32; M; Wife; 309; Yes; Yes; Unallotted

313; Bradley, Elsie; F; 7/25/26-5; N.C. Cherokee; 21/64; S; Daughter; 310; Yes; Yes; Unallotted

314; Bradley, Erma Louise; F; 4/6/29-3; N.C. Cherokee; 21/64; S; Daughter; 311; Yes; Yes; Unallotted

315; Bradley, Sarah; F; 3/26/02-30; N.C. Cherokee; 1/2; S; Head; 312; Yes; Yes; Unallotted

316; Bradley, Thomas; M; 12/21/08-23; N.C. Cherokee; 1/4; S; Head; 313; Yes; Yes; Unallotted

317; Bradley, Wm. Amos; M; 9/21/96-35; N.C. Cherokee; 1/4; M; Head; 314; Yes; Yes; Unallotted

318; Bradley, Sarah Powell; F; 11/7/98-33; N.C. Cherokee; 3/4; M; Wife; 315; Yes; Yes; Unallotted

319; Bradley, Richard; M; 6/10/18-13; N.C. Cherokee; 1/2; S; Son; 316; Yes; Yes; Unallotted

320; Bradley, Albert F.; M; 1/23/23-9; N.C. Cherokee; 1/2; S; Son; 317; Yes; Yes; Unallotted

321; Bradley, Constance; F; 2/17/31-1; N.C. Cherokee; 1/2; S; Daughter; 318; Yes; Yes; Unallotted

322; Brady, Susie Smith; F; 3/1/86-46; N.C. Cherokee; 1/4; M; Wife; 319; Yes; Yes; Unallotted

323; Brady, James Lowen; M; 3/17/10-21; N.C. Cherokee; 3/8; S; Son; 320; Yes; Yes; Unallotted

324; Brady, Samuel; M; 11/12/11-20; N.C. Cherokee; 3/8; S; Son; 321; Yes; Yes; Unallotted

325; Brady, William; M; 11/7/13-18; N.C. Cherokee; 3/8; S; Son; 322; Yes; Yes; Unallotted

326; Brady, Mary T.; F; 9/23/17-14; N.C. Cherokee; 3/8; S; Daughter; 323; Yes; Yes; Unallotted

327; Brady, Floyd; M; 2/18/20-12; N.C. Cherokee; 3/8; S; Son; 324; Yes; Yes; Unallotted

328; Brady, Arthur; M; 1/30/23-9; N.C. Cherokee; 3/8; S; Son; 325; Yes; Yes; Unallotted

329; Brady, Ralph; M; 1/20/26-6; N.C. Cherokee; 3/8; S; Son; 326; Yes; Yes; Unallotted

19

Census of the **Eastern Cherokee** reservation of the **Cherokee, N.C.** jurisdiction, as of **April 1**, **1932**, taken by **R. L. Spalsbury**, Superintendent.

Key: Number; Surname, Given; Sex; Date of Birth-Age at Last Birthday; Tribe; Degree of Blood; Marital Status; Relationship to Head of Family; Last C. Roll No.; At Jurisdiction Where Enrolled (Yes/No); (If no – Where); Ward (Yes/No); Allotment, Annuity and Identification Numbers (if given).

330; Brady, Baby Male; M; 6/26/31-9/12; N.C. Cherokee; 3/8; S; Son; ---; Yes; Yes; Unallotted

331; Breckenridge (Anderson, Cora), Cora O.; F; 7/19/04-27; N.C. Cherokee; 1/16; M; Wife; 327; Yes; Yes; Unallotted

332; Brewster, Linnie L.J.; F; 1890-42; N.C. Cherokee; 1/14; M; Wife; 328; Yes; Yes; Unallotted

333; Brock (Mashburn, Minnie), Minnie M.; F; 6/1/01-30; N.C. Cherokee; 3/32; M; Wife; 329; Yes; Yes; Unallotted

334; Brock, Ruby Lee; F; 9/19/22-10; N.C. Cherokee; 3/64; S; Daughter; 330; Yes; Yes; Unallotted

335; Brown, Jonah; M; 9/5/80-51; N.C. Cherokee; F; M; Head; 331; Yes; Yes; Unallotted

336; Brown, Mollie; F; 1/5/81-51; N.C. Cherokee; F; M; Wife; 332; Yes; Yes; Unallotted

337; Brown, Mark; M; 6/11/10-21; N.C. Cherokee; F; S; Son; 333; Yes; Yes; Unallotted

338; Brown, Lizzie; F; 3/21/12-20; N.C. Cherokee; F; S; Daughter; 334; Yes; Yes; Unallotted

339; Brown, Sam; M; 3/21/15-17; N.C. Cherokee; F; S; Son; 335; Yes; Yes; Unallotted

340; Brown, Lydia; F; 12/17/47-84; N.C. Cherokee; F; Wd; Head; 336; Yes; Yes; Unallotted

341; Brown, Peter; M; 3/3/89-42; N.C. Cherokee; F; Wd.; Head; 337; Yes; Yes; Unallotted

342; Brown, Nora; F; 6/7/17-14; N.C. Cherokee; F; S; Daughter; 338; Yes; Yes; Unallotted

343; Bruce, Arthur; M; 7/21/88-43; N.C. Cherokee; 1/16; M; Head; 339; No; Sweet Gum, Fannin, Ga.; Yes; Unallotted

344; Bruce, Corrie; F; 7/19/14-17; N.C. Cherokee; 1/32; S; Daughter; 340; No; Sweet Gum, Fannin, Ga.; Yes; Unallotted

345; Bruce, Alice; F; 8/11/15-16; N.C. Cherokee; 1/32; S; Daughter; 341; No; Sweet Gum, Fannin, Ga.; Yes; Unallotted

346; Bruce (Raper, Elzie), Elzie R.; F; 4/30/95-37; N.C. Cherokee; 1/32; M; Wife; 342; No; San Angelo, Tom Green, Tex.; Yes; Unallotted

347; Bryant (Garland, Elizabeth), Elizabeth H.G.; F; 3/21/61-71; N.C. Cherokee; 1/8; M; Wife; 343; Yes; Yes; Unallotted

Census of the **Eastern Cherokee** reservation of the **Cherokee, N.C.** jurisdiction, as of **April 1**, 19**32,** taken by **R. L. Spalsbury**, Superintendent.

Key: Number; Surname, Given; Sex; Date of Birth-Age at Last Birthday; Tribe; Degree of Blood; Marital Status; Relationship to Head of Family; Last C. Roll No.; At Jurisdiction Where Enrolled (Yes/No); (If no – Where); Ward (Yes/No); Allotment, Annuity and Identification Numbers (if given).

348; Bryant (Patterson, Ethel), Ethel; F; 12/21/98-34; N.C. Cherokee; 1/32; M; Wife; 344; No; Hemp, Fannin, Ga.; Yes; Unallotted

349; Bryant, Thelma; F; 11/3/17-13[sic]; N.C. Cherokee; 1/64; S; Daughter; 345; No; Hemp, Fannin, Ga.; Yes; Unallotted

350; Bryant, Dennis; M; 2/12/19-13; N.C. Cherokee; 1/64; S; Son; 346; No; Hemp, Fannin, Ga.; Yes; Unallotted

351; Bryant, Edna; F; 4/28/21-10; N.C. Cherokee; 1/64; S; Daughter; 347; No; Hemp, Fannin, Ga.; Yes; Unallotted

352; Bryant, Lillian; F; 1/6/23-9; N.C. Cherokee; 1/64; S; Daughter; 348; No; Hemp, Fannin, Ga.; Yes; Unallotted

353; Bryson (Adams, Martha E.), Martha Edna; F; 2/25/86-46; N.C. Cherokee; 1/32; M; Wife; 349; Yes; Yes; Unallotted

354; Bryson, Fred; M; 2/7/08-24; N.C. Cherokee; 1/64; S; Son; 350; Yes; Yes; Unallotted

355; Bryson, Thelma; M; 8/14/11-22; N.C. Cherokee; 1/64; S; Daughter; 351; Yes; Yes; Unallotted

356; Burgess, Georgia Ann; F; 6/10/69-63; N.C. Cherokee; 1/4; M; Wife; 352; Yes; Yes; Unallotted

357; Burgess, George Alger; M; 10/7/06-26; N.C. Cherokee; 1/8; S; Son; 353; Yes; Yes; Unallotted

358; Burgess, Nellie; F; 6/24/09-22; N.C. Cherokee; 1/8; S; Daughter; 354; Yes; Yes; Unallotted

359; Burgess, Frederic Homer; M; 4/24/12-19; N.C. Cherokee; 1/8; S; Son; 355; Yes; Yes; Unallotted

360; Burgess, Mary C.; F; 1/5/31-1; N.C. Cherokee; 3/16; S; Granddaughter; 356; Yes; Yes; Unallotted

361; Burgess, James; M; 8/6/99-32; N.C. Cherokee; 1/64; S; Head; 357; Yes; Yes; Unallotted

362; Burgess, Martha; F; 10/30/03-28; N.C. Cherokee; 1/64; S; Head; 358; Yes; Yes; Unallotted

363; Burgess, Myrtle; F; 11/19/98-33; N.C. Cherokee; 1/64; M; Wife; 359; Yes; Yes; Unallotted

364; Burgess, Sue; F; 9/21/19-12; N.C. Cherokee; 1/128; S; Daughter; 360; Yes; Yes; Unallotted

365; Burgess, Truman; M; 11/22/21-11; N.C. Cherokee; 1/128; S; Son; 361; Yes; Yes; Unallotted

366; Burgess, Troy Jackson; M; 12/24/23-8; N.C. Cherokee; 1/128; S; Son; 362; Yes; Yes; Unallotted

Census of the **Eastern Cherokee** reservation of the **Cherokee, N.C.** jurisdiction, as of **April 1** , 19**32,** taken by **R. L. Spalsbury** , Superintendent.

Key: Number; Surname, Given; Sex; Date of Birth-Age at Last Birthday; Tribe; Degree of Blood; Marital Status; Relationship to Head of Family; Last C. Roll No.; At Jurisdiction Where Enrolled (Yes/No); (If no – Where); Ward (Yes/No); Allotment, Annuity and Identification Numbers (if given).

367; Burgess, Ollie; F; 12/30/75-56; N.C. Cherokee; 1/32; M; Wife; 363; Yes; Yes; Unallotted

368; Burgess, John; M; 4/3/06-25; N.C. Cherokee; 1/64; S; Son; 364; Yes; Yes; Unallotted

369; Burgess, Arthur; M; 11/16/07-24; N.C. Cherokee; 1/64; S; Son; 365; Yes; Yes; Unallotted

370; Burgess, Winslow; M; 2/4/10-22; N.C. Cherokee; 1/64; S; Son; 366; Yes; Yes; Unallotted

371; Burgess, Rose; F; 3/15/12-20; N.C. Cherokee; 1/64; S; Daughter; 367; Yes; Yes; Unallotted

372; Burgess, Raburn; M; 12/31/14-17; N.C. Cherokee; 1/64; S; Son; 368; Yes; Yes; Unallotted

373; Burgess, Ada; F; 4/11/16-16; N.C. Cherokee; 1/64; S; Daughter; 369; Yes; Yes; Unallotted

374; Burrell (Stiles, Emma), Emma; F; 9/24/96-35; N.C. Cherokee; 1/32; M; Wife; 370; Yes; Yes; Unallotted

375; Busheyhead, Ben; M; 5/14/86-45; N.C. Cherokee; 7/8; M; Head; 371; Yes; Yes; Unallotted

376; Busheyhead, Nancy; F; 12/23/86-45; N.C. Cherokee; 4/4; M; Wife; 372; Yes; Yes; Unallotted

377; Busheyhead, Joel; M; 6/6/11-20; N.C. Cherokee; 15/16; S; Son; 373; Yes; Yes; Unallotted

378; Busheyhead, Robert; M; 10/29/14-17; N.C. Cherokee; 15/16; S; Son; 374; Yes; Yes; Unallotted

379; Butler (Payne, Clara), Clara; F; 7/25/03-29; N.C. Cherokee; 1/64; M; Wife; 375; Yes; Yes; Unallotted

380; Calhoun, Henry; M; 3/6/19-13; N.C. Cherokee; 1/2; S; Alone; 376; Yes; Yes; Unallotted

381; Calhoun, Lawyer; M; 5/7/60-71; N.C. Cherokee; F; Wd; Head; 377; Yes; Yes; Unallotted

382; Calhoun, Sallie Ann; F; 2/15/77-55; N.C. Cherokee; F; Wd; Head; 378; Yes; Yes; Unallotted

383; Calhoun, Lawson; M; 5/27/02-29; N.C. Cherokee; F; S; Son; 379; Yes; Yes; Unallotted

384; Calhoun, Henry; M; 4/25/04-27; N.C. Cherokee; F; S; Son; 380; Yes; Yes; Unallotted

385; Calhoun, Lawyer; M; 4/30/06-25; N.C. Cherokee; F; S; Son; 381; Yes; Yes; Unallotted

Census of the **Eastern Cherokee** reservation of the **Cherokee, N.C.** jurisdiction, as of **April 1**, 19**32**, taken by **R. L. Spalsbury**, Superintendent.

Key: Number; Surname, Given; Sex; Date of Birth-Age at Last Birthday; Tribe; Degree of Blood; Marital Status; Relationship to Head of Family; Last C. Roll No.; At Jurisdiction Where Enrolled (Yes/No); (If no – Where); Ward (Yes/No); Allotment, Annuity and Identification Numbers (if given).

386; Calhoun, Smathers; M; 6/28/12-19; N.C. Cherokee; F; S; Son; 382; Yes; Yes; Unallotted

387; Calhoun, Katie; F; 9/12/15-16; N.C. Cherokee; F; S; Daughter; 383; Yes; Yes; Unallotted

388; Calhoun, Hewitt; M; 5/12/18-13; N.C. Cherokee; F; S; Son; 384; Yes; Yes; Unallotted

389; Camp (Murphy, Isabella), Isabella; F; 1/7/92-40; N.C. Cherokee; 1/8; M; Head (Divorced); 385; No; Murphy, Cherokee, N.C.; Yes; Unallotted

390; Camp, Bettie; F; 12/8/13-18; N.C. Cherokee; 1/16; S; Daughter; 386; No; Murphy, Cherokee, N.C.; Yes; Unallotted

391; Campbell (Lunsford, Callie), Callie; F; 6/12/05-26; N.C. Cherokee; 1/64; M; Wife; 387; Yes; Yes; Unallotted

392; Cannaut, Columbus; M; 12/17/82-49; N.C. Cherokee; F; M; Head; 388; Yes; Yes; Unallotted

393; Cannaut, Maggie; F; 11/17/89-42; N.C. Cherokee; F; Div.; Wife (Divorced); 389; Yes; Yes; Unallotted

394; Cannaut, Addison; M; 9/4/09-22; N.C. Cherokee; F; S; Son; 390; Yes; Yes; Unallotted

395; Cantrell (Payne, Stella), Stella; F; 6/3/08-23; N.C. Cherokee; 1/64; M; Wife; 391; Yes; Yes; Unallotted

396; Cantrell, William; M; 9/23/21-10; N.C. Cherokee; 1/128; S; Son; 392; Yes; Yes; Unallotted

397; Carroll, Newton; M; 2/8/73-59; N.C. Cherokee; 3/16; M; Head; 393; Yes; Yes; Unallotted

398; Carter, Belvia A.L.; F; 12/12/01-30; N.C. Cherokee; 1/32; M; Wife; 394; Yes; Yes; Unallotted

399; Carter, Mabel; F; 12/10/21-10; N.C. Cherokee; 1/64; S; Daughter; 395; Yes; Yes; Unallotted

400; Carter, Wallace; M; 6/12/23-8; N.C. Cherokee; 1/64; S; Son; 396; Yes; Yes; Unallotted

401; Carver (Whitaker, Ada), Ada; F; 8/17/98-33; N.C. Cherokee; 1/32; M; Wife; 397; Yes; Yes; Unallotted

402; Carver, Bernette; F; 8/14/19-12; N.C. Cherokee; 1/64; S; Daughter; 398; Yes; Yes; Unallotted

403; Carver, James; M; 3/21/21-11; N.C. Cherokee; 1/64; S; Son; 399; Yes; Yes; Unallotted

404; Carver, Wayne; M; 4/7/23-9; N.C. Cherokee; 1/64; S; Son; 400; Yes; Yes; Unallotted

Key: Number; Surname, Given; Sex; Date of Birth-Age at Last Birthday; Tribe; Degree of Blood; Marital Status; Relationship to Head of Family; Last C. Roll No.; At Jurisdiction Where Enrolled (Yes/No); (If no – Where); Ward (Yes/No); Allotment, Annuity and Identification Numbers (if given).

405;   Carver (Raper, Hattie), Hattie; F; 7/8/81-50; N.C. Cherokee; 1/16; M; Wife; 401; Yes; Yes; Unallotted

406;   Catolster, Carson J.; M; 4/28/79-52; N.C. Cherokee; F; M; Head; 402; Yes; Yes; Unallotted

407;   Catolster, Josie S.; F; 7/21/92-39; N.C. Cherokee; F; M; Wife; 403; Yes; Yes; Unallotted

408;   Catolster, Johnson; M; 9/28/08-23; N.C. Cherokee; F; S; Son; 404; Yes; Yes; Unallotted

409;   Catolster, David; M; 2/16/11-21; N.C. Cherokee; F; S; Son; 405; Yes; Yes; Unallotted

410;   Catolster, Margaret; F; 12/18/13-18; N.C. Cherokee; F; S; Daughter; 406; Yes; Yes; Unallotted

411;   Catolster, Rebecca; F; 1/12/17-15; N.C. Cherokee; F; S; Daughter; 407; Yes; Yes; Unallotted

412;   Catolster, Benjamin; M; 5/1/19-12; N.C. Cherokee; F; S; Son; 408; Yes; Yes; Unallotted

413;   Catolster, Emma; F; 5/12/24-7; N.C. Cherokee; F; S; Daughter; 409; Yes; Yes; Unallotted

414;   Catolster, Eva Louisa; F; 3/29/28-4; N.C. Cherokee; F; S; Daughter; 410; Yes; Yes; Unallotted

415;   Catolster, Wallace; M; 1/1/78[sic]-56; N.C. Cherokee; F; M; Head; 411; Yes; Yes; Unallotted

416;   Catolster, Elsie Feather; F; 12/24/87-43; N.C. Cherokee; 1/2; M; Wife; 412; Yes; Yes; Unallotted

417;   Catolster, Eliza F.; F; 10/3/13-18; N.C. Cherokee; 3/4; S; Daughter; 413; Yes; Yes; Unallotted

418;   Catolster, Boyd; M; 5/31/16-15; N.C. Cherokee; 3/4; S; Son; 414; Yes; Yes; Unallotted

419;   Catolster, William; M; 6/15/75-56; N.C. Cherokee; F; M; Head; 415; Yes; Yes; Unallotted

420;   Catolster, Sally; F; 7/15/86-45; N.C. Cherokee; 7/8; M; Wife; 416; Yes; Yes; Unallotted

421;   Catolster, Alexander; M; 12/23/05-26; N.C. Cherokee; F; S; Step Son; 417; Yes; Yes; Unallotted

422;   Catolster, Nannie; F; 4/21/07-23; N.C. Cherokee; F; S; Step Dau.; 418; Yes; Yes; Unallotted

423;   Catolster, Guyon; M; 8/18/10-21; N.C. Cherokee; F; S; Step Son; 419; Yes; Yes; Unallotted

424;   Catolster, Lucy; F; 6/12/12-19; N.C. Cherokee; F; S; Step Dau.; 420; Yes; Yes; Unallotted

425;   Catolster, Bessie; F; 3/2/16-15; N.C. Cherokee; 15/16; S; Daughter; 422; Yes; Yes; Unallotted

Census of the **Eastern Cherokee** reservation of the **Cherokee, N.C.** jurisdiction, as of **April 1** , **1932,** taken by **R. L. Spalsbury** , Superintendent.

Key: Number; Surname, Given; Sex; Date of Birth-Age at Last Birthday; Tribe; Degree of Blood; Marital Status; Relationship to Head of Family; Last C. Roll No.; At Jurisdiction Where Enrolled (Yes/No); (If no – Where); Ward (Yes/No); Allotment, Annuity and Identification Numbers (if given).

426; Catolster, Codaskey; M; 3/13/19-13; N.C. Cherokee; 15/16; S; Son; 421; Yes; Yes; Unallotted

427; Catolster, Malinda; F; 12/21/29-2; N.C. Cherokee; 1/4; S; Granddaugh.; 423; Yes; Yes; Unallotted

428; Catt, Benjamin; M; 11/1/62-69; N.C. Cherokee; F; Wd.; Head; 424; Yes; Yes; Unallotted

429; Catt, Jesse; M; 6/6/95-36; N.C. Cherokee; F; S; Head; 425; Yes; Yes; Unallotted

430; Catt, Mary Ellen; F; 8/9/15-16; N.C. Cherokee; 1/2; S; Alone; 426; Yes; Yes; Unallotted

431; Catt, Willie; M; 3/3/84-48; N.C. Cherokee; F; M; Head; 427; Yes; Yes; Unallotted

432; Catt, Sarah P.; F; 1/11/10-22; N.C. Cherokee; 15/16; M; Wife 2nd; 428; Yes; Yes; Unallotted

433; Catt, David; M; 4/18/09-22; N.C. Cherokee; F; S; Son; 429; Yes; Yes; Unallotted

434; Catt, Robert; M; 4/12/11-20; N.C. Cherokee; F; S; Son; 430; Yes; Yes; Unallotted

435; Catt, Paul J.; M; 12/25/15-16; N.C. Cherokee; F; S; Son; 431; Yes; Yes; Unallotted

436; Catt, Boyd; M; 8/22/18-13; N.C. Cherokee; F; S; Son; 432; Yes; Yes; Unallotted

437; Catt, Sarah; F; 1/5/21-11; N.C. Cherokee; F; S; Daughter; 433; Yes; Yes; Unallotted

438; Catt, Alice; F; 10/15/29-2; N.C. Cherokee; 31/32; S; Daughter; 434; Yes; Yes; Unallotted

439; Cearley, Emery L.; M; 8/24/02-29; N.C. Cherokee; 1/16; M; Head; 435; Yes; Yes; Unallotted

440; Cearley (Raper, Lucy), Lucy Emmaline; F; 8/18/79-52; N.C. Cherokee; 1/8; M; Wife; 436; Yes; Yes; Unallotted

441; Cearley, Robert Astor; M; 2/10/05-27; N.C. Cherokee; 1/16; S; Son; 437; Yes; Yes; Unallotted

442; Cearley, John Patrick; M; 8/27/11-20; N.C. Cherokee; 1/16; S; Son; 438; Yes; Yes; Unallotted

443; Cearley, Henry T.; M; 1/31/14-18; N.C. Cherokee; 1/16; S; Son; 439; Yes; Yes; Unallotted

444; Cearley, Jetter C.; M; 4/13/16-15; N.C. Cherokee; 1/16; S; Son; 440; Yes; Yes; Unallotted

25

Census of the **Eastern Cherokee** reservation of the **Cherokee, N.C.** jurisdiction, as of **April 1**, 19**32,** taken by **R. L. Spalsbury**, Superintendent.

Key: Number; Surname, Given; Sex; Date of Birth-Age at Last Birthday; Tribe; Degree of Blood; Marital Status; Relationship to Head of Family; Last C. Roll No.; At Jurisdiction Where Enrolled (Yes/No); (If no – Where); Ward (Yes/No); Allotment, Annuity and Identification Numbers (if given).

445;   Cearley, Charlie E.; M; 6/11/20-11; N.C. Cherokee; 1/16; S; Son; 441; Yes; Yes; Unallotted

446;   Cearley, William L.; M; 1/13/900[sic]-31; N.C. Cherokee; 1/16; M; Head; 442; Yes; Yes; Unallotted

447;   Cearley, Nebraska T.; F; 5/21/01-30; N.C. Cherokee; 1/16; M; Wife; 443; Yes; Yes; Unallotted

448;   Chatmon (Robinson, Martha), Martha; F; 9/27/75-56; N.C. Cherokee; 1/4; M; Wife; 444; No; Adairsville, Bartow, Ga.; Yes; Unallotted

449;   Chavlas, Minda Reed; F; 1/25/94-38; N.C. Cherokee; 7/8; M; Wife; 445; Yes; Yes; Unallotted

450;   Chekelelee, Andy; M; 12/16/84-47; N.C. Cherokee; F; M; Head; 446; Yes; Yes; Unallotted

451;   Chekelelee, Betty Catt; F; 8/28/87-44; N.C. Cherokee; F; M; Head[sic]; 447; Yes; Yes; Unallotted

452;   Chekelelee, Bessie; F; 4/13/10-21; N.C. Cherokee; F; S; Daughter; 448; Yes; Yes; Unallotted

453;   Chekelelee, Bertha; F; 4/27/12-19; N.C. Cherokee; F; S; Daughter; 449; Yes; Yes; Unallotted

454;   Chekelelee, Lilly; F; 11/21/14-17; N.C. Cherokee; F; S; Daughter; 450; Yes; Yes; Unallotted

455;   Chekelelee, Emma May; F; 9/30/20-11; N.C. Cherokee; F; S; Daughter; 451; Yes; Yes; Unallotted

456;   Chekelelee, Simon; M; 1/15/99-32; N.C. Cherokee; F; M; Head; 452; Yes; Yes; Unallotted

457;   Chekelelee, Lizzie Smoker; F; 5/3/04-27; N.C. Cherokee; F; M; Wife; 453; Yes; Yes; Unallotted

458;   Chekelelee, Ed; M; 5/21/29-2; N.C. Cherokee; F; S; Son; ---; Yes; Yes; Unallotted

459;   Chekelelee, Boyd; M; 7/16/31-8/12; N.C. Cherokee; F; S; Son; ---; Yes; Yes; Unallotted

460;   Chekelelee, Stone; M; 1/5/72-60; N.C. Cherokee; F; Wd.; Head; 454; Yes; Yes; Unallotted

461;   Chekelelee, Tom; M; 8/16/73-58; N.C. Cherokee; F; M; Head; 455; Yes; Yes; Unallotted

462;   Childers (Lambert, Lula), Lula Frances; F; 5/10/82-49; N.C. Cherokee; 1/16; M; Wife; 456; Yes; Yes; Unallotted

Census of the **Eastern Cherokee** reservation of the **Cherokee, N.C.** jurisdiction, as of **April 1** , 19**32,** taken by **R. L. Spalsbury** , Superintendent.

Key: Number; Surname, Given; Sex; Date of Birth-Age at Last Birthday; Tribe; Degree of Blood; Marital Status; Relationship to Head of Family; Last C. Roll No.; At Jurisdiction Where Enrolled (Yes/No); (If no – Where); Ward (Yes/No); Allotment, Annuity and Identification Numbers (if given).

463; Childers, Robert M.; M; 5/27/05-26; N.C. Cherokee; 1/32; S; Son; 457; Yes; Yes; Unallotted

464; Childers, Stella Lovada; F; 12/7/08-23; N.C. Cherokee; 1/32; S; Daughter; 458; Yes; Yes; Unallotted

465; Childers, Maud M.; F; 3/9/11-21; N.C. Cherokee; 1/32; S; Daughter; 459; Yes; Yes; Unallotted

466; Childers, Clifford E.; M; 6/18/13-18; N.C. Cherokee; 1/32; S; Son; 460; Yes; Yes; Unallotted

467; Childers, Russell Daniel; M; 3/3/17-15; N.C. Cherokee; 1/32; S; Son; 461; Yes; Yes; Unallotted

468; Childers, Julius W.; M; 4/13/20-11; N.C. Cherokee; 1/32; S; Son; 462; Yes; Yes; Unallotted

469; Chiltoskie, Wahdih; M; 6/6/99-32; N.C. Cherokee; 15/16; M; Head; 463; Yes; Yes; Unallotted

470; Chiltoskie, Tennie Smith; F; 4/12/05-26; N.C. Cherokee; 7/16; M; Wife; 464; Yes; Yes; Unallotted

471; Chiltoskie, Lavina May; F; 4/14/28-4; N.C. Cherokee; 22/32; S; Daughter; 465; Yes; Yes; Unallotted

472; Chiltoskie, Charlotte; F; 10/19/68-63; N.C. Cherokee; 7/8; Wd.; Head; 466; Yes; Yes; Unallotted

473; Chiltoskie, Goingback; M; 4/9/07-24; N.C. Cherokee; 15/16; S; Son; 467; Yes; Yes; Unallotted

474; Clark (Raper, Ivy Ann), Ivy Ann; F; 12/17/97-34; N.C. Cherokee; 1/16; M; Wife; 468; Yes; Yes; Unallotted

475; Clark, Paul; M; 7/4/15-16; N.C. Cherokee; 1/32; S; Son; 469; Yes; Yes; Unallotted

476; Clark, Lottie A. Smith; F; 2/13/69-63; N.C. Cherokee; 3/8; M; Wife; 470; Yes; Yes; Unallotted

477; Clay, Timpson; M; 12/17/73-58; N.C. Cherokee; F; Wd.; Head; 471; Yes; Yes; Unallotted

478; Climbingbear, Deleskie; M; 12/12/75-56; N.C. Cherokee; F; M; Head; 472; Yes; Yes; Unallotted

479; Climbingbear, Nancy Tooni; F; 3/22/77-55; N.C. Cherokee; F; M; Wife; 473; Yes; Yes; Unallotted

480; Climbingbear, Ollie; F; 10/13/12-19; N.C. Cherokee; F; S; Daughter; 474; Yes; Yes; Unallotted

481; Climbingbear, Henderson; M; 10/19/22-9; N.C. Cherokee; F; S; Son; 475; Yes; Yes; Unallotted

Census of the **Eastern Cherokee** reservation of the **Cherokee, N.C.** jurisdiction, as of **April 1** , 19**32,** taken by **R. L. Spalsbury** , Superintendent.

Key: Number; Surname, Given; Sex; Date of Birth-Age at Last Birthday; Tribe; Degree of Blood; Marital Status; Relationship to Head of Family; Last C. Roll No.; At Jurisdiction Where Enrolled (Yes/No); (If no – Where); Ward (Yes/No); Allotment, Annuity and Identification Numbers (if given).

482; Climbingbear, Ollie; F; 6/17/53-78; N.C. Cherokee; F; Wd.; Head; 476; Yes; Yes; Unallotted

483; Coffey (Adams, Ethel), Ethel; F; 3/23/90-42; N.C. Cherokee; 1/32; M; Wife; 477; Yes; Yes; Unallotted

484; Coffey, Stella; F; 1/24/12-20; N.C. Cherokee; 1/64; S; Daughter; 478; Yes; Yes; Unallotted

485; Coffey, Blanche; F; 4/20/15-16; N.C. Cherokee; 1/64; S; Daughter; 479; Yes; Yes; Unallotted

486; Coffey, John Lee; M; 10/19/17-14; N.C. Cherokee; 1/64; S; Son; 480; Yes; Yes; Unallotted

487; Coffey, Clyde; M; 3/3/20-12; N.C. Cherokee; 1/64; S; Son; 481; Yes; Yes; Unallotted

488; Cole, Alvah; M; 9/10/13-18; N.C. Cherokee; 1/16; S; Son; 482; No; Culberson, Cherokee, N.C.; Yes; Unallotted

489; Cole, George E.; M; 2/23/91-41; N.C. Cherokee; 1/8; S; Head; 483; Yes; Yes; Unallotted

490; Cole, John; M; 1/22/24-28; N.C. Cherokee; 1/16; M; Head; 484; Yes; Yes; Unallotted

491; Cole, Robert T.; M; 6/17/86-45; N.C. Cherokee; 1/8; M; Head; 485; No; P.O. 1420 E. Airline St. Gastonia, Gaston, N.C.; Yes; Unallotted

492; Cole, Reed; M; 1/12/13-19; N.C. Cherokee; 1/16; S; Son; 486; No; P.O. 1420 E. Airline St. Gastonia, Gaston, N.C.; Yes; Unallotted

493; Cole, Grace; F; 1/22/15-17; N.C. Cherokee; 1/16; S; Daughter; 487; No; P.O. 1420 E. Airline St. Gastonia, Gaston, N.C.; Yes; Unallotted

494; Cole, Cora; F; 4/10/17-14; N.C. Cherokee; 1/16; S; Daughter; 488; No; P.O. 1420 E. Airline St. Gastonia, Gaston, N.C.; Yes; Unallotted

495; Cole, Beulah; F; 2/14/19-13; N.C. Cherokee; 1/16; S; Daughter; 489; No; P.O. 1420 E. Airline St. Gastonia, Gaston, N.C.; Yes; Unallotted

496; Cole, Wm. Olis; M; 1/9/22-10; N.C. Cherokee; 1/16; S; Son; 490; No; P.O. 1420 E. Airline St. Gastonia, Gaston, N.C.; Yes; Unallotted

497; Cole, Walter; M; 5/24/98-33; N.C. Cherokee; 1/16; M; Head; 491; No; Culberson, Cherokee, N.C.; Yes; Unallotted

498; Cole, Howard; M; 12/12/20-11; N.C. Cherokee; 1/32; S; Son; 492; No; Culberson, Cherokee, N.C.; Yes; Unallotted

499; Cole, Hazel; F; 9/4/22-9; N.C. Cherokee; 1/32; S; Daughter; 493; No; Culberson, Cherokee, N.C.; Yes; Unallotted

500; Cole, William A.; M; 6/17/79-52; N.C. Cherokee; 1/8; M; Head; 494; No; White, Bartow, Ga.; Yes; Unallotted

Census of the **Eastern Cherokee** reservation of the **Cherokee, N.C.** jurisdiction, as of **April 1** , **1932,** taken by **R. L. Spalsbury** , Superintendent.

Key: Number; Surname, Given; Sex; Date of Birth-Age at Last Birthday; Tribe; Degree of Blood; Marital Status; Relationship to Head of Family; Last C. Roll No.; At Jurisdiction Where Enrolled (Yes/No); (If no – Where); Ward (Yes/No); Allotment, Annuity and Identification Numbers (if given).

501; Cole, Arley; M; 6/9/05-26; N.C. Cherokee; 1/16; S; Son; 495; No; White, Bartow, Ga.; Yes; Unallotted

502; Cole, Hollie; M; 1/26/07-25; N.C. Cherokee; 1/16; S; Son; 496; No; White, Bartow, Ga.; Yes; Unallotted

503; Cole, Ollie; F; 9/25/09-22; N.C. Cherokee; 1/16; S; Daughter; 497; No; White, Bartow, Ga.; Yes; Unallotted

504; Cole, Irene; F; 3/21/14-18; N.C. Cherokee; 1/16; S; Daughter; 498; No; White, Bartow, Ga.; Yes; Unallotted

505; Cole, Remus; M; 12/18/17-14; N.C. Cherokee; 1/16; S; Son; 499; No; White, Bartow, Ga.; Yes; Unallotted

506; Cole, Ruby; F; 3/1/19-13; N.C. Cherokee; 1/16; S; Daughter; 500; No; White, Bartow, Ga.; Yes; Unallotted

507; Cole, Edward; M; 6/26/21-10; N.C. Cherokee; 1/16; S; Son; 501; No; White, Bartow, Ga.; Yes; Unallotted

508; Coleman, Mae Timpson; F; 1/24/93-39; N.C. Cherokee; 3/16; Div; Head; 502; Yes; Yes; Unallotted

509; Coleman, Ida E.; F; 7/11/13-18; N.C. Cherokee; 3/32; S; Daughter; 503; Yes; Yes; Unallotted

510; Coleman, Bailey B.; M; 12/18/16-15; N.C. Cherokee; 3/32; S; Son; 504; Yes; Yes; Unallotted

511; Conley, Jennie Lossie; F; 12/22/69-62; N.C. Cherokee; F; Wd.; Head; 505; Yes; Yes; Unallotted

512; Conley, John Jr.; M; 10/14/90-41; N.C. Cherokee; F; M; Head; 506; Yes; Yes; Unallotted

513; Conley, Sallie S.; F; 7/21/01-30; N.C. Cherokee; 7/8; M; Wife; 507; Yes; Yes; Unallotted

514; Conley, Elister; F; 6/29/27-4; N.C. Cherokee; 15/16; S; Daughter; 508; Yes; Yes; Unallotted

515; Conley, Selma; F; 4/21/30-1; N.C. Cherokee; 15/16; S; Daughter; 509; Yes; Yes; Unallotted

516; Conley, Richard; M; 2/28/32-1/12; N.C. Cherokee; 15/16; S; Son; ---; Yes; Yes; Unallotted

517; Conley, Luke; M; 2/9/96-35; N.C. Cherokee; F; S; Head; 510; Yes; Yes; Unallotted

518; Conseen, Annie; F; 7/13/12-19; N.C. Cherokee; F; S; Head; 511; Yes; Yes; Unallotted

519; Conseen, Mark; M; 4/23/30-1; N.C. Cherokee; 1/2; S; Son (Illeg.); 512; Yes; Yes; Unallotted

520; Conseen, George; M; 4/23/30-1; N.C. Cherokee; 1/2; S; Son (Illeg.); 513; Yes; Yes; Unallotted

29

Census of the **Eastern Cherokee** reservation of the **Cherokee, N.C.** jurisdiction, as of **April 1** , 19**32**, taken by **R. L. Spalsbury** , Superintendent.

Key: Number; Surname, Given; Sex; Date of Birth-Age at Last Birthday; Tribe; Degree of Blood; Marital Status; Relationship to Head of Family; Last C. Roll No.; At Jurisdiction Where Enrolled (Yes/No); (If no – Where); Ward (Yes/No); Allotment, Annuity and Identification Numbers (if given).

521;   Conseen, Brest; M; 7/15/61-70; N.C. Cherokee; F; Wd.; Head; 514; Yes; Yes; Unallotted

522;   Conseen, Buck; M; 5/14/06-25; N.C. Cherokee; F; M; Head; 515; Yes; Yes; Unallotted

523;   Conseen, Dinah Queen; F; 6/17/09-22; N.C. Cherokee; 5/8; M; Wife; 516; Yes; Yes; Unallotted

524;   Conseen, Eul[sic] Eliz.; F; 12/26/24-7; N.C. Cherokee; 13/16; S; Daughter; 517; Yes; Yes; Unallotted

525;   Conseen, James; M; 6/9/88-43; N.C. Cherokee; F; M; Head; 518; Yes; Yes; Unallotted

526;   Conseen, Carolina T.; F; 8/22/94-37; N.C. Cherokee; F; M; Wife (2nd); 519; Yes; Yes; Unallotted

527;   Conseen, Lucy Ann; F; 4/24/17-14; N.C. Cherokee; F; S; Daughter; 520; Yes; Yes; Unallotted

528;   Conseen, Emily; F; 4/7/25-7; N.C. Cherokee; F; S; Daughter; 521; Yes; Yes; Unallotted

529;   Conseen, Adam; M; 3/12/27-5; N.C. Cherokee; F; S; Son; 522; Yes; Yes; Unallotted

530;   Conseen, Nancy; F; 8/12/29-2; N.C. Cherokee; F; S; Daughter; 523; Yes; Yes; Unallotted

531;   Conseen, Erwin; M; 9/6/31-6/12; N.C. Cherokee; F; S; Son; ---; Yes; Yes; Unallotted

532;   Conseen, Peter; M; 8/15/79-52; N.C. Cherokee; F; M; Head; 524; Yes; Yes; Unallotted

533;   Conseen, Nancy; F; 4/15/77-54; N.C. Cherokee; F; M; Wife; 525; Yes; Yes; Unallotted

534;   Conseen, Harry; M; 11/20/04-27; N.C. Cherokee; F; S; Son; 526; Yes; Yes; Unallotted

535;   Conseen, Joe (Job); M; 10/30/06-25; N.C. Cherokee; F; S; Son; 527; Yes; Yes; Unallotted

536;   Conseen, Ida; F; 7/27/08-23; N.C. Cherokee; F; S; Daughter; 528; Yes; Yes; Unallotted

537;   Conseen, Nessie; F; 7/22/12-19; N.C. Cherokee; F; S; Daughter; 529; Yes; Yes; Unallotted

538;   Conseen, Amanda; F; 5/22/19-12; N.C. Cherokee; F; S; Daughter; 530; Yes; Yes; Unallotted

539;   Conseen, Anna; F; 7/19/21-10; N.C. Cherokee; F; S; Daughter; 531; Yes; Yes; Unallotted

540;   Conseen, Thompson; M; 5/8/88-43; N.C. Cherokee; F; M; Head; 532; Yes; Yes; Unallotted

Census of the **Eastern Cherokee** reservation of the **Cherokee, N.C.** jurisdiction, as of **April 1** , **1932,** taken by **R. L. Spalsbury** , Superintendent.

Key: Number; Surname, Given; Sex; Date of Birth-Age at Last Birthday; Tribe; Degree of Blood; Marital Status; Relationship to Head of Family; Last C. Roll No.; At Jurisdiction Where Enrolled (Yes/No); (If no – Where); Ward (Yes/No); Allotment, Annuity and Identification Numbers (if given).

541; Conseen, Irene Arch; F; 12/17/74-57; N.C. Cherokee; F; M; Wife; 533; Yes; Yes; Unallotted

542; Conseen, Willie; M; 6/28/99-32; N.C. Cherokee; F; S; Head; 534; Yes; Yes; Unallotted

543; Cook (Raper, Jessie L.), Jessie Leora; F; 14/13/91-40; N.C. Cherokee; 1/16; M; Wife; 535; No; Culberson, Cherokee, N.C.; Yes; Unallotted

544; Cook, Vernie Lee; F; 5/7/09-22; N.C. Cherokee; 1/32; S; Daughter; 536; No; Culberson, Cherokee, N.C.; Yes; Unallotted

545; Cook, Inez G.; F; 2/24/11-21; N.C. Cherokee; 1/32; S; Daughter; 537; No; Culberson, Cherokee, N.C.; Yes; Unallotted

546; Cook, Randall E.; M; 1/13/13-19; N.C. Cherokee; 1/32; S; Son; 538; No; Culberson, Cherokee, N.C.; Yes; Unallotted

547; Cook, Arvel C.; M; 1/11/15-17; N.C. Cherokee; 1/32; S; Son; 539; No; Culberson, Cherokee, N.C.; Yes; Unallotted

548; Cook, Leona Ruby; F; 2/23/17-15; N.C. Cherokee; 1/32; S; Daughter; 540; No; Culberson, Cherokee, N.C.; Yes; Unallotted

549; Cook, Rosie May; F; 1/19/19-12; N.C. Cherokee; 1/32; S; Daughter; 541; No; Culberson, Cherokee, N.C.; Yes; Unallotted

550; Cooper, Arnold E.; M; 9/7/93-38; N.C. Cherokee; 1/16; M; Head; 542; Yes; Yes; Unallotted

551; Cooper, Jessie; F; 6/14/22-9; N.C. Cherokee; 1/32; S; Daughter; 543; Yes; Yes; Unallotted

552; Cooper, Ida Lee; F; 10/19/23-8; N.C. Cherokee; 1/32; S; Daughter; 544; Yes; Yes; Unallotted

553; Cooper, Curtis; M; 5/20/95-35; N.C. Cherokee; 1/16; M; Head; 545; Yes; Yes; Unallotted

554; Cooper, Mack; M; 3/11/80-52; N.C. Cherokee; 1/32; M; Head; 546; Yes; Yes; Unallotted

555; Cooper, Catherine L.; F; 9/4/05-26; N.C. Cherokee; 1/64; S; Daughter; 547; Yes; Yes; Unallotted

556; Cooper, Stacy Jane; F; 12/12/67-64; N.C. Cherokee; 1/8; M; Wife; 548; Yes; Yes; Unallotted

557; Cooper, Mary Joe; F; 7/4/10-21; N.C. Cherokee; 1/16; S; Daughter; 549; Yes; Yes; Unallotted

558; Cornsilk, Annie; F; 1/5/59-73; N.C. Cherokee; F; Wd; Head; 550; Yes; Yes; Unallotted

Census of the **Eastern Cherokee** reservation of the **Cherokee, N.C.** jurisdiction, as of **April 1** , 1932, taken by **R. L. Spalsbury** , Superintendent.

Key: Number; Surname, Given; Sex; Date of Birth-Age at Last Birthday; Tribe; Degree of Blood; Marital Status; Relationship to Head of Family; Last C. Roll No.; At Jurisdiction Where Enrolled (Yes/No); (If no – Where); Ward (Yes/No); Allotment, Annuity and Identification Numbers (if given).

559; Cornsilk, Lorenzo D.; M; 1/11/80-52; N.C. Cherokee; F; M; Head; 551; Yes; Yes; Unallotted

560; Cornsilk, Nancy; F; 11/10/82-49; N.C. Cherokee; F; M; Wife; 552; Yes; Yes; Unallotted

561; Cornsilk, Woodie; F; 11/9/09-22; N.C. Cherokee; F; S; Daughter; 553; Yes; Yes; Unallotted

562; Cornsilk, Emma; F; 11/7/11-20; N.C. Cherokee; F; S; Daughter; 554; Yes; Yes; Unallotted

563; Cornsilk, Jacob; M; 3/5/14-18; N.C. Cherokee; F; S; Son; 555; Yes; Yes; Unallotted

564; Craig, Elvira; F; 6/2/97-34; N.C. Cherokee; 1/8; M; Wife; 556; Yes; Yes; Unallotted

565; Craig, Robert Lee; M; 1/9/16-16; N.C. Cherokee; 1/8; S; Son; 557; Yes; Yes; Unallotted

566; Craig, Winona J.; F; 4/26/17-14; N.C. Cherokee; 1/8; S; Daughter; 558; Yes; Yes; Unallotted

567; Craig, Wm. T.; M; 3/2/19-13; N.C. Cherokee; 1/16; S; Son; 559; Yes; Yes; Unallotted

568; Craig, Charles E.; M; 8/31/21-10; N.C. Cherokee; 1/16; S; Son; 560; Yes; Yes; Unallotted

569; Craig, Naomi K.; F; 5/12/25-6; N.C. Cherokee; 1/16; S; Daughter; 561; Yes; Yes; Unallotted

570; Craig (Lambert, Georgia M.), Georgia M.; F; 12/28/04-27; N.C. Cherokee; 1/32; M; Wife; 562; Yes; Yes; Unallotted

571; Craig, Gladys; F; 9/4/20-11; N.C. Cherokee; 1/64; S; Daughter; 563; Yes; Yes; Unallotted

572; Craig, Garnalee; M; 2/9/23-9; N.C. Cherokee; 1/64; S; Son; 564; Yes; Yes; Unallotted

573; Craig, Robert Donley; M; 4/12/05-26; N.C. Cherokee; 1/16; M; Head; 565; Yes; Yes; Unallotted

574; Craig, Bertha A.B.; F; 1/1/10-22; N.C. Cherokee; 1/4; M; Wife; 566; Yes; Yes; Unallotted

575; Craig, Bettie Ann; F; 6/23/29-2; N.C. Cherokee; 3/16; S; Daughter; 567; Yes; Yes; Unallotted

576; Craig, Jean Donley; F; 5/12/31-10/12; N.C. Cherokee; 3/16; S; Daughter; 5--; Yes; Yes; Unallotted

577; Craig, William W.; M; 8/20/86-45; N.C. Cherokee; 1/8; M; Head; 568; Yes; Yes; Unallotted

578; Craig, Lillie V.; F; 11/18/14-17; N.C. Cherokee; 1/16; S; Daughter; 569; Yes; Yes; Unallotted

Census of the **Eastern Cherokee** reservation of the **Cherokee, N.C.** jurisdiction, as of **April 1**, 19**32,** taken by **R. L. Spalsbury**, Superintendent.

Key: Number; Surname, Given; Sex; Date of Birth-Age at Last Birthday; Tribe; Degree of Blood; Marital Status; Relationship to Head of Family; Last C. Roll No.; At Jurisdiction Where Enrolled (Yes/No); (If no – Where); Ward (Yes/No); Allotment, Annuity and Identification Numbers (if given).

579; Crawford, Oma; F; 6/10/16-15; N.C. Cherokee; 1/64; S; Alone; 570; Yes; Yes; Unallotted

580; Crawford, Fred; M; 4/17/18-13; N.C. Cherokee; 1/64; S; Brother; 571; Yes; Yes; Unallotted

581; Cromwell, Margaret P.; F; 7/12/44-87; N.C. Cherokee; 1/16; Wd.; Head; 572; Yes; Yes; Unallotted

582; Crooks (Meroney, Bessie), Bessie M.; F; 3/4/81-51; N.C. Cherokee; 1/8; M; Wife; 573; Yes; Yes; Unallotted

583; Crowe, Aquishoe; M; 12/18/88-43; N.C. Cherokee; 7/8; M; Head; 574; Yes; Yes; Unallotted

584; Crowe, Nannie; F; 12/18/84-47; N.C. Cherokee; 7/8; M; Wife; 575; Yes; Yes; Unallotted

585; Crowe, Enoch; M; 5/10/17-14; N.C. Cherokee; 7/8; S; Son; 576; Yes; Yes; Unallotted

586; Crowe, Boyd; M; 2/7/93-35; N.C. Cherokee; 7/8; M; Head; 577; Yes; Yes; Unallotted

587; Crowe, David; M; 6/26/84-47; N.C. Cherokee; 3/4; M; Head; 578; Yes; Yes; Unallotted

588; Crowe, Sallie; F; 1/7/87-45; N.C. Cherokee; 4/4; M; Wife; 579; Yes; Yes; Unallotted

589; Crowe, Rachel; F; 11/24/07-24; N.C. Cherokee; 7/8; S; Daughter; 580; Yes; Yes; Unallotted

590; Crowe, Sevier; M; 9/17/14-17; N.C. Cherokee; 7/8; S; Son; 581; Yes; Yes; Unallotted

591; Crowe, Elnora; F; 2/3/15-17; N.C. Cherokee; 7/8; S; Daughter; 582; Yes; Yes; Unallotted

592; Crowe, Luzene; F; 1/13/17-15; N.C. Cherokee; 7/8; S; Daughter; 583; Yes; Yes; Unallotted

593; Crowe, Nellie; F; 2/29/20-12; N.C. Cherokee; 7/8; S; Daughter; 584; Yes; Yes; Unallotted

594; Crowe, John Henry; M; 8/17/22-9; N.C. Cherokee; 7/8; S; Son; 585; Yes; Yes; Unallotted

595; Crowe, Dora Crow; F; 7/30/28-3; N.C. Cherokee; 7/8; S; Daughter; 586; Yes; Yes; Unallotted

596; Crowe, John; M; 12/18/82-49; N.C. Cherokee; 3/4; M; Head; 587; Yes; Yes; Unallotted

597; Crowe, Mary; F; 12/24/84-47; N.C. Cherokee; 4/4; M; Wife; 588; Yes; Yes; Unallotted

Census of the **Eastern Cherokee** reservation of the **Cherokee, N.C.** jurisdiction, as of **April 1** , 1**932,** taken by **R. L. Spalsbury** , Superintendent.

Key: Number; Surname, Given; Sex; Date of Birth-Age at Last Birthday; Tribe; Degree of Blood; Marital Status; Relationship to Head of Family; Last C. Roll No.; At Jurisdiction Where Enrolled (Yes/No); (If no – Where); Ward (Yes/No); Allotment, Annuity and Identification Numbers (if given).

598; Crowe, Callie; F; 5/26/04-27; N.C. Cherokee; 7/8; S; Daughter; 589; Yes; Yes; Unallotted

599; Crowe, Lucy; F; 4/18/11-20; N.C. Cherokee; 7/8; S; Daughter; 590; Yes; Yes; Unallotted

600; Crowe, Iva; F; 6/26/13-18; N.C. Cherokee; 7/8; S; Daughter; 591; Yes; Yes; Unallotted

601; Crowe, Leuna; F; 4/30/16-15; N.C. Cherokee; 7/8; S; Daughter; 592; Yes; Yes; Unallotted

602; Crowe, Betty; F; 6/23/18-13; N.C. Cherokee; 7/8; S; Daughter; 593; Yes; Yes; Unallotted

603; Crowe, Charles E.; M; 7/10/25-6; N.C. Cherokee; 7/8; S; Son; 594; Yes; Yes; Unallotted

604; Crowe, Albert; M; 6/28/06-25; N.C. Cherokee; 7/8; Wd.; Head; 595; Yes; Yes; Unallotted

605; Hornbuckle, Alberta; F; 5/16/26-5; N.C. Cherokee; 1/16; S; Daughter (Illeg.); 596; Yes; Yes; Unallotted

606; Crowe, John Wesley; M; 2/8/89-43; N.C. Cherokee; 1/2; M; Head; 597; Yes; Yes; Unallotted

607; Crowe, Mollie W.E.; F; 8/6/78-53; N.C. Cherokee; 3/4; M; Wife; 598; Yes; Yes; Unallotted

608; Crowe, Joseph; M; 3/2/12-20; N.C. Cherokee; 5/8; S; Son; 599; Yes; Yes; Unallotted

609; Crowe, James D.; M; 6/11/14-17; N.C. Cherokee; 5/8; S; Son; 600; Yes; Yes; Unallotted

610; Crowe, John A.; M; 10/7/17-14; N.C. Cherokee; 5/8; S; Son; 601; Yes; Yes; Unallotted

611; Crowe, E. Thelma; F; 10/7/17-14; N.C. Cherokee; 5/8; S; Daughter; 602; Yes; Yes; Unallotted

612; Crowe, Warren H.; M; 11/8/20-11; N.C. Cherokee; 5/8; S; Son; 603; Yes; Yes; Unallotted

613; Crowe, Joseph; M; 3/8/65-67; N.C. Cherokee; 3/4; Wd.; Head; 604; Yes; Yes; Unallotted

614; Crowe, Luther; M; 4/18/98-33; N.C. Cherokee; 5/16; S; Head; 605; Yes; Yes; Unallotted

615; Crowe, Ossie; M; 5/29/82-49; N.C. Cherokee; 7/8; M; Head; 606; Yes; Yes; Unallotted

616; Crowe, Martha; F; 7/24/89-42; N.C. Cherokee; 4/4; M; Wife; 607; Yes; Yes; Unallotted

617; Crowe, Dinah; F; 9/23/13-18; N.C. Cherokee; 15/16; S; Daughter; 608; Yes; Yes; Unallotted

Census of the **Eastern Cherokee** reservation of the **Cherokee, N.C.** jurisdiction, as of **April 1**, **1932**, taken by **R. L. Spalsbury**, Superintendent.

Key: Number; Surname, Given; Sex; Date of Birth-Age at Last Birthday; Tribe; Degree of Blood; Marital Status; Relationship to Head of Family; Last C. Roll No.; At Jurisdiction Where Enrolled (Yes/No); (If no – Where); Ward (Yes/No); Allotment, Annuity and Identification Numbers (if given).

618; Crowe, Stacy; F; 1/2/16-16; N.C. Cherokee; 15/16; S; Daughter; 609; Yes; Yes; Unallotted

619; Crowe, Katie; F; 10/12/20-11; N.C. Cherokee; 15/16; S; Daughter; 610; Yes; Yes; Unallotted

620; Crowe, Guyon; M; 3/31/23-9; N.C. Cherokee; 15/16; S; Son; 611; Yes; Yes; Unallotted

621; Crowe, John Dobson; M; 10/9/27-3; N.C. Cherokee; 15/16; S; Son; 612; Yes; Yes; Unallotted

622; Crowe, Robert; M; 12/25/93-38; N.C. Cherokee; 15/16; M; Head; 613; Yes; Yes; Unallotted

623; Crowe, Samuel; M; 9/26/05-26; N.C. Cherokee; 7/8; M; Head; 614; Yes; Yes; Unallotted

624; Crowe, Josephine L.; F; 9/26/09-22; N.C. Cherokee; 3/32; M; Wife; 615; Yes; Yes; Unallotted

625; Crowe, Alyne; F; 10/9/27-4; N.C. Cherokee; 31/64; S; Daughter; 616; Yes; Yes; Unallotted

626; Crowe, Ann Lee; F; 3/21/31-1; N.C. Cherokee; 17/32; S; Daughter; 617; Yes; Yes; Unallotted

627; Crowe, Sevier; M; 12/18/60-71; N.C. Cherokee; 5/8; M; Head; 618; Yes; Yes; Unallotted

628; Crowe, Nancy S.; F; 12/24/51-80; N.C. Cherokee; 4/4; M; Wife; 619; Yes; Yes; Unallotted

629; Crowe, Ute; M; 6/18/87-44; N.C. Cherokee; 15/16; M; Head; 620; Yes; Yes; Unallotted

630; Crowe, Sallie S.; F; 5/24/03-28; N.C. Cherokee; 4/4; M; Wife; 621; Yes; Yes; Unallotted

631; Crowe, William; M; 4/24/21-10; N.C. Cherokee; 31/32; S; Son; 622; Yes; Yes; Unallotted

632; Crowe, Robert Henry; M; 7/24/14-17; N.C. Cherokee; 15/32; S; Son; 623; Yes; Yes; Unallotted

633; Crowe, Mandy; F; 7/16/22-9; N.C. Cherokee; 15/32; S; Daughter; 624; Yes; Yes; Unallotted

634; Crowe, Nora; F; 8/25/24-8; N.C. Cherokee; 15/32; S; Daughter; 625; Yes; Yes; Unallotted

635; Crowe, Richard; M; 7/7/27-4; N.C. Cherokee; 15/32; S; Son; 626; Yes; Yes; Unallotted

636; Crowe, Lucinda; F; 11/19/29-2; N.C. Cherokee; 31/32; S; Daughter; 627; Yes; Yes; Unallotted

637; Crowe, Wesley; M; 10/18/75-56; N.C. Cherokee; 3/4; S; Head; 628; Yes; Yes; Unallotted

Census of the **Eastern Cherokee** reservation of the **Cherokee, N.C.** jurisdiction, as of **April 1** , 19**32,** taken by **R. L. Spalsbury** , Superintendent.

Key: Number; Surname, Given; Sex; Date of Birth-Age at Last Birthday; Tribe; Degree of Blood; Marital Status; Relationship to Head of Family; Last C. Roll No.; At Jurisdiction Where Enrolled (Yes/No); (If no – Where); Ward (Yes/No); Allotment, Annuity and Identification Numbers (if given).

638; Crowe, Wesley; M; 5/12/02-29; N.C. Cherokee; 5/16; M; Head; 629; Yes; Yes; Unallotted

639; Crowe, Minnie A.; F; 12/5/04-27; N.C. Cherokee; 1/32; M; Wife; 630; Yes; Yes; Unallotted

640; Crowe, Forrest Sm.; M; 1/4/22-10; N.C. Cherokee; 11/64; S; Son; 631; Yes; Yes; Unallotted

641; Crowe, Juanita; F; 3/28/24-8; N.C. Cherokee; 11/64; S; Daughter; 632; Yes; Yes; Unallotted

642; Crowe, Junior; M; 5/3/26-5; N.C. Cherokee; 11/64; S; Son; 633; Yes; Yes; Unallotted

643; Cucumber, Arch; M; 3/27/90-42; N.C. Cherokee; 4/4; M; Head; 634; Yes; Yes; Unallotted

644; Cucumber, Ollie Y.; F; 9/18/69-62; N.C. Cherokee; 4/4; M; Wife; 635; Yes; Yes; Unallotted

645; Cucumber, Arch; M; 3/21/07-25; N.C. Cherokee; 4/4; S; Head; 636; Yes; Yes; Unallotted

646; Cucumber, Katie; F; 5/2/82-52; N.C. Cherokee; 4/4; Wd.; Wife; 637; Yes; Yes; Unallotted

647; Cucumber, Spencer; M; 5/10/10-21; N.C. Cherokee; 4/4; S; Son; 638; Yes; Yes; Unallotted

648; Cucumber, Jack; M; 3/7/12-20; N.C. Cherokee; 4/4; S; Son; 639; Yes; Yes; Unallotted

649; Cucumber, Delliske; M; 4/27/20-11; N.C. Cherokee; 4/4; S; Son; 640; Yes; Yes; Unallotted

650; Cucumber, James; M; 8/9/91-40; N.C. Cherokee; 4/4; M; Head; 641; Yes; Yes; Unallotted

651; Cucumber, Lizzie Reed; F; 3/10/93-39; N.C. Cherokee; 7/8; M; Wife; 642; Yes; Yes; Unallotted

652; Cucumber, Jennie; F; 8/11/11-20; N.C. Cherokee; 15/16; S; Daughter; 643; Yes; Yes; Unallotted

653; Cucumber, Mason; M; 1/18/13-19; N.C. Cherokee; 15/16; S; Son; 644; Yes; Yes; Unallotted

654; Cucumber, Amanda; F; 3/1/16-16; N.C. Cherokee; 15/16; S; Daughter; 645; Yes; Yes; Unallotted

655; Cucumber, David; M; 2/27/18-14; N.C. Cherokee; 15/16; S; Son; 646; Yes; Yes; Unallotted

656; Cucumber, Madeline; F; 6/15/24-7; N.C. Cherokee; 15/16; S; Daughter; 647; Yes; Yes; Unallotted

657; Cucumber, John D.; M; 3/2/08-26; N.C. Cherokee; 4/4; S; Head; 648; Yes; Yes; Unallotted

Census of the **Eastern Cherokee** reservation of the **Cherokee, N.C.** jurisdiction, as of **April 1**, 19**32**, taken by **R. L. Spalsbury**, Superintendent.

Key: Number; Surname, Given; Sex; Date of Birth-Age at Last Birthday; Tribe; Degree of Blood; Marital Status; Relationship to Head of Family; Last C. Roll No.; At Jurisdiction Where Enrolled (Yes/No); (If no – Where); Ward (Yes/No); Allotment, Annuity and Identification Numbers (if given).

658;   Cucumber, Noah; M; 4/2/08-26; N.C. Cherokee; 4/4; M; Head; 649; Yes; Yes; Unallotted

659;   Cucumber, Emmaline L.; F; 10/10/09-22; N.C. Cherokee; 4/4; M; Wife; 650; Yes; Yes; Unallotted

660;   Cucumber, Alfred G.; M; 2/18/29-3; N.C. Cherokee; 4/4; S; Son; 651; Yes; Yes; Unallotted

661;   Culberson, Sarah J.; F; 7/30/90-41; N.C. Cherokee; 1/4; M; Wife; 652;   No; Kingston, Bartow, Ga.; Yes; Unallotted

662;   Culwell (Raper, Bertha), Bertha; F; 3/20/96-36; N.C. Cherokee; 1/16; M; Wife; 653; No; Drumright, Creek, Okla.; Yes; Unallotted

663;   Dailey (Robinson, Guita I.), Guita I.; F; 8/1/91-40; N.C. Cherokee; 1/16; M; Wife; 654; Yes; Yes; Unallotted

664;   Dailey, Mattie Jane; F; 1/15/13-19; N.C. Cherokee; 1/32; S; Daughter; 655; Yes; Yes; Unallotted

665;   Dailey, Noah; M; 11/26/16-15; N.C. Cherokee; 1/32; S; Son; 656; Yes; Yes; Unallotted

666;   Dailey, Leonard; M; 7/1/18-13; N.C. Cherokee; 1/32; S; Son; 657; Yes; Yes; Unallotted

667;   Dailey, Wilma; F; 11/1/20-11; N.C. Cherokee; 1/32; S; Daughter; 658; Yes; Yes; Unallotted

668;   Darlon, Mack; M; 12/10/92-39; N.C. Cherokee; 1/64; M; Head; 659; Yes; Yes; Unallotted

669;   Darlon, Sherley; F; 9/20/15-16; N.C. Cherokee; 1/128; S; Daughter; 660; Yes; Yes; Unallotted

670;   Darlon, Parlee; F; 4/6/19-12; N.C. Cherokee; 1/128; S; Daughter; 661; Yes; Yes; Unallotted

671;   Darlon, Minnie; F; 8/22/21-10; N.C. Cherokee; 1/128; S; Daughter; 662; Yes; Yes; Unallotted

672;   Darlon, Nettie; F; 12/27/23-8; N.C. Cherokee; 1/128; S; Daughter; 663; Yes; Yes; Unallotted

673;   Davis, Anita; F; 4/15/97-34; N.C. Cherokee; 4/4; S; Head; 664; Yes; Yes; Unallotted

674;   Davis, David; M; 5/18/01-31; N.C. Cherokee; 4/4; S; Head; 665; Yes; Yes; Unallotted

675;   Davis, George; M; 7/5/05-26; N.C. Cherokee; 4/4; S; Brother; 666; Yes; Yes; Unallotted

676;   Davis, Elizabeth; F; 2/19/01-31; N.C. Cherokee; 1/64; M; Wife; 667; Yes; Yes; Unallotted

Census of the **Eastern Cherokee** reservation of the **Cherokee, N.C.** jurisdiction, as of **April 1** , 19**32**, taken by **R. L. Spalsbury** , Superintendent.

Key: Number; Surname, Given; Sex; Date of Birth-Age at Last Birthday; Tribe; Degree of Blood; Marital Status; Relationship to Head of Family; Last C. Roll No.; At Jurisdiction Where Enrolled (Yes/No); (If no – Where); Ward (Yes/No); Allotment, Annuity and Identification Numbers (if given).

677;   Davis, Mary Delle; F; 6/5/21-10; N.C. Cherokee; 1/128; S; Daughter; 668; Yes; Yes; Unallotted

678;   Davis, Martha Jane; F; 3/29/23-9; N.C. Cherokee; 1/128; S; Daughter; 669; Yes; Yes; Unallotted

679;   Davis, Isaac; M; 9/27/99-32; N.C. Cherokee; 4/4; M; Head; 670; Yes; Yes; Unallotted

680;   Davis, Lena Long; F; 2/10/08-24; N.C. Cherokee; 3/4; M; Wife; 671; Yes; Yes; Unallotted

681;   Davis, Israel; M; 6/6/94-37; N.C. Cherokee; 4/4; M; Head; 672; Yes; Yes; Unallotted

682;   Davis, Margaret Bradley; F; 4/24/00-31; N.C. Cherokee; 1/4; M; Wife; 673; Yes; Yes; Unallotted

683;   Davis, Cornelius; M; 5/19/22-9; N.C. Cherokee; 5/8; S; Son; 674; Yes; Yes; Unallotted

684;   Davis, Joe; M; 7/21/73-58; N.C. Cherokee; 4/4; Wd.; Head; 675; Yes; Yes; Unallotted

685;   Davis (Payne, Lydia), Lydia M.; F; 3/7/06-26; N.C. Cherokee; 1/32; M; Wife; 676; Yes; Yes; Unallotted

686;   Dean, Sybil D.; F; 4/18/07-24; N.C. Cherokee; 3/16; M; Wife; 677; Yes; Yes; Unallotted

687;   Davis, Henry L.; M; 9/13/23-8; N.C. Cherokee; 3/32; S; Son; 678; Yes; Yes; Unallotted

688;   Deaton, Calcina S.; F; 4/26/93-38; N.C. Cherokee; 1/8; M; Wife; 679; Yes; Yes; Unallotted

689;   Davis, Woodrow; M; 2/20/28-4; N.C. Cherokee; 1/16; S; Son; 680; Yes; Yes; Unallotted

690;   Deaver (Robinson, Mary E.), Mary E.; F; 9/23/74-57; N.C. Cherokee; 1/16; M; Wife; 681; No; Culberson, Cherokee, N.C.; Yes; Unallotted

691;   Deaver, John Robert; M; 10/18/08-23; N.C. Cherokee; 1/32; S; Son; 682; No; Culberson, Cherokee, N.C.; Yes; Unallotted

692;   Delegeskie or Taylor, John; M; 12/21/59-72; N.C. Cherokee; 4/4; Wd.; Head; 683; Yes; Yes; Unallotted

693;   Denton (Smith, Bessie), Bessie; F; 3/20/04-28; N.C. Cherokee; 1/8; M; Wife; 684; Yes; Yes; Unallotted

Census of the **Eastern Cherokee** reservation of the **Cherokee, N.C.** jurisdiction, as of **April 1** , 19**32,** taken by **R. L. Spalsbury** , Superintendent.

Key: Number; Surname, Given; Sex; Date of Birth-Age at Last Birthday; Tribe; Degree of Blood; Marital Status; Relationship to Head of Family; Last C. Roll No.; At Jurisdiction Where Enrolled (Yes/No); (If no – Where); Ward (Yes/No); Allotment, Annuity and Identification Numbers (if given).

694; Dillard (Adams, Nora), Nora; F; 5/24/04-27; N.C. Cherokee; 1/64; M; Wife; 685; Yes; Yes; Unallotted

695; Dillard, Windle; M; 8/13/22-9; N.C. Cherokee; 1/128; S; Son; 686; Yes; Yes; Unallotted

696; Dillingham (Wakefield, Bettie), Bettie; F; 12/23/69-62; N.C. Cherokee; 1/32; M; Head; 687; Yes; Yes; Unallotted

697; Dills (Rogers, Villa), Villa; F; 6/24/99-32; N.C. Cherokee; 1/8; M; Wife; 688; Yes; Yes; Unallotted

698; Dills, Ruby; F; 6/28/15-16; N.C. Cherokee; 1/16; S; Daughter; 689; Yes; Yes; Unallotted

699; Dills, Louise; F; 5/8/18-13; N.C. Cherokee; 1/16; S; Daughter; 690; Yes; Yes; Unallotted

700; Dills, Turner; M; 8/4/21-10; N.C. Cherokee; 1/16; S; Son; 691; Yes; Yes; Unallotted

701; Dills, Lyle; M; 1/22/24-8; N.C. Cherokee; 1/16; S; Son; 692; Yes; Yes; Unallotted

702; Dockery (Payne, Emma), Emma J.; F; 10/7/81-50; N.C. Cherokee; 1/16; M; Wife; 693; Yes; Yes; Unallotted

703; Dockery, Ralph B.; M; 6/8/07-24; N.C. Cherokee; 1/32; S; Son; 694; Yes; Yes; Unallotted

704; Dockery, Dora Lee; F; 5/2/13-18; N.C. Cherokee; 1/32; S; Daughter; 695; Yes; Yes; Unallotted

705; Dockery, Roscoe A.; M; 7/11/16-15; N.C. Cherokee; 1/32; S; Son; 696; Yes; Yes; Unallotted

706; Dockery, Josephine; F; 8/31/19-12; N.C. Cherokee; 1/32; S; Daughter; 697; Yes; Yes; Unallotted

707; Dockery, Grace A.; F; 5/4/22-9; N.C. Cherokee; 1/32; S; Daughter; 698; Yes; Yes; Unallotted

708; Donley, Robert L.; M; 3/23/73-59; N.C. Cherokee; 1/8; Wd.; Head; 699; Yes; Yes; Unallotted

709; Driver, Betty; F; 12/21/44-87; N.C. Cherokee; 4/4; Wd.; Head; 700; Yes; Yes; Unallotted

710; Driver, Checkelelee; M; 9/15/81-50; N.C. Cherokee; 4/4; Wd.; Head; 701; Yes; Yes; Unallotted

711; Driver, Mason; M; 9/23/09-22; N.C. Cherokee; 4/4; S; Son; 702; Yes; Yes; Unallotted

712; Driver, Amanda; F; 3/3/16-16; N.C. Cherokee; 4/4; S; Daughter; 703; Yes; Yes; Unallotted

Census of the **Eastern Cherokee** reservation of the **Cherokee, N.C.** jurisdiction, as of **April 1** , **1932,** taken by **R. L. Spalsbury** , Superintendent.

Key: Number; Surname, Given; Sex; Date of Birth-Age at Last Birthday; Tribe; Degree of Blood; Marital Status; Relationship to Head of Family; Last C. Roll No.; At Jurisdiction Where Enrolled (Yes/No); (If no – Where); Ward (Yes/No); Allotment, Annuity and Identification Numbers (if given).

713; Driver, James; M; 7/24/21-10; N.C. Cherokee; 4/4; S; Son; 704; Yes; Yes; Unallotted

714; Driver, Dickey; M; 6/21/47-84; N.C. Cherokee; 4/4; Wd.; Head; 705; Yes; Yes; Unallotted

715; Driver, John; M; 12/26/13-19; N.C. Cherokee; 9/16; S; Son; 706; Yes; Yes; Unallotted

716; Driver, George; M; 3/23/03-29; N.C. Cherokee; 4/4; M; Head; 707; Yes; Yes; Unallotted

717; Driver, Annie Bird; F; 1/14/07-25; N.C. Cherokee; 4/4; M; Wife; 708; Yes; Yes; Unallotted

718; Driver, John; M; 3/29/27-5; N.C. Cherokee; 4/4; S; Son; 709; Yes; Yes; Unallotted

719; Driver, Waidsutte; F; 6/7/30-1; N.C. Cherokee; 4/4; S; Daughter; 710; Yes; Yes; Unallotted

720; Driver, James G.; M; 4/25/77-54; N.C. Cherokee; 4/4; M; Head; 711; Yes; Yes; Unallotted

721; Driver, John; M; 12/15/98-33; N.C. Cherokee; 4/4; M; Head; 712; Yes; Yes; Unallotted

722; Driver, Nannie T.; F; 12/18/02-29; N.C. Cherokee; 4/4; M; Wife; 713; Yes; Yes; Unallotted

723; Driver, Nicodemus; M; 3/23/20-12; N.C. Cherokee; 4/4; S; Son; 714; Yes; Yes; Unallotted

724; Driver, Quincy; M; 2/26/22-10; N.C. Cherokee; 4/4; S; Son; 715; Yes; Yes; Unallotted

725; Driver, Watty; M; 3/11/29-3; N.C. Cherokee; 4/4; S; Son; 716; Yes; Yes; Unallotted

726; Driver, Tom; M; 3/11/29-3; N.C. Cherokee; 4/4; S; Son; 717; Yes; Yes; Unallotted

727; Driver, Judas; M; 8/1/66-65; N.C. Cherokee; 4/4; M; Head; 718; Yes; Yes; Unallotted

728; Driver, Eliza; F; 7/4/66-65; N.C. Cherokee; 4/4; M; Wife; 719; Yes; Yes; Unallotted

729; Driver, Ned; M; 8/9/00-31; N.C. Cherokee; 7/8; Div.; Head; 720; Yes; Yes; Unallotted

730; Driver, Adam West; M; 5/17/17-14; N.C. Cherokee; 15/16; S; Son; 721; Yes; Yes; Unallotted

731; Driver, Richard T.; M; 8/11/18-13; N.C. Cherokee; 15/16; S; Son; 722; Yes; Yes; Unallotted

Census of the **Eastern Cherokee** reservation of the **Cherokee, N.C.** jurisdiction, as of **April 1** , 19**32**, taken by **R. L. Spalsbury** , Superintendent.

Key: Number; Surname, Given; Sex; Date of Birth-Age at Last Birthday; Tribe; Degree of Blood; Marital Status; Relationship to Head of Family; Last C. Roll No.; At Jurisdiction Where Enrolled (Yes/No); (If no – Where); Ward (Yes/No); Allotment, Annuity and Identification Numbers (if given).

732; Driver, MacAdoo; M; 2/19/20-12; N.C. Cherokee; 15/16; S; Son; 723; Yes; Yes; Unallotted

733; Driver, Ruth; F; 12/15/22-9; N.C. Cherokee; 15/16; S; Daughter; 724; Yes; Yes; Unallotted

734; Driver, Russel B.; M; 2/15/74-58; N.C. Cherokee; 4/4; M; Head; 725; No; Newton, Bucks, Pa.; Yes; Unallotted

735; Driver, Wesley; M; 2/23/71-61; N.C. Cherokee; 4/4; M; Head; 726; Yes; Yes; Unallotted

736; Driver, Agnes; F; 12/21/70-61; N.C. Cherokee; 4/4; M; Wife; 727; Yes; Yes; Unallotted

737; Driver, William; M; 8/21/73-58; N.C. Cherokee; 4/4; Wd.; Head; 728; Yes; Yes; Unallotted

738; Dunlap (Wolfe, Delia Ann), Delia Ann; F; 2/10/91-41; N.C. Cherokee; 1/8; M; Wife; 729; Yes; Yes; Unallotted

739; Dunlap, David H.; M; 12/21/22-9; N.C. Cherokee; 1/16; S; Son; 730; Yes; Yes; Unallotted

740; Dunlap, Mary Matilda; F; 7/9/13-18; N.C. Cherokee; 1/16; S; Alone; 731; Yes; Yes; Unallotted

741; Dunlap, John Robert; M; 11/13/15-16; N.C. Cherokee; 1/16; S; Brother; 732; Yes; Yes; Unallotted

742; Dunlap, Robert L.; M; 1/8/90-42; N.C. Cherokee; 1/8; M; Head; 733; Yes; Yes; Unallotted

743; Dunlap, Odell; M; 11/14/21-10; N.C. Cherokee; 1/16; S; Son; 734; Yes; Yes; Unallotted

744; Enloe, Fallen L.; F; 4/24/15-16; N.C. Cherokee; 1/16; M; Wife; 735; Yes; Yes; Unallotted

745; Eller (Patterson, Josie), Josie P.; F; 11/11/00-31; N.C. Cherokee; 1/32; M; Wife; 736; Yes; Yes; Unallotted

746; Ellis (Hardin, Celia), Celia H.; F; 5/17/94-37; N.C. Cherokee; 1/16; M; Wife; 737; Yes; Yes; Unallotted

747; Ellis, Magdalene E.; F; 5/12/17-14; N.C. Cherokee; 1/32; S; Daughter; 738; Yes; Yes; Unallotted

748; Ellis, Wm. Samuel; M; 10/27/18-13; N.C. Cherokee; 1/32; S; Son; 739; Yes; Yes; Unallotted

749; Ellis, Thomas J.; M; 7/9/20-11; N.C. Cherokee; 1/32; S; Son; 740; Yes; Yes; Unallotted

Census of the **Eastern Cherokee** reservation of the **Cherokee, N.C.** jurisdiction, as of **April 1**, 19**32**, taken by **R. L. Spalsbury**, Superintendent.

Key: Number; Surname, Given; Sex; Date of Birth-Age at Last Birthday; Tribe; Degree of Blood; Marital Status; Relationship to Head of Family; Last C. Roll No.; At Jurisdiction Where Enrolled (Yes/No); (If no – Where); Ward (Yes/No); Allotment, Annuity and Identification Numbers (if given).

750; Ellis (Tatham, Olive), Olive T.; F; 4/1/04-28; N.C. Cherokee; 1/16; M; Wife; 741; Yes; Yes; Unallotted

751; Endros, Edwin; M; 2/1/08-24; N.C. Cherokee; 3/8; S; Head; 742; Yes; Yes; Unallotted

752; Enloe (Lambert, Mintha), Mintha D.; F; 10/9/12-19; N.C. Cherokee; 1/32; M; Wife; 743; Yes; Yes; Unallotted

753; Ewart, Tiney L.; F; 10/4/05-26; N.C. Cherokee; 1/4; M; Wife; 744; Yes; Yes; Unallotted

754; Ewart, Samuel; M; 10/21/25-6; N.C. Cherokee; 1/8; S; Son; 745; Yes; Yes; Unallotted

755; Eubank, Lillie; F; 1888-45; N.C. Cherokee; 1/4; M; Wife; 746; Yes; Yes; Unallotted

756; Feather, William; M; 5/2/20-11; N.C. Cherokee; 4/4; S; Alone; 747; Yes; Yes; Unallotted

757; Feather, Hettie; F; 3/24/98-34; N.C. Cherokee; 4/4; S; Head; 748; No; Philadelphia, Philadelphia, Pa; Yes; Unallotted

758; Feather, Lawyer; M; 12/12/68-63; N.C. Cherokee; 4/4; M; Head; 749; Yes; Yes; Unallotted

759; Feather, Mary; F; 12/12/67-64; N.C. Cherokee; 4/4; M; Wife; 750; Yes; Yes; Unallotted

760; Feather, Jonah; M; 7/5/05-26; N.C. Cherokee; 4/4; S; Son; 751; Yes; Yes; Unallotted

761; Featherhead, Wilson; M; 12/21/72-59; N.C. Cherokee; 4/4; Wd.; Head; 752; Yes; Yes; Unallotted

762; Falls, Bettie B.; F; 1900-32; N.C. Cherokee; 1/4; M; Wife; 754; Yes; Yes; Unallotted

763; Finger, Sophronia; F; 11/2/76-55; N.C. Cherokee; 1/4; M; Wife; 755; Yes; Yes; Unallotted

764; Finger, Samuel A.; M; 2/20/98-34; N.C. Cherokee; 1/8; S; Son; 756; Yes; Yes; Unallotted

765; Finger, Leonia; F; 7/5/05-26; N.C. Cherokee; 1/8; S; Daughter; 757; Yes; Yes; Unallotted

766; Finger, Elmer E.; M; 4/26/08-23; N.C. Cherokee; 1/8; S; Son; 758; Yes; Yes; Unallotted

Census of the **Eastern Cherokee** reservation of the **Cherokee, N.C.** jurisdiction, as of **April 1** , 19**32,** taken by **R. L. Spalsbury** , Superintendent.

Key: Number; Surname, Given; Sex; Date of Birth-Age at Last Birthday; Tribe; Degree of Blood; Marital Status; Relationship to Head of Family; Last C. Roll No.; At Jurisdiction Where Enrolled (Yes/No); (If no – Where); Ward (Yes/No); Allotment, Annuity and Identification Numbers (if given).

767; Finger, Ruby Irene; F; 9/6/11-20; N.C. Cherokee; 1/8; S; Daughter; 759; Yes; Yes; Unallotted

768; Finger, Cora J.; F; 8/5/17-14; N.C. Cherokee; 1/8; S; Daughter; 760; Yes; Yes; Unallotted

769; Fisher (McLeymore, Elsie), Elsie McL.; F; 6/15/08-23; N.C. Cherokee; 5/16; M; Wife; 761; Yes; Yes; Unallotted

770; Fisher, Frankie C.; F; 10/3/96-35; N.C. Cherokee; 1/16; M; Wife; 762; Yes; Yes; Unallotted

771; Fisher, Stacey A.; F; 4/28/22-9; N.C. Cherokee; 1/32; S; Daughter; 763; Yes; Yes; Unallotted

772; Fortner (Raper, Delia), Delia; F; 5/14/99-32; N.C. Cherokee; 1/16; M; Wife; 764; Yes; Yes; Unallotted

773; Fortner, June; F; 6/5/18-13; N.C. Cherokee; 1/32; S; Daughter; 765; Yes; Yes; Unallotted

774; Fortner, Sis; F; 12/24/1876-56; N.C. Cherokee; 1/4; M; Wife; 766; Yes; Yes; Unallotted

775; Foster (Raper, Alice), Alice; F; 5/29/74-57; N.C. Cherokee; 1/8; M; Wife; 767; Yes; Yes; Unallotted

776; Foster, Robert; M; 4/16/01-30; N.C. Cherokee; 1/16; S; Son; 768; Yes; Yes; Unallotted

777; Foster, Burton; M; 7/26/03-28; N.C. Cherokee; 1/16; S; Son; 769; Yes; Yes; Unallotted

778; Foster, Leroy; M; 2/4/06-26; N.C. Cherokee; 1/16; S; Son; 770; Yes; Yes; Unallotted

779; Foster, William E.; M; 10/17/13-18; N.C. Cherokee; 1/16; S; Son; 771; Yes; Yes; Unallotted

780; French, Meroney; M; 12/15/98-33; N.C. Cherokee; 4/4; M; Head; 772; Yes; Yes; Unallotted

781; French, Callie R.; F; 10/28/10-21; N.C. Cherokee; 4/4; M; Wife 2nd; 773; Yes; Yes; Unallotted

782; French, Roy Daniel; M; 8/19/22-9; N.C. Cherokee; 4/4; S; Son; 774; Yes; Yes; Unallotted

783; French, John K.; M; 1/7/24-8; N.C. Cherokee; 4/4; S; Son; 775; Yes; Yes; Unallotted

784; French, Manuel M.; M; 4/23/28-3; N.C. Cherokee; 4/4; S; Son; 776; Yes; Yes; Unallotted

785; French, Morgan; M; 12/15/98-33; N.C. Cherokee; 4/4; M; Head; 777; Yes; Yes; Unallotted

Census of the **Eastern Cherokee** reservation of the **Cherokee, N.C.** jurisdiction, as of **April 1** , 19**32,** taken by **R. L. Spalsbury** , Superintendent.

Key: Number; Surname, Given; Sex; Date of Birth-Age at Last Birthday; Tribe; Degree of Blood; Marital Status; Relationship to Head of Family; Last C. Roll No.; At Jurisdiction Where Enrolled (Yes/No); (If no – Where); Ward (Yes/No); Allotment, Annuity and Identification Numbers (if given).

786; French, Ned; M; 11/8/99-32; N.C. Cherokee; 4/4; S; Head; 778; Yes; Yes; Unallotted

787; French, Jesse; M; 3/17/05-27; N.C. Cherokee; 4/4; S; Brother; 779; Yes; Yes; Unallotted

788; French, Samuel; M; 11/6/16-15; N.C. Cherokee; 4/4; S; Alone; 780; Yes; Yes; Unallotted

789; French, Gerry; M; 5/18/18-13; N.C. Cherokee; 4/4; S; Brother; 781; Yes; Yes; Unallotted

790; French, Judy; F; 5/29/21-10; N.C. Cherokee; 4/4; S; Sister; 782; Yes; Yes; Unallotted

791; French, Saughee; M; 3/28/00-32; N.C. Cherokee; 4/4; S; Head; 783; Yes; Yes; Unallotted

792; French, George; M; 5/25/02-29; N.C. Cherokee; 4/4; S; Brother; 784; Yes; Yes; Unallotted

793; Frye (Bauer, Owenah), Owenah A.; F; 10/17/95-36; N.C. Cherokee; 3/8; M; Wife; 785; Yes; Yes; Unallotted

794; Garland, Jesse L.; M; 8/31/56-75; N.C. Cherokee; 1/8; M; Head; 786 ; Yes; Yes; Unallotted

795; Garland, Emory; M; 4/23/2/19/03-29; N.C. Cherokee; 1/16; S; Son; 787; Yes; Yes; Unallotted

796; Garland, Radia Elmer; F; 9/11/05-26; N.C. Cherokee; 1/16; S; Daughter; 788; Yes; Yes; Unallotted

797; Garland, John B.; M; 1/22/79-53; N.C. Cherokee; 1/16; M; Head; 789; Yes; Yes; Unallotted

798; Garland, Frank; M; 3/10/06-26; N.C. Cherokee; 1/32; S; Son; 790; Yes; Yes; Unallotted

799; Garland, Fred; M; 7/12/08-23; N.C. Cherokee; 1/32; S; Son; 791; Yes; Yes; Unallotted

800; Garland, Edgar; M; 8/11/11-20; N.C. Cherokee; 1/32; S; Son; 792; Yes; Yes; Unallotted

801; Garland, Aud; M; 5/6/19-12; N.C. Cherokee; 1/32; S; Son; 793; Yes; Yes; Unallotted

802; Garland, Leonzo[sic]; M; 5/22/85-46; N.C. Cherokee; 1/16; M; Head; 794; No; Culberson, Cherokee, N.C.; Yes; Unallotted

803; Garland, Homer; M; 1/14/10-22; N.C. Cherokee; 1/32; S; Son; 795; No; Culberson, Cherokee, N.C.; Yes; Unallotted

804; Garland, Ruth; F; 10/17/13-18; N.C. Cherokee; 1/32; S; Daughter; 796; No; Culberson, Cherokee, N.C.; Yes; Unallotted

Census of the **Eastern Cherokee** reservation of the **Cherokee, N.C.** jurisdiction, as of **April 1** , 19**32**, taken by **R. L. Spalsbury** , Superintendent.

Key: Number; Surname, Given; Sex; Date of Birth-Age at Last Birthday; Tribe; Degree of Blood; Marital Status; Relationship to Head of Family; Last C. Roll No.; At Jurisdiction Where Enrolled (Yes/No); (If no – Where); Ward (Yes/No); Allotment, Annuity and Identification Numbers (if given).

805; Garland, Charlie; M; 1/14/15-17; N.C. Cherokee; 1/32; S; Son; 797; No; Culberson, Cherokee, N.C.; Yes; Unallotted

806; Garland, Edith; F; 4/21/18-13; N.C. Cherokee; 1/32; S; Daughter; 798; No; Culberson, Cherokee, N.C.; Yes; Unallotted

807; Garland, Nettie; F; 4/11/20-11; N.C. Cherokee; 1/32; S; Daughter; 799; No; Culberson, Cherokee, N.C.; Yes; Unallotted

808; Garland, Dora; F; 7/4/22-9; N.C. Cherokee; 1/32; S; Daughter; 800; No; Culberson, Cherokee, N.C.; Yes; Unallotted

809; Garland, Emma; F; 3/28/24-8; N.C. Cherokee; 1/32; S; Daughter; 801; No; Culberson, Cherokee, N.C.; Yes; Unallotted

810; Garland, Roxanna; F; 3/12/58-74; N.C. Cherokee; 1/8; S; Head; 802; No; Culberson, Cherokee, N.C.; Yes; Unallotted

811; Garland, William S.; M; 6/27/66-65; N.C. Cherokee; 1/8; S; Head; 803; No; Culberson, Cherokee, N.C.; Yes; Unallotted

812; Garren (Cole, Ida), Ida C.; F; 6/13/91-40; N.C. Cherokee; 1/16; M; Wife; 804; Yes; Yes; Unallotted

813; Garren, Elmer; M; 10/9/14-17; N.C. Cherokee; 1/32; S; Son; 805; Yes; Yes; Unallotted

814; Garren, Rosa; F; 3/27/20-12; N.C. Cherokee; 1/32; S; Daughter; 806; Yes; Yes; Unallotted

815; George, Bessie T.; F; 5/8/97-34; N.C. Cherokee; 3/4; Wd.; Head; 807; Yes; Yes; Unallotted

816; George, Florence; F; 8/15/16-15; N.C. Cherokee; 3/8; S; Daughter; 808; Yes; Yes; Unallotted

817; George, Rosie E.B.; F; 7/14/79-52; N.C. Cherokee; 1/8; Wd.; Head; 809; Yes; Yes; Unallotted

818; George, Margaret; F; 1/17/17-15; N.C. Cherokee; 9/16; S; Daughter; 810; Yes; Yes; Unallotted

819; George, Dawson; M; 6/14/60-71; N.C. Cherokee; 4/4; M; Head; 811; Yes; Yes; Unallotted

820; George, Mary; F; 6/24/60-71; N.C. Cherokee; 7/8; M; Wife; 812; Yes; Yes; Unallotted

821; George, Annie; F; 12/30/83-48; N.C. Cherokee; 15/16; S; Daughter; 813; No; Little Neck, Long Island, N.Y.; Yes; Unallotted

822; George, Elijah; M; 4/1/74-58; N.C. Cherokee; 4/4; M; Head; 814; Yes; Yes; Unallotted

823; George, Nicey Wilnoty; F; 4/13/89-42; N.C. Cherokee; 4/4; M; Wife; 815; Yes; Yes; Unallotted

Census of the **Eastern Cherokee** reservation of the **Cherokee, N.C.** jurisdiction, as of **April 1** , 19**32,** taken by **R. L. Spalsbury** , Superintendent.

Key: Number; Surname, Given; Sex; Date of Birth-Age at Last Birthday; Tribe; Degree of Blood; Marital Status; Relationship to Head of Family; Last C. Roll No.; At Jurisdiction Where Enrolled (Yes/No); (If no – Where); Ward (Yes/No); Allotment, Annuity and Identification Numbers (if given).

824; George, Lewis; M; 8/28/05-26; N.C. Cherokee; 4/4; S; Son; 816; Yes; Yes; Unallotted

825; George, Martha; F; 5/16/07-24; N.C. Cherokee; 4/4; S; Daughter; 817; Yes; Yes; Unallotted

826; George, Cornelia; F; 1/28/08-24; N.C. Cherokee; 4/4; S; Daughter; 818; Yes; Yes; Unallotted

827; George, Annie; F; 4/13/16-15; N.C. Cherokee; 4/4; S; Daughter; 819; Yes; Yes; Unallotted

828; George, Bessie; F; 6/19/17-14; N.C. Cherokee; 4/4; S; Daughter; 820; Yes; Yes; Unallotted

829; George, Joseph; M; 5/14/19-12; N.C. Cherokee; 4/4; S; Son; 821; Yes; Yes; Unallotted

830; George, Guy; M; 4/13/21-10; N.C. Cherokee; 4/4; S; Son; 822; Yes; Yes; Unallotted

831; George, Janie; F; 3/10/25-7; N.C. Cherokee; 4/4; S; Daughter; 823; Yes; Yes; Unallotted

832; George, Davis D.; M; 5/12/27-4; N.C. Cherokee; 4/4; S; Son; 824; Yes; Yes; Unallotted

833; George, Lucy; F; 5/12/27-4; N.C. Cherokee; 4/4; S; Daughter; 825; Yes; Yes; Unallotted

834; George, Ollie; F; 9/14/29-2; N.C. Cherokee; 4/4; S; Daughter; 826; Yes; Yes; Unallotted

835; George, Elijah; M; 4/1/78-54; N.C. Cherokee; 4/4; S; Head; 827; Yes; Yes; Unallotted

836; George, Elizabeth; F; 12/21/60-71; N.C. Cherokee; 4/4; Wd.; Head; 828; Yes; Yes; Unallotted

837; George, Elmo Don; M; 5/8/03-28; N.C. Cherokee; 15/16; S; Head; 829; Yes; Yes; Unallotted

838; George, Goliath; M; 9/20/01-30; N.C. Cherokee; 4/4; M; Head; 830; Yes; Yes; Unallotted

839; George, Bessie B.; F; 11/5/00-31; N.C. Cherokee; 15/16; M; Wife; 831; Yes; Yes; Unallotted

840; George, Paulina; F; 8/27/20-11; N.C. Cherokee; 31/32; S; Daughter; 832; Yes; Yes; Unallotted

841; George, Green; M; 6/2/00-31; N.C. Cherokee; 4/4; S; Head; 833; Yes; Yes; Unallotted

842; George, Jackson; M; 8/5/02-29; N.C. Cherokee; 4/4; S; Head; 834; Yes; Yes; Unallotted

Census of the **Eastern Cherokee** reservation of the **Cherokee, N.C.** jurisdiction, as of **April 1**, **1932,** taken by **R. L. Spalsbury**, Superintendent.

Key: Number; Surname, Given; Sex; Date of Birth-Age at Last Birthday; Tribe; Degree of Blood; Marital Status; Relationship to Head of Family; Last C. Roll No.; At Jurisdiction Where Enrolled (Yes/No); (If no – Where); Ward (Yes/No); Allotment, Annuity and Identification Numbers (if given).

843; George, Jacob; M; 3/9/94-38; N.C. Cherokee; 4/4; M; Head; 835; Yes; Yes; Unallotted

844; George, Nola S.; F; 11/17/97-34; N.C. Cherokee; 4/4; M; Wife; 836; Yes; Yes; Unallotted

845; George, Ammons; M; 6/12/15-16; N.C. Cherokee; 4/4; S; Son; 837; Yes; Yes; Unallotted

846; George, Sherman; M; 12/22/16-15; N.C. Cherokee; 4/4; S; Son; 838; Yes; Yes; Unallotted

847; George, Jonah; M; 2/16/19-13; N.C. Cherokee; 4/4; S; Son; 839; Yes; Yes; Unallotted

848; George, Callie; F; 2/1/23-9; N.C. Cherokee; 4/4; S; Daughter; 840; Yes; Yes; Unallotted

849; George, Josie; F; 10/16/23-8; N.C. Cherokee; 4/4; S; Alone; 841; Yes; Yes; Unallotted

850; George (Lee, Julia), Julia V.; F; 2/22/75-57; N.C. Cherokee; 1/16; M; Wife; 842; Yes; Yes; Unallotted

851; George, Logan; M; 7/21/88-43; N.C. Cherokee; 4/4; S; Head; 843; Yes; Yes; Unallotted

852; George, Maggie R.; F; 3/24/89-43; N.C. Cherokee; 7/8; M; Wife; 844; Yes; Yes; Unallotted

853; George, Manley; M; 5/29/89-42; N.C. Cherokee; 15/16; M; Head; 845; Yes; Yes; Unallotted

854; George, Savannah P.; F; 9/2/07-24; N.C. Cherokee; 4/4; M; Wife; 846; Yes; Yes; Unallotted

855; George, Annie; F; 8/10/25-6; N.C. Cherokee; 31/32; S; Daughter; 847; Yes; Yes; Unallotted

856; George, Columbus; M; 6/18/27-4; N.C. Cherokee; 31/32; S; Son; 848; Yes; Yes; Unallotted

857; George, Hoover; M; 2/6/29-3; N.C. Cherokee; 31/32; S; Son; 849; Yes; Yes; Unallotted

858; George, Sallie; F; 6/6/30-1; N.C. Cherokee; 31/32; S; Daughter; 850; Yes; Yes; Unallotted

859; George, Martha; F; 11/4/91-40; N.C. Cherokee; 15/16; M; Wife (Div.); 851; Yes; Yes; Unallotted

860; George, Ben; M; 10/21/13-18; N.C. Cherokee; 15/32; S; Son; 852; Yes; Yes; Unallotted

861; George, Tom; M; 3/21/18-14; N.C. Cherokee; 15/32; S; Son; 853; Yes; Yes; Unallotted

Census of the **Eastern Cherokee** reservation of the **Cherokee, N.C.** jurisdiction, as of **April 1** , 19**32,** taken by **R. L. Spalsbury** , Superintendent.

Key: Number; Surname, Given; Sex; Date of Birth-Age at Last Birthday; Tribe; Degree of Blood; Marital Status; Relationship to Head of Family; Last C. Roll No.; At Jurisdiction Where Enrolled (Yes/No); (If no – Where); Ward (Yes/No); Allotment, Annuity and Identification Numbers (if given).

862; George, Sam; M; 8/5/20-11; N.C. Cherokee; 15/32; S; Son; 854; Yes; Yes; Unallotted

863; George, Shell; M; 3/21/60-72; N.C. Cherokee; 4/4; S; Head; 855; Yes; Yes; Unallotted

864; George, Shon; M; 9/18/72-59; N.C. Cherokee; 4/4; S; Head; 856; Yes; Yes; Unallotted

865; Gilbert (Robinson, Emmaline), Emmaline; F; 10/9/97-34; N.C. Cherokee; 1/16; M; Wife; 857; Yes; Yes; Unallotted

866; Gilbert, Paul A.; M; 12/24/22-9; N.C. Cherokee; 1/32; S; Son; 858; Yes; Yes; Unallotted

867; Gilreath (Raper, Georgia), Georgia; F; 1/28/91-41; N.C. Cherokee; 1/16; M; Wife; 859; Yes; Yes; Unallotted

868; Gilreath, Albert B.; M; 10/6/13-18; N.C. Cherokee; 1/32; S; Son; 860; Yes; Yes; Unallotted

869; Gilreath, Rubia; F; 8/25/15-16; N.C. Cherokee; 1/32; S; Daughter; 861; Yes; Yes; Unallotted

870; Gilreath, Roxie; F; 5/29/17-14; N.C. Cherokee; 1/32; S; Daughter; 862; Yes; Yes; Unallotted

871; Gilreath, Cecil; M; 11/17/21-10; N.C. Cherokee; 1/32; S; Son; 863; Yes; Yes; Unallotted

872; Gilreath, Rittie; F; 5/18/23-8; N.C. Cherokee; 1/32; S; Daughter; 864; Yes; Yes; Unallotted

873; Gloyne, Lula O.; F; 12/27/91-40; N.C. Cherokee; 1/2; Wd.; Head; 865; Yes; Yes; Unallotted

874; Gloyne, Roberta; F; 4/19/19-12; N.C. Cherokee; 1/4; S; Daughter; 866; Yes; Yes; Unallotted

875; Gloyne, John H.; M; 4/10/21-10; N.C. Cherokee; 1/4; S; Son; 867; Yes; Yes; Unallotted

876; Gloyne, Daniel D.; M; 5/17/23-8; N.C. Cherokee; 1/4; S; Son; 868; Yes; Yes; Unallotted

877; Gloyne, Mary T.; F; 8/30/28-4; N.C. Cherokee; 1/4; S; Daughter; 869; Yes; Yes; Unallotted

878; Goforth, Arthur; M; 3/8/11-21; N.C. Cherokee; 3/32; M; Head; 870; Yes; Yes; Unallotted

879; Goin, Sallie; F; 12/21/49-82; N.C. Cherokee; 3/4; S; Single; 871; Yes; Yes; Unallotted

Census of the **Eastern Cherokee** reservation of the **Cherokee, N.C.** jurisdiction, as of **April 1**, **1932,** taken by **R. L. Spalsbury**, Superintendent.

Key: Number; Surname, Given; Sex; Date of Birth-Age at Last Birthday; Tribe; Degree of Blood; Marital Status; Relationship to Head of Family; Last C. Roll No.; At Jurisdiction Where Enrolled (Yes/No); (If no – Where); Ward (Yes/No); Allotment, Annuity and Identification Numbers (if given).

880;   Going, Birdchopper; M; 12/21/69-62; N.C. Cherokee; 4/4; M; Head; 872; Yes; Yes; Unallotted

881;   Going, Ollie; F; 8/21/72-59; N.C. Cherokee; 4/4; M; Wife; 873; Yes; Yes; Unallotted

882;   Going, Emmaline; F; 3/5/09-23; N.C. Cherokee; 4/4; S; Daughter; 874; Yes; Yes; Unallotted

883;   Going, Emerson J.; M; 5/15/28-3; N.C. Cherokee; 1/2; S; Grandson (Illeg.); 875; Yes; Yes; Unallotted

884;   Going, George; M; 9/12/21-10; N.C. Cherokee; 4/4; S; Alone; 876; Yes; Yes; Unallotted

885;   Graves (Murphy, Inez), Inez; F; 10/14/93-38; N.C. Cherokee; 1/8; M; Wife; 877; No; Unaka, Cherokee, N.C.; Yes; Unallotted

886;   Graves, Fred; M; 8/25/13-18; N.C. Cherokee; 1/16; S; Son; 878; No; Unaka, Cherokee, N.C.; Yes; Unallotted

887;   Graves, Myrtle; F; 4/2/16-15; N.C. Cherokee; 1/16; S; Daughter; 879; No; Unaka, Cherokee, N.C.; Yes; Unallotted

888;   Graves, Mary; F; 8/28/18-13; N.C. Cherokee; 1/16; S; Daughter; 880; No; Unaka, Cherokee, N.C.; Yes; Unallotted

889;   Graves, Eva; F; 11/15/20-11; N.C. Cherokee; 1/16; S; Daughter; 881; No; Unaka, Cherokee, N.C.; Yes; Unallotted

890;   Graves, Hoyt; M; 1/15/23-9; N.C. Cherokee; 1/16; S; Son; 882; No; Unaka, Cherokee, N.C.; Yes; Unallotted

891;   Green (Payne, Cora), Cora E.; F; 4/8/84-47; N.C. Cherokee; 1/16; M; Wife; 883; No; Letitia, Cherokee, N.C.; Yes; Unallotted

892;   Green, Lurlie B.; F; 12/22/06-25; N.C. Cherokee; 1/32; S; Daughter; 884; No; Letitia, Cherokee, N.C.; Yes; Unallotted

893;   Green, Bonnie Lee; F; 9/10/09-22; N.C. Cherokee; 1/32; S; Daughter; 885; No; Letitia, Cherokee, N.C.; Yes; Unallotted

894;   Green, Blanche; F; 8/2/12-19; N.C. Cherokee; 1/32; S; Daughter; 886; No; Letitia, Cherokee, N.C.; Yes; Unallotted

895;   Green, Millie; F; 12/27/14-17; N.C. Cherokee; 1/32; S; Daughter; 887; No; Letitia, Cherokee, N.C.; Yes; Unallotted

896;   Green, Alfred; M; 8/12/18-13; N.C. Cherokee; 1/32; S; Son; 888; No; Letitia, Cherokee, N.C.; Yes; Unallotted

897;   Green, Margaret H.; F; 2/25/24-8; N.C. Cherokee; 1/32; S; Daughter; 889; No; Letitia, Cherokee, N.C.; Yes; Unallotted

898;   Green, Lena B.; F; 1904-28; N.C. Cherokee; 1/4; M; Wife; 890; No; Ensley, Jefferson, Ala.; Yes; Unallotted

899;   Green (Rogers, Martha C.), Martha; F; 2/12/78-54; N.C. Cherokee; 1/16; M; Wife; 891; Yes; Yes; Unallotted

Census of the **Eastern Cherokee** reservation of the **Cherokee, N.C.** jurisdiction, as of **April 1** , 1932, taken by **R. L. Spalsbury** , Superintendent.

Key: Number; Surname, Given; Sex; Date of Birth-Age at Last Birthday; Tribe; Degree of Blood; Marital Status; Relationship to Head of Family; Last C. Roll No.; At Jurisdiction Where Enrolled (Yes/No); (If no – Where); Ward (Yes/No); Allotment, Annuity and Identification Numbers (if given).

900;   Greene (Baker, Stella), Stella B.; F; 3/13/98-34; N.C. Cherokee; 1/16; M; Wife; 892; Yes; Yes; Unallotted

901;   Greene, Samuel P.; M; 3/17/22-10; N.C. Cherokee; 1/32; S; Son; 893; Yes; Yes; Unallotted

902;   Greybeard, Sallie ; F; 3/14/99-33; N.C. Cherokee; 1/2; S; Head; 894; No; Philadelphia, Philadelphia, Pa.; Yes; Unallotted

903;   Griffin, Ima; F; 12/15/12-19; N.C. Cherokee; 1/32; S; Alone; 895; Yes; Yes; Unallotted

904;   Griffin, Iowa; F; 4/14/18-13; N.C. Cherokee; 1/32; S; Sister; 896; Yes; Yes; Unallotted

905;   Griffin, Frankie; F; 9/23/20-11; N.C. Cherokee; 1/32; S; Sister; 897; Yes; Yes; Unallotted

906;   Griffin (Murphy, Jane), Jane M.; F; 4/16/77-54; N.C. Cherokee; 1/8; M; Wife; 898; Yes; Yes; Unallotted

907;   Griffin, Minnie Goforth; F; 1/4/87-45; N.C. Cherokee; 3/16; M; Wife; 899; Yes; Yes; Unallotted

908;   Hagood (Meroney, Mayes), Mayes M.; F; 11/7/96-35; N.C. Cherokee; 1/16; M; Wife; 900; Yes; Yes; Unallotted

909;   Haigler, Cora McL.; F; 5/29/05-26; N.C. Cherokee; 5/16; M; Wife; 901; Yes; Yes; Unallotted

910;   Haigler, Frank W.; M; 2/12/24-8; N.C. Cherokee; 5/32; S; Son; 902; Yes; Yes; Unallotted

911;   Hamby (Raper, Edna), Edna R.; F; 11/19/09-22; N.C. Cherokee; 1/32; M; Wife; 903; No; Oak Park, Cherokee, N.C.; Yes; Unallotted

912;   Hamilton, Leona Jordan; F; 1876-56; N.C. Cherokee; -1/4; M; Wife; 904; Yes; Yes; Unallotted

913;   Hardin, Dillard; M; 10/20/01-30; N.C. Cherokee; 1/32; M; Head; 905; Yes; Yes; Unallotted

914;   Hardin, Dorothy; F; 9/5/23-9; N.C. Cherokee; 1/64; S; Daughter; 906; Yes; Yes; Unallotted

915;   Hardin, Dock; M; 8/10/86-45; N.C. Cherokee; 1/16; M; Head; 907; Yes; Yes; Unallotted

916;   Hardin, Cluria; F; 6/10/07-24; N.C. Cherokee; 1/32; S; Daughter; 908; Yes; Yes; Unallotted

Census of the **Eastern Cherokee** reservation of the **Cherokee, N.C.** jurisdiction, as of **April 1**, 19**32,** taken by **R. L. Spalsbury**, Superintendent.

Key: Number; Surname, Given; Sex; Date of Birth-Age at Last Birthday; Tribe; Degree of Blood; Marital Status; Relationship to Head of Family; Last C. Roll No.; At Jurisdiction Where Enrolled (Yes/No); (If no – Where); Ward (Yes/No); Allotment, Annuity and Identification Numbers (if given).

917; Hardin, Essie; F; 7/24/09-22; N.C. Cherokee; 1/32; S; Daughter; 909; Yes; Yes; Unallotted

918; Hardin, Gay; M; 2/14/12-19; N.C. Cherokee; 1/32; S; Son; 910; Yes; Yes; Unallotted

919; Hardin, Lury; F; 4/14/15-16; N.C. Cherokee; 1/32; S; Daughter; 911; Yes; Yes; Unallotted

920; Hardin, Arlie; M; 4/26/18-13; N.C. Cherokee; 1/32; S; Son; 912; Yes; Yes; Unallotted

921; Hardin, James O.; M; 11/4/03-28; N.C. Cherokee; 1/32; S; Head; 913; Yes; Yes; Unallotted

922; Hardin, Glenson; M; 12/18/07-24; N.C. Cherokee; 1/32; S; Brother; 914; Yes; Yes; Unallotted

923; Hardin, Garfield; M; 11/19/09-22; N.C. Cherokee; 1/32; S; Brother; 915; Yes; Yes; Unallotted

924; Hardin, Giles; M; 3/28/12-20; N.C. Cherokee; 1/32; S; Brother; 916; Yes; Yes; Unallotted

925; Hardin, Raymond; M; 1/31/15-17; N.C. Cherokee; 1/32; S; Brother; 917; Yes; Yes; Unallotted

926; Hardin, Elizabeth; F; 6/25/46-85; N.C. Cherokee; 1/8; M; Wife; 918; Yes; Yes; Unallotted

927; Hardin, Frank J.; M; 4/5/77-54; N.C. Cherokee; 1/16; M; Head; 919; Yes; Yes; Unallotted

928; Hardin, Herbert; M; 4/30/06-25; N.C. Cherokee; 1/32; S; Son; 920; Yes; Yes; Unallotted

929; Hardin, Mae; F; 5/10/09-22; N.C. Cherokee; 1/32; S; Daughter; 921; Yes; Yes; Unallotted

930; Hardin, Vernon; M; 1/17/11-21; N.C. Cherokee; 1/32; S; Son; 922; Yes; Yes; Unallotted

931; Hardin, Geneva; F; 6/30/14-17; N.C. Cherokee; 1/32; S; Daughter; 923; Yes; Yes; Unallotted

932; Hardin, Marvin; M; 7/17/16-15; N.C. Cherokee; 1/32; S; Son; 924; Yes; Yes; Unallotted

933; Hardin, James W.; M; 6/11/91-40; N.C. Cherokee; 1/32; S; Head; 925; Yes; Yes; Unallotted

934; Hardin, Odis; M; 7/21/09-22; N.C. Cherokee; 1/64; S; Son; 926; Yes; Yes; Unallotted

935; Hardin, Luke; M; 7/25/12-19; N.C. Cherokee; 1/64; S; Son; 927; Yes; Yes; Unallotted

936; Hardin, Monie; F; 1/29/15-17; N.C. Cherokee; 1/64; S; Daughter; 928; Yes; Yes; Unallotted

Census of the **Eastern Cherokee** reservation of the **Cherokee, N.C.** jurisdiction, as of **April 1** , 19**32,** taken by **R. L. Spalsbury** , Superintendent.

Key: Number; Surname, Given; Sex; Date of Birth-Age at Last Birthday; Tribe; Degree of Blood; Marital Status; Relationship to Head of Family; Last C. Roll No.; At Jurisdiction Where Enrolled (Yes/No); (If no – Where); Ward (Yes/No); Allotment, Annuity and Identification Numbers (if given).

937;   Hardin, Arlecy; F; 10/3/17-14; N.C. Cherokee; 1/64; S; Daughter; 929; Yes; Yes; Unallotted

938;   Hardin, Edward; M; 9/18/21-10; N.C. Cherokee; 1/64; S; Son; 930; Yes; Yes; Unallotted

939;   Hardin, Lonaino; M; 2/28/96-36; N.C. Cherokee; 1/32; M; Head; 931; Yes; Yes; Unallotted

940;   Hardin, Arnold E.; M; 3/1/24-8; N.C. Cherokee; 1/64; S; Son; 932; Yes; Yes; Unallotted

941;   Hardin, Loyd; M; 5/10/83-48; N.C. Cherokee; 1/16; M; Head; 933; Yes; Yes; Unallotted

942;   Hardin, Pearly; M; 6/20/03-28; N.C. Cherokee; 1/32; S; Son; 934; Yes; Yes; Unallotted

943;   Hardin, Romelus; M; 10/26/05-26; N.C. Cherokee; 1/32; S; Son; 935; Yes; Yes; Unallotted

944;   Hardin, Bertie; M; 4/22/11-20; N.C. Cherokee; 1/32; S; Son; 936; Yes; Yes; Unallotted

945;   Hardin, Ernest; M; 3/4/14-18; N.C. Cherokee; 1/32; S; Son; 937; Yes; Yes; Unallotted

946;   Hardin, Nellie Audry; F; 7/5/16-15; N.C. Cherokee; 1/32; S; Daughter; 938; Yes; Yes; Unallotted

947;   Hardin, Edith; F; 9/13/18-13; N.C. Cherokee; 1/32; S; Daughter; 939; Yes; Yes; Unallotted

948;   Hardin, Richard; M; 1/12/93-39; N.C. Cherokee; 1/32; S; Head; 940; Yes; Yes; Unallotted

949;   Hardin, Beula; F; 5/29/08-23; N.C. Cherokee; 1/32; S; Sister; 941; Yes; Yes; Unallotted

950;   Hardin, Guion; M; 5/5/11-20; N.C. Cherokee; 1/32; S; Brother; 942; Yes; Yes; Unallotted

951;   Hardin, Flora; F; 11/27/12-19; N.C. Cherokee; 1/32; S; Sister; 943; Yes; Yes; Unallotted

952;   Hardin, Willard; M; 4/29/15-16; N.C. Cherokee; 1/32; S; Brother; 944; Yes; Yes; Unallotted

953;   Creasman, Golman; M; 12/7/18-13; N.C. Cherokee; 1/64; S; Nephew; 945; Yes; Yes; Unallotted

954;   Hardin, Thomas J.; M; 8/1/96-35; N.C. Cherokee; 1/32; M; Head; 946; Yes; Yes; Unallotted

955;   Hardin, Wyley; M; 11/18/17-14; N.C. Cherokee; 1/64; S; Son; 947; Yes; Yes; Unallotted

956;   Hardin, Pauline R.; F; 9/12/19-12; N.C. Cherokee; 1/64; S; Daughter; 948; Yes; Yes; Unallotted

Census of the **Eastern Cherokee** reservation of the **Cherokee, N.C.** jurisdiction, as of **April 1**, **1932,** taken by **R. L. Spalsbury**, Superintendent.

Key: Number; Surname, Given; Sex; Date of Birth-Age at Last Birthday; Tribe; Degree of Blood; Marital Status; Relationship to Head of Family; Last C. Roll No.; At Jurisdiction Where Enrolled (Yes/No); (If no – Where); Ward (Yes/No); Allotment, Annuity and Identification Numbers (if given).

957; Hardin, Ada; F; 6/16/21-10; N.C. Cherokee; 1/64; S; Daughter; 949; Yes; Yes; Unallotted

958; Hardin, Virgil; M; 3/13/98-34; N.C. Cherokee; 1/32; M; Head; 950; Yes; Yes; Unallotted

959; Hardin, Frances; F; 4/13/22-9; N.C. Cherokee; 1/64; S; Daughter; 951; Yes; Yes; Unallotted

960; Hardin, William; M; 8/19/04-27; N.C. Cherokee; 1/64; S; Head; 952; Yes; Yes; Unallotted

961; Hardin, Grant; M; 9/9/05-26; N.C. Cherokee; 1/64; S; Brother; 953; Yes; Yes; Unallotted

962; Hardin, Ruby; F; 4/23/07-24; N.C. Cherokee; 1/64; S; Sister; 954; Yes; Yes; Unallotted

963; Hardin, Noah; M; 3/25/11-21; N.C. Cherokee; 1/64; S; Brother; 955; Yes; Yes; Unallotted

964; Hardin, Guy; M; 3/20/13-19; N.C. Cherokee; 1/64; S; Brother; 956; Yes; Yes; Unallotted

965; Hardin, Fotch; M; 9/11/18-13; N.C. Cherokee; 1/64; S; Brother; 957; Yes; Yes; Unallotted

966; Hardin, William J.; M; 1/5/72-60; N.C. Cherokee; 1/16; M; Head; 958; Yes; Yes; Unallotted

967; Hardin, Hardie; M; 5/4/00-31; N.C. Cherokee; 1/32; S; Son; 959; Yes; Yes; Unallotted

968; Hardin, Roy; M; 11/18/04-27; N.C. Cherokee; 1/32; S; Son; 960; Yes; Yes; Unallotted

969; Hardin, Paul; M; 3/6/11-21; N.C. Cherokee; 1/32; S; Son; 961; Yes; Yes; Unallotted

970; Hardin, Vincent; M; 11/9/13-18; N.C. Cherokee; 1/32; S; Son; 962; Yes; Yes; Unallotted

971; Hardin, Gurley; M; 11/9/13-18; N.C. Cherokee; 1/32; S; Son; 963; Yes; Yes; Unallotted

972; Harding, Mary J.C.; F; 6/18/77-54; N.C. Cherokee; 1/8; M; Wife; 964; Yes; Yes; Unallotted

973; Harding, Harold; M; 5/28/12-19; N.C. Cherokee; 1/16; S; Son; 965; Yes; Yes; Unallotted

974; Harding, Florence S.; F; 11/27/13-18; N.C. Cherokee; 1/16; S; Daughter; 966; Yes; Yes; Unallotted

[Note: 975-986, Missing page left off film. Check 1930, 1931 & 1933 Censuses]

987; Hartness, Girty L.; F; 8/3/06-25; N.C. Cherokee; 1/64; S; Daughter; 979; Yes; Yes; Unallotted

53

Census of the **Eastern Cherokee** reservation of the **Cherokee, N.C.** jurisdiction, as of **April 1** , 1932, taken by **R. L. Spalsbury** , Superintendent.

Key: Number; Surname, Given; Sex; Date of Birth-Age at Last Birthday; Tribe; Degree of Blood; Marital Status; Relationship to Head of Family; Last C. Roll No.; At Jurisdiction Where Enrolled (Yes/No); (If no – Where); Ward (Yes/No); Allotment, Annuity and Identification Numbers (if given).

988; Hartness, Icey; F; 1/30/08-24; N.C. Cherokee; 1/64; S; Daughter; 980; Yes; Yes; Unallotted

989; Hawkins (Raper, Dora P.), Dora P.; F; 4/20/82-49; N.C. Cherokee; 1/8; M; Wife; 981; No; Copperhill, Polk, Tenn.; Yes; Unallotted

990; Hawkins, Charles L.; M; 9/27/03-28; N.C. Cherokee; 1/16; S; Son; 982; No; Copperhill, Polk, Tenn.; Yes; Unallotted

991; Hawkins, Luther; M; 1/29/09-23; N.C. Cherokee; 1/16; S; Son; 983; No; Copperhill, Polk, Tenn.; Yes; Unallotted

992; Hawkins, Della May; F; 12/26/10-21; N.C. Cherokee; 1/16; S; Daughter; 984; No; Copperhill, Polk, Tenn.; Yes; Unallotted

993; Hawkins, Hammond Lee; M; 12/26/12-19; N.C. Cherokee; 1/16; S; Son; 985; No; Copperhill, Polk, Tenn.; Yes; Unallotted

994; Hawkins, Ruth; F; 7/30/15-16; N.C. Cherokee; 1/16; S; Daughter; 986; No; Copperhill, Polk, Tenn.; Yes; Unallotted

995; Hawkins, Maud; F; 6/17/18-13; N.C. Cherokee; 1/16; S; Daughter; 987; No; Copperhill, Polk, Tenn.; Yes; Unallotted

996; Hawkins, James; M; 8/3/21-10; N.C. Cherokee; 1/16; S; Son; 988; No; Copperhill, Polk, Tenn.; Yes; Unallotted

997; Hayes (Mashburn, Mattie), Mattie M.; F; 1/21/03-29; N.C. Cherokee; 3/32; M; Wife; 989; Yes; Yes; Unallotted

998; Hayes (Mashburn, Nina), Nina M.; F; 8/22/07-24; N.C. Cherokee; 3/32; M; Wife; 990; Yes; Yes; Unallotted

999; Haymon, Bessie Burgess; F; 4/20/96-35; N.C. Cherokee; 1/8; M; Wife; 991; Yes; Yes; Unallotted

1000; Hensley, Grace Smith; F; 4/21/05-27; N.C. Cherokee; 3/16; M; Wife; 992; Yes; Yes; Unallotted

1001; Hensley, Naomi M.; F; 5/25/25-6; N.C. Cherokee; 3/32; S; Daughter; 993; Yes; Yes; Unallotted

1002; Hensley (Smith, Louisa), Louisa S.; F; 11/5/81-50; N.C. Cherokee; 1/4; M; Wife; 994; No; Maryville, Blount, Tenn.; Yes; Unallotted

1003; Hensley (Lambert, Oney), Oney L.; F; 6/11/06-25; N.C. Cherokee; 1/16; M; Wife; 995; Yes; Yes; Unallotted

1004; Henson, Everett; M; 12/25/16-15; N.C. Cherokee; 1/64; S; Alone; 966; No; Ducktown, Polk, Tenn.; Yes; Unallotted

1005; Herron (Wolfe, Amanda), Amanda J.W.; F; 9/22/99-32; N.C. Cherokee; 1/8; M; Wife; 997; Yes; Yes; Unallotted

Census of the **Eastern Cherokee** reservation of the **Cherokee, N.C.** jurisdiction, as of **April 1** , **1932,** taken by **R. L. Spalsbury** , Superintendent.

Key: Number; Surname, Given; Sex; Date of Birth-Age at Last Birthday; Tribe; Degree of Blood; Marital Status; Relationship to Head of Family; Last C. Roll No.; At Jurisdiction Where Enrolled (Yes/No); (If no – Where); Ward (Yes/No); Allotment, Annuity and Identification Numbers (if given).

1006; Higgins (Smith, Emma), Emma; F; 9/26/88-43; N.C. Cherokee; 1/4; M; Wife; 998; No; Maryville, Blount, Tenn.; Yes; Unallotted

1007; Higgins, Rose; F; 12/7/09-22; N.C. Cherokee; 1/8; S; Daughter; 999; No; Maryville, Blount, Tenn.; Yes; Unallotted

1008; Higgins, Lillie; F; 3/6/10-22; N.C. Cherokee; 1/8; S; Daughter; 1000; No; Maryville, Blount, Tenn.; Yes; Unallotted

1009; Higgins, Charles; M; 2/5/13-19; N.C. Cherokee; 1/8; S; Son; 1001; No; Maryville, Blount, Tenn.; Yes; Unallotted

1010; Higgins, Thelma; F; 9/12/14-17; N.C. Cherokee; 1/8; S; Daughter; 1002; No; Maryville, Blount, Tenn.; Yes; Unallotted

1011; Higgins, Henry; M; 12/23/18-13; N.C. Cherokee; 1/8; S; Son; 1003; No; Maryville, Blount, Tenn.; Yes; Unallotted

1012; Higgins, Willie; M; 12/31/22-9; N.C. Cherokee; 1/8; S; Son; 1004; No; Maryville, Blount, Tenn.; Yes; Unallotted

1013; Hill, Abraham; M; 5/15/64-67; N.C. Cherokee; 4/4; M; Head; 1005; Yes; Yes; Unallotted

1014; Hill, Annie; F; 9/20/72-59; N.C. Cherokee; 4/4; M; Wife; 1006; Yes; Yes; Unallotted

1015; Hill, Blaine; M; 7/20/86-45; N.C. Cherokee; 15/16; M; Head; 1007; Yes; Yes; Unallotted

1016; Hill, Luzene; F; 6/12/80-51; N.C. Cherokee; 4/4; M; Wife; 1008; Yes; Yes; Unallotted

1017; Hill, Viola N.; F; 9/27/09-22; N.C. Cherokee; 31/32; S; Daughter; 1009; Yes; Yes; Unallotted

1018; Hill, Elizabeth; F; 12/23/13-18; N.C. Cherokee; 31/32; S; Daughter; 1010; Yes; Yes; Unallotted

1019; Hill, Blaine Jr.; M; 10/7/15-16; N.C. Cherokee; 31/32; S; Son; 1011; Yes; Yes; Unallotted

1020; Hill, Lloyd; M; 8/23/17-14; N.C. Cherokee; 31/32; S; Son; 1012; Yes; Yes; Unallotted

1021; Hill (Mr. Viola N.), James R.; M; 13/14/27-5; N.C. Cherokee; 1/4+; S; Grandson; 1013; Yes; Yes; Unallotted

1022; Hill (Mr.[sic] Viola N,), Amelia; F; 8/31/28-3; N.C. Cherokee; 1/4+; S; Granddau.; 1014; Yes; Yes; Unallotted

1023; Hill, John; M; 6/21/56-75; N.C. Cherokee; 4/4; Wd.; Head; 1015; Yes; Yes; Unallotted

1024; Hill, Laura J. Wolfe; F; 4/2/90-41; N.C. Cherokee; 4/4; Wd.; Head; 1016; Yes; Yes; Unallotted

1025; Hill, Ned; M; 9/18/13-18; N.C. Cherokee; 31/32; S; Son; 1017; Yes; Yes; Unallotted

Census of the **Eastern Cherokee** reservation of the **Cherokee, N.C.** jurisdiction, as of **April 1**, 19**32,** taken by **R. L. Spalsbury**, Superintendent.

Key: Number; Surname, Given; Sex; Date of Birth-Age at Last Birthday; Tribe; Degree of Blood; Marital Status; Relationship to Head of Family; Last C. Roll No.; At Jurisdiction Where Enrolled (Yes/No); (If no – Where); Ward (Yes/No); Allotment, Annuity and Identification Numbers (if given).

1026; Hill, Rufus Scott; M; 10/4/15-16; N.C. Cherokee; 31/32; S; Son; 1018; Yes; Yes; Unallotted

1027; Hill, Jake; M; 7/7/25-6; N.C. Cherokee; 31/32; S; Son; 1019; Yes; Yes; Unallotted

1028; Hill, Jesse; M; 10/5/27-4; N.C. Cherokee; 31/32; S; Son; 1020; Yes; Yes; Unallotted

1029; Hill, Ned; M; 3/28/88-43; N.C. Cherokee; 15/16; S; Head; 1021; Yes; Yes; Unallotted

1030; Hill, Etta; F; 12/26/74-57; N.C. Cherokee; 4/4; Wd.; Head; 1022; Yes; Yes; Unallotted

1031; Hipps (Lambert, Nannie), Nannie; F; 11/5/92-39; N.C. Cherokee; 1/16; M; Wife; 1023; Yes; Yes; Unallotted

1032; Hipps, Nina Marie; F; 3/22/13-19; N.C. Cherokee; 1/32; S; Daughter; 1024; Yes; Yes; Unallotted

1033; Hipps, James D.; M; 6/15/17-14; N.C. Cherokee; 1/32; S; Son; 1025; Yes; Yes; Unallotted

1034; Hipps, Emmaline; F; 5/15/20-11; N.C. Cherokee; 1/32; S; Daughter; 1026; Yes; Yes; Unallotted

1035; Hipps, Joshua B.; M; 9/26/23-8; N.C. Cherokee; 1/32; S; Son; 1027; Yes; Yes; Unallotted

1036; Hipps (Lambert, Verdie), Verdie L.; F; 4/28/94-37; N.C. Cherokee; 1/16; M; Wife; 1028; Yes; Yes; Unallotted

1037; Hipps, Bernice Lee; F; 2/24/22-10; N.C. Cherokee; 1/32; S; Daughter; 1029; Yes; Yes; Unallotted

1038; Hipps, Joseph F.; M; 12/3/23-8; N.C. Cherokee; 1/32; S; Son; 1030; Yes; Yes; Unallotted

1039; Hodges, Ollie Jane; F; 1876-56; N.C. Cherokee; 1/4-; M; Wife; 1031; Yes; Yes; Unallotted

1040; Hodges, Ollie; F; 1901-31; N.C. Cherokee; 1/4-; S; Daughter; 1032; Yes; Yes; Unallotted

1041; Hogan (Lee, Edith), Edith L.; F; 6/28/96-35; N.C. Cherokee; 1/16; M; Wife; 1033; Yes; Yes; Unallotted

1042; Hogan, Wayne; M; 12/6/16-15; N.C. Cherokee; 1/32; S; Son; 1034; Yes; Yes; Unallotted

1043; Hogan, Floyd; M; 8/11/18-13; N.C. Cherokee; 1/32; S; Son; 1035; Yes; Yes; Unallotted

1044; Hogan, Norma; F; 11/10/21-10; N.C. Cherokee; 1/32; S; Daughter; 1036; Yes; Yes; Unallotted

Census of the **Eastern Cherokee** reservation of the **Cherokee, N.C.** jurisdiction, as of **April 1**, **1932,** taken by **R. L. Spalsbury**, Superintendent.

Key: Number; Surname, Given; Sex; Date of Birth-Age at Last Birthday; Tribe; Degree of Blood; Marital Status; Relationship to Head of Family; Last C. Roll No.; At Jurisdiction Where Enrolled (Yes/No); (If no – Where); Ward (Yes/No); Allotment, Annuity and Identification Numbers (if given).

1045; Hogan, Faye; F; 5/18/23-8; N.C. Cherokee; 1/32; S; Daughter; 1037; Yes; Yes; Unallotted

1046; Holland, David; M; 11/7/08-23; N.C. Cherokee; 3/8; S; Head; 1038; Yes; Yes; Unallotted

1047; Holland, Jesse; M; 3/12/58-74; N.C. Cherokee; 1/8; M; Head; 1039; Yes; Yes; Unallotted

1048; Hornbuckle, Andy; M; 7/9/03-28; N.C. Cherokee; 3/4; S; Head; 1040; Yes; Yes; Unallotted

1049; Hornbuckle, Charles; M; 4/11/17-14; N.C. Cherokee; 3/32; S; Alone; 1041; Yes; Yes; Unallotted
1050; Hornbuckle, Lottie; F; 3/28/20-12; N.C. Cherokee; 3/32; S; Sister; 1042; Yes; Yes; Unallotted

1051; Hornbuckle, Daniel; M; 7/7/96-35; N.C. Cherokee; 3/4; M; Head; 1043; Yes; Yes; Unallotted
1052; Hornbuckle, Nannie; F; 5/17/05-26; N.C. Cherokee; 9/16; M; Wife; 1044; Yes; Yes; Unallotted

1053; Hornbuckle, Fred; M; 7/11/97-34; N.C. Cherokee; 1/8; S; Head; 1045; Yes; Yes; Unallotted

1054; Hornbuckle, George; M; 5/4/77-54; N.C. Cherokee; 1/4; M; Head; 1046; Yes; Yes; Unallotted
1055; Hornbuckle, Hartman; M; 4/16/01-30; N.C. Cherokee; 1/8; S; Son; 1047; Yes; Yes; Unallotted
1056; Hornbuckle, Wm. Allen; M; 9/29/07-24; N.C. Cherokee; 1/8; S; Son; 1048; Yes; Yes; Unallotted
1057; Hornbuckle, Clifford; M; 7/1/10-21; N.C. Cherokee; 1/8; S; Son; 1049; Yes; Yes; Unallotted
1058; Hornbuckle, Thurman; M; 8/12/12-19; N.C. Cherokee; 1/8; S; Son; 1050; Yes; Yes; Unallotted
1059; Hornbuckle, Clyda May; F; 7/22/15-16; N.C. Cherokee; 1/8; S; Daughter; 1051; Yes; Yes; Unallotted
1060; Hornbuckle, Benjamin; M; 7/19/18-13; N.C. Cherokee; 1/8; S; Son; 1052; Yes; Yes; Unallotted

1061; Hornbuckle, Israel; M; 6/9/87-44; N.C. Cherokee; 7/8; M; Head; 1053; Yes; Yes; Unallotted
1062; Hornbuckle, Addie Queen; F; 2/5/02-30; N.C. Cherokee; 5/8; M; Wife; 1054; Yes; Yes; Unallotted

Census of the **Eastern Cherokee** reservation of the **Cherokee, N.C.** jurisdiction, as of **April 1** , 1**932,** taken by   **R. L. Spalsbury**   , Superintendent.

Key: Number; Surname, Given; Sex; Date of Birth-Age at Last Birthday; Tribe; Degree of Blood; Marital Status; Relationship to Head of Family; Last C. Roll No.; At Jurisdiction Where Enrolled (Yes/No); (If no – Where); Ward (Yes/No); Allotment, Annuity and Identification Numbers (if given).

1063;   Hornbuckle, Jeff D.; M; 5/4/64-67; N.C. Cherokee; 1/2; M; Head; 1055; Yes; Yes; Unallotted

1064;   Hornbuckle, Aninih B.; F; 12/21/48-83; N.C. Cherokee; 4/4; M; Wife; 1056; Yes; Yes; Unallotted

1065;   Hornbuckle, Jeff D. Jr.; M; 9/27/92-39; N.C. Cherokee; 3/4; M; Head; 1057; Yes; Yes; Unallotted

1066;   Hornbuckle, Sallie Otter; F; 11/9/01-30; N.C. Cherokee; 4/4; M; Wife; 1058; Yes; Yes; Unallotted

1067;   Hornbuckle, Callie; F; 1/2/22-10; N.C. Cherokee; 7/8; S; Daughter; 1059; Yes; Yes; Unallotted

1068;   Hornbuckle, Mattie; F; 12/21/63-68; N.C. Cherokee; 4/4; Wd.; Head; 1060; Yes; Yes; Unallotted

1069;   Hornbuckle, John R.; M; 9/16/05-26; N.C. Cherokee; 1/8; M; Head; 1061; Yes; Yes; Unallotted

1070;   Hornbuckle, Stacy C.; F; 11/29/09-22; N.C. Cherokee; 7/8; M; Wife; 1062; Yes; Yes; Unallotted

1071;   Hornbuckle, Larens; M; 2/13/28-4; N.C. Cherokee; 1/2; S; Son; 1063; Yes; Yes; Unallotted

1072;   Hornbuckle, Jean E.; F; 10/23/29-2; N.C. Cherokee; 1/2; S; Daughter; 1064; Yes; Yes; Unallotted

1073;   Hornbuckle, Johnson; M; 11/19/01-30; N.C. Cherokee; 1/2; S; Head; 1065; Yes; Yes; Unallotted

1074;   Hornbuckle, Julius; M; 2/2/00-32; N.C. Cherokee; 1/4; S; Head; 1066; Yes; Yes; Unallotted

1075;   Hornbuckle, Maggie; F; 5/1/80-51; N.C. Cherokee; 7/8; S; Head; 1067; Yes; Yes; Unallotted

1076;   Hornbuckle, William; M; 1/20/69-63; N.C. Cherokee; 1/4; M; Head; 1068; Yes; Yes; Unallotted

1077;   Hornbuckle, Mary Maney; F; 6/19/04-27; N.C. Cherokee; 1/2; M; Wife; 1069; Yes; Yes; Unallotted

1078;   Hornbuckle, Jennie; F; 3/6/11-21; N.C. Cherokee; 1/8; S; Daughter; 1070; Yes; Yes; Unallotted

1079;   Hornbuckle, Minnie May; F; 9/4/21-10; N.C. Cherokee; 3/8; S; Daughter; 1071; Yes; Yes; Unallotted

1080;   Hornbuckle, John S.; M; 5/9/25-6; N.C. Cherokee; 3/8; S; Son; 1072; Yes; Yes; Unallotted

1081;   Hornbuckle, Evelyn N.; F; 1/22/30-2; N.C. Cherokee; 3/8; S; Daughter; 1073; Yes; Yes; Unallotted

Census of the **Eastern Cherokee** reservation of the **Cherokee, N.C.** jurisdiction, as of **April 1** , 19**32,** taken by **R. L. Spalsbury** , Superintendent.

Key: Number; Surname, Given; Sex; Date of Birth-Age at Last Birthday; Tribe; Degree of Blood; Marital Status; Relationship to Head of Family; Last C. Roll No.; At Jurisdiction Where Enrolled (Yes/No); (If no – Where); Ward (Yes/No); Allotment, Annuity and Identification Numbers (if given).

1082; Hornbuckle, William; M; 12/25/81-50; N.C. Cherokee; 7/8; M; Head; 1074; Yes; Yes; Unallotted

1083; Hornbuckle, Annie O.; F; 5/31/94-37; N.C. Cherokee; 15/16; M; Wife; 1075; Yes; Yes; Unallotted

1084; Hornbuckle, Polly B.; F; 11/28/06-24; N.C. Cherokee; 1/16; Wd.; Head; 1077; Yes; Yes; Unallotted

1085; Hunter (Patterson, Celia), Celia; F; 6/12/01-30; N.C. Cherokee; 1/32; M; Wife; 1078; Yes; Yes; Unallotted

1086; Hornbuckle, Agnes; F; 1/21/24-8; N.C. Cherokee; 1/64; S; Daughter; 1079; Yes; Yes; Unallotted

1087; Huskey, Birdie C.H.; F; 4/12/11-20; N.C. Cherokee; 31/32; M; Wife; 1080; Yes; Yes; Unallotted

1088; Hyde (Rose, Carrie), Carrie R.; F; 4/10/04-27; N.C. Cherokee; 1/16; M; Wife; 1081; Yes; Yes; Unallotted

1089; Jackson (Raper, Dovie), Dovie; F; 3/15/03-29; N.C. Cherokee; 1/16; M; Wife; 1082; Yes; Yes; Unallotted

1090; Jackson, Thelma Lee; F; 10/29/22-9; N.C. Cherokee; 1/32; S; Daughter; 1083; Yes; Yes; Unallotted

1091; Jackson, Carl; M; 5/19/24-7; N.C. Cherokee; 1/32; S; Son; 1084; Yes; Yes; Unallotted

1092; Jackson, Eddie; M; 3/10/04-28; N.C. Cherokee; 4/4; M; Head; 1085; Yes; Yes; Unallotted

1093; Jackson, Margaret A.; F; 6/15/06-25; N.C. Cherokee; 15/16; M; Wife; 1086; Yes; Yes; Unallotted

1094; Jackson, Edward; M; 8/30/26-5; N.C. Cherokee; 29/32; S; Son; 1087; Yes; Yes; Unallotted

1095; Jackson, Lula; F; 3/13/32-18 days; N.C. Cherokee; 29/32; S; Daughter; ---; Yes; Yes; Unallotted

1096; Jackson, Jack; M; 2/2/92-40; N.C. Cherokee; 7/16; M; Head; 1089; Yes; Yes; Unallotted

1097; Jackson, Mary Queen; F; 3/15/03-29; N.C. Cherokee; 5/8; M; Wife; 1090; Yes; Yes; Unallotted

1098; Jackson, Walter S.; M; 5/29/23-8; N.C. Cherokee; 17/32; S; Son; 1091; Yes; Yes; Unallotted

1099; Jackson, John S.; M; 1/21/25-7; N.C. Cherokee; 17/32; S; Son; 1092; Yes; Yes; Unallotted

1100; Jackson, Boyd S.; M; 3/7/27-5; N.C. Cherokee; 17/32; S; Son; 1093; Yes; Yes; Unallotted

Census of the **Eastern Cherokee** reservation of the **Cherokee, N.C.** jurisdiction, as of **April 1** , 19**32**, taken by **R. L. Spalsbury** , Superintendent.

Key: Number; Surname, Given; Sex; Date of Birth-Age at Last Birthday; Tribe; Degree of Blood; Marital Status; Relationship to Head of Family; Last C. Roll No.; At Jurisdiction Where Enrolled (Yes/No); (If no – Where); Ward (Yes/No); Allotment, Annuity and Identification Numbers (if given).

1101; Jackson, Neoma E.; F; 2/26/29-3; N.C. Cherokee; 17/32; S; Daughter; 1094; Yes; Yes; Unallotted

1102; Jackson, Mary E.; F; 8/12/31-7/12; N.C. Cherokee; 17/32; S; Daughter; ---; Yes; Yes; Unallotted

1103; Jackson, Jacob; M; 12/22/00-31; N.C. Cherokee; 4/4; M; Head; 1095; Yes; Yes; Unallotted

1104; Jackson, Olivan B.; F; 7/18/01-30; N.C. Cherokee; 4/4; M; Wife; 1096; Yes; Yes; Unallotted

1105; Jackson, Elijah; M; 5/16/18-13; N.C. Cherokee; 4/4; S; Son; 1097; Yes; Yes; Unallotted

1106; Jackson, Bessie; F; 6/22/24-7; N.C. Cherokee; 4/4; S; Daughter; 1098; Yes; Yes; Unallotted

1107; Jackson, John; M; 2/1/29-3; N.C. Cherokee; 4/4; S; Son; 1099; Yes; Yes; Unallotted

1108; Jackson, Jennie A.H.; F; 5/25/86-45; N.C. Cherokee; 3/4; M; Wife; 1100; Yes; Yes; Unallotted

1109; Jackson, Lawyer; M; 5/9/72-59; N.C. Cherokee; 4/4; M; Head; 1101; Yes; Yes; Unallotted

1110; Jackson, Dekie; F; 10/5/71-60; N.C. Cherokee; 4/4; M; Wife; 1102; Yes; Yes; Unallotted

1111; Jackson, Florence; F; 5/19/02-29; N.C. Cherokee; 4/4; S; Daughter; 1103; Yes; Yes; Unallotted

1112; Jackson (Murphy, Margaret), Margaret M.; F; 4/17/89-42; N.C. Cherokee; 1/8; M; Wife; 1104; Yes; Yes; Unallotted

1113; Hipps, Willard; M; 3/3/07-25; N.C. Cherokee; 1/16; S; Son; 1105; Yes; Yes; Unallotted

1114; Jackson, Robert; M; 10/24/75-56; N.C. Cherokee; 4/4; M; Head; 1106; Yes; Yes; Unallotted

1115; Jackson, Caroline; F; 4/30/77-54; N.C. Cherokee; 4/4; M; Wife; 1107; Yes; Yes; Unallotted

1116; Jackson, Isaac; M; 8/30/08-23; N.C. Cherokee; 4/4; S; Son; 1108; Yes; Yes; Unallotted

1117; Jackson, Stacey; F; 1/18/60-72; N.C. Cherokee; 4/4; Wd.; Head; 1109; Yes; Yes; Unallotted

1118; Jackson, Wesley; M; 10/17/99-32; N.C. Cherokee; 4/4; Div.; Head; 1110; Yes; Yes; Unallotted

Census of the **Eastern Cherokee** reservation of the **Cherokee, N.C.** jurisdiction, as of **April 1** , **1932,** taken by **R. L. Spalsbury** , Superintendent.

Key: Number; Surname, Given; Sex; Date of Birth-Age at Last Birthday; Tribe; Degree of Blood; Marital Status; Relationship to Head of Family; Last C. Roll No.; At Jurisdiction Where Enrolled (Yes/No); (If no – Where); Ward (Yes/No); Allotment, Annuity and Identification Numbers (if given).

1119; Jacobs (Driver, Helen), Helen E.; F; 6/7/08-23; N.C. Cherokee; 1/2; M; Wife; 1111; Yes; Yes; Unallotted

1120; James, Allen; M; 3/29/98-34; N.C. Cherokee; 1/64; S; Head; 1112; Yes; Yes; Unallotted

1121; James, Asa; M; 6/25/87-44; N.C. Cherokee; 1/64; M; Head; 1113; Yes; Yes; Unallotted

1122; James, Annie; F; 1/21/09-23; N.C. Cherokee; 1/128; S; Daughter; 1114; Yes; Yes; Unallotted

1123; James, Frank; M; 12/8/11-20; N.C. Cherokee; 1/128; S; Son; 1115; Yes; Yes; Unallotted

1124; James, Geneva; F; 8/5/14-17; N.C. Cherokee; 1/128; S; Daughter; 1116; Yes; Yes; Unallotted

1125; James, Sheridan; M; 4/29/17-14; N.C. Cherokee; 1/128; S; Son; 1117; Yes; Yes; Unallotted

1126; James, Dorothy; F; 11/27/19-12; N.C. Cherokee; 1/128; S; Daughter; 1118; Yes; Yes; Unallotted

1127; James, Roscoe; M; 3/11/22-10; N.C. Cherokee; 1/128; S; Son; 1119; Yes; Yes; Unallotted

1128; Jenkins (Cooper, Myrtle), Myrtle; F; 10/6/02-29; N.C. Cherokee; 1/16; M; Wife; 1120; Yes; Yes; Unallotted

1129; Jessan, Nellie W.; F; 6/2/96-35; N.C. Cherokee; 7/8; Wd.; Head; 1121; Yes; Yes; Unallotted

1130; Jessan, Elnora; F; 6/16/08-23; N.C. Cherokee; 13/16; S; Step-dau.; 1122; Yes; Yes; Unallotted

1131; Jessan, Lillian; F; 8/10/10-21; N.C. Cherokee; 13/16; S; Step-dau.; 1123; Yes; Yes; Unallotted

1132; Jessan, John J.; M; 5/10/13-18; N.C. Cherokee; 13/16; S; Step-son; 1124; Yes; Yes; Unallotted

1133; James, Mary Holt; F; 9/10/18-13; N.C. Cherokee; 7/8; S; Daughter; 1125; Yes; Yes; Unallotted

1134; Jessan, Sim DeHart; M; 1/3/03-29; N.C. Cherokee; 4/4; M; Head; 1126; Yes; Yes; Unallotted

1135; Jessan, Agnes Long; F; 1/19/04-24[sic]; N.C. Cherokee; 4/4; M; Wife; 1127; Yes; Yes; Unallotted

1136; Johnson, Addison; M; 6/28/86-45; N.C. Cherokee; 3/8; M; Head; 1128; Yes; Yes; Unallotted

1137; Johnson, Isaac; M; 7/14/93-38; N.C. Cherokee; 1/4; S; Head; 1129; Yes; Yes; Unallotted

Census of the **Eastern Cherokee** reservation of the **Cherokee, N.C.** jurisdiction, as of **April 1** , 19**32,** taken by **R. L. Spalsbury** , Superintendent.

Key: Number; Surname, Given; Sex; Date of Birth-Age at Last Birthday; Tribe; Degree of Blood; Marital Status; Relationship to Head of Family; Last C. Roll No.; At Jurisdiction Where Enrolled (Yes/No); (If no – Where); Ward (Yes/No); Allotment, Annuity and Identification Numbers (if given).

1138; Johnson (Loudermilk, Rebecca), Rebecca; F; 8/23/99-32; N.C. Cherokee; 1/16; M; Wife; 1130; Yes; Yes; Unallotted

1139; Johnson, Tom; M; 5/16/09-22; N.C. Cherokee; 4/4; S; Head; 1131; Yes; Yes; Unallotted

1140; Johnson, Jonah; M; 6/27/11-20; N.C. Cherokee; 4/4; S; Brother; 1132; Yes; Yes; Unallotted

1141; Johnson, Tuskegie; M; 12/22/78-54; N.C. Cherokee; 4/4; M; Head; 1133; Yes; Yes; Unallotted

1142; Johnson, Sally O.; F; 12/22/84-47; N.C. Cherokee; 4/4; M; Wife; 1134; Yes; Yes; Unallotted

1143; Johnson, Charles; M; 11/17/14-17; N.C. Cherokee; 4/4; S; Son; 1135; Yes; Yes; Unallotted

1144; Johnson, Yona; M; 12/25/79-52; N.C. Cherokee; 4/4; M; Head; 1137; Yes; Yes; Unallotted

1145; Johnson, Margaret G.; F; 9/14/12-19; N.C. Cherokee; 15/16; S; Daughter; 1138; Yes; Yes; Unallotted

1146; Johnson, Joseph L.; M; 11/16/16-15; N.C. Cherokee; 15/16; S; Son; 1139; Yes; Yes; Unallotted

1147; Johnson, Lloyd H.; M; 11/5/19-12; N.C. Cherokee; 15/16; S; Son; 1140; Yes; Yes; Unallotted

1148; Jones (Hardin, Verdia), Virdie; F; 2/18/04-28; N.C. Cherokee; 1/32; M; Wife; 1141; Yes; Yes; Unallotted

1149; Jones, Lyle; M; 6/14/23-9; N.C. Cherokee; 1/64; S; Son; 1142; Yes; Yes; Unallotted

1150; Jordan (Lambert, Julia), Julia; F; 4/22/01-30; N.C. Cherokee; 1/16; M; Wife; 1143; Yes; Yes; Unallotted

1151; Jordan, Wm. Carson; M; 3/5/20-12; N.C. Cherokee; 1/32; S; Son; 1144; Yes; Yes; Unallotted

1152; Jordan, Mary E.; F; 1/3/23-9; N.C. Cherokee; 1/32; S; Daughter; 1145; Yes; Yes; Unallotted

1153; Jordan, Clyde; M; 1880-52; N.C. Cherokee; 1/4-; M; Head; 1146; Yes; Added by letter 1/27/31; Yes; Unallotted

1154; Jordan, Jake A.; M; 1890-42; N.C. Cherokee; 1/4-; M; Husband; 1147; Yes; Added by letter 1/27/31; Yes; Unallotted

1155; Jordan, John J.; M; 1886-46; N.C. Cherokee; 1/4-; M; Husband; 1148; Yes; Added by letter 1/27/31; Yes; Unallotted

1156; Jordan, John M.; M; 1893-39; N.C. Cherokee; 1/4-; S; Single; 1149; Yes; Added by letter 1/27/31; Yes; Unallotted

Census of the **Eastern Cherokee** reservation of the **Cherokee, N.C.** jurisdiction, as of **April 1** , 19**32,** taken by **R. L. Spalsbury** , Superintendent.

Key: Number; Surname, Given; Sex; Date of Birth-Age at Last Birthday; Tribe; Degree of Blood; Marital Status; Relationship to Head of Family; Last C. Roll No.; At Jurisdiction Where Enrolled (Yes/No); (If no – Where); Ward (Yes/No); Allotment, Annuity and Identification Numbers (if given).

1157; Jordan, Mark; M; 1873-59; N.C. Cherokee; 1/4-; M; Husband; 1150; Yes; Added by letter 1/27/31; Yes; Unallotted

1158; Jordan, Della; F; 1915-17; N.C. Cherokee; 1/4-; S; Daughter; 1151; Yes; Added by letter 1/27/31; Yes; Unallotted

1159; Jordan, Leona; F; 1920-12; N.C. Cherokee; 1/4-; S; Daughter; 1152; Yes; Added by letter 1/27/31; Yes; Unallotted

1160; Jordan, Zora; F; 1921-11; N.C. Cherokee; 1/4-; S; Daughter; 1153; Yes; Added by letter 1/27/31; Yes; Unallotted

1161; Jordan, Wm. A.; M; 1889-43; N.C. Cherokee; 1/4-; M; Husband; 1154; Yes; Added by letter 1/27/31; Yes; Unallotted

1162; Jumper, Edward; M; 12/25/00-31; N.C. Cherokee; 4/4; M; Head; 1155; Yes; Yes; Unallotted

1163; Jumper, Nancy W.; F; 7/4/06-25; N.C. Cherokee; 4/4; M; Wife; 1156; Yes; Yes; Unallotted

1164; Jumper, Ute; M; 7/21/23-8; N.C. Cherokee; 4/4; S; Son; 1157; Yes; Yes; Unallotted

1165; Jumper, Stancill; M; 10/24/99-32; N.C. Cherokee; 4/4; M; Head; 1158; Yes; Yes; Unallotted

1166; Jumper, Nola Long; F; 6/27/99-32; N.C. Cherokee; 4/4; M; Wife; 1159; Yes; Yes; Unallotted

1167; Jumper, Leona; F; 1/10/26-6; N.C. Cherokee; 4/4; S; Daughter; 1160; Yes; Yes; Unallotted

1168; Jumper, Nellie; F; 11/15/27-4; N.C. Cherokee; 4/4; S; Daughter; 1161; Yes; Yes; Unallotted

1169; Jumper, Stancill Jr.; M; 2/15/30-2; N.C. Cherokee; 4/4; S; Son; 1162; Yes; Yes; Unallotted

1170; Jumper, Ute; M; 5/10/71-60; N.C. Cherokee; 4/4; M; Head; 1163; Yes; Yes; Unallotted

1171; Jumper, Betsy; F; 12/22/72-59; N.C. Cherokee; 4/4; M; Wife; 1164; Yes; Yes; Unallotted

1172; Jumper, James; M; 3/24/04-28; N.C. Cherokee; 4/4; S; Son; 1165; Yes; Yes; Unallotted

1173; Jumper, Thomas; M; 6/18/06-25; N.C. Cherokee; 4/4; S; Son; 1166; Yes; Yes; Unallotted

1174; Jumper, Henry; M; 6/21/08-23; N.C. Cherokee; 4/4; S; Son; 1167; Yes; Yes; Unallotted

1175; Jumper, Ella; F; 10/23/09-22; N.C. Cherokee; 4/4; S; Daughter; 1168; Yes; Yes; Unallotted

1176; Junaluskie, Emmaline; F; 11/8/98-33; N.C. Cherokee; 15/16; Wd.; Head; 1170; Yes; Yes; Unallotted

Census of the **Eastern Cherokee** reservation of the **Cherokee, N.C.** jurisdiction, as of **April 1** , 19**32,** taken by **R. L. Spalsbury** , Superintendent.

Key: Number; Surname, Given; Sex; Date of Birth-Age at Last Birthday; Tribe; Degree of Blood; Marital Status; Relationship to Head of Family; Last C. Roll No.; At Jurisdiction Where Enrolled (Yes/No); (If no – Where); Ward (Yes/No); Allotment, Annuity and Identification Numbers (if given).

1177; Junaluskie, Martha; F; 9/5/16-15; N.C. Cherokee; 31/32; S; Daughter; 1171; Yes; Yes; Unallotted

1178; Junaluskie, Mark; M; 9/19/17-14; N.C. Cherokee; 31/32; S; Son; 1172; Yes; Yes; Unallotted

1179; Junaluskie, Winnie; F; 5/5/19-12; N.C. Cherokee; 31/32; S; Daughter; 1173; Yes; Yes; Unallotted

1180; Junaluskie, Sallie Ann; F; 2/1/21-11; N.C. Cherokee; 31/32; S; Daughter; 1174; Yes; Yes; Unallotted

1181; Junaluskie, Arch; M; 2/19/23-9; N.C. Cherokee; 31/32; S; Son; 1175; Yes; Yes; Unallotted

1182; Junaluskie, Lillian; F; 1/25/32-2/12; N.C. Cherokee; 31/32; S; Daughter; ---; Yes; Yes; Unallotted

1183; Kalonuheskie, Abraham; M; 8/1/84-47; N.C. Cherokee; 4/4; M; Head; 1176; Yes; Yes; Unallotted

1184; Kalonuheskie, Charles; M; 1/19/87-45; N.C. Cherokee; 1/2; M; Head; 1177; Yes; Yes; Unallotted

1185; Kalonuheskie, Sallie L.; F; 1/19/78-54; N.C. Cherokee; 1/2; M; Wife; 1178; Yes; Yes; Unallotted

1186; Kalonuheskie, Styles; M; 1/19/17-15; N.C. Cherokee; 1/2; S; Son; 1179; Yes; Yes; Unallotted

1187; Kalonuheskie, Edith; F; 8/16/08-20; N.C. Cherokee; 1/2; S; Alone; 1180; Yes; Yes; Unallotted

1188; Kalonuheskie, Esiah; M; 9/15/55-76; N.C. Cherokee; 4/4; Wd.; Head; 1181; Yes; Yes; Unallotted

1189; Kalonuheskie, Martha; F; 11/26/02-29; N.C. Cherokee; 1/2; S; Head; 1182; Yes; Yes; Unallotted

1190; Kalonuheskie, Nannie; F; 1/19/98-34; N.C. Cherokee; 4/4; S; Head; 1183; Yes; Yes; Unallotted

1191; Kalonuheskie, Philip; M; 12/1/18-13; N.C. Cherokee; 13/16; S; Son; 1184; Yes; Yes; Unallotted

1192; Kalonuheskie, Tahow; M; 3/11/25-6; N.C. Cherokee; 1/2; S; Son; 1185; Yes; Yes; Unallotted

1193; Queen, Bascom; M; 1/18/32-2/12; N.C. Cherokee; 15/16; S; Son; ---; Yes; Yes; Unallotted

1194; Kalonuheskie, Tom; M; 12/25/88-43; N.C. Cherokee; 1/2; M; Head; 1186; Yes; Yes; Unallotted

1195; Kalonuheskie, Awee S.; F; 11/13/98-33; N.C. Cherokee; 4/4; M; Wife; 1187; Yes; Yes; Unallotted

Census of the **Eastern Cherokee** reservation of the **Cherokee, N.C.** jurisdiction, as of **April 1** , **1932,** taken by   **R. L. Spalsbury**   , Superintendent.

Key: Number; Surname, Given; Sex; Date of Birth-Age at Last Birthday; Tribe; Degree of Blood; Marital Status; Relationship to Head of Family; Last C. Roll No.; At Jurisdiction Where Enrolled (Yes/No); (If no – Where); Ward (Yes/No); Allotment, Annuity and Identification Numbers (if given).

1196; Junaluskie, Leone; F; 11/17/16-15; N.C. Cherokee; 3/4; S; Daughter; 1188; Yes; Yes; Unallotted

1197; Kalonuheskie, Gwynn; M; 10/27/18-13; N.C. Cherokee; 3/4; S; Son; 1189; Yes; Yes; Unallotted

1198; Kalonuheskie, Simon; M; 11/27/22-9; N.C. Cherokee; 3/4; S; Son; 1190; Yes; Yes; Unallotted

1199; Keg, Matthews; M; 3/25/66-66; N.C. Cherokee; 3/4; M; Head; 1191; Yes; Yes; Unallotted

1200; Keg, Kiney Ben; F; 12/24/82-49; N.C. Cherokee; 4/4; M; Wife; 1192; Yes; Yes; Unallotted

1201; Quince, Jennie; F; 7/20/14-17; N.C. Cherokee; 4/4; S; Step-dau.; 1193; Yes; Yes; Unallotted

1202; Kidd, David; M; 6/23/66-65; N.C. Cherokee; 1/32; M; Head; 1194; Yes; Yes; Unallotted

1203; Kidd, Goffrey; M; 6/6/18-13; N.C. Cherokee; 1/64; S; Son; 1195; Yes; Yes; Unallotted

1204; Kidd, Luther; M; 7/15/04-27; N.C. Cherokee; 1/64; S; Head; 1196; Yes; Yes; Unallotted

1205; Kidd, Walter; M; 2/8/89-43; N.C. Cherokee; 1/64; M; Head; 1197; Yes; Yes; Unallotted

1206; Kidd, Marcus; M; 5/22/14-17; N.C. Cherokee; 1/128; S; Son; 1198; Yes; Yes; Unallotted

1207; Kidd, Crawford; M; 5/16/16-15; N.C. Cherokee; 1/128; S; Son; 1199; Yes; Yes; Unallotted

1208; Kidd, Wm. H.; M; 5/26/97-34; N.C. Cherokee; 1/64; M; Head; 1200; Yes; Yes; Unallotted

1209; Killian (Raper, Viola), Viola E.; F; 12/19/03-28; N.C. Cherokee; 1/16; M; Wife; 1201; Yes; Yes; Unallotted

1210; Killingsworth (Thompson, Iris), Viola E.; F; 7/3/05-26; N.C. Cherokee; 1/16; M; Wife; 1202; Yes; Yes; Unallotted

1211; Killpatrick, Lydia; F; 3/19/00-32; N.C. Cherokee; 1/64; M; Wife; 1203; Yes; Yes; Unallotted

1212; King, (Tommy) Frederick; M; 11/18/18-13; N.C. Cherokee; 1/32; S; Alone; 1204; Yes; Yes; Unallotted

Census of the **Eastern Cherokee** reservation of the **Cherokee, N.C.** jurisdiction, as of **April 1** , 1932, taken by **R. L. Spalsbury** , Superintendent.

Key: Number; Surname, Given; Sex; Date of Birth-Age at Last Birthday; Tribe; Degree of Blood; Marital Status; Relationship to Head of Family; Last C. Roll No.; At Jurisdiction Where Enrolled (Yes/No); (If no – Where); Ward (Yes/No); Allotment, Annuity and Identification Numbers (if given).

1213; Kunteeskih, Sahwahohi; F; 12/22/47-84; N.C. Cherokee; 4/4; Wd.; Wife; 1205; Yes; Yes; Unallotted

1214; Kurry, Mandy Axe; F; 1/13/99-33; N.C. Cherokee; 4/4; M; Wife; 1206; Yes; Yes; Unallotted

1215; Kyker (Anderson, Bessie), Bessie; F; 8/11/02-29; N.C. Cherokee; 1/16; M; Wife; 1207; Yes; Yes; Unallotted

1216; Ladd (Rogers, Bonnie), Bonnie; F; 1/13/92-40; N.C. Cherokee; 1/8; M; Wife; 1208; Yes; Yes; Unallotted
1217; Ladd, Max; M; 3/9/11-21; N.C. Cherokee; 1/16; S; Son; 1209; Yes; Yes; Unallotted
1218; Ladd, Fay; F; 11/17/13-18; N.C. Cherokee; 1/16; S; Daughter; 1210; Yes; Yes; Unallotted
1219; Ladd, Fern; F; 1/1/16-16; N.C. Cherokee; 1/16; S; Daughter; 1211; Yes; Yes; Unallotted

1220; Lambert, Andrew J.; M; 1/20/01-31; N.C. Cherokee; 1/32; M; Head; 1212; Yes; Yes; Unallotted
1221; Lambert, Nola Griffin; F; 9/27/10-21; N.C. Cherokee; 1/32; M; Wife; 1213; Yes; Yes; Unallotted

1222; Lambert, Charley; M; 11/14/85-46; N.C. Cherokee; 9/16; Wd.; Head; 1214; Yes; Yes; Unallotted
1223; Lambert, Jackson; M; 1/10/06-26; N.C. Cherokee; 21/32; S; Son; 1215; Yes; Yes; Unallotted
1224; Lambert, John Adam; M; 2/28/11-21; N.C. Cherokee; 21/32; S; Son; 1216; Yes; Yes; Unallotted
1225; Lambert, Luvenia; F; 5/20/15-16; N.C. Cherokee; 21/32; S; Daughter; 1217; Yes; Yes; Unallotted
1226; Lambert, Guy; M; 10/20/17-14; N.C. Cherokee; 21/32; S; Son; 1218; Yes; Yes; Unallotted
1227; Lambert, Mianna; F; 12/27/19-12; N.C. Cherokee; 25/32; S; Daughter; 1219; Yes; Yes; Unallotted
1228; Lambert, Lucinda; F; 4/13/22-9; N.C. Cherokee; 25/32; S; Daughter; 1220; Yes; Yes; Unallotted

1229; Lambert, Charlie; M; 3/20/89-43; N.C. Cherokee; 1/16; M; Head; 1221; Yes; Yes; Unallotted
1230; Lambert, MaggieW.; F; 9/9/00-31; N.C. Cherokee; 3/4; M; Wife; 1222; Yes; Yes; Unallotted
1231; Lambert, Joseph R.; M; 11/27/25-6; N.C. Cherokee; 13/32; S; Son; 1223; Yes; Yes; Unallotted

Census of the **Eastern Cherokee** reservation of the **Cherokee, N.C.** jurisdiction, as of **April 1** , 19**32,** taken by **R. L. Spalsbury** , Superintendent.

Key: Number; Surname, Given; Sex; Date of Birth-Age at Last Birthday; Tribe; Degree of Blood; Marital Status; Relationship to Head of Family; Last C. Roll No.; At Jurisdiction Where Enrolled (Yes/No); (If no – Where); Ward (Yes/No); Allotment, Annuity and Identification Numbers (if given).

1232; Lambert, William N.; M; 3/18/28-4; N.C. Cherokee; 13/32; S; Son; 1224; Yes; Yes; Unallotted

1233; Lambert, Herbert A.; M; 6/7/31-9/12; N.C. Cherokee; 13/32; S; Son; ---; Yes; Yes; Unallotted

1234; Lambert, Claude; M; 1/2/91-41; N.C. Cherokee; 1/16; M; Head; 1225; Yes; Yes; Unallotted

1235; Lambert, Ibeuria; F; 2/16/13-19; N.C. Cherokee; 1/32; S; Daughter; 1226; Yes; Yes; Unallotted

1236; Lambert, Georgia; F; 7/8/17-14; N.C. Cherokee; 1/32; S; Daughter; 1227; Yes; Yes; Unallotted

1237; Lambert, Jack Wm.; M; 2/11/20-12; N.C. Cherokee; 1/32; S; Son; 1228; Yes; Yes; Unallotted

1238; Lambert, Samuel D.; M; 11/11/22-9; N.C. Cherokee; 1/32; S; Son; 1229; Yes; Yes; Unallotted

1239; Lambert, Columbus; M; 12/25/71-60; N.C. Cherokee; 1/16; M; Head; 1230; Yes; Yes; Unallotted

1240; Howard (Lambert, Cora), Cora P.; F; 2/21/06-27; N.C. Cherokee; 1/32; M; Wife; 1231; Yes; Yes; Unallotted

1241; Lambert, Leonard C.; M; 1/25/08-24; N.C. Cherokee; 1/32; S; Head; 1232; Yes; Yes; Unallotted

1242; Lambert, Willard; M; 7/6/10-21; N.C. Cherokee; 1/32; S; Brother; 1233; Yes; Yes; Unallotted

1243; Lambert, Gillian; M; 7/4/12-19; N.C. Cherokee; 1/32; S; Brother; 1234; Yes; Yes; Unallotted

1244; Lambert, Leona; F; 2/19/15-17; N.C. Cherokee; 1/32; S; Sister; 1235; Yes; Yes; Unallotted

1245; Lambert, Philip; M; 1/31/18-14; N.C. Cherokee; 1/32; S; Brother; 1236; Yes; Yes; Unallotted

1246; Lambert, Corbett; M; 3/12/97-35; N.C. Cherokee; 1/16; M; Head; 1237; Yes; Yes; Unallotted

1247; Lambert, Robert; M; 10/3/20-11; N.C. Cherokee; 1/32; S; Son; 1238; Yes; Yes; Unallotted

1248; Lambert, Samuel C.; M; 1/19/23-9; N.C. Cherokee; 1/32; S; Son; 1239; Yes; Yes; Unallotted

1249; Lambert, Edward; M; 3/21/85-45; N.C. Cherokee; 1/16; M; Head; 1240; Yes; Yes; Unallotted

1250; Lambert, Edward Monroe; M; 11/15/08-23; N.C. Cherokee; 1/32; S; Head; 1241; Yes; Yes; Unallotted

Census of the **Eastern Cherokee** reservation of the **Cherokee, N.C.** jurisdiction, as of **April 1** , 19**32,** taken by **R. L. Spalsbury** , Superintendent.

Key: Number; Surname, Given; Sex; Date of Birth-Age at Last Birthday; Tribe; Degree of Blood; Marital Status; Relationship to Head of Family; Last C. Roll No.; At Jurisdiction Where Enrolled (Yes/No); (If no – Where); Ward (Yes/No); Allotment, Annuity and Identification Numbers (if given).

1251; Lambert, Fitzsimmons; M; 5/19/96-35; N.C. Cherokee; 1/16; M; Head; 1242; Yes; Yes; Unallotted

1252; Lambert, Fred G.; M; 8/1/91-41; N.C. Cherokee; 1/16; M; Head; 1243; Yes; Yes; Unallotted

1253; Lambert, Wymer Holt; M; 12/18/15-16; N.C. Cherokee; 1/32; S; Son; 1244; Yes; Yes; Unallotted

1254; Lambert, Venoia; F; 5/17/17-14; N.C. Cherokee; 1/32; S; Daughter; 1245; Yes; Yes; Unallotted

1255; Lambert, Joyce; F; 9/13/23-8; N.C. Cherokee; 1/32; S; Daughter; 1246; Yes; Yes; Unallotted

1256; Lambert, Henry H.; M; 1/11/04-28; N.C. Cherokee; 1/32; M; Head; 1247; Yes; Yes; Unallotted

1257; Lambert, Amanda G.; F; 5/29/11-20; N.C. Cherokee; 7/8; M; Wife; 1248; Yes; Yes; Unallotted

1258; Lambert, Tom H.; M; 8/20/28-3; N.C. Cherokee; 29/64; S; Son; 1249; Yes; Yes; Unallotted

1259; Lambert, David; M; 11/22/30-1; N.C. Cherokee; 29/64; S; Son; ---; Yes; Yes; Unallotted

1260; Lambert, Hugh H.; M; 1/10/02-30; N.C. Cherokee; 1/32; M; Head; 1250; Yes; Yes; Unallotted

1261; Lambert, Hugh J.; M; 4/19/74-57; N.C. Cherokee; 1/16; M; Head; 1251; Yes; Yes; Unallotted

1262; Lambert, Isaac; M; 4/20/04-27; N.C. Cherokee; 1/32; S; Son; 1252; Yes; Yes; Unallotted

1263; Lambert, George; M; 10/15/09-22; N.C. Cherokee; 1/32; S; Son; 1253; Yes; Yes; Unallotted

1264; Lambert, Ethel; F; 8/1/13-18; N.C. Cherokee; 1/32; S; Daughter; 1254; Yes; Yes; Unallotted

1265; Lambert, Cato; M; 2/6/16-16; N.C. Cherokee; 1/32; S; Son; 1255; Yes; Yes; Unallotted

1266; Lambert, Vaniela; F; 4/10/18-13; N.C. Cherokee; 1/32; S; Daughter; 1256; Yes; Yes; Unallotted

1267; Lambert, Hugh N.; M; 12/26/80-51; N.C. Cherokee; 1/16; Wd.; Head; 1257; Yes; Yes; Unallotted

1268; Lambert, Paul Leroy; M; 5/25/09-22; N.C. Cherokee; 7/32; S; Son; 1258; Yes; Yes; Unallotted

1269; Lambert, Arthur; M; 7/15/11-20; N.C. Cherokee; 7/32; S; Son; 1259; Yes; Yes; Unallotted

1270; Lambert, Albert S.; M; 1/24/14-18; N.C. Cherokee; 7/32; S; Son; 1260; Yes; Yes; Unallotted

Census of the **Eastern Cherokee** reservation of the **Cherokee, N.C.** jurisdiction, as of **April 1** , **1932,** taken by **R. L. Spalsbury** , Superintendent.

Key: Number; Surname, Given; Sex; Date of Birth-Age at Last Birthday; Tribe; Degree of Blood; Marital Status; Relationship to Head of Family; Last C. Roll No.; At Jurisdiction Where Enrolled (Yes/No); (If no – Where); Ward (Yes/No); Allotment, Annuity and Identification Numbers (if given).

1271; Lambert, Mary Ann; F; 2/15/16-16; N.C. Cherokee; 7/32; S; Daughter; 1261; Yes; Yes; Unallotted

1272; Lambert, Virginia C.; F; 7/21/18-13; N.C. Cherokee; 7/32; S; Daughter; 1262; Yes; Yes; Unallotted

1273; Lambert, Hugh N.; M; 4/14/21-10; N.C. Cherokee; 7/32; S; Son; 1263; Yes; Yes; Unallotted

1274; Lambert, Jesse L.; M; 1/7/24-8; N.C. Cherokee; 7/32; S; Son; 1264; Yes; Yes; Unallotted

1275; Lambert, James W.; M; 5/25/75-56; N.C. Cherokee; 1/16; M; Head; 1265; Yes; Yes; Unallotted

~~1276; Enloe (Lambert), Mintha; F; 10/9/12-19; N.C. Cherokee; 1/32; M; Daughter; 1266;~~ Yes; Note: see page 251.; Yes; Unallotted

1277; Lambert, Felix; M; 5/25/17-14; N.C. Cherokee; 1/32; S; Son; 1267; Yes; Yes; Unallotted

1278; Lambert, Mary H.; F; 9/26/19-12; N.C. Cherokee; 1/32; S; Daughter; 1268; Yes; Yes; Unallotted

1279; Lambert, Jesse; M; 3/8/93-39; N.C. Cherokee; 1/16; M; Head; 1269; Yes; Yes; Unallotted

1280; Lambert, Lelia L.; F; 4/20/19-12; N.C. Cherokee; 1/32; S; Daughter; 1270; Yes; Yes; Unallotted

1281; Lambert, Cleo.; F; 3/30/21-11; N.C. Cherokee; 1/32; S; Daughter; 1271; Yes; Yes; Unallotted

1282; Lambert, Floy Lilly; F; 4/24/23-8; N.C. Cherokee; 1/32; S; Daughter; 1272; Yes; Yes; Unallotted

1283; Lambert, Jesse B.; M; 1/13/77-55; N.C. Cherokee; 1/16; M; Head; 1273; Yes; Yes; Unallotted

1284; Lambert, Minnie E.S.; F; 11/5/90-41; N.C. Cherokee; 1/32; M; Wife; 1274; Yes; Yes; Unallotted

1285; Lambert, Carl G.; M; 6/11/11-20; N.C. Cherokee; 3/64; S; Son; 1275; Yes; Yes; Unallotted

1286; Lambert, Jesse E.; F; 2/28/14-18; N.C. Cherokee; 3/64; S; Daughter; 1276; Yes; Yes; Unallotted

1287; Lambert, Ralph P.; M; 1/20/18-14; N.C. Cherokee; 3/64; S; Son; 1277; Yes; Yes; Unallotted

1288; Lambert, John H.; M; 2/14/97-35; N.C. Cherokee; 1/32; M; Head; 1278; Yes; Yes; Unallotted

1289; Lambert, Joseph G.; M; 10/20/02-29; N.C. Cherokee; 1/32; M; Head; 1279; Yes; Yes; Unallotted

1290; Lambert, Louisa G.; F; 5/3/08-23; N.C. Cherokee; 3/32; M; Wife; 1280; Yes; Yes; Unallotted

Key: Number; Surname, Given; Sex; Date of Birth-Age at Last Birthday; Tribe; Degree of Blood; Marital Status; Relationship to Head of Family; Last C. Roll No.; At Jurisdiction Where Enrolled (Yes/No); (If no – Where); Ward (Yes/No); Allotment, Annuity and Identification Numbers (if given).

1291; Lambert, Dorothy P.; F; 9/23/27-4; N.C. Cherokee; 4/64; S; Daughter; 1281; Yes; Yes; Unallotted

1292; Lambert, Lloyd; M; 8/28/82-49; N.C. Cherokee; 9/16; M; Head; 1282; Yes; Yes; Unallotted

1293; Lambert, Sallie; F; 4/4/77-54; N.C. Cherokee; 3/4; M; Wife; 1283; Yes; Yes; Unallotted

1294; Lambert, Luzene; F; 7/18/01-31; N.C. Cherokee; 3/8; S; Step-dau.; 1284; Yes; Yes; Unallotted

1295; Lambert, Nellie; F; 1/7/07-24; N.C. Cherokee; 21/32; S; Daughter; 1285; Yes; Yes; Unallotted

1296; Lambert, Jesse; M; 1/7/09-23; N.C. Cherokee; 21/32; S; Son; 1286; Yes; Yes; Unallotted

1297; Lambert, Ruth; F; 6/28/13-18; N.C. Cherokee; 21/32; S; Daughter; 1287; Yes; Yes; Unallotted

1298; Lambert, Freeman; M; 10/19/18-13; N.C. Cherokee; 21/32; S; Son; 1288; Yes; Yes; Unallotted

1299; Lambert, Edna; F; 5/2/24-7; N.C. Cherokee; 21/32; S; Daughter; 1289; Yes; Yes; Unallotted

1300; Lambert, Gwendolyn; F; 10/31/29-3; N.C. Cherokee; --; S; Granddau. (Illeg.); 1290; Yes; Yes; Unallotted

1301; Lambert, Lucy; F; 3/25/23-9; N.C. Cherokee; 7/8; S; Alone; 1291; Yes; Yes; Unallotted

1302; Lambert, Samuel D.; M; 4/15/25-6; N.C. Cherokee; --; S; Brother; 1292; Yes; Yes; Unallotted

1303; Lambert, Ollie; F; 5/12/04-27; N.C. Cherokee; 21/32; S; Head; 1293; Yes; Yes; Unallotted

1304; Lambert, Winford; M; 3/11/22-10; N.C. Cherokee; 21/64; S; Son; 1294; Yes; Yes; Unallotted

1305; Lambert, Pearson; M; 7/4/00-31; N.C. Cherokee; 1/32; M; Head; 1295; Yes; Yes; Unallotted

1306; Lambert, Fannie M.; F; 12/24/18-13; N.C. Cherokee; 1/64; S; Daughter; 1296; Yes; Yes; Unallotted

1307; Lambert, Wm. Russel; M; 1/6/21-11; N.C. Cherokee; 1/64; S; Son; 1297; Yes; Yes; Unallotted

1308; Lambert, Josephine; F; 4/24/23-8; N.C. Cherokee; 1/64; S; Daughter; 1298; Yes; Yes; Unallotted

1309; Lambert, Samuel C.; M; 11/27/59-72; N.C. Cherokee; 1/8; M; Head; 1299; Yes; Yes; Unallotted

1310; Lambert, Theodore; M; 5/9/03-28; N.C. Cherokee; 1/16; S; Son; 1300; Yes; Yes; Unallotted

Census of the **Eastern Cherokee** reservation of the **Cherokee, N.C.** jurisdiction, as of **April 1** , 19**32,** taken by **R. L. Spalsbury** , Superintendent.

Key: Number; Surname, Given; Sex; Date of Birth-Age at Last Birthday; Tribe; Degree of Blood; Marital Status; Relationship to Head of Family; Last C. Roll No.; At Jurisdiction Where Enrolled (Yes/No); (If no – Where); Ward (Yes/No); Allotment, Annuity and Identification Numbers (if given).

1311; Lambert, Gaylord; M; 12/31/09-22; N.C. Cherokee; 1/16; S; Son; 1301; Yes; Yes; Unallotted

1312; Lambert, Lillian; F; 3/13/13-19; N.C. Cherokee; 1/16; S; Daughter; 1302; Yes; Yes; Unallotted

1313; Lambert, Russell; M; 2/25/16-16; N.C. Cherokee; 1/16; S; Son; 1303; Yes; Yes; Unallotted

1314; Lambert (McCoy, Stella), Stella; F; 11/25/05-27; N.C. Cherokee; 1/16; Div.; Head; 1304; Yes; Yes; Unallotted

1315; Lambert, Thomas O.; M; 2/12/79-53; N.C. Cherokee; 1/16; M; Head; 1305; Yes; Yes; Unallotted

1316; Lambert, John A.; M; 6/5/05-26; N.C. Cherokee; 1/32; S; Son; 1306; Yes; Yes; Unallotted

1317; Lambert, Cora H.; F; 6/30/13-18; N.C. Cherokee; 1/32; S; Daughter; 1307; Yes; Yes; Unallotted

1318; Lambert, Gracie N.; F; 6/15/15-16; N.C. Cherokee; 1/32; S; Daughter; 1308; Yes; Yes; Unallotted

1319; Lambert, Julia E.; F; 3/12/20-12; N.C. Cherokee; 1/32; S; Daughter; 1309; Yes; Yes; Unallotted

1320; Lambert, Thomas R.; M; 1/1/83-49; N.C. Cherokee; 1/16; M; Head; 1310; Yes; Yes; Unallotted

1321; Lambert, Nannie Y.; F; 7/18/90-41; N.C. Cherokee; 1/16; M; Wife; 1311; Yes; Yes; Unallotted

1322; Lambert, Seymour; M; 8/9/09-22; N.C. Cherokee; 1/16; S; Son; 1312; Yes; Yes; Unallotted

1323; Lambert, Amos; M; 12/23/17-14; N.C. Cherokee; 1/16; S; Son; 1313; Yes; Yes; Unallotted

1324; Lambert, Mary; F; 5/10/20-11; N.C. Cherokee; 1/16; S; Daughter; 1314; Yes; Yes; Unallotted

1325; Lambert, Willard; M; 5/27/24-7; N.C. Cherokee; 1/16; S; Son; 1315; Yes; Yes; Unallotted

1326; Larch, David; M; 4/24/81-50; N.C. Cherokee; 4/4; M; Head; 1316; Yes; Yes; Unallotted

1327; Larch, Winnie O.; F; 12/22/78-53; N.C. Cherokee; 4/4; M; Wife; 1317; Yes; Yes; Unallotted

1328; Larch, William D.; M; 8/11/74-57; N.C. Cherokee; 4/4; M; Head; 1318; Yes; Yes; Unallotted

1329; Larch, Anita Davis; F; 1897-35; N.C. Cherokee; 4/4; M; Wife; 1319; Yes; Yes; Unallotted

1330; Larch, Wm. Jr.; M; 10/25/29-2; N.C. Cherokee; 4/4; S; Son; 1320; Yes; Yes; Unallotted

71

Census of the **Eastern Cherokee** reservation of the **Cherokee, N.C.** jurisdiction, as of **April 1**, 19**32**, taken by **R. L. Spalsbury**, Superintendent.

Key: Number; Surname, Given; Sex; Date of Birth-Age at Last Birthday; Tribe; Degree of Blood; Marital Status; Relationship to Head of Family; Last C. Roll No.; At Jurisdiction Where Enrolled (Yes/No); (If no – Where); Ward (Yes/No); Allotment, Annuity and Identification Numbers (if given).

1331; Larch, Florence; F; 5/25/31-10/12; N.C. Cherokee; 4/4; S; Daughter; ---; Yes; Yes; Unallotted

1332; Ledford, Allen; M; 6/24/04-27; N.C. Cherokee; 4/4; S; Head; 1321; Yes; Yes; Unallotted

1333; Ledford (Rogers, Catherine), Catherine; F; 7/12/74-57; N.C. Cherokee; 1/16; M; Wife; 1322; No; Culberson, Cherokee, N.C.; Yes; Unallotted
1334; Ledford, Cora; F; 7/22/02-29; N.C. Cherokee; 1/32; S; Daughter; 1323; No; Culberson, Cherokee, N.C.; Yes; Unallotted
1335; Ledford, Adkins; M; 7/19/05-26; N.C. Cherokee; 1/32; S; Son; 1324; No; Culberson, Cherokee, N.C.; Yes; Unallotted
1336; Ledford, Charles A.; M; 1/31/08-24; N.C. Cherokee; 1/32; S; Son; 1325; No; Culberson, Cherokee, N.C.; Yes; Unallotted
1337; Ledford, Bonnie M.; F; 5/21/10-21; N.C. Cherokee; 1/32; S; Daughter; 1326; No; Culberson, Cherokee, N.C.; Yes; Unallotted
1338; Ledford, Cyrus Atlas; M; 6/18/12-19; N.C. Cherokee; 1/32; S; Son; 1327; No; Culberson, Cherokee, N.C.; Yes; Unallotted
1339; Ledford, Dorothy; F; 9/17/16-15; N.C. Cherokee; 1/32; S; Daughter; 1328; No; Culberson, Cherokee, N.C.; Yes; Unallotted

1340; Ledford, Charley; M; 5/5/83-48; N.C. Cherokee; 4/4; M; Head; 1329; Yes; Yes; Unallotted
1341; Ledford, Maggie W.; F; 9/16/92-39; N.C. Cherokee; 4/4; M; Wife; 1330; Yes; Yes; Unallotted

1342; Ledford, Jake; M; 3/25/77-55; N.C. Cherokee; 4/4; M; Head; 1331; Yes; Yes; Unallotted
1343; Ledford, Mary; F; 5/5/75-56; N.C. Cherokee; 4/4; M; Wife; 1332; Yes; Yes; Unallotted
1344; Ledford, Amy; F; 3/29/08-24; N.C. Cherokee; 4/4; S; Daughter; 1333; Yes; Yes; Unallotted

1345; Ledford (Patterson, Lura), Lura; F; 3/20/04-28; N.C. Cherokee; 1/32; M; Wife; 1334; No; Shooting Creek, Clay, N.C.; Yes; Unallotted
1346; Ledford, Helen; F; 2/22/23-9; N.C. Cherokee; 1/64; S; Daughter; 1335; No; Shooting Creek, Clay, N.C.; Yes; Unallotted

1347; Ledford (McDonald, Mae), Mae; F; 12/13/99-32; N.C. Cherokee; 1/64; M; Wife; 1336; Yes; Yes; Unallotted
1348; Ledford, Jodie; M; 12/5/22-9; N.C. Cherokee; 1/128; S; Son; 1337; Yes; Yes; Unallotted

1349; Ledford, Riley; M; 3/25/77-55; N.C. Cherokee; 4/4; Wd.; Head; 1338; Yes; Yes; Unallotted

Census of the **Eastern Cherokee** reservation of the **Cherokee, N.C.** jurisdiction, as of **April 1** , **1932,** taken by **R. L. Spalsbury** , Superintendent.

Key: Number; Surname, Given; Sex; Date of Birth-Age at Last Birthday; Tribe; Degree of Blood; Marital Status; Relationship to Head of Family; Last C. Roll No.; At Jurisdiction Where Enrolled (Yes/No); (If no – Where); Ward (Yes/No); Allotment, Annuity and Identification Numbers (if given).

1350; Ledford, Caroline; F; 1/25/07-25; N.C. Cherokee; 4/4; S; Daughter; 1339; Yes; Yes; Unallotted

1351; Ledford, Moses; M; 6/8/12-19; N.C. Cherokee; 4/4; S; Son; 1340; Yes; Yes; Unallotted

1352; Ledford, Nancy; F; 3/27/14-18; N.C. Cherokee; 4/4; S; Daughter; 1341; Yes; Yes; Unallotted

1353; Ledford, James; M; 4/3/17-14; N.C. Cherokee; 4/4; S; Son; 1342; Yes; Yes; Unallotted

1354; Ledford, Elnora; F; 4/27/19-12; N.C. Cherokee; 4/4; S; Daughter; 1343; Yes; Yes; Unallotted

1355; Ledford, Noah; M; 5/9/21-10; N.C. Cherokee; 4/4; S; Son; 1344; Yes; Yes; Unallotted

1356; Ledford, Nellie M.; F; 3/21/32-10 days; N.C. Cherokee; 1/2; S; Granddau. (Ill.); ---; Yes; Yes; Unallotted

1357; Ledford, Billy J.; M; 6/19/31-9/12; N.C. Cherokee; 1/2; S; Grandson (Ill.); ---; Yes; Yes; Unallotted

1358; Ledford, Ruby; F; 9/17/18-13; N.C. Cherokee; 1/32; S; Alone; 1345; No; Culberson, Cherokee, N.C.; Yes; Unallotted

1359; Ledford, Jewel; F; 12/29/21-10; N.C. Cherokee; 1/32; S; Sister; 1346; No; Culberson, Cherokee, N.C.; Yes; Unallotted

1360; Ledford, Sampson; M; 6/8/85-46; N.C. Cherokee; 4/4; M; Head; 1347; Yes; Yes; Unallotted

1361; Ledford, Nancy W.; F; 11/15/93-38; N.C. Cherokee; 4/4; M; Wife; 1348; Yes; Yes; Unallotted

1362; Ledford, Nicey; F; 1/24/16-16; N.C. Cherokee; 4/4; S; Daughter; 1349; Yes; Yes; Unallotted

1363; Ledford, Mason; M; 9/9/17-14; N.C. Cherokee; 4/4; S; Son; 1350; Yes; Yes; Unallotted

1364; Ledford, Wilson; M; 12/8/19-12; N.C. Cherokee; 4/4; S; Son; 1351; Yes; Yes; Unallotted

1365; Lee, Alonzo; M; 1/9/74-58; N.C. Cherokee; 1/16; M; Head; 1352; No; Silver Lake, Wyoming, N.Y.; Yes; Unallotted

1366; Lee, Ramona F.; F; 3/18/96-36; N.C. Cherokee; 1/8; M; Wife; 1353; Yes; Yes; Unallotted

1367; Lee, Ruby I.; F; 10/3/12-19; N.C. Cherokee; 1/16; S; Daughter; 1354; Yes; Yes; Unallotted

1368; Lee, Pearl A.; F; 7/1/15-16; N.C. Cherokee; 1/16; S; Daughter; 1355; Yes; Yes; Unallotted

1369; Lee, Ruth C.; F; 8/22/17-14; N.C. Cherokee; 1/16; S; Daughter; 1356; Yes; Yes; Unallotted

Census of the **Eastern Cherokee** reservation of the **Cherokee, N.C.** jurisdiction, as of **April 1** , 19**32,** taken by **R. L. Spalsbury** , Superintendent.

Key: Number; Surname, Given; Sex; Date of Birth-Age at Last Birthday; Tribe; Degree of Blood; Marital Status; Relationship to Head of Family; Last C. Roll No.; At Jurisdiction Where Enrolled (Yes/No); (If no – Where); Ward (Yes/No); Allotment, Annuity and Identification Numbers (if given).

1370; Lee, Naomi M.; F; 10/24/19-12; N.C. Cherokee; 1/16; S; Daughter; 1357; Yes; Yes; Unallotted

1371; Lee, William C.; M; 6/14/13-18; N.C. Cherokee; 1/32; S; Alone; 1358; Yes; Yes; Unallotted

1372; Lee, James F.; M; 6/3/15-16; N.C. Cherokee; 1/32; S; Brother; 1359; Yes; Yes; Unallotted

1373; Le Fevers (Garland, Tamoxzena), Tamoxzena; F; 3/10/81-51; N.C. Cherokee; 1/16; M; Wife; 1360; Yes; Yes; Unallotted

1374; Le Fevers, Linnie; F; 11/14/99-32; N.C. Cherokee; 1/32; S; Daughter; 1361; Yes; Yes; Unallotted

1375; Le Fevers, William; M; 6/15/01-30; N.C. Cherokee; 1/32; S; Son; 1362; Yes; Yes; Unallotted

1376; Lillard (Crowe, Dora), Dora C.; F; 7/6/95-36; N.C. Cherokee; 3/16; M; Wife; 1363; Yes; Yes; Unallotted

1377; Littlejohn, Edison; M; 8/3/14-17; N.C. Cherokee; 15/16; S; Alone; 1364; Yes; Yes; Unallotted

1378; Littlejohn, Elowih; M; 2/15/76-56; N.C. Cherokee; 4/4; M; Head; 1365; Yes; Yes; Unallotted

1379; Littlejohn, Annie; F; 9/15/81-50; N.C. Cherokee; 4/4; M; Wife; 1366; Yes; Yes; Unallotted

1380; Littlejohn, Sherman; M; 4/12/04-27; N.C. Cherokee; 4/4; S; Son; 1367; Yes; Yes; Unallotted

1381; Littlejohn, Jefferson; M; 7/7/07-24; N.C. Cherokee; 4/4; S; Son; 1368; Yes; Yes; Unallotted

1382; Littlejohn, Lizzie; F; 3/5/13-19; N.C. Cherokee; 4/4; S; Daughter; 1369; Yes; Yes; Unallotted

1383; Littlejohn, George; M; 3/16/14-18; N.C. Cherokee; 4/4; S; Son; 1370; Yes; Yes; Unallotted

1384; Littlejohn, Ned; M; 1/2/19-12; N.C. Cherokee; 4/4; S; Son; 1371; Yes; Yes; Unallotted

1385; Littlejohn, Richard; M; 4/14/21-10; N.C. Cherokee; 4/4; S; Son; 1372; Yes; Yes; Unallotted

1386; Littlejohn, Guy; M; 5/11/96-35; N.C. Cherokee; 7/8; S; Head; 1373; Yes; Yes; Unallotted

1387; Littlejohn, Garret; M; 5/11/06-25; N.C. Cherokee; 7/8; S; Brother; 1374; Yes; Yes; Unallotted

1388; Littlejohn, Henson; M; 5/27/98-33; N.C. Cherokee; 4/4; M; Head; 1375; Yes; Yes; Unallotted

Census of the **Eastern Cherokee** reservation of the **Cherokee, N.C.** jurisdiction, as of **April 1** , 1932, taken by **R. L. Spalsbury** , Superintendent.

Key: Number; Surname, Given; Sex; Date of Birth-Age at Last Birthday; Tribe; Degree of Blood; Marital Status; Relationship to Head of Family; Last C. Roll No.; At Jurisdiction Where Enrolled (Yes/No); (If no – Where); Ward (Yes/No); Allotment, Annuity and Identification Numbers (if given).

1389; Littlejohn, Lewee Long; F; 7/1/98-33; N.C. Cherokee; 4/4; M; Wife; 1376; Yes; Yes; Unallotted

1390; Littlejohn, Alice; F; 9/15/20-11; N.C. Cherokee; 4/4; S; Step-dau.; 1377; Yes; Yes; Unallotted

1391; Littlejohn, Boyd; M; 4/12/22-9; N.C. Cherokee; 4/4; S; Stepson; 1378; Yes; Yes; Unallotted

1392; Littlejohn, Amanda; F; 1/18/24-8; N.C. Cherokee; 4/4; S; Step-dau.; 1379; Yes; Yes; Unallotted

1393; Littlejohn, Thomas; M; 7/5/20-12; N.C. Cherokee; 4/4; S; Son; 1380; Yes; Yes; Unallotted

1394; Littlejohn, Salina; F; 4/4/26-5; N.C. Cherokee; 4/4; S; Daughter; 1381; Yes; Yes; Unallotted

1395; Littlejohn, Isaac; M; 5/28/00-31; N.C. Cherokee; 7/8; M; Head; 1382; Yes; Yes; Unallotted

1396; Littlejohn, Eliza C.; F; 5/28/03-28; N.C. Cherokee; 15/16; M; Wife; 1383; Yes; Yes; Unallotted

1397; Littlejohn, Johnson; M; 3/23/22-9; N.C. Cherokee; 29/32; S; Son; 1384; Yes; Yes; Unallotted

1398; Littlejohn, Maggie D.; F; 12/6/25-6; N.C. Cherokee; 29/32; S; Daughter; 1385; Yes; Yes; Unallotted

1399; Littlejohn, John; M; 6/1/01-30; N.C. Cherokee; 4/4; S; Head; 1386; Yes; Yes; Unallotted

1400; Littlejohn, Owen; M; 3/19/05-27; N.C. Cherokee; 4/4; S; Head; 1387; Yes; Yes; Unallotted

1401; Littlejohn, Ropetwister; M; 3/15/67-65; N.C. Cherokee; 3/4; M; Head; 1388; Yes; Yes; Unallotted

1402; Littlejohn, Annie; F; 10/5/77-54; N.C. Cherokee; 3/4; M; Wife; 1389; Yes; Yes; Unallotted

1403; Littlejohn, Sallie; F; 4/5/03-28; N.C. Cherokee; 3/4; S; Daughter; 1390; Yes; Yes; Unallotted

1404; Littlejohn, Isaac; M; 12/29/05-26; N.C. Cherokee; 3/4; S; Son; 1391; Yes; Yes; Unallotted

1405; Littlejohn, Eugene; M; 2/25/12-20; N.C. Cherokee; 3/4; S; Son; 1392; Yes; Yes; Unallotted

1406; Littlejohn, Bessie; F; 1/29/14-18; N.C. Cherokee; 3/4; S; Daughter; 1393; Yes; Yes; Unallotted

1407; Littlejohn, Saunooke; M; 12/16/62-69; N.C. Cherokee; 4/4; M; Head; 1394; Yes; Yes; Unallotted

1408; Littlejohn, Anna E.; F; 3/27/68-64; N.C. Cherokee; 4/4; M; Wife; 1395; Yes; Yes; Unallotted

Census of the **Eastern Cherokee** reservation of the **Cherokee, N.C.** jurisdiction, as of **April 1** , 19**32,** taken by **R. L. Spalsbury** , Superintendent.

Key: Number; Surname, Given; Sex; Date of Birth-Age at Last Birthday; Tribe; Degree of Blood; Marital Status; Relationship to Head of Family; Last C. Roll No.; At Jurisdiction Where Enrolled (Yes/No); (If no – Where); Ward (Yes/No); Allotment, Annuity and Identification Numbers (if given).

1409; Littlejohn, Addie; F; 8/9/07-24; N.C. Cherokee; 4/4; S; Daughter; 1396; Yes; Yes; Unallotted

1410; Locust, Lewis; M; 8/5/01-30; N.C. Cherokee; 1/4; M; Head; 1397; Yes; Yes; Unallotted

1411; Locust, Jennie B.; F; 7/21/02-29; N.C. Cherokee; 1/16; M; Wife; 1398; Yes; Yes; Unallotted

1412; Locust, Harding; M; 2/6/21-11; N.C. Cherokee; 5/32; S; Son; 1399; Yes; Yes; Unallotted

1413; Locust, Alzino May; F; 11/20/25-6; N.C. Cherokee; 5/32; S; Daughter; 1400; Yes; Yes; Unallotted

1414; Locust, Noah; M; 7/8/83-48; N.C. Cherokee; 1/2; M; Head; 1401; Yes; Yes; Unallotted

1415; Locust, Homer; M; 3/22/11-21; N.C. Cherokee; 1/4; S; Son; 1402; Yes; Yes; Unallotted

1416; Locust, Josephine; F; 12/17/14-17; N.C. Cherokee; 1/4; S; Daughter; 1403; Yes; Yes; Unallotted

1417; Locust, Wm. Arthur; M; 6/5/15-16; N.C. Cherokee; 1/4; S; Son; 1404; Yes; Yes; Unallotted

1418; Locust, Wm. Russel; M; 6/4/17-14; N.C. Cherokee; 1/4; S; Son; 1405; Yes; Yes; Unallotted

1419; Locust, Noah A.; M; 11/3/22-9; N.C. Cherokee; 1/4; S; Son; 1406; Yes; Yes; Unallotted

1420; Locust, Herbert F.; M; 4/17/28-3; N.C. Cherokee; 1/4; S; Son; 1407; Yes; Yes; Unallotted

1421; Loma, Dinah S.; F; 9/20/01-30; N.C. Cherokee; 4/4; M; Wife; 1408; Yes; Yes; Unallotted

1422; Long, Adam; M; 12/22/57-74; N.C. Cherokee; 4/4; M; Head; 1409; Yes; Yes; Unallotted

1423; Long, Polly; F; 12/22/56-75; N.C. Cherokee; 4/4; M; Wife; 1410; Yes; Yes; Unallotted

1424; Long, Charles B.; M; 12/22/89-42; N.C. Cherokee; 4/4; M; Head; 1411; Yes; Yes; Unallotted

1425; Long, Rosa D.; F; 11/22/03-28; N.C. Cherokee; 4/4; M; Wife; 1412; Yes; Yes; Unallotted

1426; Long, Fred; M; 5/21/20-11; N.C. Cherokee; 4/4; S; Son; 1413; Yes; Yes; Unallotted

1427; Long, Agnes; F; 8/23/22-9; N.C. Cherokee; 4/4; S; Daughter; 1414; Yes; Yes; Unallotted

1428; Long, Jackson; M; 11/8/27-4; N.C. Cherokee; 4/4; S; Son; 1415; Yes; Yes; Unallotted

Census of the **Eastern Cherokee** reservation of the **Cherokee, N.C.** jurisdiction, as of **April 1** , **1932,** taken by **R. L. Spalsbury** , Superintendent.

Key: Number; Surname, Given; Sex; Date of Birth-Age at Last Birthday; Tribe; Degree of Blood; Marital Status; Relationship to Head of Family; Last C. Roll No.; At Jurisdiction Where Enrolled (Yes/No); (If no – Where); Ward (Yes/No); Allotment, Annuity and Identification Numbers (if given).

1429; Long, Dobson; M; 1/22/62-70; N.C. Cherokee; 4/4; M; Head; 1416; Yes; Yes; Unallotted

1430; Long, Sallie; F; 12/22/65-66; N.C. Cherokee; 4/4; M; Wife; 1417; Yes; Yes; Unallotted

1431; Long, Elizabeth; F; 12/7/01-30; N.C. Cherokee; 4/4; S; Daughter; 1418; Yes; Yes; Unallotted

1432; Long, Edna M.; F; 8/15/16-15; N.C. Cherokee; 7/8; S; Alone; 1419; Yes; Yes; Unallotted

1433; Long, Isaac; M; 12/22/06-25; N.C. Cherokee; 3/4; S; Head; 1420; Yes; Yes; Unallotted

1434; Long, Martha; F; 12/22/12-19; N.C. Cherokee; 3/4; S; Sister; 1421; Yes; Yes; Unallotted

1435; Long, Joe; M; 12/22/65-66; N.C. Cherokee; 4/4; M; Head; 1422; Yes; Yes; Unallotted

1436; Long, Nancy G.; F; 12/22/41-90; N.C. Cherokee; 4/4; M; Wife; 1423; Yes; Yes; Unallotted

1437; Long, Charley; M; 5/10/94-37; N.C. Cherokee; 4/4; S; Son; 1424; No; Address unknown, Fla.; Yes; Unallotted

1438; Long, John; M; 12/22/74-57; N.C. Cherokee; 4/4; M; Head; 1425; Yes; Yes; Unallotted

1439; Long, Eve; F; 12/22/65-66; N.C. Cherokee; 4/4; M; Wife; 1426; Yes; Yes; Unallotted

1440; Long, Johnson; M; 12/22/63-68; N.C. Cherokee; 4/4; M; Head; 1427; Yes; Yes; Unallotted

1441; Long, Maggie; F; 4/18/76-55; N.C. Cherokee; 4/4; M; Wife; 1428; Yes; Yes; Unallotted

1442; Long, Annie; F; 4/10/07-24; N.C. Cherokee; 4/4; S; Daughter; 1429; Yes; Yes; Unallotted

1443; Long, Martha; F; 4/10/15-16; N.C. Cherokee; 4/4; S; Daughter; 1430; Yes; Yes; Unallotted

1444; Long, Joseph B.; M; 4/7/71-60; N.C. Cherokee; 4/4; M; Head; 1431; Yes; Yes; Unallotted

1445; Long, Sallie; F; 4/24/76-54; N.C. Cherokee; 13/16; M; Wife; 1432; Yes; Yes; Unallotted

1446; Long, Lucy; F; 7/13/05-26; N.C. Cherokee; 29/32; S; Daughter; 1433; Yes; Yes; Unallotted

1447; Long, Edna; F; 4/3/07-24; N.C. Cherokee; 29/32; S; Daughter; 1434; Yes; Yes; Unallotted

Census of the **Eastern Cherokee** reservation of the **Cherokee, N.C.** jurisdiction, as of **April 1** , 19**32,** taken by **R. L. Spalsbury** , Superintendent.

Key: Number; Surname, Given; Sex; Date of Birth-Age at Last Birthday; Tribe; Degree of Blood; Marital Status; Relationship to Head of Family; Last C. Roll No.; At Jurisdiction Where Enrolled (Yes/No); (If no – Where); Ward (Yes/No); Allotment, Annuity and Identification Numbers (if given).

1448; Long, Lloyd; M; 4/19/09-22; N.C. Cherokee; 29/32; S; Son; 1435; Yes; Yes; Unallotted

1449; Long, Peter; M; 8/3/79-52; N.C. Cherokee; 4/4; M; Head; 1436; Yes; Yes; Unallotted

1450; Long, Anona C.; F; 10/31/91-40; N.C. Cherokee; 9/16; M; Wife; 1437; Yes; Yes; Unallotted

1451; Long, Joseph G.; M; 12/5/12-19; N.C. Cherokee; 9/32; S; Stepson; 1438; Yes; Yes; Unallotted

1452; Long, Temotzema; F; 4/15/14-17; N.C. Cherokee; 25/32; S; Daughter; 1439; Yes; Yes; Unallotted

1453; Long, Stephen G.; M; 11/28/15-16; N.C. Cherokee; 25/32; S; Son; 1440; Yes; Yes; Unallotted

1454; Long, Wilbur; M; 4/16/18-13; N.C. Cherokee; 25/32; S; Son; 1441; Yes; Yes; Unallotted

1455; Long, William; M; 1/8/21-11; N.C. Cherokee; 25/32; S; Son; 1442; Yes; Yes; Unallotted

1456; Long, Rachel; F; 1/8/21-11; N.C. Cherokee; 25/32; S; Daughter; 1443; Yes; Yes; Unallotted

1457; Long, Laura; F; 8/30/23-8; N.C. Cherokee; 25/32; S; Daughter; 1444; Yes; Yes; Unallotted

1458; Long, Johnnie; M; 5/25/27-4; N.C. Cherokee; 25/32; S; Son; 1445; Yes; Yes; Unallotted

1459; Long, Robert E.; M; 4/8/30-2; N.C. Cherokee; 25/32; S; Son; 1446; Yes; Yes; Unallotted

1460; Long, Rachel; F; 12/22/74-57; N.C. Cherokee; 4/4; S; Head; 1447; Yes; Yes; Unallotted

1461; Long, Will West; M; 1/25/70-62; N.C. Cherokee; 4/4; M; Head; 1448; Yes; Yes; Unallotted

1462; Long, Mary W.; F; 12/7/70-61; N.C. Cherokee; 4/4; M; Wife; 1449; Yes; Yes; Unallotted

1463; Long, Allen W.; M; 6/2/17-14; N.C. Cherokee; 4/4; S; Son; 1450; Yes; Yes; Unallotted

1464; Long, William G.; M; 5/15/97-34; N.C. Cherokee; 4/4; M; Head; 1451; Yes; Yes; Unallotted

1465; Long, Susie W.; F; 9/15/96-35; N.C. Cherokee; 4/4; M; Wife; 1452; Yes; Yes; Unallotted

1466; Long, Ella; F; 11/1/19-12; N.C. Cherokee; 4/4; S; Daughter; 1453; Yes; Yes; Unallotted

1467; Long, Mary; F; 3/31/21-10; N.C. Cherokee; 4/4; S; Daughter; 1454; Yes; Yes; Unallotted

Census of the **Eastern Cherokee** reservation of the **Cherokee, N.C.** jurisdiction, as of **April 1** , **1932,** taken by **R. L. Spalsbury** , Superintendent.

Key: Number; Surname, Given; Sex; Date of Birth-Age at Last Birthday; Tribe; Degree of Blood; Marital Status; Relationship to Head of Family; Last C. Roll No.; At Jurisdiction Where Enrolled (Yes/No); (If no – Where); Ward (Yes/No); Allotment, Annuity and Identification Numbers (if given).

1468; Long, Adam; M; 3/9/23-8; N.C. Cherokee; 4/4; S; Son; 1455; Yes; Yes; Unallotted

1469; Lossie, Candy; M; 3/10/98-33; N.C. Cherokee; 4/4; S; Head; 1456; Yes; Yes; Unallotted

1470; Lossie, John R.; M; 2/25/03-29; N.C. Cherokee; 4/4; S; Brother; 1457; Yes; Yes; Unallotted

1471; Lossie, Hayes; M; 3/22/05-27; N.C. Cherokee; 4/4; S; Brother; 1458; Yes; Yes; Unallotted

1472; Lossie, David; M; 6/16/93-38; N.C. Cherokee; 4/4; M; Head; 1459; Yes; Yes; Unallotted

1473; Lossie, Lydia W.; F; 4/21/13-18; N.C. Cherokee; 4/4; M; Wife; 1460; Yes; Yes; Unallotted

1474; Lossie, Sampson; M; 4/7/26-5; N.C. Cherokee; 4/4; S; Son; 1461; Yes; Yes; Unallotted

1475; Lossie, Charlie; M; 2/19/29-3; N.C. Cherokee; 4/4; S; Son; 1462; Yes; Yes; Unallotted

1476; Lossie, Annie; F; 11/2/31-4/12; N.C. Cherokee; 4/4; S; Daughter; ---; Yes; Yes; Unallotted

1477; Lossie, Katy L.; F; 12/28/98-33; N.C. Cherokee; 7/8; Wd.; Head; 1463; Yes; Yes; Unallotted

1478; Lossie, Solomon; M; 9/4/99-32; N.C. Cherokee; 4/4; S; Head; 1464; Yes; Yes; Unallotted

1479; Lossih, Dom Thomas; M; 3/12/96-36; N.C. Cherokee; 4/4; M; Head; 1465; Yes; Yes; Unallotted

1480; Lossih, Bettie G.; F; 2/15/03-29; N.C. Cherokee; 3/4; M; Wife; 1466; Yes; Yes; Unallotted

1481; George, Judas; M; 10/29/20-11; N.C. Cherokee; 7/8; S; Stepson; 1467; Yes; Yes; Unallotted

1482; Lossih, Henry; M; 8/15/70-59; N.C. Cherokee; 4/4; M; Head; 1468; Yes; Yes; Unallotted

1483; Lossih, Aggie; F; 4/8/80-51; N.C. Cherokee; 4/4; M; Wife; 1469; Yes; Yes; Unallotted

1484; Lossih, Rosy; F; 6/26/07-24; N.C. Cherokee; 4/4; S; Daughter; 1470; Yes; Yes; Unallotted

1485; Lossih, Calvin S.; M; 6/30/09-22; N.C. Cherokee; 4/4; S; Son; 1471; Yes; Yes; Unallotted

1486; Lossih, Abel; M; 6/10/11-20; N.C. Cherokee; 4/4; S; Son; 1472; Yes; Yes; Unallotted

Census of the **Eastern Cherokee** reservation of the **Cherokee, N.C.** jurisdiction, as of **April 1** , 19**32**, taken by **R. L. Spalsbury** , Superintendent.

Key: Number; Surname, Given; Sex; Date of Birth-Age at Last Birthday; Tribe; Degree of Blood; Marital Status; Relationship to Head of Family; Last C. Roll No.; At Jurisdiction Where Enrolled (Yes/No); (If no – Where); Ward (Yes/No); Allotment, Annuity and Identification Numbers (if given).

1487; Lossih, Mary; F; 9/25/13-18; N.C. Cherokee; 4/4; S; Daughter; 1473; Yes; Yes; Unallotted

1488; Lossih, Adam Ross; M; 5/27/21-10; N.C. Cherokee; 4/4; S; Son; 1474; Yes; Yes; Unallotted

1489; Lossih (Mr. Rosy), Jonas Eli; M; 3/21/29-3; N.C. Cherokee; 1/4-; S; Grandson; 1475; Yes; Yes; Unallotted

1490; Lossih, John D.; M; 6/14/70-61; N.C. Cherokee; 4/4; M; Head; 1476; Yes; Yes; Unallotted

1491; Lossih, Laura; F; 5/2/69-62; N.C. Cherokee; 7/8; M; Wife; 1477; Yes; Yes; Unallotted

1492; Lossih, John Jr.; M; 4/8/98-33; N.C. Cherokee; 15/16; S; Son; 1478; Yes; Yes; Unallotted

1493; Lossih, Jesse J.; M; 4/1/07-25; N.C. Cherokee; 15/16; S; Son; 1479; Yes; Yes; Unallotted

1494; Lossih, Jonas; M; 3/26/73-59; N.C. Cherokee; 4/4; M; Head; 1480; Yes; Yes; Unallotted

1495; Lossih, Nicey W.; F; 10/8/80-51; N.C. Cherokee; 4/4; M; Wife; 1481; Yes; Yes; Unallotted

1496; Lossih, Sarah; F; 4/18/23-8; N.C. Cherokee; 4/4; S; Alone; 1482; Yes; Yes; Unallotted

1497; Loudermilk (Raper, Cynthia), Cynthia A.; F; 7/31/62-69; N.C. Cherokee; 1/8; M; Wife; 1483; No; Culberson, Cherokee, N.C.; Yes; Unallotted

1498; Loudermilk, Elmer; M; 5/22/04-27; N.C. Cherokee; 1/32; M; Head; 1484; No; Ducktown, Polk, Tenn.; Yes; Unallotted

1499; Loudermilk, John R.; M; 7/7/79-52; N.C. Cherokee; 1/16; M; Head; 1485; Yes; Yes; Unallotted

1500; Loudermilk, Leroy; M; 9/13/09-22; N.C. Cherokee; 1/32; S; Son; 1486; Yes; Yes; Unallotted

1501; Loudermilk , Wilford T.; M; 1/5/13-19; N.C. Cherokee; 1/32; S; Son; 1487; Yes; Yes; Unallotted

1502; Loudermilk (Garland, Josephine), Josephine; F; 11/11/76-55; N.C. Cherokee; 1/16; M; Wife; 1488; No; Ducktown, Polk, Tenn.; Yes; Unallotted

1503; Loudermilk, Clinton; M; 6/12/08-23; N.C. Cherokee; 1/32; S; Son; 1489; No; Ducktown, Polk, Tenn.; Yes; Unallotted

1504; Loudermilk, Luther; M; 11/7/10-21; N.C. Cherokee; 1/32; S; Son; 1490; No; Ducktown, Polk, Tenn.; Yes; Unallotted

1505; Loudermilk, Willard L.; M; 6/12/15-16; N.C. Cherokee; 1/32; S; Son; 1491; No; Ducktown, Polk, Tenn.; Yes; Unallotted

Census of the **Eastern Cherokee** reservation of the **Cherokee, N.C.** jurisdiction, as of **April 1** , 19**32,** taken by **R. L. Spalsbury** , Superintendent.

Key: Number; Surname, Given; Sex; Date of Birth-Age at Last Birthday; Tribe; Degree of Blood; Marital Status; Relationship to Head of Family; Last C. Roll No.; At Jurisdiction Where Enrolled (Yes/No); (If no – Where); Ward (Yes/No); Allotment, Annuity and Identification Numbers (if given).

1506; Loudermilk, Thomas L.; M; 7/31/00-31; N.C. Cherokee; 1/32; M; Head; 1492; No; Copperhill, Polk, Tenn.; Yes; Unallotted

1507; Loudermilk, Cecil S.; M; 11/14/22-9; N.C. Cherokee; 1/64; S; Son; 1493; No; Copperhill, Polk, Tenn.; Yes; Unallotted

1508; Lovingood (Dockery, Elsie), Elsie A.; F; 1/20/05-27; N.C. Cherokee; 1/32; M; Wife; 1494; Yes; Yes; Unallotted

1509; Lowen, John; M; 12/22/60-71; N.C. Cherokee; 4/4; Wd.; Head; 1495; Yes; Yes; Unallotted

1510; Lowen, John B.; M; 5/22/60-71; N.C. Cherokee; 4/4; S; Head; 1496; Yes; Yes; Unallotted

1511; Ludwig, Bessie N.; F; 5/1/87-44; N.C. Cherokee; 1/4; M; Wife; 1497; Yes; Yes; Unallotted

1512; Lunsford (Rogers, Inez), Inez; F; 4/22/07-24; N.C. Cherokee; 1/8; M; Wife; 1498; Yes; Yes; Unallotted

1513; Lunsford, Ted; M; 6/23/07-24; N.C. Cherokee; 1/64; S; Head; 1499; Yes; Yes; Unallotted

1514; Lunsford, Dee; M; 6/23/09-22; N.C. Cherokee; 1/64; S; Brother; 1500; Yes; Yes; Unallotted

1515; Lunsford, Woodrow; M; 6/23/11-20; N.C. Cherokee; 1/64; S; Brother; 1501; Yes; Yes; Unallotted

1516; Lunsford, Ausloo; M; 6/23/13-18; N.C. Cherokee; 1/64; S; Brother; 1502; Yes; Yes; Unallotted

1517; Lunsford, Jane; F; 6/23/15-16; N.C. Cherokee; 1/64; S; Sister; 1503; Yes; Yes; Unallotted

1518; Lunsford, May; F; 6/23/20-11; N.C. Cherokee; 1/64; S; Sister; 1504; Yes; Yes; Unallotted

1519; Lunsford, Vernon; M; 6/23/21-10; N.C. Cherokee; 1/64; S; Brother; 1505; Yes; Yes; Unallotted

1520; McAllister (Garland, Harriet), Harriet A.; F; 6/27/66-65; N.C. Cherokee; 1/8; M; Wife; 1506; Yes; Yes; Unallotted

1521; McCoy, David; M; 7/13/73-58; N.C. Cherokee; 1/8; M; Head; 1507; Yes; Yes; Unallotted

1522; McCoy, Bessie; F; 9/12/11-20; N.C. Cherokee; 1/16; S; Daughter; 1508; Yes; Yes; Unallotted

1523; McCoy, Eva; F; 8/22/13-19; N.C. Cherokee; 1/16; S; Daughter; 1509; Yes; Yes; Unallotted

Census of the **Eastern Cherokee** reservation of the **Cherokee, N.C.** jurisdiction, as of **April 1** , 19**32,** taken by **R. L. Spalsbury** , Superintendent.

Key: Number; Surname, Given; Sex; Date of Birth-Age at Last Birthday; Tribe; Degree of Blood; Marital Status; Relationship to Head of Family; Last C. Roll No.; At Jurisdiction Where Enrolled (Yes/No); (If no – Where); Ward (Yes/No); Allotment, Annuity and Identification Numbers (if given).

1524; McCoy, Edna; F; 1/8/16-16; N.C. Cherokee; 1/16; S; Daughter; 1510; Yes; Yes; Unallotted

1525; McCoy, James; M; 12/1/81-50; N.C. Cherokee; 1/8; M; Head; 1511; Yes; Yes; Unallotted

1526; McCoy, William T.; M; 3/6/06-26; N.C. Cherokee; 1/16; S; Son; 1512; Yes; Yes; Unallotted

1527; McCoy, Joseph H.; M; 11/24/07-24; N.C. Cherokee; 1/16; S; Son; 1513; Yes; Yes; Unallotted

1528; McCoy, Frank; M; 12/28/12-19; N.C. Cherokee; 1/16; S; Son; 1514; Yes; Yes; Unallotted

1529; McCoy, Edith; F; 4/22/14-17; N.C. Cherokee; 1/16; S; Daughter; 1515; Yes; Yes; Unallotted

1530; McCoy, Olive; F; 8/26/16-15; N.C. Cherokee; 1/16; S; Daughter; 1516; Yes; Yes; Unallotted

1531; McCoy, Lola A.; F; 4/27/19-12; N.C. Cherokee; 1/16; S; Daughter; 1517; Yes; Yes; Unallotted

1532; McCoy, Russell D.; M; 8/4/22-9; N.C. Cherokee; 1/16; S; Son; 1518; Yes; Yes; Unallotted

1533; McCoy, Helen; F; 12/5/24-7; N.C. Cherokee; 1/16; S; Daughter; 1519; Yes; Yes; Unallotted

1534; McCoy, James; M; 10/6/04-27; N.C. Cherokee; 1/16; S; Head; 1520; Yes; Yes; Unallotted

1535; McCoy, James W.R.; M; 8/7/01-30; N.C. Cherokee; 1/16; M; Head; 1521; Yes; Yes; Unallotted

1536; McCoy, Eunice M.; F; 12/28/21-10; N.C. Cherokee; 1/32; S; Daughter; 1522; Yes; Yes; Unallotted

1537; McCoy, Margaret J.; F; 2/1/23-9; N.C. Cherokee; 1/32; S; Daughter; 1523; Yes; Yes; Unallotted

1538; McCoy, Jesse; M; 12/22/09-22; N.C. Cherokee; 1/16; M; Head; 1524; Yes; Yes; Unallotted

1539; McCoy, John C.; M; 2/3/77-55; N.C. Cherokee; 1/8; M; Head; 1525; Yes; Yes; Unallotted

1540; McCoy, Walter; M; 5/20/09-22; N.C. Cherokee; 1/16; S; Son; 1526; Yes; Yes; Unallotted

1541; McCoy, Pearson; M; 4/19/98-33; N.C. Cherokee; 1/16; M; Head; 1527; Yes; Yes; Unallotted

1542; McCoy, Sallie L.; F; 7/7/09-22; N.C. Cherokee; 1/32; M; Wife; 1528; Yes; Yes; Unallotted

Census of the **Eastern Cherokee** reservation of the **Cherokee, N.C.** jurisdiction, as of **April 1** , **1932,** taken by **R. L. Spalsbury** , Superintendent.

Key: Number; Surname, Given; Sex; Date of Birth-Age at Last Birthday; Tribe; Degree of Blood; Marital Status; Relationship to Head of Family; Last C. Roll No.; At Jurisdiction Where Enrolled (Yes/No); (If no – Where); Ward (Yes/No); Allotment, Annuity and Identification Numbers (if given).

1543; McDaniel, Andy; M; 11/10/79-52; N.C. Cherokee; 1/32; M; Head; 1529; Yes; Yes; Unallotted

1544; McDaniel, Bob; M; 2/13/06-26; N.C. Cherokee; 1/64; S; Son; 1530; Yes; Yes; Unallotted

1545; McDaniel, Onie; F; 9/30/08-23; N.C. Cherokee; 1/64; S; Daughter; 1531; Yes; Yes; Unallotted

1546; McDaniel, Burgan; M; 2/23/11-21; N.C. Cherokee; 1/64; S; Son; 1532; Yes; Yes; Unallotted

1547; McDaniel, Dottie; F; 2/14/13-19; N.C. Cherokee; 1/64; S; Daughter; 1533; Yes; Yes; Unallotted

1548; McDaniel, Nina; F; 1/16/18-14; N.C. Cherokee; 1/64; S; Daughter; 1534; Yes; Yes; Unallotted

1549; McDaniel, Mary Lou; F; 12/2/21-10; N.C. Cherokee; 1/64; S; Daughter; 1535; Yes; Yes; Unallotted

1550; McDaniel, Belva; M; 11/15/88-43; N.C. Cherokee; 1/32; M; Head; 1536; Yes; Yes; Unallotted

1551; McDaniel, Fannie; F; 4/25/08-23; N.C. Cherokee; 1/64; S; Daughter; 1537; Yes; Yes; Unallotted

1552; McDaniel, Hobart; M; 3/5/05-27; N.C. Cherokee; 1/64; S; Head; 1538; Yes; Yes; Unallotted

1553; McDaniel, Dee; M; 6/23/07-24; N.C. Cherokee; 1/64; S; Brother; 1536; Yes; Yes; Unallotted

1554; McDaniel, Pearl; F; 12/8/09-22; N.C. Cherokee; 1/64; S; Sister; 1540; Yes; Yes; Unallotted

1555; McDaniel, Behaden; M; 6/10/11-20; N.C. Cherokee; 1/64; S; Brother; 1541; Yes; Yes; Unallotted

1556; McDaniel, Louisel; M; 12/23/13-18; N.C. Cherokee; 1/64; S; Brother; 1542; Yes; Yes; Unallotted

1557; McDaniel, Glin; M; 5/15/15-16; N.C. Cherokee; 1/64; S; Brother; 1543; Yes; Yes; Unallotted

1558; McDonald, Addie; F; 12/3/01-30; N.C. Cherokee; 1/64; M; Wife; 1544; Yes; Yes; Unallotted

1559; McDonald, Eva Mae; F; 11/10/21-10; N.C. Cherokee; 1/128; S; Daughter; 1545; Yes; Yes; Unallotted

1560; McDonald, Harrison H.; M; 12/17/89-42; N.C. Cherokee; 1/32; M; Head; 1546; Yes; Yes; Unallotted

1561; McDonald, Bonnie; F; 6/20/11-20; N.C. Cherokee; 1/64; S; Daughter; 1547; Yes; Yes; Unallotted

1562; McDonald, Vesta; F; 8/27/13-18; N.C. Cherokee; 1/64; S; Daughter; 1548; Yes; Yes; Unallotted

Census of the **Eastern Cherokee** reservation of the **Cherokee, N.C.** jurisdiction, as of **April 1**, 19**32,** taken by **R. L. Spalsbury**, Superintendent.

Key: Number; Surname, Given; Sex; Date of Birth-Age at Last Birthday; Tribe; Degree of Blood; Marital Status; Relationship to Head of Family; Last C. Roll No.; At Jurisdiction Where Enrolled (Yes/No); (If no – Where); Ward (Yes/No); Allotment, Annuity and Identification Numbers (if given).

1563; McDonald, Lawton; M; 12/21/15-16; N.C. Cherokee; 1/64; S; Son; 1549; Yes; Yes; Unallotted

1564; McDonald, Irene; F; 8/8/18-13; N.C. Cherokee; 1/64; S; Daughter; 1550; Yes; Yes; Unallotted

1565; McDonald, Lillian; F; 1/14/21-11; N.C. Cherokee; 1/64; S; Daughter; 1551; Yes; Yes; Unallotted

1566; McDonald, James; M; 12/30/76-55; N.C. Cherokee; 1/32; M; Head; 1552; Yes; Yes; Unallotted

1567; McDonald, May; F; 4/2/07-23; N.C. Cherokee; 1/64; S; Daughter; 1553; Yes; Yes; Unallotted

1568; McDonald, Tommie; M; 1/1/13-19; N.C. Cherokee; 1/64; S; Son; 1554; Yes; Yes; Unallotted

1569; McDonald, John; M; 6/12/73-59; N.C. Cherokee; 1/32; M; Head; 1555; Yes; Yes; Unallotted

1570; McDonald, Charlie; M; 1/23/08-24; N.C. Cherokee; 1/64; S; Son; 1556; Yes; Yes; Unallotted

1571; McDonald, Boyd; M; 5/28/12-19; N.C. Cherokee; 1/64; S; Son; 1557; Yes; Yes; Unallotted

1572; McDonald, Leonard; M; 11/10/14-17; N.C. Cherokee; 1/64; S; Son; 1558; Yes; Yes; Unallotted

1573; McGillis, Nellie F.; F; 9/2/01-30; N.C. Cherokee; 4/4; M; Wife; 1559; Yes; Yes; Unallotted

1574; McLeymore, Morrell; M; 9/9/00-31; N.C. Cherokee; 5/16; S; Head; 1560; Yes; Yes; Unallotted

1575; McLeymore, Samuel R.; M; 3/6/06-26; N.C. Cherokee; 5/16; S; Brother; 1561; Yes; Yes; Unallotted

1576; McLeymore, Wm. Glen; M; 11/10/10-21; N.C. Cherokee; 5/16; S; Brother; 1562; Yes; Yes; Unallotted

1577; McLeymore, Kermit C.; M; 1/13/13-19; N.C. Cherokee; 5/16; S; Brother; 1563; Yes; Yes; Unallotted

1578; Madrano, Agnes Owl; F; 10/19/97-34; N.C. Cherokee; 1/2; M; Wife; 1564; Yes; Yes; Unallotted

1579; Maney, Bruce; M; 8/27/08-23; N.C. Cherokee; 1/32; S; Head; 1565; Yes; Yes; Unallotted

1580; Maney (Matthews, Eva), Eva A.; F; 11/13/04-27; N.C. Cherokee; 1/32; M; Wife; 1566; Yes; Yes; Unallotted

1581; Maney, Lillian R.; F; 8/20/20-11; N.C. Cherokee; 1/64; S; Daughter; 1567; Yes; Yes; Unallotted

Census of the **Eastern Cherokee** reservation of the **Cherokee, N.C.** jurisdiction, as of **April 1**, **1932,** taken by **R. L. Spalsbury** , Superintendent.

Key: Number; Surname, Given; Sex; Date of Birth-Age at Last Birthday; Tribe; Degree of Blood; Marital Status; Relationship to Head of Family; Last C. Roll No.; At Jurisdiction Where Enrolled (Yes/No); (If no – Where); Ward (Yes/No); Allotment, Annuity and Identification Numbers (if given).

1582; Maney, Cecil; M; 12/26/22-9; N.C. Cherokee; 1/64; S; Son; 1568; Yes; Yes; Unallotted

1583; Maney, John; M; 5/10/06-25; N.C. Cherokee; 1/2; M; Head; 1569; Yes; Yes; Unallotted

1584; Maney, John Wm. Jr.; M; 2/2/31-1; N.C. Cherokee; 3/4; S; Son; 15704; Yes; Yes; Unallotted

1585; Maney, Jacob; M; 5/26/08-23; N.C. Cherokee; 1/2; S; Head; 1570; Yes; Yes; Unallotted

1586; Maney, Caroline; F; 11/6/13-18; N.C. Cherokee; 1/2; S; Daughter; 1571; Yes; Yes; Unallotted

1587; Maney, Simon P.; M; 3/11/14-18; N.C. Cherokee; 1/2; S; Son; 1572; Yes; Yes; Unallotted

1588; Maney, Jesse J.; M; 6/7/16-15; N.C. Cherokee; 1/2; S; Son; 1573; Yes; Yes; Unallotted

1589; Maney, Rachel A.; F; 11/30/01-30; N.C. Cherokee; 4/4; M; Wife; 1575; Yes; Yes; Unallotted

1590; Maney, Richard; M; 3/5/12-20; N.C. Cherokee; 1/4; S; Son (Fr. white); 1576; Yes; Yes; Unallotted

1591; Maney, James O.; M; 10/26/13-18; N.C. Cherokee; 1/4; S; Son; 1577; Yes; Yes; Unallotted

1592; Maney, Shufford; M; 2/29/16-16; N.C. Cherokee; 1/4; S; Son; 1578; Yes; Yes; Unallotted

1593; Maney, Frank D.; M; 6/30/17-14; N.C. Cherokee; 1/4; S; Son; 1579; Yes; Yes; Unallotted

1594; Martin, Lucy; F; 8/15/72-59; N.C. Cherokee; 4/4; Wd.; Head; 1580; Yes; Yes; Unallotted

1595; Martin, Charles; M; 12/19/08-23; N.C. Cherokee; 4/4; S; Son; 1581; Yes; Yes; Unallotted

1596; Martin (Lambert, Ida), Ida; F; 12/25/08-23; N.C. Cherokee; 1/32; M; Wife; 1582; Yes; Yes; Unallotted

1597; Martin, Thomas; M; 12/25/87-44; N.C. Cherokee; 4/4; Wd.; Head; 1583; Yes; Yes; Unallotted

1598; Martin, Sarah; F; 3/31/22-10; N.C. Cherokee; 4/4; S; Daughter; 1584; Yes; Yes; Unallotted

1599; Martin, Andy; M; 2/8/24-8; N.C. Cherokee; 4/4; S; Son; 1585; Yes; Yes; Unallotted

1600; Martin, Jesse T.; M; 12/15/28-3; N.C. Cherokee; 4/4; S; Son; 1586; Yes; Yes; Unallotted

Census of the **Eastern Cherokee** reservation of the **Cherokee, N.C.** jurisdiction, as of **April 1**, 19**32**, taken by **R. L. Spalsbury**, Superintendent.

Key: Number; Surname, Given; Sex; Date of Birth-Age at Last Birthday; Tribe; Degree of Blood; Marital Status; Relationship to Head of Family; Last C. Roll No.; At Jurisdiction Where Enrolled (Yes/No); (If no – Where); Ward (Yes/No); Allotment, Annuity and Identification Numbers (if given).

1601; Martin, Wesley; M; 7/10/96-35; N.C. Cherokee; 4/4; M; Head; 1587; Yes; Yes; Unallotted

1602; Martin, Louisa M.; F; 1/21/86-46; N.C. Cherokee; 1/8; M; Wife; 1588; Yes; Yes; Unallotted

1603; Mashburn (Stiles, Alma), Alma; F; 3/23/02-30; N.C. Cherokee; 1/32; M; Wife; 1589; No; Birch, Cherokee, N.C.; Yes; Unallotted

1604; Mashburn, Pearl N.; F; 3/26/23-9; N.C. Cherokee; 1/64; S; Daughter; 1590; No; Birch, Cherokee, N.C.; Yes; Unallotted

1605; Mashburn, Frank; M; 1/21/00-32; N.C. Cherokee; 3/32; M; Head; 1591; Yes; Yes; Unallotted

1606; Mashburn, Fred; M; 10/27/20-11; N.C. Cherokee; 3/64; S; Son; 1592; Yes; Yes; Unallotted

1607; Mashburn, Claude; M; 12/9/22-9; N.C. Cherokee; 3/64; S; Son; 1593; Yes; Yes; Unallotted

1608; Mashburn (Timpson, Harriett), Harriett A.; F; 9/23/78-54; N.C. Cherokee; 3/16; M; Wife; 1594; Yes; Yes; Unallotted

1609; Mashburn, Bessie; F; 7/23/01-30; N.C. Cherokee; 3/32; S; Daughter; 1595; Yes; Yes; Unallotted

1610; Mashburn, James L.; M; 10/17/03-28; N.C. Cherokee; 3/32; S; Son; 1596; Yes; Yes; Unallotted

1611; Mashburn, Sarah A.; F; 1/25/06-26; N.C. Cherokee; 3/32; S; Daughter; 1597; Yes; Yes; Unallotted

1612; Mashburn, Thomas R.; M; 6/26/11-20; N.C. Cherokee; 3/32; S; Son; 1598; Yes; Yes; Unallotted

1613; Mashburn, Lorraine; F; 8/22/15-16; N.C. Cherokee; 3/32; S; Daughter; 1599; Yes; Yes; Unallotted

1614; Mashburn, Lydia M.; F; 7/23/19-12; N.C. Cherokee; 3/32; S; Daughter; 1600; Yes; Yes; Unallotted

1615; Mashburn, Cynthia N.; F; 5/9/23-9; N.C. Cherokee; 3/32; S; Daughter; 1601; Yes; Yes; Unallotted

1616; Mashburn (Timpson, Leora), Leora; F; 5/10/83-48; N.C. Cherokee; 3/16; M; Wife; 1602; Yes; Yes; Unallotted

1617; Mashburn, Bertha; F; 8/17/05-26; N.C. Cherokee; 3/32; S; Daughter; 1603; Yes; Yes; Unallotted

1618; Mashburn, Myrtle; F; 10/21/09-22; N.C. Cherokee; 3/32; S; Daughter; 1604; Yes; Yes; Unallotted

1619; Matheson (Hardin, Odin), Odin; F; 12/2/03-28; N.C. Cherokee; 1/32; M; Wife; 1605; Yes; Yes; Unallotted

Census of the **Eastern Cherokee** reservation of the **Cherokee, N.C.** jurisdiction, as of **April 1** , 1932, taken by **R. L. Spalsbury** , Superintendent.

Key: Number; Surname, Given; Sex; Date of Birth-Age at Last Birthday; Tribe; Degree of Blood; Marital Status; Relationship to Head of Family; Last C. Roll No.; At Jurisdiction Where Enrolled (Yes/No); (If no – Where); Ward (Yes/No); Allotment, Annuity and Identification Numbers (if given).

1620; Matthews (Lambert, Lillian), Lillian I.; F; 10/3/81-50; N.C. Cherokee; 1/16; M; Wife; 1606; Yes; Yes; Unallotted

1621; Matthews, Marshall; M; 12/22/13-18; N.C. Cherokee; 1/32; S; Son; 1607; Yes; Yes; Unallotted

1622; Matthews, Seaborne; M; 11/9/16-15; N.C. Cherokee; 1/32; S; Son; 1608; Yes; Yes; Unallotted

1623; Matthews, Ollie; F; 9/14/17-14; N.C. Cherokee; 1/64; S; Alone; 1609; Yes; Yes; Unallotted

1624; Meroney, Bailey B.; M; 10/21/66-65; N.C. Cherokee; 1/8; M; Head; 1610; Yes; Yes; Unallotted

1625; Meroney, Bailey B.; M; 8/18/01-30; N.C. Cherokee; 1/16; M; Head; 1611; Yes; Yes; Unallotted

1626; Meroney, Della; F; 5/6/06-25; N.C. Cherokee; 1/16; S; Head; 1612; Yes; Yes; Unallotted

1627; Meroney, Felix P.; M; 3/27/05-27; N.C. Cherokee; 1/16; M; Head; 1613; Yes; Yes; Unallotted

1628; Meroney, Richard B.; M; 7/21/01-30; N.C. Cherokee; 1/16; M; Head; 1614; Yes; Yes; Unallotted

1629; Meroney, Barbara; F; 4/28/23-8; N.C. Cherokee; 1/32; S; Daughter; 1615; Yes; Yes; Unallotted

1630; Meroney, Wm. H.; M; 2/10/77-55; N.C. Cherokee; 1/8; M; Head; 1616; Yes; Yes; Unallotted

1631; Meroney, Raymond; M; 5/27/13-18; N.C. Cherokee; 1/16; S; Son; 1617; Yes; Yes; Unallotted

1632; Meroney, Martha D.; F; 7/25/14-17; N.C. Cherokee; 1/16; S; Daughter; 1618; Yes; Yes; Unallotted

1633; Meroney, David W.; M; 1/15/16-16; N.C. Cherokee; 1/16; S; Son; 1619; Yes; Yes; Unallotted

1634; Meroney, Wm. H.; M; 12/27/17-14; N.C. Cherokee; 1/16; S; Son; 1620; Yes; Yes; Unallotted

1635; Meroney, Louise M.; F; 5/29/20-11; N.C. Cherokee; 1/16; S; Daughter; 1621; Yes; Yes; Unallotted

1636; Miller (Rogers, Flonnie), Flonnie; F; 4/15/89-42; N.C. Cherokee; 1/8; M; Wife; 1622; Yes; Yes; Unallotted

1637; Miller, Lissie; F; 8/2/08-23; N.C. Cherokee; 1/16; S; Daughter; 1623; Yes; Yes; Unallotted

Census of the **Eastern Cherokee** reservation of the **Cherokee, N.C.** jurisdiction, as of **April 1**, 19**32**, taken by **R. L. Spalsbury**, Superintendent.

Key: Number; Surname, Given; Sex; Date of Birth-Age at Last Birthday; Tribe; Degree of Blood; Marital Status; Relationship to Head of Family; Last C. Roll No.; At Jurisdiction Where Enrolled (Yes/No); (If no – Where); Ward (Yes/No); Allotment, Annuity and Identification Numbers (if given).

1638; Miller, Bessie; F; 1/21/10-22; N.C. Cherokee; 1/16; S; Daughter; 1624; Yes; Yes; Unallotted

1639; Miller, Vertie; F; 9/11/11-20; N.C. Cherokee; 1/16; S; Daughter; 1625; Yes; Yes; Unallotted

1640; Miller, Vernon; M; 2/3/13-19; N.C. Cherokee; 1/16; S; Son; 1626; Yes; Yes; Unallotted

1641; Miller, Adelle; F; 8/3/14-17; N.C. Cherokee; 1/16; S; Daughter; 1627; Yes; Yes; Unallotted

1642; Miller, Baskey; M; 1/7/16-16; N.C. Cherokee; 1/16; S; Son; 1628; Yes; Yes; Unallotted

1643; Miller, Atlas; FM; 11/3/17-14; N.C. Cherokee; 1/16; S; Daughter[sic]; 1629; Yes; Yes; Unallotted

1644; Miller, Arnold; M; 10/27/19-12; N.C. Cherokee; 1/16; S; Son; 1630; Yes; Yes; Unallotted

1645; Miller, Alanerd; F; 3/7/23-9; N.C. Cherokee; 1/16; S; Daughter; 1631; Yes; Yes; Unallotted

1646; Miller, Bedonard; F; 3/7/23-9; N.C. Cherokee; 1/16; S; Daughter; 1632; Yes; Yes; Unallotted

1647; Miller (Porter, Iris), Iris P.; F; 8/1/92-39; N.C. Cherokee; 1/16; M; Wife; 1633; Yes; Yes; Unallotted

1648; Monroe (Lee, Nora), Nora A.; F; 7/12/80-51; N.C. Cherokee; 1/16; M; Wife; 1634; Yes; Yes; Unallotted

1649; Moody, Callie O.; F; 9/30/87-44; N.C. Cherokee; 1/4; M; Wife; 1635; Yes; Yes; Unallotted

1650; Moody, Harlin; M; 7/2/14-17; N.C. Cherokee; 1/8; S; Son; 1636; Yes; Yes; Unallotted

1651; Moody, Garland; M; 12/24/15-16; N.C. Cherokee; 1/8; S; Son; 1637; Yes; Yes; Unallotted

1652; Moody, Russell P.; M; 3/26/18-14; N.C. Cherokee; 1/8; S; Son; 1638; Yes; Yes; Unallotted

1653; Moody, Solomon; M; 12/31/19-12; N.C. Cherokee; 1/8; S; Son; 1639; Yes; Yes; Unallotted

1654; Moody, Bonnie Lee; F; 2/8/22-10; N.C. Cherokee; 1/8; S; Daughter; 1640; Yes; Yes; Unallotted

1655; Moody, Ruth P.; F; 5/6/24-7; N.C. Cherokee; 1/8; S; Daughter; 1641; Yes; Yes; Unallotted

1656; Moore, Georgia C.; F; 10/28/82-49; N.C. Cherokee; 1/8; M; Wife; 1642; Yes; Yes; Unallotted

1657; Moore (Tallent, Luretta), Luretta C.; F; 7/4/89-42; N.C. Cherokee; 1/64; M; Wife; 1643; Yes; Yes; Unallotted

Census of the **Eastern Cherokee** reservation of the **Cherokee, N.C.** jurisdiction, as of **April 1**, **1932,** taken by **R. L. Spalsbury**, Superintendent.

Key: Number; Surname, Given; Sex; Date of Birth-Age at Last Birthday; Tribe; Degree of Blood; Marital Status; Relationship to Head of Family; Last C. Roll No.; At Jurisdiction Where Enrolled (Yes/No); (If no – Where); Ward (Yes/No); Allotment, Annuity and Identification Numbers (if given).

1658; Morgan, Mary A.; F; 5/2/12-19; N.C. Cherokee; 1/32; S; Dau. (Fr. white); 1644; Yes; Yes; Unallotted

1659; Morgan, Rena C.; F; 5/27/14-17; N.C. Cherokee; 1/32; S; Daughter; 1645; Yes; Yes; Unallotted

1660; Morgan, Wm. Albert; M; 10/27/16-15; N.C. Cherokee; 1/32; S; Son; 1646; Yes; Yes; Unallotted

1661; Morgan, Stella G.; F; 1/30/18-14; N.C. Cherokee; 1/32; S; Daughter; 1647; Yes; Yes; Unallotted

1662; Morgan, Carroll V.; F; 8/27/21-10; N.C. Cherokee; 1/32; S; Daughter; 1648; Yes; Yes; Unallotted

1663; Morrison, Fred; M; 2/22/02-32; N.C. Cherokee; 1/64; M; Head; 1649; Yes; Yes; Unallotted

1664; Morrison, Bruce; M; 1909-23; N.C. Cherokee; 1/4-; M; Head; 1650; Yes; Yes; Unallotted

1665; Morrison, Ollie; F; 2/20/81-51; N.C. Cherokee; 1/32; M; Wife; 1651; Yes; Yes; Unallotted

1666; Morrison, Blanche; F; 6/11/05-26; N.C. Cherokee; 1/64; S; Daughter; 1652; Yes; Yes; Unallotted

1667; Morrison, Beulah; F; 6/11/05-26; N.C. Cherokee; 1/64; S; Daughter; 1653; Yes; Yes; Unallotted

1668; Morrison, Marie; F; 2/20/12-22; N.C. Cherokee; 1/64; S; Daughter; 1654; Yes; Yes; Unallotted

1669; Morrow (Baker, Dona), Dona; F; 3/12/95-37; N.C. Cherokee; 1/16; M; Wife; 1655; No; Culberson, Cherokee, N.C,; Yes; Unallotted

1670; Morrow, Harford; M; 3/27/16-16; N.C. Cherokee; 1/32; S; Son; 1656; No; Culberson, Cherokee, N.C,; Yes; Unallotted

1671; Mull (Raper, Effie), Effie; F; 3/28/94-38; N.C. Cherokee; 1/16; M; Wife; 1657; No; Kannapolis, Caburrus, N.C,; Yes; Unallotted

1672; Mull, Bertha M.; F; 12/16/11-20; N.C. Cherokee; 1/32; S; Daughter; 1658; No; Kannapolis, Caburrus, N.C,; Yes; Unallotted

1673; Mull, Wm. Roy; M; 3/26/14-18; N.C. Cherokee; 1/32; S; Son; 1659; No; Kannapolis, Caburrus, N.C,; Yes; Unallotted

1674; Mull, John R.; M; 6/26/20-11; N.C. Cherokee; 1/32; S; Son; 1660; No; Kannapolis, Caburrus, N.C,; Yes; Unallotted

1675; Mull, Ruth E.; F; 12/4/21-10; N.C. Cherokee; 1/32; S; Daughter; 1661; No; Kannapolis, Caburrus, N.C,; Yes; Unallotted

1676; Mumblehead, James W.; M; 10/5/88-43; N.C. Cherokee; 4/4; M; Head; 1662; Yes; Yes; Unallotted

Census of the **Eastern Cherokee** reservation of the **Cherokee, N.C.** jurisdiction, as of **April 1**, **1932,** taken by **R. L. Spalsbury**, Superintendent.

Key: Number; Surname, Given; Sex; Date of Birth-Age at Last Birthday; Tribe; Degree of Blood; Marital Status; Relationship to Head of Family; Last C. Roll No.; At Jurisdiction Where Enrolled (Yes/No); (If no – Where); Ward (Yes/No); Allotment, Annuity and Identification Numbers (if given).

1677; Mumblehead, Lorena S.; F; 10/6/64-65; N.C. Cherokee; 1/4; Wd.; Head; 1663; Yes; Yes; Unallotted

1678; Murphy, Fred; M; 4/16/07-24; N.C. Cherokee; 1/4; S; Head; 1664; Yes; Yes; Unallotted

1679; Murphy, Gay; M; 1/29/06-26; N.C. Cherokee; 1/8; M; Head; 1665; No; Violet, Cherokee, N.C.; Yes; Unallotted

1680; Murphy, Greeley; M; 1/29/06-26; N.C. Cherokee; 1/8; S; Head; 1666; No; Violet, Cherokee, N.C.; Yes; Unallotted

1681; Murphy, Howard; M; 1/7/95-37; N.C. Cherokee; 1/8; M; Head; 1667; Yes; Yes; Unallotted

1682; Murphy, Jesse; M; 12/23/63-68; N.C. Cherokee; 1/4; M; Head; 1668; Yes; Yes; Unallotted

1683; Murphy, Mary M.; F; 6/25/69-62; N.C. Cherokee; 1/8; M; Wife; 1669; Yes; Yes; Unallotted

1684; Murphy, Joseph L.; M; 4/16/93-38; N.C. Cherokee; 1/8; M; Head; 1670; No; Struthers, Mahoning, Ohio; Yes; Unallotted

1685; Murphy, Sadie; F; 10/24/16-15; N.C. Cherokee; 1/16; S; Daughter; 1671; No; Struthers, Mahoning, Ohio; Yes; Unallotted

1686; Murphy, Joseph M.; M; 3/25/65-67; N.C. Cherokee; 1/4; M; Head; 1672; Yes; Yes; Unallotted

1687; Murphy, Ella; F; 8/8/12-19; N.C. Cherokee; 1/8; S; Alone; 1673; Yes; Yes; Unallotted

1688; Murphy, Cordelia; F; 1/26/15-17; N.C. Cherokee; 1/8; S; Sister; 1674; Yes; Yes; Unallotted

1689; Murphy, Ralph; M; 10/26/29-2; N.C. Cherokee; --; S; Nephew; 1675; Yes; Yes; Unallotted

1690; Murphy, Leander, Jr.; M; 7/19/95-36; N.C. Cherokee; 1/8; M; Head; 1676; Yes; Yes; Unallotted

1691; Murphy, Hollis; F; 3/1/21-11; N.C. Cherokee; 1/16; S; Daughter; 1677; Yes; Yes; Unallotted

1692; Murphy, Dale; F; 12/28/22-9; N.C. Cherokee; 1/16; S; Daughter; 1678; Yes; Yes; Unallotted

1693; Murphy, Manco, Jr.; M; 3/29/93-39; N.C. Cherokee; 1/8; M; Head; 1679; Yes; Yes; Unallotted

Census of the **Eastern Cherokee** reservation of the **Cherokee, N.C.** jurisdiction, as of **April 1** , **1932,** taken by **R. L. Spalsbury** , Superintendent.

Key: Number; Surname, Given; Sex; Date of Birth-Age at Last Birthday; Tribe; Degree of Blood; Marital Status; Relationship to Head of Family; Last C. Roll No.; At Jurisdiction Where Enrolled (Yes/No); (If no – Where); Ward (Yes/No); Allotment, Annuity and Identification Numbers (if given).

1694; Murphy, Walter; M; 4/16/00-31; N.C. Cherokee; 1/16; M; Head; 1680; Yes; Yes; Unallotted

1695; Murphy, Marinda M.; F; 1/28/00-32; N.C. Cherokee; 1/16; M; Wife; 1681; Yes; Yes; Unallotted

1696; Murphy, Ethel; F; 4/18/16-15; N.C. Cherokee; 1/16; S; Daughter; 1682; Yes; Yes; Unallotted

1697; Murphy, Alice; F; 4/17/17-14; N.C. Cherokee; 1/16; S; Daughter; 1683; Yes; Yes; Unallotted

1698; Murphy, William; M; 1/6/90-42; N.C. Cherokee; 3/16; M; Head; 1684; Yes; Yes; Unallotted

1699; Murphy, Manco L.; M; 4/9/10-21; N.C. Cherokee; 3/32; S; Son; 1685; Yes; Yes; Unallotted

1700; Murphy, Robert; M; 1/28/12-20; N.C. Cherokee; 3/32; S; Son; 1686; Yes; Yes; Unallotted

1701; Murphy, Luther; M; 6/15/15-16; N.C. Cherokee; 3/32; S; Son; 1687; Yes; Yes; Unallotted

1702; Murphy, Lawrence; M; 6/14/18-13; N.C. Cherokee; 3/32; S; Son; 1688; Yes; Yes; Unallotted

1703; Murphy, Clarence; M; 6/14/18-13; N.C. Cherokee; 3/32; S; Son; 1689; Yes; Yes; Unallotted

1704; Murphy, Mary Etta; F; 3/28/21-11; N.C. Cherokee; 3/32; S; Daughter; 1690; Yes; Yes; Unallotted

1705; Ned, Ezekiel; M; 8/15/64-67; N.C. Cherokee; 4/4; M; Head; 1691; Yes; Yes; Unallotted

1706; Ned, Susan; F; 3/1/63-69; N.C. Cherokee; 4/4; M; Wife; 1692; Yes; Yes; Unallotted

1707; Newton, James D.; M; 8/1/72-59; N.C. Cherokee; 1/16; M; Head; 1693; Yes; Yes; Unallotted

1708; Nick, Chiltoskey; M; 1/6/83-49; N.C. Cherokee; 1/4; S; Head; 1694; No; Ohio; Yes; Unallotted

1709; Nottytom, Peter; M; 6/20/69-62; N.C. Cherokee; 4/4; Wd.; Head; 1695; Yes; Yes; Unallotted

1710; Okwataga, Elizabeth; F; 12/23/42-89; N.C. Cherokee; 4/4; Wd.; Head; 1696; Yes; Yes; Unallotted

1711; Oocumma, Alex; M; 12/23/66-65; N.C. Cherokee; 7/8; M; Head; 1697; Yes; Yes; Unallotted

1712; Oocumma, Annie; F; 12/23/86-45; N.C. Cherokee; 4/4; M; Wife; 1698; Yes; Yes; Unallotted

91

Census of the **Eastern Cherokee** reservation of the **Cherokee, N.C.** jurisdiction, as of **April 1** , 19**32**, taken by **R. L. Spalsbury** , Superintendent.

Key: Number; Surname, Given; Sex; Date of Birth-Age at Last Birthday; Tribe; Degree of Blood; Marital Status; Relationship to Head of Family; Last C. Roll No.; At Jurisdiction Where Enrolled (Yes/No); (If no – Where); Ward (Yes/No); Allotment, Annuity and Identification Numbers (if given).

1713; Oocumma, John; M; 1/20/12-20; N.C. Cherokee; 15/16; S; Son; 1699; Yes; Yes; Unallotted

~~1714; Oocumma, Samuel; M; 2/29/18-14; N.C. Cherokee; 15/16; S; Son; 1700; Yes;~~ Note. See page 251.; Yes; Unallotted

1715; Oocumma, Joseph; M; 6/19/21-10; N.C. Cherokee; 15/16; S; Son; 1701; Yes; Yes; Unallotted

1716; Oocumma, Andy; M; 4/24/24-7; N.C. Cherokee; 15/16; S; Son; 1702; Yes; Yes; Unallotted

1717; Oocumma, Enoch; M; 12/1/90-41; N.C. Cherokee; 15/16; M; Head; 1703; Yes; Yes; Unallotted

1718; Oocumma, Malinda Q.; F; 6/20/04-27; N.C. Cherokee; 5/8; M; Wife; 1704; Yes; Yes; Unallotted

1719; Oocumma, Wilson; M; 5/30/24-7; N.C. Cherokee; 25/32; S; Son; 1705; Yes; Yes; Unallotted

1720; Oocumma, Wilson; M; 9/12/77-54; N.C. Cherokee; 15/16; M; Head; 1706; Yes; Yes; Unallotted

1721; Oocumma, Rachel W.R.; F; 1/23/85-47; N.C. Cherokee; 4/4; M; Wife; 1707; Yes; Yes; Unallotted

1722; Oosowee, David S.; M; 5/7/72-59; N.C. Cherokee; 4/4; M; Head; 1708; Yes; Yes; Unallotted

1723; Oosowee, Susie; F; 6/20/76-55; N.C. Cherokee; 4/4; M; Wife; 1709; Yes; Yes; Unallotted

1724; Oosowee, Tahquette; M; 6/27/99-32; N.C. Cherokee; 4/4; M; Head; 1710; Yes; Yes; Unallotted

1725; Oosowee, Nancy S.; F; 12/23/83-48; N.C. Cherokee; 4/4; M; Wife; 1711; Yes; Yes; Unallotted

1726; Otter, Andrew; M; 10/11/67-64; N.C. Cherokee; 4/4; Wd.; Head; 1712; Yes; Yes; Unallotted

1727; Otter, Jackson; M; 11/23/97-34; N.C. Cherokee; 4/4; M; Head; 1713; Yes; Yes; Unallotted

1728; Otter, Mary S.; F; 4/10/03-28; N.C. Cherokee; 4/4; M; Wife; 1714; Yes; Yes; Unallotted

1729; Otter, Sallie T.; F; 12/18/20-11; N.C. Cherokee; 4/4; S; Daughter; 1715; Yes; Yes; Unallotted

1730; Otter, Samuel Wm.; M; 12/13/22-9; N.C. Cherokee; 4/4; S; Son; 1716; Yes; Yes; Unallotted

1731; Otter, Henry D.; M; 5/21/25-7; N.C. Cherokee; 4/4; S; Son; 1717; Yes; Yes; Unallotted

Census of the **Eastern Cherokee** reservation of the **Cherokee, N.C.** jurisdiction, as of **April 1** , 19**32,** taken by **R. L. Spalsbury** , Superintendent.

Key: Number; Surname, Given; Sex; Date of Birth-Age at Last Birthday; Tribe; Degree of Blood; Marital Status; Relationship to Head of Family; Last C. Roll No.; At Jurisdiction Where Enrolled (Yes/No); (If no – Where); Ward (Yes/No); Allotment, Annuity and Identification Numbers (if given).

1732; Otter, Oliver; M; 8/3/29-2; N.C. Cherokee; 4/4; S; Son; 1718; Yes; Yes; Unallotted

1733; Owenby (Wakefield, Kate), Kate; F; 5/7/08-23; N.C. Cherokee; 1/64; M; Wife; 1719; Yes; Yes; Unallotted

1734; Owenby, Ruth; F; 9/6/23-8; N.C. Cherokee; 1/128; S; Daughter; 1720; Yes; Yes; Unallotted

1735; Owl, Adam; M; 1/27/60-72; N.C. Cherokee; 1/2; M; Head; 1721; Yes; Yes; Unallotted

1736; Owl, Cornelia; F; 12/23/63-68; N.C. Cherokee; 4/4; M; Wife; 1722; Yes; Yes; Unallotted

1737; Owl, Quincy; M; 12/1/04-27; N.C. Cherokee; 3/4; S; Son; 1723; Yes; Yes; Unallotted

1738; Owl, Allen; M; 2/26/90-42; N.C. Cherokee; 4/4; M; Head; 1724; Yes; Yes; Unallotted

1739; Owl, Martha; F; 2/8/14-18; N.C. Cherokee; 1/2; S; Daughter; 1725; Yes; Yes; Unallotted

1740; Owl, Noah; M; 3/31/16-15; N.C. Cherokee; 1/2; S; Son; 1726; Yes; Yes; Unallotted

1741; Owl, Ammons; M; 2/24/90-42; N.C. Cherokee; 4/4; M; Head; 1727; Yes; Yes; Unallotted

1742; Owl, Elizabeth; F; 6/22/86-45; N.C. Cherokee; 4/4; M; Wife; 1728; Yes; Yes; Unallotted

1743; Owl, Gertrude E.; F; 9/7/14-17; N.C. Cherokee; 4/4; S; Daughter; 1729; Yes; Yes; Unallotted

1744; Owl, Raymond; M; 1/5/18-14; N.C. Cherokee; 4/4; S; Son; 1730; Yes; Yes; Unallotted

1745; Owl, Alice C.; F; 4/6/24-7; N.C. Cherokee; 4/4; S; Daughter; 1731; Yes; Yes; Unallotted

1746; Owl, Charlotte; F; 3/8/09-23; N.C. Cherokee; 1/2; S; Head; 1732; Yes; Yes; Unallotted

1747; Owl, Dahney; F; 9/30/81-50; N.C. Cherokee; 15/16; Div.; Head; 1733; Yes; Yes; Unallotted

1748; Owl, David; M; 7/11/93-39; N.C. Cherokee; 1/2; M; Head; 1734; Yes; Yes; Unallotted

1749; Owl, David; M; 10/17/97-34; N.C. Cherokee; 3/4; M; Head; 1735; Yes; Yes; Unallotted

Census of the **Eastern Cherokee** reservation of the **Cherokee, N.C.** jurisdiction, as of **April 1** , 19**32,** taken by **R. L. Spalsbury** , Superintendent.

Key: Number; Surname, Given; Sex; Date of Birth-Age at Last Birthday; Tribe; Degree of Blood; Marital Status; Relationship to Head of Family; Last C. Roll No.; At Jurisdiction Where Enrolled (Yes/No); (If no – Where); Ward (Yes/No); Allotment, Annuity and Identification Numbers (if given).

1750; Owl, Elizabeth; F; 2/17/02-30; N.C. Cherokee; 7/16; M; Wife; 1736; Yes; Yes; Unallotted

1751; Owl, Caledonia; F; 6/11/18-13; N.C. Cherokee; 19/32; S; Daughter; 1737; Yes; Yes; Unallotted

1752; Owl, Lloyd J.; M; 6/9/20-11; N.C. Cherokee; 19/32; S; Son; 1738; Yes; Yes; Unallotted

1753; Owl, Dinah; F; 12/22/58-73; N.C. Cherokee; 4/14; Wd.; Head; 1739; Yes; Yes; Unallotted

1754; Owl, William; M; 2/16/92-40; N.C. Cherokee; 4/4; S; Son; 1740; Yes; Yes; Unallotted

1755; Owl, Enoch; M; 3/9/99-33; N.C. Cherokee; 4/4; M; Head; 1741; Yes; Yes; Unallotted

1756; Owl, Ollie Q.; F; 2/28/99-33; N.C. Cherokee; 5/8; M; Wife; 1742; Yes; Yes; Unallotted

1757; Owl, Frell; M; 3/1/99-33; N.C. Cherokee; 1/2; S; Head; 1743; Yes; Yes; Unallotted

1758; Owl, George; M; 12/26/95-36; N.C. Cherokee; 1/2; M; Head; 1744; Yes; Yes; Unallotted

1759; Owl, George Jr.; M; 8/1/20-11; N.C. Cherokee; 1/4; S; Son; 1745; Yes; Yes; Unallotted

1760; Owl, Rebecca; F; 4/27/23-8; N.C. Cherokee; 1/4; S; Daughter; 1746; Yes; Yes; Unallotted

1761; Owl, Hilary S.; M; 4/5/26-5; N.C. Cherokee; 1/4; S; Son; 1747; Yes; Yes; Unallotted

1762; Owl, Henry; M; 8/1/97-34; N.C. Cherokee; 1/2; S; Head; 1748; Yes; Yes; Unallotted

1763; Owl, James; M; 10/20/86-45; N.C. Cherokee; 4/4; M; Head; 1749; Yes; Yes; Unallotted

1764; Owl, Charlotte; F; 8/13/94-37; N.C. Cherokee; 4/4; M; Wife; 1750; Yes; Yes; Unallotted

1765; Owl, Lloyd; M; 11/21/09-22; N.C. Cherokee; 4/4; S; Son; 1751; Yes; Yes; Unallotted

1766; Owl, Jefferson; M; 10/30/14-17; N.C. Cherokee; 4/4; S; Son; 1752; Yes; Yes; Unallotted

1767; Owl, Charles; M; 2/2/20-12; N.C. Cherokee; 4/4; S; Son; 1753; Yes; Yes; Unallotted

1768; Owl, Harriett N.; F; 7/15/30-1; N.C. Cherokee; 4/4; S; Daughter; 1754; Yes; Yes; Unallotted

Census of the **Eastern Cherokee** reservation of the **Cherokee, N.C.** jurisdiction, as of **April 1** , **1932,** taken by **R. L. Spalsbury** , Superintendent.

Key: Number; Surname, Given; Sex; Date of Birth-Age at Last Birthday; Tribe; Degree of Blood; Marital Status; Relationship to Head of Family; Last C. Roll No.; At Jurisdiction Where Enrolled (Yes/No); (If no – Where); Ward (Yes/No); Allotment, Annuity and Identification Numbers (if given).

1769; Owl, Johnson; M; 5/27/79-52; N.C. Cherokee; 4/4; M; Head; 1755; Yes; Yes; Unallotted

1770; Owl, Stacey; F; 3/29/80-52; N.C. Cherokee; 4/4; M; Wife; 1756; Yes; Yes; Unallotted

1771; Owl, Joseph; M; 8/10/13-18; N.C. Cherokee; 4/4; S; Son; 1757; Yes; Yes; Unallotted

1772; Owl, Jonah; M; 4/25/79-52; N.C. Cherokee; 4/4; M; Head; 1758; Yes; Yes; Unallotted

1773; Owl, Sallie S.; F; 12/15/88-43; N.C. Cherokee; 4/4; M; Wife; 1759; Yes; Yes; Unallotted

1774; Owl (Mr. Julia Sanders), Philip; M; 6/29/09-22; N.C. Cherokee; 11/16; S; Son; 1760; Yes; Yes; Unallotted

1775; Owl, Ellis; M; 11/13/13-18; N.C. Cherokee; 11/16; S; Son; 1761; Yes; Yes; Unallotted

1776; Owl, Lloyd; M; 8/22/99-32; N.C. Cherokee; 1/4; M; Head; 1762; Yes; Yes; Unallotted

1777; Owl, Jessie E.; F; 6/16/22-9; N.C. Cherokee; 5/8; S; Daughter; 1763; Yes; Yes; Unallotted

1778; Owl, Robert E.; M; 4/27/24-7; N.C. Cherokee; 5/8; S; Son; 1764; Yes; Yes; Unallotted

1779; Owl, Louis; M; 2/28/08-24; N.C. Cherokee; 4/4; S; Head; 1765; Yes; Yes; Unallotted

1780; Owl, Mark; M; 6/2/92-39; N.C. Cherokee; 1/4; M; Head; 1766; Yes; Yes; Unallotted

1781; Owl, Belva S.; F; 2/28/92-40; N.C. Cherokee; 1/4; M; Wife; 1767; Yes; Yes; Unallotted

1782; Owl, Jarrett; M; 6/28/11-20; N.C. Cherokee; 1/4; S; Son; 1768; Yes; Yes; Unallotted

1783; Owl, Oscar; M; 11/5/12-19; N.C. Cherokee; 1/4; S; Son; 1769; Yes; Yes; Unallotted

1784; Owl, Ralph; M; 3/19/15-17; N.C. Cherokee; 1/4; S; Son; 1770; Yes; Yes; Unallotted

1785; Owl, Eugene; M; 8/22/17-14; N.C. Cherokee; 1/4; S; Son; 1771; Yes; Yes; Unallotted

1786; Owl, Clifton; M; 3/20/20-12; N.C. Cherokee; 1/4; S; Son; 1772; Yes; Yes; Unallotted

1787; Owl, Clifford; M; 3/20/20-12; N.C. Cherokee; 1/4; S; Son; 1773; Yes; Yes; Unallotted

1788; Owl, Edna; F; 8/25/21-10; N.C. Cherokee; 1/4; S; Daughter; 1774; Yes; Yes; Unallotted

Key: Number; Surname, Given; Sex; Date of Birth-Age at Last Birthday; Tribe; Degree of Blood; Marital Status; Relationship to Head of Family; Last C. Roll No.; At Jurisdiction Where Enrolled (Yes/No); (If no – Where); Ward (Yes/No); Allotment, Annuity and Identification Numbers (if given).

1789; Owl, Viola; F; 5/8/26-5; N.C. Cherokee; 1/4; S; Daughter; 1775; Yes; Yes; Unallotted

1790; Owl, Rosie E.; F; 1/10/28-4; N.C. Cherokee; 1/4; S; Daughter; 1776; Yes; Yes; Unallotted

1791; Owl, Nettie E.; F; 5/14/31-10/12; N.C. Cherokee; 1/4; S; Daughter; ---; Yes; Yes; Unallotted

1792; Owl, Moses; M; 3/26/89-43; N.C. Cherokee; 3/4; M; Head; 1777; Yes; Yes; Unallotted

1793; Owl, Sampson; M; 11/17/54-77; N.C. Cherokee; 4/4; M; Head; 1778; Yes; Yes; Unallotted

1794; Owl, Samuel; M; 10/28/97-34; N.C. Cherokee; 3/4; M; Head; 1779; Yes; Yes; Unallotted

1795; Owl, Callie S.; F; 3/23/01-31; N.C. Cherokee; 3/16; M; Wife; 1780; Yes; Yes; Unallotted

1796; Owl, Samuel F.; M; 9/2/18-13; N.C. Cherokee; 15/32; S; Son; 1781; Yes; Yes; Unallotted

1797; Owl, Ethlyn R.; F; 4/10/20-11; N.C. Cherokee; 15/32; S; Daughter; 1782; Yes; Yes; Unallotted

1798; Owl, John L.; M; 6/22/22-9; N.C. Cherokee; 15/32; S; Son; 1783; Yes; Yes; Unallotted

1799; Owl, Dora; F; 10/23/24-7; N.C. Cherokee; 15/32; S; Daughter; 1784; Yes; Yes; Unallotted

1800; Owl, Bennie L.; M; 7/18/30-1; N.C. Cherokee; 15/32; S; Son; 1785; Yes; Yes; Unallotted

1801; Owl, Solomon; M; 8/22/63-68; N.C. Cherokee; 1/2; M; Head; 1786; Yes; Yes; Unallotted

1802; Owl, Alfred B.; M; 4/18/97-34; N.C. Cherokee; 1/4; S; Son; 1787; Yes; Yes; Unallotted

1803; Owl, Cornelius; M; 3/24/02-30; N.C. Cherokee; 1/4; S; Son; 1788; Yes; Yes; Unallotted

1804; Owl, Ethel R.; F; 10/19/04-27; N.C. Cherokee; 1/4; S; Daughter; 1789; Yes; Yes; Unallotted

1805; Owl, William D.; M; 2/18/07-25; N.C. Cherokee; 1/4; S; Son; 1790; Yes; Yes; Unallotted

1806; Owl, DeWitt; M; 6/7/08-23; N.C. Cherokee; 1/4; S; Son; 1791; Yes; Yes; Unallotted

1807; Owl, Edward; M; 3/27/10-22; N.C. Cherokee; 1/4; S; Son; 1792; Yes; Yes; Unallotted

1808; Owl (Mr[sic] Evy McCoy), Bessie E.; F; 10/11/30-1; N.C. Cherokee; 1/4; S; Granddau.; 1793; Yes; Yes; Unallotted

Census of the **Eastern Cherokee** reservation of the **Cherokee, N.C.** jurisdiction, as of **April 1** , 19**32,** taken by **R. L. Spalsbury** , Superintendent.

Key: Number; Surname, Given; Sex; Date of Birth-Age at Last Birthday; Tribe; Degree of Blood; Marital Status; Relationship to Head of Family; Last C. Roll No.; At Jurisdiction Where Enrolled (Yes/No); (If no – Where); Ward (Yes/No); Allotment, Annuity and Identification Numbers (if given).

1809; Owl, Thomas; M; 3/19/87-45; N.C. Cherokee; 3/4; M; Head; 1794; Yes; Yes; Unallotted

1810; Owl, W. Thomas; M; 1/25/05-27; N.C. Cherokee; 1/2; S; Head; 1795; Yes; Yes; Unallotted

1811; Owl, William; M; 4/20/84-47; N.C. Cherokee; 3/4; M; Head; 1796; Yes; Yes; Unallotted

1812; Palmer, Dora Owl; F; 1/23/90-42; N.C. Cherokee; 1/4; M; Wife; 1797; Yes; Yes; Unallotted

1813; Palmer, Ledford; M; 1/17/12-20; N.C. Cherokee; 1/8; S; Son; 1798; Yes; Yes; Unallotted

1814; Palmer, Haddington; M; 10/1/13-18; N.C. Cherokee; 1/8; S; Son; 1799; Yes; Yes; Unallotted

1815; Palmer, Nettie M.; F; 10/16/15-16; N.C. Cherokee; 1/8; S; Daughter; 1800; Yes; Yes; Unallotted

1816; Palmer, Holt; M; 9/17/17-14; N.C. Cherokee; 1/8; S; Son; 1801; Yes; Yes; Unallotted

1817; Palmer, Theodore; M; 5/31/19-12; N.C. Cherokee; 1/8; S; Son; 1802; Yes; Yes; Unallotted

1818; Palmer, Irene; F; 4/1/21-10; N.C. Cherokee; 1/8; S; Daughter; 1803; Yes; Yes; Unallotted

1819; Palmer, Martin L.; M; 4/16/23-8; N.C. Cherokee; 1/8; S; Son; 1804; Yes; Yes; Unallotted

1820; Palmer, James; M; 5/22/25-6; N.C. Cherokee; 1/8; S; Son; 1805; Yes; Yes; Unallotted

1821; Palmer, Edward; M; 4/24/27-4; N.C. Cherokee; 1/8; S; Son; 1806; Yes; Yes; Unallotted

1822; Palmer, Lewis; M; 9/19/29-2; N.C. Cherokee; 1/8; S; Son; 1807; Yes; Yes; Unallotted

1823; Panther, Mark; M; 11/22/75-56; N.C. Cherokee; 4/4; M; Head; 1808; Yes; Yes; Unallotted

1824; Panther, Windy L.; F; 8/1/88-43; N.C. Cherokee; 4/4; M; Wife; 1809; Yes; Yes; Unallotted

1825; Panther, Samuel; M; 4/4/13-18; N.C. Cherokee; 4/4; S; Son; 1810; Yes; Yes; Unallotted

1826; Panther, Juanita; F; 1/17/17-15; N.C. Cherokee; 4/4; S; Daughter; 1811; Yes; Yes; Unallotted

1827; Panther, Olivan; F; 4/30/22-9; N.C. Cherokee; 4/4; S; Daughter; 1812; Yes; Yes; Unallotted

1828; Parker (Lambert, Cora), Cora L.; F; 4/23/99-32; N.C. Cherokee; 1/16; M; Wife; 1813; Yes; Yes; Unallotted

Census of the **Eastern Cherokee** reservation of the **Cherokee, N.C.** jurisdiction, as of **April 1** , 19**32,** taken by **R. L. Spalsbury** , Superintendent.

Key: Number; Surname, Given; Sex; Date of Birth-Age at Last Birthday; Tribe; Degree of Blood; Marital Status; Relationship to Head of Family; Last C. Roll No.; At Jurisdiction Where Enrolled (Yes/No); (If no – Where); Ward (Yes/No); Allotment, Annuity and Identification Numbers (if given).

1829; Parker, John W.; M; 1/10/24-8; N.C. Cherokee; 1/32; S; Son; 1814; Yes; Yes; Unallotted

1830; Parker (Lambert, Flora), Flora L.; F; 9/9/02-29; N.C. Cherokee; 1/4; M; Wife; 1815; Yes; Yes; Unallotted

1831; Parker, Helen K.; F; 9/2/21-10; N.C. Cherokee; 1/8; S; Daughter; 1816; Yes; Yes; Unallotted

1832; Parker, Mary K.; F; 12/3/22-9; N.C. Cherokee; 1/8; S; Daughter; 1817; Yes; Yes; Unallotted

1833; Parker, Edgar K.; M; 9/2/24-7; N.C. Cherokee; 1/8; S; Son; 1818; Yes; Yes; Unallotted

1834; Parker, Jerome; M; 8/26/28-3; N.C. Cherokee; 1/8; S; Son; 1819; Yes; Yes; Unallotted

1835; Parker (Voiles, Josie), Josie; F; 11/24/77-54; N.C. Cherokee; 1/16; M; Wife; 1820; Yes; Yes; Unallotted

1836; Parris, Lola (Lula); F; 2/4/12-18; N.C. Cherokee; 1/16; S; Alone; 1821; No; 441 W. 37th St., Chattanooga, Hamilton, Tenn.; Yes; Unallotted

1837; Parton (Baker, Crickett), Crickett; F; 3/13/02-30; N.C. Cherokee; 1/16; M; Wife; 1822; No; Culberson, Cherokee, N. C.; Yes; Unallotted

1838; Parton, Thelma; F; 7/23/23-9; N.C. Cherokee; 1/32; S; Daughter; 1823; No; Culberson, Cherokee, N. C.; Yes; Unallotted

1839; Partridge, Bessie; F; 7/20/10-21; N.C. Cherokee; 4/4; S; Head; 1824; Yes; Yes; Unallotted

1840; Partridge, Bird; M; 8/4/79-52; N.C. Cherokee; 4/4; M; Head; 1825; Yes; Yes; Unallotted

1841; Partridge, Elsie G.; F; 10/11/84-47; N.C. Cherokee; 7/8; M; Wife; 1826; Yes; Yes; Unallotted

1842; Partridge, John; M; 6/17/11-20; N.C. Cherokee; 15/16; S; Son; 1827; Yes; Yes; Unallotted

1843; Partridge, Dahney; F; 12/14/13-18; N.C. Cherokee; 15/16; S; Daughter; 1828; Yes; Yes; Unallotted

1844; Partridge, Sallie; F; 12/13/17-14; N.C. Cherokee; 15/16; S; Daughter; 1829; Yes; Yes; Unallotted

1845; Partridge, Nora; F; 4/12/19-12; N.C. Cherokee; 15/16; S; Daughter; 1830; Yes; Yes; Unallotted

1846; Partridge, Mollie; F; 3/10/22-10; N.C. Cherokee; 15/16; S; Daughter; 1831; Yes; Yes; Unallotted

1847; Patterson, Alonzo; M; 12/29/96-35; N.C. Cherokee; 1/32; M; Head; 1832; No; Loving, Fannin, Ga.; Yes; Unallotted

Census of the **Eastern Cherokee** reservation of the **Cherokee, N.C.** jurisdiction, as of **April 1** , 1**932,** taken by **R. L. Spalsbury** , Superintendent.

Key: Number; Surname, Given; Sex; Date of Birth-Age at Last Birthday; Tribe; Degree of Blood; Marital Status; Relationship to Head of Family; Last C. Roll No.; At Jurisdiction Where Enrolled (Yes/No); (If no – Where); Ward (Yes/No); Allotment, Annuity and Identification Numbers (if given).

1848; Patterson, Leonard; M; 9/4/16-15; N.C. Cherokee; 1/64; S; Son; 1833; No; Loving, Fannin, Ga.; Yes; Unallotted

1849; Patterson, Zell; F; 5/23/18-13; N.C. Cherokee; 1/64; S; Daughter; 1834; No; Loving, Fannin, Ga.; Yes; Unallotted

1850; Patterson, Alyne; F; 12/23/19-12; N.C. Cherokee; 1/64; S; Daughter; 1835; No; Loving, Fannin, Ga.; Yes; Unallotted

1851; Patterson, Clyta; F; 8/31/21-10; N.C. Cherokee; 1/64; S; Daughter; 1836; No; Loving, Fannin, Ga.; Yes; Unallotted

1852; Patterson, L.C.; M; 3/12/23-9; N.C. Cherokee; 1/64; S; Son; 1837; No; Loving, Fannin, Ga.; Yes; Unallotted

1853; Patterson (Cole, Ella), Ella C.; F; 5/22/77-54; N.C. Cherokee; 1/16; M; Wife; 1838; No; Lewner, Union, Ga.; Yes; Unallotted

1854; Patterson, Arvil; M; 3/12/06-26; N.C. Cherokee; 1/32; S; Son; 1839; No; Lewner, Union, Ga.; Yes; Unallotted

1855; Patterson, Beadie; F; 12/30/08-23; N.C. Cherokee; 1/32; S; Daughter; 1840; No; Lewner, Union, Ga.; Yes; Unallotted

1856; Patterson, Zida; F; 11/11/10-21; N.C. Cherokee; 1/32; S; Daughter; 1841; No; Lewner, Union, Ga.; Yes; Unallotted

1857; Patterson, Redie; F; 8/21/12-19; N.C. Cherokee; 1/32; S; Daughter; 1842; No; Lewner, Union, Ga.; Yes; Unallotted

1858; Patterson, Clifton; M; 4/22/14-17; N.C. Cherokee; 1/32; S; Son; 1843; No; Lewner, Union, Ga.; Yes; Unallotted

1859; Patterson, Ruby; F; 3/26/16-16; N.C. Cherokee; 1/32; S; Daughter; 1844; No; Lewner, Union, Ga.; Yes; Unallotted

1860; Patterson, L.J.; M; 11/12/18-13; N.C. Cherokee; 1/32; S; Son; 1845; No; Lewner, Union, Ga.; Yes; Unallotted

1861; Patterson, Hobart; M; 11/11/03-28; N.C. Cherokee; 1/32; M; Head; 1846; No; Hayesville, Clay, N.C.; Yes; Unallotted

1862; Patterson, Delmer; M; 8/20/23-8; N.C. Cherokee; 1/64; S; Son; 1847; No; Hayesville, Clay, N.C.; Yes; Unallotted

1863; Patterson (Raper, Iowa), Iowa; F; 3/6/81-51; N.C. Cherokee; 1/16; M; Wife; 1848; No; Hayesville, Clay, N.C.; Yes; Unallotted

1864; Patterson , Eunice; F; 2/14/07-25; N.C. Cherokee; 1/32; S; Daughter; 1849; No; Hayesville, Clay, N.C.; Yes; Unallotted

1865; Patterson , Eula; F; 1/3/10-22; N.C. Cherokee; 1/32; S; Daughter; 1850; No; Hayesville, Clay, N.C.; Yes; Unallotted

1866; Patterson, Ray; M; 11/29/12-19; N.C. Cherokee; 1/32; S; Son; 1851; No; Hayesville, Clay, N.C.; Yes; Unallotted

1867; Patterson, Lyle; M; 7/11/15-16; N.C. Cherokee; 1/32; S; Son; 1852; No; Hayesville, Clay, N.C.; Yes; Unallotted

1868; Patterson, John; M; 3/13/18-14; N.C. Cherokee; 1/32; S; Son; 1853; No; Hayesville, Clay, N.C.; Yes; Unallotted

Census of the **Eastern Cherokee** reservation of the **Cherokee, N.C.** jurisdiction, as of **April 1** , 19**32**, taken by **R. L. Spalsbury** , Superintendent.

Key: Number; Surname, Given; Sex; Date of Birth-Age at Last Birthday; Tribe; Degree of Blood; Marital Status; Relationship to Head of Family; Last C. Roll No.; At Jurisdiction Where Enrolled (Yes/No); (If no – Where); Ward (Yes/No); Allotment, Annuity and Identification Numbers (if given).

1869; Patterson, Mary Joe; F; 2/29/24-8; N.C. Cherokee; 1/32; S; Daughter; 1854; No; Hayesville, Clay, N.C.; Yes; Unallotted

1870; Patterson, Oldham; M; 7/5/01-30; N.C. Cherokee; 1/16; S; Head; 1855; No; Gastonia, Gaston, N.C.; Yes; Unallotted

1871; Patterson, Almer; M; 4/12/06-25; N.C. Cherokee; 1/16; S; Brother; 1856; No; Gastonia, Gaston, N.C.; Yes; Unallotted

1872; Patterson, Alwain; M; 5/16/10-21; N.C. Cherokee; 1/16; S; Brother; 1857; No; Gastonia, Gaston, N.C.; Yes; Unallotted

1873; Passmore (Lee, Nancy), Nancy J.; F; 9/8/77-54; N.C. Cherokee; 1/16; M; Wife; 1858; Yes; Yes; Unallotted

1874; Passmore, Thomas N.; M; 4/12/02-29; N.C. Cherokee; 1/32; S; Son; 1859; Yes; Yes; Unallotted

1875; Passmore, Charles A.; M; 6/16/03-28; N.C. Cherokee; 1/32; S; Son; 1860; Yes; Yes; Unallotted

1876; Passmore, Rose C.; F; 5/28/05-26; N.C. Cherokee; 1/32; S; Daughter; 1861; Yes; Yes; Unallotted

1877; Passmore, Oscar; M; 9/22/07-24; N.C. Cherokee; 1/32; S; Son; 1862; Yes; Yes; Unallotted

1878; Passmore, David; M; 3/26/12-20; N.C. Cherokee; 1/32; S; Son; 1863; Yes; Yes; Unallotted

1879; Passmore, Mary; F; 9/20/13-18; N.C. Cherokee; 1/32; S; Daughter; 1864; Yes; Yes; Unallotted

1880; Passmore, Sarah; F; 8/11/15-16; N.C. Cherokee; 1/32; S; Daughter; 1865; Yes; Yes; Unallotted

1881; Passmore, Palace; F; 7/26/18-13; N.C. Cherokee; 1/32; S; Daughter; 1866; Yes; Yes; Unallotted

1882; Passmore, Alice; F; 7/26/18-13; N.C. Cherokee; 1/32; S; Daughter; 1867; Yes; Yes; Unallotted

1883; Passmore, Belvia; F; 5/3/21-10; N.C. Cherokee; 1/32; S; Daughter; 1868; Yes; Yes; Unallotted

1884; Payne, Albert F.; M; 8/1/99-32; N.C. Cherokee; 1/32; M; Head; 1869; Yes; Yes; Unallotted

1885; Payne, David L.; M; 12/12/74-57; N.C. Cherokee; 1/32; M; Head; 1870; Yes; Yes; Unallotted

1886; Payne, Clarence; M; 9/25/14-17; N.C. Cherokee; 1/64; S; Son; 1871; Yes; Yes; Unallotted

1887; Payne, Rosa Mae; F; 5/31/16-15; N.C. Cherokee; 1/64; S; Daughter; 1872; Yes; Yes; Unallotted

1888; Payne, Desser L.; M; 5/28/18-13; N.C. Cherokee; 1/64; S; Son; 1873; Yes; Yes; Unallotted

Census of the **Eastern Cherokee** reservation of the **Cherokee, N.C.** jurisdiction, as of **April 1** , 19**32,** taken by **R. L. Spalsbury** , Superintendent.

Key: Number; Surname, Given; Sex; Date of Birth-Age at Last Birthday; Tribe; Degree of Blood; Marital Status; Relationship to Head of Family; Last C. Roll No.; At Jurisdiction Where Enrolled (Yes/No); (If no – Where); Ward (Yes/No); Allotment, Annuity and Identification Numbers (if given).

1889; Payne, Georgia; F; 5/10/20-11; N.C. Cherokee; 1/64; S; Daughter; 1874; Yes; Yes; Unallotted

1890; Payne, Oveliva; F; 3/18/22-10; N.C. Cherokee; 1/64; S; Daughter; 1875; Yes; Yes; Unallotted

1891; Payne, Elisha; M; 2/6/85-47; N.C. Cherokee; 1/32; M; Head; 1876; No; Hiawassee, Cherokee, N.C.; Yes; Unallotted

1892; Payne, Buster; M; 6/14/08-23; N.C. Cherokee; 1/64; S; Son; 1877; No; Hiawassee, Cherokee, N.C.; Yes; Unallotted

1893; Payne, Lou Belle; F; 3/2/12-20; N.C. Cherokee; 1/64; S; Daughter; 1878; No; Hiawassee, Cherokee, N.C.; Yes; Unallotted

1894; Payne, Cuba; F; 11/14/14-17; N.C. Cherokee; 1/64; S; Daughter; 1879; No; Hiawassee, Cherokee, N.C.; Yes; Unallotted

1895; Payne, Manda; F; 9/7/16-15; N.C. Cherokee; 1/64; S; Daughter; 1880; No; Hiawassee, Cherokee, N.C.; Yes; Unallotted

1896; Payne (Taylor, Estie), Estie T.; F; 10/9/00-31; N.C. Cherokee; 1/32; M; Wife; 1881; No; Hiawassee, Cherokee, N.C.; Yes; Unallotted

1897; Payne, Walter; M; 5/28/21-10; N.C. Cherokee; 1/64; S; Son; 1882; No; Hiawassee, Cherokee, N.C.; Yes; Unallotted

1898; Payne, Earl; M; 4/1/23-9; N.C. Cherokee; 1/64; S; Son; 1883; No; Hiawassee, Cherokee, N.C.; Yes; Unallotted

1899; Payne, James M.; M; 2/25/76-56; N.C. Cherokee; 1/16; M; Head; 1884; No; Ranger, Cherokee, N.C.; Yes; Unallotted

1900; Payne, Carrie; F; 6/4/10-21; N.C. Cherokee; 1/32; S; Daughter; 1885; No; Ranger, Cherokee, N.C.; Yes; Unallotted

1901; Payne, Margie E.; F; 9/19/13-18; N.C. Cherokee; 1/32; S; Daughter; 1886; No; Ranger, Cherokee, N.C.; Yes; Unallotted

1902; Payne, Jim; M; 12/20/88-43; N.C. Cherokee; 1/32; M; Head; 1887; Yes; Yes; Unallotted

1903; Payne, Clifford; M; 6/14/10-21; N.C. Cherokee; 1/64; S; Son; 1888; Yes; Yes; Unallotted

1904; Payne, Jaunita; F; 7/16/14-17; N.C. Cherokee; 1/64; S; Daughter; 1889; Yes; Yes; Unallotted

1905; Payne, Thelma; F; 10/8/16-15; N.C. Cherokee; 1/64; S; Daughter; 1890; Yes; Yes; Unallotted

1906; Payne, James; M; 12/11/18-13; N.C. Cherokee; 1/64; S; Son; 1891; Yes; Yes; Unallotted

1907; Payne, Calvin; M; 12/2/20-11; N.C. Cherokee; 1/64; S; Son; 1892; Yes; Yes; Unallotted

1908; Payne, Pauline; F; 5/15/23-8; N.C. Cherokee; 1/64; S; Daughter; 1893; Yes; Yes; Unallotted

Census of the **Eastern Cherokee** reservation of the **Cherokee, N.C.** jurisdiction, as of **April 1** , 1932, taken by **R. L. Spalsbury** , Superintendent.

Key: Number; Surname, Given; Sex; Date of Birth-Age at Last Birthday; Tribe; Degree of Blood; Marital Status; Relationship to Head of Family; Last C. Roll No.; At Jurisdiction Where Enrolled (Yes/No); (If no – Where); Ward (Yes/No); Allotment, Annuity and Identification Numbers (if given).

1909; Payne, Oliver C.; M; 1/1/92-40; N.C. Cherokee; 1/16; M; Head; 1894; No; Birch, Cherokee, N.C.; Yes; Unallotted

1910; Payne, Mabel J.; F; 2/16/14-18; N.C. Cherokee; 1/32; S; Daughter; 1895; No; Birch, Cherokee, N.C.; Yes; Unallotted

1911; Payne, Claude H.; M; 12/4/15-16; N.C. Cherokee; 1/32; S; Son; 1896; No; Birch, Cherokee, N.C.; Yes; Unallotted

1912; Payne, Lois E.; F; 12/30/17-14; N.C. Cherokee; 1/32; S; Daughter; 1897; No; Birch, Cherokee, N.C.; Yes; Unallotted

1913; Payne, Ralph G.; M; 2/7/22-10; N.C. Cherokee; 1/32; S; Son; 1898; No; Birch, Cherokee, N.C.; Yes; Unallotted

1914; Payne, Ohlen; M; 7/19/23-8; N.C. Cherokee; 1/32; S; Son; 1899; No; Birch, Cherokee, N.C.; Yes; Unallotted

1915; Payne, Poley E.; M; 6/23/96-35; N.C. Cherokee; 1/32; M; Head; 1900; No; Kinsey, Cherokee, N.C.; Yes; Unallotted

1916; Payne, Neil; M; 8/8/20-11; N.C. Cherokee; 1/64; S; Son; 1901; No; Kinsey, Cherokee, N.C.; Yes; Unallotted

1917; Payne, Lucy; F; 3/27/22-10; N.C. Cherokee; 1/64; S; Daughter; 1902; No; Kinsey, Cherokee, N.C.; Yes; Unallotted

1918; Payne, Rollin T.; M; 1/28/97-34; N.C. Cherokee; 1/32; M; Head; 1903; No; Etowah, McMinn, Tenn.; Yes; Unallotted

1919; Payne, William E.; M; 4/10/72-59; N.C. Cherokee; 1/16; M; Head; 1904; No; Gastonia, Gaston, N.C.; Yes; Unallotted

1920; Payne, William A.; M; 11/11/03-28; N.C. Cherokee; 1/32; S; Son; 1905; No; Gastonia, Gaston, N.C.; Yes; Unallotted

1921; Payne, Cynthia; F; 12/29/07-24; N.C. Cherokee; 1/32; S; Daughter; 1906; No; Gastonia, Gaston, N.C.; Yes; Unallotted

1922; Payne, Gertrude; F; 3/19/10-22; N.C. Cherokee; 1/32; S; Daughter; 1907; No; Gastonia, Gaston, N.C.; Yes; Unallotted

1923; Payne, Annie Lee; F; 12/31/16-15; N.C. Cherokee; 1/32; S; Daughter; 1908; No; Gastonia, Gaston, N.C.; Yes; Unallotted

1924; Peckerwood, McKinley; M; 10/6/02-30; N.C. Cherokee; 4/4; M; Head; 1909; Yes; Yes; Unallotted

1925; Peckerwood, Mary A.; F; 3/27/88-44; N.C. Cherokee; 3/4; M; Wife; 1910; Yes; Yes; Unallotted

1926; Peckerwood, Tom Ross; M; 3/19/31-1; N.C. Cherokee; 7/8; S; Son; 1911; Yes; Yes; Unallotted

1927; Pheasant, William; M; 4/25/80-51; N.C. Cherokee; 4/4; M; Head; 1912; Yes; Yes; Unallotted

1928; Pheasant, Rachel W.; F; 3/15/92-40; N.C. Cherokee; 4/4; M; Wife; 1913; Yes; Yes; Unallotted

Census of the **Eastern Cherokee** reservation of the **Cherokee, N.C.** jurisdiction, as of **April 1** , 19**32,** taken by **R. L. Spalsbury** , Superintendent.

Key: Number; Surname, Given; Sex; Date of Birth-Age at Last Birthday; Tribe; Degree of Blood; Marital Status; Relationship to Head of Family; Last C. Roll No.; At Jurisdiction Where Enrolled (Yes/No); (If no – Where); Ward (Yes/No); Allotment, Annuity and Identification Numbers (if given).

1929; Pheasant, Wallie; M; 12/26/17-14; N.C. Cherokee; 4/4; S; Son; 1914; Yes; Yes; Unallotted

1930; Pheasant, Driver; M; 3/11/20-11; N.C. Cherokee; 4/4; S; Son; 1915; Yes; Yes; Unallotted

1931; Pheasant, Ellie; F; 11/4/22-9; N.C. Cherokee; 4/4; S; Daughter; 1916; Yes; Yes; Unallotted

1932; Pheasant, Irene; F; 6/3/26-5; N.C. Cherokee; 4/4; S; Daughter; 1917; Yes; Yes; Unallotted

1933; Pike, Lillie A.; F; 2/8/70-62; N.C. Cherokee; 3/32; Wd.; Head; 1918; Yes; Yes; Unallotted

1934; Pope (Patterson, Elizabeth), Elizabeth; F; 4/20/00-31; N.C. Cherokee; 1/32; M; Wife; 1919; Yes; Yes; Unallotted

1935; Porter (Meroney, Florence), Florence; F; 3/16/63-69; N.C. Cherokee; 1/8; M; Wife; 1920; Yes; Yes; Unallotted

1936; Porter, James D.; M; 4/30/89-42; N.C. Cherokee; 1/16; M; Head; 1921; Yes; Yes; Unallotted

1937; Potter, Thomas R.; M; 11/5/95-36; N.C. Cherokee; 3/16; M; Head; 1922; Yes; Yes; Unallotted

1938; Potts (Smith, Rosanna), Rosanna; F; 3/22/00-32; N.C. Cherokee; 1/8; M; Wife; 1923; Yes; Yes; Unallotted

1939; Powell, Doogah; F; 12/23/71-60; N.C. Cherokee; 4/4; Wd.; Head; 1924; Yes; Yes; Unallotted

1940; Powell, Holmes; M; 2/9/02-30; N.C. Cherokee; 3/4; S; Son; 1925; Yes; Yes; Unallotted

1941; Powell, Noah; M; 3/10/08-24; N.C. Cherokee; 3/4; S; Son; 1926; Yes; Yes; Unallotted

1942; Powell, Moses; M; 6/7/88-43; N.C. Cherokee; 3/4; M; Head; 1927; Yes; Yes; Unallotted

1943; Powell, Elnora; F; 1/16/98-34; N.C. Cherokee; 4/4; M; Wife; 1928; Yes; Yes; Unallotted

1944; Powell, Emma; F; 5/1/15-17; N.C. Cherokee; 7/8; S; Daughter; 1929; Yes; Yes; Unallotted

1945; Powell, Catherine; F; 8/27/25-7; N.C. Cherokee; 7/8; S; Daughter; 1930; Yes; Yes; Unallotted

1946; Powell, Beulah L.; F; 12/8/27-4; N.C. Cherokee; 7/8; S; Daughter; 1931; Yes; Yes; Unallotted

Census of the **Eastern Cherokee** reservation of the **Cherokee, N.C.** jurisdiction, as of **April 1** , 19**32,** taken by **R. L. Spalsbury** , Superintendent.

Key: Number; Surname, Given; Sex; Date of Birth-Age at Last Birthday; Tribe; Degree of Blood; Marital Status; Relationship to Head of Family; Last C. Roll No.; At Jurisdiction Where Enrolled (Yes/No); (If no – Where); Ward (Yes/No); Allotment, Annuity and Identification Numbers (if given).

1947; Powell, Berdina A.; F; 4/21/30-2; N.C. Cherokee; 7/8; S; Daughter; 1932; Yes; Yes; Unallotted

1948; Powell, Stancill; M; 12/17/91-40; N.C. Cherokee; 3/4; M; Head; 1933; Yes; Yes; Unallotted

1949; Powell, Kina S.; F; 2/11/99-33; N.C. Cherokee; 4/4; M; Wife; 1934; Yes; Yes; Unallotted

1950; Powell, Dorothy H.; F; 9/22/29-2; N.C. Cherokee; 7/8; S; Daughter; 1935; Yes; Yes; Unallotted

1951; Price, Grace H.; F; 1/3/07-25; N.C. Cherokee; 3/8; M; Wife; 1936; Yes; Yes; Unallotted

1952; Pullium, Carolina; F; 6/29/80-51; N.C. Cherokee; 1/32; M; Wife; 1937; Yes; Yes; Unallotted

1953; Pullium, John; M; 9/26/06-25; N.C. Cherokee; 1/64; S; Son; 1938; Yes; Yes; Unallotted

1954; Pullium, Decatur; M; 11/22/03-28; N.C. Cherokee; 1/64; S; Head; 1939; Yes; Yes; Unallotted

1955; Pullium, Galusha; M; 5/21/99-32; N.C. Cherokee; 1/64; S; Head; 1940; Yes; Yes; Unallotted

1956; Pittman, Ella B.; F; 1909-23; N.C. Cherokee; 1/4-; S; Head; 1941; Yes; Yes; Added in accordance with letter v1/27/31; Unallotted

1957; Queen, Jasper; M; 2/23/94-38; N.C. Cherokee; 5/8; M; Head; 1942; Yes; Yes; Unallotted

1958; Queen, Luzene R.; F; 2/28/99-33; N.C. Cherokee; 15/16; M; Wife; 1943; Yes; Yes; Unallotted

1959; Queen, Kina; F; 2/22/20-12; N.C. Cherokee; 25/32; S; Daughter; 1944; Yes; Yes; Unallotted

1960; Queen, Blaine; M; 1/29/21-11; N.C. Cherokee; 25/32; S; Son; 1945; Yes; Yes; Unallotted

1961; Queen, Awee; F; 7/24/22-9; N.C. Cherokee; 25/32; S; Daughter; 1946; Yes; Yes; Unallotted

1962; Queen, Minnie; F; 6/26/26-5; N.C. Cherokee; 25/32; S; Daughter; 1947; Yes; Yes; Unallotted

1963; Queen, Louis; M; 7/30/28-3; N.C. Cherokee; 25/32; S; Son; 1948; Yes; Yes; Unallotted

1964; Queen, Jessie; F; 7/9/30-1; N.C. Cherokee; 25/32; S; Daughter; 1949; Yes; Yes; Unallotted

Census of the **Eastern Cherokee** reservation of the **Cherokee, N.C.** jurisdiction, as of **April 1**, 19**32,** taken by **R. L. Spalsbury**, Superintendent.

Key: Number; Surname, Given; Sex; Date of Birth-Age at Last Birthday; Tribe; Degree of Blood; Marital Status; Relationship to Head of Family; Last C. Roll No.; At Jurisdiction Where Enrolled (Yes/No); (If no – Where); Ward (Yes/No); Allotment, Annuity and Identification Numbers (if given).

1965;   Queen (Lambert, Lora), Lora; F; 10/18/07-24; N.C. Cherokee; 1/32; M; Wife; 1950; Yes; Yes; Unallotted

1966;   Queen, Lelia C.; F; 8/25/98-33; N.C. Cherokee; 1/16; M; Wife; 1951; Yes; Yes; Unallotted

1967;   Queen, Lois R.; F; 1/5/23-9; N.C. Cherokee; 1/32; S; Daughter; 1952; Yes; Yes; Unallotted

1968;   Queen, Levi; M; 6/7/70-61; N.C. Cherokee; 1/4; M; Head; 1953; Yes; Yes; Unallotted

1969;   Queen, Mary; F; 2/10/80-52; N.C. Cherokee; 4/4; M; Wife; 1954; Yes; Yes; Unallotted

1970;   Queen, Abraham; M; 7/11/99-32; N.C. Cherokee; 5/8; S; Son; 1955; Yes; Yes; Unallotted

1971;   Queen, Lillian; F; 12/11/12-19; N.C. Cherokee; 5/8; S; Daughter; 1956; Yes; Yes; Unallotted

1972;   Queen, Martha; F; 5/30/14-17; N.C. Cherokee; 5/8; S; Daughter; 1957; Yes; Yes; Unallotted

1973;   Queen, Stacey; F; 10/31/16-15; N.C. Cherokee; 5/8; S; Daughter; 1958; Yes; Yes; Unallotted

1974;   Queen, Cowan; M; 7/23/19-12; N.C. Cherokee; 5/8; S; Son; 1959; Yes; Yes; Unallotted

1975;   Queen, Simpson; M; 9/15/73-58; N.C. Cherokee; 1/4; M; Head; 1960; Yes; Yes; Unallotted

1976;   Queen, John; M; 5/15/07-24; N.C. Cherokee; 5/8; S; Son; 1961; Yes; Yes; Unallotted

1977;   Queen, Rachel; F; 8/19/09-22; N.C. Cherokee; 5/8; S; Daughter; 1962; Yes; Yes; Unallotted

1978;   Queen, Lucy; F; 3/24/12-20; N.C. Cherokee; 5/8; S; Daughter; 1963; Yes; Yes; Unallotted

1979;   Queen, Solomon; M; 11/17/15-16; N.C. Cherokee; 5/8; S; Son; 1964; Yes; Yes; Unallotted

1980;   Queen, Nolan; M; 1/27/01-31; N.C. Cherokee; 5/8; M; Head; 1965; Yes; Yes; Unallotted

1981;   Queen, Golinda A.; F; 4/10/07-24; N.C. Cherokee; 4/4; M; Wife; 1966; Yes; Yes; Unallotted

1982;   Queen, Sam; M; 5/2/27-4; N.C. Cherokee; 13/16; S; Son; 1967; Yes; Yes; Unallotted

1983;   Quinlan, Mary C.; F; 1899-33; N.C. Cherokee; 1/4-; M; Wife; 1968; Yes; Yes; Unallotted

Census of the **Eastern Cherokee** reservation of the **Cherokee, N.C.** jurisdiction, as of **April 1**, **1932,** taken by **R. L. Spalsbury**, Superintendent.

Key: Number; Surname, Given; Sex; Date of Birth-Age at Last Birthday; Tribe; Degree of Blood; Marital Status; Relationship to Head of Family; Last C. Roll No.; At Jurisdiction Where Enrolled (Yes/No); (If no – Where); Ward (Yes/No); Allotment, Annuity and Identification Numbers (if given).

1984; Rakestraw, Lena B.; F; 2/25/05-27; N.C. Cherokee; 1/64; M; Wife; 1969; Yes; Yes; Unallotted

1985; Ramsey, Roxey W.; F; 2/11/09-23; N.C. Cherokee; 1/16; S; Head; 1970; Yes; Yes; Unallotted

1986; Raper, Alexander; M; 2/27/44-88; N.C. Cherokee; 1/4; M; Head; 1971; Yes; Yes; Unallotted

1987; Raper, Alonzo; M; 5/2/95-34; N.C. Cherokee; 1/16; M; Head; 1972; Yes; Yes; Unallotted

1988; Raper, Bonetta; F; 2/25/19-13; N.C. Cherokee; 1/32; S; Daughter; 1973; Yes; Yes; Unallotted

1989; Raper, Jeanette; F; 2/6/21-11; N.C. Cherokee; 1/32; S; Daughter; 1974; Yes; Yes; Unallotted

1990; Raper, Opal; F; 3/1/23-9; N.C. Cherokee; 1/32; S; Daughter; 1975; Yes; Yes; Unallotted

1991; Raper, Myrtle; F; 5/28/24-7; N.C. Cherokee; 1/32; S; Daughter; 1976; Yes; Yes; Unallotted

1992; Raper, Alvin; M; 4/9/92-39; N.C. Cherokee; 1/16; M; Head; 1977; Yes; Yes; Unallotted

1993; Raper, Clifton; M; 7/31/16-15; N.C. Cherokee; 1/32; S; Son; 1978; Yes; Yes; Unallotted

1994; Raper, Carmen; F; 12/11/18-13; N.C. Cherokee; 1/32; S; Daughter; 1979; Yes; Yes; Unallotted

1995; Raper, Pearl; F; 4/12/20-11; N.C. Cherokee; 1/32; S; Daughter; 1980; Yes; Yes; Unallotted

1996; Raper, Clarence; M; 7/1/23-8; N.C. Cherokee; 1/32; S; Son; 1981; Yes; Yes; Unallotted

1997; Raper (children Marshall Raper), Amos Lloyd; M; 12/3/14-17; N.C. Cherokee; 1/16; S; Son; 1982; Yes; Yes; Unallotted

1998; Raper, Atha G.; F; 1/1/17-15; N.C. Cherokee; 1/16; S; Daughter; 1983; Yes; Yes; Unallotted

1999; Raper, Howard H.; M; 4/16/19-13; N.C. Cherokee; 1/16; S; Son; 1984; Yes; Yes; Unallotted

2000; Raper, Verdie H.; F; 3/27/21-11; N.C. Cherokee; 1/16; S; Daughter; 1985; Yes; Yes; Unallotted

2001; Raper, James H.; M; 3/31/23-9; N.C. Cherokee; 1/16; S; Son; 1986; Yes; Yes; Unallotted

2002; Raper, Asa; M; 3/1/86-45; N.C. Cherokee; 1/16; M; Head; 1987; Yes; Yes; Unallotted

Census of the **Eastern Cherokee** reservation of the **Cherokee, N.C.** jurisdiction, as of **April 1**, **1932,** taken by **R. L. Spalsbury**, Superintendent.

Key: Number; Surname, Given; Sex; Date of Birth-Age at Last Birthday; Tribe; Degree of Blood; Marital Status; Relationship to Head of Family; Last C. Roll No.; At Jurisdiction Where Enrolled (Yes/No); (If no – Where); Ward (Yes/No); Allotment, Annuity and Identification Numbers (if given).

2003; Raper, Augustus; M; 5/27/02-29; N.C. Cherokee; 1/16; M; Head; 1988; Yes; Yes; Unallotted

2004; Raper, Norma W.; F; 12/27/02-29; N.C. Cherokee; 1/16; M; Wife; 1989; Yes; Yes; Unallotted

2005; Raper, Berry B.B.; M; 3/20/59-73; N.C. Cherokee; 1/8; M; Head; 1990; Yes; Yes; Unallotted

2006; Raper, Charles B.; M; 9/17/75-56; N.C. Cherokee; 1/8; M; Head; 1991; No; Culberson, Cherokee, N.C.; Yes; Unallotted

2007; Raper, Homer W.; M; 1/10/11-21; N.C. Cherokee; 1/16; S; Son; 1992; No; Culberson, Cherokee, N.C.; Yes; Unallotted

2008; Raper, Lela; F; 2/16/13-19; N.C. Cherokee; 1/16; S; Daughter; 1993; No; Culberson, Cherokee, N.C.; Yes; Unallotted

2009; Raper, Cleaston; M; 5/17/18-13; N.C. Cherokee; 1/16; S; Son; 1994; No; Culberson, Cherokee, N.C.; Yes; Unallotted

2010; Raper, Austin; M; 1/25/23-9; N.C. Cherokee; 1/16; S; Son; 1995; No; Culberson, Cherokee, N.C.; Yes; Unallotted

2011; Raper, Clarence A.; M; 1/4/00-32; N.C. Cherokee; 1/16; M; Head; 1996; Yes; Yes; Unallotted

2012; Raper, Juanita; F; 12/15/23-8; N.C. Cherokee; 1/32; S; Daughter; 1997; Yes; Yes; Unallotted

2013; Raper, Cly Victor; M; 10/3/97-34; N.C. Cherokee; 1/16; M; Head; 1998; No; Culberson, Cherokee, N.C.; Yes; Unallotted

2014; Raper, James V.; M; 3/3/18-14; N.C. Cherokee; 1/32; S; Son; 1999; No; Culberson, Cherokee, N.C.; Yes; Unallotted

2015; Raper, Dewey E.; M; 9/18/20-11; N.C. Cherokee; 1/32; S; Son; 2000; No; Culberson, Cherokee, N.C.; Yes; Unallotted

2016; Raper, Delta C.; M; 5/30/00-31; N.C. Cherokee; 1/16; M; Head; 2001; No; Culberson, Cherokee, N.C.; Yes; Unallotted

2017; Raper, Claude; M; 12/28/18-13; N.C. Cherokee; 1/32; S; Son; 2002; No; Culberson, Cherokee, N.C.; Yes; Unallotted

2018; Raper, Clifford; M; 12/16/20-11; N.C. Cherokee; 1/32; S; Son; 2003; No; Culberson, Cherokee, N.C.; Yes; Unallotted

2019; Raper, Denver Lee; M; 6/19/98-33; N.C. Cherokee; 1/16; M; Head; 2004; No; Culberson, Cherokee, N.C.; Yes; Unallotted

2020; Raper, Marie; F; 12/12/14-17; N.C. Cherokee; 1/32; S; Daughter; 2005; No; Culberson, Cherokee, N.C.; Yes; Unallotted

2021; Raper, Dewey; M; 7/14/22-9; N.C. Cherokee; 1/32; S; Son; 2006; No; Culberson, Cherokee, N.C.; Yes; Unallotted

Census of the **Eastern Cherokee** reservation of the **Cherokee, N.C.** jurisdiction, as of **April 1** , 1932, taken by **R. L. Spalsbury** , Superintendent.

Key: Number; Surname, Given; Sex; Date of Birth-Age at Last Birthday; Tribe; Degree of Blood; Marital Status; Relationship to Head of Family; Last C. Roll No.; At Jurisdiction Where Enrolled (Yes/No); (If no – Where); Ward (Yes/No); Allotment, Annuity and Identification Numbers (if given).

2022; Raper, Edgar; M; 5/2/94-37; N.C. Cherokee; 1/16; M; Head; 2007; Yes; Yes; Unallotted

2023; Raper, Carrie W.; F; 3/3/00-32; N.C. Cherokee; 1/16; M; Wife; 2008; Yes; Yes; Unallotted

2024; Raper, Wm. Roy; M; 11/4/21-10; N.C. Cherokee; 1/16; S; Son; 2009; Yes; Yes; Unallotted

2025; Raper, Robert L.; M; 1/18/24-8; N.C. Cherokee; 1/16; S; Son; 2010; Yes; Yes; Unallotted

2026; Raper, Fred; M; 3/20/03-29; N.C. Cherokee; 1/16; S; Head; 2011; No; Wichita Falls, Wichita, Tex.; Yes; Unallotted

2027; Raper, Gano; M; 5/15/83-48; N.C. Cherokee; 1/16; M; Head; 2012; No; Douglas, Coffee, Ga.; Yes; Unallotted

2028; Raper, Harley; M; 3/20/86-46; N.C. Cherokee; 1/16; M; Head; 2013; No; Hale Center, Hale, Tex.; Yes; Unallotted

2029; Raper, Henry J.; M; 12/23/86-45; N.C. Cherokee; 1/8; M; Head; 2014; No; Clover, York, S.C.; Yes; Unallotted

2030; Raper, Ivan; M; 4/27/05-26; N.C. Cherokee; 1/16; S; Son; 2015; No; Clover, York, S.C.; Yes; Unallotted

2031; Raper, Delia; F; 1/22/08-24; N.C. Cherokee; 1/16; S; Daughter; 2016; No; Clover, York, S.C.; Yes; Unallotted

2032; Raper, Ira; M; 12/21/10-21; N.C. Cherokee; 1/16; S; Son; 2017; No; Clover, York, S.C.; Yes; Unallotted

2033; Raper, Clyde; M; 12/29/16-15; N.C. Cherokee; 1/16; S; Son; 2018; No; Clover, York, S.C.; Yes; Unallotted

2034; Raper, Dewey; M; 2/5/20-12; N.C. Cherokee; 1/16; S; Son; 2019; No; Clover, York, S.C.; Yes; Unallotted

2035; Raper, Harford; M; 10/11/22-9; N.C. Cherokee; 1/16; S; Son; 2020; No; Clover, York, S.C.; Yes; Unallotted

2036; Raper, James; M; 3/31/95-37; N.C. Cherokee; 1/16; M; Head; 2021; No; Oak Park, Cherokee, N.C.; Yes; Unallotted

2037; Raper, Marcus; M; 5/3/16-15; N.C. Cherokee; 1/32; S; Son; 2022; No; Oak Park, Cherokee, N.C.; Yes; Unallotted

2038; Raper, Lillian; F; 11/15/17-14; N.C. Cherokee; 1/32; S; Daughter; 2023; No; Yes; Oak Park, Cherokee, N.C.; Yes; Unallotted

2039; Raper, Thomas; M; 11/14/19-12; N.C. Cherokee; 1/32; S; Son; 2024; No; Oak Park, Cherokee, N.C.; Yes; Unallotted

2040; Raper, Windell; M; 11/9/21-10; N.C. Cherokee; 1/32; S; Son; 2025; No; Oak Park, Cherokee, N.C.; Yes; Unallotted

Census of the **Eastern Cherokee** reservation of the **Cherokee, N.C.** jurisdiction, as of **April 1** , 19**32,** taken by **R. L. Spalsbury** , Superintendent.

Key: Number; Surname, Given; Sex; Date of Birth-Age at Last Birthday; Tribe; Degree of Blood; Marital Status; Relationship to Head of Family; Last C. Roll No.; At Jurisdiction Where Enrolled (Yes/No); (If no – Where); Ward (Yes/No); Allotment, Annuity and Identification Numbers (if given).

2041; Raper, James W.; M; 11/9/63-68; N.C. Cherokee; 1/8; M; Head; 2026; No; R.R. #2 Clever, Christian, Mo.; Yes; Unallotted

2042; Raper, Jesse L.; M; 8/21/70-61; N.C. Cherokee; 1/8; M; Head; 2027; Yes; Yes; Unallotted
2043; Raper, Claude E.; M; 6/15/99-32; N.C. Cherokee; 1/16; S; Son; 2028; Yes; Yes; Unallotted
2044; Raper, Curley C.; M; 6/3/01-30; N.C. Cherokee; 1/16; S; Son; 2029; Yes; Yes; Unallotted
2045; Raper, Minnie C.; F; 7/5/07-24; N.C. Cherokee; 1/16; S; Daughter; 2030; Yes; Yes; Unallotted
2046; Raper, William C.; M; 6/4/12-19; N.C. Cherokee; 1/16; S; Son; 2031; Yes; Yes; Unallotted

2047; Raper, John H.; M; 4/30/83-48; N.C. Cherokee; 1/16; M; Head; 2032; No; Bradenton, Manatee, Fla.; Yes; Unallotted
2048; Raper, Lillie M.; F; 4/30/07-24; N.C. Cherokee; 1/32; S; Daughter; 2033; No; Bradenton, Manatee, Fla.; Yes; Unallotted
2049; Raper, Herman E.; M; 4/30/09-22; N.C. Cherokee; 1/32; S; Son; 2034; No; Bradenton, Manatee, Fla.; Yes; Unallotted
2050; Raper, Ralph J.; M; 4/30/17-14; N.C. Cherokee; 1/32; S; Son; 2035; No; Bradenton, Manatee, Fla.; Yes; Unallotted
2051; Raper, Nellie A.; F; 4/30/20-11; N.C. Cherokee; 1/32; S; Daughter; 2036; No; Bradenton, Manatee, Fla.; Yes; Unallotted

2052; Raper, Lich; M; 5/3/89-42; N.C. Cherokee; 1/16; M; Head; 2037; Yes; Yes; Unallotted

2053; Raper, Lon; M; 3/30/81-51; N.C. Cherokee; 1/16; M; Head; 2038; No; Oak Park, Cherokee, N.C.; Yes; Unallotted
2054; Raper, Marseilla; F; 10/28/12-19; N.C. Cherokee; 1/32; S; Daughter; 2039; No; Oak Park, Cherokee, N.C.; Yes; Unallotted
2055; Raper, Vivian; F; 12/20/14-17; N.C. Cherokee; 1/32; S; Daughter; 2040; No; Oak Park, Cherokee, N.C.; Yes; Unallotted
2056; Raper, Merideth; M; 11/15/16-15; N.C. Cherokee; 1/32; S; Son; 2041; No; Oak Park, Cherokee, N.C.; Yes; Unallotted
2057; Raper, Thelma; F; 1/4/19-13; N.C. Cherokee; 1/32; S; Daughter; 2042; No; Oak Park, Cherokee, N.C.; Yes; Unallotted
2058; Raper, Jesse Willar.; M; 5/30/22-9; N.C. Cherokee; 1/32; S; Son; 2043; No; Oak Park, Cherokee, N.C.; Yes; Unallotted

2059; Raper, Marshall; M; 1/4/73-59; N.C. Cherokee; 1/8; M; Head; 2044; No; Culberson, Cherokee, N.C.; Yes; Unallotted
2060; Raper, Clinton; M; 1/6/02-30; N.C. Cherokee; 1/16; S; Son; 2045; No; Culberson, Cherokee, N.C.; Yes; Unallotted

Census of the **Eastern Cherokee** reservation of the **Cherokee, N.C.** jurisdiction, as of **April 1**, 19**32,** taken by **R. L. Spalsbury**, Superintendent.

Key: Number; Surname, Given; Sex; Date of Birth-Age at Last Birthday; Tribe; Degree of Blood; Marital Status; Relationship to Head of Family; Last C. Roll No.; At Jurisdiction Where Enrolled (Yes/No); (If no – Where); Ward (Yes/No); Allotment, Annuity and Identification Numbers (if given).

2061; Raper, Bonnie B.; F; 1/14/07-25; N.C. Cherokee; 1/16; S; Daughter; 2046; No; Culberson, Cherokee, N.C.; Yes; Unallotted

2062; Raper, Wm. Taft; M; 2/9/09-23; N.C. Cherokee; 1/16; S; Son; 2047; No; Culberson, Cherokee, N.C.; Yes; Unallotted

2063; Raper, Rose Ella; F; 9/9/11-20; N.C. Cherokee; 1/16; S; Daughter; 2048; No; Culberson, Cherokee, N.C.; Yes; Unallotted

2064; Raper, Martin; M; 5/23/89-42; N.C. Cherokee; 1/16; M; Head; 2049; No; Patrick, Cherokee, N.C.; Yes; Unallotted

2065; Raper, Glenn; M; 11/14/14-17; N.C. Cherokee; 1/32; S; Son; 2050; No; Patrick, Cherokee, N.C.; Yes; Unallotted

2066; Raper, Lois; F; 12/31/17-14; N.C. Cherokee; 1/32; S; Daughter; 2051; No; Patrick, Cherokee, N.C.; Yes; Unallotted

2067; Raper, Blanche; F; 3/5/20-12; N.C. Cherokee; 1/32; S; Daughter; 2052; No; Patrick, Cherokee, N.C.; Yes; Unallotted

2068; Raper, Charley; M; 3/4/22-10; N.C. Cherokee; 1/32; S; Son; 2053; No; Patrick, Cherokee, N.C.; Yes; Unallotted

2069; Raper, Marty A.; M; 10/2/92-39; N.C. Cherokee; 1/16; M; Head; 2054; Yes; Yes; Unallotted

2070; Raper, Everett G.; M; 5/8/18-13; N.C. Cherokee; 1/32; S; Son; 2055; Yes; Yes; Unallotted

2071; Raper, Edna D.; F; 1/22/20-12; N.C. Cherokee; 1/32; S; Daughter; 2056; Yes; Yes; Unallotted

2072; Raper, Clarence W.; M; 7/24/22-9; N.C. Cherokee; 1/32; S; Son; 2057; Yes; Yes; Unallotted

2073; Raper, Oscar; M; 3/20/86-46; N.C. Cherokee; 1/16; M; Head; 2058; Yes; Yes; Unallotted

2074; Raper, Robert; M; 3/20/99-33; N.C. Cherokee; 1/16; M; Head; 2059; Yes; Yes; Unallotted

2075; Raper, Rosa May; F; 3/20/01-31; N.C. Cherokee; 1/16; S; Head; 2060; No; Marietta, Cobb, Ga.; Yes; Unallotted

2076; Raper, Thomas; M; 12/23/58-73; N.C. Cherokee; 1/8; M; Head; 2061; No; Oak Park, Cherokee, N.C.; Yes; Unallotted

2077; Raper, Clifton; M; 4/15/06-25; N.C. Cherokee; 1/16; S; Son; 2062; No; Oak Park, Cherokee, N.C.; Yes; Unallotted

2078; Raper, Earnest; M; 9/13/12-19; N.C. Cherokee; 1/16; S; Son; 2063; No; Oak Park, Cherokee, N.C.; Yes; Unallotted

2079; Raper, Whoola B.; M; 3/23/88-44; N.C. Cherokee; 1/16; M; Head; 2064; No; Birch, Cherokee, N.C.; Yes; Unallotted

Census of the **Eastern Cherokee** reservation of the **Cherokee, N.C.** jurisdiction, as of **April 1**, **1932,** taken by **R. L. Spalsbury**, Superintendent.

Key: Number; Surname, Given; Sex; Date of Birth-Age at Last Birthday; Tribe; Degree of Blood; Marital Status; Relationship to Head of Family; Last C. Roll No.; At Jurisdiction Where Enrolled (Yes/No); (If no – Where); Ward (Yes/No); Allotment, Annuity and Identification Numbers (if given).

2080; Raper, Jefferson; M; 8/16/20-11; N.C. Cherokee; 1/32; S; Son; 2065; No; Birch, Cherokee, N.C.; Yes; Unallotted

2081; Raper, William A.; M; 6/15/84-47; N.C. Cherokee; 1/16; M; Head; 2066; No; Clever, Christian, Mo.; Yes; Unallotted

2082; Raper, William; M; 2/21/08-24; N.C. Cherokee; 1/16; S; Head; 2067; No; Culberson, Cherokee, N.C.; Yes; Unallotted

2083; Raper, William B.; M; 1/3/79-53; N.C. Cherokee; 1/16; M; Head; 2068; No; Brasstown, Clay, N.C.; Yes; Unallotted
2084; Raper, William P.; M; 11/18/11-20; N.C. Cherokee; 1/32; S; Son; 2069; No; Brasstown, Clay, N.C.; Yes; Unallotted

2085; Raper, William T.; M; 4/7/68-63; N.C. Cherokee; 1/8; M; Head; 2070; No; Culberson, Cherokee, N.C.; Yes; Unallotted
2086; Raper, James G.; M; 1/24/04-28; N.C. Cherokee; 1/16; S; Son; 2071; No; Culberson, Cherokee, N.C.; Yes; Unallotted
2087; Raper, William A.; M; 4/27/08-23; N.C. Cherokee; 1/16; S; Son; 2072; No; Culberson, Cherokee, N.C.; Yes; Unallotted
2088; Raper, Bertha M.; F; 1/11/10-22; N.C. Cherokee; 1/16; S; Daughter; 2073; No; Culberson, Cherokee, N.C.; Yes; Unallotted
2089; Raper, Melba L.; F; 8/18/21-10; N.C. Cherokee; 1/16; S; Daughter; 2074; No; Culberson, Cherokee, N.C.; Yes; Unallotted
2090; Raper, Ruby L.; F; 6/15/23-8; N.C. Cherokee; 1/16; S; Daughter; 2075; No; Culberson, Cherokee, N.C.; Yes; Unallotted

2091; Rattler, George W.; M; 3/15/73-59; N.C. Cherokee; 4/4; M; Head; 2076; Yes; Yes; Unallotted
2092; Rattler, Hettie S.; F; 12/25/98-33; N.C. Cherokee; 4/4; M; Wife; 2077; Yes; Yes; Unallotted
2093; Rattler, Ammons; M; 5/30/11-20; N.C. Cherokee; 4/4; S; Son; 2078; Yes; Yes; Unallotted
2094; Rattler, Iva R.; F; 1/3/30-2; N.C. Cherokee; 4/4; S; Daughter; 2079; Yes; Yes; Unallotted

2095; Rattler, Henson; M; 12/7/02-29; N.C. Cherokee; 4/4; M; Head; 2080; Yes; Yes; Unallotted
2096; Rattler, Fanny O.; F; 3/6/09-23; N.C. Cherokee; 4/4; M; Wife; 2081; Yes; Yes; Unallotted

2097; Rattler, John; M; 12/14/84-47; N.C. Cherokee; 4/4; M; Head; 2082; Yes; Yes; Unallotted
2098; Rattler, Emmaline; F; 3/29/87-45; N.C. Cherokee; 4/4; M; Wife; 2083; Yes; Yes; Unallotted

Census of the **Eastern Cherokee** reservation of the **Cherokee, N.C.** jurisdiction, as of **April 1** , 19**32**, taken by **R. L. Spalsbury** , Superintendent.

Key: Number; Surname, Given; Sex; Date of Birth-Age at Last Birthday; Tribe; Degree of Blood; Marital Status; Relationship to Head of Family; Last C. Roll No.; At Jurisdiction Where Enrolled (Yes/No); (If no – Where); Ward (Yes/No); Allotment, Annuity and Identification Numbers (if given).

2099; Rattler (Illeg.), John W.; M; 12/20/06-25; N.C. Cherokee; 1/2; S; Son; 2084; Yes; Yes; Unallotted

2100; Rattler, Lucy; F; 6/3/09-22; N.C. Cherokee; 4/4; S; Daughter; 2085; Yes; Yes; Unallotted

2101; Rattler, Willie; M; 8/7/11-20; N.C. Cherokee; 4/4; S; Son; 2086; Yes; Yes; Unallotted

2102; Rattler, Joseph; M; 5/11/14-17; N.C. Cherokee; 4/4; S; Son; 2087; Yes; Yes; Unallotted

2103; Rattler, Wilson; M; 11/16/16-15; N.C. Cherokee; 4/4; S; Son; 2088; Yes; Yes; Unallotted

2104; Rattler, Mike; M; 7/21/19-12; N.C. Cherokee; 4/4; S; Son; 2089; Yes; Yes; Unallotted

2105; Rattler, Roxie; F; 6/19/21-10; N.C. Cherokee; 4/4; S; Daughter; 2090; Yes; Yes; Unallotted

2106; Rattler, Morgan; M; 1/5/05-27; N.C. Cherokee; 4/4; Wd.; Head; 2091; Yes; Yes; Unallotted

2107; Rattler, Nancy; F; 12/31/46-85; N.C. Cherokee; 4/4; Wd.; Head; 2092; Yes; Yes; Unallotted

2108; Rattler, Jonah; M; 3/15/89-43; N.C. Cherokee; 4/4; S; Son; 2093; Yes; Yes; Unallotted

2109; Rattler, Walter; M; 4/9/04-27; N.C. Cherokee; 1/2; M; Head; 2094; Yes; Yes; Unallotted

2110; Rattler, Charles; M; 10/18/22-9; N.C. Cherokee; 1/4; S; Son; 2095; Yes; Yes; Unallotted

2111; Ratliff, Lawyer; M; 3/15/75-57; N.C. Cherokee; 1/8; Wd.; Head; 2096; No; Andrews, Cherokee, N.C.; Yes; Unallotted

2112; Ratliff, Emma; F; 4/15/29-2; N.C. Cherokee; 1/16; S; Daughter; 2097; No; Andrews, Cherokee, N.C.; Yes; Unallotted

2113; Ratliff, William B.; M; 6/1/73-58; N.C. Cherokee; 1/8; M; Head; 2098; Yes; Yes; Unallotted

2114; Ratliff, Elizabeth; F; 5/1/76-55; N.C. Cherokee; 4/4; M; Wife; 2099; Yes; Yes; Unallotted

2115; Ratliff, Emma C.; F; 5/26/01-30; N.C. Cherokee; 9/16; S; Daughter; 2100; Yes, Yes; Unallotted

2116; Ratliff, Jacob R.; M; 1/23/04-28; N.C. Cherokee; 9/16; S; Son; 2101; Yes, Yes; Unallotted

2117; Ratliff, Ella Mae; F; 11/15/06-25; N.C. Cherokee; 9/16; S; Daughter; 2102; Yes, Yes; Unallotted

2118; Rattliff, Jonah A.; M; 7/6/10-21; N.C. Cherokee; 9/16; S; Son; 2103; Yes, Yes; Unallotted

Census of the **Eastern Cherokee** reservation of the **Cherokee, N.C.** jurisdiction, as of **April 1** , 19**32,** taken by **R. L. Spalsbury** , Superintendent.

Key: Number; Surname, Given; Sex; Date of Birth-Age at Last Birthday; Tribe; Degree of Blood; Marital Status; Relationship to Head of Family; Last C. Roll No.; At Jurisdiction Where Enrolled (Yes/No); (If no – Where); Ward (Yes/No); Allotment, Annuity and Identification Numbers (if given).

2119; Ratliff, Myrtle M.; F; 2/6/12-20; N.C. Cherokee; 9/16; S; Daughter; 2104; Yes, Yes; Unallotted

2120; Ratliff, Isaac W.; M; 9/6/15-16; N.C. Cherokee; 9/16; S; Son; 2105; Yes, Yes; Unallotted

2121; Rave, Martha C.; F; 3/7/85-47; N.C. Cherokee; 4/4; M; Wife; 2106; Yes; Yes; Unallotted

2122; Rave, Maurice W.; M; 2/22/13-19; N.C. Cherokee; 1/2; S; Son; 2107; Yes, Yes; Unallotted

2123; Rave, Wilma[sic] A.; M; 3/3/15-17; N.C. Cherokee; 1/2; S; Son; 2108; Yes, Yes; Unallotted

2124; Reagan (Lambert, Hester), Hester L.; F; 4/15/87-44; N.C. Cherokee; 1/16; M; Wife; 2109; Yes; Yes; Unallotted

2125; Reagan, Emmet; M; 2/19/08-24; N.C. Cherokee; 1/32; S; Son; 2110; Yes, Yes; Unallotted

2126; (Knight), Paulina; F; 1/21/10-22; N.C. Cherokee; 1/32; M𝘚; Daughter; 2111; Yes, Yes; Unallotted

2127; Reagan, Pollard; M; 3/11/12-20; N.C. Cherokee; 1/32; S; Son; 2112; Yes, Yes; Unallotted

2128; Reagan, Mary E.; F; 10/8/14-17; N.C. Cherokee; 1/32; S; Daughter; 2113; Yes, Yes; Unallotted

2129; Reagan, Stella S.; F; 2/21/16-16; N.C. Cherokee; 1/32; S; Daughter; 2114; Yes, Yes; Unallotted

2130; Reagan, John P.; M; 7/4/18-13; N.C. Cherokee; 1/32; S; Son; 2115; Yes, Yes; Unallotted

2131; Reagan, Hubert; M; 3/22/20-12; N.C. Cherokee; 1/32; S; Son; 2116; Yes, Yes; Unallotted

2132; Reagan, Daniel; M; 4/13/24-7; N.C. Cherokee; 1/32; S; Son; 2117; Yes, Yes; Unallotted

2133; Reed, Adam; M; 11/11/75-46; N.C. Cherokee; 7/8; M; Head; 2118; Yes; Yes; Unallotted

2134; Reed, Margaret; F; 4/20/91-41; N.C. Cherokee; 4/4; M; Wife; 2119; Yes; Yes; Unallotted

2135; Reed, Mooday[sic]; M; 12/22/14-17; N.C. Cherokee; 7/8; S; Son; 2120; Yes, Yes; Unallotted

2136; Reed, Gladys M.; F; 2/3/20-12; N.C. Cherokee; 15/16; S; Daughter; 2121; Yes; Yes; Unallotted

2137; Reed, Sallie S.; F; 11/11/22-9; N.C. Cherokee; 15/16; S; Daughter; 2122; Yes; Yes; Unallotted

2138; Reed, Nellie A.; F; 3/17/25-8; N.C. Cherokee; 15/16; S; Daughter; 2123; Yes; Yes; Unallotted

2139; Reed, Charlotte; F; 3/30/29-3; N.C. Cherokee; 15/16; S; Daughter; 2124; Yes; Yes; Unallotted

Census of the **Eastern Cherokee** reservation of the **Cherokee, N.C.** jurisdiction, as of **April 1** , 1932, taken by **R. L. Spalsbury** , Superintendent.

Key: Number; Surname, Given; Sex; Date of Birth-Age at Last Birthday; Tribe; Degree of Blood; Marital Status; Relationship to Head of Family; Last C. Roll No.; At Jurisdiction Where Enrolled (Yes/No); (If no – Where); Ward (Yes/No); Allotment, Annuity and Identification Numbers (if given).

2140; Reed, David; M; 3/15/61-71; N.C. Cherokee; 3/4; S; Head; 2125; Yes; Yes; Unallotted

2141; Reed, Deweese; M; 5/31/79-52; N.C. Cherokee; 7/8; M; Head; 2126; Yes; Yes; Unallotted

2142; Reed, Minda Q.; F; 10/27/95-36; N.C. Cherokee; 5/8; M; Wife; 2127; Yes; Yes; Unallotted

2143; Reed, Robert; M; 7/4/19-12; N.C. Cherokee; 12/16; S; Son; 2128; Yes, Yes; Unallotted

2144; Reed (Raper, Elizabeth), Elizabeth; F; 7/9/98-33; N.C. Cherokee; 1/16; M; Wife; 2129; No; Firestone Park Sta., Akron, Summit, Ohio; Yes; Unallotted

2145; Reed, Frances H.; M; 10/12/21-10; N.C. Cherokee; 1/32; S; Son; 2130; No; Firestone Park Sta., Akron, Summit, Ohio; Yes; Unallotted

2146; Reed, Fidele; M; 9/12/69-62; N.C. Cherokee; 3/4; M; Head; 2131; Yes; Yes; Unallotted

2147; Reed, Addie H.; F; 1/17/92-40; N.C. Cherokee; 1/8; M; Wife; 2132; Yes; Yes; Unallotted

2148; Reed, Rachel; F; 3/25/14-18; N.C. Cherokee; 7/16; S; Daughter; 2133; Yes; Yes; Unallotted

2149; Reed, Cinda; F; 2/2/16-16; N.C. Cherokee; 7/16; S; Daughter; 2134; Yes; Yes; Unallotted

2150; Reed, Lula; F; 3/21/19-13; N.C. Cherokee; 7/16; S; Daughter; 2135; Yes; Yes; Unallotted

2151; Reed, Wilson; M; 3/21/21-11; N.C. Cherokee; 7/16; S; Son; 2136; Yes, Yes; Unallotted

2152; Reed, Anna M.; F; 9/6/23-8; N.C. Cherokee; 7/16; S; Daughter; 2137; Yes; Yes; Unallotted

2153; Reed, Maggie M.; F; 1/12/26-6; N.C. Cherokee; 7/16; S; Daughter; 2138; Yes; Yes; Unallotted

2154; Reed, Henry J.; M; 2/2/28-4; N.C. Cherokee; 7/16; S; Son; 2139; Yes, Yes; Unallotted

2155; Reed, James; M; 5/2/90-41; N.C. Cherokee; 7/8; M; Head; 2141; Yes; Yes; Unallotted

2156; Reed, Minda L.; F; 5/30/93-38; N.C. Cherokee; 8/8; M; Wife; 2142; Yes; Yes; Unallotted

2157; Reed, Margaret; F; 8/30/17-14; N.C. Cherokee; 15/16; S; Daughter; 2143; Yes; Yes; Unallotted

2158; Reed, Martha; F; 7/29/19-12; N.C. Cherokee; 15/16; S; Daughter; 2144; Yes; Yes; Unallotted

2159; Reed, Ollie; F; 4/10/22-9; N.C. Cherokee; 15/16; S; Daughter; 2145; Yes; Yes; Unallotted

Census of the **Eastern Cherokee** reservation of the **Cherokee, N.C.** jurisdiction, as of **April 1**, **1932,** taken by **R. L. Spalsbury**, Superintendent.

Key: Number; Surname, Given; Sex; Date of Birth-Age at Last Birthday; Tribe; Degree of Blood; Marital Status; Relationship to Head of Family; Last C. Roll No.; At Jurisdiction Where Enrolled (Yes/No); (If no – Where); Ward (Yes/No); Allotment, Annuity and Identification Numbers (if given).

2160; Reed, Malone; M; 7/11/25-6; N.C. Cherokee; 15/16; S; Son; 2146; Yes; Yes; Unallotted

2161; Reed, James; M; 12/23/52-79; N.C. Cherokee; 3/4; S; Head; 2147; Yes; Yes; Unallotted

2162; Reed, James W.; M; 4/30/67-64; N.C. Cherokee; 3/4; M; Head; 2148; No; Salisbury, Rowan, N.C.; Yes; Unallotted

2163; Reed, Johnson; M; 3/5/05-27; N.C. Cherokee; 15/16; M; Head; 2149; Yes; Yes; Unallotted

2164; Reed, Dinah; F; 10/20/05-26; N.C. Cherokee; 4/4; M; Wife; 2150; Yes; Yes; Unallotted

2165; Reed, Peter; M; 5/17/25-6; N.C. Cherokee; 31/32; S; Son; 2151; Yes; Yes; Unallotted

2166; Reed, Helen; F; 4/2/27-4; N.C. Cherokee; 31/32; S; Daughter; 2152; Yes; Yes; Unallotted

2167; Reed, Lloyd; M; 4/15/89-42; N.C. Cherokee; 7/8; M; Head; 2153; Yes; Yes; Unallotted

2168; Reed, Rachel; F; 12/23/51-80; N.C. Cherokee; 3/4; Wd.; Head; 2154; Yes; Yes; Unallotted

2169; Reed, Samuel; M; 3/7/11-21; N.C. Cherokee; 7/8; S; Head; 2155; Yes; Yes; Unallotted

2170; Reed, Matilda; F; 2/6/16-16; N.C. Cherokee; 7/8; S; Sister; 2156; Yes; Yes; Unallotted

2171; Reed, Mark; M; 4/11/20-11; N.C. Cherokee; 7/8; S; Brother; 2157; Yes; Yes; Unallotted

2172; Reed, Sarah; F; 6/19/12-19; N.C. Cherokee; 7/8; S; Alone; 2158; Yes; Yes; Unallotted

2173; Reed, Sarah J.; F; 5/8/15-16; N.C. Cherokee; 7/16; S; Alone; 2159; Yes; Yes; Unallotted

2174; Reed, Theodore; M; 8/29/85-46; N.C. Cherokee; 1/4; M; Head; 2160; Yes; Yes; Unallotted

2175; Reed, Theodore E.; M; 6/29/16-15; N.C. Cherokee; 1/8; S; Son; 2161; Yes; Yes; Unallotted

2176; Reed, William; M; 4/15/82-49; N.C. Cherokee; 7/8; M; Head; 2162; Yes; Yes; Unallotted

Census of the **Eastern Cherokee** reservation of the **Cherokee, N.C.** jurisdiction, as of **April 1** , 19**32**, taken by **R. L. Spalsbury** , Superintendent.

Key: Number; Surname, Given; Sex; Date of Birth-Age at Last Birthday; Tribe; Degree of Blood; Marital Status; Relationship to Head of Family; Last C. Roll No.; At Jurisdiction Where Enrolled (Yes/No); (If no – Where); Ward (Yes/No); Allotment, Annuity and Identification Numbers (if given).

2177; Reed, Katie K.; F; 12/23/90-41; N.C. Cherokee; 1/2; M; Wife; 2163; Yes; Yes; Unallotted

2178; Reed, Jackson; M; 1/4/09-23; N.C. Cherokee; 11/16; S; Son; 2164; Yes; Yes; Unallotted

2179; Reed, Cornelia; F; 11/13/11-20; N.C. Cherokee; 11/16; S; Daughter; 2165; Yes; Yes; Unallotted

2180; Reed, Esther; F; 4/30/13-18; N.C. Cherokee; 11/16; S; Daughter; 2166; Yes; Yes; Unallotted

2181; Reed, Noah; M; 1/26/18-14; N.C. Cherokee; 11/16; S; Son; 2167; Yes; Yes; Unallotted

2182; Reed, David; M; 7/26/20-11; N.C. Cherokee; 11/16; S; Son; 2168; Yes; Yes; Unallotted

2183; Reed, McKinley; M; 7/3/23-8; N.C. Cherokee; 11/16; S; Son; 2169; Yes; Yes; Unallotted

2184; Reed, Susie; F; 2/18/29-3; N.C. Cherokee; 11/16; S; Daughter; 2170; Yes; Yes; Unallotted

2185; Reed, Alexander; M; 4/28/31-11/12; N.C. Cherokee; 11/16; S; Son; ---; Yes; Yes; Unallotted

2186; Reynolds (Raper, Eva), Eva R.; F; 2/12/04-28; N.C. Cherokee; 1/16; M; Wife; 2171; No; Akron, Summit, Ohio; Yes; Unallotted

2187; Reynolds, Artie G.; M; 1/22/23-9; N.C. Cherokee; 1/32; S; Son; 2172; No; Akron, Summit, Ohio; Yes; Unallotted

2188; Reynolds, Geneva; F; 5/10/24-7; N.C. Cherokee; 1/32; S; Daughter; 2173; No; Akron, Summit, Ohio; Yes; Unallotted

2189; Richards, Mamie P.; F; 1/27/87-45; N.C. Cherokee; 1/16; M; Wife; 2174; Yes; Yes; Unallotted

2190; Richards, Ruby K.; F; 9/11/06-25; N.C. Cherokee; 1/32; S; Daughter; 2175; Yes; Yes; Unallotted

2191; Richards (Cole, Orney), Orney; F; 11/7/93-38; N.C. Cherokee; 1/16; M; Wife; 2176; Yes; Yes; Unallotted

2192; Richards, Doyle; M; 8/24/15-16; N.C. Cherokee; 1/32; S; Son; 2177; Yes; Yes; Unallotted

2193; Richards, Zelzie; M; 8/13/17-14; N.C. Cherokee; 1/32; S; Son; 2178; Yes; Yes; Unallotted

2194; Richards, Edward; M; 8/10/19-12; N.C. Cherokee; 1/32; S; Son; 2179; Yes; Yes; Unallotted

2195; Riffey (Wolfe, Eliza), Eliza P.; F; 9/30/02-29; N.C. Cherokee; 1/8; M; Wife; 2180; Yes; Yes; Unallotted

2196; Riley, James; M; 5/3/01-30; N.C. Cherokee; 1/4; S; Head; 2181; Yes; Yes; Unallotted

Census of the **Eastern Cherokee** reservation of the **Cherokee, N.C.** jurisdiction, as of **April 1** , **1932,** taken by **R. L. Spalsbury** , Superintendent.

Key: Number; Surname, Given; Sex; Date of Birth-Age at Last Birthday; Tribe; Degree of Blood; Marital Status; Relationship to Head of Family; Last C. Roll No.; At Jurisdiction Where Enrolled (Yes/No); (If no – Where); Ward (Yes/No); Allotment, Annuity and Identification Numbers (if given).

2197; Roberts (Smith, Josephine), Josephine; F; 9/30/95-36; N.C. Cherokee; 1/8; M; Wife; 2182; Yes; Yes; Unallotted
2198; Roberts, Pauline; F; 7/15/14-17; N.C. Cherokee; 1/16; S; Daughter; 2183; Yes; Yes; Unallotted
2199; Roberts, Leroy; M; 1/5/17-15; N.C. Cherokee; 1/16; S; Son; 2184; Yes; Yes; Unallotted
2200; Roberts, Wane; M; 11/2/19-12; N.C. Cherokee; 1/16; S; Son; 2185; Yes; Yes; Unallotted
2201; Roberts, Glenn; M; 2/27/21-11; N.C. Cherokee; 1/16; S; Son; 2186; Yes; Yes; Unallotted

2202; Roberts (Smith, Lottie), Lottie; F; 9/26/83-48; N.C. Cherokee; 3/8; M; Wife; 2187; No; Sweetwater, Monroe, Tenn.; Yes; Unallotted
2203; Roberts, Walter; M; 6/20/03-28; N.C. Cherokee; 3/16; S; Son; 2188; No; Sweetwater, Monroe, Tenn.; Yes; Unallotted
2204; Roberts, Fred; M; 5/12/05-26; N.C. Cherokee; 3/16; S; Son; 2189; No; Sweetwater, Monroe, Tenn.; Yes; Unallotted
2205; Roberts, Lula; F; 5/6/07-24; N.C. Cherokee; 3/16; S; Daughter; 2190; No; Sweetwater, Monroe, Tenn.; Yes; Unallotted
2206; Roberts, G.W.; M; 8/15/13-18; N.C. Cherokee; 3/16; S; Son; 2191; No; Sweetwater, Monroe, Tenn.; Yes; Unallotted
2207; Roberts, Emma; F; 1/7/18-14; N.C. Cherokee; 3/16; S; Daughter; 2192; No; Sweetwater, Monroe, Tenn.; Yes; Unallotted
2208; Roberts, Leona; F; 8/5/21-10; N.C. Cherokee; 3/16; S; Daughter; 2193; No; Sweetwater, Monroe, Tenn.; Yes; Unallotted

2209; Roberson (Raper, Iowa), Iowa; F; 12/2/88-43; N.C. Cherokee; 1/8; M; Wife; 2194; No; Culberson, Cherokee, N.C.; Yes; Unallotted
2210; Roberson, A.J.; M; 8/12/12-19; N.C. Cherokee; 1/16; S; Son; 2195; No; Culberson, Cherokee, N.C.; Yes; Unallotted
2211; Roberson, Walter A.; M; 9/5/14-17; N.C. Cherokee; 1/16; S; Son; 2196; No; Culberson, Cherokee, N.C.; Yes; Unallotted
2212; Roberson, Wayne C.; M; 7/5/17-14; N.C. Cherokee; 1/16; S; Son; 2197; No; Culberson, Cherokee, N.C.; Yes; Unallotted
2213; Roberson, Nona D.; F; 2/25/23-9; N.C. Cherokee; 1/16; S; Daughter; 2198; No; Culberson, Cherokee, N.C.; Yes; Unallotted

2214; Robinson, Birgie; F; 1883-49; N.C. Cherokee; 1/4-; M; Wife; 2199; No; Rossville, Walker, Ga.; Yes; Unallotted

2215; Robinson, Charles H.; M; 1/13/05-27; N.C. Cherokee; 1/32; S; Head; 2200; No; Schoolfield, Pitsylvania, Pa.; Yes; Unallotted
2216; Robinson, Howard G.; M; 5/5/07-24; N.C. Cherokee; 1/32; S; Brother; 2201; No; Schoolfield, Pitsylvania, Pa.; Yes; Unallotted

Census of the **Eastern Cherokee** reservation of the **Cherokee, N.C.** jurisdiction, as of **April 1** , 19**32,** taken by **R. L. Spalsbury** , Superintendent.

Key: Number; Surname, Given; Sex; Date of Birth-Age at Last Birthday; Tribe; Degree of Blood; Marital Status; Relationship to Head of Family; Last C. Roll No.; At Jurisdiction Where Enrolled (Yes/No); (If no – Where); Ward (Yes/No); Allotment, Annuity and Identification Numbers (if given).

2217; Robinson, Henry H.; M; 5/30/10-21; N.C. Cherokee; 1/32; S; Brother; 2202; No; Schoolfield, Pitsylvania, Pa.; Yes; Unallotted

2218; Robinson, Alvin W.; M; 4/6/12-19; N.C. Cherokee; 1/32; S; Brother; 2203; No; Schoolfield, Pitsylvania, Pa.; Yes; Unallotted

2219; Robinson, Malvin O.; M; 3/14/14-18; N.C. Cherokee; 1/32; S; Brother; 2204; No; Schoolfield, Pitsylvania, Pa.; Yes; Unallotted

2220; Robinson, Bessie I.; F; 11/28/16-15; N.C. Cherokee; 1/32; S; Sister; 2205; No; Schoolfield, Pitsylvania, Pa.; Yes; Unallotted

2221; Robinson (Raper, Ellen), Ellen; F; 2/4/66-66; N.C. Cherokee; 1/8; M; Wife; 2206; No; Murphy, Cherokee, N.C.; Yes; Unallotted

2222; Robinson, Hadley; M; 2/26/99-33; N.C. Cherokee; 1/16; S; Son; 2207; No; Murphy, Cherokee, N.C.; Yes; Unallotted

2223; Robinson, Thomas L.; M; 7/15/83-48; N.C. Cherokee; 1/16; M; Head; 2208; No; Murphy, Cherokee, N.C.; Yes; Unallotted

2224; Robinson, William R.; M; 11/19/05-26; N.C. Cherokee; 1/32; S; Son; 2209; No; Murphy, Cherokee, N.C.; Yes; Unallotted

2225; Robinson, Harley T.; M; 12/30/08-23; N.C. Cherokee; 1/32; S; Son; 2210; No; Murphy, Cherokee, N.C.; Yes; Unallotted

2226; Robinson, Sarah E.; F; 4/18/12-19; N.C. Cherokee; 1/32; S; Daughter; 2211; No; Murphy, Cherokee, N.C.; Yes; Unallotted

2227; Robinson, Luther; M; 4/14/14-17; N.C. Cherokee; 1/32; S; Son; 2212; No; Murphy, Cherokee, N.C.; Yes; Unallotted

2228; Robinson, Clara N.; F; 1/2/17-15; N.C. Cherokee; 1/32; S; Daughter; 2213; No; Murphy, Cherokee, N.C.; Yes; Unallotted

2229; Robinson, Edward; M; 2/2/19-13; N.C. Cherokee; 1/32; S; Son; 2214; No; Murphy, Cherokee, N.C.; Yes; Unallotted

2230; Robinson, Susie M.; F; 7/15/22-9; N.C. Cherokee; 1/32; S; Daughter; 2215; No; Murphy, Cherokee, N.C.; Yes; Unallotted

2231; Robinson, Rose Bell; F; 6/2/24-7; N.C. Cherokee; 1/32; S; Daughter; 2216; No; Murphy, Cherokee, N.C.; Yes; Unallotted

2232; Robinson, Willis O.; M; 10/3/80-51; N.C. Cherokee; 1/16; M; Head; 2217; No; Murphy, Cherokee, N.C.; Yes; Unallotted

2233; Robinson, Fred A.; M; 1/16/19-13; N.C. Cherokee; 1/32; S; Son; 2218; No; Murphy, Cherokee, N.C.; Yes; Unallotted

2234; Rogers, Astor; M; 5/23/05-26; N.C. Cherokee; 1/8; S; Head; 2219; Yes; Yes; Unallotted

2235; Rogers, Junior C.; M; 4/7/26-8[sic]; N.C. Cherokee; 1/16; S; Son; 2220; Yes; Yes; Unallotted

2236; Rogers, Floyd; M; 4/4/02-29; N.C. Cherokee; 1/8; M; Head; 2221; Yes; Yes; Unallotted

Census of the **Eastern Cherokee** reservation of the **Cherokee, N.C.** jurisdiction, as of **April 1**, **1932,** taken by **R. L. Spalsbury**, Superintendent.

Key: Number; Surname, Given; Sex; Date of Birth-Age at Last Birthday; Tribe; Degree of Blood; Marital Status; Relationship to Head of Family; Last C. Roll No.; At Jurisdiction Where Enrolled (Yes/No); (If no – Where); Ward (Yes/No); Allotment, Annuity and Identification Numbers (if given).

2237; Rogers, Maud S.; F; 11/11/98-33; N.C. Cherokee; 1/8; M; Wife; 2222; Yes; Yes; Unallotted

2238; Rogers, Samuel R.; M; 1/27/22-10; N.C. Cherokee; 1/8; S; Son; 2223; Yes; Yes; Unallotted

2239; Rogers, Irwin; M; 7/21/90-41; N.C. Cherokee; 1/16; M; Head; 2224; No; Adairsville, Bartow, Ga. Yes; Unallotted

2240; Rogers (Cole, Lula), Lula; F; 1/17/07-25; N.C. Cherokee; 1/16; M; Wife; 2225; Yes; Yes; Unallotted

2241; Rogers, Oscar; M; 8/7/96-35; N.C. Cherokee; 1/8; M; Head; 2226; Yes; Yes; Unallotted

2242; Rogers, Clarence; M; 5/5/15-16; N.C. Cherokee; 1/16; S; Son; 2227; Yes; Yes; Unallotted

2243; Rogers, Elsie; F; 7/24/17-14; N.C. Cherokee; 1/16; S; Daughter; 2228; Yes; Yes; Unallotted

2244; Rogers, Shirley; M[sic]; 11/12/19-12; N.C. Cherokee; 1/16; S; Son[sic]; 2229; Yes; Yes; Unallotted

2245; Rogers, Ruth M.; F; 3/24/24-8; N.C. Cherokee; 1/16; S; Daughter; 2230; Yes; Yes; Unallotted

2246; Rogers, Charles F.; M; 3/31/31-1; N.C. Cherokee; 1/16; S; Son; 2231; Yes; Yes; Unallotted

2247; Rollins, Dovie; F; 4/17/62-69; N.C. Cherokee; 1/8; M; Wife; 2232; No; Rossville, Walker, Ga.; Yes; Unallotted

2248; Rose (Sneed, Florence), Florence; F; 11/20/69-62; N.C. Cherokee; 1/8; M; Wife; 2233; Yes; Yes; Unallotted

2249; Rose, Benjamin T.; M; 6/30/07-24; N.C. Cherokee; 1/16; S; Son; 2234; Yes; Yes; Unallotted

2250; Rose, Thurman; M; 3/16/10-22; N.C. Cherokee; 1/16; S; Son; 2235; Yes; Yes; Unallotted

2251; Rose, Wayne; M; 1/17/13-19; N.C. Cherokee; 1/16; S; Son; 2236; Yes; Yes; Unallotted

2252; Rose, Jake; M; 4/8/95-36; N.C. Cherokee; 1/16; M; Head; 2237; Yes; Yes; Unallotted

2253; Rose, Velma; F; 6/8/19-12; N.C. Cherokee; 1/32; S; Daughter; 2238; Yes; Yes; Unallotted

2254; Rose, Thelma; F; 2/22/22-10; N.C. Cherokee; 1/32; S; Daughter; 2239; Yes; Yes; Unallotted

2255; Rose, William; M; 8/31/92-39; N.C. Cherokee; 1/16; M; Head; 2240; Yes; Yes; Unallotted

Census of the **Eastern Cherokee** reservation of the **Cherokee, N.C.** jurisdiction, as of **April 1** , 1932, taken by **R. L. Spalsbury** , Superintendent.

Key: Number; Surname, Given; Sex; Date of Birth-Age at Last Birthday; Tribe; Degree of Blood; Marital Status; Relationship to Head of Family; Last C. Roll No.; At Jurisdiction Where Enrolled (Yes/No); (If no – Where); Ward (Yes/No); Allotment, Annuity and Identification Numbers (if given).

2256; Rose, Horace J.; M; 2/8/22-10; N.C. Cherokee; 1/32; S; Son; 2241; Yes; Yes; Unallotted

2257; Rose, Nora Lee; F; 6/1/24-7; N.C. Cherokee; 1/32; S; Daughter; 2242; Yes; Yes; Unallotted

2258; ~~Ross, Adam; M; 7/26/82-49; N.C. Cherokee; 4/4; M; Head; 2243~~; Yes; Note – see page 251; Yes; Unallotted

2259; Ross, Katie; F; 1/6/13-19; N.C. Cherokee; 7/8; S; Daughter; 2244; Yes; Yes; Unallotted

2260; Ross, Olive E.; F; 3/9/18-14; N.C. Cherokee; 7/8; S; Daughter; 2245; Yes; Yes; Unallotted

2261; Ross, Leroy; M; 7/14/20-11; N.C. Cherokee; 7/8; S; Son; 2246; Yes; Yes; Unallotted

2262; Ross, Kane T.; M; 2/28/88-44; N.C. Cherokee; 4/4; M; Head; 2247; Yes; Yes; Unallotted

2263; Ross, Josie T.; F; 2/3/08-24; N.C. Cherokee; 4/4; M; Wife; 2248; Yes; Yes; Unallotted

2264; Ross, William; M; 4/8/90-41; N.C. Cherokee; 4/4; M; Head; 2249; Yes; Yes; Unallotted

2265; Ross, Malinda O.; F; 5/8/93-38; N.C. Cherokee; 4/4; M; Wife; 2250; Yes; Yes; Unallotted

2266; Ross, Isaac; M; 2/2/17-15; N.C. Cherokee; 4/4; S; Son; 2251; Yes; Yes; Unallotted

2267; Ross, Minnie; F; 3/7/20-12; N.C. Cherokee; 4/4; S; Daughter; 2252; Yes; Yes; Unallotted

2268; Ross, Russell; M; 3/19/23-9; N.C. Cherokee; 4/4; S; Son; 2253; Yes; Yes; Unallotted

2269; Ross, Wilson M.; M; 2/16/28-4; N.C. Cherokee; 4/4; S; Son; 2254; Yes; Yes; Unallotted

2270; Ross, Deedanuskie; M; 2/19/32-1/12; N.C. Cherokee; 4/4; S; Son; ---; Yes; Yes; Unallotted

2271; Ross, McKinley; M; 12/25/99-32; N.C. Cherokee; 1/2; S; Head; 2255; Yes; Yes; Unallotted

2272; Runion (Raper, Julia), Julia R.; F; 12/23/00-31; N.C. Cherokee; 1/16; M; Wife; 2256; No; Farner, Polk, Tenn.; Yes; Unallotted

2273; Runion, Charlie; M; 8/14/17-14; N.C. Cherokee; 1/32; S; Son; 2257; No; Farner, Polk, Tenn.; Yes; Unallotted

2274; Runion, Pauline; F; 9/26/19-12; N.C. Cherokee; 1/32; S; Daughter; 2258; No; Farner, Polk, Tenn.; Yes; Unallotted

2275; Runion, Lake; M; 9/14/22-9; N.C. Cherokee; 1/32; S; Son; 2259; No; Farner, Polk, Tenn.; Yes; Unallotted

Census of the **Eastern Cherokee** reservation of the **Cherokee, N.C.** jurisdiction, as of **April 1** , 19**32,** taken by **R. L. Spalsbury** , Superintendent.

Key: Number; Surname, Given; Sex; Date of Birth-Age at Last Birthday; Tribe; Degree of Blood; Marital Status; Relationship to Head of Family; Last C. Roll No.; At Jurisdiction Where Enrolled (Yes/No); (If no – Where); Ward (Yes/No); Allotment, Annuity and Identification Numbers (if given).

2276; Salerno, Lucinda W.; F; 12/23/83-48; N.C. Cherokee; 4/4; M; Wife; 2260; Yes; Yes; Unallotted

2277; Sampson, James; M; 1/18/53-79; N.C. Cherokee; 4/4; M; Head; 2261; Yes; Yes; Unallotted

2278; Sampson, Sallie; F; 1/10/63-69; N.C. Cherokee; 4/4; M; Wife; 2262; Yes; Yes; Unallotted

2279; Sanders, Cudge; M; 6/10/61-70; N.C. Cherokee; 1/4; M; Head; 2263; Yes; Yes; Unallotted

2280; Sanders, Polly; F; 8/27/57-74; N.C. Cherokee; 1/2; M; Wife; 2264; Yes; Yes; Unallotted

2281; Sanders, Moses; M; 10/4/96-35; N.C. Cherokee; 3/8; M; Head; 2265; Yes; Yes; Unallotted

2282; Sanders, Jennie M.; F; 6/11/15-16; N.C. Cherokee; 3/16; S; Daughter; 2266; Yes; Yes; Unallotted

2283; Sanders, Wm. Adron; M; 11/24/18-13; N.C. Cherokee; 3/16; S; Son; 2267; Yes; Yes; Unallotted

2284; Sanders, Theodore; M; 4/27/22-9; N.C. Cherokee; 3/16; S; Son; 2268; Yes; Yes; Unallotted

2285; Sanders, Vernon; M; 4/26/24-7; N.C. Cherokee; 3/16; S; Son; 2269; Yes; Yes; Unallotted

2286; Satterfield (Loudermilk, Julia), Julia L.; F; 6/6/06-25; N.C. Cherokee; 1/32; M; Wife; 2270; No; Culberson, Cherokee, N.C.,; Yes; Unallotted

2287; Satterfield, Lottie; F; 2/3/24-8; N.C. Cherokee; 1/64; S; Daughter; 2271; No; Culberson, Cherokee, N.C.,; Yes; Unallotted

2288; Saunooke, Amoneeta; M; 1/17/94-38; N.C. Cherokee; 4/4; M; Head; 2272; Yes; Yes; Unallotted

2289; Saunooke, Nancy T.; F; 8/10/01-30; N.C. Cherokee; 4/4; M; Wife; 2273; Yes; Yes; Unallotted

2290; Saunooke, Lydia T.; F; 4/18/31-11/12; N.C. Cherokee; 4/4; S; Daughter; ---; Yes; Yes; Unallotted

2291; Saunooke, Anderson; M; 1/1/04-28; N.C. Cherokee; 1/2; M; Head; 2274; Yes; Yes; Unallotted

2292; Saunooke, Stacy E.P.; F; 10/28/29-22; N.C. Cherokee; 7/8; M; Wife; 2275; Yes; Yes; Unallotted

2293; Saunooke, Edna V.; F; 7/18/29-2; N.C. Cherokee; 11/16; S; Daughter; 2276; Yes; Yes; Unallotted

2294; Saunooke, Robert G.; M; 8/5/31-7/12; N.C. Cherokee; 11/16; S; Son; ---; Yes; Yes; Unallotted

Census of the **Eastern Cherokee** reservation of the **Cherokee, N.C.** jurisdiction, as of **April 1** , 19**32,** taken by **R. L. Spalsbury** , Superintendent.

Key: Number; Surname, Given; Sex; Date of Birth-Age at Last Birthday; Tribe; Degree of Blood; Marital Status; Relationship to Head of Family; Last C. Roll No.; At Jurisdiction Where Enrolled (Yes/No); (If no – Where); Ward (Yes/No); Allotment, Annuity and Identification Numbers (if given).

2295; Saunooke, Cain; M; 12/2/07-25; N.C. Cherokee; 4/4; Wd.; Head; 2277; Yes; Yes; Unallotted

2296; (Smith), Margaret; F; 6/12/11-20; N.C. Cherokee; 1/8; S; (Mr.[sic] Golinda); 2436; Yes; Yes; Unallotted

2297; Saunooke, Golinda; F; 10/17/31-5/12; N.C. Cherokee; 5/8; S; Daughter; ---; Yes; Yes; Unallotted

2298; Saunooke, Edward; M; 9/2/00-31; N.C. Cherokee; 1/2; M; Head; 2278; Yes; Yes; Unallotted

2299; Saunooke, Jackson; M; 3/30/83-52; N.C. Cherokee; 4/4; S; Head; 2279; No; Preston, Richardson, Neb.; Yes; Unallotted

2300; Saunooke, James; M; 6/18/87-44; N.C. Cherokee; 4/4; M; Head; 2280; Yes; Yes; Unallotted

2301; Saunooke, Rachel T.; F; 9/21/95-36; N.C. Cherokee; 4/4; M; Wife; 2281; Yes; Yes; Unallotted

2302; Saunooke, Nicodemus; M; 8/11/18-13; N.C. Cherokee; 4/4; S; Son; 2282; Yes; Yes; Unallotted

2303; Saunooke, Jackson; M; 3/8/28-4; N.C. Cherokee; 4/4; S; Son; 2283; Yes; Yes; Unallotted

2304; Saunooke, Joseph; M; 9/4/72-59; N.C. Cherokee; 4/4; Wd.; Head; 2284; Yes; Yes; Unallotted

2305; Saunooke, Emma; F; 11/25/10-21; N.C. Cherkee; 31/32; S; Daughter; 2285; Yes; Yes; Unallotted

2306; Saunooke, Richard; M; 8/6/15-16; N.C. Cherokee; 31/32; S; Son; 2286; Yes; Yes; Unallotted

2307; Saunooke, Edison J.; M; 9/22/18-13; N.C. Cherokee; 31/32; S; Son; 2287; Yes; Yes; Unallotted

2308; Saunooke, Welch Lee; M; 3/31/20-12; N.C. Cherokee; 31/32; S; Son; 2288; Yes; Yes; Unallotted

2309; Saunooke, Thelma M.; F; 1/25/24-8; N.C. Cherokee; 31/32; S; Daughter; 2289; Yes; Yes; Unallotted

2310; Saunooke, Malinda; F; 2/18/86-46; N.C. Cherokee; 4/4; S; Head; 2290; Yes; Yes; Unallotted

2311; Saunooke, Stephen; M; 12/25/97-34; N.C. Cherokee; 4/4; M; Head; 2291; Yes; Yes; Unallotted

2312; Saunooke, Callie D.; F; 7/5/08-23; N.C. Cherokee; 4/4; M; Wife; 2292; Yes; Yes; Unallotted

2313; Saunooke, Samuel; M; 12/15/78-53; N.C. Cherokee; 7/8; M; Head; 2293; Yes; Yes; Unallotted

122

Census of the **Eastern Cherokee** reservation of the **Cherokee, N.C.** jurisdiction, as of **April 1**, 19**32**, taken by **R. L. Spalsbury**, Superintendent.

Key: Number; Surname, Given; Sex; Date of Birth-Age at Last Birthday; Tribe; Degree of Blood; Marital Status; Relationship to Head of Family; Last C. Roll No.; At Jurisdiction Where Enrolled (Yes/No); (If no – Where); Ward (Yes/No); Allotment, Annuity and Identification Numbers (if given).

2314; Saunooke, Harvey S.; M; 7/30/20-11; N.C. Cherokee; 7/16; S; Son; 2294; Yes; Yes; Unallotted

2315; Saunooke, Stillwell; M; 9/1/91-40; N.C. Cherokee; 7/8; S; Head; 2295; Yes; Yes; Unallotted

2316; Saunooke, William; M; 7/4/70-61; N.C. Cherokee; 4/4; M; Head; 2296; Yes; Yes; Unallotted
2317; Saunooke, Osler; M; 7/19/06-25; N.C. Cherokee; 1/2; S; Son; 2297; Yes; Yes; Unallotted
2318; Saunooke, Cowanah; M; 4/6/09-22; N.C. Cherokee; 1/2; S; Son; 2298; Yes; Yes; Unallotted
2319; Saunooke, Freeman; M; 2/8/11-21; N.C. Cherokee; 1/2; S; Son; 2299; Yes; Yes; Unallotted
2320; Saunooke, Nettie; F; 7/11/13-18; N.C. Cherokee; 1/2; S; Daughter; 2300; Yes; Yes; Unallotted
2321; Saunooke, Cora; F; 2/22/15-17; N.C. Cherokee; 1/2; S; Daughter; 2301; Yes; Yes; Unallotted
2322; Saunooke, Matilda; F; 1/2/18-14; N.C. Cherokee; 1/2; S; Daughter; 2302; Yes; Yes; Unallotted

2323; Saunooke (Standingdeer), William; M; 4/13/14-17; N.C. Cherokee; 31/32; S; Alone; 2303; Yes; Yes; Unallotted

2324; Sauve, Minnie E.; F; 5/4/81-50; N.C. Cherokee; 1/4; M; Wife; 2304; Yes; Yes; Unallotted

2325; Sawyer, Allen; M; 5/3/77-54; N.C. Cherokee; 4/4; M; Head; 2305; Yes; Yes; Unallotted
2326; Sawyer, Kiney; F; 5/17/84-47; N.C. Cherokee; 4/4; M; Wife; 2306; Yes; Yes; Unallotted
2327; Sawyer, Thomas; M; 6/25/05-26; N.C. Cherokee; 4/4; S; Son; 2307; Yes; Yes; Unallotted

2328; Sawyer (Hardin, Inez), Inez E.; F; 7/8/05-26; N.C. Cherokee; 1/32; M; Wife; 2308; Yes; Yes; Unallotted
2329; Nichols, Thelma; F; 3/16/20-12; N.C. Cherokee; 1/64; S; Daughter; 2309; Yes; Yes; Unallotted

2330; Screamer, Cornelia; F; 5/13/22-9; N.C. Cherokee; 4/4; S; Daughter; 2310; Yes; Yes; Unallotted
2331; Screamer, Nellie; F; 2/13/24-8; N.C. Cherokee; 4/4; S; Daughter; 2311; Yes; Yes; Unallotted

Census of the **Eastern Cherokee** reservation of the **Cherokee, N.C.** jurisdiction, as of **April 1** , 19**32,** taken by **R. L. Spalsbury** , Superintendent.

Key: Number; Surname, Given; Sex; Date of Birth-Age at Last Birthday; Tribe; Degree of Blood; Marital Status; Relationship to Head of Family; Last C. Roll No.; At Jurisdiction Where Enrolled (Yes/No); (If no – Where); Ward (Yes/No); Allotment, Annuity and Identification Numbers (if given).

2332; Screamer, James; M; 12/23/59-72; N.C. Cherokee; 4/4; M; Head; 2312; Yes; Yes; Unallotted

2333; Screamer, Cinda; F; 10/15/71-60; N.C. Cherokee; 4/4; M; Wife; 2313; Yes; Yes; Unallotted

2334; Screamer, Soggie; M; 7/31/93-38; N.C. Cherokee; 4/4; S; Son; 2314; No; Okla.; Yes; Unallotted

2335; Screamer, Kane; M; 9/19/91-40; N.C. Cherokee; 4/4; M; Head; 2315; Yes; Yes; Unallotted

2336; Screamer, Polly S.; F; 12/26/06-25; N.C. Cherokee; 15/16; M; Wife; 2316; Yes; Yes; Unallotted

2337; Screamer, Annie R.; F; 8/14/25-7; N.C. Cherokee; 31/32; S; Daughter; 2317; Yes; Yes; Unallotted

2338; Screamer, James; M; 1/28/29-3; N.C. Cherokee; 31/32; S; Son; 2318; Yes; Yes; Unallotted

2339; Screamer, Jennie L.; F; 3/2/32-29 days; N.C. Cherokee; 31/32; S; Daughter; ---; Yes; Yes; Unallotted

2340; Screamer, Manus; M; 9/19/82-49; N.C. Cherokee; 4/4; M; Head; 2319; Yes; Yes; Unallotted

2341; Screamer, Nannie; F; 5/18/77-54; N.C. Cherokee; 4/4; M; Wife; 2320; Yes; Yes; Unallotted

2342; Screamer, Mianna; F; 11/3/12-19; N.C. Cherokee; 4/4; S; Daughter; 2321; Yes; Yes; Unallotted

2343; Screamer, Manus, Jr.; M; 9/12/14-17; N.C. Cherokee; 4/4; S; Son; 2322; Yes; Yes; Unallotted

2344; Scruggs (Keg, Rebecca), Rebecca; F; 2/10/10-22; N.C. Cherokee; 7/8; M; Wife; 2323; Yes; Yes; Unallotted

2345; Sequoyah (Runningwolf), Ammons; M; 8/23/02-29; N.C. Cherokee; 4/4; M; Head; Separated, 2324; No; In Navy,; Yes; Unallotted

2346; Sequoyah, Ollick O.; F; 6/17/03-28; N.C. Cherokee; 4/4; M; Wife; Separated, 2325; Yes; Yes; Unallotted

2347; Sequoyah, Mable; F; 1/6/22-10; N.C. Cherokee; 4/4; S; Daughter; 2326;Yes; Yes; Unallotted

2348; Sequoyah, Ammons; M; 4/3/05-26; N.C. Cherokee; 7/8; M; Head; 2327; Yes; Yes; Unallotted

2349; Sequoyah, Kina L.L.; F; 12/4/02-29; N.C. Cherokee; 4/4; M; Wife; 2328; Yes; Yes; Unallotted

2350; Sequoyah, Willie L.; F; 2/9/30-2; N.C. Cherokee; 15/16; S; Daughter; 2329; Yes; Yes; Unallotted

Census of the **Eastern Cherokee** reservation of the **Cherokee, N.C.** jurisdiction, as of **April 1**, **1932,** taken by **R. L. Spalsbury**, Superintendent.

Key: Number; Surname, Given; Sex; Date of Birth-Age at Last Birthday; Tribe; Degree of Blood; Marital Status; Relationship to Head of Family; Last C. Roll No.; At Jurisdiction Where Enrolled (Yes/No); (If no – Where); Ward (Yes/No); Allotment, Annuity and Identification Numbers (if given).

2351; Sequoyah, Lloyd; M; 6/30/99-32; N.C. Cherokee; 4/4; M; Head; 2330; Yes; Yes; Unallotted

2352; Sequoyah, Lizzy W.; F; 7/6/01-30; N.C. Cherokee; 4/4; M; Wife; 2331; Yes; Yes; Unallotted

2353; Sequoyah, Edward; M; 6/16/19-12; N.C. Cherokee; 4/4; S; Son; 2332; Yes; Yes; Unallotted

2354; Sequoyah, Lucy; F; 12/23/22-9; N.C. Cherokee; 4/4; S; Daughter; 2333;Yes; Yes; Unallotted

2355; Sequoyah (Runningwolf) Sequoia; M; 5/15/78-53; N.C. Cherokee; 4/4; M; Head; Separated, 2334; Yes; Yes; Unallotted

2356; Sequoyah, Mollie; F; 6/11/82-49; N.C. Cherokee; 4/4; M; Wife; 2335; Yes; Yes; Unallotted

2357; Sequoyah, Minda E.; F; 6/21/18-13; N.C. Cherokee; 4/4; S; Daughter; 2336; Yes; Yes; Unallotted

2358; Sequoyah, Amanda; F; 10/27/21-10; N.C. Cherokee; 4/4; S; Daughter; 2337; Yes; Yes; Unallotted

2359; Sequoyah, Louise H.; F; 6/8/59-72; N.C. Cherokee; 7/8; Wd.; Head; 2338; Yes; Yes; Unallotted

2360; Shake-ear, Fidella; M; 12/23/71-60; N.C. Cherokee; 4/4; M; Head; 2339; Yes; Yes; Unallotted

2361; Sequoyah, Lizzie; F; 12/23/64-67; N.C. Cherokee; 4/4; M; Wife; 2340; Yes; Yes; Unallotted

2362; Shell, John; M; 12/23/58-73; N.C. Cherokee; 4/4; Wd.; Head; 2341; Yes; Yes; Unallotted

2363; Shell, Ute; M; 6/18/77-54; N.C. Cherokee; 4/4; Wd.; Head; 2342; Yes; Yes; Unallotted

2364; Shell, Joseph; M; 9/5/01-30; N.C. Cherokee; 4/4; S; Son; 2343; Yes; Yes; Unallotted

2365; Shell, Joshua; M; 8/23/08-23; N.C. Cherokee; 4/4; S; Son; 2344; Yes; Yes; Unallotted

2366; Shell, Boyd; M; 3/23/11-21; N.C. Cherokee; 4/4; S; Son; 2345; Yes; Yes; Unallotted

2367; Shell, Nancy; F; 7/20/15-16; N.C. Cherokee; 4/4; S; Daughter; 2346; Yes; Yes; Unallotted

2368; Shell, Lilly; F; 3/7/16-16; N.C. Cherokee; 4/4; S; Daughter; 2347; Yes; Yes; Unallotted

2369; Shell, Celia; F; 12/18/18-13; N.C. Cherokee; 4/4; S; Daughter; 2348; Yes; Yes; Unallotted

2370; Shell, Couney; M; 5/3/26-5; N.C. Cherokee; 4/4; S; Son; 2349; Yes; Yes; Unallotted

Census of the **Eastern Cherokee** reservation of the **Cherokee, N.C.** jurisdiction, as of **April 1** , 19**32,** taken by **R. L. Spalsbury** , Superintendent.

Key: Number; Surname, Given; Sex; Date of Birth-Age at Last Birthday; Tribe; Degree of Blood; Marital Status; Relationship to Head of Family; Last C. Roll No.; At Jurisdiction Where Enrolled (Yes/No); (If no – Where); Ward (Yes/No); Allotment, Annuity and Identification Numbers (if given).

2371; Sherrill, John; M; 11/10/73-59; N.C. Cherokee; 3/4; M; Head; 2350; Yes; Yes; Unallotted

2372; Sherrill, Mollie; F; 12/11/80-51; N.C. Cherokee; 4/4; M; Wife; 2351; Yes; Yes; Unallotted

2373; Sherrill, Julia; F; 5/27/06-25; N.C. Cherokee; 7/8; S; Daughter; 2352; Yes; Yes; Unallotted

2374; Sherrill, Samuel; M; 8/29/08-23; N.C. Cherokee; 7/8; S; Son; 2353; Yes; Yes; Unallotted

2375; Sherrill, Alice; F; 12/29/11-20; N.C. Cherokee; 7/8; S; Daughter; 2354; Yes; Yes; Unallotted

2376; Sherrill, Andy; M; 4/5/13-18; N.C. Cherokee; 7/8; S; Son; 2355; Yes; Yes; Unallotted

2377; Sherrill, Dinah; F; 7/5/15-16; N.C. Cherokee; 7/8; S; Daughter; 2356; Yes; Yes; Unallotted

2378; Sherrill (Maney, Ruth), Ruth; F; 12/06/06-25; N.C. Cherokee; 1/32; M; Wife; 2357; No; 412 N. Green St., Winston-Salem, Forsyth, N.C.; Yes; Unallotted

2379; Shook (Fr. white), Ollie May; F; 3/29/09-23; N.C. Cherokee; 1/16; S; Daughter; 2358; Yes; Yes; Unallotted

2380; Shook, Ethel; F; 5/16/11-20; N.C. Cherokee; 1/16; S; Daughter; 2359; Yes; Yes; Unallotted

2381; Shook, Clifford; M; 10/21/15-16; N.C. Cherokee; 1/16; S; Son; 2360; Yes; Yes; Unallotted

2382; Shook, Clarence; M; 3/22/19-13; N.C. Cherokee; 1/16; S; Son; 2361; Yes; Yes; Unallotted

2383; Shook, Boyd; M; 10/26/23-8; N.C. Cherokee; 1/16; S; Son; 2362; Yes; Yes; Unallotted

2384; Simpson, Martha O.; F; 1/21/76-56; N.C. Cherokee; 4/4; M; Wife; 2363; No; Cal.; Yes; Unallotted

2385; Skaggs, Nora; F; 2/15/88-44; N.C. Cherokee; 1/16; M; Wife; 2364; No; Ozark, Christian, Mo.; Yes; Unallotted

2386; Skitty, Sevier; M; 12/23/48-83; N.C. Cherokee; 4/4; S; Head; 2365; Yes; Yes; Unallotted

2387; Smith, Annie; F; 7/17/11-20; N.C. Cherokee; 5/8; S; Alone; 2366; Yes; Yes; Unallotted

2388; Smith, Rosie; F; 7/3/13-18; N.C. Cherokee; 5/8; S; Sister; 2367; Yes; Yes; Unallotted

2389; Smith, Mary; F; 2/3/15-17; N.C. Cherokee; 5/8; S; Sister; 2368; Yes; Yes; Unallotted

Census of the **Eastern Cherokee** reservation of the **Cherokee, N.C.** jurisdiction, as of **April 1** , **1932,** taken by **R. L. Spalsbury** , Superintendent.

Key: Number; Surname, Given; Sex; Date of Birth-Age at Last Birthday; Tribe; Degree of Blood; Marital Status; Relationship to Head of Family; Last C. Roll No.; At Jurisdiction Where Enrolled (Yes/No); (If no – Where); Ward (Yes/No); Allotment, Annuity and Identification Numbers (if given).

2390; Shone, Mary; F; 1876-56; N.C. Cherokee; 1/4-; M; Wife; 2369; No; (Added by O.L. 1/27/31) Yes; Unallotted

2391; Smith, Arthur; M; 4/4/85-46; N.C. Cherokee; 1/4; M; Head; 2370; No; Knoxville, Knox, Tenn.; Yes; Unallotted

2392; Smith, Oveda; F; 11/15/20-11; N.C. Cherokee; 1/8; S; Daughter; 2371; No; Knoxville, Knox, Tenn.; Yes; Unallotted

2393; Smith, Louise; F; 6/15/23-8; N.C. Cherokee; 1/8; S; Daughter; 2372; No; Knoxville, Knox, Tenn.; Yes; Unallotted

2394; Smith, David M.; M; 1/20/00-32; N.C. Cherokee; 1/4; M; Head; 2373; No; In army,; Yes; Unallotted

2395; Smith, Duffy; M; 11/26/80-51; N.C. Cherokee; 1/2; S; Head; 2374; Yes; Yes; Unallotted

2396; Smith, Frances E.; M; 3/23/86-46; N.C. Cherokee; 1/2; M; Head; 2375; Yes; Yes; Unallotted

2397; Smith, Betty W.; F; 4/1/81-50; N.C. Cherokee; 7/8; M; Wife; 2376; Yes; Yes; Unallotted

2398; Smith, Victor C.; M; 4/11/11-20; N.C. Cherokee; 11/16; S; Son; 2377; Yes; Yes; Unallotted

2399; Smith, Edgar A.; M; 9/18/12-19; N.C. Cherokee; 11/16; S; Son; 2378; Yes; Yes; Unallotted

2400; Smith, Clifford; M; 4/12/14-17; N.C. Cherokee; 11/16; S; Son; 2379; Yes; Yes; Unallotted

2401; Smith, Alvin E.; M; 6/5/16-15; N.C. Cherokee; 11/16; S; Son; 2380; Yes; Yes; Unallotted

2402; Smith, Sheridan; M; 11/24/17-14; N.C. Cherokee; 11/16; S; Son; 2381; Yes; Yes; Unallotted

2403; Smith, Frances; F; 8/6/20-11; N.C. Cherokee; 11/16; S; Daughter; 2382; Yes; Yes; Unallotted

2404; Smith, Leta B.; F; 11/27/24-7; N.C. Cherokee; 11/16; S; Daughter; 2383; Yes; Yes; Unallotted

2405; Smith, George L.; M; 12/25/80-51; N.C. Cherokee; 3/8; M; Head; 2384; No; Bristol, Bucks, Pa.; Yes; Unallotted

2406; Smith, Harley; M; 3/26/13-19; N.C. Cherokee; 1/8; S; Alone; 2385; Yes; Yes; Unallotted

2407; Smith, Hartman; M; 10/15/97-34; N.C. Cherokee; 3/16; M; Head; 2386; Yes; Yes; Unallotted

Census of the **Eastern Cherokee** reservation of the **Cherokee, N.C.** jurisdiction, as of **April 1** , 19**32,** taken by **R. L. Spalsbury** , Superintendent.

Key: Number; Surname, Given; Sex; Date of Birth-Age at Last Birthday; Tribe; Degree of Blood; Marital Status; Relationship to Head of Family; Last C. Roll No.; At Jurisdiction Where Enrolled (Yes/No); (If no – Where); Ward (Yes/No); Allotment, Annuity and Identification Numbers (if given).

2408; Smith (Mr. white[sic]); Russel; M; 8/2/04-27; N.C. Cherokee; 3/8; S; Head; 2387; Yes; Yes; Unallotted

2409; Smith, Myrtle; F; 12/13/08-23; N.C. Cherokee; 3/8; S; Sister; 2388; Yes; Yes; Unallotted

2410; Smith, Bessie; F; 9/29/13-18; N.C. Cherokee; 3/8; S; Sister; 2389; Yes; Yes; Unallotted

2411; Smith, Henry; M; 9/12/91-40; N.C. Cherokee; 1/4; M; Head; 2390; No; Maryville, Blount, Tenn.; Yes; Unallotted

2412; Smith, Juanetta; F; 2/28/21-11; N.C. Cherokee; 1/8; S; Daughter; 2391; No; Maryville, Blount, Tenn.; Yes; Unallotted

2413; Smith, Henry H. Jr.; M; 5/16/24-8; N.C. Cherokee; 1/8; S; Son; 2392; No; Maryville, Blount, Tenn.; Yes; Unallotted

2414; Smith, Jacob L.; M; 12/23/79-52; N.C. Cherokee; 5/8; M; Head; 2393; Yes; Yes; Unallotted

2415; Smith, Ollie; F; 8/12/76-55; N.C. Cherokee; 4/4; M; Wife; 2394; Yes; Yes; Unallotted

2416; Smith, Lawrence; M; 3/20/07-25; N.C. Cherokee; 13/16; S; Son; 2395; Yes; Yes; Unallotted

2417; Smith, Charles H.; M; 1/11/11-21; N.C. Cherokee; 13/16; S; Son; 2396; Yes; Yes; Unallotted

2418; Smith, Arthur; M; 11/30/12-19; N.C. Cherokee; 13/16; S; Son; 2397; Yes; Yes; Unallotted

2419; Smith, Bernice; F; 4/26/16-15; N.C. Cherokee; 13/16; S; Daughter; 2398; Yes; Yes; Unallotted

2420; Smith, James D.; M; 4/25/78-53; N.C. Cherokee; 1/2; M; Head; 2399; Yes; Yes; Unallotted

2421; Smith, Bertha; F; 1/23/14-18; N.C. Cherokee; 1/4; S; Daughter; 2400; Yes; Yes; Unallotted

2422; Smith, John Ross; M; 4/25/16-15; N.C. Cherokee; 1/4; S; Son; 2401; Yes; Yes; Unallotted

2423; Smith, Ethel L.; F; 11/25/31-4/12; N.C. Cherokee; 1/4; S; Daughter; ---; Yes; Yes; Unallotted

2424; Smith, James G.W.; M; 3/26/94-38; N.C. Cherokee; 1/8; M; Head; 2402; Yes; Yes; Unallotted

2425; Smith, Zelma R.; F; 11/25/14-17; N.C. Cherokee; 1/16; S; Daughter; 2403; Yes; Yes; Unallotted

2426; Smith, Gladys; F; 6/18/17-14; N.C. Cherokee; 1/16; S; Daughter; 2404; Yes; Yes; Unallotted

2427; Smith, John D.; M; 11/17/06-25; N.C. Cherokee; 7/16; M; Head; 2405; Yes; Yes; Unallotted

Census of the **Eastern Cherokee** reservation of the **Cherokee, N.C.** jurisdiction, as of **April 1**, 1932, taken by **R. L. Spalsbury**, Superintendent.

Key: Number; Surname, Given; Sex; Date of Birth-Age at Last Birthday; Tribe; Degree of Blood; Marital Status; Relationship to Head of Family; Last C. Roll No.; At Jurisdiction Where Enrolled (Yes/No); (If no – Where); Ward (Yes/No); Allotment, Annuity and Identification Numbers (if given).

2428; Smith, Mary M.; F; 2/10/30-2; N.C. Cherokee; 7/32; S; Daughter; 2406; Yes; Yes; Unallotted

2429; Smith, John Q.A.; M; 8/12/70-61; N.C. Cherokee; 1/4; M; Head; 2407; Yes; Yes; Unallotted

2430; Smith, Robert S.; M; 4/1/04-27; N.C. Cherokee; 1/8; S; Son; 2408; Yes; Yes; Unallotted

2431; Smith, Ross B.; M; 12/25/07-24; N.C. Cherokee; 1/8; S; Son; 2409; Yes; Yes; Unallotted

2432; Smith, (Bates, Lizzie), Lizzie; F; 7/28/02-29; N.C. Cherokee; 1/16; S; Head; 2410; Yes; Yes; Unallotted

2433; Smith, Oscar G.; M; 6/21/21-10; N.C. Cherokee; 1/32; S; Son; 2411; Yes; Yes; Unallotted

2434; Smith, Lloyd H.; M; 2/25/73-59; N.C. Cherokee; 7/8; M; Head; 2412; Yes; Yes; Unallotted

2435; Smith, Dovi; F; 2/22/09-23; N.C. Cherokee; 7/16; S; Daughter; 2413; Yes; Yes; Unallotted

2436; Smith, Nancy; F; 12/23/51-80; N.C. Cherokee; 4/4; Wd.; Head; 2414; Yes; Yes; Unallotted

2437; Smith, Margaret; F; 2/9/12-20; N.C. Cherokee; 1/64; S; Daughter; 2415; Yes; Yes; Unallotted

2438; Smith, Earlie; M; 5/6/14-17; N.C. Cherokee; 1/64; S; Son; 2416; Yes; Yes; Unallotted

2439; Smith, Marshall; M; 9/12/97-34; N.C. Cherokee; 1/16; S; Head; 2417; Yes; Yes; Unallotted

2440; Smith, (Raper, Mary), Mary; F; 4/30/01-30; N.C. Cherokee; 1/16; M; Wife; 2418; Yes; Yes; Unallotted

2441; Smith, Edna; F; 8/30/20-11; N.C. Cherokee; 1/32; S; Daughter; 2419; Yes; Yes; Unallotted

2442; Smith, Mary M.; F; 6/18/52-79; N.C. Cherokee; 1/4; Wd.; Head; 2420; Yes; Yes; Unallotted

2443; Smith, Minnie; F; 12/3/17-14; N.C. Cherokee; 1/8; S; Alone; 2421; Yes; Yes; Unallotted

2444; Smith, Noah; M; 9/5/03-28; N.C. Cherokee; 7/16; M; Head; 2422; Yes; Yes; Unallotted

2445; Smith, Stella A.; F; 11/7/07-24; N.C. Cherokee; 1/16; M; Wife; 2423; Yes; Yes; Unallotted

129

Census of the **Eastern Cherokee** reservation of the **Cherokee, N.C.** jurisdiction, as of **April 1** , 19**32,** taken by **R. L. Spalsbury** , Superintendent.

Key: Number; Surname, Given; Sex; Date of Birth-Age at Last Birthday; Tribe; Degree of Blood; Marital Status; Relationship to Head of Family; Last C. Roll No.; At Jurisdiction Where Enrolled (Yes/No); (If no – Where); Ward (Yes/No); Allotment, Annuity and Identification Numbers (if given).

2446; Smith, Philip H.; M; 6/24/29-2; N.C. Cherokee; 1/4; S; Son; 2424; Yes; Yes; Unallotted

2447; Smith, Noah Ed.; M; 3/27/83-49; N.C. Cherokee; 1/2; M; Head; 2425; No; Wis.; Yes; Unallotted

2448; Smith, Oliver; M; 10/31/96-35; N.C. Cherokee; 1/2; M; Head; 2426; Yes; Yes; Unallotted

2449; Smith, Nan S.; F; 8/7/90-41; N.C. Cherokee; 4/4; M; Wife; 2427; Yes; Yes; Unallotted

2450; Smith, Charlotte; F; 8/28/16-15; N.C. Cherokee; 3/4; S; Daughter; 2428; Yes; Yes; Unallotted

2451; Smith, Milton P.; M; 4/27/19-12; N.C. Cherokee; 3/4; S; Son; 2429; Yes; Yes; Unallotted

2452; Smith, Roberson; M; 5/2/00-31; N.C. Cherokee; 7/16; M; Head; 2430; Yes; Yes; Unallotted

2453; Smith, Jarret J.; M; 6/3/23-8; N.C. Cherokee; 7/32; S; Son; 2431; Yes; Yes; Unallotted

2454; Smith, Joseph A.; M; 5/31/25-6; N.C. Cherokee; 7/32; S; Son; 2432; Yes; Yes; Unallotted

2455; Smith, Samuel A.; M; 2/25/64-68; N.C. Cherokee; 1/4; M; Head; 2433; Yes; Yes; Unallotted

2456; Smith, Goldman; M; 12/14/98-33; N.C. Cherokee; 1/4; S; Son; 2434; Yes; Yes; Unallotted

2457; Smith, Jesse H.; M; 4/14/03-28; N.C. Cherokee; 1/4; S; Son; 2435; Yes; Yes; Unallotted

2458; Smith, Martin; M; 11/7/12-19; N.C. Cherokee; 1/8; S; Son; 2437; Yes; Yes; Unallotted

2459; Smith, Sallie; F; 3/7/14-18; N.C. Cherokee; 1/8; S; Daughter; 2438; Yes; Yes; Unallotted

2460; Smith, Franklin; M; 1/11/16-16; N.C. Cherokee; 1/8; S; Son; 2439; Yes; Yes; Unallotted

2461; Smith, James; M; 9/8/17-14; N.C. Cherokee; 1/8; S; Son; 2440; Yes; Yes; Unallotted

2462; Smith, Toddie; F; 4/3/20-11; N.C. Cherokee; 1/8; S; Daughter; 2441; Yes; Yes; Unallotted

2463; Smith, Tiney Mae; F; 5/20/22-9; N.C. Cherokee; 1/8; S; Daughter; 2442; Yes; Yes; Unallotted

2464; Smith, Henry; M; 4/7/24-7; N.C. Cherokee; 1/8; S; Son; 2443; Yes; Yes; Unallotted

2465; Smith, Levi; M; 7/4/28-3; N.C. Cherokee; 1/8; S; Son; 2444; Yes; Yes; Unallotted

Census of the **Eastern Cherokee** reservation of the **Cherokee, N.C.** jurisdiction, as of **April 1**, **1932**, taken by **R. L. Spalsbury**, Superintendent.

Key: Number; Surname, Given; Sex; Date of Birth-Age at Last Birthday; Tribe; Degree of Blood; Marital Status; Relationship to Head of Family; Last C. Roll No.; At Jurisdiction Where Enrolled (Yes/No); (If no – Where); Ward (Yes/No); Allotment, Annuity and Identification Numbers (if given).

2466; Smith, Thaddeus S.; M; 8/13/78-53; N.C. Cherokee; 3/8; M; Head; 2445; Yes; Yes; Unallotted

2467; Smith, Muriel; F; 12/31/09-22; N.C. Cherokee; 3/16; S; Daughter; 2446; Yes; Yes; Unallotted

2468; Smith, Helen; F; 11/3/12-19; N.C. Cherokee; 3/16; S; Daughter; 2447; Yes; Yes; Unallotted

2469; Smith, Carrie E.; F; 2/19/15-17; N.C. Cherokee; 3/16; S; Daughter; 2448; Yes; Yes; Unallotted

2470; Smith, Ruby M.; F; 4/12/18-13; N.C. Cherokee; 3/16; S; Daughter; 2449; Yes; Yes; Unallotted

2471; Smith, Phoebe E.; F; 9/27/21-10; N.C. Cherokee; 3/16; S; Daughter; 2450; Yes; Yes; Unallotted

2472; Smith, Sibbald; M; 2/3/29-3; N.C. Cherokee; 3/16; S; Son; 2451; Yes; Yes; Unallotted

2473; Smith, Zona F.; F; 2/5/31-1; N.C. Cherokee; 3/16; S; Daughter; 2452; Yes; Yes; Unallotted

2474; Smith, Thomas; M; 4/15/83-48; N.C. Cherokee; 7/8; M; Head; 2453; Yes; Yes; Unallotted

2475; Smith, Budford; M; 7/10/09-22; N.C. Cherokee; 7/16; S; Son; 2454; Yes; Yes; Unallotted

2476; Smith, Leuna; F; 4/10/11-20; N.C. Cherokee; 7/16; S; Daughter; 2455; Yes; Yes; Unallotted

2477; Smith, Hosea G.; M; 4/15/13-18; N.C. Cherokee; 7/16; S; Son; 2456; Yes; Yes; Unallotted

2478; Smith, Gertrude; F; 11/6/16-15; N.C. Cherokee; 7/16; S; Daughter; 2457; Yes; Yes; Unallotted

2479; Smith, Rachel; F; 6/13/20-11; N.C. Cherokee; 7/16; S; Daughter; 2458; Yes; Yes; Unallotted

2480; Smith, James E.; M; 4/13/23-8; N.C. Cherokee; 7/16; S; Son; 2459; Yes; Yes; Unallotted

2481; Smith, Alyne; F; 12/28/30-1; N.C. Cherokee; 1/4; S; Granddau.; 2460; Yes; Yes; Unallotted

2482; Smoker, Charles; M; 1/5/04-28; N.C. Cherokee; 4/4; S; Head; 2461; Yes; Yes; Unallotted

2483; Smoker (Mr.[sic] Hettie Smoker Rattler), Dinah; F; 3/19/21-11; N.C. Cherokee; 4/4; S; Daughter; 2462; Yes; Yes; Unallotted

2484; Smoker, Davidson; M; 12/13/11-20; N.C. Cherokee; 4/4; S; Son; 2463; Yes; Yes; Unallotted

2485; Smoker, Owen; M; 2/24/14-18; N.C. Cherokee; 4/4; S; Son; 2464; Yes; Yes; Unallotted

Census of the **Eastern Cherokee** reservation of the **Cherokee, N.C.** jurisdiction, as of **April 1** , 19**32,** taken by **R. L. Spalsbury** , Superintendent.

Key: Number; Surname, Given; Sex; Date of Birth-Age at Last Birthday; Tribe; Degree of Blood; Marital Status; Relationship to Head of Family; Last C. Roll No.; At Jurisdiction Where Enrolled (Yes/No); (If no – Where); Ward (Yes/No); Allotment, Annuity and Identification Numbers (if given).

2486; Smoker, Lloyd; M; 1/18/71-61; N.C. Cherokee; 4/4; Wd.; Head; 2465; Yes; Yes; Unallotted

2487; Smoker, Moses (Ross); M; 11/27/97-34; N.C. Cherokee; 4/4; Wd.; Head; 2466; Yes; Yes; Unallotted

2488; Smoker, Will S.; M; 1/5/71-61; N.C. Cherokee; 4/4; M; Head; 2467; Yes; Yes; Unallotted
2489; Smoker, Alkinney; F; 1/5/78-54; N.C. Cherokee; 4/4; M; Wife; 2468; Yes; Yes; Unallotted
2490; Smoker, Lucy; F; 1/7/07-25; N.C. Cherokee; 4/4; S; Daughter; 2469; Yes; Yes; Unallotted
2491; Smoker, Martha B.; F; 6/9/09-22; N.C. Cherokee; 4/4; S; Daughter; 2470; Yes; Yes; Unallotted
2492; Smoker, Ute; M; 3/20/12-20; N.C. Cherokee; 4/4; S; Son; 2471; Yes; Yes; Unallotted
2493; Smoker, Bessie; F; 5/30/14-17; N.C. Cherokee; 4/4; S; Daughter; 2472; Yes; Yes; Unallotted
2494; Smoker, Amanda; F; 12/13/16-15; N.C. Cherokee; 4/4; S; Daughter; 2473; Yes; Yes; Unallotted
2495; Smoker, Jack C.; M; 8/28/19-12; N.C. Cherokee; 4/4; S; Son; 2474; Yes; Yes; Unallotted

2496; Sneed, Annie L.; F; 11/30/97-34; N.C. Cherokee; 1/8; S; Mother; 2475; Yes; Yes; Unallotted
2497; Sneed, Gladys E.; F; 4/29/23-8; N.C. Cherokee; 1/16; S; Daughter (Illeg.); 2476; Yes; Yes; Unallotted

2498; Sneed, Blakely; M; 11/1/04-27; N.C. Cherokee; 1/16; M; Head; 2477; Yes; Yes; Unallotted

2499; Sneed, Campbell; M; 11/20/87-44; N.C. Cherokee; 1/8; M; Head; 2478; Yes; Yes; Unallotted
2500; Sneed, Minda B.; F; 11/28/89-42; N.C. Cherokee; 1/2; M; Wife; 2479; Yes; Yes; Unallotted
2501; Sneed, Carrie; F; 7/18/08-23; N.C. Cherokee; 5/16; S; Daughter; 2480; Yes; Yes; Unallotted
2502; Sneed, Ernest; M; 4/20/10-21; N.C. Cherokee; 5/16; S; Son; 2481; Yes; Yes; Unallotted
2503; Sneed, Pocahontas; F; 11/12/11-20; N.C. Cherokee; 5/16; S; Daughter; 2482; Yes; Yes; Unallotted
2504; Sneed, Patrick; M; 4/25/13-18; N.C. Cherokee; 5/16; S; Son; 2483; Yes; Yes; Unallotted
2505; Sneed, Claudia M.; F; 4/20/15-16; N.C. Cherokee; 5/16; S; Daughter; 2484; Yes; Yes; Unallotted

Census of the **Eastern Cherokee** reservation of the **Cherokee, N.C.** jurisdiction, as of **April 1** , 19**32,** taken by **R. L. Spalsbury** , Superintendent.

Key: Number; Surname, Given; Sex; Date of Birth-Age at Last Birthday; Tribe; Degree of Blood; Marital Status; Relationship to Head of Family; Last C. Roll No.; At Jurisdiction Where Enrolled (Yes/No); (If no – Where); Ward (Yes/No); Allotment, Annuity and Identification Numbers (if given).

2506; Sneed, Marie; F; 10/18/17-14; N.C. Cherokee; 5/16; S; Daughter; 2485; Yes; Yes; Unallotted

2507; Sneed, Virginia; F; 12/29/20-11; N.C. Cherokee; 5/16; S; Daughter; 2486; Yes; Yes; Unallotted

2508; Sneed, Vernon; M; 1/7/22-10; N.C. Cherokee; 5/16; S; Son; 2487; Yes; Yes; Unallotted

2509; Sneed, Winifred; F; 3/25/24-7; N.C. Cherokee; 5/16; S; Daughter; 2488; Yes; Yes; Unallotted

2510; Sneed, Priscilla; F; 10/8/28-3; N.C. Cherokee; 5/16; S; Daughter; 2489; Yes; Yes; Unallotted

2511; Sneed, Gertha; F; 3/13/32-18 days; N.C. Cherokee; 5/16; S; Granddau.; ---; Yes; Yes; Unallotted

2512; Sneed, James P.; M; 9/7/61-70; N.C. Cherokee; 1/4; M; Head; 2490; Yes; Yes; Unallotted

2513; Sneed, Manco; M; 2/18/85-47; N.C. Cherokee; 1/8; M; Head; 2491; Yes; Yes; Unallotted

2514; Sneed, Rosebud; F; 3/29/91-41; N.C. Cherokee; 1/8; M; Wife; 2492; Yes; Yes; Unallotted

2515; Sneed, Lawrence; M; 6/13/12-19; N.C. Cherokee; 1/8; S; Son; 2493; Yes; Yes; Unallotted

2516; Sneed, Dakota; F; 9/22/15-16; N.C. Cherokee; 1/8; S; Daughter; 2494; Yes; Yes; Unallotted

2517; Sneed, Mary; F; 8/29/17-14; N.C. Cherokee; 1/8; S; Daughter; 2495; Yes; Yes; Unallotted

2518; Sneed, Martha; F; 8/29/17-14; N.C. Cherokee; 1/8; S; Daughter; 2496; Yes; Yes; Unallotted

2519; Sneed, Ella; F; 7/10/20-11; N.C. Cherokee; 1/8; S; Daughter; 2497; Yes; Yes; Unallotted

2520; Sneed, Russell; M; 10/2/24-7; N.C. Cherokee; 1/8; S; Son; 2498; Yes; Yes; Unallotted

2521; Sneed, Irene; F; 4/6/27-4; N.C. Cherokee; 1/8; S; Daughter; 2499; Yes; Yes; Unallotted

2522; Sneed, Osco; M; 3/10/79-53; N.C. Cherokee; 1/8; M; Head; 2500; Yes; Yes; Unallotted

2523; Sneed, Thomas M.; M; 2/20/07-25; N.C. Cherokee; 1/16; S; Son; 2501; Yes; Yes; Unallotted

2524; Sneed, John G.; M; 5/29/14-17; N.C. Cherokee; 1/16; S; Son; 2502; Yes; Yes; Unallotted

2525; Sneed, Charlotte; F; 2/28/17-15; N.C. Cherokee; 1/16; S; Daughter; 2503; Yes; Yes; Unallotted

2526; Sneed, Elba; F; 2/15/19-13; N.C. Cherokee; 1/16; S; Daughter; 2504; Yes; Yes; Unallotted

Census of the **Eastern Cherokee** reservation of the **Cherokee, N.C.** jurisdiction, as of **April 1** , 19**32,** taken by **R. L. Spalsbury** , Superintendent.

Key: Number; Surname, Given; Sex; Date of Birth-Age at Last Birthday; Tribe; Degree of Blood; Marital Status; Relationship to Head of Family; Last C. Roll No.; At Jurisdiction Where Enrolled (Yes/No); (If no – Where); Ward (Yes/No); Allotment, Annuity and Identification Numbers (if given).

2527; Sneed, Kenneth O.; M; 3/21/22-10; N.C. Cherokee; 1/16; S; Son; 2505; Yes; Yes; Unallotted

2528; Sneed, Peco; M; 9/25/75-56; N.C. Cherokee; 1/8; M; Head; 2506; Yes; Yes; Unallotted

2529; Sneed, Lillian K.; F; 4/12/10-21; N.C. Cherokee; 1/16; S; Daughter; 2507; Yes; Yes; Unallotted

2530; Sneed, Woodrow; M; 2/10/13-19; N.C. Cherokee; 1/16; S; Son; 2508; Yes; Yes; Unallotted

2531; Sneed, Mildred R.; F; 3/28/16-16; N.C. Cherokee; 1/16; S; Daughter; 2509; Yes; Yes; Unallotted

2532; Sneed, Savannah; F; 4/13/19-12; N.C. Cherokee; 1/16; S; Daughter; 2510; Yes; Yes; Unallotted

2533; Sneed, John B.; M; 12/5/22-9; N.C. Cherokee; 1/16; S; Son; 2511; Yes; Yes; Unallotted

2534; Sneed, William S.; M; 3/28/62-70; N.C. Cherokee; 1/4; M; Head; 2512; Yes; Yes; Unallotted

2535; Souther (Cole, Dora), Dora C.; F; 6/15/88-43; N.C. Cherokee; 1/8; M; Wife; 2513; No; Blairsville, Union, Ga.; Yes; Unallotted

2536; Souther, Delpha; F; 9/19/08-23; N.C. Cherokee; 1/16; S; Daughter; 2514; No; Blairsville, Union, Ga.; Yes; Unallotted

2537; Souther, Hartford; M; 9/7/10-21; N.C. Cherokee; 1/16; S; Son; 2515; No; Blairsville, Union, Ga.; Yes; Unallotted

2538; Souther, Myrtle; F; 1/23/13-19; N.C. Cherokee; 1/16; S; Daughter; 2516; No; Blairsville, Union, Ga.; Yes; Unallotted

2539; Souther, Deva; F; 7/2/15-16; N.C. Cherokee; 1/16; S; Daughter; 2517; No; Blairsville, Union, Ga.; Yes; Unallotted

2540; Souther, Vaughn; M; 7/11/17-14; N.C. Cherokee; 1/16; S; Son; 2518; No; Blairsville, Union, Ga.; Yes; Unallotted

2541; Souther, Ina; F; 3/30/20-12; N.C. Cherokee; 1/16; S; Daughter; 2519; No; Blairsville, Union, Ga.; Yes; Unallotted

2542; Spencer, Roxie S.; F; 5/5/87-44; N.C. Cherokee; 7/8; M; Wife; 2520; Yes; Yes; Unallotted

2543; Spray, Gertrude S.; F; 6/17/94-37; N.C. Cherokee; 7/8; S; Head; 2521; Yes; Yes; Unallotted

2544; Squirrel, Daniel; M; 2/4/04-28; N.C. Cherokee; 4/4; S; Head; 2522; Yes; Yes; Unallotted

2545; Squirrel, Ollie; F; 3/22/06-26; N.C. Cherokee; 4/4; S; Sister; 2523; Yes; Yes; Unallotted

Census of the **Eastern Cherokee** reservation of the **Cherokee, N.C.** jurisdiction, as of **April 1** , **1932,** taken by **R. L. Spalsbury** , Superintendent.

Key: Number; Surname, Given; Sex; Date of Birth-Age at Last Birthday; Tribe; Degree of Blood; Marital Status; Relationship to Head of Family; Last C. Roll No.; At Jurisdiction Where Enrolled (Yes/No); (If no – Where); Ward (Yes/No); Allotment, Annuity and Identification Numbers (if given).

2546; Squirrel, Sheperd; M; 4/28/08-23; N.C. Cherokee; 4/4; S; Brother; 2524; Yes; Yes; Unallotted

2547; Squirrel, Abel; M; 5/20/10-21; N.C. Cherokee; 4/4; S; Brother; 2525; Yes; Yes; Unallotted

2548; Squirrel, David; M; 7/6/14-17; N.C. Cherokee; 4/4; S; Brother; 2526; Yes; Yes; Unallotted

2549; Squirrel, George; M; 4/15/68-63; N.C. Cherokee; 4/4; M; Head; 2527; Yes; Yes; Unallotted

2550; Squirrel, Rebecca; F; 5/17/72-59; N.C. Cherokee; 4/4; M; Wife; 2528; Yes; Yes; Unallotted

2551; Squirrel, Sequechee; M; 5/8/00-31; N.C. Cherokee; 4/4; S; Son; 2529; Yes; Yes; Unallotted

2552; Squirrel, Kinsey; M; 4/8/96-35; N.C. Cherokee; 4/4; M; Head; 2530; Yes; Yes; Unallotted

2553; Squirrel, Lydia T.W.; F; 1/20/91-41; N.C. Cherokee; 13/16; M; Wife; 2531; Yes; Yes; Unallotted

2554; Squirrel, Emma; F; 7/4/20-11; N.C. Cherokee; 29/32; S; Daughter; 2532; Yes; Yes; Unallotted

2555; Squirrel, Adam; M; 8/10/24-7; N.C. Cherokee; 1/4+; S; Son; 2533; Yes; Yes; Unallotted

2556; Squirrel, Abel; M; 8/15/27-4; N.C. Cherokee; 1/4+; S; Son; 2534; Yes; Yes; Unallotted

2557; Squirrel, Gene T.; M; 3/26/30-2; N.C. Cherokee; 29/32; S; Son; 2535; Yes; Yes; Unallotted

2558; Stalcup (Thompson, Atha), Atha W.; F; 12/19/02-29; N.C. Cherokee; 1/16; M; Wife; 2536; No; Taft, Kern, Cal.; Yes; Unallotted

2559; Standingdeer, Margaret; F; 11/15/54-77; N.C. Cherokee; 4/4; Wd.; Head; 2537; Yes; Yes; Unallotted

2560; Standingdeer, Carl; M; 12/12/81-50; N.C. Cherokee; 4/4; M; Head; 2538; Yes; Yes; Unallotted

2561; Standingdeer, Anna Tooni; F; 11/14/76-55; N.C. Cherokee; 4/4; M; Wife 2nd; 2539; Yes; Yes; Unallotted

2562; Standingdeer, Roxanna; F; 10/9/11-20; N.C. Cherokee; 13/16; S; Daughter; 2540; Yes; Yes; Unallotted

2563; Standingdeer, Virginia; F; 4/14/08-23; N.C. Cherokee; 13/16; S; Daughter; 2541; Yes; Yes; Unallotted

2564; Standingdeer, Mary Janet; F; 9/26/13-18; N.C. Cherokee; 13/16; S; Daughter; 2542; Yes; Yes; Unallotted

2565; Standingdeer, Carl, Jr.; M; 1/11/15-17; N.C. Cherokee; 13/16; S; Son; 2543; Yes; Yes; Unallotted

Census of the **Eastern Cherokee** reservation of the **Cherokee, N.C.** jurisdiction, as of **April 1** , 19**32,** taken by **R. L. Spalsbury** , Superintendent.

Key: Number; Surname, Given; Sex; Date of Birth-Age at Last Birthday; Tribe; Degree of Blood; Marital Status; Relationship to Head of Family; Last C. Roll No.; At Jurisdiction Where Enrolled (Yes/No); (If no – Where); Ward (Yes/No); Allotment, Annuity and Identification Numbers (if given).

2566; Standingdeer, Junaluska; M; 12/12/81-50; N.C. Cherokee; 4/4; M; Head; 2544; No; Minneapolis, Hennepin, Minn.; Yes; Unallotted

2567; Standingdeer, Lowen; M; 11/14/82-49; N.C. Cherokee; 4/4; M; Head; 2545; Yes; Yes; Unallotted

2568; Standingdeer, Nannie S.; F; 4/18/94-37; N.C. Cherokee; 15/16; M; Wife; 2546; Yes; Yes; Unallotted

2569; Standingdeer, Simon; M; 7/14/21-10; N.C. Cherokee; 31/32; S; Son; 2547; Yes; Yes; Unallotted

2570; Standingdeer, Alex; M; 12/24/58-73; N.C. Cherokee; 4/4; Wd.; Head; 2548; Yes; Yes; Unallotted

2571; Standingdeer (Lambert), Sallie Ann; F; 4/28/09-22; N.C. Cherokee; 1/2; M; Wife; 2549; Yes; Yes; Unallotted

2572; Standingdeer, Caroline S.; F; 9/17/28-3; N.C. Cherokee; 1/4; S; Daughter; 2550; Yes; Yes; Unallotted

2573; Lambert, Dorothy; F; 9/19/30-1; N.C. Cherokee; 17/64; S; Daughter; 2551; Yes; Yes; Unallotted

2574; Stamper, Ned; M; 7/12/68-63; N.C. Cherokee; 3/4; M; Head; 2552; Yes; Yes; Unallotted

2575; Stamper, Sallie Ann; F; 5/15/75-56; N.C. Cherokee; 3/4; M; Wife; 2553; Yes; Yes; Unallotted

2576; Stamper, Sarah; F; 10/15/07-24; N.C. Cherokee; 3/4; S; Daughter; 2554; Yes; Yes; Unallotted

2577; Stamper, Robertson; M; 2/13/12-20; N.C. Cherokee; 3/4; S; Son; 2555; Yes; Yes; Unallotted

2578; Stamper, Margaret; F; 7/8/14-17; N.C. Cherokee; 3/4; S; Daughter; 2556; Yes; Yes; Unallotted

2579; Stamper, William; M; 2/14/01-30; N.C. Cherokee; 3/4; M; Head; 2557; Yes; Yes; Unallotted

2580; Stamper, Lottie Q.; F; 1/4/07-25; N.C. Cherokee; 5/8; M; Wife; 2558; Yes; Yes; Unallotted

2581; Stepp, Ida M.A.; F; 6/27/08-23; N.C. Cherokee; 1/32; M; Wife; 2559; Yes; Yes; Unallotted

2582; Stiles, Gilbert; M; 6/6/93-38; N.C. Cherokee; 1/32; M; Head; 2560; No; Marble, Cherokee, N.C.; Yes; Unallotted

2583; Stiles, Annie P.; F; 8/30/18-13; N.C. Cherokee; 1/64; S; Daughter; 2561; No; Marble, Cherokee, N.C.; Yes; Unallotted

2584; Stiles, Forrest J.; M; 10/19/19-12; N.C. Cherokee; 1/64; S; Son; 2562; No; Marble, Cherokee, N.C.; Yes; Unallotted

Census of the **Eastern Cherokee** reservation of the **Cherokee, N.C.** jurisdiction, as of **April 1** , **1932,** taken by **R. L. Spalsbury** , Superintendent.

Key: Number; Surname, Given; Sex; Date of Birth-Age at Last Birthday; Tribe; Degree of Blood; Marital Status; Relationship to Head of Family; Last C. Roll No.; At Jurisdiction Where Enrolled (Yes/No); (If no – Where); Ward (Yes/No); Allotment, Annuity and Identification Numbers (if given).

2585; Stiles, Jessie E.; F; 5/1/21-10; N.C. Cherokee; 1/64; S; Daughter; 2563; No; Marble, Cherokee, N.C.; Yes; Unallotted

2586; Stiles (Loudermilk, Hollie), Hollie L.; F; 9/24/88-43; N.C. Cherokee; 1/16; M; Wife; 2564; No; Culberson, Cherokee, N.C.; Yes; Unallotted

2587; Stiles, Floyd; M; 9/10/10-21; N.C. Cherokee; 1/32; S; Son; 2565; No; Culberson, Cherokee, N.C.; Yes; Unallotted

2588; Stiles, Sadie Lee; F; 8/10/12-19; N.C. Cherokee; 1/32; S; Daughter; 2566; No; Culberson, Cherokee, N.C.; Yes; Unallotted

2589; Stiles, Wm. S.; M; 8/26/15-16; N.C. Cherokee; 1/32; S; Son; 2567; No; Culberson, Cherokee, N.C.; Yes; Unallotted

2590; Stiles, Elsie V.; F; 12/4/17-14; N.C. Cherokee; 1/32; S; Daughter; 2568; No; Culberson, Cherokee, N.C.; Yes; Unallotted

2591; Stiles, Beulah R.; F; 2/22/20-12; N.C. Cherokee; 1/32; S; Daughter; 2569; No; Culberson, Cherokee, N.C.; Yes; Unallotted

2592; Stiles, Hazel; F; 9/15/22-9; N.C. Cherokee; 1/32; S; Daughter; 2570; No; Culberson, Cherokee, N.C.; Yes; Unallotted

2593; Stiles, Floyd; M; 3/16/05-27; N.C. Cherokee; 1/32; M; Head; 2571; Yes; Yes; Unallotted

2594; Stiles, Lester T.; M; 10/7/98-33; N.C. Cherokee; 1/32; M; Head; 2572; No; Gastonia, Gaston, N.C.; Yes; Unallotted

2595; Stiles, Evelyn E.; F; 2/24/21-11; N.C. Cherokee; 1/64; S; Daughter; 2573; No; Gastonia, Gaston, N.C.; Yes; Unallotted

2596; Stiles, Mary C.; F; 2/31/23-9; N.C. Cherokee; 1/64; S; Daughter; 2574; No; Gastonia, Gaston, N.C.; Yes; Unallotted

2597; Stiles (Raper, Lula), Lula; F; 12/8/08-23; N.C. Cherokee; 1/16; M; Wife; 2575; No; Oak Park, Cherokee, N.C.; Yes; Unallotted

2598; Stiles (Payne, Mary), Mary; F; 12/22/69-62; N.C. Cherokee; 1/16; M; Wife; 2576; Yes; Yes; Unallotted

2599; Stiles, Clem O.; M; 9/6/03-28; N.C. Cherokee; 1/32; S; Son; 2577; Yes; Yes; Unallotted

2600; Stiles, Hal V.; M; 3/5/06-26; N.C. Cherokee; 1/32; S; Son; 2578; Yes; Yes; Unallotted

2601; Stiles, Oliver; M; 2/22/98-34; N.C. Cherokee; 1/32; M; Head; 2579; No; Marble, Cherokee, N.C.; Yes; Unallotted

2602; Stiles, Herman; M; 10/20/19-12; N.C. Cherokee; 1/64; S; Son; 2580; No; Marble, Cherokee, N.C.; Yes; Unallotted

2603; Stiles, Kenneth; M; 6/20/21-10; N.C. Cherokee; 1/64; S; Son; 2581; No; Marble, Cherokee, N.C.; Yes; Unallotted

Census of the **Eastern Cherokee** reservation of the **Cherokee, N.C.** jurisdiction, as of **April 1**, 19**32**, taken by **R. L. Spalsbury**, Superintendent.

Key: Number; Surname, Given; Sex; Date of Birth-Age at Last Birthday; Tribe; Degree of Blood; Marital Status; Relationship to Head of Family; Last C. Roll No.; At Jurisdiction Where Enrolled (Yes/No); (If no – Where); Ward (Yes/No); Allotment, Annuity and Identification Numbers (if given).

2604; Stiles, Homer; M; 8/8/23-7; N.C. Cherokee; 1/64; S; Son; 2582; No; Marble, Cherokee, N.C.; Yes; Unallotted

2605; Stiles (Payne, Theodocia[sic]), F; 6/22/78-53; N.C. Cherokee; 1/16; M; Wife; 2583; Yes; Yes; Unallotted

2606; Stiles, Ella; F; 5/16/07-24; N.C. Cherokee; 1/32; S; Daughter; 2584; Yes; Yes; Unallotted

2607; Stiles, Wilfred; M; 9/20/09-22; N.C. Cherokee; 1/32; S; Son; 2585; Yes; Yes; Unallotted

2608; Stiles, Noah Neil; M; 12/2/12-19; N.C. Cherokee; 1/32; S; Son; 2586; Yes; Yes; Unallotted

2609; Stiles, Virgil R.; M; 12/25/00-31; N.C. Cherokee; 1/32; M; Head; 2587; No; Box 491, Etowah, McMinn, Tenn.; Yes; Unallotted

2610; Stiles, Fay E.; F; 11/21/20-11; N.C. Cherokee; 1/64; S; Daughter; 2588; No; Box 491, Etowah, McMinn, Tenn.; Yes; Unallotted

2611; Stiles, Blanche; F; 11/13/22-9; N.C. Cherokee; 1/64; S; Daughter; 2589; No; Box 491, Etowah, McMinn, Tenn.; Yes; Unallotted

2612; St. Jermain, Nicie; F; 3/4/70-62; N.C. Cherokee; 1/4; M; Wife; 2590; Yes; Yes; Unallotted

2613; Sutaga, Mary; F; 1/19/61-71; N.C. Cherokee; 4/4; Wd.; Head; 2591; Yes; Yes; Unallotted

2614; Swafford (Lee, Debrader), Debrader; F; 2/21/97-35; N.C. Cherokee; 1/16; M; Wife; 2592; Yes; Yes; Unallotted

2615; Swafford, Wm. Tray; M; 2/19/14-18; N.C. Cherokee; 1/32; S; Son; 2593; Yes; Yes; Unallotted

2616; Swafford, Ruby E.; F; 12/18/15-16; N.C. Cherokee; 1/32; S; Daughter; 2594; Yes; Yes; Unallotted

2617; Swafford, James R.; M; 10/2/17-14; N.C. Cherokee; 1/32; S; Son; 2595; Yes; Yes; Unallotted

2618; Swafford, Edwin Lee; M; 7/8/19-12; N.C. Cherokee; 1/32; S; Son; 2596; Yes; Yes; Unallotted

2619; Swafford, Rachel L.; F; 7/1/21-10; N.C. Cherokee; 1/32; S; Daughter; 2597; Yes; Yes; Unallotted

2620; Swafford, John H.; M; 11/1/22-9; N.C. Cherokee; 1/32; S; Son; 2598; Yes; Yes; Unallotted

2621; Swafford (Thompson, Verdie), Verdie T.; F; 9/16/02-29; N.C. Cherokee; 1/16; M; Wife; 2599; Yes; Yes; Unallotted

2622; Swanson (Loudermilk, Cora), Cora; F; 5/18/06-25; N.C. Cherokee; 1/32; M; Wife; 2600; Yes; Yes; Unallotted

Census of the **Eastern Cherokee** reservation of the **Cherokee, N.C.** jurisdiction, as of **April 1** , **1932,** taken by **R. L. Spalsbury** , Superintendent.

Key: Number; Surname, Given; Sex; Date of Birth-Age at Last Birthday; Tribe; Degree of Blood; Marital Status; Relationship to Head of Family; Last C. Roll No.; At Jurisdiction Where Enrolled (Yes/No); (If no – Where); Ward (Yes/No); Allotment, Annuity and Identification Numbers (if given).

2623; Swayney, Jesse W.; M; 8/2/88-43; N.C. Cherokee; 1/8; M; Head; 2601; Yes;
        Yes; Unallotted
2624; Swayney, Laura J.; F; 2/28/16-16; N.C. Cherokee; 1/16; S; Daughter; 2602;
        Yes; Yes; Unallotted
2625; Swayney, Jesse L.; M; 7/22/17-14; N.C. Cherokee; 1/16; S; Son; 2603; Yes;
        Yes; Unallotted
2626; Swayney, Leonard; M; 10/24/21-10; N.C. Cherokee; 1/16; S; Son; 2604; Yes;
        Yes; Unallotted
2627; Swayney, David W.; M; 6/14/28-3; N.C. Cherokee; 1/16; S; Son; 2605; Yes;
        Yes; Unallotted
2628; Swayney, Edith B.; F; 9/26/30-1; N.C. Cherokee; 1/16; S; Daughter; 2606;
        Yes; Yes; Unallotted

2629; Swayney, John W.; M; 1/9/83-49; N.C. Cherokee; 1/8; M; Head; 2607; Yes;
        Yes; Unallotted
2630; Swayney, Alvin W.; M; 11/5/10-21; N.C. Cherokee; 1/16; S; Son; 2608; Yes;
        Yes; Unallotted
2631; Swayney, Laura J.; F; 9/17/12-19; N.C. Cherokee; 1/16; S; Daughter; 2609;
        Yes; Yes; Unallotted
2632; Swayney, Winona L.; F; 6/8/15-16; N.C. Cherokee; 1/16; S; Daughter; 2610;
        Yes; Yes; Unallotted
2633; Swayney, James H.; M; 3/4/18-14; N.C. Cherokee; 1/16; S; Son; 2611; Yes;
        Yes; Unallotted
2634; Swayney, Roxana A.; F; 3/17/21-11; N.C. Cherokee; 1/16; S; Daughter; 2612;
        Yes; Yes; Unallotted
2635; Swayney, Allegra L.; F; 10/3/23-8; N.C. Cherokee; 1/16; S; Daughter; 2613;
        Yes; Yes; Unallotted

2636; Swayney, Laura J.; F; 12/6/57-74; N.C. Cherokee; 1/4; Wd.; Head; 2614;
        Yes; Yes; Unallotted

2637; Swayney, Lorenzo D.; M; 10/5/78-53; N.C. Cherokee; 1/8; M; Head; 2615;
        No; Cramerton, Gaston, N.C.; Yes; Unallotted
2638; Swayney, Frank D.; M; 2/14/05-27; N.C. Cherokee; 1/16; S; Son; 2616;
        No; Cramerton, Gaston, N.C.; Yes; Unallotted
2639; Swayney, Grace; F; 2/1/10-22; N.C. Cherokee; 1/16; S; Daughter; 2617;
        No; Cramerton, Gaston, N.C.; Yes; Unallotted
2640; Swayney, Dora E.; F; 5/6/12-19; N.C. Cherokee; 1/16; S; Daughter; 2618;
        No; Cramerton, Gaston, N.C.; Yes; Unallotted
2641; Swayney, Chiltoskey; M; 5/2/15-16; N.C. Cherokee; 1/16; S; Son; 2619;
        No; Cramerton, Gaston, N.C.; Yes; Unallotted
2642; Swayney, Nathaniel; M; 3/28/17-15; N.C. Cherokee; 1/16; S; Son; 2620;
        No; Cramerton, Gaston, N.C.; Yes; Unallotted

Census of the **Eastern Cherokee** reservation of the **Cherokee, N.C.** jurisdiction, as of **April 1** , 19**32,** taken by **R. L. Spalsbury** , Superintendent.

Key: Number; Surname, Given; Sex; Date of Birth-Age at Last Birthday; Tribe; Degree of Blood; Marital Status; Relationship to Head of Family; Last C. Roll No.; At Jurisdiction Where Enrolled (Yes/No); (If no – Where); Ward (Yes/No); Allotment, Annuity and Identification Numbers (if given).

2643; Swayney, Thurman; M; 10/14/07-24; N.C. Cherokee; 1/16; M; Head; 2621; No; Cramerton, Gaston, N.C.; Yes; Unallotted

2644; Swayney, Walter D.; M; 4/13/17-14; N.C. Cherokee; 1/16; S; Son (Illeg.); 2622; Yes; Yes; Unallotted

2645; Swimmer, Lucy; F; 6/18/86-45; N.C. Cherokee; 4/4; Wd.; Head; 2623; Yes; Yes; Unallotted

2646; Swimmer, Grace; F; 6/15/07-24; N.C. Cherokee; 4/4; S; Daughter; 2624; Yes; Yes; Unallotted

2647; Swimmer, Luke; M; 3/17/10-22; N.C. Cherokee; 4/4; S; Son; 2625; Yes; Yes; Unallotted

2648; Swimmer, Thomas; M; 4/2/14-17; N.C. Cherokee; 4/4; S; Son; 2626; Yes; Yes; Unallotted

2649; Swimmer (Mr. Grace), David; M; 7/31/25-6; N.C. Cherokee; 4/4; S; Grandson; 2627; Yes; Yes; Unallotted

2650; Swimmer, Sarah J.; F; 4/19/12-19; N.C. Cherokee; 4/4; Wd.; Head; 2628; Yes; Yes; Unallotted

2651; Swimmer, Lucy Ann; F; 9/12/28-3; N.C. Cherokee; 4/4; S; Daughter; 2629; Yes; Yes; Unallotted

2652; Swimmer, Runaway; M; 8/7/77-54; N.C. Cherokee; 4/4; M; Head; 2630; Yes; Yes; Unallotted

2653; Swimmer, Anna; F; 5/15/80-51; N.C. Cherokee; 4/4; M; Wife; 2631; Yes; Yes; Unallotted

2654; Swimmer, Thomas; M; 12/14/55-76; N.C. Cherokee; 4/4; M; Head; 2632; Yes; Yes; Unallotted

2655; Swimmer, Anna; F; 2/1/62-69; N.C. Cherokee; 4/4; M; Wife; 2633; Yes; Yes; Unallotted

2656; Tahlala, Homer W.; M; 6/5/17-14; N.C. Cherokee; 1/2; S; Son (Illeg.); 2634; Yes; Yes; Unallotted

2657; Tahquette, John; M; 12/4/54-77; N.C. Cherokee; 4/4; M; Head; 2635; No; Hulbert, Cherokee, Okla.; Yes; Unallotted

2658; Tahquette, John A.; M; 4/27/70-61; N.C. Cherokee; 1/2; Wd.; Head; 2636; Yes; Yes; Unallotted

2659; Tahquette, Frank G.; M; 1/3/07-25; N.C. Cherokee; 3/4; S; Son; 2637; Yes; Yes; Unallotted

2660; Tahquette, Howard W.; M; 11/13/09-22; N.C. Cherokee; 3/4; S; Son; 2638; Yes; Yes; Unallotted

2661; Tahquette, Amy E.; F; 1/9/11-20; N.C. Cherokee; 3/4; S; Daughter; 2639; Yes; Yes; Unallotted

Census of the **Eastern Cherokee** reservation of the **Cherokee, N.C.** jurisdiction, as of **April 1** , **1932,** taken by **R. L. Spalsbury** , Superintendent.

Key: Number; Surname, Given; Sex; Date of Birth-Age at Last Birthday; Tribe; Degree of Blood; Marital Status; Relationship to Head of Family; Last C. Roll No.; At Jurisdiction Where Enrolled (Yes/No); (If no – Where); Ward (Yes/No); Allotment, Annuity and Identification Numbers (if given).

2662; Tahquette, Marion P.; F; 1/9/11-20; N.C. Cherokee; 3/4; S; Daughter; 2640; Yes; Yes; Unallotted

2663; Tahquette, Ernest D.; M; 5/7/16-15; N.C. Cherokee; 3/4; S; Son; 2641; Yes; Yes; Unallotted

2664; Tahquette, Martha; F; 12/24/63-68; N.C. Cherokee; 4/4; S; Head; 2642; Yes; Yes; Unallotted

2665; Tatham, Mary; F; 11/18/06-25; N.C. Cherokee; 1/16; S; Head; 2643; Yes; Yes; Unallotted

2666; Tatham, Leunia; F; 4/11/11-20; N.C. Cherokee; 1/16; S; Sister; 2644; Yes; Yes; Unallotted

2667; Taylor, Eliza; F; 12/4/56-75; N.C. Cherokee; 1/4; Wd.; Head; 2645; Yes; Yes; Unallotted

2668; Taylor, David; M; 6/29/03-28; N.C. Cherokee; 5/8; S; Son; 2646; Yes; Yes; Unallotted

2669; Taylor (Mr.[sic] Mary Sneed Adkins), Inez C.; F; 5/24/14-17; N.C. Cherokee; 1/16; S; Daughter; 2647; Yes; Yes; Unallotted

2670; Taylor, Gerald F.; M; 7/23/21-10; N.C. Cherokee; 1/16; S; Son; 2648; Yes; Yes; Unallotted

2671; Taylor, Jack; M; 6/8/88-43; N.C. Cherokee; 5/8; M; Head; 2649; Yes; Yes; Unallotted

2672; Taylor, Rebecca; F; 5/28/97-34; N.C. Cherokee; 4/4; M; Wife; 2650; Yes; Yes; Unallotted

2673; Taylor, Bettie J.; F; 10/2/17-14; N.C. Cherokee; 13/16; S; Daughter; 2651; Yes; Yes; Unallotted

2674; Taylor, Celia; F; 5/15/20-11; N.C. Cherokee; 13/16; S; Daughter; 2652; Yes; Yes; Unallotted

2675; Taylor, Annie; F; 3/28/22-10; N.C. Cherokee; 13/16; S; Daughter; 2653; Yes; Yes; Unallotted

2676; Taylor, Philip; M; 5/6/24-7; N.C. Cherokee; 13/16; S; Son; 2654; Yes; Yes; Unallotted

2677; Taylor, James; M; 6/15/04-27; N.C. Cherokee; 13/16; S; Head; 2655; Yes; Yes; Unallotted

2678; Taylor, John; M; 12/4/90-41; N.C. Cherokee; 5/8; M; Head; 2656; Yes; Yes; Unallotted

2679; Taylor, Nora S.; F; 9/14/98-33; N.C. Cherokee; 4/4; M; Wife; 2657; Yes; Yes; Unallotted

2680; Taylor, George; M; 12/14/16-15; N.C. Cherokee; 13/16; S; Son; 2658; Yes; Yes; Unallotted

Census of the **Eastern Cherokee** reservation of the **Cherokee, N.C.** jurisdiction, as of **April 1** , 19**32,** taken by **R. L. Spalsbury** , Superintendent.

Key: Number; Surname, Given; Sex; Date of Birth-Age at Last Birthday; Tribe; Degree of Blood; Marital Status; Relationship to Head of Family; Last C. Roll No.; At Jurisdiction Where Enrolled (Yes/No); (If no – Where); Ward (Yes/No); Allotment, Annuity and Identification Numbers (if given).

2681; Taylor, Jesse; M; 6/6/25-6; N.C. Cherokee; 13/16; S; Son; 2659; Yes; Yes; Unallotted

2682; Taylor, Herbert; M; 9/19/29-2; N.C. Cherokee; 13/16; S; Son; 2660; Yes; Yes; Unallotted

2683; Taylor, Julius; M; 1/3/78-54; N.C. Cherokee; 3/4; M; Head; 2661; Yes; Yes; Unallotted

2684; Taylor, Stacey; F; 6/6/76-55; N.C. Cherokee; 7/8; M; Wife; 2662; Yes; Yes; Unallotted

2685; Taylor, Julius; M; 12/20/98-33; N.C. Cherokee; 5/8; M; Head; 2663; Yes; Yes; Unallotted

2686; Taylor, Julia Ned; F; 9/17/02-29; N.C. Cherokee; 4/4; M; Wife; 2664; Yes; Yes; Unallotted

2687; Taylor, Rachel; F; 2/12/22-9; N.C. Cherokee; 13/16; S; Daughter; 2665; Yes; Yes; Unallotted

2688; Taylor, Sallie; F; 10/21/24-7; N.C. Cherokee; 13/16; S; Daughter; 2666; Yes; Yes; Unallotted

2689; Taylor, Mary; F; 2/17/27-5; N.C. Cherokee; 13/16; S; Daughter; 2667; Yes; Yes; Unallotted

2690; Taylor, Jarrett; M; 10/23/31-5/12; N.C. Cherokee; 13/16; S; Son; ---; Yes; Yes; Unallotted

2691; Taylor, John; M; 3/16/09-23; N.C. Cherokee; 5/8; S; Head; 2668; Yes; Yes; Unallotted

2692; Taylor (Meroney, Lula), Lula M.; F; 9/9/91-40; N.C. Cherokee; 1/16; M; Wife; 2669; Yes; Yes; Unallotted

2693; Taylor, Fred, Jr.; M; 1/1/06-26; N.C. Cherokee; 1/32; S; Son; 2670; Yes; Yes; Unallotted

2694; Taylor, James A.; M; 3/15/16-16; N.C. Cherokee; 1/32; S; Son; 2671; Yes; Yes; Unallotted

2695; Taylor, Gertrude A.; F; 7/24/18-13; N.C. Cherokee; 1/32; S; Daughter; 2672; Yes; Yes; Unallotted

2696; Taylor, Nancy W.; F; 6/17/94-37; N.C. Cherokee; 4/4; Div.; Head; 2673; Yes; Yes; Unallotted

2697; Taylor, Eva K.; F; 4/2/11-20; N.C. Cherokee; 13/16; S; Daughter; 2674; Yes; Yes; Unallotted

2698; Taylor, Simeon; M; 12/20/14-17; N.C. Cherokee; 13/16; S; Son; 2675; Yes; Yes; Unallotted

2699; Taylor, Sally Ann; F; 6/16/22-9; N.C. Cherokee; 29/32; S; Daughter; 2676; Yes; Yes; Unallotted

Census of the **Eastern Cherokee** reservation of the **Cherokee, N.C.** jurisdiction, as of **April 1** , **1932,** taken by **R. L. Spalsbury** , Superintendent.

Key: Number; Surname, Given; Sex; Date of Birth-Age at Last Birthday; Tribe; Degree of Blood; Marital Status; Relationship to Head of Family; Last C. Roll No.; At Jurisdiction Where Enrolled (Yes/No); (If no – Where); Ward (Yes/No); Allotment, Annuity and Identification Numbers (if given).

2700; Taylor, Sherman; M; 7/6/82-49; N.C. Cherokee; 3/4; Wd.; Head; 2677; Yes; Yes; Unallotted

2701; Taylor (Saunooke), Eva; F; 4/22/11-20; N.C. Cherokee; 7/8; S; Daughter; 2678; Yes; Yes; Unallotted

2702; Taylor, Larch; M; 11/6/14-17; N.C. Cherokee; 7/8; S; Son; 2679; Yes; Yes; Unallotted

2703; Taylor, Hettie; F; 4/23/16-15; N.C. Cherokee; 7/8; S; Daughter; 2680; Yes; Yes; Unallotted

2704; Taylor, Cindy; F; 3/17/19-12; N.C. Cherokee; 7/8; S; Daughter; 2681; Yes; Yes; Unallotted

2705; Taylor, Julius; M; 7/9/21-10; N.C. Cherokee; 7/8; S; Son; 2682; Yes; Yes; Unallotted

2706; Taylor, Stacy; F; 6/8/27-4; N.C. Cherokee; 7/8; S; Daughter; 2683; Yes; Yes; Unallotted

2707; Taylor, Stacey; F; 12/4/60-71; N.C. Cherokee; 4/4; Wd.; Head; 2684; Yes; Yes; Unallotted

2708; Taylor, Thomas E.; M; 3/30/77-55; N.C. Cherokee; 1/16; M; Head; 2685; No; Hiawassee, Cherokee, N.C.; Yes; Unallotted

2709; Taylor, Oliver; M; 8/2/06-25; N.C. Cherokee; 1/32; S; Son; 2686; No; Hiawassee, Cherokee, N.C.; Yes; Unallotted

2710; Taylor, Alvin; M; 3/24/08-24; N.C. Cherokee; 1/32; S; Son; 2687; No; Hiawassee, Cherokee, N.C.; Yes; Unallotted

2711; Taylor, Howard; M; 10/12/11-20; N.C. Cherokee; 1/32; S; Son; 2688; No; Hiawassee, Cherokee, N.C.; Yes; Unallotted

2712; Taylor, Molt; M; 1/19/13-19; N.C. Cherokee; 1/32; S; Son; 2689; No; Hiawassee, Cherokee, N.C.; Yes; Unallotted

2713; Taylor, Elmer; M; 6/30/15-16; N.C. Cherokee; 1/32; S; Son; 2690; No; Hiawassee, Cherokee, N.C.; Yes; Unallotted

2714; Taylor, Timpson; M; 1/15/00-32; N.C. Cherokee; 5/8; M; Head; 2691; Yes; Yes; Unallotted

2715; Taylor, Cinda R.; F; 4/17/97-34; N.C. Cherokee; 7/8; M; Wife; 2692; Yes; Yes; Unallotted

2716; Taylor, Richard; M; 4/13/21-10; N.C. Cherokee; 3/4; S; Son; 2693; Yes; Yes; Unallotted

2717; Taylor, Reuben E.; M; 11/7/25-6; N.C. Cherokee; 3/4; S; Son; 2694; Yes; Yes; Unallotted

2718; Taylor, Remus E.; M; 4/11/29-2; N.C. Cherokee; 3/4; S; Son; 2695; Yes; Yes; Unallotted

2719; Taylor, Helen E.; F; 7/31/31-8/12; N.C. Cherokee; 3/4; S; Daughter; ---; Yes; Yes; Unallotted

Census of the **Eastern Cherokee** reservation of the **Cherokee, N.C.** jurisdiction, as of **April 1** , 1932, taken by **R. L. Spalsbury** , Superintendent.

Key: Number; Surname, Given; Sex; Date of Birth-Age at Last Birthday; Tribe; Degree of Blood; Marital Status; Relationship to Head of Family; Last C. Roll No.; At Jurisdiction Where Enrolled (Yes/No); (If no – Where); Ward (Yes/No); Allotment, Annuity and Identification Numbers (if given).

2720; Taylor, William; M; 11/8/06-25; N.C. Cherokee; 5/8; M; Head; 2696; Yes; Yes; Unallotted

2721; Taylor, Cecelia; F; 10/28/06-25; N.C. Cherokee; 13/16; M; Wife; 2697; Yes; Yes; Unallotted

2722; Taylor, William Jr.; M; 1/11/26-6; N.C. Cherokee; 13/32; S; Son; 2698; Yes; Yes; Unallotted

2723; Taylor, Wilmer; M; 11/30/28-3; N.C. Cherokee; 13/32; S; Son; 2699; Yes; Yes; Unallotted

2724; Taylor, Lucy F.; F; 8/30/30-1; N.C. Cherokee; 13/32; S; Daughter; 2700; Yes; Yes; Unallotted

2725; Teague, Mable; F; 9/12/14-17; N.C. Cherokee; 1/32; S; Alone; 2701; No; Ducktown, Polk, Tenn.; Yes; Unallotted

2726; Teague, Wade; M; 2/17/16-16; N.C. Cherokee; 1/32; S; Brother; 2702; No; Ducktown, Polk, Tenn.; Yes; Unallotted

2727; Teesateskie, Jesse; M; 5/14/86-45; N.C. Cherokee; 4/4; M; Head; 2703; Yes; Yes; Unallotted

2728; Teesateskie, Polly Bird; F; 1/5/84-48; N.C. Cherokee; 4/4; M; Wife; 2704; Yes; Yes; Unallotted

2729; Teesateskie, Sarah; F; 5/25/12-19; N.C. Cherokee; 4/4; S; Daughter; 2705; Yes; Yes; Unallotted

2730; Teesateskie, Joseph; M; 7/10/14-17; N.C. Cherokee; 4/4; S; Son; 2706; Yes; Yes; Unallotted

2731; Teesateskie, Lee; M; 9/29/18-13; N.C. Cherokee; 4/4; S; Son; 2707; Yes; Yes; Unallotted

2732; Teesateskie, Lilly; F; 3/26/20-12; N.C. Cherokee; 4/4; S; Daughter; 2708; Yes; Yes; Unallotted

2733; Teesateskie, Susie; F; 6/29/22-9; N.C. Cherokee; 4/4; S; Daughter; 2709; Yes; Yes; Unallotted

2734; Teesateskie, Dinah; F; 4/27/24-7; N.C. Cherokee; 4/4; S; Daughter; 2710; Yes; Yes; Unallotted

2735; Teesateskie, John; M; 1/5/50-82; N.C. Cherokee; 4/4; M; Head; 2711; Yes; Yes; Unallotted

2736; Teesateskie, Betty B.; F; 2/26/00-32; N.C. Cherokee; 4/4; M; Wife; 2712; Yes; Yes; Unallotted

2737; Teesateskie, Chicoah; F; 5/3/21-10; N.C. Cherokee; 4/4; S; Daughter; 2713; Yes; Yes; Unallotted

2738; Teesateskie, Ida; F; 8/3/23-8; N.C. Cherokee; 4/4; S; Daughter; 2714; Yes; Yes; Unallotted

2739; Teesateskie, Rogers; M; 8/3/23-8; N.C. Cherokee; 4/4; S; Son; 2715; Yes; Yes; Unallotted

Census of the **Eastern Cherokee** reservation of the **Cherokee, N.C.** jurisdiction, as of **April 1** , 19**32,** taken by **R. L. Spalsbury** , Superintendent.

Key: Number; Surname, Given; Sex; Date of Birth-Age at Last Birthday; Tribe; Degree of Blood; Marital Status; Relationship to Head of Family; Last C. Roll No.; At Jurisdiction Where Enrolled (Yes/No); (If no – Where); Ward (Yes/No); Allotment, Annuity and Identification Numbers (if given).

2740; Teesateskie, Jonah; M; 1/20/04-28; N.C. Cherokee; 4/4; M; Head; 2716; Yes; Yes; Unallotted

2741; Teesateskie, Josiah E.; M; 8/2/30-1; N.C. Cherokee; 4/4; S; Son; ---; Yes; Yes; Unallotted

2742; Teesateskie, Noah; M; 1/5/85-46; N.C. Cherokee; 4/4; M; Head; 2717; Yes; Yes; Unallotted

2743; Teesateskie, Winnie W.; F; 8/15/07-24; N.C. Cherokee; 4/4; M; Wife 2nd; 2718; Yes; Yes; Unallotted

2744; Teesateskie, George; M; 5/9/11-20; N.C. Cherokee; 4/4; S; Son; 2719; Yes; Yes; Unallotted

2745; Teesateskie, Mary; F; 2/9/14-18; N.C. Cherokee; 4/4; S; Daughter; 2720; Yes; Yes; Unallotted

2746; Teesateskie, Matthew; M; 12/17/15-16; N.C. Cherokee; 4/4; S; Son; 2721; Yes; Yes; Unallotted

2747; Teesateskie, Sampson; M; 10/15/91-40; N.C. Cherokee; 4/4; M; Head; 2722; Yes; Yes; Unallotted

2748; Teesateskie, Nessie W.; F; 2/15/82-50; N.C. Cherokee; 4/4; M; Wife; 2723; Yes; Yes; Unallotted

2749; Teesateskie, Welch; M; 1/18/99-33; N.C. Cherokee; 3/4; M; Head; 2724; Yes; Yes; Unallotted

2750; Teesateskie, Tommie; M; 7/10/23-8; N.C. Cherokee; 7/8; S; Son; 2725; Yes; Yes; Unallotted

2751; Teesateskie, Nessih; F; 4/17/55-76; N.C. Cherokee; 4/4; Wd.; Head; 2726; Yes; Yes; Unallotted

2752; Teesateskie, Willie; M; 7/14/07-24; N.C. Cherokee; 4/4; M; Head; 2727; Yes; Yes; Unallotted

2753; Teesateskie, Lillian S.; F; 7/8/07-24; N.C. Cherokee; 4/4; M; Wife; 2728; Yes; Yes; Unallotted

2754; Teleskie, Jesse; M; 12/4/90-41; N.C. Cherokee; 4/4; M; Head; 2729; Yes; Yes; Unallotted

2755; Teleskie, Sallie L.; F; 4/17/80-51; N.C. Cherokee; 4/4; M; Wife; 2730; Yes; Yes; Unallotted

2756; Thompson, Ahsinnah; M; 9/5/83-48; N.C. Cherokee; 4/4; M; Head; 2731; Yes; Yes; Unallotted

2757; Thompson, Mary E.; F; 1/1/83-49; N.C. Cherokee; 1/2; M; Wife; 2732; Yes; Yes; Unallotted

2758; Thompson, Jefferson; M; 2/12/17-15; N.C. Cherokee; 3/4; S; Son; 2733; Yes; Yes; Unallotted

Census of the **Eastern Cherokee** reservation of the **Cherokee, N.C.** jurisdiction, as of **April 1** , 1932, taken by **R. L. Spalsbury** , Superintendent.

Key: Number; Surname, Given; Sex; Date of Birth-Age at Last Birthday; Tribe; Degree of Blood; Marital Status; Relationship to Head of Family; Last C. Roll No.; At Jurisdiction Where Enrolled (Yes/No); (If no – Where); Ward (Yes/No); Allotment, Annuity and Identification Numbers (if given).

2759; Thompson, Allene; F; 10/7/18-13; N.C. Cherokee; 3/4; S; Daughter; 2734; Yes; Yes; Unallotted

2760; Thompson, Pearl C.; F; 8/11/20-11; N.C. Cherokee; 3/4; S; Daughter; 2735; Yes; Yes; Unallotted

2761; Thompson, Reginald R.; M; 3/12/23-9; N.C. Cherokee; 3/4; S; Son; 2736; Yes; Yes; Unallotted

2762; Thompson, Annie; F; 3/30/06-26; N.C. Cherokee; 4/4; S; Head; 2737; Yes; Yes; Unallotted

2763; Thompson (Loudermilk, Daffney Raper), Daffney; F; 3/29/98-34; N.C. Cherokee; 1/16; M; Wife; 2738; Yes; Yes; Unallotted

2764; Thompson, Sanford D.; M; 5/24/20-11; N.C. Cherokee; 1/32; S; Son; 2739; Yes; Yes; Unallotted

2765; Thompson, Greeley; M; 4/11/99-32; N.C. Cherokee; 1/16; M; Head; 2740; Yes; Yes; Unallotted

2766; Thompson, Jackson; M; 1/7/03-29; N.C. Cherokee; 4/4; M; Head; 2741; Yes; Yes; Unallotted

2767; Thompson, Alice W.; F; 3/12/06-26; N.C. Cherokee; 4/4; M; Wife; 2742; Yes; Yes; Unallotted

2768; Thompson, Joseph W.; M; 6/9/27-4; N.C. Cherokee; 4/4; S; Son; 2743; Yes; Yes; Unallotted

2769; Thompson, McKinley; M; 6/25/31-9/12; N.C. Cherokee; 4/4; S; Son; ---; Yes; Yes; Unallotted

2770; Thompson, Johnson; M; 4/12/68-63; N.C. Cherokee; 4/4; M; Head; 2744; Yes; Yes; Unallotted

2771; Thompson, Nancy; F; 12/7/69-62; N.C. Cherokee; 4/4; M; Wife; 2745; Yes; Yes; Unallotted

2772; Thompson, Simon; M; 6/1/94-37; N.C. Cherokee; 4/4; S; Son; 2746; Yes; Yes; Unallotted

2773; Thompson, David; M; 12/21/96-35; N.C. Cherokee; 4/4; S; Son; 2747; Yes; Yes; Unallotted

2774; Thompson, Jonah; M; 10/17/00-31; N.C. Cherokee; 4/4; M; Head; 2748; Yes; Yes; Unallotted

2775; Thompson, Lucinda; F; 2/10/10-22; N.C. Cherokee; 4/4; M; Wife; 2749; Yes; Yes; Unallotted

2776; Thompson, Abe; M; 9/12/30-1; N.C. Cherokee; 4/4; S; Son; 2750; Yes; Yes; Unallotted

2777; Thompson (Webster, Martha), Martha; F; 2/11/74-57; N.C. Cherokee; 1/8; M; Wife; 2751; No; Culberson, Cherokee, N.C.; Yes; Unallotted

Census of the **Eastern Cherokee** reservation of the **Cherokee, N.C.** jurisdiction, as of **April 1**, **1932,** taken by **R. L. Spalsbury**, Superintendent.

2778;   Thompson, William; M; 12/4/94-37; N.C. Cherokee; 1/16; S; Son; 2752; No; Culberson, Cherokee, N.C.; Yes; Unallotted

2779;   Thompson, Minnie; F; 5/22/98-33; N.C. Cherokee; 1/16; S; Daughter; 2753; No; Culberson, Cherokee, N.C.; Yes; Unallotted

2780;   Thompson, Elbert; M; 12/1/99-32; N.C. Cherokee; 1/16; S; Son; 2754; No; Culberson, Cherokee, N.C.; Yes; Unallotted

2781;   Thompson, Jewel; M; 1/23/05-27; N.C. Cherokee; 1/16; S; Son; 2755; No; Culberson, Cherokee, N.C.; Yes; Unallotted

2782;   Thompson, Marvin; M; 4/25/06-25; N.C. Cherokee; 1/16; S; Son; 2756; No; Culberson, Cherokee, N.C.; Yes; Unallotted

2783;   Thompson, Walter; M; 1/22/08-24; N.C. Cherokee; 1/16; S; Son; 2757; No; Culberson, Cherokee, N.C.; Yes; Unallotted

2784;   Thompson (Webster, Mary), Mary W.; F; 10/22/76-55; N.C. Cherokee; 1/8; M; Wife; 2758; No; Alton Park, Hamilton, Tenn.; Yes; Unallotted

2785;   Thompson, Lawrence; M; 12/3/08-23; N.C. Cherokee; 1/16; S; Son; 2759; No; Alton Park, Hamilton, Tenn.; Yes; Unallotted

2786;   Thompson, Willard; M; 10/31/11-20; N.C. Cherokee; 1/16; S; Son; 2760; No; Alton Park, Hamilton, Tenn.; Yes; Unallotted

2787;   Thompson, Rosa; F; 10/9/17-14; N.C. Cherokee; 1/16; S; Daughter; 2761; No; Alton Park, Hamilton, Tenn.; Yes; Unallotted

2788;   Thompson, Claude; M; 5/10/20-11; N.C. Cherokee; 1/16; S; Son; 2762; No; Alton Park, Hamilton, Tenn.; Yes; Unallotted

2789;   Thompson, Olin; M; 2/26/97-35; N.C. Cherokee; 1/16; M; Head; 2763; Yes; Yes; Unallotted

2790;   Thompson, Peter; M; 7/18/86-45; N.C. Cherokee; 13/16; S; Head; 2764; Yes; Yes; Unallotted

2791;   Thompson, Goliath; M; 8/17/98-33; N.C. Cherokee; 13/16; S; Brother; 2765; Yes; Yes; Unallotted

2792;   Thompson, Ruth V.; F; 2/8/83-49; N.C. Cherokee; 3/16; M; Wife; 2766; Yes; Yes; Unallotted

2793;   Thompson (Wolf, Sophronia I.), Sophronia; F; 7/16/96-35; N.C. Cherokee; 1/8; M; Wife; 2767; Yes; Yes; Unallotted

2794;   Thompson, Paul L.; M; 4/17/15-16; N.C. Cherokee; 1/16; S; Son; 2768; Yes; Yes; Unallotted

2795;   Thompson, Nola B.; F; 4/11/17-14; N.C. Cherokee; 1/16; S; Daughter; 2769; Yes; Yes; Unallotted

2796;   Thompson, Charles B.; M; 3/27/19-12; N.C. Cherokee; 1/16; S; Son; 2770; Yes; Yes; Unallotted

Census of the **Eastern Cherokee** reservation of the **Cherokee, N.C.** jurisdiction, as of **April 1**, 19**32,** taken by **R. L. Spalsbury**, Superintendent.

Key: Number; Surname, Given; Sex; Date of Birth-Age at Last Birthday; Tribe; Degree of Blood; Marital Status; Relationship to Head of Family; Last C. Roll No.; At Jurisdiction Where Enrolled (Yes/No); (If no – Where); Ward (Yes/No); Allotment, Annuity and Identification Numbers (if given).

2797; Thompson, Wilson; M; 8/13/92-39; N.C. Cherokee; 13/16; M; Head; 2771; Yes; Yes; Unallotted

2798; Thompson, Martha Owl; F; 7/11/99-32; N.C. Cherokee; 3/4; M; Wife; 2772; Yes; Yes; Unallotted

2799; Thompson, Enos; M; 11/8/24-7; N.C. Cherokee; 25/32; S; Son; 2773; Yes; Yes; Unallotted

2800; Thompson, Not Given; M; 9/5/27-4; N.C. Cherokee; 25/32; S; Son; 2774; Yes; Yes; Unallotted

2801; Thompson, Lawrence; M; 4/2/31-11/12; N.C. Cherokee; 25/32; S; Son; ---; Yes; Yes; Unallotted

2802; Timpson, Bertha; F; 12/28/96-35; N.C. Cherokee; 1/64; M; Wife; 2775; Yes; Yes; Unallotted

2803; Timpson, Humphrey P.; M; 12/26/58-73; N.C. Cherokee; 3/8; S; Head; 2776; Yes; Yes; Unallotted

2804; Timpson, James; M; 12/1/52-79; N.C. Cherokee; 3/8; S; Head; 2777; Yes; Yes; Unallotted

2805; Timpson, James A.; M; 12/1/80-51; N.C. Cherokee; 3/16; M; Head; 2778; Yes; Yes; Unallotted

2806; Timpson, Lawrence A.; M; 8/9/09-22; N.C. Cherokee; 3/32; S; Son; 2779; Yes; Yes; Unallotted

2807; Timpson, Lexie; F; 2/27/12-19; N.C. Cherokee; 3/32; S; Daughter; 2780; Yes; Yes; Unallotted

2808; Timpson, Glenn; M; 3/23/14-18; N.C. Cherokee; 3/32; S; Son; 2781; Yes; Yes; Unallotted

2809; Timpson, Flora; F; 7/25/16-15; N.C. Cherokee; 3/32; S; Daughter; 2782; Yes; Yes; Unallotted

2810; Timpson, Cecil; M; 5/15/18-13; N.C. Cherokee; 3/32; S; Son; 2783; Yes; Yes; Unallotted

2811; Timpson, Coy; M; 9/20/20-11; N.C. Cherokee; 3/32; S; Son; 2784; Yes; Yes; Unallotted

2812; Timpson, John S.; M; 8/8/85-46; N.C. Cherokee; 3/16; M; Head; 2785; Yes; Yes; Unallotted

2813; Timpson, Vestraex; F; 9/10/13-18; N.C. Cherokee; 13/128; S; Daughter; 2786; Yes; Yes; Unallotted

2814; Timpson, Elsie; F; 8/29/15-16; N.C. Cherokee; 13/128; S; Daughter; 2787; Yes; Yes; Unallotted

2815; Timpson, Wilma; F; 5/29/20-11; N.C. Cherokee; 13/128; S; Daughter; 2788; Yes; Yes; Unallotted

2816; Tincher (Sneed, Lula), Lula S.; F; 12/14/87-44; N.C. Cherokee; 1/8; M; Wife; 2789; Yes; Yes; Unallotted

Census of the **Eastern Cherokee** reservation of the **Cherokee, N.C.** jurisdiction, as of **April 1** , 19**32,** taken by **R. L. Spalsbury** , Superintendent.

Key: Number; Surname, Given; Sex; Date of Birth-Age at Last Birthday; Tribe; Degree of Blood; Marital Status; Relationship to Head of Family; Last C. Roll No.; At Jurisdiction Where Enrolled (Yes/No); (If no – Where); Ward (Yes/No); Allotment, Annuity and Identification Numbers (if given).

2817;   Toe, Campbell; M; 4/4/67-64; N.C. Cherokee; 4/4; M; Head; 2790; Yes; Yes; Unallotted

2818;   Toineeta, Arneach; M; 7/3/93-38; N.C. Cherokee; 4/4; M; Head; 2791; Yes; Yes; Unallotted

2819;   Toineeta, Martha Y.; F; 5/15/92-39; N.C. Cherokee; 4/4; M; Wife; 2792; Yes; Yes; Unallotted

2820;   Toineeta, Jefferson; M; 2/27/17-15; N.C. Cherokee; 4/4; S; Son; 2793; Yes; Yes; Unallotted

2821;   Toineeta, Jeremiah; M; 2/14/21-11; N.C. Cherokee; 4/4; S; Son; 2794; Yes; Yes; Unallotted

2822;   Toineeta, Alice; F; 4/3/23-8; N.C. Cherokee; 4/4; S; Daughter; 2795; Yes; Yes; Unallotted

2823;   Toineeta, Joseph; M; 2/14/27-4; N.C. Cherokee; 4/4; S; Son; 2797; Yes; Yes; Unallotted

2824;   Toineeta, Joshua; M; 10/15/28-3; N.C. Cherokee; 4/4; S; Son; 2798; Yes; Yes; Unallotted

2825;   Toineeta, Geneva; F; 9/7/30-1; N.C. Cherokee; 4/4; S; Daughter; 2799; Yes; Yes; Unallotted

2826;   Toineeta, Edwin T.; M; 9/10/08-23; N.C. Cherokee; 3/16; S; Head; 2800; Yes; Yes; Unallotted

2827;   Toineeta, George; M; 1/18/83-49; N.C. Cherokee; 4/4; M; Head; 2801; Yes; Yes; Unallotted

2828;   Toineeta, Pearl W.; F; 12/22/88-43; N.C. Cherokee; 1/2; M; Wife; 2802; Yes; Yes; Unallotted

2829;   Toineeta, F. Geneva; F; 6/17/10-21; N.C. Cherokee; 11/16; S; Daughter; 2803; Yes; Yes; Unallotted

2830;   Toineeta, Loney; M; 6/1/13-18; N.C. Cherokee; 11/16; S; Son; 2804; Yes; Yes; Unallotted

2831;   Toineeta, George H.; M; 8/2/17-14; N.C. Cherokee; 3/4; S; Son; 2805; Yes; Yes; Unallotted

2832;   Toineeta, Margaret; F; 10/3/19-12; N.C. Cherokee; 3/4; S; Daughter; 2806; Yes; Yes; Unallotted

2833;   Toineeta, Dorothy; F; 11/2/27-5; N.C. Cherokee; 3/4; S; Daughter; 2807; Yes; Yes; Unallotted

2834;   Toineeta, Sally; F; 12/24/60-71; N.C. Cherokee; 4/4; Wd.; Head; 2808; Yes; Yes; Unallotted

2835;   Toineeta, West; M; 12/10/81-50; N.C. Cherokee; 4/4; S; Son; 2809; Yes; Yes; Unallotted

2836;   Toineeta, Nick; M; 4/22/67-64; N.C. Cherokee; 4/4; M; Head; 2810; Yes; Yes; Unallotted

149

Census of the **Eastern Cherokee** reservation of the **Cherokee, N.C.** jurisdiction, as of **April 1** , 1932, taken by **R. L. Spalsbury** , Superintendent.

Key: Number; Surname, Given; Sex; Date of Birth-Age at Last Birthday; Tribe; Degree of Blood; Marital Status; Relationship to Head of Family; Last C. Roll No.; At Jurisdiction Where Enrolled (Yes/No); (If no – Where); Ward (Yes/No); Allotment, Annuity and Identification Numbers (if given).

2837; Toineeta, Betty; F; 12/24/62-69; N.C. Cherokee; 4/4; M; Wife; 2811; Yes; Yes; Unallotted

2838; Toineeta, Suagih; M; 3/21/89-43; N.C. Cherokee; 4/4; S; Son; 2812; Yes; Yes; Unallotted

2839; Tollie (Bradley, Lizzie), Lizzie; F; 6/13/87-44; N.C. Cherokee; 1/2; M; Wife; 2813; Yes; Yes; Unallotted

2840; Tooni, Elijah; M; 12/27/99-32; N.C. Cherokee; 4/4; M; Head; 2814; Yes; Yes; Unallotted

2841; Tooni, Aggie G.; F; 6/8/04-27; N.C. Cherokee; 4/4; M; Wife; 2815; Yes; Yes; Unallotted

2842; George, Dinah; F; 8/1/22-9; N.C. Cherokee; 4/4; S; Step-dau.; 2816; Yes; Yes; Unallotted

2843; Tooni, Ike; M; 2/8/26-6; N.C. Cherokee; 4/4; S; Son; 2817; Yes; Yes; Unallotted

2844; Tooni, Annie; F; 4/5/30-1; N.C. Cherokee; 4/4; S; Daughter; 2818; Yes; Yes; Unallotted

2845; Tooni, Stan; M; 1/26/32-2/12; N.C. Cherokee; 4/4; S; Son; ---; Yes; Yes; Unallotted

2846; Tooni, Lizzie D.; F; 1/30/82-49; N.C. Cherokee; 4/4; Wd.; Head; 2819; Yes; Yes; Unallotted

2847; Tooni, Rachel; F; 9/28/08-23; N.C. Cherokee; 4/4; S; Daughter; 2820; Yes; Yes; Unallotted

2848; Tooni, Russel; M; 10/30/11-20; N.C. Cherokee; 4/4; S; Son; 2821; Yes; Yes; Unallotted

2849; Tooni, Michael; M; 12/17/13-18; N.C. Cherokee; 4/4; S; Son; 2822; Yes; Yes; Unallotted

2850; Tooni, Rebecca; F; 11/1/18-13; N.C. Cherokee; 4/4; S; Daughter; 2823; Yes; Yes; Unallotted

2851; Tooni, Mary; F; 4/13/21-10; N.C. Cherokee; 4/4; S; Daughter; 2824; Yes; Yes; Unallotted

2852; Tooni (Mr. Annie Standingdeer), Tom; M; 10/20/13-18; N.C. Cherokee; 4/4; S; Son; 2825; Yes; Yes; Unallotted

2853; Tooni, Ollie Ann; F; 10/5/16-15; N.C. Cherokee; 4/4; S; Daughter; 2826; Yes; Yes; Unallotted

2854; Tramper, Amineeta; M; 6/12/86-45; N.C. Cherokee; 4/4; M; Head; 2827; Yes; Yes; Unallotted

2855; Tramper, Lucinda; F; 8/4/93-38; N.C. Cherokee; 9/16; M; Wife; 2828; Yes; Yes; Unallotted

2856; Tramper, Elziney; F; 9/30/17-14; N.C. Cherokee; 25/32; S; Daughter; 2829; Yes; Yes; Unallotted

Census of the **Eastern Cherokee** reservation of the **Cherokee, N.C.** jurisdiction, as of **April 1**, 19**32,** taken by **R. L. Spalsbury**, Superintendent.

Key: Number; Surname, Given; Sex; Date of Birth-Age at Last Birthday; Tribe; Degree of Blood; Marital Status; Relationship to Head of Family; Last C. Roll No.; At Jurisdiction Where Enrolled (Yes/No); (If no – Where); Ward (Yes/No); Allotment, Annuity and Identification Numbers (if given).

2857; Tramper, Sallie; F; 8/11/23-8; N.C. Cherokee; 25/32; S; Daughter; 2830; Yes; Yes; Unallotted

2858; Tramper, John A.; M; 8/26/28-3; N.C. Cherokee; 25/32; S; Son; 2831; Yes; Yes; Unallotted

2859; Tramper, Chiltoskey; M; 4/10/82-49; N.C. Cherokee; 4/4; M; Head; 2832; Yes; Yes; Unallotted

2860; Tramper, Emma Axe; F; 8/20/97-34; N.C. Cherokee; 4/4; M; Wife; 2833; Yes; Yes; Unallotted

2861; Tramper, Welch; M; 11/2/18-13; N.C. Cherokee; 4/4; S; Son; 2834; Yes; Yes; Unallotted

2862; Tramper, Lillian; F; 1/8/23-9; N.C. Cherokee; 4/4; S; Daughter; 2835; Yes; Yes; Unallotted

2863; Tramper, Tonie; M; 5/20/28-3; N.C. Cherokee; 4/4; S; Son; 2836; Yes; Yes; Unallotted

2864; Tramper, Kahlie; F; 4/17/30-1; N.C. Cherokee; 4/4; S; Daughter; 2837; Yes; Yes; Unallotted

2865; Treadway, Mary L.; F; 9/26/10-21; N.C. Cherokee; 1/32; M; Wife; 2838; Yes; Yes; Unallotted

2866; Truett, Reuben; M; 8/16/10-21; N.C. Cherokee; 1/32; S; Head; 2839; Yes; Yes; Unallotted

2867; Truett, Vinson; M; 3/9/13-19; N.C. Cherokee; 1/32; S; Brother; 2840; Yes; Yes; Unallotted

2868; Truett, Edward; M; 3/14/17-15; N.C. Cherokee; 1/32; S; Brother; 2841; Yes; Yes; Unallotted

2869; Truett, Clara B.; F; 9/27/20-11; N.C. Cherokee; 1/32; S; Sister; 2842; Yes; Yes; Unallotted

2870; Twin, Viola; F; 3/10/10-22; N.C. Cherokee; 3/8; S; Alone; 2843; Yes; Yes; Unallotted

2871; Lindsey (Mr. Viola Twin), Jackie; M; 5/27/31-10/12; N.C. Cherokee; 3/16; S; Son; ---; Yes; Yes; Unallotted

2872; Voiles, Jane; F; 5/10/57-74; N.C. Cherokee; 1/8; M; Wife; 2844; No; Rossville, Walker, Ga.; Yes; Unallotted

2873; Voiles, Vinson; M; 4/10/79-52; N.C. Cherokee; 1/16; M; Head; 2845; No; Lookout Mtn., Hamilton, Tenn.; Yes; Unallotted

2874; Voiles, William; M; 6/10/81-50; N.C. Cherokee; 1/16; M; Head; 2846; No; Rossville, Walker, Ga.; Yes; Unallotted

Census of the **Eastern Cherokee** reservation of the **Cherokee, N.C.** jurisdiction, as of **April 1** , 19**32,** taken by **R. L. Spalsbury** , Superintendent.

Key: Number; Surname, Given; Sex; Date of Birth-Age at Last Birthday; Tribe; Degree of Blood; Marital Status; Relationship to Head of Family; Last C. Roll No.; At Jurisdiction Where Enrolled (Yes/No); (If no – Where); Ward (Yes/No); Allotment, Annuity and Identification Numbers (if given).

2875; Wachacha, Charles; M; 4/30/90-41; N.C. Cherokee; 4/4; Wd.; Head; 2847; Yes; Yes; Unallotted

2876; Wachacha, Moses; M; 12/22/21-10; N.C. Cherokee; 4/4; S; Son; 2848; Yes; Yes; Unallotted

2877; Wachacha, Jack; M; 11/15/93-38; N.C. Cherokee; 4/4; M; Head; 2849; Yes; Yes; Unallotted

2878; Wachacha, Dinah C.; F; 8/10/96-35; N.C. Cherokee; 4/4; M; Wife; 2850; Yes; Yes; Unallotted

2879; Wachacha, Claude; M; 1/17/23-9; N.C. Cherokee; 4/4; S; Son; 2851; Yes; Yes; Unallotted

2880; Wachacha, James; M; 12/25/83-48; N.C. Cherokee; 4/4; M; Head; 2852; Yes; Yes; Unallotted

2881; Wachacha, Sarah Axe; F; 9/12/97-34; N.C. Cherokee; 4/4; M; Wife; 2853; Yes; Yes; Unallotted

2882; Wachacha, Carrie; F; 6/10/21-10; N.C. Cherokee; 4/4; S; Daughter; 2854; Yes; Yes; Unallotted

2883; Wachacha, Henry; M; 3/25/23-9; N.C. Cherokee; 4/4; S; Son; 2855; Yes; Yes; Unallotted

2884; Wachacha, Jarret; M; 12/15/84-47; N.C. Cherokee; 4/4; M; Head; 2856; Yes; Yes; Unallotted

2885; Wachacha, Amanda T.; F; 9/28/94-37; N.C. Cherokee; 4/4; M; Wife; 2857; Yes; Yes; Unallotted

2886; Wachacha, Linda; F; 2/10/13-19; N.C. Cherokee; 4/4; S; Daughter; 2858; Yes; Yes; Unallotted

2887; Wachacha, Raleigh; M; 8/21/15-16; N.C. Cherokee; 4/4; S; Son; 2859; Yes; Yes; Unallotted

2888; Wachacha, Mollie; F; 5/22/18-13; N.C. Cherokee; 4/4; S; Daughter; 2860; Yes; Yes; Unallotted

2889; Wachacha, John W.; M; 10/15/98-33; N.C. Cherokee; 4/4; M; Head; 2861; Yes; Yes; Unallotted

2890; Wachacha, Martha W.; F; 4/26/10-21; N.C. Cherokee; 4/4; M; Wife; 2862; Yes; Yes; Unallotted

2891; Wachacha, Posey; M; 3/15/94-40; N.C. Cherokee; 4/4; Wd.; Head; 2863; Yes; Yes; Unallotted

2892; Wachacha, Sarah; M; 4/15/89-42; N.C. Cherokee; 4/4; S; Head; 2864; Yes; Yes; Unallotted

2893; Wachacha, Oney; F; 5/15/04-27; N.C. Cherokee; 4/4; S; Sister; 2865; Yes; Yes; Unallotted

Census of the **Eastern Cherokee** reservation of the **Cherokee, N.C.** jurisdiction, as of **April 1**, **1932,** taken by **R. L. Spalsbury**, Superintendent.

Key: Number; Surname, Given; Sex; Date of Birth-Age at Last Birthday; Tribe; Degree of Blood; Marital Status; Relationship to Head of Family; Last C. Roll No.; At Jurisdiction Where Enrolled (Yes/No); (If no – Where); Ward (Yes/No); Allotment, Annuity and Identification Numbers (if given).

2894; Wahyahneetah, Allen; M; 5/5/73-42; N.C. Cherokee; 4/4; M; Head; 2866; Yes; Yes; Unallotted

2895; Wahyahneetah, Sallie; F; 7/10/69-62; N.C. Cherokee; 4/4; M; Wife; 2867; Yes; Yes; Unallotted

2896; Wahyahneetah, Awee; F; 12/24/53-78; N.C. Cherokee; 4/4; Wd.; Head; 2868; Yes; Yes; Unallotted

2897; Wahyahneetah, Posey; M; 12/4/00-31; N.C. Cherokee; 4/4; Wd.; Head; 2869; Yes; Yes; Unallotted

2898; Wahyahneetah, William; M; 8/13/70-61; N.C. Cherokee; 4/4; M; Head; 2870; Yes; Yes; Unallotted

2899; Wahyahneetah, Kamie; F; 9/28/77-54; N.C. Cherokee; 1/2; M; Wife; 2871; Yes; Yes; Unallotted

2900; Wahyahneetah, Samuel; M; 7/5/03-28; N.C. Cherokee; 3/4; S; Son; 2872; Yes; Yes; Unallotted

2901; Wahyahneetah, Leroy; M; 7/22/06-25; N.C. Cherokee; 3/4; S; Son; 2873; Yes; Yes; Unallotted

2902; Wahyahneetah, Ethel; F; 3/12/11-21; N.C. Cherokee; 3/4; S; Daughter; 2874; Yes; Yes; Unallotted

2903; Wahyahneetah, Robert; M; 11/10/13-18; N.C. Cherokee; 3/4; S; Son; 2875; Yes; Yes; Unallotted

2904; Wahyahneetah, John; M; 4/5/19-12; N.C. Cherokee; 3/4; S; Son; 2876; Yes; Yes; Unallotted

2905; Waidsutte, Bird; M; 12/14/77-54; N.C. Cherokee; 4/4; M; Head; 2877; Yes; Yes; Unallotted

2906; Waidsutte, Mary; F; 12/14/70-61; N.C. Cherokee; 4/4; M; Wife; 2878; Yes; Yes; Unallotted

2907; Waidsutte, Lee; M; 1/7/03-29; N.C. Cherokee; 3/4; S; Son; 2879; Yes; Yes; Unallotted

2908; Waidsutte, Davis; M; 12/21/67-64; N.C. Cherokee; 4/4; M; Head; 2880; Yes; Yes; Unallotted

2909; Waidsutte, Nancy; F; 5/5/71-60; N.C. Cherokee; 4/4; M; Wife; 2881; Yes; Yes; Unallotted

2910; Waidsutte, Bird; M; 6/10/01-30; N.C. Cherokee; 3/4; S; Son; 2882; Yes; Yes; Unallotted

2911; Waidsutte, Addison; M; 10/15/10-21; N.C. Cherokee; 4/4; S; Son; 2883; Yes; Yes; Unallotted

2912; Waidsutte, Margaret; F; 2/4/12-20; N.C. Cherokee; 4/4; S; Alone; 2884; Yes; Yes; Unallotted

Census of the **Eastern Cherokee** reservation of the **Cherokee, N.C.** jurisdiction, as of **April 1**, 19**32**, taken by **R. L. Spalsbury**, Superintendent.

Key: Number; Surname, Given; Sex; Date of Birth-Age at Last Birthday; Tribe; Degree of Blood; Marital Status; Relationship to Head of Family; Last C. Roll No.; At Jurisdiction Where Enrolled (Yes/No); (If no – Where); Ward (Yes/No); Allotment, Annuity and Identification Numbers (if given).

2913; Wakefield, Albert; M; 4/7/79-52; N.C. Cherokee; 1/32; M; Head; 2885; Yes; Yes; Unallotted

2914; Wakefield, Charlie; M; 6/6/74-57; N.C. Cherokee; 1/32; M; Head; 2886; Yes; Yes; Unallotted

2915; Wakefield, Ruth; F; 4/12/10-21; N.C. Cherokee; 1/64; S; Daughter; 2887; Yes; Yes; Unallotted

2916; Wakefield, Elizabeth; F; 7/29/13-18; N.C. Cherokee; 1/64; S; Daughter; 2888; Yes; Yes; Unallotted

2917; Wakefield, Charles Jr.; M; 11/23/15-16; N.C. Cherokee; 1/64; S; Son; 2889; Yes; Yes; Unallotted

2918; Wakefield, Annie; F; 4/24/17-14; N.C. Cherokee; 1/64; S; Daughter; 2890; Yes; Yes; Unallotted

2919; Wakefield, Luther; M; 4/24/20-11; N.C. Cherokee; 1/64; S; Son; 2891; Yes; Yes; Unallotted

2920; Wakefield, Ralph; M; 8/1/23-8; N.C. Cherokee; 1/64; S; Son; 2892; Yes; Yes; Unallotted

2921; Wakefield, David Lee; M; 3/4/14-18; N.C. Cherokee; 1/64; S; Son (Mr. White); 2893; Yes; Yes; Unallotted

2922; Wakefield, Marie; F; 1/13/16-16; N.C. Cherokee; 1/64; S; Daughter; 2894; Yes; Yes; Unallotted

2923; Wakefield, Kathleen; F; 11/12/17-14; N.C. Cherokee; 1/64; S; Daughter; 2895; Yes; Yes; Unallotted

2924; Wakefield, Maxine; F; 11/23/19-12; N.C. Cherokee; 1/64; S; Daughter; 2896; Yes; Yes; Unallotted

2925; Wakefield, Kenneth; M; 3/17/22-10; N.C. Cherokee; 1/64; S; Son; 2897; Yes; Yes; Unallotted

2926; Wakefield, Edmond S.; M; 2/22/77-55; N.C. Cherokee; 1/32; S; Head; 2898; Yes; Yes; Unallotted

2927; Wakefield, Esco; M; 10/16/66-65; N.C. Cherokee; 1/32; M; Head; 2899; Yes; Yes; Unallotted

2928; Wakefield, Thomas; M; 12/9/05-26; N.C. Cherokee; 1/64; S; Son; 2900; Yes; Yes; Unallotted

2929; Wakefield, Wiley E.; M; 12/4/09-22; N.C. Cherokee; 1/64; S; Son; 2901; Yes; Yes; Unallotted

2930; Wakefield, Lycurgus; M; 5/13/81-50; N.C. Cherokee; 1/32; S; Head; 2902; Yes; Yes; Unallotted

2931; Wakefield, Lucy; F; 5/11/95-36; N.C. Cherokee; 1/64; S; Head; 2903; Yes; Yes; Unallotted

Census of the **Eastern Cherokee** reservation of the **Cherokee, N.C.** jurisdiction, as of **April 1**, **1932,** taken by **R. L. Spalsbury**, Superintendent.

Key: Number; Surname, Given; Sex; Date of Birth-Age at Last Birthday; Tribe; Degree of Blood; Marital Status; Relationship to Head of Family; Last C. Roll No.; At Jurisdiction Where Enrolled (Yes/No); (If no – Where); Ward (Yes/No); Allotment, Annuity and Identification Numbers (if given).

2932; Wakefield, Virginia; F; 5/13/81-50; N.C. Cherokee; 1/32; S; Head; 2904; Yes; Yes; Unallotted

2933; Walker, Amanda C.; F; 12/7/98-33; N.C. Cherokee; 4/4; M; Wife; 2905; Yes; Yes; Unallotted
2934; Walker, Lucile; F; 12/31/21-10; N.C. Cherokee; 1/2; S; Daughter; 2906; Yes; Yes; Unallotted
2935; Walker, George Wm.; M; 5/11/23-8; N.C. Cherokee; 1/2; S; Son; 2907; Yes; Yes; Unallotted
2936; Walker, Eugene; M; 6/2/28-3; N.C. Cherokee; 1/2; S; Son; 2908; Yes; Yes; Unallotted
2937; Walker, Pauline; F; 7/3/30-1; N.C. Cherokee; 1/2; S; Daughter; 2909; Yes; Yes; Unallotted

2938; Walker (Taylor, Edith), Edith; F; 5/5/04-27; N.C. Cherokee; 1/32; M; Wife; 2910; No; Hiwassee, Cherokee, N.C.; Yes; Unallotted
2939; Walker, D.O.; M; 10/12/23-8; N.C. Cherokee; 1/64; M; Son; 2911; No; Hiwassee, Cherokee, N.C.; Yes; Unallotted

2940; Walkingstick, Bascomb; M; 8/13/88-43; N.C. Cherokee; 4/4; M; Head; 2912; Yes; Yes; Unallotted
2941; Walkingstick, Alice S.; F; 4/1/03-29; N.C. Cherokee; 15/16; M; Wife; 2913; Yes; Yes; Unallotted
2942; Walkingstick, William; M; 8/28/14-17; N.C. Cherokee; 4/4; S; Son; 2914; Yes; Yes; Unallotted
2943; Walkingstick, Henry; M; 8/10/16-15; N.C. Cherokee; 4/4; S; Son; 2915; Yes; Yes; Unallotted
2944; Walkingstick, Wayne; M; 4/20/21-10; N.C. Cherokee; 4/4; S; Son; 2916; Yes; Yes; Unallotted
2945; Walkingstick, Virgil; M; 11/7/31-4/12; N.C. Cherokee; 4/4; S; Son; ---; Yes; Yes; Unallotted

2946; Walkingstick, James; M; 12/28/85-46; N.C. Cherokee; 4/4; M; Head; 2917; Yes; Yes; Unallotted
2947; Walkingstick, Mandy T.; F; 11/12/90-41; N.C. Cherokee; 4/4; M; Wife; 2918; Yes; Yes; Unallotted

2948; Walkingstick, Jasper; M; 10/14/72-59; N.C. Cherokee; 4/4; Wd.; Head; 2919; Yes; Yes; Unallotted
2949; Walkingstick, Willie; M; 10/1/06-25; N.C. Cherokee; 4/4; S; Son; 2919a; Yes; Yes; Unallotted
2950; Walkingstick, John; M; 8/13/11-20; N.C. Cherokee; 4/4; S; Son; 2920; Yes; Yes; Unallotted
2951; Walkingstick, Samuel; M; 11/13/13-18; N.C. Cherokee; 4/4; S; Son; 2921; Yes; Yes; Unallotted

Census of the **Eastern Cherokee** reservation of the **Cherokee, N.C.** jurisdiction, as of **April 1** , 19**32,** taken by **R. L. Spalsbury** , Superintendent.

Key: Number; Surname, Given; Sex; Date of Birth-Age at Last Birthday; Tribe; Degree of Blood; Marital Status; Relationship to Head of Family; Last C. Roll No.; At Jurisdiction Where Enrolled (Yes/No); (If no – Where); Ward (Yes/No); Allotment, Annuity and Identification Numbers (if given).

2952; Walkingstick, John; M; 12/23/52-79; N.C. Cherokee; 4/4; Wd.; Head; 2922; Yes; Yes; Unallotted

2953; Walkingstick, Enoch; M; 7/2/09-22; N.C. Cherokee; 4/4; S; Son; 2923; Yes; Yes; Unallotted

2954; Walkingstick, Maggie Axe; F; 9/12/94-37; N.C. Cherokee; 4/4; Div.; Head; 2924; Yes; Yes; Unallotted

2955; Walkingstick, Mason; M; 1/6/03-29; N.C. Cherokee; 4/4; M; Head; 2925; Yes; Yes; Unallotted

2956; Walkingstick, Lucy Bird; F; 4/6/08-23; N.C. Cherokee; 4/4; M; Wife; 2926; Yes; Yes; Unallotted

2957; Walkingstick, Mike; M; 2/20/02-30; N.C. Cherokee; 4/4; M; Head; 2928; Yes; Yes; Unallotted

2958; Walkingstick, Emily T.; F; 9/24/05-26; N.C. Cherokee; 3/4; M; Wife; 2929; Yes; Yes; Unallotted

2959; Walkingstick, Alfred K.; M; 5/3/27-4; N.C. Cherokee; 7/8; S; Son; 2930; Yes; Yes; Unallotted

2960; Walkingstick, Moses; M; 3/25/96-36; N.C. Cherokee; 4/4; M; Head; 2931; Yes; Yes; Unallotted

2961; Walkingstick, Jennie W.; F; 12/24/90-41; N.C. Cherokee; 4/4; M; Wife; 2932; Yes; Yes; Unallotted

2962; Walkingstick, Ancy; F; 3/20/20-12; N.C. Cherokee; 4/4; S; Daughter; 2933; Yes; Yes; Unallotted

2963; Walkingstick, Emmaline; F; 2/5/24-8; N.C. Cherokee; 4/4; S; Daughter; 2934; Yes; Yes; Unallotted

2964; Walkingstick, Linda G.; F; 3/5/85-47; N.C. Cherokee; 4/4; Wd.; Head; 2935; Yes; Yes; Unallotted

2965; Walkingstick, Lydia; F; 6/10/13-18; N.C. Cherokee; 4/4; S; Daughter; 2936; Yes; Yes; Unallotted

2966; Walkingstick, Minda; F; 9/10/19-12; N.C. Cherokee; 4/4; S; Daughter; 2937; Yes; Yes; Unallotted

2967; Walkingstick, Edward; M; 3/14/21-10; N.C. Cherokee; 4/4; S; Son; 2938; Yes; Yes; Unallotted

2968; Walkingstick, Abraham; M; 8/30/24-7; N.C. Cherokee; 4/4; S; Son; 2939; Yes; Yes; Unallotted

2969; Walkingstick, Tom; M; 1/17/08-24; N.C. Cherokee; 4/4; S; Head; 2940; Yes; Yes; Unallotted

2970; Wallace, James; M; 1/15/78-55; N.C. Cherokee; 4/4; M; Head; 2941; Yes; Yes; Unallotted

Census of the **Eastern Cherokee** reservation of the **Cherokee, N.C.** jurisdiction, as of **April 1** , **1932,** taken by **R. L. Spalsbury** , Superintendent.

Key: Number; Surname, Given; Sex; Date of Birth-Age at Last Birthday; Tribe; Degree of Blood; Marital Status; Relationship to Head of Family; Last C. Roll No.; At Jurisdiction Where Enrolled (Yes/No); (If no – Where); Ward (Yes/No); Allotment, Annuity and Identification Numbers (if given).

2971; Wallace, Sallie L.; F; 12/10/64-67; N.C. Cherokee; 4/4; M; Wife; 2942; Yes; Yes; Unallotted

2972; Wallace, Tahquette; M; 10/14/03-28; N.C. Cherokee; 15/16; M; Head; 2943; Yes; Yes; Unallotted

2973; Wallace, Margarind; F; 10/10/12-19; N.C. Cherokee; 4/4; M; Wife 2nd; 2944; Yes; Yes; Unallotted

2974; Wallace, Stacy; F; 10/14/21-10; N.C. Cherokee; 31/32; S; Daughter; 2945; Yes; Yes; Unallotted

2975; Wallace, Marjorie; F; 8/10/22-9; N.C. Cherokee; 31/32; S; Daughter; 2946; Yes; Yes; Unallotted

2976; Wallace, Ollie; F; 10/8/29-2; N.C. Cherokee; 31/32; S; Daughter; ---; Yes; Yes; Unallotted

2977; Warrick, Selma C.; F; 2/22/08-24; N.C. Cherokee; 1/16; M; Wife; 2947; Yes; Yes; Unallotted

2978; Washington, Jesse; M; 3/5/73-59; N.C. Cherokee; 4/4; M; Head; 2948; Yes; Yes; Unallotted

2979; Washington, Ollie; F; 12/26/76-55; N.C. Cherokee; 7/8; M; Wife; 2949; Yes; Yes; Unallotted

2980; Washington, Emma; F; 8/16/04-27; N.C. Cherokee; 15/16; S; Daughter; 2950; Yes; Yes; Unallotted

2981; Washington, George; M; 7/6/06-25; N.C. Cherokee; 15/16; S; Son; 2951; Yes; Yes; Unallotted

2982; Washington, Jonas; M; 3/9/09-23; N.C. Cherokee; 15/16; S; Son; 2952; Yes; Yes; Unallotted

2983; Washington, Joseph; M; 2/20/82-50; N.C. Cherokee; 4/4; M; Head; 2953; Yes; Yes; Unallotted

2984; Washington, Stella B.; F; 3/17/84-48; N.C. Cherokee; 1/2; M; Wife; 2954; Yes; Yes; Unallotted

2985; Washington, Richard; M; 9/27/10-21; N.C. Cherokee; 3/4; S; Son; 2955; Yes; Yes; Unallotted

2986; Washington, Josephine; F; 4/29/13-18; N.C. Cherokee; 3/4; S; Daughter; 2956; Yes; Yes; Unallotted

2987; Washington, Erma L.; F; 2/5/16-16; N.C. Cherokee; 3/4; S; Daughter; 2957; Yes; Yes; Unallotted

2988; Watson (Foster, Elsie), Elsie; F; 6/17/99-32; N.C. Cherokee; 1/16; M; Wife; 2958; No; Culberson, Cherokee, N.C.; Yes; Unallotted

2989; Watson, Virginia; F; 8/13/21-10; N.C. Cherokee; 1/32; S; Daughter; 2959; No; Culberson, Cherokee, N.C.; Yes; Unallotted

2990; Watson, James H.; M; 2/13/22-10; N.C. Cherokee; 1/32; S; Son; 2960; No; Culberson, Cherokee, N.C.; Yes; Unallotted

Census of the **Eastern Cherokee** reservation of the **Cherokee, N.C.** jurisdiction, as of **April 1** , 19**32,** taken by **R. L. Spalsbury** , Superintendent.

Key: Number; Surname, Given; Sex; Date of Birth-Age at Last Birthday; Tribe; Degree of Blood; Marital Status; Relationship to Head of Family; Last C. Roll No.; At Jurisdiction Where Enrolled (Yes/No); (If no – Where); Ward (Yes/No); Allotment, Annuity and Identification Numbers (if given).

2991; Watty, Goolarche; M; 12/20/76-55; N.C. Cherokee; 4/4; M; Head; 2961; Yes; Yes; Unallotted

2992; Watty, Nessih; F; 12/15/76-55; N.C. Cherokee; 4/4; M; Wife; 2962; Yes; Yes; Unallotted

2993; Watty, Stephen; M; 1/25/98-34; N.C. Cherokee; 4/4; S; Son; 2963; Yes; Yes; Unallotted

2994; Watty, Jessan; M; 3/17/16-16; N.C. Cherokee; 4/4; S; Son; 2964; Yes; Yes; Unallotted

2995; Watty, Ollie; F; 12/23/09-22; N.C. Cherokee; 4/4; S; Daughter; 2965; Yes; Yes; Unallotted

2996; Wayne, Will; M; 12/26/75-56; N.C. Cherokee; 4/4; Wd.; Head; 2966; Yes; Yes; Unallotted

2997; Wayne, Agnes; F; 8/20/11-20; N.C. Cherokee; 4/4; S; Daughter; 2967; Yes; Yes; Unallotted

2998; Wayne, Sara; F; 8/22/30-1; N.C. Cherokee; 4/4; S; Grand-dau.(Illeg.); ---; Yes; Yes; Unallotted

2999; Webb, Fannie C.; F; 9/17/00-31; N.C. Cherokee; 1/16; M; Wife; 2968; Yes; Yes; Unallotted

3000; Webb, Winifred C.; F; 10/25/22-9; N.C. Cherokee; 1/32; S; Daughter; 2969; Yes; Yes; Unallotted

3001; Webster, Galer B.; M; 4/2/71-60; N.C. Cherokee; 1/8; M; Head; 2970; No; Choteau, Hayes[sic], Okla.; Yes; Unallotted

3002; Webster, Harry T.; M; 4/2/98-33; N.C. Cherokee; 1/16; S; Head; 2971; No; Choteau, Hayes, Okla.; Yes; Unallotted

3003; Webster, Rachel A.; F; 2/16/41-91; N.C. Cherokee; 1/4; Wd.; Head; 2972; Yes; Yes; Unallotted

3004; Webster, Ralph W.; M; 4/2/96-35; N.C. Cherokee; 1/16; M; Head; 2973; No; Wetumka, Hughes, Okla.; Yes; Unallotted

3005; Webster, William; M; 10/10/69-62; N.C. Cherokee; 1/8; M; Head; 2974; No; Culberson, Cherokee, N.C.; Yes; Unallotted

3006; Webster, Jetter C.; M; 2/19/97-35; N.C. Cherokee; 1/16; S; Son; 2975; No; Culberson, Cherokee, N.C.; Yes; Unallotted

3007; Webster, William R.; M; 2/22/06-26; N.C. Cherokee; 1/16; S; Son; 2976; No; Culberson, Cherokee, N.C.; Yes; Unallotted

3008; Webster, William L.; M; 7/2/12-19; N.C. Cherokee; 1/16; S; Son; 2977; No; Culberson, Cherokee, N.C.; Yes; Unallotted

3009; Webster, Thomas D.; M; 11/14/14-17; N.C. Cherokee; 1/16; S; Son; 2978; No; Culberson, Cherokee, N.C.; Yes; Unallotted

Census of the **Eastern Cherokee** reservation of the **Cherokee, N.C.** jurisdiction, as of **April 1**, **1932**, taken by **R. L. Spalsbury**, Superintendent.

Key: Number; Surname, Given; Sex; Date of Birth-Age at Last Birthday; Tribe; Degree of Blood; Marital Status; Relationship to Head of Family; Last C. Roll No.; At Jurisdiction Where Enrolled (Yes/No); (If no – Where); Ward (Yes/No); Allotment, Annuity and Identification Numbers (if given).

3010; Welch, Adam; M; 12/4/84-47; N.C. Cherokee; 4/4; M; Head; 2979; Yes; Yes; Unallotted

3011; Welch, Anna P.; F; 12/25/93-38; N.C. Cherokee; 13/16; M; Wife; 2980; Yes; Yes; Unallotted

3012; Welch, Charlotte; F; 10/9/13-18; N.C. Cherokee; 29/32; S; Daughter; 2981; Yes; Yes; Unallotted

3013; Welch, Wilson; M; 10/14/14-17; N.C. Cherokee; 29/32; S; Son; 2982; Yes; Yes; Unallotted

3014; Welch, Elijah; M; 12/27/17-14; N.C. Cherokee; 29/32; S; Son; 2983; Yes; Yes; Unallotted

3015; Welch, Simpson; M; 7/14/21-10; N.C. Cherokee; 29/32; S; Son; 2984; Yes; Yes; Unallotted

3016; Welch, John; M; 4/11/30-1; N.C. Cherokee; 29/32; S; Son; 2985; Yes; Yes; Unallotted

3017; Welch, Akin; M; 4/11/27-4; N.C. Cherokee; 29/32; S; Son; 2986; Yes; Yes; Unallotted

3018; Welch, Cornetta; M; 10/15/80-51; N.C. Cherokee; 4/4; M; Head; 2987; Yes; Yes; Unallotted

3019; Welch, Nicey T.; F; 2/16/73-56; N.C. Cherokee; 4/4; M; Wife; 2988; Yes; Yes; Unallotted

3020; Welch (Mr. Liddy Squirrell), David; M; 11/16/11-20; N.C. Cherokee; 29/32; S; Son; 2989; Yes; Yes; Unallotted

3021; Welch, Lucinda; F; 5/4/14-17; N.C. Cherokee; 29/32; S; Daughter; 2990; Yes; Yes; Unallotted

3022; Welch, Awee; F; 5/15/80-51; N.C. Cherokee; 4/4; Wd.; Head; 2991; Yes; Yes; Unallotted

3023; Welch, James B.; M; 4/25/91-40; N.C. Cherokee; 4/4; S; Son; 2992; Yes; Yes; Unallotted

3024; Welch, Jane; F; 7/16/08-23; N.C. Cherokee; 4/4; S; Daughter; 2993; Yes; Yes; Unallotted

3025; Welch, Edward; M; 10/14/02-29; N.C. Cherokee; 7/8; S; Head; 2994; Yes; Yes; Unallotted

3026; Welch, Elijah; M; 12/26/62-69; N.C. Cherokee; 4/4; Wd.; Head; 2995; Yes; Yes; Unallotted

3027; Welch, Ephesus; M; 10/19/83-48; N.C. Cherokee; 4/4; M; Head; 2996; Yes; Yes; Unallotted

3028; Welch, Stacy; F; 2/26/90-42; N.C. Cherokee; 4/4; M; Wife; 2997; Yes; Yes; Unallotted

Census of the **Eastern Cherokee** reservation of the **Cherokee, N.C.** jurisdiction, as of **April 1**, 19**32,** taken by **R. L. Spalsbury**, Superintendent.

Key: Number; Surname, Given; Sex; Date of Birth-Age at Last Birthday; Tribe; Degree of Blood; Marital Status; Relationship to Head of Family; Last C. Roll No.; At Jurisdiction Where Enrolled (Yes/No); (If no – Where); Ward (Yes/No); Allotment, Annuity and Identification Numbers (if given).

3029; Welch, Juna; M; 10/19/07-24; N.C. Cherokee; 4/4; S; Son; 2998; Yes; Yes; Unallotted

3030; Welch, Isaac; M; 10/6/19-12; N.C. Cherokee; 4/4; S; Son; 2999; Yes; Yes; Unallotted

3031; Welch, Mike; M; 2/4/23-9; N.C. Cherokee; 4/4; S; Son; 3000; Yes; Yes; Unallotted

3032; Welch, Nannie; F; 1/29/26-6; N.C. Cherokee; 4/4; S; Daughter; 3001; Yes; Yes; Unallotted

3033; Welch, James Blue; M; 7/19/29-2; N.C. Cherokee; 4/4; S; Son; 3002; Yes; Yes; Unallotted

3034; Welch, Frank C.; M; 4/17/09-22; N.C. Cherokee; 29/32; M; Head; 3003; Yes; Yes; Unallotted

3035; Welch, Dinah C.; F; 4/24/10-21; N.C. Cherokee; 4/4; M; Wife; 3004; Yes; Yes; Unallotted

3036; Welch, Henderson; M; 4/20/29-2; N.C. Cherokee; 61/64; S; Son; 3005; Yes; Yes; Unallotted

3037; Welch, James B.; M; 5/12/75-56; N.C. Cherokee; 1/4; M; Head; 3006; Yes; Yes; Unallotted

3038; Welch, Yihginneh; F; 3/27/00-32; N.C. Cherokee; 4/4; Wd.; Head; 3007; Yes; Yes; Unallotted

3039; Welch, Adam; M; 5/22/25-6; N.C. Cherokee; 4/4; S; Son; 3008; Yes; Yes; Unallotted

3040; Welch, Daniel; M; 10/7/27-4; N.C. Cherokee; 4/4; S; Son; 3009; Yes; Yes; Unallotted

3041; Welch, Mary Bell; F; 12/15/29-2; N.C. Cherokee; 4/4; S; Daughter; 3010; Yes; Yes; Unallotted

3042; Welch, James G.; M; 5/23/91-40; N.C. Cherokee; 9/16; M; Head; 3011; Yes; Yes; Unallotted

3043; Welch, Lottie T.; F; 10/28/90-41; N.C. Cherokee; 4/4; M; Wife; 3012; Yes; Yes; Unallotted

3044; Welch, Elizabeth; F; 7/5/13-19; N.C. Cherokee; 25/32; S; Daughter; 3013; Yes; Yes; Unallotted

3045; Welch, Amy; F; 10/28/15-16; N.C. Cherokee; 25/32; S; Daughter; 3014; Yes; Yes; Unallotted

3046; Welch, Irving; M; 3/19/18-14; N.C. Cherokee; 25/32; S; Son; 3015; Yes; Yes; Unallotted

3047; Welch, Oscar; M; 5/24/21-10; N.C. Cherokee; 25/32; S; Son; 3016; Yes; Yes; Unallotted

3048; Welch, Myrtle; F; 4/2/24-7; N.C. Cherokee; 25/32; S; Daughter; 3017; Yes; Yes; Unallotted

Census of the **Eastern Cherokee** reservation of the **Cherokee, N.C.** jurisdiction, as of **April 1** , **1932,** taken by **R. L. Spalsbury** , Superintendent.

Key: Number; Surname, Given; Sex; Date of Birth-Age at Last Birthday; Tribe; Degree of Blood; Marital Status; Relationship to Head of Family; Last C. Roll No.; At Jurisdiction Where Enrolled (Yes/No); (If no – Where); Ward (Yes/No); Allotment, Annuity and Identification Numbers (if given).

3049; Welch, Mary Jane; F; 5/3/27-4; N.C. Cherokee; 25/32; S; Daughter; 3018; Yes; Yes; Unallotted

3050; Welch, Charlotte; F; 11/10/29-2; N.C. Cherokee; 25/32; S; Daughter; 3019; Yes; Yes; Unallotted

3051; Welch, John; M; 9/26/93-38; N.C. Cherokee; 7/8; M; Head; 3020; Yes; Yes; Unallotted

3052; Welch, Mary; F; 6/12/91-40; N.C. Cherokee; 7/8; M; Wife; 3021; Yes; Yes; Unallotted

3053; Welch, Lloyd; M; 8/18/95-36; N.C. Cherokee; 5/16; M; Head; 3022; Yes; Yes; Unallotted

3054; Welch, Mark; M; 5/21/00-31; N.C. Cherokee; 4/4; M; Head; 3023; Yes; Yes; Unallotted

3055; Welch, Polly C.; F; 3/19/94-38; N.C. Cherokee; 4/4; M; Wife; 3024; Yes; Yes; Unallotted

3056; Welch, Sally; F; 5/29/21-10; N.C. Cherokee; 4/4; S; Daughter; 3025; Yes; Yes; Unallotted

3057; Welch, Mark G.; M; 4/21/77-54; N.C. Cherokee; 3/4; S; Head; 3026; Yes; Yes; Unallotted

3058; Welch, Moses; M; 3/1/86-46; N.C. Cherokee; 4/4; M; Head; 3027; Yes; Yes; Unallotted

3059; Welch, Cindy; F; 6/15/98-33; N.C. Cherokee; 4/4; M; Wife; 3028; Yes; Yes; Unallotted

3060; Welch, Nancy; F; 12/25/65-66; N.C. Cherokee; 4/4; Wd.; Head; 3029; Yes; Yes; Unallotted

3061; Welch, Ned; M; 4/16/03-28; N.C. Cherokee; 4/4; Div.; Head; 3030; Yes; Yes; Unallotted

3062; Welch, Elizabeth; F; 5/25/09-22; N.C. Cherokee; 1/2; Div.; Wife (Div.); 3031; Yes; Yes; Unallotted

3063; Welch, Richard; M; 6/30/03-28; N.C. Cherokee; 11/16; S; Head; 3032; Yes; Yes; Unallotted

3064; Welch, Sampson; M; 8/4/61-70; N.C. Cherokee; 4/4; M; Head; 3033; Yes; Yes; Unallotted

3065; Welch, Lizzie; F; 12/4/62-69; N.C. Cherokee; 4/4; M; Wife; 3034; Yes; Yes; Unallotted

Census of the **Eastern Cherokee** reservation of the **Cherokee, N.C.** jurisdiction, as of **April 1** , 19**32,** taken by **R. L. Spalsbury** , Superintendent.

Key: Number; Surname, Given; Sex; Date of Birth-Age at Last Birthday; Tribe; Degree of Blood; Marital Status; Relationship to Head of Family; Last C. Roll No.; At Jurisdiction Where Enrolled (Yes/No); (If no – Where); Ward (Yes/No); Allotment, Annuity and Identification Numbers (if given).

3066; Welch, Tempe J.; F; 1/22/88-44; N.C. Cherokee; 1/4; M; Wife; 3035; Yes; Yes; Unallotted

3067; Welch, Theodore; M; 7/1/97-34; N.C. Cherokee; 5/16; M; Head; 3036; Yes; Yes; Unallotted

3068; Welch, Willie; M; 7/14/89-42; N.C. Cherokee; 9/16; M; Head; 3037; Yes; Yes; Unallotted

3069; Welch, Maude F.; F; 5/24/94-37; N.C. Cherokee; 4/4; M; Wife; 3038; Yes; Yes; Unallotted

3070; Welch, Elliott; M; 3/29/15-17; N.C. Cherokee; 25/32; S; Son; 3039; Yes; Yes; Unallotted

3071; Welch, Edna; F; 9/25/16-15; N.C. Cherokee; 25/32; S; Daughter; 3040; Yes; Yes; Unallotted

3072; Welch, Edith; F; 9/30/18-13; N.C. Cherokee; 25/32; S; Daughter; 3041; Yes; Yes; Unallotted

3073; Wesley, Judas; M; 12/16/78-53; N.C. Cherokee; 7/8; M; Head; 3042; Yes; Yes; Unallotted

3074; Wesley, Jennie; F; 12/20/55-76; N.C. Cherokee; 4/4; M; Wife; 3043; Yes; Yes; Unallotted

3075; West, Buck; M; 4/11/98-33; N.C. Cherokee; 7/8; M; Head; 3044; Yes; Yes; Unallotted

3076; West, Susan B.; F; 7/6/01-30; N.C. Cherokee; 15/16; M; Wife; 3045; Yes; Yes; Unallotted

3077; West, Alfred; M; 4/24/21-10; N.C. Cherokee; 29/32; S; Son; 3046; Yes; Yes; Unallotted

3078; West, Cecil; M; 4/20/23-8; N.C. Cherokee; 29/32; S; Son; 3047; Yes; Yes; Unallotted

3079; West, Doris; F; 6/1/25-6; N.C. Cherokee; 29/32; S; Daughter; 113; Yes; Yes; Unallotted

3080; West, James; M; 11/2/94-37; N.C. Cherokee; 7/8; S; Head; 3048; Yes; Yes; Unallotted

3081; Whip-poor-will, Manley; M; 6/15/84-47; N.C. Cherokee; 4/4; S; Head; 3049; Yes; Yes; Unallotted

3082; Whitaker, James M.; M; 8/23/46-85; N.C. Cherokee; 1/16; S; Head; 3050; Yes; Yes; Unallotted

3083; Whitaker, Jud; M; 5/19/00-31; N.C. Cherokee; 1/32; M; Head; 3051; Yes; Yes; Unallotted

Census of the **Eastern Cherokee** reservation of the **Cherokee, N.C.** jurisdiction, as of **April 1** , **1932,** taken by **R. L. Spalsbury** , Superintendent.

Key: Number; Surname, Given; Sex; Date of Birth-Age at Last Birthday; Tribe; Degree of Blood; Marital Status; Relationship to Head of Family; Last C. Roll No.; At Jurisdiction Where Enrolled (Yes/No); (If no – Where); Ward (Yes/No); Allotment, Annuity and Identification Numbers (if given).

3084; Whitaker, Willard; M; 4/27/21-10; N.C. Cherokee; 1/64; S; Son; 3052; Yes; Yes; Unallotted

3085; Whitaker, Herman; M; 11/19/22-9; N.C. Cherokee; 1/64; S; Son; 3053; Yes; Yes; Unallotted

3086; Whitaker (Harden, Rutha), Rutha; F; 3/4/79-53; N.C. Cherokee; 1/16; M; Wife; 3054; Yes; Yes; Unallotted

3087; Whitaker, Ross; M; 2/8/11-21; N.C. Cherokee; 1/32; S; Son; 3055; Yes; Yes; Unallotted

3088; Whitaker, Stephen; M; 8/12/55-76; N.C. Cherokee; 1/16; M; Head; 3056; Yes; Yes; Unallotted

3089; White (Harden, Bettie), Bettie; F; 3/4/89-42; N.C. Cherokee; 1/16; M; Wife; 3057; No; Lorey Mills Station, Gastonia, Gaston, N.C.; Yes; Unallotted

3090; White, Mary; F; 6/14/09-22; N.C. Cherokee; 1/32; S; Daughter; 3058; No; Lorey Mills Station, Gastonia, Gaston, N.C.; Yes; Unallotted

3091; White, Robert; M; 3/26/13-19; N.C. Cherokee; 1/32; S; Son; 3059; No; Lorey Mills Station, Gastonia, Gaston, N.C.; Yes; Unallotted

3092; White, John; M; 5/20/17-14; N.C. Cherokee; 1/32; S; Son; 3060; No; Lorey Mills Station, Gastonia, Gaston, N.C.; Yes; Unallotted

3093; White, Inez; F; 12/19/19-12; N.C. Cherokee; 1/32; S; Daughter; 3061; No; Lorey Mills Station, Gastonia, Gaston, N.C.; Yes; Unallotted

3094; White, Pink; M; 8/13/22-9; N.C. Cherokee; 1/32; S; Son; 3062; No; Lorey Mills Station, Gastonia, Gaston, N.C.; Yes; Unallotted

3095; White, Dee; M; 4/17/06-25; N.C. Cherokee; 1/32; M; Head; 3063; Yes; Yes; Unallotted

3096; White, Dillard; M; 6/17/04-27; N.C. Cherokee; 1/32; M; Head; 3064; Yes; Yes; Unallotted

3097; White-tree, Floy B.; F; 7/1/99-32; N.C. Cherokee; 1/8; M; Wife; 3065; Yes; Yes; Unallotted

3098; White-tree, F. Wenonah; F; 7/11/16-15; N.C. Cherokee; 1/16; S; Daughter; 3066; Yes; Yes; Unallotted

3099; White-tree, John; M; 8/3/20-11; N.C. Cherokee; 1/16; S; Son; 3067; Yes; Yes; Unallotted

3100; White-tree, Alva E.; M; 10/29/22-9; N.C. Cherokee; 1/16; S; Son; 3068; Yes; Yes; Unallotted

3101; Wildcat, Dahnola; M; 1/8/81-50; N.C. Cherokee; 4/4; M; Head; 3069; Yes; Yes; Unallotted

3102; Wildcat, Sallie; F; 2/16/81-51; N.C. Cherokee; 4/4; M; Wife; 3070; Yes; Yes; Unallotted

Census of the **Eastern Cherokee** reservation of the **Cherokee, N.C.** jurisdiction, as of **April 1** , 19**32,** taken by **R. L. Spalsbury** , Superintendent.

Key: Number; Surname, Given; Sex; Date of Birth-Age at Last Birthday; Tribe; Degree of Blood; Marital Status; Relationship to Head of Family; Last C. Roll No.; At Jurisdiction Where Enrolled (Yes/No); (If no – Where); Ward (Yes/No); Allotment, Annuity and Identification Numbers (if given).

3103; Wildcat, Addison; M; 2/21/20-12; N.C. Cherokee; 4/4; S; Son; 3071; Yes; Yes; Unallotted

3104; Wildcat, Boyman; M; 2/21/20-12; N.C. Cherokee; 4/4; S; Son; 3072; Yes; Yes; Unallotted

3105; Will, John; M; 12/26/62-69; N.C. Cherokee; 4/4; M; Head; 3073; Yes; Yes; Unallotted

3106; Will, Jane; F; 12/20/73-58; N.C. Cherokee; 4/4; M; Wife; 3074; Yes; Yes; Unallotted

3107; Will, James; M; 2/2/01-31; N.C. Cherokee; 4/4; S; Son; 3075; Yes; Yes; Unallotted

3108; Will, David; M; 10/29/06-25; N.C. Cherokee; 4/4; S; Son; 3076; Yes; Yes; Unallotted

3109; Will (Thompson), Luzene; F; 1/7/09-23; N.C. Cherokee; 4/4; S; Daughter; 3077; Yes; Yes; Unallotted

3110; Will, Nellie; F; 10/15/11-20; N.C. Cherokee; 4/4; S; Daughter; 3078; Yes; Yes; Unallotted

3111; Wilnoty, Joseph; M; 5/5/94-37; N.C. Cherokee; 3/4; M; Head; 3079; Yes; Yes; Unallotted

3112; Wilnoty, Ned; M; 9/9/96-35; N.C. Cherokee; 3/4; S; Brother; 3080; Yes; Yes; Unallotted

3113; Wilnoty, Tidmarsh; M; 8/11/31-7/12; N.C. Cherokee; 7/16; S; Son; ---; Yes; Yes; Unallotted

3114; Wilnoty, Moses; M; 8/23/83-48; N.C. Cherokee; 4/4; M; Head; 3081; Yes; Yes; Unallotted

3115; Wilnoty, Alice M.; F; 6/1/98-33; N.C. Cherokee; 1/8; M; Wife; 3082; Yes; Yes; Unallotted

3116; Wilnoty, Julius; M; 12/18/09-22; N.C. Cherokee; 9/16; S; Son; 3083; Yes; Yes; Unallotted

3117; Wilnoty, Elizabeth; F; 2/23/14-18; N.C. Cherokee; 9/16; S; Daughter; 3084; Yes; Yes; Unallotted

3118; Wilnoty, Fred; M; 8/8/28-3; N.C. Cherokee; 9/16; S; Son; 3085; Yes; Yes; Unallotted

3119; Wilnoty, Sallie; F; 12/26/50-81; N.C. Cherokee; 4/4; Wd.; Head; 3086; Yes; Yes; Unallotted

3120; Wilnoty, Simon; M; 6/19/92-39; N.C. Cherokee; 4/4; M; Head; 3087; Yes; Yes; Unallotted

3121; Wilnoty, Josephine; F; 6/5/06-25; N.C. Cherokee; 1/2; M; Wife; 3088; Yes; Yes; Unallotted

3122; Wilnoty, Bettie Lou; F; 8/28/28-3; N.C. Cherokee; 3/4; S; Daughter; 3089; Yes; Yes; Unallotted

Census of the **Eastern Cherokee** reservation of the **Cherokee, N.C.** jurisdiction, as of **April 1** , **1932,** taken by **R. L. Spalsbury** , Superintendent.

Key: Number; Surname, Given; Sex; Date of Birth-Age at Last Birthday; Tribe; Degree of Blood; Marital Status; Relationship to Head of Family; Last C. Roll No.; At Jurisdiction Where Enrolled (Yes/No); (If no – Where); Ward (Yes/No); Allotment, Annuity and Identification Numbers (if given).

3123; Wilnoty, Paul R.; M; 4/18/31-11/12; N.C. Cherokee; 3/4; S; Son; ---; Yes; Yes; Unallotted

3124; Winkler, Maybelle; F; 5/12/13-18; N.C. Cherokee; 1/32; S; Daughter (Fr. white); 3090; Yes; Yes; Unallotted

3125; Winkler, Dennis; M; 1/9/16-16; N.C. Cherokee; 1/32; S; Son; 3091; Yes; Yes; Unallotted

3126; Winkler, Hazel; F; 8/28/18-13; N.C. Cherokee; 1/32; S; Daughter; 3092; Yes; Yes; Unallotted

3127; Winkler, Lois; F; 11/15/20-11; N.C. Cherokee; 1/32; S; Daughter; 3093; Yes; Yes; Unallotted

3128; Winkler, Harrell; M; 1/4/23-9; N.C. Cherokee; 1/32; S; Son; 3094; Yes; Yes; Unallotted

3129; Wolfe, Callie; F; 7/4/77-54; N.C. Cherokee; 4/4; Wd.; Head; 3095; Yes; Yes; Unallotted

3130; Wolfe, Charles; M; 8/22/92-39; N.C. Cherokee; 1/2; S; Head; 3096; Yes; Yes; Unallotted

3131; Wolfe, David; M; 1/2/40-92; N.C. Cherokee; 1/2; M; Head; 3097; Yes; Yes; Unallotted

3132; Wolfe, Dawson; M; 8/15/87-44; N.C. Cherokee; 4/4; M; Head; 3098; Yes; Yes; Unallotted

3133; Wolfe, Polly W.; F; 9/1/04-27; N.C. Cherokee; 4/4; M; Wife; 3099; Yes; Yes; Unallotted

3134; Wolfe, Dinah; F; 3/15/14-18; N.C. Cherokee; 4/4; S; Daughter; 3100; Yes; Yes; Unallotted

3135; Wolfe, James; M; 3/16/15-17; N.C. Cherokee; 4/4; S; Son; 3101; Yes; Yes; Unallotted

3136; Wolfe, Ina; F; 7/3/23-8; N.C. Cherokee; 4/4; S; Daughter; 3102; Yes; Yes; Unallotted

3137; Wolfe, Edward; M; 11/8/91-40; N.C. Cherokee; 7/8; M; Head; 3103; Yes; Yes; Unallotted

3138; Wolfe, George L.; M; 5/10/67-64; N.C. Cherokee; 1/4; M; Head; 3104; Yes; Yes; Unallotted

3139; Wolfe, Jacob; M; 4/2/71-60; N.C. Cherokee; 4/4; M; Head; 3105; No; Decatur, Benyon[sic], Ark.; Yes; Unallotted

3140; Wolfe, Jesse; M; 7/21/00-31; N.C. Cherokee; 4/4; S; Son; 3106; Yes; Yes; Unallotted

Census of the **Eastern Cherokee** reservation of the **Cherokee, N.C.** jurisdiction, as of **April 1** , 19**32,** taken by **R. L. Spalsbury** , Superintendent.

Key: Number; Surname, Given; Sex; Date of Birth-Age at Last Birthday; Tribe; Degree of Blood; Marital Status; Relationship to Head of Family; Last C. Roll No.; At Jurisdiction Where Enrolled (Yes/No); (If no – Where); Ward (Yes/No); Allotment, Annuity and Identification Numbers (if given).

3141; Wolfe, Jacob; M; 3/15/13-19; N.C. Cherokee; 4/4; S; Son; 3109; Yes; Yes; Unallotted

3142; Wolfe, James T.; M; 8/5/85-46; N.C. Cherokee; 1/2; M; Head; 3110; Yes; Yes; Unallotted

3143; Wolfe, Bettie S.; F; 10/15/96-35; N.C. Cherokee; 1/2; M; Wife; 3111; Yes; Yes; Unallotted

3144; Wolfe, Wm. Wallace; M; 2/18/12-20; N.C. Cherokee; 1/2; S; Son; 3112; Yes; Yes; Unallotted

3145; Wolfe, Edwin W.; M; 4/18/14-17; N.C. Cherokee; 1/2; S; Son; 3113; Yes; Yes; Unallotted

3146; Wolfe, Donald G.; M; 9/6/16-15; N.C. Cherokee; 1/2; S; Son; 3114; Yes; Yes; Unallotted

3147; Wolfe, Robert W.; M; 2/13/19-13; N.C. Cherokee; 1/2; S; Son; 3115; Yes; Yes; Unallotted

3148; Wolfe, Wade H.; M; 3/11/21-11; N.C. Cherokee; 1/2; S; Son; 3116; Yes; Yes; Unallotted

3149; Wolfe, Mary Iva; F; 12/29/23-8; N.C. Cherokee; 1/2; S; Daughter; 3117; Yes; Yes; Unallotted

3150; Wolfe, Bettie W.; F; 6/17/26-5; N.C. Cherokee; 1/2; S; Daughter; 3118; Yes; Yes; Unallotted

3151; Wolfe, James T.; M; 5/14/30-1; N.C. Cherokee; 1/2; S; Son; 3119; Yes; Yes; Unallotted

3152; Wolfe, John; M; 9/12/71-60; N.C. Cherokee; 4/4; M; Head; 3120; Yes; Yes; Unallotted

3153; Wolfe, Linda; F; 6/10/78-53; N.C. Cherokee; 4/4; M; Wife; 3121; Yes; Yes; Unallotted

3154; Wolfe, Walker; M; 4/21/05-26; N.C. Cherokee; 4/4; S; Son; 3122; Yes; Yes; Unallotted

3155; Wolfe, Salkinney; F; 7/16/11-20; N.C. Cherokee; 4/4; S; Daughter; 3123; Yes; Yes; Unallotted

3156; Wolfe, Josephine; F; 2/22/13-19; N.C. Cherokee; 4/4; S; Daughter; 3124; Yes; Yes; Unallotted

3157; Wolfe, Rebecca; F; 3/17/15-17; N.C. Cherokee; 4/4; S; Daughter; 3125; Yes; Yes; Unallotted

3158; Wolfe, John R.; M; 5/3/03-28; N.C. Cherokee; 1/8; S; Head; 3126; Yes; Yes; Unallotted

3159; Wolfe, William H.; M; 3/23/05-27; N.C. Cherokee; 1/8; S; Head; 3127; Yes; Yes; Unallotted

3160; Wolfe, Charles; M; 9/5/10-21; N.C. Cherokee; 1/8; S; Head; 3129; Yes; Yes; Unallotted

Census of the **Eastern Cherokee** reservation of the **Cherokee, N.C.** jurisdiction, as of **April 1** , 1932, taken by **R. L. Spalsbury** , Superintendent.

Key: Number; Surname, Given; Sex; Date of Birth-Age at Last Birthday; Tribe; Degree of Blood; Marital Status; Relationship to Head of Family; Last C. Roll No.; At Jurisdiction Where Enrolled (Yes/No); (If no – Where); Ward (Yes/No); Allotment, Annuity and Identification Numbers (if given).

3161; Wolfe, Jessie M.; M; 7/15/09-22; N.C. Cherokee; 1/8; S; Head; 3128; Yes; Yes; Unallotted

3162; Wolfe, Marian E.; F; 4/22/29-2; N.C. Cherokee; 1/16; S; Daughter; 3130; Yes; Yes; Unallotted

3163; Wolfe, Jonah; M; 9/16/93-38; N.C. Cherokee; 4/4; M; Head; 3131; Yes; Yes; Unallotted

3164; Wolfe, Minda H.; F; 10/6/98-33; N.C. Cherokee; 15/16; M; Wife; 3132; Yes; Yes; Unallotted

3165; Wolfe, Ned W.; M; 4/4/20-11; N.C. Cherokee; 31/32; S; Son; 3133; Yes; Yes; Unallotted

3166; Wolfe, Katherine; F; 12/26/23-8; N.C. Cherokee; 31/32; S; Daughter; 3134; Yes; Yes; Unallotted

3167; Wolfe, Ollie; F; 6/4/26-6; N.C. Cherokee; 31/32; S; Daughter; 3135; Yes; Yes; Unallotted

3168; Wolfe, Maggie; F; 4/8/29-2; N.C. Cherokee; 31/32; S; Daughter; 3136; Yes; Yes; Unallotted

3169; Wolfe, Lillian; F; 11/15/31-4/12; N.C. Cherokee; 31/32; S; Daughter; ---; Yes; Yes; Unallotted

3170; Wolfe, Joseph H.; M; 2/23/71-61; N.C. Cherokee; 4/4; M; Head; 3137; Yes; Yes; Unallotted

3171; Wolfe, Jennie; F; 2/16/69-63; N.C. Cherokee; 4/4; M; Wife; 3138; Yes; Yes; Unallotted

3172; Wolfe, Joseph J.; M; 11/15/97-34; N.C. Cherokee; 4/4; M; Head; 3139; Yes; Yes; Unallotted

3173; Wolfe, Lizzie W.; F; 6/8/05-26; N.C. Cherokee; 4/4; M; Wife; 3140; Yes; Yes; Unallotted

3174; Wolfe, Amble S.; M; 6/8/21-10; N.C. Cherokee; 4/4; S; Son; 3141; Yes; Yes; Unallotted

3175; Wolfe, Richard; M; 6/22/23-8; N.C. Cherokee; 4/4; S; Son; 3142; Yes; Yes; Unallotted

3176; Wolfe, Morgan C.; M; 7/29/26-6; N.C. Cherokee; 4/4; S; Son; 3143; Yes; Yes; Unallotted

3177; Wolfe, Lula M.; F; 6/20/30-1; N.C. Cherokee; 4/4; S; Daughter; 3144; Yes; Yes; Unallotted

3178; Wolfe, Junaluska; M; 3/15/86-46; N.C. Cherokee; 4/4; M; Head; 3145; Yes; Yes; Unallotted

3179; Wolfe, Mary T.; F; 10/3/99-32; N.C. Cherokee; 4/4; M; Wife; 3146; Yes; Yes; Unallotted

3180; Wolfe, Bird; M; 4/24/18-13; N.C. Cherokee; 4/4; S; Son; 3147; Yes; Yes; Unallotted

Census of the **Eastern Cherokee** reservation of the **Cherokee, N.C.** jurisdiction, as of **April 1** , 19**32,** taken by **R. L. Spalsbury** , Superintendent.

Key: Number; Surname, Given; Sex; Date of Birth-Age at Last Birthday; Tribe; Degree of Blood; Marital Status; Relationship to Head of Family; Last C. Roll No.; At Jurisdiction Where Enrolled (Yes/No); (If no – Where); Ward (Yes/No); Allotment, Annuity and Identification Numbers (if given).

3181; Wolfe, Nancy; F; 4/24/25-6; N.C. Cherokee; 4/4; S; Daughter; 3148; Yes; Yes; Unallotted

3182; Wolfe, Lewis D.; M; 9/22/93-38; N.C. Cherokee; 1/8; M; Head; 3149; Yes; Yes; Unallotted

3183; Wolfe, Lewis H.; M; 12/24/71-60; N.C. Cherokee; 1/4; M; Head; 3150; Yes; Yes; Unallotted

3184; Wolfe, James W.; M; 3/25/06-26; N.C. Cherokee; 1/8; S; Son; 3151; Yes; Yes; Unallotted

3185; Wolfe, Frederick; M; 7/8/09-22; N.C. Cherokee; 1/8; S; Son; 3152; Yes; Yes; Unallotted

3186; Wolfe, Dessie C.; F; 6/19/13-18; N.C. Cherokee; 1/8; S; Daughter; 3153; Yes; Yes; Unallotted

3187; Wolfe, Jane; F; 3/4/58-73; N.C. Cherokee; 4/4; Wd.; Head; 3155; Yes; Yes; Unallotted

3188; Wolfe, Owen; M; 12/18/84-47; N.C. Cherokee; 4/4; M; Head; 3156; Yes; Yes; Unallotted

3189; Wolfe, Lucy A.D.; F; 12/1/90-41; N.C. Cherokee; 4/4; M; Wife; 3157; Yes; Yes; Unallotted

3190; Wolfe, Jeremiah; M; 8/28/24-7; N.C. Cherokee; 4/4; S; Son; 3158; Yes; Yes; Unallotted

3191; Wolfe, Ward; M; 9/26/90-41; N.C. Cherokee; 4/4; M; Head; 3159; Yes; Yes; Unallotted

3192; Wolfe, Carolina; F; 11/1/98-33; N.C. Cherokee; 4/4; M; Wife; 3160; Yes; Yes; Unallotted

3193; Wolfe, Elnora; F; 7/12/16-15; N.C. Cherokee; 4/4; S; Daughter; 3161; Yes; Yes; Unallotted

3194; Wolfe, William; M; 3/2/20-12; N.C. Cherokee; 4/4; S; Son; 3162; Yes; Yes; Unallotted

3195; Wolfe, Daniel; M; 8/28/22-9; N.C. Cherokee; 4/4; S; Son; 3163; Yes; Yes; Unallotted

3196; Wolfe, William J.; M; 12/30/77-54; N.C. Cherokee; 4/4; Wd.; Head; 3164; Yes; Yes; Unallotted

3197; Wolfe, Joe; M; 7/29/02-29; N.C. Cherokee; 4/4; S; Son; 3165; No; Canton Asylum, Canton, Lincoln, S.D.; Yes; Unallotted

3198; Wolfe, Addison; M; 12/25/06-25; N.C. Cherokee; 4/4; S; Son; 3166; Yes; Yes; Unallotted

3199; Wolfe, Lilly; F; 7/25/09-22; N.C. Cherokee; 4/4; S; Daughter; 3167; Yes; Yes; Unallotted

Census of the **Eastern Cherokee** reservation of the **Cherokee, N.C.** jurisdiction, as of **April 1** , 19**32,** taken by **R. L. Spalsbury** , Superintendent.

Key: Number; Surname, Given; Sex; Date of Birth-Age at Last Birthday; Tribe; Degree of Blood; Marital Status; Relationship to Head of Family; Last C. Roll No.; At Jurisdiction Where Enrolled (Yes/No); (If no – Where); Ward (Yes/No); Allotment, Annuity and Identification Numbers (if given).

3200; Wolfe, Eli; M; 12/25/12-19; N.C. Cherokee; 4/4; S; Son; 3168; Yes; Yes; Unallotted

3201; Wright (Parris, Laura), Laura M.; F; 5/15/06-25; N.C. Cherokee; 1/16; M; Wife; 3169; No; Culberson, Cherokee, N.C.; Yes; Unallotted

3202; Yonce (Lambert, Nancy), Nancy; F; 3/18/52-80; N.C. Cherokee; 1/8; M; Wife; 3170; Yes; Yes; Unallotted

3203; Young, Catherine; F; 8/13/86-45; N.C. Cherokee; 7/8; M; Wife; 3171; Yes; Yes; Unallotted

3204; Young, Willie B.; F; 9/14/02-29; N.C. Cherokee; 1/8; M; Wife; 3172; Yes; Yes; Unallotted

3205; Young, William E.; M; 9/3/27-4; N.C. Cherokee; 1/16; S; Son; 3173; Yes; Yes; Unallotted

3206; Young, Robert; M; 10/8/30-1; N.C. Cherokee; 1/16; S; Son; 3174; Yes; Yes; Unallotted

3207; Youngbird, Rufus; M; 4/8/87-44; N.C. Cherokee; 7/8; M; Head; 3175; Yes; Yes; Unallotted

3208; Youngbird, Amanda W.; F; 8/15/90-41; N.C. Cherokee; 1/2; M; Wife; 3176; Yes; Yes; Unallotted

3209; Youngbird, Carol; F; 7/23/16-15; N.C. Cherokee; 15/16; S; Daughter; 3177; Yes; Yes; Unallotted

3210; Youngbird, Myrtle E.; F; 10/18/19-12; N.C. Cherokee; 15/16; S; Daughter; 3178; Yes; Yes; Unallotted

3211; Youngbird, Ruth; F; 12/12/22-9; N.C. Cherokee; 15/16; S; Daughter; 3179; Yes; Yes; Unallotted

3212; Youngbird, Saughee; M; 8/20/91-40; N.C. Cherokee; 7/8; M; Head; 3180; Yes; Yes; Unallotted

3213; Youngbird, Lizzie; F; 4/8/03-28; N.C. Cherokee; 7/8; M; Wife; 3181; Yes; Yes; Unallotted

3214; Youngbird, Edmond; M; 2/26/22-10; N.C. Cherokee; 7/8; S; Son; 3182; Yes; Yes; Unallotted

3215; Youngbird, John A.; M; 8/13/24-7; N.C. Cherokee; 7/8; S; Son; 3183; Yes; Yes; Unallotted

3216; Youngbird, James; M; 1/21/26-6; N.C. Cherokee; 7/8; S; Son; 3184; Yes; Yes; Unallotted

3217; Youngbird, David; M; 10/26/27-4; N.C. Cherokee; 7/8; S; Son; 3185; Yes; Yes; Unallotted

3218; Youngbird, Ned; M; 11/24/29-2; N.C. Cherokee; 7/8; S; Son; 3186; Yes; Yes; Unallotted

Census of the **Eastern Cherokee** reservation of the **Cherokee, N.C.** jurisdiction, as of **April 1**, 19**32**, taken by **R. L. Spalsbury**, Superintendent.

Key: Number; Surname, Given; Sex; Date of Birth-Age at Last Birthday; Tribe; Degree of Blood; Marital Status; Relationship to Head of Family; Last C. Roll No.; At Jurisdiction Where Enrolled (Yes/No); (If no – Where); Ward (Yes/No); Allotment, Annuity and Identification Numbers (if given).

3219; Youngbird, Yohnih; M; 5/30/92-39; N.C. Cherokee; 7/8; S; Head; 3187; Yes; Yes; Unallotted

3220; Youngbird, Wesley; M; 3/25/94-38; N.C. Cherokee; 7/8; S; Brother; 3188; Yes; Yes; Unallotted

3221; Youngbird, Wah-kin-nih; F; 3/4/04-28; N.C. Cherokee; 7/8; S; Sister; 3189; Yes; Yes; Unallotted

3222; Youngdeer, Jacob; M; 7/20/72-59; N.C. Cherokee; 4/4; Wd.; Head; 3190; Yes; Yes; Unallotted

3223; Youngdeer, Jesse; M; 5/7/84-47; N.C. Cherokee; 4/4; M; Head; 3191; Yes; Yes; Unallotted

3224; Youngdeer, Martha; F; 8/12/94-37; N.C. Cherokee; 1/4; M; Wife; 3192; Yes; Yes; Unallotted

3225; Youngdeer, Jesse H.; M; 10/2/17-14; N.C. Cherokee; 5/8; S; Son; 3193; Yes; Yes; Unallotted

3226; Youngdeer, Robert S.; M; 4/13/22-10; N.C. Cherokee; 5/8; S; Son; 3194; Yes; Yes; Unallotted

3227; Youngdeer, Betsy; F; 7/7/49-82; N.C. Cherokee; 4/4; Wd.; Head; 3195; Yes; Yes; Unallotted

3228; Youngdeer, Eli; M; 7/20/81-50; N.C. Cherokee; 4/4; S; Son; 3196; Yes; Yes; Unallotted

3229; Youngdeer, Jonah; M; 6/29/83-48; N.C. Cherokee; 4/4; S; Son; 3197; Yes; Yes; Unallotted

3230; Youngdeer, Moody; M; 6/30/99-32; N.C. Cherokee; 4/4; S; Son; 3198; Yes; Yes; Unallotted

3231; Zimmerman, Norma; F; 2/1/03-29; N.C. Cherokee; 1/64; M; Wife; 3199; Yes; Yes; Unallotted

3232; Arch (Fr. Horace Arch), Wm. Howard; M; 11/22/31-4/12; N.C. Cherokee; 6/8; S; Son; ---; Yes; Yes; Unallotted

3233; McCoy (Fr. Jesse McCoy), Edwin; M; 10/15/31-5/12; N.C. Cherokee; 5/32; S; Son; ---; Yes; Yes; Unallotted

3230; Correct Census – as of Apr. 1, 1932
    Note: 1932 census #2258, Ross, Adam (died 11/9/31) Page 176 should be omitted from census 1932 Death Report #9.
    "   "   #1714, Occumma, Samuel (died 2/29/32) Page 135 should be omitted from census 1932 Death Report #7.
    "   "   #1276, Lambert, (Enloe), Mintha, duplicated by #752 page 59

ADDITIONS -

Made to 1932 Census from 1930 Census

Census of the **Eastern Cherokee** reservation of the **Cherokee, N.C.** jurisdiction, as of **April 1** , 19**32,** taken by **R. L. Spalsbury** , Superintendent.

Key: Census Number; Surname, Given; Sex; Date of Birth - Age; Tribe; Degree of Blood; Marital Status; Relationship to Head of Family; Where Enrolled (Yes/No); (If no – Where); Ward (Yes/No); Allotment, Annuity and Identification Numbers (if given).

1932   (1) ADDITIONS made to 1932 Census over 1930 Census and reasons

9;	Adams, Emma Lee; F; 3/12/24-8; N.C. Cherokee; 1/64; S; Daughter; Yes; O.L. 1/27/31; Yes; Unallotted
89;	Armachain, Jesse; M; 1/28/96-37; N.C. Cherokee; 4/4; M; Husband; Yes; Omitted on 1930 Census; Yes; Unallotted
90;	Armachain, Lucy Long; F; 1/16/99-34; N.C. Cherokee; 3/4; M; Wife; Yes; Omitted on 1930 Census; Yes; Unallotted
91;	Armachain, Stella E.; F; 5/28/21-11; N.C. Cherokee; 7/8; S; Daughter; Yes; Omitted on 1930 Census; Yes; Unallotted
92;	Armachain, Jesse James; M; 1/5/29-3; N.C. Cherokee; 7/8; S; Son; Yes; Omitted on 1930 Census; Yes; Unallotted
93;	Armachain, Stacy; F; 3/6/31-1; N.C. Cherokee; 7/8; S; Daughter; Yes; Listed under births-1931 Census; Yes; Unallotted
106;	Armachain, Wayne L.; M; 6/28/30-1; N.C. Cherokee; 9/16; S; Son; Yes; Listed under births-1931 Census; Yes; Unallotted
117;	Ashe, Margie L.; F; 10/14/30-1; N.C. Cherokee; 1/8; S; Daughter; Yes; Listed under births-1931 Census; Yes; Unallotted
119;	Austin, Howard; M; 7/5/11-22; N.C. Cherokee; 1/4-; S; Son; No; O.L. 1/27/31, Hiland[sic] Park, Hamilton, Tenn.; Yes; Unallotted
120;	Austin, Jack; M; 8/10/00-32; N.C. Cherokee; 1/4-; S; Son; No; O.L. 1/27/31, Hiland Park, Hamilton, Tenn.; Yes; Unallotted
121;	Austin, James; M; 5/11/90-42; N.C. Cherokee; 1/4-; S; Son; No; O.L. 1/27/31, Hiland Park, Hamilton, Tenn.; Yes; Unallotted
122;	Austin, Lelia; F; 5/19/97-34; N.C. Cherokee; 1/4-; S; Daughter; No; O.L. 1/27/31, Hiland Park, Hamilton, Tenn.; Yes; Unallotted
123;	Jones, Alice A.; F; 7/16/03-28; N.C. Cherokee; 1/4-; M; Daughter; No; O.L. 1/27/31, Hiland Park, Hamilton, Tenn.; Yes; Unallotted
124;	Mullins, Maggie A.; F; 5/11/95-37; N.C. Cherokee; 1/4-; S; Daughter; No; O.L. 1/27/31, Hiland Park, Hamilton, Tenn.; Yes; Unallotted
215;	Bishop, Lillie; F; 1870-62; N.C. Cherokee; 1/8; M; Wife; Yes; O.L. 1/27/31; Yes; Unallotted
216;	Bishop, Hattie B.; F; 1912-20; N.C. Cherokee; 1/16; S; Daughter; Yes; O.L. 1/27/31; Yes; Unallotted
243;	Blythe (Johnson), Alta M.; F; 10/22/31-5/12; N.C. Cherokee; 1/2; S; Daughter; Yes; Listed under births -1932 Census; Yes; Unallotted
301;	Moles (Bradley), Racheal M.; F; 6/23/31-9/12; N.C. Cherokee; 1/8; S; Daughter; Yes; Listed under births -1932 Census; Yes; Unallotted
308;	Bradley, Rachel; F; 7/15/06-26; N.C. Cherokee; 1/4; S; Daughter; Yes; Omitted on 1930 Census; Yes; Unallotted
321;	Bradley, Constance; F; 2/17/31-1; N.C. Cherokee; 1/2; S; Daughter; Yes; Listed under births -1931 Census; Yes; Unallotted
330;	Brady, Baby Male; M; 6/26/31-9/12; N.C. Cherokee; 3/8; S; Son; Yes; Listed under births -1932 Census; Yes; Unallotted

Census of the **Eastern Cherokee** reservation of the **Cherokee, N.C.** jurisdiction, as of **April 1**, 19**32,** taken by **R. L. Spalsbury**, Superintendent.

Key: Census Number; Surname, Given; Sex; Date of Birth - Age; Tribe; Degree of Blood; Marital Status; Relationship to Head of Family; Where Enrolled (Yes/No); (If no - Where); Ward (Yes/No); Allotment, Annuity and Identification Numbers (if given).

332;   Brewster, Linnie L.J.; F; 1890-42; N.C. Cherokee; 1/4; M; Wife; Yes; O.L. 1/27/31; Yes; Unallotted

360;   Burgess, Mary C.; F; 1/5/31-1; N.C. Cherokee; 3/16; S; Daughter; Yes; Listed under births -1931 Census; Yes; Unallotted

458;   Chekelelee, Ed; M; 5/21/29-2; N.C. Cherokee; 4/4; S; Son; Yes; Unreported birth -1931 Census; Yes; Unallotted

459;   Chekelelee, Boyd; M; 7/16/31-8/12; N.C. Cherokee; 4/4; S; Son; Yes; Listed under births -1932 Census; Yes; Unallotted

515;   Conley, Selma; F; 4/21/30-1; N.C. Cherokee; 15/16; S; Daughter; Yes; Listed under births -1931 Census; Yes; Unallotted

516;   Conley, Richard; M; 2/28/32-1/12; N.C. Cherokee; 15/16; S; Son; Yes; Listed under births -1932 Census; Yes; Unallotted

519;   Conseen, Mark; M; 4/23/30-1; N.C. Cherokee; 1/2; S; Son; Yes; Listed under births -1931 Census; Yes; Unallotted

520;   Conseen, George; M; 4/23/30-1; N.C. Cherokee; 1/2; S; Son; Yes; Listed under births -1931 Census; Yes; Unallotted

531;   Conseen, Erwin; M; 9/6/31-6/12; N.C. Cherokee; 4/4; S; Son; Yes; Listed under births -1932 Census; Yes; Unallotted

575;   Craig, Bettie Ann; F; 6/23/29-2; N.C. Cherokee; 3/16; S; Daughter; Yes; Unreported birth -1931 Census; Yes; Unallotted

576;   Craig, Jean Donley; F; 5/12/31-10/12; N.C. Cherokee; 3/16; S; Daughter; Yes; Listed under births -1932 Census; Yes; Unallotted

626;   Crowe, Ann Lee; F; 3/21/31-1; N.C. Cherokee; 17/32; S; Daughter; Yes; Listed under births -1931 Census; Yes; Unallotted

674;   Davis, David; M; 5/18/01-31; N.C. Cherokee; 4/4; S; Son; Yes; Omitted on 1930 Census; Yes; Unallotted

675;   Davis, George; M; 7/5/05-26; N.C. Cherokee; 4/4; S; Son; Yes; Omitted on 1930 Census; Yes; Unallotted

719;   Driver, Waidsutte; F; 6/7/30-1; N.C. Cherokee; 4/4; S; Daughter; Yes; Listed under births -1931 Census; Yes; Unallotted

755;   Eubank, Lillie; F; 1888-45; N.C. Cherokee; 1/4; M; Wife; Yes; O.L. 1/27/31; Yes; Unallotted

762;   Falls, Bettie B.; F; 1900-32; N.C. Cherokee; 1/4; M; Wife; Yes; O.L. 1/27/31; Yes; Unallotted

774;   Fortner, Sis; F; 12/24/76-56; N.C. Cherokee; 1/4; M; Wife; Yes; O.L. 1/27/31; Yes; Unallotted

858;   George, Sallie; F; 6/6/30-1; N.C. Cherokee; 31/32; S; Daughter; Yes; Listed under births -1931 Census; Yes; Unallotted

898;   Green, Lena B.; F; 1904-28; N.C. Cherokee; 1/4-; M; Wife; No; O.L. 1/27/31; Ensley, Jefferson, Ala. Yes; Unallotted

912;   Hamilton, Leona J.; F; 1876-56; N.C. Cherokee; 1/4-; M; Wife; Yes; O.L. 1/27/31; Yes; Unallotted

1039;   Hodges, Ollie J.; F; 1876-56; N.C. Cherokee; 1/4-; M; Wife; Yes; O.L. 1/27/31; Yes; Unallotted

Census of the **Eastern Cherokee** reservation of the **Cherokee, N.C.** jurisdiction, as of **April 1** , 19**32,** taken by **R. L. Spalsbury** , Superintendent.

Key: Census Number; Surname, Given; Sex; Date of Birth - Age; Tribe; Degree of Blood; Marital Status; Relationship to Head of Family; Where Enrolled (Yes/No); (If no – Where); Ward (Yes/No); Allotment, Annuity and Identification Numbers (if given).

1040;   Hodges, Ollie; F; 1901-31; N.C. Cherokee; 1/4-; S; Daughter; Yes; O.L. 1/27/31; Yes; Unallotted

1095;   Jackson, Lula; F; 3/13/32-18 days; N.C. Cherokee; 29/32; S; Daughter; Yes; Listed under births – 1932 Census; Yes; Unallotted

1102;   Jackson, Mary E.; F; 8/12/31-7/12; N.C. Cherokee; 17/32; S; Daughter; Yes; Listed under births – 1932 Census; Yes; Unallotted

1153;   Jordan, Clyde; M; 1880-52; N.C. Cherokee; 1/4-; M; Husband; Yes; O. L. 1/27/31; Yes; Unallotted

1154;   Jordan, Jake A.; M; 1890-42; N.C. Cherokee; 1/4-; M; Husband; Yes; O. L. 1/27/31; Yes; Unallotted

1155;   Jordan, John J.; M; 1886-46; N.C. Cherokee; 1/4-; M; Husband; Yes; O. L. 1/27/31; Yes; Unallotted

1156;   Jordan, John M.; M; 1893-39; N.C. Cherokee; 1/4-; S; Son; Yes; O. L. 1/27/31; Yes; Unallotted

1157;   Jordan, Mark; M; 1873-59; N.C. Cherokee; 1/4-; M; Husband; Yes; O. L. 1/27/31; Yes; Unallotted

1158;   Jordan, Della; F; 1915-17; N.C. Cherokee; 1/4-; S; Daughter; Yes; O. L. 1/27/31; Yes; Unallotted

1159;   Jordan, Leona; F; 1920-12; N.C. Cherokee; 1/4-; S; Daughter; Yes; O. L. 1/27/31; Yes; Unallotted

1160;   Jordan, Zora; F; 1921-11; N.C. Cherokee; 1/4-; S; Daughter; Yes; O. L. 1/27/31; Yes; Unallotted

1161;   Jordan, Wm. A.; M; 1889-43; N.C. Cherokee; 1/4-; M; Husband; Yes; O. L. 1/27/31; Yes; Unallotted

1182;   Junaluskie, Lillian; F; 1/25/32-2/12; N.C. Cherokee; 31/32; S; Daughter; Yes; Listed under births - 1932 census; Yes; Unallotted

1193;   Queen (Kalonuheskie), Bascom; M; 1/18/32-2/12; N.C. Cherokee; 15/16; S; Son; Yes; Listed under births - 1932 census; Yes; Unallotted

1233;   Lambert, Herbert A.; M; 6/7/31-9/12; N.C. Cherokee; 13/32; S; Son; Yes; Listed under births - 1932 census; Yes; Unallotted

1259;   Lambert, David; M; 11/22/30-1; N.C. Cherokee; 29/64; S; Son; Yes; Listed under births - 1931 census; Yes; Unallotted

1314;   Lambert, (McCoy), Stella; F; 11/25/05-27; N.C. Cherokee; 1/16; Div.; Wife; Yes; Omitted from1930 Census; Yes; Unallotted

1331;   Larch, Florence; F; 5/25/31-10/12; N.C. Cherokee; 4/4; S; Daughter; Yes; Listed under births - 1932 census; Yes; Unallotted

1356;   Ledford, Nellie M.; F; 3/21/32-10 days; N.C. Cherokee; 1/2; S; Daughter; Yes; Listed under births - 1932 census; Yes; Unallotted

1357;   Ledford, Billy J.; M; 6/19/31-9/12; N.C. Cherokee; 1/2; S; Son; Yes; Listed under births - 1932 census; Yes; Unallotted

1459;   Long, Robt. E.; M; 4/8/30-2; N.C. Cherokee; 25/32; S; Son; Yes; Listed under births - 1931 census; Yes; Unallotted

1474;   Lossie, Sampson; M; 4/7/26-5; N.C. Cherokee; 4/4; S; Son; Yes; Omitted from 1930 census; Yes; Unallotted

Census of the **Eastern Cherokee** reservation of the **Cherokee, N.C.** jurisdiction, as of **April 1** , 19**32**, taken by **R. L. Spalsbury** , Superintendent.

Key: Census Number; Surname, Given; Sex; Date of Birth - Age; Tribe; Degree of Blood; Marital Status; Relationship to Head of Family; Where Enrolled (Yes/No); (If no – Where); Ward (Yes/No); Allotment, Annuity and Identification Numbers (if given).

1475;   Lossie, Charlie; M; 2/19/29-3; N.C. Cherokee; 4/4; S; Son; Yes; Omitted from 1930 census; Yes; Unallotted

1476;   Lossie, Annie; F; 11/2/31-4/12; N.C. Cherokee; 4/4; S; Daughter; Yes; Listed under births - 1932 census; Yes; Unallotted

1584;   Maney, John Jr.; M; 2/2/31-1; N.C. Cherokee; 3/4; S; Son; Yes; Listed under births - 1931 census; Yes; Unallotted

1664;   Morrison, Bruce; M; 1909-23; N.C. Cherokee; 1/4-; M; Husband; Yes; O. L. 1/27/31; Yes; Unallotted

1768;   Owl, Harriet; F; 7/15/30-1; N.C. Cherokee; 4/4; S; Daughter; Yes; Listed under births - 1931 census; Yes; Unallotted

1791;   Owl, Nettie E.; F; 5/14/31-10/12; N.C. Cherokee; 1/4; S; Daughter; Yes; Listed under births - 1932 census; Yes; Unallotted

1800;   Owl, Bennie L.; M; 7/18/30-1; N.C. Cherokee; 15/32; S; Son; Yes; Listed under births - 1931 census; Yes; Unallotted

1808;   Owl, Bessie E.; F; 10/11/30-1; N.C. Cherokee; 1/4; S; Daughter; Yes; Listed under births - 1931 census; Yes; Unallotted

1926;   Peckerwood, Tom Ross; M; 3/19/31-1; N.C. Cherokee; 7/8; S; Son; Yes; Listed under births - 1931 census; Yes; Unallotted

1947;   Powell, Berdina; F; 4/21/30-2; N.C. Cherokee; 7/8; S; Daughter; Yes; Listed under births - 1931 census; Yes; Unallotted

1956;   Pittman, Ella B.; F; 1909-23; N.C. Cherokee; 1/4-; S; Daughter; Yes; O. L. 1/27/31; Yes; Unallotted

1964;   Queen, Jessie; F; 7/9/30-1; N.C. Cherokee; 25/32; S; Daughter; Yes; Listed under births - 1931 census; Yes; Unallotted

1983;   Quinlan, Mary C.; F; 1899-33; N.C. Cherokee; 1/4-; M; Wife; Yes; O. L. 1/27/31; Yes; Unallotted

2161;   Reed, James; M; 12/23/52-79; N.C. Cherokee; 3/4; S; Head; Yes; Omitted from 1930 census; Yes; Unallotted

2185;   Reed, Alexander; M; 4/28/31-11/12; N.C. Cherokee; 11/16; S; Son; Yes; Listed under births - 1932 census; Yes; Unallotted

2214;   Robinson, Birgie; F; 1883-49; N.C. Cherokee; 1/4-; M; Wife; No; O. L. 1/27/31; Rossville, Walker, Ga.; Yes; Unallotted

2246;   Rogers, Chas.; M; 3/31/31-1; N.C. Cherokee; 1/16; S; Son; Yes; Listed under births - 1931 census; Yes; Unallotted

2270;   Ross, Deedanuskie; M; 2/19/32-1/12; N.C. Cherokee; 4/4; S; Son; Yes; Listed under births - 1932 census; Yes; Unallotted

2290;   Saunooke, Lydia; F; 4/18/31-11/12; N.C. Cherokee; 4/4; S; Daughter; Yes; Listed under births - 1932 census; Yes; Unallotted

2294;   Saunooke, Robt.; M; 8/5/31-7/12; N.C. Cherokee; 11/16; S; Son; Yes; Listed under births - 1932 census; Yes; Unallotted

2297;   Saunooke, Golinda; F; 10/17/31-5/12; N.C. Cherokee; 5/8; S; Daughter; Yes; Listed under births - 1932 census; Yes; Unallotted

2313;   Saunooke, Samuel; M; 12/15/78-53; N.C. Cherokee; 7/8; M; Husband; Yes; Omitted on 1930 census; Yes; Unallotted

Census of the **Eastern Cherokee** reservation of the **Cherokee, N.C.** jurisdiction, as of **April 1**, **1932**, taken by **R. L. Spalsbury**, Superintendent.

Key: Census Number; Surname, Given; Sex; Date of Birth - Age; Tribe; Degree of Blood; Marital Status; Relationship to Head of Family; Where Enrolled (Yes/No); (If no - Where); Ward (Yes/No); Allotment, Annuity and Identification Numbers (if given).

2314; Saunooke, Harvey; M; 7/30/20-11; N.C. Cherokee; 7/16; S; Son; Yes; Omitted on 1930 census; Yes; Unallotted

2339; Screamer, Jennie L.; F; 3/2/32-29 days; N.C. Cherokee; 31/32; S; Daughter; Yes; Listed under births - 1932 census; Yes; Unallotted

2390; Shone, Mary; F; 1876-56; N.C. Cherokee; 1/4-; M; Wife; No; O. L. 1/27/31; Ensley, Jefferson, Ala.; Yes; Unallotted

2423; Smith, Ethel L.; F; 11/25/31-4/12; N.C. Cherokee; 1/4; S; Daughter; Yes; Listed under births - 1932 census; Yes; Unallotted

2473; Smith, Zona F.; F; 2/5/31-1; N.C. Cherokee; 3/16; S; Daughter; Yes; Listed under births - 1931 census; Yes; Unallotted

2481; Smith, Alyne; F; 12/28/30-1; N.C. Cherokee; 1/4; S; Daughter; Yes; Listed under births - 1931 census; Yes; Unallotted

2511; Sneed, Gertha; F; 3/13/32-18 da.; N.C. Cherokee; 5/16; S; Daughter; Yes; Listed under births - 1932 census; Yes; Unallotted

2573; Lambert (Standingdeer), Dorothy; F; 9/19/30-1; N.C. Cherokee; 17/64; S; Daughter; Yes; Listed under births - 1931 census; Yes; Unallotted

2628; Swayney, Edith; F; 9/26/30-1; N.C. Cherokee; 1/16; S; Daughter; Yes; Listed under births - 1931 census; Yes; Unallotted

2690; Taylor, Jarrett; M; 10/23/31-5/12; N.C. Cherokee; 13/16; S; Son; Yes; Listed under births - 1932 census; Yes; Unallotted

2719; Taylor, Helen E.; F; 7/31/31-8/12; N.C. Cherokee; 3/4; S; Daughter; Yes; Listed under births - 1932 census; Yes; Unallotted

2724; Taylor, Lucy; F; 8/30/30-1; N.C. Cherokee; 13/32; S; Daughter; Yes; Listed under births - 1931 census; Yes; Unallotted

2741; Teesateskie, Josiah; M; 8/2/30-1; N.C. Cherokee; 4/4; S; Son; Yes; Listed under births - 1931 census; Yes; Unallotted

2769; Thompson, McKinley; M; 6/25/31-9/12; N.C. Cherokee; 4/4; S; Son; Yes; Listed under births - 1932 census; Yes; Unallotted

2776; Thompson, Abe; M; 9/12/30-1; N.C. Cherokee; 4/4; S; Son; Yes; Listed under births - 1931 census; Yes; Unallotted

2801; Thompson, Lawrence; M; 4/2/31-11/12; N.C. Cherokee; 25/32; S; Son; Yes; Listed under births - 1932 census; Yes; Unallotted

2825; Toineeta, Geneva; F; 9/7/30-1; N.C. Cherokee; 4/4; S; Daughter; Yes; Listed under births - 1931 census; Yes; Unallotted

2844; Tooni, Annie; F; 4/5/30-1; N.C. Cherokee; 4/4; S; Daughter; Yes; Listed under births - 1931 census; Yes; Unallotted

2845; Tooni, Stan; M; 1/26/32-2/12; N.C. Cherokee; 4/4; S; Son; Yes; Listed under births - 1932 census; Yes; Unallotted

2864; Tramper, Kahlie; F; 4/17/30-1; N.C. Cherokee; 4/4; S; Daughter; Yes; Listed under births - 1931 census; Yes; Unallotted

2871; Lindsay (Mr. Twin, Viola), Jackie; M; 5/27/31-10/12; N.C. Cherokee; 3/16; S; Son; Yes; Listed under births - 1932 census; Yes; Unallotted

2887; Wachacha, Raleigh; M; 8/21/15-16; N.C. Cherokee; 4/4; S; Son; Yes; Omitted on 1930 census; Yes; Unallotted

Census of the **Eastern Cherokee** reservation of the **Cherokee, N.C.** jurisdiction, as of **April 1** , 19**32,** taken by **R. L. Spalsbury** , Superintendent.

Key: Census Number; Surname, Given; Sex; Date of Birth - Age; Tribe; Degree of Blood; Marital Status; Relationship to Head of Family; Where Enrolled (Yes/No); (If no – Where); Ward (Yes/No); Allotment, Annuity and Identification Numbers (if given).

2888;   Wachacha, Mollie; F; 5/22/18-13; N.C. Cherokee; 4/4; S; Daughter; Yes; Omitted on 1930 census; Yes; Unallotted

2937;   Walker, Pauline; F; 7/3/30-1; N.C. Cherokee; 1/2; S; Daughter; Yes; Listed under births - 1931 census; Yes; Unallotted

2945;   Walkingstick, Virgil; M; 11/7/31-4/12; N.C. Cherokee; 4/4; S; Son; Yes; Listed under births - 1932 census; Yes; Unallotted

2976;   Wallace, Ollie; F; 10/8/29-2; N.C. Cherokee; 31/32; S; Daughter; Yes; Unreported birth 1931 census; Yes; Unallotted

2998;   Wayne, Sara; F; 8/22/30-1; N.C. Cherokee; 4/4; S; Daughter; Yes; Listed under births - 1931 census; Yes; Unallotted

3016;   Welch, John; M; 4/11/30-1; N.C. Cherokee; 29/32; S; Son; Yes; Listed under births - 1931 census; Yes; Unallotted

3017;   Welch, Akin; M; 4/11/27-4; N.C. Cherokee; 29/32; S; Son; Yes; Unreported birth 1931 census; Yes; Unallotted

3113;   Wilnoty, Tidmarsh; M; 8/11/31-7/12; N.C. Cherokee; 7/16; S; Son; Yes; Listed under births - 1932 census; Yes; Unallotted

3123;   Wilnoty, Paul R.; M; 4/18/31-11/12; N.C. Cherokee; 3/4; S; Son; Yes; Listed under births - 1932 census; Yes; Unallotted

3151;   Wolfe, James T.; M; 5/14/30-1; N.C. Cherokee; 1/2; S; Son; Yes; Listed under births - 1931 census; Yes; Unallotted

3169;   Wolfe, Lillian; F; 11/15/31-4/12; N.C. Cherokee; 31/32; S; Daughter; Yes; Listed under births - 1932 census; Yes; Unallotted

3177;   Wolfe, Lula M.; F; 6/20/30-1; N.C. Cherokee; 4/4; S; Daughter; Yes; Listed under births - 1931 census; Yes; Unallotted

3206;   Young, Robert; M; 10/8/30-1; N.C. Cherokee; 1/16; S; Son; Yes; Listed under births - 1931 census; Yes; Unallotted

3232;   Arch, Wm. Howard; M; 11/2/31-4/12; N.C. Cherokee; 6/8; S; Son; Yes; Listed under births - 1932 census; Yes; Unallotted

3233;   McCoy, Edwin; M; 10/15/31-5/12; N.C. Cherokee; 5/12[sic]; S; Son; Yes; Listed under births - 1932 census; Yes; Unallotted

SUBTRACTIONS -

Made on 1932 Census from 1930 Census

Census of the **Eastern Cherokee** reservation of the **Cherokee, N.C.** jurisdiction, as of **April 1** , 19**32**, taken by **R. L. Spalsbury** , Superintendent.

Key: Census Number; Surname, Given; Sex; Age at Last Date of Birth; Tribe; Degree of Blood; Marital Status; Relationship to Head of Family; Where Enrolled (Yes/No); (If no – Where); Ward (Yes/No); Allotment, Annuity and Identification Numbers (if given).

1930   (1) SUBTRACTIONS made on 1932 census from 1930 census and reasons

38;   Allen, Lorena; F; 5; N.C. Cherokee; 1/16-; S; Daughter; No; O.L. 5/9/31; Violet, Cherokee, N.C.; Yes; Unallotted

141;   Bates, Willard; M; 5; N.C. Cherokee; 1/16-; S; Son; Yes; O.L. 5/9/31; Yes; Unallotted

156;   Beck, Gady E.; F; 5; N.C. Cherokee; 1/16-; S; Daughter; Yes; O.L. 5/9/31; Yes; Unallotted

189;   Bird, David; M; 36; N.C. Cherokee; 1/4; M; Husband; Yes; death – 1931 census; Yes; Unallotted

239;   Bowman, Jacob T.; M; 3; N.C. Cherokee; 1/16-; S; Son; Yes; O.L. 5/9/31; Yes; Unallotted

240;   Bowman, Willie; M; 10/12; N.C. Cherokee; 1/16-; S; Son; Yes; O.L. 5/9/31; Yes; Unallotted

249;   Bradley, Pauline; F; 5; N.C. Cherokee; 1/16-; S; Daughter; Yes; O.L. 5/9/31; Yes; Unallotted

250;   Bradley, Estella; F; 3; N.C. Cherokee; 1/16-; S; Daughter; Yes; O.L. 5/9/31; Yes; Unallotted

283;   Bradley, Doris; F; 5; N.C. Cherokee; 1/16-; S; Daughter; Yes; O.L. 5/9/31; Yes; Unallotted

284;   Bradley, Vivian; F; 5/12; N.C. Cherokee; 1/16-; S; Daughter; Yes; O.L. 5/9/31; Yes; Unallotted

288;   Bradley, Virginia; F; 4; N.C. Cherokee; 1/16-; S; Daughter; Yes; O.L. 5/9/31; Yes; Unallotted

303;   Bradley, John; M; 4; N.C. Cherokee; 1/16-; S; Son; Yes; O.L. 5/9/31; Yes; Unallotted

348;   Bryson, Clifford; M; 11; N.C. Cherokee; 1/4-; S; Son; Yes; O.L. 1/27/31; Yes; Unallotted

349;   Bryson, Robert; M; 9; N.C. Cherokee; 1/4-; S; Son; Yes; O.L. 1/27/31; Yes; Unallotted

368;   Burrell, Hugh; M; 16; N.C. Cherokee; 1/4-; S; Son; NO; O.L. 1/27/31; Pamplin, Appomatox, Va.; Yes; Unallotted

369;   Burrell, Ernest; M; 15; N.C. Cherokee; 1/4-; S; Son; NO; O.L. 1/27/31; Pamplin, Appomatox, Va.; Yes; Unallotted

542;   Cooper, Helen; F; 4; N.C. Cherokee; 1/16-; S; Daughter; Yes; O.L. 5/9/31; Yes; Unallotted

543;   Cooper, Wilma; F; 3; N.C. Cherokee; 1/16-; S; Daughter; Yes; O.L. 5/9/31; Yes; Unallotted

544;   Cooper, James; M; 10/12; N.C. Cherokee; 1/16-; S; Son; Yes; O.L. 5/9/31; Yes; Unallotted

546;   Cooper, Curtis Jr.; M; 4; N.C. Cherokee; 1/16-; S; Son; Yes; O.L. 5/9/31; Yes; Unallotted

547;   Cooper, Thos. K.; M; 2; N.C. Cherokee; 1/16-; S; Son; Yes; O.L. 5/9/31; Yes; Unallotted

Census of the **Eastern Cherokee** reservation of the **Cherokee, N.C.** jurisdiction, as of **April 1** , 19**32,** taken by **R. L. Spalsbury** , Superintendent.

Key: Census Number; Surname, Given; Sex; Age at Last Date of Birth; Tribe; Degree of Blood; Marital Status; Relationship to Head of Family; Where Enrolled (Yes/No); (If no – Where); Ward (Yes/No); Allotment, Annuity and Identification Numbers (if given).

548; Cooper, Harry; M; 11/12; N.C. Cherokee; 1/16-; S; Son; Yes; O.L. 5/9/31; Yes; Unallotted

597; Crowe, Maggie H.E.; F; 24; N.C. Cherokee; 1/4; M; Wife; Yes; Died 11/4/28; Yes; Unallotted

729; Key (Dunlap), Wm. H.; M; 19; N.C. Cherokee; 1/4-; S; Son; Yes; O.L. 1/27/31; Yes; Unallotted

730; Key, Clarence; M; 17; N.C. Cherokee; 1/4-; S; Son; Yes; O.L. 1/27/31; Yes; Unallotted

731; Key, Nola May; F; 14; N.C. Cherokee; 1/4-; S; Daughter; Yes; O.L. 1/27/31; Yes; Unallotted

743; Enloe, Alberta H.; F; 3; N.C. Cherokee; 1/4-; S; Daughter; Yes; Duplicated – also shown #598 on 1930 census; Yes; Unallotted

752; Featherhead, Ella J.; F; 70; N.C. Cherokee; F; M; Wife; Yes; Death – 1932 census; Yes; Unallotted

782; French, Jonah; M; 26; N.C. Cherokee; F; S; Son; Yes; Death – 1931 census; Yes; Unallotted

1027; Hipps, Nellie Sue; F; 4; N.C. Cherokee; 1/16-; S; Daughter; Yes; O.L. 5/9/31; Yes; Unallotted

1071; Hornbuckle, Wilson; M; 28; N.C. Cherokee; 1/4-; M; Husband; Yes; Death – 1932 census; Yes; Unallotted

1115; Jenkins, Lucile; F; 5; N.C. Cherokee; 1/16-; S; Daughter; Yes; O.L. 5/9/31; Yes; Unallotted

1131; Johnson, Gussie; F; 11; N.C. Cherokee; F; S; Daughter; Yes; Death – 1932 census; Yes; Unallotted

1155; Jumper, Sarah; F; 17; N.C. Cherokee; F; S; Daughter; Yes; Duplicated - also on 1930 census #2638; Yes; Unallotted

1200; Lambert, Hugh; M; 2; N.C. Cherokee; 1/16-; S; Son; Yes; O.L. 5/9/31; Yes; Unallotted

1217; Lambert, Eugene; M; 4; N.C. Cherokee; 1/16-; S; Son; Yes; O.L. 5/9/31; Yes; Unallotted

1218; Lambert, Alice; F; 2; N.C. Cherokee; 1/16-; S; Daughter; Yes; O.L. 5/9/31; Yes; Unallotted

1221; Howard (Lambert), David; M; 5; N.C. Cherokee; 1/16-; S; Son; Yes; O.L. 5/9/31; Yes; Unallotted

1222; Howard, Katie; F; 3; N.C. Cherokee; 1/16-; S; Daughter; Yes; O.L. 5/9/31; Yes; Unallotted

1223; Howard, Mary; F; 1; N.C. Cherokee; 1/16-; S; Daughter; Yes; O.L. 5/9/31; Yes; Unallotted

1235; Lambert, Miles; M; 4; N.C. Cherokee; 1/16-; S; Son; Yes; O.L. 5/9/31; Yes; Unallotted

1236; Lambert, Hoover; M; 1; N.C. Cherokee; 1/16-; S; Son; Yes; O.L. 5/9/31; Yes; Unallotted

1241; Lambert, Cape; M; 3; N.C. Cherokee; 1/16-; S; Son; Yes; O.L. 5/9/31; Yes; Unallotted

Census of the **Eastern Cherokee** reservation of the **Cherokee, N.C.** jurisdiction, as of **April 1**, **1932,** taken by **R. L. Spalsbury**, Superintendent.

Key: Census Number; Surname, Given; Sex; Age at Last Date of Birth; Tribe; Degree of Blood; Marital Status; Relationship to Head of Family; Where Enrolled (Yes/No); (If no – Where); Ward (Yes/No); Allotment, Annuity and Identification Numbers (if given).

1263; Enloe (Lambert), Edith; F; 1; N.C. Cherokee; 1/16-; S; Daughter; Yes; O.L. 5/9/31; Yes; Unallotted

1270; Lambert, Eula; F; 4; N.C. Cherokee; 1/16-; S; Daughter; Yes; O.L. 5/9/31; Yes; Unallotted

1271; Lambert, Daniel; M; 3; N.C. Cherokee; 1/16-; S; Son; Yes; O.L. 5/9/31; Yes; Unallotted

1277; Lambert, Frederick; M; 3; N.C. Cherokee; 1/16-; S; Son; Yes; O.L. 5/9/31; Yes; Unallotted

1300; Lambert, James; M; 5; N.C. Cherokee; 1/16-; S; Son; Yes; O.L. 5/9/31; Yes; Unallotted

1347; Ledford, Mary; F; 6; N.C. Cherokee; F; S; Daughter; Yes; Death – 1931 census; Yes; Unallotted

1361; Lee, Virginia; F; 7; N.C. Cherokee; 1/4-; S; Daughter; Yes; O.L. 1/27/31; Yes; Unallotted

1525; McCoy, Eleanor; F; 5; N.C. Cherokee; 1/16-; S; Daughter; Yes; O.L. 5/9/31; Yes; Unallotted

1526; McCoy, James; M; 3; N.C. Cherokee; 1/16-; S; Son; Yes; O.L. 5/9/31; Yes; Unallotted

1528; McCoy, Jessie; F; 2; N.C. Cherokee; 1/16-; S; Daughter; Yes; O.L. 5/9/31; Yes; Unallotted

1573; Maney, Olive; F; 4; N.C. Cherokee; 1/16-; S; Daughter; Yes; O.L. 5/9/31; Yes; Unallotted

1574; Maney, Ralph; M; 2; N.C. Cherokee; 1/16-; S; Son; Yes; O.L. 5/9/31; Yes; Unallotted

1577; Maney, Alice; F; 19; N.C. Cherokee; 1/4; S; Daughter; Yes; Death – 1931 census; Yes; Unallotted

1589; Martin, Roxie; F; 4; N.C. Cherokee; 1/16-; S; Daughter; Yes; O.L. 5/9/31; Yes; Unallotted

1591; Martin, Emmaline; F; 32; N.C. Cherokee; F; M; Wife; Yes; Death – 1931 census; Yes; Unallotted

1599; Mashburn, David; M; 21; N.C. Cherokee; 1/4-; S; Son; Yes; O.L. 1/27/31; Yes; Unallotted

1600; Mashburn, Mary W.; F; 17; N.C. Cherokee; 1/4-; S; Daughter; Yes; O.L. 1/27/31; Yes; Unallotted

1601; Mashburn, Jesse Jr.; M; 16; N.C. Cherokee; 1/4-; S; Son; Yes; O.L. 1/27/31; Yes; Unallotted

1602; Mashburn, Milton B.; M; 15; N.C. Cherokee; 1/4-; S; Son; Yes; O.L. 1/27/31; Yes; Unallotted

1603; Mashburn, Ned T.; M; 10; N.C. Cherokee; 1/4-; S; Son; Yes; O.L. 1/27/31; Yes; Unallotted

1604; Mashburn, Annie L.; F; 8; N.C. Cherokee; 1/4-; S; Daughter; Yes; O.L. 1/27/31; Yes; Unallotted

1605; Mashburn, Ed. T.; M; 7; N.C. Cherokee; 1/4-; S; Son; Yes; O.L. 1/27/31; Yes; Unallotted

Census of the **Eastern Cherokee** reservation of the **Cherokee, N.C.** jurisdiction, as of **April 1** , 19**32,** taken by **R. L. Spalsbury** , Superintendent.

Key: Census Number; Surname, Given; Sex; Age at Last Date of Birth; Tribe; Degree of Blood; Marital Status; Relationship to Head of Family; Where Enrolled (Yes/No); (If no – Where); Ward (Yes/No); Allotment, Annuity and Identification Numbers (if given).

1606;   Mashburn, Fred H.; M; 7; N.C. Cherokee; 1/4-; S; Son; Yes; O.L. 1/27/31; Yes; Unallotted

1639;   Miller, Agnes R.; F; 24; N.C. Cherokee; 1/4; M; Wife; Yes; O.L. 1/27/31; Yes; Unallotted

1640;   Miller, Charles; M; 6; N.C. Cherokee; 1/4-; S; Son; Yes; O.L. 1/27/31; Yes; Unallotted

1718;   Oocumma, Samuel; M; 12; N.C. Cherokee; 1/4; S; Son; Yes; Death – 1932 census; Yes; Unallotted

1830;   Parker, Harold Lee; M; 4; N.C. Cherokee; 1/16-; S; Son; Yes; O.L. 5/9/31; Yes; Unallotted

1971;   Queen, Sallie; F; 47; N.C. Cherokee; F; M; Wife; Yes; Died 7/25/25; Yes; Unallotted

2128;   Knight (Reagan), James; M; 4; N.C. Cherokee; 1/16-; S; Son; Yes; O.L. 5/9/31; Yes; Unallotted

2158;   Reed, Wm. Elmer; M; 21; N.C. Cherokee; 1/4; S; Son; No; O.L. 1/27/31; Salisbury, Rowan, N.C.; Yes; Unallotted

2159;   Reed, Meekerson; M; 19; N.C. Cherokee; 1/4; S; Son; No; O.L. 1/27/31; Salisbury, Rowan, N.C.; Yes; Unallotted

2254;   Ross, Adam; M; 47; N.C. Cherokee; F; Wd.; Widower; Yes; Death – 1932 census; Yes; Unallotted

2249;   Rose, Glenn; M; 2; N.C. Cherokee; 1/16-; S; Son; Yes; O.L. 5/9/31; Yes; Unallotted

2250;   Rose, Wm. P.; M; 10/12; N.C. Cherokee; 1/16-; S; Son; Yes; O.L. 5/9/31; Yes; Unallotted

2304;   Saunooke, Larseen (Lorena); F; 11/12; N.C. Cherokee; F; S; Daughter; Yes; Death – 1931 census; Yes; Unallotted

2307;   Saunooke, Anderson; M; 26; N.C. Cherokee; 1/4; S; Son; Yes; Duplicated – shown on 1930 census #2285; Yes; Unallotted

2434;   Sneed, Georgia; F; 4; N.C. Cherokee; 1/16-; S; Daughter; Yes; O.L. 5/9/31; Yes; Unallotted

2510;   Sneed, Wilburn; M; 21; N.C. Cherokee; 1/4-; S; Son; Yes; Death – 1931 census; Yes; Unallotted

2569;   Stepp, Luther; M; 2; N.C. Cherokee; 1/16-; S; Son; Yes; O.L. 5/9/31; Yes; Unallotted

2614;   Swayney, Ethel; F; 10; N.C. Cherokee; 1/4-; S; Daughter; Yes; Death – 1931 census; Yes; Unallotted

2803;   Toineeta, Johnny; M; 4; N.C. Cherokee; F; S; Son; Yes; Died 7/1/25; Yes; Unallotted

2928;   Walkingstick, Rufus; M; 8/12; N.C. Cherokee; F; S; Son; Yes; Death – 1932 census; Yes; Unallotted

2936;   Walkingstick, Owen; M; 40; N.C. Cherokee; F; M; Husband; Yes; Died – 11/20/29; Yes; Unallotted

3107;   Wolfe, Able; M; 26; N.C. Cherokee; F; S; Son; Yes; Death – 1932 census; Yes; Unallotted

Census of the **Eastern Cherokee** reservation of the **Cherokee, N.C.** jurisdiction, as of **April 1** , **1932,** taken by **R. L. Spalsbury** , Superintendent.

Key: Census Number; Surname, Given; Sex; Age at Last Date of Birth; Tribe; Degree of Blood; Marital Status; Relationship to Head of Family; Where Enrolled (Yes/No); (If no – Where); Ward (Yes/No); Allotment, Annuity and Identification Numbers (if given).

3152;   Wolfe, Lloyd L.; M; 37; N.C. Cherokee; F; S; Son; Yes; Death – 1931 census; Yes; Unallotted

Census of the Cherokee Tribe

Eastern Cherokee Agency, N.C.

As of April 1, 1933

Taken by R. L. Spalsbury, Superintendent.

Census of the **Eastern Cherokee** reservation of the **Cherokee, N.C.** jurisdiction, as of **April 1** , **1933,** taken by **R. L. Spalsbury** , Superintendent.

Key: Number; Surname, Given; Sex; Date of Birth-Age at Last Birthday; Tribe; Degree of Blood; Marital Status; Relationship to Head of Family; Last C. Roll No.; At Jurisdiction Where Enrolled (Yes/No); (If no – Where); Ward (Yes/No); Allotment, Annuity and Identification Numbers (if given).

1; Abernathy (Meroney, Sallie Belle), Sallie Belle; F; 10/16/94-38; N.C. Cherokee; 1/16; M; Head; 1; Yes; Yes; Unallotted

2; Abernathy, Miles Henry; M; 1/29/15-18; N.C. Cherokee; 1/32; S; Son; 2; Yes; Yes; Unallotted

3; Abernathy, Tabitha Dell; F; 5/3/19-12; N.C. Cherokee; 1/32; S; Dau.; 3; Yes; Yes; Unallotted

4; Abernathy, Fannie Bell; F; 8/12/23-9; N.C. Cherokee; 1/32; S; Dau.; 4; Yes; Yes; Unallotted

5; Adams, Adeline; F; 7/10/83-48; N.C. Cherokee; 1/32; M; Head; 5; Yes; Yes; Unallotted

6; Adams, Lionel; M; 2/6/08-25; N.C. Cherokee; 1/64; S; Son; 6; Yes; Yes; Unallotted

7; Adams, Stephen; M; 6/25/14-18; N.C. Cherokee; 1/64; S; Son; 7; Yes; Yes; Unallotted

8; Adams, Ever (Eva); F; 10/23/02-30; N.C. Cherokee; 1/32; M; Wife; 8; Yes; Yes; Unallotted

9; Adams, Emma Lee; F; 3/12/24-9; N.C. Cherokee; 1/64; S; Dau.; 9; Yes; Yes; Unallotted

10; Adams, Gudger; M; 9/16/01-31; N.C. Cherokee; 1/64; S; Head; 10; Yes; Yes; Unallotted

11; Adams, John V.; M; 6/11/93-39; N.C. Cherokee; 1/32; M; Head; 11; Yes; Yes; Unallotted

12; Adams, Trilba; F; 6/13/16-16; N.C. Cherokee; 1/64; S; Dau.; 12; Yes; Yes; Unallotted

13; Adams, Stanley; M; 8/20/19-13; N.C. Cherokee; 1/64; S; Son; 13; Yes; Yes; Unallotted

14; Adams, Juanita; F; 4/2/22-10; N.C. Cherokee; 1/64; S; Dau.; 14; Yes; Yes; Unallotted

15; Adams, Lewis; M; 4/8/04-28; N.C. Cherokee; 1/64; S; Head; 15; Yes; Yes; Unallotted

16; Adams, Monell; M; 10/15/04-28; N.C. Cherokee; 1/64; S; Head; 16; No; Culberson, Cherokee, N.C. Yes; Unallotted

17; Adams, Parrie; M; 12/5/03-29; N.C. Cherokee; 1/64; S; Head; 17; Yes; Yes; Unallotted

18; Adams, Rollins E.; M; 6/11/84-48; N.C. Cherokee; 1/32; M; Head; 18; Yes; Yes; Unallotted

Census of the **Eastern Cherokee** reservation of the **Cherokee, N.C.** jurisdiction, as of **April 1** , 19**33,** taken by **R. L. Spalsbury** , Superintendent.

Key: Number; Surname, Given; Sex; Date of Birth-Age at Last Birthday; Tribe; Degree of Blood; Marital Status; Relationship to Head of Family; Last C. Roll No.; At Jurisdiction Where Enrolled (Yes/No); (If no – Where); Ward (Yes/No); Allotment, Annuity and Identification Numbers (if given).

19; Adams, Quincy; M; 3/14/07-26; N.C. Cherokee; 1/64; S; Son; 19; Yes; Yes; Unallotted

20; Adams, Rollins Jr.; M; 6/11/10-22; N.C. Cherokee; 1/64; S; Son; 20; Yes; Yes; Unallotted

21; Adams, Mattie; F; 2/15/12-21; N.C. Cherokee; 1/64; S; Dau.; 21; Yes; Yes; Unallotted

22; Adams, Walter; M; 5/23/81-51; N.C. Cherokee; 1/32; M; Head; 22; Yes; Yes; Unallotted

23; Adams, Frank; M; 3/16/06-27; N.C. Cherokee; 1/64; S; Son; 23; Yes; Yes; Unallotted

24; Adams Belvia; F; 10/11/08-24; N.C. Cherokee; 1/64; S; Dau.; 24; Yes; Yes; Unallotted

25; Adams, Marion; M; 12/8/11-21; N.C. Cherokee; 1/64; S; Son; 25; Yes; Yes; Unallotted

26; Adams, Posey; M; 7/16/14-18; N.C. Cherokee; 1/64; S; Son; 26; Yes; Yes; Unallotted

27; Adams, Mary; F; 5/10/16-16; N.C. Cherokee; 1/64; S; Dau.; 27; Yes; Yes; Unallotted

28; Adams, Jesse; M; 10/5/19-13; N.C. Cherokee; 1/64; S; Son; 28; Yes; Yes; Unallotted

29; Adams, Ruth; F; 8/6/21-12; N.C. Cherokee; 1/64; S; Dau.; 29; Yes; Yes; Unallotted

30; Adams, Willard; M; 10/15/01-30; N.C. Cherokee; 1/64; M; Head; 30; Yes; Yes; Unallotted

31; Adkins, Mary Sneed; F; 2/19/95-38; N.C. Cherokee; 1/8; M; Wife; 31; Yes; Yes; Unallotted

32; Adkins, Mary L.; F; 5/28/24-8; N.C. Cherokee; 1/16; S; Dau.; 32; Yes; Yes; Unallotted

33; Akin (Meroney, Margaret), Margaret A.; F; 7/16/99-33; N.C. Cherokee; 1/16; M; Head; 33; Yes; Yes; Unallotted

34; Akin, Jack Barton; M; 1/11/22-11; N.C. Cherokee; 1/32; S; Son; 34; Yes; Yes; Unallotted

35; Allen, John T.; M; 3/8/71-61; N.C. Cherokee; 4/4; M; Head; 35; Yes; Yes; Unallotted

36; Allen, Eva; F; 12/16/81-51; N.C. Cherokee; 4/4; M; Wife; 36; Yes; Yes; Unallotted

37; Allen (Murphy, Lillie B.), Lillie B.; F; 2/12/03-30; N.C. Cherokee; 1/8; M; Wife; 37; No; Violet, Cherokee, N.C.; Yes; Unallotted

Census of the **Eastern Cherokee** reservation of the **Cherokee, N.C.** jurisdiction, as of **April 1**, **1933,** taken by **R. L. Spalsbury**, Superintendent.

Key: Number; Surname, Given; Sex; Date of Birth-Age at Last Birthday; Tribe; Degree of Blood; Marital Status; Relationship to Head of Family; Last C. Roll No.; At Jurisdiction Where Enrolled (Yes/No); (If no – Where); Ward (Yes/No); Allotment, Annuity and Identification Numbers (if given).

38;   Allen, Guion; M; 11/26/22-10; N.C. Cherokee; 1/16; S; Son; 38; No; Violet, Cherokee, N.C.; Yes; Unallotted

39;   Allison, Maggie P.; F; 7/16/22-10; N.C. Cherokee; 1/64; S; Dau.; 39; Yes; Yes; Unallotted

40;   Allison, Roy Robert; M; 2/13/04-29; N.C. Cherokee; 1/32; S; Son; 41; Yes; (Father, white); Yes; Unallotted

41;   Allison, Albert M.; M; 4/30/06-26; N.C. Cherokee; 1/32; S; Son; 42; Yes; Yes; Unallotted

42;   Allison, Felix W.; M; 2/6/12-21; N.C. Cherokee; 1/32; S; Son; 43; Yes; Yes; Unallotted

43;   Allison, Boyce J.; M; 8/12/14-18; N.C. Cherokee; 1/32; S; Son; 44; Yes; Yes; Unallotted

44;   Allison, Nora M.; F; 12/19/16-16; N.C. Cherokee; 1/32; S; Dau.; 45; Yes; Yes; Unallotted

45;   Anderson (Garland, Addie L.), Addie L.G.; F; 5/8/88-44; N.C. Cherokee; 1/16; M; Wife; 46; Yes; Yes; Unallotted

46;   Anderson, Gertie; F; 7/16/11-21; N.C. Cherokee; 1/32; S; Dau.; 47; Yes; Yes; Unallotted

47;   Anderson, Elbert; M; 4/23/14-18; N.C. Cherokee; 1/32; S; Son; 48; Yes; Yes; Unallotted

48;   Anderson, Marie; F; 3/6/17-16; N.C. Cherokee; 1/32; S; Dau.; 49; Yes; Yes; Unallotted

49;   Anderson, Emory; M; 9/28/21-11; N.C. Cherokee; 1/32; S; Dau[sic]; 50; Yes; Yes; Unallotted

50;   Anderson (Raper, Dona), Dona; F; 3/20/89-44; N.C. Cherokee; 1/16; M; Wife; 46; No; Atlanta, Fulton, Ga.; Yes; Unallotted

51;   Anderson, Ella Mary; F; 3/14/10-23; N.C. Cherokee; 1/16; S; Head; 52; No; Culberson, Cherokee, N.C.; Yes; Unallotted

52;   Anderson, Wm. Burl; M; 12/3/12-20; N.C. Cherokee; 1/16; S; Bro.; 53; No; Culberson, Cherokee, N.C.; Yes; Unallotted

53;   Anderson (Payne, Erma), Erma Za Payne; F; 3/7/07-26; N.C. Cherokee; 1/32; M; Wife; 54; No; Blue Ridge, Fannin, Ga.; Yes; Unallotted

54;   Anderson, James Olen; M; 5/5/24-8; N.C. Cherokee; 1/64; S; Son; 55; No; Blue Ridge, Fannin, Ga.; Yes; Unallotted

55;   Anderson, Lloyd; M; 6/21/17-15; N.C. Cherokee; 1/64; S; Son; 56; No; Culberson, Cherokee, N.C.; Yes; Unallotted

56;   Anderson, Earnest; M; 6/25/19-13; N.C. Cherokee; 1/64; S; Son; 57; No; Culberson, Cherokee, N.C.; Yes; Unallotted

Census of the **Eastern Cherokee** reservation of the **Cherokee, N.C.** jurisdiction, as of **April 1** , 1933, taken by **R. L. Spalsbury** , Superintendent.

Key: Number; Surname, Given; Sex; Date of Birth-Age at Last Birthday; Tribe; Degree of Blood; Marital Status; Relationship to Head of Family; Last C. Roll No.; At Jurisdiction Where Enrolled (Yes/No); (If no – Where); Ward (Yes/No); Allotment, Annuity and Identification Numbers (if given).

57;   Anderson, Evelyn; F; 7/25/21-11; N.C. Cherokee; 1/64; S; Dau.; 58; No; Culberson, Cherokee, N.C.; Yes; Unallotted

58;   Anderson, (Raper, Pearl), Pearl Raper; F; 1/4/05-28; N.C. Cherokee; 1/16; M; Wife; 59; Yes; Yes; Unallotted

59;   Arch, Codaskie; M; 6/2/99-33; N.C. Cherokee; F; S; Head; 60; Yes; Yes; Unallotted

60;   Arch, Winnie; F; 3/6/07-26; N.C. Cherokee; 15/16; S; Sister; 61; Yes; Yes; Unallotted

61;   Arch, Anna; F; 3/28/10-23; N.C. Cherokee; 15/16; S; Sister; 62; Yes; Yes; Unallotted

62;   Arch, Johnson; M; 12/25/83-49; N.C. Cherokee; 3/4; M; Head; 63; Yes; Yes; Unallotted

63;   Arch, Ella; F; 9/1/89-43; N.C. Cherokee; 1/2; M; Wife; 64; Yes; Yes; Unallotted

~~64;   Arch, Cora; F; 9/2/07-26; N.C. Cherokee; 5/8; M; Dau.; 65; Yes; Yes; Unallotted~~

64;   Arch, Horace; M; 5/16/09-23; N.C. Cherokee; 5/8; M; Son; 66; Yes; Yes; Unallotted

65;   Arch, Elma Cleona; F; 2/28/11-22; N.C. Cherokee; 5/8; M; Dau.; 67; Yes; Yes; Unallotted

66;   Arch, Bessie; F; 6/2/15-17; N.C. Cherokee; 5/8; S; Dau.; 68; Yes; Yes; Unallotted

67;   Arch, Ethlyn; F; 12/31/19-13; N.C. Cherokee; 5/8; S; Dau.; 69; Yes; Yes; Unallotted

68;   Arch, Johnson Jr.; M; 8/22/22-10; N.C. Cherokee; 5/8; S; Son; 70; Yes; Yes; Unallotted

69;   Arch, William H.; M; 11/2/31-1; N.C. Cherokee; 13/16; S; G-Son 3232; Yes; Yes; Unallotted

70;   Arch, Charles Edward; M; 2/14/33-1/12; N.C. Cherokee; 13/16; S; Son; --; Yes; Yes; Unallotted

71;   Arch, Martha; F; 6/16/84-48; N.C. Cherokee; F; Wd.; Head; 71; Yes; Yes; Unallotted

72;   Arch, Jesse; M; 6/8/08-24; N.C. Cherokee; F; S; Son; 72; Yes; Yes; Unallotted

73;   Arch, Jimme; M; 11/16/10-22; N.C. Cherokee; F; S; Son; 73; Yes; Yes; Unallotted

74;   Arch, Eva Stella; F; 9/16/13-19; N.C. Cherokee; F; S; Dau.; 74; Yes; Yes; Unallotted

75;   Arch, Joseph Lee; M; 11/12/20-12; N.C. Cherokee; F; S; Son; 75; Yes; Yes; Unallotted

76;   Arch, Edna; F; 2/12/25-8; N.C. Cherokee; F; S; Dau.; 76; Yes; Yes; Unallotted

Census of the **Eastern Cherokee** reservation of the **Cherokee, N.C.** jurisdiction, as of **April 1** , **1933,** taken by **R. L. Spalsbury** , Superintendent.

Key: Number; Surname, Given; Sex; Date of Birth-Age at Last Birthday; Tribe; Degree of Blood; Marital Status; Relationship to Head of Family; Last C. Roll No.; At Jurisdiction Where Enrolled (Yes/No); (If no – Where); Ward (Yes/No); Allotment, Annuity and Identification Numbers (if given).

77; Arch, Noah; M; 2/28/92-41; N.C. Cherokee; F; M; Head; 77; Yes; Yes; Unallotted

78; Arch, Cinda S.; F; 5/3/00-32; N.C. Cherokee; F; M; Wife; 78; Yes; Yes; Unallotted

79; Arch, Elizabeth B.; F; 9/15/19-13; N.C. Cherokee; F; S; Dau.; 79; Yes; Yes; Unallotted

80; Arch, Elsie Jennie; F; 3/28/22-11; N.C. Cherokee; F; S; Dau.; 80; Yes; Yes; Unallotted

81; Arch, Lulu Edith; F; 5/17/24-8; N.C. Cherokee; F; S; Dau.; 81; Yes; Yes; Unallotted

82; Arch, Wm. Wayne; M; 2/28/30-3; N.C. Cherokee; F; S; Son; 82; Yes; Yes; Unallotted

83; Arch, Olivan; F; 3/20/95-38; N.C. Cherokee; 3/4; M; Head; 83; Yes; Yes; Unallotted

84; Arch, Pauline B.; F; 1/1/17-16; N.C. Cherokee; 3/8; S; Dau.; 84; Yes; Yes; Unallotted

85; Arch, Nellie; F; 6/27/20-12; N.C. Cherokee; 5/8; S; Dau.; 85; Yes; Yes; Unallotted

86; Armachain, Chewinih; F; 11/4/41-91; N.C. Cherokee; F; Wd; Head; 86; Yes; Yes; Unallotted

87; Armachain, Davis; M; 1/4/51-81; N.C. Cherokee; F; Wd; Head; 87; Yes; Yes; Unallotted

88; Armachain, Sevier; M; 1/22/04-29; N.C. Cherokee; F; S; Son; 88; Yes; Yes; Unallotted

89; Armachain, Jesse; M; 1/28/96-38; N.C. Cherokee; F; M; Head; 89; Yes; Yes; Unallotted

90; Armachain, Lucy Long; F; 1/16/99-34; N.C. Cherokee; 3/4; M; Wife; 90; Yes; Yes; Unallotted

91; Armachain, Stella E.; F; 5/28/21-12; N.C. Cherokee; 7/8; S; Dau.; 91; Yes; Yes; Unallotted

92; Armachain, Jesse James; M; 1/5/29-4; N.C. Cherokee; 7/8; S; Son; 92; Yes; Yes; Unallotted

93; Armachain, Stacy; F; 3/6/31-2; N.C. Cherokee; 7/8; S; Dau.; 93; Yes; Yes; Unallotted

94; Armachain, Jonah; M; 8/6/95-37; N.C. Cherokee; F; M; Head; 94; Yes; Yes; Unallotted

95; Armachain, Kiney Watty; F; 8/7/99-33; N.C. Cherokee; F; M; Wife; 95; Yes; Yes; Unallotted

96; Armachain, Jim; M; 10/10/21-11; N.C. Cherokee; F; S; Son; 96; Yes; Yes; Unallotted

Census of the **Eastern Cherokee** reservation of the **Cherokee, N.C.** jurisdiction, as of **April 1** , 1933, taken by **R. L. Spalsbury** , Superintendent.

Key: Number; Surname, Given; Sex; Date of Birth-Age at Last Birthday; Tribe; Degree of Blood; Marital Status; Relationship to Head of Family; Last C. Roll No.; At Jurisdiction Where Enrolled (Yes/No); (If no – Where); Ward (Yes/No); Allotment, Annuity and Identification Numbers (if given).

97;   Armachain, DeHart; M; 5/22/23-9; N.C. Cherokee; F; S; Son; 97; Yes; Yes; Unallotted

98;   Armachain, Lacy; M; 10/5/77-55; N.C. Cherokee; F; M; Head; 98; Yes; Yes; Unallotted

99;   Armachain, Anna (Annie); F; 4/1/72-62; N.C. Cherokee; F; M; Wife; 99; Yes; Yes; Unallotted

100;   Armachain, James; M; 6/21/10-22; N.C. Cherokee; F; S; Son; 100; Yes; Yes; Unallotted

101;   Armachain, Louis; M; 6/12/99-33; N.C. Cherokee; F; M; Head; 101; Yes; Yes; Unallotted

102;   Armachain, Dora; F; 2/18/99-34; N.C. Cherokee; 1/8; M; Wife; 102; Yes; Yes; Unallotted

103;   Armachain, Emma; F; 4/30/19-13; N.C. Cherokee; 9/16; S; Dau.; 103; Yes; Yes; Unallotted

104;   Armachain, Wm. Davis; M; 9/24/21-11; N.C. Cherokee; 9/16; S; Son; 104; Yes; Yes; Unallotted

105;   Armachain, Calvin; M; 10/23/25-7; N.C. Cherokee; 9/16; S; Son; 105; Yes; Yes; Unallotted

106;   Armachain, Wayne Lewis; M; 6/28/30-1; N.C. Cherokee; 9/16; S; Son; 106; Yes; Yes; Unallotted

107;   Armachain, Ruth; F; 5/24/32-10/12; N.C. Cherokee; 9/16; S; Dau.; ---; Yes; Yes; Unallotted

108;   Arneach, Jefferson; M; 4/7/74-58; N.C. Cherokee; F; M; Head; 107; Yes; Yes; Unallotted

109;   Arneach, Sarah; F; 1/17/75-57; N.C. Cherokee; 7/8; M; Wife; 108; Yes; Yes; Unallotted

110;   Arneach, Samuel; M; 12/26/08-24; N.C. Cherokee; 15/16; S; Son; 109; Yes; Yes; Unallotted

111;   Arneach, John E.H.; M; 5/1/11-21; N.C. Cherokee; 15/16; S; Son; 110; Yes; Yes; Unallotted

112;   Arneach, Stella P.; F; 2/23/13-20; N.C. Cherokee; 15/16; S; Dau.; 111; Yes; Yes; Unallotted

113;   Arneach, Sylvester; M; 12/4/14-18; N.C. Cherokee; 15/16; S; Son; 112; Yes; Yes; Unallotted

114;   Arneach, Francis N.; M; 11/7/17-15; N.C. Cherokee; 15/16; S; Son; 113; Yes; Yes; Unallotted

115;   Ashe (Locust, Bessie), Bessie; F; 6/21/03-29; N.C. Cherokee; 1/4; M; Wife; 114; Yes; Yes; Unallotted

116;   Ashe (Locust, Martha), Martha L.; F; 12/2/09-22; N.C. Cherokee; 1/4; M; Wife; 115; Yes; Yes; Unallotted

Census of the **Eastern Cherokee** reservation of the **Cherokee, N.C.** jurisdiction, as of **April 1** , **1933,** taken by **R. L. Spalsbury** , Superintendent.

Key: Number; Surname, Given; Sex; Date of Birth-Age at Last Birthday; Tribe; Degree of Blood; Marital Status; Relationship to Head of Family; Last C. Roll No.; At Jurisdiction Where Enrolled (Yes/No); (If no – Where); Ward (Yes/No); Allotment, Annuity and Identification Numbers (if given).

117; Ashe, Joseph H.; M; 4/28/28-4; N.C. Cherokee; 1/8; S; Son; 116; Yes; Yes; Unallotted

118; Ashe, Margie L.; F; 10/14/30-2; N.C. Cherokee; 1/8; S; Dau.; 117; Yes; Yes; Unallotted

119; Austin, Vianey; F; 10/20/70-62; N.C. Cherokee; 1/16; M; Head; 118; No; Hiland[sic] Park, Hamilton, Tenn.; Yes; Unallotted

120; Austin, Howard; M; 7/5/11-23; N.C. Cherokee; 1/4-; S; Son; 119; No; Hiland Park, Hamilton, Tenn.; Yes; Unallotted

121; Austin, Jack; M; 8/10/00-32; N.C. Cherokee; 1/4-; S; Son; 120; No; Hiland Park, Hamilton, Tenn.; Yes; Unallotted

122; Austin, James; M; 5/11/90-42; N.C. Cherokee; 1/4-; S; Son; 121; No; Hiland Park, Hamilton, Tenn.; Yes; Unallotted

123; Austin, Lelia; F; 5/19/97-35; N.C. Cherokee; 1/4-; S; Dau.; 122; No; Hiland Park, Hamilton, Tenn.; Yes; Unallotted

124; Jones, Alice Austin; F; 7/16/03-29; N.C. Cherokee; 1/4-; M; Dau.; 123; No; Hiland Park, Hamilton, Tenn.; Yes; Unallotted

125; Mullins, Maggie Austin; F; 5/11/95-38; N.C. Cherokee; 1/4-; S; Dau.; 124; No; Hiland Park, Hamilton, Tenn.; Yes; Unallotted

126; Axe, John D.; M; 12/16/62-70; N.C. Cherokee; F; M; Head; 125; Yes; Yes; Unallotted

127; Axe, Eva; F; 12/16/64-68; N.C. Cherokee; F; M; Wife; 126; Yes; Yes; Unallotted

128; Axe, Josiah Long; M; 6/16/64-68; N.C. Cherokee; F; M; Head; 127; Yes; Yes; Unallotted

129; Axe, Ella; F; 7/2/05-28; N.C. Cherokee; F; S; Dau.; 128; Yes; Yes; Unallotted

130; Axe, Dora; F; 2/21/13-20; N.C. Cherokee; F; S; Dau.; 129; Yes; Yes; Unallotted

131; Axe, Posey; M; 6/15/15-14; N.C. Cherokee; F; S; Son; 130; Yes; Yes; Unallotted

132; Axe, Lucindy; F; 4/29/22-10; N.C. Cherokee; F; S; Dau.; 131; Yes; Yes; Unallotted

133; Axe, Willie; M; 2/16/72-61; N.C. Cherokee; F; Wd; Head; 132; Yes; Yes; Unallotted

134; Baker (Webster, Bonnie F.), Bonnie Fair; F; 12/18/96-36; N.C. Cherokee; 1/16; M; Wife; 133; No; Wagoner, Wagoner, Okla.; Yes; Unallotted

135; Baker (Cole, Elizabeth), Elizabeth B.; F; 12/16/62-70; N.C. Cherokee; 1/8; M; Wife; 134; Yes; Yes; Unallotted

Census of the **Eastern Cherokee** reservation of the **Cherokee, N.C.** jurisdiction, as of **April 1** , 19**33,** taken by **R. L. Spalsbury** , Superintendent.

Key: Number; Surname, Given; Sex; Date of Birth-Age at Last Birthday; Tribe; Degree of Blood; Marital Status; Relationship to Head of Family; Last C. Roll No.; At Jurisdiction Where Enrolled (Yes/No); (If no – Where); Ward (Yes/No); Allotment, Annuity and Identification Numbers (if given).

136; Baker (Churchill, Ella McCoy), Ella McCoy; F; 1/13/78-55; N.C. Cherokee; 1/8; M; Wife; 135; Yes; Yes; Unallotted

137; Baker, Mary R.; F; 4/24/05-26; N.C. Cherokee; 1/16; S; Dau.; 136; Yes; Yes; Unallotted

138; Baker, Cora; F; 10/5/10-22; N.C. Cherokee; 1/16; S; Dau.; 137; Yes; Yes; Unallotted

139; Baker, Alice; F; 3/19/13-20; N.C. Cherokee; 1/16; S; Dau.; 138; Yes; Yes; Unallotted

140; Baker, Thomas, Jr.; M; 2/23/16-17; N.C. Cherokee; 1/16; S; Son; 139; Yes; Yes; Unallotted

141; Baker (Cole, Elmira), Elmire Cole; F; 1/1/72-61; N.C. Cherokee; 1/8; M; Wife; 140; No; Culberson, Cherokee, N.C.; Yes; Unallotted

142; Baker, Ada; F; 3/13/10-23; N.C. Cherokee; 1/16; S; Dau.; 141; No; Culberson, Cherokee, N.C.; Yes; Unallotted

143; Baker, Homer; M; 3/12/12-21; N.C. Cherokee; 1/16; S; Son; 142; No; Culberson, Cherokee, N.C.; Yes; Unallotted

144; Baker, Luther; M; 3/13/95-38; N.C. Cherokee; 1/16; M; Head; 143; No; Culberson, Cherokee, N.C.; Yes; Unallotted

145; Baker, Howard; M; 3/12/20-13; N.C. Cherokee; 1/32; S; Son; 144; No; Culberson, Cherokee, N.C.; Yes; Unallotted

146; Baker, Lloyd; M; 9/1/23-9; N.C. Cherokee; 1/32; S; Son; 145; No; Culberson, Cherokee, N.C.; Yes; Unallotted

147; Barnes (Payne, Grace Lee), Grace Lee; F; 9/22/03-29; N.C. Cherokee; 1/32; M; Wife; 146; No; Benham, Harlan, Ky.; Yes; Unallotted

148; Barnett (Mashburn, Kate), Kate; F; 1/13/99-34; N.C. Cherokee; 1/64; M; Wife; 147; Yes; Yes; Unallotted

149; Barnett, Clinton; M; 11/25/15-17; N.C. Cherokee; 1/128; S; Son; 148; Yes; Yes; Unallotted

150; Barnett, Irene; F; 5/25/19-13; N.C. Cherokee; 1/128; S; Dau.; 149; Yes; Yes; Unallotted

151; Barnett, Wilburn; M; 8/8/22-10; N.C. Cherokee; 1/128; S; Son; 150; Yes; Yes; Unallotted

152; Barnett, Ruby; F; 12/1/18-14; N.C. Cherokee; 1/128; S; Niece; 151; Yes; Yes; Unallotted

153; Bates (Raper, Dessie), Dessie; F; 11/9/05-27; N.C. Cherokee; 1/16; M; Wife; 152; Yes; Yes; Unallotted

154; Batson (Crow, Henrietta), Henrietta C.; F; 9/15/86-46; N.C. Cherokee; 1/4; M; Wife; 153; Yes; Yes; Unallotted

Census of the **Eastern Cherokee** reservation of the **Cherokee, N.C.** jurisdiction, as of **April 1** , **1933,** taken by **R. L. Spalsbury** , Superintendent.

Key: Number; Surname, Given; Sex; Date of Birth-Age at Last Birthday; Tribe; Degree of Blood; Marital Status; Relationship to Head of Family; Last C. Roll No.; At Jurisdiction Where Enrolled (Yes/No); (If no – Where); Ward (Yes/No); Allotment, Annuity and Identification Numbers (if given).

155; Battle, Adeline; F; 4/30/52-80; N.C. Cherokee; 1/16; M; Wife; 154; Yes; Yes; Unallotted

156; Battle, Bruce W.; M; 9/28/76-56; N.C. Cherokee; 1/32; M; Head; 155; Yes; Yes; Unallotted

157; Battle, Daisy L.; F; 5/23/09-23; N.C. Cherokee; 1/64; S; Dau.; 156; Yes; Yes; Unallotted

158; Battle, Addie Lee; F; 12/27/10-22; N.C. Cherokee; 1/64; S; Dau.; 157; Yes; Yes; Unallotted

159; Battle, Bruce W. Jr.; M; 5/19/13-19; N.C. Cherokee; 1/64; S; Son; 158; Yes; Yes; Unallotted

160; Battle, Joan; F; 11/25/20-12; N.C. Cherokee; 1/64; S; Dau.; 159; Yes; Yes; Unallotted

161; Battle, Wm. M.; M; 11/23/83-49; N.C. Cherokee; 1/32; S; Head; 160; Yes; Yes; Unallotted

162; Bauer, Fred; M; 12/27/96-36; N.C. Cherokee; 3/8; M; Head; 161; Yes; Yes; Unallotted

163; Beavers (Robinson, Fannie), Fannie R.; F; 4/23/94-38; N.C. Cherokee; 1/16; M; Wife; 162; Yes; Yes; Unallotted

164; Beavers, Cliffie; F; 10/5/13-19; N.C. Cherokee; 1/32; S; Dau.; 163; Yes; Yes; Unallotted

165; Beavers, Lexie; F; 2/3/16-17; N.C. Cherokee; 1/32; S; Dau.; 164; Yes; Yes; Unallotted

166; Beck, Eugene; M; 5/18/89-43; N.C. Cherokee; 1/8; M; Head; 165; Yes; Yes; Unallotted

167; Beck (Matthews, Gady), Gady M.; F; 11/27/07-25; N.C. Cherokee; 1/32; M; Wife; 166; Yes; Yes; Unallotted

168; Beck, Samuel; M; 4/11/90-41; N.C. Cherokee; 1/8; M; Head; 167; Yes; Yes; Unallotted

169; Beck, Sarah Sneed; F; 9/4/01-31; N.C. Cherokee; 1/16; M; Wife; 168; Yes; Yes; Unallotted

170; Beck, Samuel Foch; M; 5/18/18-14; N.C. Cherokee; 3/32; S; Son; 169; Yes; Yes; Unallotted

171; Beck, John Quentin; M; 8/11/20-12; N.C. Cherokee; 3/32; S; Son; 170; Yes; Yes; Unallotted

172; Beck, Wilma Lee; F; 1/19/23-10; N.C. Cherokee; 3/32; S; Dau.; 171; Yes; Yes; Unallotted

173; Beck, Paul Kevia[sic]; M; 5/29/29-3; N.C. Cherokee; 3/32; S; Son; 172; Yes; Yes; Unallotted

Census of the **Eastern Cherokee** reservation of the **Cherokee, N.C.** jurisdiction, as of **April 1**, 1933, taken by **R. L. Spalsbury**, Superintendent.

Key: Number; Surname, Given; Sex; Date of Birth-Age at Last Birthday; Tribe; Degree of Blood; Marital Status; Relationship to Head of Family; Last C. Roll No.; At Jurisdiction Where Enrolled (Yes/No); (If no – Where); Ward (Yes/No); Allotment, Annuity and Identification Numbers (if given).

174; Beck, James Timothy; M; 5/27/32-8/12; N.C. Cherokee; 3/32; S; Son; ---; Yes; Yes; Unallotted

175; Ben, Cheick; M; 1/14/65-68; N.C. Cherokee; F; M; Head; 173; Yes; Yes; Unallotted

176; Ben, Ollie; F; 7/18/84-48; N.C. Cherokee; F; M; Wife; 174; Yes; Yes; Unallotted

177; Ben, Stan; M; 1/15/04-29; N.C. Cherokee; F; S; Son; 175; Yes; Yes; Unallotted

178; Ben, Callie; F; 4/1/13-20; N.C. Cherokee; F; S; Dau.; 176; Yes; Yes; Unallotted

179; Ben, Nannie; F; 4/18/15-17; N.C. Cherokee; F; S; Dau.; 177; Yes; Yes; Unallotted

180; Ben, Louisa; F; 6/22/18-15; N.C. Cherokee; F; S; Dau.; 178; Yes; Yes; Unallotted

181; Ben, Lucy; F; 7/12/21-11; N.C. Cherokee; F; S; Dau.; 179; Yes; Yes; Unallotted

182; Biggers (Adams, Daisy), Daisy; F; 5/18/88-44; N.C. Cherokee; 1/32; M; Wife; 180; Yes; Yes; Unallotted

183; Bigmeat, Isaiah; M; 12/16/78-54; N.C. Cherokee; F; M; Head; 181; Yes; Yes; Unallotted

184; Bigmeat, Sarah; F; 8/20/80-52; N.C. Cherokee; F; M; Wife; 182; Yes; Yes; Unallotted

185; Bigmeat, John; M; 12/7/12-19; N.C. Cherokee; F; S; Son; 183; Yes; Yes; Unallotted

186; Bigmeat, Richard; M; 6/20/18-14; N.C. Cherokee; F; S; Son; 184; Yes; Yes; Unallotted

187; Bigmeat, Nicodemus; M; 12/16/75-57; N.C. Cherokee; F; M; Head; 185; Yes; Yes; Unallotted

188; Bigmeat, Robert; M; 2/16/92-41; N.C. Cherokee; 7/8; M; Head; 186; Yes; Yes; Unallotted

189; Bigmeat, Charlotte L.; F; 6/12/87-45; N.C. Cherokee; 9/16; M; Wife; 187; Yes; Yes; Unallotted

190; Bigmeat, Tinie C.; F; 7/16/13-19; N.C. Cherokee; 23/32; S; Dau.; 188; Yes; Yes; Unallotted

191; Bigmeat, Ethel; F; 11/9/16-16; N.C. Cherokee; 23/32; S; Dau.; 189; Yes; Yes; Unallotted

192; Bigmeat, Elizabeth; F; 6/21/19-13; N.C. Cherokee; 23/32; S; Dau.; 190; Yes; Yes; Unallotted

193; Bigmeat, Mark Welch; M; 12/9/21-11; N.C. Cherokee; 23/32; S; Son; 191; Yes; Yes; Unallotted

Census of the **Eastern Cherokee** reservation of the **Cherokee, N.C.** jurisdiction, as of **April 1** , **1933,** taken by **R. L. Spalsbury** , Superintendent.

Key: Number; Surname, Given; Sex; Date of Birth-Age at Last Birthday; Tribe; Degree of Blood; Marital Status; Relationship to Head of Family; Last C. Roll No.; At Jurisdiction Where Enrolled (Yes/No); (If no – Where); Ward (Yes/No); Allotment, Annuity and Identification Numbers (if given).

194; Bigmeat, Mabel; F; 1/15/25-8; N.C. Cherokee; 23/32; S; Dau.; 192; Yes; Yes; Unallotted

195; Bigmeat, Welch; M; 3/8/29-4; N.C. Cherokee; 23/32; S; Son; 193; Yes; Yes; Unallotted

196; Bigmeat, Yona; M; 12/16/77-55; N.C. Cherokee; F; S; Head; 194; Yes; Yes; Unallotted

197; Birchfield (Harden, Willie Pearl), Willie P.; F; 12/25/98-33; N.C. Cherokee; 1/64; M; Wife; 195; Yes; Yes; Unallotted

198; Birchfield, Odis; M; 9/25/20-12; N.C. Cherokee; 1/128; S; Son; 196; Yes; Yes; Unallotted

199; Birchfield, Willie Belle; F; 5/31/22-9; N.C. Cherokee; 1/128; S; Dau.; 197; Yes; Yes; Unallotted

200; Birchfield, Wanda; F; 2/7/24-8; N.C. Cherokee; 1/128; S; Dau.; 198; Yes; Yes; Unallotted

201; Bird, Annie Bradley; F; 6/15/02-30; N.C. Cherokee; 1/4; Wd; Head; 199; Yes; Yes; Unallotted

202; Bird, Eli; M; 4/7/92-40; N.C. Cherokee; F; F[sic]; Head; 200; Yes; Yes; Unallotted

203; Bird, Amanda Swayney; F; 1/12/01-33; N.C. Cherokee; 1/16; M; Wife; 201; Yes; Yes; Unallotted

204; Bird, Jerome J.; M; 10/8/21-11; N.C. Cherokee; 17/32; S; Son; 202; Yes; Yes; Unallotted

205; Bird, Bernardina L.; F; 7/30/23-9; N.C. Cherokee; 17/32; S; Dau.; 203; Yes; Yes; Unallotted

206; Bird, Carl Henry; M; 3/16/25-8; N.C. Cherokee; 17/32; S; Son; 204; Yes; Yes; Unallotted

207; Bird, Octa Iona; F; 5/30/26-6; N.C. Cherokee; 17/32; S; Dau.; 205; Yes; Yes; Unallotted

208; Bird, Going; M; 8/25/66-66; N.C. Cherokee; F; Wd; Head; 206; Yes; Yes; Unallotted

209; Bird, Solomon; M; 7/15/02-30; N.C. Cherokee; F; M; Head; 207; Yes; Yes; Unallotted

210; Bird, Minnie Rattler; F; 4/17/07-25; N.C. Cherokee; F; M; Wife; 208; Yes; Yes; Unallotted

211; Bird, Stephen; M; 4/27/55-77; N.C. Cherokee; F; Wd; Head; 209; Yes; Yes; Unallotted

Census of the **Eastern Cherokee** reservation of the **Cherokee, N.C.** jurisdiction, as of **April 1** , 1933, taken by **R. L. Spalsbury** , Superintendent.

Key: Number; Surname, Given; Sex; Date of Birth-Age at Last Birthday; Tribe; Degree of Blood; Marital Status; Relationship to Head of Family; Last C. Roll No.; At Jurisdiction Where Enrolled (Yes/No); (If no – Where); Ward (Yes/No); Allotment, Annuity and Identification Numbers (if given).

212; Bird, Timpson; M; 12/18/85-47; N.C. Cherokee; F; M; Head; 210; Yes; Yes; Unallotted

213; Bird, Alkinney T.; F; 6/29/04-28; N.C. Cherokee; 7/8; M; Wife; 211; Yes; Yes; Unallotted

214; Bird, Annie; F; 11/27/19-13; N.C. Cherokee; 15/16; S; Dau.; 212; Yes; Yes; Unallotted

215; Bird, Lucinda; F; 9/20/21-10; N.C. Cherokee; 15/16; S; Dau.; 213; Yes; Yes; Unallotted

216; Bird, William; M; 5/17/24-8; N.C. Cherokee; 15/16; S; Son; 214; Yes; Yes; Unallotted

217; Bishop, Lillie; F; 1870-63; N.C. Cherokee; 1/8; M; Head; 215; Yes; Yes; Unallotted

218; Bishop, Hattie Bell; F; 1912-20; N.C. Cherokee; 1/16; S; Dau.; 216; Yes; Yes; Unallotted

219; Blackfox, Charley; M; 1/13/81-52; N.C. Cherokee; 7/8; M; Head; 217; Yes; Yes; Unallotted

220; Blackfox, Nancy; F; 10/2/83-49; N.C. Cherokee; F; M; Wife; 218; Yes; Yes; Unallotted

~~Blackfox, Nancy; F; 3/1/12-21; N.C. Cherokee; 15/16; S; Dau.; 219; Yes; Yes; Unallotted~~

221; Blackfox, Ross; M; 5/2/15-17; N.C. Cherokee; 15/16; S; Son; 220; Yes; Yes; Unallotted

222; Blackfox, Joe; M; 1/17/21-12; N.C. Cherokee; 15/16; S; Son; 221; Yes; Yes; Unallotted

223; Blackfox, Dinah C.; F; 12/17/57-76; N.C. Cherokee; F; Wd; Head; 222; Yes; Yes; Unallotted

224; Blankenship, Arizona; F; 5/13/75-57; N.C. Cherokee; 1/8; M; Wife; 223; Yes; Yes; Unallotted

225; Blankenship, Lillian J.; F; 4/22/09-24; N.C. Cherokee; 1/16; S; Dau.; 224; Yes; Yes; Unallotted

226; Blankenship, Fred Turner; M; 1/18/11-22; N.C. Cherokee; 1/16; S; Son; 225; Yes; Yes; Unallotted

227; Blankenship, Helen K.; F; 11/8/12-20; N.C. Cherokee; 1/16; S; Dau.; 226; Yes; Yes; Unallotted

228; Blankenship, Leroy E.; M; 4/27/14-18; N.C. Cherokee; 1/16; S; Son; 227; Yes; Yes; Unallotted

229; Blythe, Arch; M; 7/19/77-55; N.C. Cherokee; 7/8; Wd; Head; 228; Yes; Yes; Unallotted

230; Blythe, Sampson; M; 6/3/03-29; N.C. Cherokee; 11/16; S; Son; 229; Yes; Yes; Unallotted

Census of the **Eastern Cherokee** reservation of the **Cherokee, N.C.** jurisdiction, as of **April 1** , 19**33**, taken by **R. L. Spalsbury** , Superintendent.

Key: Number; Surname, Given; Sex; Date of Birth-Age at Last Birthday; Tribe; Degree of Blood; Marital Status; Relationship to Head of Family; Last C. Roll No.; At Jurisdiction Where Enrolled (Yes/No); (If no – Where); Ward (Yes/No); Allotment, Annuity and Identification Numbers (if given).

231; Blythe, Birdie B.; F; 5/21/10-22; N.C. Cherokee; 11/16; S; Dau.; 230; Yes; Yes; Unallotted

232; Blythe, Francis M.; M; 2/13/13-20; N.C. Cherokee; 11/16; S; Son; 231; Yes; Yes; Unallotted

233; Blythe, Susannah; F; 2/11/16-17; N.C. Cherokee; 11/16; S; Dau.; 232; Yes; Yes; Unallotted

234; Blythe, Freddie; M; 8/21/18-14; N.C. Cherokee; 11/16; S; Son; 233; Yes; Yes; Unallotted

235; Blythe, Pauline T.; F; 3/3/22-11; N.C. Cherokee; 11/16; S; Dau.; 234; Yes; Yes; Unallotted

236; Blythe, David; M; 9/30/62-70; N.C. Cherokee; 5/8; M; Head; 235; Yes; Yes; Unallotted

237; Blythe, Nancy; F; 7/6/72-61; N.C. Cherokee; 7/8; M; Wife; 236; Yes; Yes; Unallotted

238; Blythe, Jarret; M; 5/30/86-46; N.C. Cherokee; 1/2; M; Head; 237; Yes; Yes; Unallotted

239; Blythe, Mary B.; F; 7/30/92-40; N.C. Cherokee; 1/8; M; Wife; 238; Yes; Yes; Unallotted

240; Blythe, Andy J.; M; 4/11/15-18; N.C. Cherokee; 5/16; S; Alone; 239; Yes; Yes; Unallotted

241; Blythe, Lloyd J.; M; 9/16/09-23; N.C. Cherokee; 5/16; M; Head; 240; Yes; Yes; Unallotted

242; Blythe, Rachel B.; F; 7/15/06-26; N.C. Cherokee; 1/4; M; Wife; 241; Yes; Yes; Unallotted

243; Blythe, Lloyd A.J.; M; 2/11/30-3; N.C. Cherokee; 1/2; S; Son; 242; Yes; Yes; Unallotted

244; Blythe, Alta Maine; F; 10/22/31-1; N.C. Cherokee; 1/2; S; Dau.; 243; Yes; Yes; Unallotted

245; Blythe, Rachel; F; 7/23/16-16; N.C. Cherokee; 5/16; S; Alone; 244; Yes; Yes; Unallotted

246; Blythe, Emma Katherine; F; 4/11/18-14; N.C. Cherokee; 5/16; S; Sister; 245; Yes; Yes; Unallotted

247; Blythe, Wm. Henry; M; 11/15/73-59; N.C. Cherokee; 5/8; S; Head; 246; Yes; Yes; Unallotted

248; Bowman (Timpson, Caldonia), Caldonia; F; 4/18/70-62; N.C. Cherokee; 3/16; M; Wife; 247; Yes; Yes; Unallotted

Census of the **Eastern Cherokee** reservation of the **Cherokee, N.C.** jurisdiction, as of **April 1**, **1933**, taken by **R. L. Spalsbury**, Superintendent.

Key: Number; Surname, Given; Sex; Date of Birth-Age at Last Birthday; Tribe; Degree of Blood; Marital Status; Relationship to Head of Family; Last C. Roll No.; At Jurisdiction Where Enrolled (Yes/No); (If no – Where); Ward (Yes/No); Allotment, Annuity and Identification Numbers (if given).

249; Bowman, Grace Rose; F; 3/31/99-34; N.C. Cherokee; 1/16; M; Wife; 248; Yes; Yes; Unallotted

250; Bowman, Paul (Harold); M; 2/9/19-14; N.C. Cherokee; 1/32; S; Son; 249; Yes; Yes; Unallotted

251; Bowman, Catherine; F; 5/12/21-11; N.C. Cherokee; 1/32; S; Dau.; 250; Yes; Yes; Unallotted

252; Bowman, Nora Rose; F; 12/21/01-31; N.C. Cherokee; 1/16; M; Wife; 251; Yes; Yes; Unallotted

253; Brackett (Thompson, Iowa), Iowa; F; 10/4/94-38; N.C. Cherokee; 1/16; M; Wife; 252; Yes; Yes; Unallotted

254; Bradley, Eliza Jane; F; 5/5/72-60; N.C. Cherokee; 1/2; M; Wife; 253; Yes; Yes; Unallotted

255; Bradley, Lydia; F; 8/19/05-27; N.C. Cherokee; 1/4; S; Dau.; 254; Yes; Yes; Unallotted

256; Bradley, Seaborne; M; 10/25/07-25; N.C. Cherokee; 1/4; S; Son; 255; Yes; Yes; Unallotted

257; Bradley, Martha I.; F; 7/29/13-19; N.C. Cherokee; 1/4; S; Dau.; 256; Yes; Yes; Unallotted

258; Bradley (Lambert, Florence), Florence; F; 7/27/07-25; N.C. Cherokee; 1/16; M; Wife; 257; Yes; Yes; Unallotted

259; Bradley, Henry; M; 9/28/83-49; N.C. Cherokee; 13/16; M; Head; 258; Yes; Yes; Unallotted

260; Bradley, Nancy T.; F; 3/15/81-51; N.C. Cherokee; F; M; Wife; 259; Yes; Yes; Unallotted

261; Bradley, James; M; 1/20/06-27; N.C. Cherokee; 29/32; S; Son; 260; Yes; Yes; Unallotted

--- ; ~~Bradley, Arnessa; F; 8/5/07-25; N.C. Cherokee; 29/32; S; Dau.; 261; Yes; Yes; Unallotted~~

262; Bradley, Dueese; M; 8/29/09-23; N.C. Cherokee; 29/32; S; Son; 262; Yes; Yes; Unallotted

263; Bradley, Shon; M; 6/5/11-21; N.C. Cherokee; 29/32; S; Son; 263; Yes; Yes; Unallotted

264; Bradley, George; M; 10/18/13-19; N.C. Cherokee; 29/32; S; Son; 264; Yes; Yes; Unallotted

265; Bradley, Ellen; F; 11/13/15-17; N.C. Cherokee; 29/32; S; Dau.; 265; Yes; Yes; Unallotted

266; Bradley, Reva; F; 3/9/18-15; N.C. Cherokee; 29/32; S; Dau.; 266; Yes; Yes; Unallotted

267; Bradley, Fred; M; 1/16/20-13; N.C. Cherokee; 29/32; S; Dau.[sic]; 267; Yes; Yes; Unallotted

Census of the **Eastern Cherokee** reservation of the **Cherokee, N.C.** jurisdiction, as of **April 1**, **1933**, taken by **R. L. Spalsbury**, Superintendent.

Key: Number; Surname, Given; Sex; Date of Birth-Age at Last Birthday; Tribe; Degree of Blood; Marital Status; Relationship to Head of Family; Last C. Roll No.; At Jurisdiction Where Enrolled (Yes/No); (If no – Where); Ward (Yes/No); Allotment, Annuity and Identification Numbers (if given).

268;   Bradley, Rowena; F; 12/16/22-10; N.C. Cherokee; 29/32; S; Dau.; 268; Yes; Yes; Unallotted

269;   Bradley, James Walter; M; 7/8/94-38; N.C. Cherokee; 1/4; M; Head; 269; Yes; Yes; Unallotted

270;   Bradley, Eva Calhoun; F; 1/16/98-35; N.C. Cherokee; F; M; Wife; 270; Yes; Yes; Unallotted

271;   Bradley, Helen; F; 7/4/22-10; N.C. Cherokee; 5/8; S; Dau.; 271; Yes; Yes; Unallotted

272;   Bradley, Juanita; F; 7/7/28-4; N.C. Cherokee; 5/8; S; Dau.; 272; Yes; Yes; Unallotted

273;   Bradley, Johnson; M; 5/18/80-52; N.C. Cherokee; 1/2; M; Head; 273; Yes; Yes; Unallotted

274;   Bradley, Ethel; F; 1/2/10-23; N.C. Cherokee; 1/4; S; Dau.; 274; Yes; Yes; Unallotted

275;   Bradley, Antoine R.; M; 12/16/11-21; N.C. Cherokee; 1/4; S; Son; 275; Yes; Yes; Unallotted

276;   Bradley, Margaret Lou; F; 9/28/13-19; N.C. Cherokee; 1/4; S; Dau.; 276; Yes; Yes; Unallotted

277;   Bradley, Ardis Elinor; F; 1/21/15-18; N.C. Cherokee; 1/4; S; Dau.; 277; Yes; Yes; Unallotted

278;   Bradley, Robert F.; M; 9/19/18-14; N.C. Cherokee; 1/4; S; Dau.[sic]; 278; Yes; Yes; Unallotted

279;   Bradley, Joseph; M; 5/28/82-50; N.C. Cherokee; 1/2; M; Head; 279; Yes; Yes; Unallotted

280;   Bradley, Johnson; M; 6/11/09-24; N.C. Cherokee; 1/4; S; Son; 280; Yes; Yes; Unallotted

281;   Bradley, Lucinda; F; 2/24/11-22; N.C. Cherokee; 1/4; S; Dau.; 281; Yes; Yes; Unallotted

282;   Bradley, Lewis; M; 4/11/13-19; N.C. Cherokee; 1/4; S; Son; 282; Yes; Yes; Unallotted

283;   Bradley, Betty; F; 1/15/15-18; N.C. Cherokee; 1/4; S; Dau.; 283; Yes; Yes; Unallotted

284;   Bradley, Raymond; M; 8/19/17-15; N.C. Cherokee; 1/4; S; Son; 284; Yes; Yes; Unallotted

285;   Bradley, Freeman; M; 8/9/20-12; N.C. Cherokee; 1/4; S; Son; 285; Yes; Yes; Unallotted

286;   Bradley, Judson; M; 8/11/02-30; N.C. Cherokee; 1/4; M; Head; 286; Yes; Yes; Unallotted

287;   Bradley (McCoy, Julia), Julia; F; 12/2/03-29; N.C. Cherokee; 1/16; M; Wife; 287; Yes; Yes; Unallotted

Census of the **Eastern Cherokee** reservation of the **Cherokee, N.C.** jurisdiction, as of **April 1**, 1933, taken by **R. L. Spalsbury**, Superintendent.

Key: Number; Surname, Given; Sex; Date of Birth-Age at Last Birthday; Tribe; Degree of Blood; Marital Status; Relationship to Head of Family; Last C. Roll No.; At Jurisdiction Where Enrolled (Yes/No); (If no – Where); Ward (Yes/No); Allotment, Annuity and Identification Numbers (if given).

288; Bradley, Wm. Lee; M; 11/11/21-11; N.C. Cherokee; 1/32; S; Son; 288; Yes; Yes; Unallotted

289; Bradley, Olene G.; F; 5/22/23-9; N.C. Cherokee; 1/32; S; Dau.; 289; Yes; Yes; Unallotted

290; Bradley (McCoy, Mary), Mary; F; 5/19/01-31; N.C. Cherokee; 1/16; M; Wife; 290; Yes; Yes; Unallotted

291; Bradley, John Winford; M; 10/14/21-12; N.C. Cherokee; 1/32; S; Son; 291; Yes; Yes; Unallotted

292; Bradley, Charles Coolidge; M; 2/2/24-9; N.C. Cherokee; 1/32; S; Dau.[sic]; 292; Yes; Yes; Unallotted

293; Bradley, Irene; F; 9/26/23-9; N.C. Cherokee; 1/4; S; Alone; 293; Yes; Yes; Unallotted

294; Bradley, Morgan; M; 2/15/26-7; N.C. Cherokee; 1/4; S; Bro.; 294; Yes; Yes; Unallotted

295; Bradley, Nancy; F; 5/20/74-58; N.C. Cherokee; 1/2; M; Wife; 295; Yes; Yes; Unallotted

296; Bradley, Minda; F; 1/6/06-27; N.C. Cherokee; 1/4; S; Dau.; 296; Yes; Yes; Unallotted

--- ; ~~Bradley, Etta L.; F; 6/22/12-20; N.C. Cherokee; 1/4; S; Daughter; 297; Yes; Yes; Unallotted~~

297; Bradley, Jerome; M; 4/16/14-18; N.C. Cherokee; 1/4; S; Son; 298; Yes; Yes; Unallotted

298; Moles, Vera Bradley, Vera W.; F; 1/5/09-24; N.C. Cherokee; 1/4; M; Dau.; 300; Yes; Yes; Unallotted

299; Bradley, Luvinia; F; 12/9/16-16; N.C. Cherokee; 1/4; S; Dau.; 299; Yes; Yes; Unallotted

300; Moles (Bradley), Racheal M.; F; 6/23/31-1; N.C. Cherokee; 1/8; S; Grand daughter; 301; Yes; Yes; Unallotted

301; Moles, Dorothy Elaine; F; 8/13/32-7/12; N.C. Cherokee; 1/8; S; G-Dau.; ---; Yes; Yes; Unallotted

302; Bradley, Nick; M; 4/13/95-37; N.C. Cherokee; 1/2; M; Head; 302; Yes; Yes; Unallotted

303; Bradley, John R.; M; 3/28/27-6; N.C. Cherokee; 1/4; S; Son; 303; Yes; Yes; Unallotted

304; Bradley, Jarret T.; M; 2/12/29-4; N.C. Cherokee; 1/4; S; Son; 304; Yes; Yes; Unallotted

305; Bradley (Lambert, Pearl), Pearl L.; F; 11/19/98-34; N.C. Cherokee; 1/32; M; Wife; 305; Yes; Yes; Unallotted

306; Bradley, Arizona; F; 10/17/19-13; N.C. Cherokee; 1/64; S; Dau.; 306; Yes; Yes; Unallotted

Census of the **Eastern Cherokee** reservation of the **Cherokee, N.C.** jurisdiction, as of **April 1**, **1933**, taken by **R. L. Spalsbury**, Superintendent.

Key: Number; Surname, Given; Sex; Date of Birth-Age at Last Birthday; Tribe; Degree of Blood; Marital Status; Relationship to Head of Family; Last C. Roll No.; At Jurisdiction Where Enrolled (Yes/No); (If no – Where); Ward (Yes/No); Allotment, Annuity and Identification Numbers (if given).

307;   Bradley, Nannie C.; F; 8/23/21-11; N.C. Cherokee; 1/64; S; Dau.; 307; Yes; Yes; Unallotted

308;   ~~Bradley, Rachel; F; 7/15/06-27; N.C. Cherokee; 1/4; S; Head; 308; Yes; Yes; Unallotted~~

309;   Bradley, Harold Calvin; M; 11/29/24-8; N.C. Cherokee; 1/16; S; Son; 309; Yes; Yes; Unallotted

310;   Bradley, Freda Anna; F; 3/29/28-5; N.C. Cherokee; 7/16; S; Dau.; 310; Yes; Yes; Unallotted

311;   Bradley, Roy; M; 6/14/04-28; N.C. Cherokee; 1/4; M; Head; 311; Yes; Yes; Unallotted

312;   Bradley, Alice Crowe; F; 6/4/98-34; N.C. Cherokee; 13/32; M; Wife; 312; Yes; Yes; Unallotted

313;   Bradley, Elsie; F; 7/25/26-6; N.C. Cherokee; 21/64; S; Dau.; 313; Yes; Yes; Unallotted

314;   Bradley, Erma Louise; F; 4/6/29-4; N.C. Cherokee; 21/64; S; Dau.; 314; Yes; Yes; Unallotted

315;   Bradley, Frances Thelma; F; 9/29/32-6/12; N.C. Cherokee; 21/64; S; Dau.; ---; Yes; Yes; Unallotted

316;   Bradley, Thomas; M; 12/21/08-24; N.C. Cherokee; 1/4; S; Head; 316; Yes; Yes; Unallotted

317;   Bradley, Wm. Amos; M; 9/21/96-36; N.C. Cherokee; 1/4; M; Head; 317; Yes; Yes; Unallotted

318;   Bradley, Sarah Powell; F; 11/7/98-34; N.C. Cherokee; 3/4; M; Wife; 318; Yes; Yes; Unallotted

319;   Bradley, Richard; M; 6/10/18-14; N.C. Cherokee; 1/2; S; Son; 319; Yes; Yes; Unallotted

320;   Bradley, Albert F.; M; 1/23/23-10; N.C. Cherokee; 1/2; S; Son; 320; Yes; Yes; Unallotted

321;   Bradley, Constance; F; 2/17/31-2; N.C. Cherokee; 1/2; S; Dau.; 321; Yes; Yes; Unallotted

322;   Brady, Susie Smith; F; 3/1/86-47; N.C. Cherokee; 1/4; M; Wife; 322; Yes; Yes; Unallotted

323;   Brady, James Lowen; M; 3/17/10-22; N.C. Cherokee; 3/8; S; Son; 323; Yes; Yes; Unallotted

324;   Brady, Samuel; M; 11/12/11-21; N.C. Cherokee; 3/8; S; Son; 324; Yes; Yes; Unallotted

325;   Brady, William; M; 11/7/13-19; N.C. Cherokee; 3/8; S; Son; 325; Yes; Yes; Unallotted

326;   Brady, Mary T.; F; 9/23/17-15; N.C. Cherokee; 3/8; S; Dau.; 326; Yes; Yes; Unallotted

Census of the **Eastern Cherokee** reservation of the **Cherokee, N.C.** jurisdiction, as of **April 1** , 1933, taken by **R. L. Spalsbury** , Superintendent.

Key: Number; Surname, Given; Sex; Date of Birth-Age at Last Birthday; Tribe; Degree of Blood; Marital Status; Relationship to Head of Family; Last C. Roll No.; At Jurisdiction Where Enrolled (Yes/No); (If no – Where); Ward (Yes/No); Allotment, Annuity and Identification Numbers (if given).

327; Brady, Floyd; M; 2/18/20-13; N.C. Cherokee; 3/8; S; Son; 327; Yes; Yes; Unallotted

328; Brady, Arthur; M; 1/30/23-10; N.C. Cherokee; 3/8; S; Son; 328; Yes; Yes; Unallotted

329; Brady, Ralph; M; 1/20/26-7; N.C. Cherokee; 3/8; S; Son; 329; Yes; Yes; Unallotted

330; Brady, Baby Male; M; 6/26/31-1; N.C. Cherokee; 3/8; S; Son; 330; Yes; Yes; Unallotted

331; Breckenridge (Anderson, Cora), Cora O.; F; 7/19/04-28; N.C. Cherokee; 1/16; M; Wife; 331; Yes; Yes; Unallotted

332; Brewster, Linnie L.J.; F; 1890-43; N.C. Cherokee; 1/14; M; Wife; 332; Yes; Yes; Unallotted

333; Brock (Mashburn, Minnie), Minnie M.; F; 6/1/01-31; N.C. Cherokee; 3/32; M; Wife; 333; Yes; Yes; Unallotted

334; Brock, Ruby Lee; F; 9/19/22-11; N.C. Cherokee; 3/64; S; Dau.; 334; Yes; Yes; Unallotted

335; Brown, Jonah; M; 9/5/80-52; N.C. Cherokee; F; M; Head; 335; Yes; Yes; Unallotted

336; Brown, Mollie; F; 1/5/81-52; N.C. Cherokee; F; M; Wife; 336; Yes; Yes; Unallotted

337; Brown, Mark; M; 6/11/10-22; N.C. Cherokee; F; S; Son; 337; Yes; Yes; Unallotted

338; Brown, Lizzie; F; 3/21/12-21; N.C. Cherokee; F; S; Dau.; 338; Yes; Yes; Unallotted

339; Brown, Sam; M; 3/21/15-18; N.C. Cherokee; F; S; Son; 339; Yes; Yes; Unallotted

340; Brown, Lydia; F; 12/17/47-85; N.C. Cherokee; F; Wd; Head; 340; Yes; Yes; Unallotted

341; Brown, Peter; M; 3/3/89-43; N.C. Cherokee; F; Wd.; Head; 341; Yes; Yes; Unallotted

342; Brown, Nora; F; 6/7/17-15; N.C. Cherokee; F; S; Dau.; 342; Yes; Yes; Unallotted

343; Bruce, Arthur; M; 7/21/88-44; N.C. Cherokee; 1/16; M; Head; 343; No; Sweet Gum, Fannin, Ga.; Yes; Unallotted

344; Bruce, Corrie; F; 7/19/14-18; N.C. Cherokee; 1/32; S; Dau.; 344; No; Sweet Gum, Fannin, Ga.; Yes; Unallotted

345; Bruce, Alice; F; 8/11/15-17; N.C. Cherokee; 1/32; S; Dau.; 345; No; Sweet Gum, Fannin, Ga.; Yes; Unallotted

Census of the **Eastern Cherokee** reservation of the **Cherokee, N.C.** jurisdiction, as of **April 1** , 19**33**, taken by **R. L. Spalsbury** , Superintendent.

Key: Number; Surname, Given; Sex; Date of Birth-Age at Last Birthday; Tribe; Degree of Blood; Marital Status; Relationship to Head of Family; Last C. Roll No.; At Jurisdiction Where Enrolled (Yes/No); (If no – Where); Ward (Yes/No); Allotment, Annuity and Identification Numbers (if given).

346;   Bruce (Raper, Elzie), Elzie R.; F; 38; N.C. Cherokee; 1/32; M; Wife; 346; No; San Angelo, Tom Green, Tex.; Yes; Unallotted

347;   Bryant (Garland, Elizabeth), Elizabeth H.G.; F; 3/21/61-72; N.C. Cherokee; 1/8; M; Wife; 347; Yes; Yes; Unallotted

348;   Bryant (Patterson, Ethel), Ethel; F; 12/21/98-35; N.C. Cherokee; 1/32; M; Wife; 348; No; Hemp, Fannin, Ga.; Yes; Unallotted

349;   Bryant, Thelma; F; 11/3/17-15; N.C. Cherokee; 1/64; S; Dau.; 349; No; Hemp, Fannin, Ga.; Yes; Unallotted

350;   Bryant, Dennis; M; 2/12/19-14; N.C. Cherokee; 1/64; S; Son; 350; No; Hemp, Fannin, Ga.; Yes; Unallotted

351;   Bryant, Edna; F; 4/28/21-11; N.C. Cherokee; 1/64; S; Dau.; 351; No; Hemp, Fannin, Ga.; Yes; Unallotted

352;   Bryant, Lillian; F; 1/6/23-10; N.C. Cherokee; 1/64; S; Dau.; 352; No; Hemp, Fannin, Ga.; Yes; Unallotted

353;   Bryson (Adams, Martha E.), Martha Edna; F; 2/25/86-47; N.C. Cherokee; 1/32; M; Wife; 353; Yes; Yes; Unallotted

354;   Bryson, Fred; M; 2/7/08-25; N.C. Cherokee; 1/64; S; Son; 354; Yes; Yes; Unallotted

355;   Bryson, Thelma; M; 8/14/11-23; N.C. Cherokee; 1/64; S; Dau.; 355; Yes; Yes; Unallotted

356;   Burgess, Georgia Ann; F; 6/10/69-64; N.C. Cherokee; 1/4; M; Wife; 356; Yes; Yes; Unallotted

357;   Burgess, Nellie; F; 6/24/09-23; N.C. Cherokee; 1/8; S; Dau.; 358; Yes; Yes; Unallotted

358;   Burgess, Frederic Homer; M; 4/24/12-20; N.C. Cherokee; 1/8; S; Son; 359; Yes; Yes; Unallotted

359;   Burgess, George Alger; M; 10/7/06-27; N.C. Cherokee; 1/8; S; Son; 357; Yes; Yes; Unallotted

360;   Burgess (Bradley, Etta L.), Etta L.; F; 6/22/12-20; N.C. Cherokee; 1/4; M; Wife; 297; Yes; Yes; Unallotted

361;   Burgess, Mary C.; F; 1/5/31-2; N.C. Cherokee; 3/16; S; Dau.; 360; Yes; Yes; Unallotted

362;   Burgess, James; M; 8/6/99-33; N.C. Cherokee; 1/64; M; Head; 361; Yes; Yes; Unallotted

363;   Burgess, Martha; F; 10/30/03-29; N.C. Cherokee; 1/64; S; Head; 362; Yes; Yes; Unallotted

Census of the **Eastern Cherokee** reservation of the **Cherokee, N.C.** jurisdiction, as of **April 1** , 19**33,** taken by **R. L. Spalsbury** , Superintendent.

Key: Number; Surname, Given; Sex; Date of Birth-Age at Last Birthday; Tribe; Degree of Blood; Marital Status; Relationship to Head of Family; Last C. Roll No.; At Jurisdiction Where Enrolled (Yes/No); (If no – Where); Ward (Yes/No); Allotment, Annuity and Identification Numbers (if given).

364;   Burgess, Myrtle; F; 11/19/98-34; N.C. Cherokee; 1/64; M; Wife; 363; Yes; Yes; Unallotted

365;   Burgess, Sue; F; 9/21/19-13; N.C. Cherokee; 1/128; S; Dau.; 364; Yes;   Yes; Unallotted

366;   Burgess, Truman; M; 11/22/21-12; N.C. Cherokee; 1/128; S; Son; 365; Yes; Yes; Unallotted

367;   Burgess, Troy Jackson; M; 12/24/23-9; N.C. Cherokee; 1/128; S; Son; 366; Yes; Yes; Unallotted

368;   Burgess, Ollie; F; 12/30/75-57; N.C. Cherokee; 1/32; M; Wife; 367; Yes; Yes; Unallotted

369;   Burgess, John; M; 4/3/06-26; N.C. Cherokee; 1/64; S; Son; 368; Yes; Yes; Unallotted

370;   Burgess, Arthur; M; 11/16/07-25; N.C. Cherokee; 1/64; S; Son; 369; Yes; Yes; Unallotted

371;   Burgess, Winslow; M; 2/4/10-23; N.C. Cherokee; 1/64; S; Son; 370; Yes; Yes; Unallotted

372;   Burgess, Rose; F; 3/15/12-21; N.C. Cherokee; 1/64; S; Dau.; 371; Yes;   Yes; Unallotted

373;   Burgess, Raburn; M; 12/31/14-18; N.C. Cherokee; 1/64; S; Son; 372; Yes; Yes; Unallotted

374;   Burgess, Ada; F; 4/11/16-17; N.C. Cherokee; 1/64; S; Dau.; 373; Yes; Yes; Unallotted

375;   Burrell (Stiles, Emma), Emma; F; 9/24/96-36; N.C. Cherokee; 1/32; M; Wife; 374; Yes; Yes; Unallotted

376;   Busheyhead, Ben; M; 5/14/86-46; N.C. Cherokee; 7/8; M; Head; 375; Yes; Yes; Unallotted

377;   Busheyhead, Nancy; F; 12/23/86-46; N.C. Cherokee; 4/4; M; Wife; 376; Yes; Yes; Unallotted

378;   Busheyhead, Joel; M; 6/6/11-21; N.C. Cherokee; 15/16; S; Son; 377; Yes; Yes; Unallotted

379;   Busheyhead, Robert; M; 10/29/14-18; N.C. Cherokee; 15/16; S; Son; 378; Yes; Yes; Unallotted

380;   Butler (Payne, Clara), Clara; F; 7/25/03-30; N.C. Cherokee; 1/64; M; Wife; 379; Yes; Yes; Unallotted

381;   Calhoun, Henry; M; 3/6/19-14; N.C. Cherokee; 1/2; S; Alone; 380; Yes; Yes; Unallotted

382;   Calhoun, Lawyer; M; 5/7/60-72; N.C. Cherokee; F; Wd; Head; 381; Yes; Yes; Unallotted

Census of the **Eastern Cherokee** reservation of the **Cherokee, N.C.** jurisdiction, as of **April 1** , **1933,** taken by **R. L. Spalsbury** , Superintendent.

Key: Number; Surname, Given; Sex; Date of Birth-Age at Last Birthday; Tribe; Degree of Blood; Marital Status; Relationship to Head of Family; Last C. Roll No.; At Jurisdiction Where Enrolled (Yes/No); (If no – Where); Ward (Yes/No); Allotment, Annuity and Identification Numbers (if given).

383; Calhoun, Sallie Ann; F; 2/15/77-56; N.C. Cherokee; F; Wd; Head; 382; Yes; Yes; Unallotted

384; Calhoun, Lawson; M; 5/27/02-30; N.C. Cherokee; F; S; Son; 383; Yes; Yes; Unallotted

385; Calhoun, Henry; M; 4/25/04-28; N.C. Cherokee; F; S; Son; 384; Yes; Yes; Unallotted

386; Calhoun, Lawyer; M; 4/30/06-26; N.C. Cherokee; F; S; Son; 385; Yes; Yes; Unallotted

387; Calhoun, Smathers; M; 6/28/12-20; N.C. Cherokee; F; S; Son; 386; Yes; Yes; Unallotted

388; Calhoun, Katie; F; 9/12/15-17; N.C. Cherokee; F; S; Dau.; 387; Yes; Yes; Unallotted

389; Calhoun, Hewitt; M; 5/12/18-14; N.C. Cherokee; F; S; Son; 388; Yes; Yes; Unallotted

390; Camp (Murphy, Isabella), Isabella; F; 1/7/92-41; N.C. Cherokee; 1/8; M; Head (Divorced); 389; No; Murphy, Cherokee, N.C.; Yes; Unallotted

391; Camp, Bettie; F; 12/8/13-19; N.C. Cherokee; 1/16; S; Dau.; 390; No; Murphy, Cherokee, N.C.; Yes; Unallotted

392; Campbell (Lunsford, Callie), Callie; F; 6/12/05-27; N.C. Cherokee; 1/64; M; Wife; 391; Yes; Yes; Unallotted

393; Cannaut, Columbus; M; 12/17/82-50; N.C. Cherokee; F; M; Head; 392; Yes; Yes; Unallotted

394; Cannaut, Maggie; F; 11/17/89-43; N.C. Cherokee; F; Div.; Head; 393; Yes; Yes; Unallotted

395; Cannaut, Addison; M; 9/4/09-23; N.C. Cherokee; F; S; Son; 394; Yes; Yes; Unallotted

396; Cantrell (Payne, Stella), Stella; F; 6/3/08-24; N.C. Cherokee; 1/64; M; Wife; 395; Yes; Yes; Unallotted

397; Cantrell, William; M; 9/23/21-11; N.C. Cherokee; 1/128; S; Son; 396; Yes; Yes; Unallotted

398; Carroll, Newton; M; 2/8/73-60; N.C. Cherokee; 3/16; M; Head; 397; Yes; Yes; Unallotted

399; Carter, Belvia A.L.; F; 12/12/01-31; N.C. Cherokee; 1/32; M; Wife; 398; Yes; Yes; Unallotted

400; Carter, Mabel; F; 12/10/21-11; N.C. Cherokee; 1/64; S; Dau.; 399; Yes; Yes; Unallotted

401; Carter, Wallace; M; 6/12/23-9; N.C. Cherokee; 1/64; S; Son; 400; Yes; Yes; Unallotted

Census of the **Eastern Cherokee** reservation of the **Cherokee, N.C.** jurisdiction, as of **April 1** , 19**33,** taken by **R. L. Spalsbury** , Superintendent.

Key: Number; Surname, Given; Sex; Date of Birth-Age at Last Birthday; Tribe; Degree of Blood; Marital Status; Relationship to Head of Family; Last C. Roll No.; At Jurisdiction Where Enrolled (Yes/No); (If no – Where); Ward (Yes/No); Allotment, Annuity and Identification Numbers (if given).

402;   Carver (Whitaker, Ada), Ada; F; 8/17/98-34; N.C. Cherokee; 1/32; M; Wife; 401; Yes; Yes; Unallotted

403;   Carver, Bernette; F; 8/14/19-13; N.C. Cherokee; 1/64; S; Dau.; 402; Yes; Yes; Unallotted

404;   Carver, James; M; 3/21/21-12; N.C. Cherokee; 1/64; S; Son; 403; Yes; Yes; Unallotted

405;   Carver, Wayne; M; 4/7/23-10; N.C. Cherokee; 1/64; S; Son; 404; Yes; Yes; Unallotted

406;   Carver (Raper, Hattie), Hattie; F; 7/8/81-51; N.C. Cherokee; 1/16; M; Wife; 405; Yes; Yes; Unallotted

407;   Catolster, Carson J.; M; 4/28/79-53; N.C. Cherokee; F; M; Head; 406; Yes; Yes; Unallotted

408;   Catolster, Josie S.; F; 7/21/92-40; N.C. Cherokee; F; M; Wife; 407; Yes; Yes; Unallotted

409;   Catolster, Johnson; M; 9/28/08-24; N.C. Cherokee; F; S; Son; 408; Yes; Yes; Unallotted

410;   Catolster, David; M; 2/16/11-22; N.C. Cherokee; F; S; Son; 409; Yes; Yes; Unallotted

411;   Catolster, Margaret; F; 12/18/13-19; N.C. Cherokee; F; S; Dau.; 410; Yes; Yes; Unallotted

412;   Catolster, Rebecca; F; 1/12/17-16; N.C. Cherokee; F; S; Dau.; 411; Yes; Yes; Unallotted

413;   Catolster, Benjamin; M; 5/1/19-13; N.C. Cherokee; F; S; Son; 412; Yes; Yes; Unallotted

414;   Catolster, Emma; F; 5/12/24-8; N.C. Cherokee; F; S; Dau.; 413; Yes; Yes; Unallotted

415;   Catolster, Eva Louisa; F; 3/29/28-5; N.C. Cherokee; F; S; Dau.; 414; Yes; Yes; Unallotted

416;   Catolster, Wallace; M; 1/1/78[sic]-57; N.C. Cherokee; F; M; Head; 415; Yes; Yes; Unallotted

417;   Catolster, Elsie Feather; F; 12/24/87-44; N.C. Cherokee; 1/2; M; Wife; 416; Yes; Yes; Unallotted

418;   Catolster, Eliza F.; F; 10/3/13-19; N.C. Cherokee; 3/4; S; Dau.; 417; Yes; Yes; Unallotted

419;   Catolster, Boyd; M; 5/31/16-16; N.C. Cherokee; 3/4; S; Son; 418; Yes; Yes; Unallotted

420;   Catolster, William; M; 6/15/75-57; N.C. Cherokee; F; M; Head; 419; Yes; Yes; Unallotted

421;   Catolster, Sally; F; 7/15/87-46; N.C. Cherokee; 7/8; M; Wife; 420; Yes; Yes; Unallotted

Census of the **Eastern Cherokee** reservation of the **Cherokee, N.C.** jurisdiction, as of **April 1** , **1933,** taken by **R. L. Spalsbury** , Superintendent.

Key: Number; Surname, Given; Sex; Date of Birth-Age at Last Birthday; Tribe; Degree of Blood; Marital Status; Relationship to Head of Family; Last C. Roll No.; At Jurisdiction Where Enrolled (Yes/No); (If no – Where); Ward (Yes/No); Allotment, Annuity and Identification Numbers (if given).

422; Catolster, Alexander; M; 12/23/05-27; N.C. Cherokee; F; S; St-Son; 421; Yes; Yes; Unallotted

423; Catolster, Nannie; F; 4/21/07-24; N.C. Cherokee; F; S; St-Dau.; 422; Yes; Yes; Unallotted

424; Catolster, Guyon; M; 8/18/10-22; N.C. Cherokee; F; S; St- Son; 423; Yes; Yes; Unallotted

425; Catolster, Lucy; F; 6/12/12-20; N.C. Cherokee; F; S; St-Dau.; 424; Yes; Yes; Unallotted

426; Catolster, Bessie; F; 3/2/16-16; N.C. Cherokee; 15/16; S; Dau.; 425; Yes; Yes; Unallotted

427; Catolster, Codaskey; M; 3/13/19-14; N.C. Cherokee; 15/16; S; Son; 426; Yes; Yes; Unallotted

428; Catolster, Malinda; F; 12/21/29-3; N.C. Cherokee; 1/4; S; Granddaugh.; 427; Yes; Yes; Unallotted

429; Catt, Benjamin; M; 11/1/62-70; N.C. Cherokee; F; Wd.; Head; 428; Yes; Yes; Unallotted

430; Catt, Jesse; M; 6/6/95-37; N.C. Cherokee; F; S; Head; 429; Yes; Yes; Unallotted

431; Catt, Mary Ellen; F; 8/9/15-17; N.C. Cherokee; 1/2; S; Alone; 430; Yes; Yes; Unallotted

432; Catt, Willie; M; 3/3/84-49; N.C. Cherokee; F; M; Head; 431; Yes; Yes; Unallotted

433; Catt, Sarah P.; F; 1/11/10-23; N.C. Cherokee; 15/16; M; 2nd wife; 432; Yes; Yes; Unallotted

434; Catt, David; M; 4/18/09-23; N.C. Cherokee; F; M; Son; 433; Yes; Yes; Unallotted

435; Catt, Robert; M; 4/12/11-21; N.C. Cherokee; F; S; Son; 434; Yes; Yes; Unallotted

436; Catt, Paul J.; M; 12/25/15-17; N.C. Cherokee; F; S; Son; 435; Yes; Yes; Unallotted

437; Catt, Boyd; M; 8/22/18-14; N.C. Cherokee; F; S; Son; 436; Yes; Yes; Unallotted

438; Catt, Sarah; F; 1/5/21-12; N.C. Cherokee; F; S; Dau.; 437; Yes; Yes; Unallotted

439; Catt, Alice; F; 10/15/29-3; N.C. Cherokee; 31/32; S; Dau.; 438; Yes; Yes; Unallotted

440; Catt, James E.; M; 8/30/31-1; N.C. Cherokee; 31/32; S; Son; ---; Yes; Yes; Unallotted

441; Cearley, Emery L.; M; 8/24/02-30; N.C. Cherokee; 1/16; M; Head; 439; Yes; Yes; Unallotted

211

Census of the **Eastern Cherokee** reservation of the **Cherokee, N.C.** jurisdiction, as of **April 1**, 19**33,** taken by **R. L. Spalsbury**, Superintendent.

Key: Number; Surname, Given; Sex; Date of Birth-Age at Last Birthday; Tribe; Degree of Blood; Marital Status; Relationship to Head of Family; Last C. Roll No.; At Jurisdiction Where Enrolled (Yes/No); (If no – Where); Ward (Yes/No); Allotment, Annuity and Identification Numbers (if given).

442; Cearley (Raper, Lucy), Lucy Emmaline; F; 8/18/79-53; N.C. Cherokee; 1/8; M; Wife; 440; Yes; Yes; Unallotted

443; Cearley, Robert Astor; M; 2/10/05-28; N.C. Cherokee; 1/16; M; Son; 441; Yes; Yes; Unallotted

444; Cearley, John Patrick; M; 8/27/11-21; N.C. Cherokee; 1/16; S; Son; 442; Yes; Yes; Unallotted

445; Cearley, Henry T.; M; 1/31/14-19; N.C. Cherokee; 1/16; S; Son; 443; Yes; Yes; Unallotted

446; Cearley, Jetter C.; M; 4/13/16-16; N.C. Cherokee; 1/16; S; Son; 444; Yes; Yes; Unallotted

447; Cearley, Charlie E.; M; 6/11/20-12; N.C. Cherokee; 1/16; S; Son; 445; Yes; Yes; Unallotted

448; Cearley, William L.; M; 1/13/00-32; N.C. Cherokee; 1/16; M; Head; 446; Yes; Yes; Unallotted

449; Cearley, Nebraska T.; F; 5/21/01-31; N.C. Cherokee; 1/16; M; Wife; 447; Yes; Yes; Unallotted

450; Chatmon (Robinson, Martha), Martha; F; 9/27/75-57; N.C. Cherokee; 1/4; M; Wife; 448; No; Adairsville, Bartow, Ga.; Yes; Unallotted

451; Chavlas, Minda Reed; F; 1/25/94-39; N.C. Cherokee; 7/8; M; Wife; 449; Yes; Yes; Unallotted

452; Chekelelee, Andy; M; 12/16/84-48; N.C. Cherokee; F; M; Head; 450; Yes; Yes; Unallotted

453; Chekelelee, Betty Catt; F; 8/28/87-45; N.C. Cherokee; F; M; Wife; 451; Yes; Yes; Unallotted

454; Chekelelee, Bessie; F; 4/13/10-22; N.C. Cherokee; F; S; Dau.; 452; Yes; Yes; Unallotted

455; Chekelelee, Bertha; F; 4/27/12-20; N.C. Cherokee; F; S; Dau.; 453; Yes; Yes; Unallotted

456; Chekelelee, Lilly; F; 11/21/14-18; N.C. Cherokee; F; S; Dau.; 454; Yes; Yes; Unallotted

457; Chekelelee, Emma May; F; 9/30/20-12; N.C. Cherokee; F; S; Dau.; 455; Yes; Yes; Unallotted

458; Chekelelee, Simon; M; 1/15/99-33; N.C. Cherokee; F; M; Head; 456; Yes; Yes; Unallotted

459; Chekelelee, Lizzie Smoker; F; 5/3/04-28; N.C. Cherokee; F; M; Wife; 457; Yes; Yes; Unallotted

460; Chekelelee, Ed; M; 5/21/29-3; N.C. Cherokee; F; S; Son; 458; Yes; Yes; Unallotted

461; Chekelelee, Boyd; M; 7/16/31-1; N.C. Cherokee; F; S; Son; 459; Yes; Yes; Unallotted

Census of the **Eastern Cherokee** reservation of the **Cherokee, N.C.** jurisdiction, as of **April 1**, **1933,** taken by **R. L. Spalsbury**, Superintendent.

Key: Number; Surname, Given; Sex; Date of Birth-Age at Last Birthday; Tribe; Degree of Blood; Marital Status; Relationship to Head of Family; Last C. Roll No.; At Jurisdiction Where Enrolled (Yes/No); (If no – Where); Ward (Yes/No); Allotment, Annuity and Identification Numbers (if given).

462; Chekelelee, Stone; M; 1/5/72-61; N.C. Cherokee; F; Wd.; Head; 460; Yes; Yes; Unallotted

463; Chekelelee, Tom; M; 8/16/73-59; N.C. Cherokee; F; M; Head; 461; Yes; Yes; Unallotted

464; Childers (Lambert, Lula), Lula Frances; F; 5/10/82-50; N.C. Cherokee; 1/16; M; Wife; 462; Yes; Yes; Unallotted

465; Childers, Robert M.; M; 5/27/05-27; N.C. Cherokee; 1/32; S; Son; 463; Yes; Yes; Unallotted

466; Childers, Stella L.; F; 12/7/08-24; N.C. Cherokee; 1/32; S; Dau.; 464; Yes; Yes; Unallotted

467; Childers, Maud M.; F; 3/9/11-22; N.C. Cherokee; 1/32; S; Dau.; 465; Yes; Yes; Unallotted

468; Childers, Clifford E.; M; 6/18/13-19; N.C. Cherokee; 1/32; S; Son; 466; Yes; Yes; Unallotted

469; Childers, Russell Daniel; M; 3/3/17-16; N.C. Cherokee; 1/32; S; Son; 467; Yes; Yes; Unallotted

470; Childers, Julius W.; M; 4/13/20-12; N.C. Cherokee; 1/32; S; Son; 468; Yes; Yes; Unallotted

471; Chiltoskie, Wahdih; M; 6/6/99-33; N.C. Cherokee; 15/16; M; Head; 469; Yes; Yes; Unallotted

472; Chiltoskie, Tennie Smith; F; 4/12/05-27; N.C. Cherokee; 7/16; M; Wife; 470; Yes; Yes; Unallotted

473; Chiltoskie, Lavina May; F; 4/14/28-5; N.C. Cherokee; 22/32; S; Dau.; 471; Yes; Yes; Unallotted

474; Chiltoskie, Charlotte; F; 10/19/68-64; N.C. Cherokee; 7/8; Wd.; Head; 472; Yes; Yes; Unallotted

475; Chiltoskie, Goingback; M; 4/9/07-25; N.C. Cherokee; 15/16; S; Son; 473; Yes; Yes; Unallotted

476; Clark (Raper, Ivy Ann), Ivy Ann; F; 12/17/97-35; N.C. Cherokee; 1/16; M; Wife; 474; Yes; Yes; Unallotted

477; Clark, Paul; M; 7/4/15-17; N.C. Cherokee; 1/32; S; Son; 475; Yes; Yes; Unallotted

478; Clark, Lottie A. Smith; F; 2/13/69-64; N.C. Cherokee; 3/8; M; Wife; 476; Yes; Yes; Unallotted

479; Clay, Timpson; M; 12/17/73-59; N.C. Cherokee; F; Wd.; Head; 477; Yes; Yes; Unallotted

213

Census of the **Eastern Cherokee** reservation of the **Cherokee, N.C.** jurisdiction, as of **April 1**, **1933,** taken by **R. L. Spalsbury**, Superintendent.

Key: Number; Surname, Given; Sex; Date of Birth-Age at Last Birthday; Tribe; Degree of Blood; Marital Status; Relationship to Head of Family; Last C. Roll No.; At Jurisdiction Where Enrolled (Yes/No); (If no – Where); Ward (Yes/No); Allotment, Annuity and Identification Numbers (if given).

480; Climbingbear, Deleskie; M; 12/12/75-57; N.C. Cherokee; F; M; Head; 478; Yes; Yes; Unallotted

481; Climbingbear, Nancy Tooni; F; 3/22/77-56; N.C. Cherokee; F; M; Wife; 479; Yes; Yes; Unallotted

482; Climbingbear, Ollie; F; 10/13/12-20; N.C. Cherokee; F; S; Dau.; 480; Yes; Yes; Unallotted

483; Climbingbear, Henderson; M; 10/19/22-10; N.C. Cherokee; F; S; Son; 481; Yes; Yes; Unallotted

484; Coffey (Adams, Ethel), Ethel; F; 3/23/90-43; N.C. Cherokee; 1/32; M; Wife; 483; Yes; Yes; Unallotted

485; Coffey, Stella; F; 1/24/12-21; N.C. Cherokee; 1/64; S; Dau.; 484; Yes; Yes; Unallotted

486; Coffey, Blanche; F; 4/20/15-17; N.C. Cherokee; 1/64; S; Dau.; 485; Yes; Yes; Unallotted

487; Coffey, John Lee; M; 10/19/17-15; N.C. Cherokee; 1/64; S; Son; 486; Yes; Yes; Unallotted

488; Coffey, Clyde; M; 3/3/20-13; N.C. Cherokee; 1/64; S; Son; 487; Yes; Yes; Unallotted

489; Cole, Alvah; M; 9/10/13-19; N.C. Cherokee; 1/16; S; Son; 488; No; Culberson, Cherokee, N.C.; Yes; Unallotted

490; Cole, George E.; M; 2/23/91-42; N.C. Cherokee; 1/8; S; Head; 489; Yes; Yes; Unallotted

491; Cole, John; M; 1/22/24-29; N.C. Cherokee; 1/16; M; Head; 490; Yes; Yes; Unallotted

492; Cole, Robert T.; M; 6/17/86-46; N.C. Cherokee; 1/8; M; Head; 491; No;1420 E. Airline St. Gastonia, Gaston, N.C.; Yes; Unallotted

493; Cole, Reed; M; 1/12/13-20; N.C. Cherokee; 1/16; S; Son; 492; No; 1420 E. Airline St. Gastonia, Gaston, N.C.; Yes; Unallotted

494; Cole, Grace; F; 1/22/15-18; N.C. Cherokee; 1/16; S; Dau.; 493; No;1420 E. Airline St. Gastonia, Gaston, N.C.; Yes; Unallotted

495; Cole, Cora; F; 4/10/17-15; N.C. Cherokee; 1/16; S; Dau.; 494; No; 1420 E. Airline St. Gastonia, Gaston, N.C.; Yes; Unallotted

496; Cole, Beulah; F; 2/14/19-14; N.C. Cherokee; 1/16; S; Dau.; 495; No; 1420 E. Airline St. Gastonia, Gaston, N.C.; Yes; Unallotted

497; Cole, Wm. Olis; M; 1/9/22-11; N.C. Cherokee; 1/16; S; Son; 496; No; 1420 E. Airline St. Gastonia, Gaston, N.C.; Yes; Unallotted

498; Cole, Walter; M; 5/24/98-34; N.C. Cherokee; 1/16; M; Head; 497; No; Culberson, Cherokee, N.C.; Yes; Unallotted

Census of the **Eastern Cherokee** reservation of the **Cherokee, N.C.** jurisdiction, as of **April 1** , **1933,** taken by **R. L. Spalsbury** , Superintendent.

Key: Number; Surname, Given; Sex; Date of Birth-Age at Last Birthday; Tribe; Degree of Blood; Marital Status; Relationship to Head of Family; Last C. Roll No.; At Jurisdiction Where Enrolled (Yes/No); (If no – Where); Ward (Yes/No); Allotment, Annuity and Identification Numbers (if given).

499; Cole, Howard; M; 12/12/20-12; N.C. Cherokee; 1/32; S; Son; 498; No; Culberson, Cherokee, N.C.; Yes; Unallotted

500; Cole, Hazel; F; 9/4/22-10; N.C. Cherokee; 1/32; S; Dau.; 499; No; Culberson, Cherokee, N.C.; Yes; Unallotted

501; Cole, William A.; M; 6/17/79-53; N.C. Cherokee; 1/8; M; Head; 500; No; White, Bartow, Ga.; Yes; Unallotted

502; Cole, Arley; M; 6/9/05-27; N.C. Cherokee; 1/16; S; Son; 501; No; White, Bartow, Ga.; Yes; Unallotted

503; Cole, Hollie; M; 1/26/07-26; N.C. Cherokee; 1/16; S; Son; 502; No; White, Bartow, Ga.; Yes; Unallotted

504; Cole, Ollie; F; 9/25/09-23; N.C. Cherokee; 1/16; S; Dau.; 503; No; White, Bartow, Ga.; Yes; Unallotted

505; Cole, Irene; F; 3/21/14-19; N.C. Cherokee; 1/16; S; Dau.; 504; No; White, Bartow, Ga.; Yes; Unallotted

506; Cole, Remus; M; 12/18/17-15; N.C. Cherokee; 1/16; S; Son; 505; No; White, Bartow, Ga.; Yes; Unallotted

507; Cole, Ruby; F; 3/1/19-14; N.C. Cherokee; 1/16; S; Dau.; 506; No; White, Bartow, Ga.; Yes; Unallotted

508; Cole, Edward; M; 6/26/21-11; N.C. Cherokee; 1/16; S; Son; 507; No; White, Bartow, Ga.; Yes; Unallotted

509; Coleman, Mae Timpson; F; 1/24/93-40; N.C. Cherokee; 3/16; Div; Head; 508; Yes; Yes; Unallotted

510; Coleman, Ida E.; F; 7/11/13-19; N.C. Cherokee; 3/32; S; Dau.; 509; Yes; Yes; Unallotted

511; Coleman, Bailey B.; M; 12/18/16-16; N.C. Cherokee; 3/32; S; Son; 510; Yes; Yes; Unallotted

512; Conley, Jennie Lossie; F; 12/22/69-63; N.C. Cherokee; F; Wd.; Head; 511; Yes; Yes; Unallotted

513; Conley, John Jr.; M; 10/14/90-42; N.C. Cherokee; F; M; Head; 512; Yes; Yes; Unallotted

514; Conley, Sallie S.; F; 7/21/01-31; N.C. Cherokee; 7/8; M; Wife; 513; Yes; Yes; Unallotted

515; Conley, Elister; F; 6/29/27-5; N.C. Cherokee; 15/16; S; Dau.; 514; Yes; Yes; Unallotted

516; Conley, Selma; F; 4/21/30-2; N.C. Cherokee; 15/16; S; Dau.; 515; Yes; Yes; Unallotted

517; Conley, Richard; M; 2/28/32-1; N.C. Cherokee; 15/16; S; Son; 516; Yes; Yes; Unallotted

518; Conley, Luke; M; 2/9/96-36; N.C. Cherokee; F; S; Head; 517; Yes; Yes; Unallotted

Census of the **Eastern Cherokee** reservation of the **Cherokee, N.C.** jurisdiction, as of **April 1** , 1933, taken by **R. L. Spalsbury** , Superintendent.

Key: Number; Surname, Given; Sex; Date of Birth-Age at Last Birthday; Tribe; Degree of Blood; Marital Status; Relationship to Head of Family; Last C. Roll No.; At Jurisdiction Where Enrolled (Yes/No); (If no – Where); Ward (Yes/No); Allotment, Annuity and Identification Numbers (if given).

519;   Conseen, Annie; F; 7/13/12-20; N.C. Cherokee; F; S; Head; 518; Yes; Yes; Unallotted

520;   Conseen, Mark; M; 4/23/30-2; N.C. Cherokee; 1/2; S; Son; 519; Yes; Yes; Unallotted

521;   Conseen, George; M; 4/23/30-2; N.C. Cherokee; 1/2; S; Son; 520; Yes; Yes; Unallotted

522;   Conseen, Brest; M; 7/15/61-71; N.C. Cherokee; F; Wd.; Head; 521; Yes; Yes; Unallotted

523;   Conseen, Buck; M; 5/14/06-26; N.C. Cherokee; F; M; Head; 522; Yes; Yes; Unallotted

524;   Conseen, Dinah Queen; F; 6/17/09-23; N.C. Cherokee; 5/8; M; Wife; 523; Yes; Yes; Unallotted

525;   Conseen, Eve Eliz.; F; 12/26/24-8; N.C. Cherokee; 13/16; S; Dau.; 524; Yes; Yes; Unallotted

526;   Conseen, James; M; 6/9/88-44; N.C. Cherokee; F; M; Head; 525; Yes; Yes; Unallotted

527;   Conseen, Carolina T.; F; 8/22/94-38; N.C. Cherokee; F; M; Wife; 526; Yes; Yes; Unallotted

528;   Conseen, Lucy Ann; F; 4/24/17-15; N.C. Cherokee; F; S; Dau.; 527; Yes; Yes; Unallotted

529;   Conseen, Emily; F; 4/7/25-8; N.C. Cherokee; F; S; Dau.; 528; Yes; Yes; Unallotted

530;   Conseen, Adam; M; 3/12/27-6; N.C. Cherokee; F; S; Son; 529; Yes; Yes; Unallotted

531;   Conseen, Nancy; F; 8/12/29-3; N.C. Cherokee; F; S; Dau.; 530; Yes; Yes; Unallotted

532;   Conseen, Erwin; M; 9/6/31-1; N.C. Cherokee; F; S; Son; 531; Yes; Yes; Unallotted

533;   Conseen, Peter; M; 8/15/79-53; N.C. Cherokee; F; M; Head; 532; Yes; Yes; Unallotted

534;   Conseen, Nancy; F; 4/15/77-55; N.C. Cherokee; F; M; Wife; 533; Yes; Yes; Unallotted

535;   Conseen, Harry; M; 11/20/04-28; N.C. Cherokee; F; S; Son; 534; Yes; Yes; Unallotted

536;   Conseen, Joe (Job); M; 10/30/06-26; N.C. Cherokee; F; S; Son; 535; Yes; Yes; Unallotted

537;   Conseen, Ida; F; 7/27/08-24; N.C. Cherokee; F; S; Dau.; 536; Yes; Yes; Unallotted

538;   Conseen, Nessie; F; 7/22/12-20; N.C. Cherokee; F; S; Dau.; 537; Yes; Yes; Unallotted

Census of the **Eastern Cherokee** reservation of the **Cherokee, N.C.** jurisdiction, as of **April 1**, **1933,** taken by **R. L. Spalsbury**, Superintendent.

Key: Number; Surname, Given; Sex; Date of Birth-Age at Last Birthday; Tribe; Degree of Blood; Marital Status; Relationship to Head of Family; Last C. Roll No.; At Jurisdiction Where Enrolled (Yes/No); (If no – Where); Ward (Yes/No); Allotment, Annuity and Identification Numbers (if given).

539; Conseen, Amanda; F; 5/22/19-13; N.C. Cherokee; F; S; Dau.; 538; Yes; Yes; Unallotted

540; Conseen, Anna; F; 7/19/21-11; N.C. Cherokee; F; S; Dau.; 539; Yes; Yes; Unallotted

541; Conseen, Thompson; M; 5/8/88-44; N.C. Cherokee; F; M; Head; 540; Yes; Yes; Unallotted

542; Conseen, Irene Arch; F; 12/17/74-58; N.C. Cherokee; F; M; Wife; 541; Yes; Yes; Unallotted

543; Conseen, Willie; M; 6/28/99-33; N.C. Cherokee; F; S; Head; 542; Yes; Yes; Unallotted

544; Cook (Raper, Jessie L.), Jessie Leora; F; 14/13/91-41; N.C. Cherokee; 1/16; M; Wife; 543; No; Culberson, Cherokee, N.C.; Yes; Unallotted

545; Cook, Vernie Lee; F; 5/7/09-23; N.C. Cherokee; 1/32; S; Dau.; 544; No; Culberson, Cherokee, N.C.; Yes; Unallotted

546; Cook, Inez G.; F; 2/24/11-22; N.C. Cherokee; 1/32; S; Dau.; 545; No; Culberson, Cherokee, N.C.; Yes; Unallotted

547; Cook, Randall E.; M; 1/13/13-20; N.C. Cherokee; 1/32; S; Son; 546; No; Culberson, Cherokee, N.C.; Yes; Unallotted

548; Cook, Arvel C.; M; 1/11/15-18; N.C. Cherokee; 1/32; S; Son; 547; No; Culberson, Cherokee, N.C.; Yes; Unallotted

549; Cook, Leona Ruby; F; 2/23/17-16; N.C. Cherokee; 1/32; S; Dau.; 548; No; Culberson, Cherokee, N.C.; Yes; Unallotted

550; Cook, Rosie May; F; 1/19/19-13; N.C. Cherokee; 1/32; S; Dau.; 549; No; Culberson, Cherokee, N.C.; Yes; Unallotted

551; Cooper, Arnold; M; 9/7/93-39; N.C. Cherokee; 1/16; M; Head; 550; Yes; Yes; Unallotted

552; Cooper, Jessie; F; 6/14/22-10; N.C. Cherokee; 1/32; S; Dau.; 551; Yes; Yes; Unallotted

553; Cooper, Ida Lee; F; 10/19/23-9; N.C. Cherokee; 1/32; S; Dau.; 552; Yes; Yes; Unallotted

554; Cooper, Curtis; M; 5/20/95-36; N.C. Cherokee; 1/16; M; Head; 553; Yes; Yes; Unallotted

555; Cooper, Mack; M; 3/11/80-53; N.C. Cherokee; 1/32; M; Head; 554; Yes; Yes; Unallotted

556; Cooper, Catherine L.; F; 9/4/05-27; N.C. Cherokee; 1/64; S; Dau.; 555; Yes; Yes; Unallotted

557; Cooper, Stacy Jane; F; 12/12/67-65; N.C. Cherokee; 1/8; M; Wife; 556; Yes; Yes; Unallotted

Census of the **Eastern Cherokee** reservation of the **Cherokee, N.C.** jurisdiction, as of **April 1**, 1933, taken by **R. L. Spalsbury**, Superintendent.

Key: Number; Surname, Given; Sex; Date of Birth-Age at Last Birthday; Tribe; Degree of Blood; Marital Status; Relationship to Head of Family; Last C. Roll No.; At Jurisdiction Where Enrolled (Yes/No); (If no – Where); Ward (Yes/No); Allotment, Annuity and Identification Numbers (if given).

558; Cooper, Mary Joe; F; 7/4/10-22; N.C. Cherokee; 1/16; S; Dau.; 557; Yes; Yes; Unallotted

559; Cornsilk, Annie; F; 1/5/59-74; N.C. Cherokee; F; Wd; Head; 558; Yes; Yes; Unallotted

560; Cornsilk, Lorenzo D.; M; 1/11/80-53; N.C. Cherokee; F; M; Head; 559; Yes; Yes; Unallotted

561; Cornsilk, Nancy; F; 11/10/82-50; N.C. Cherokee; F; M; Wife; 560; Yes; Yes; Unallotted

562; Cornsilk, Woodie; F; 11/9/09-23; N.C. Cherokee; F; S; Dau.; 561; Yes; Yes; Unallotted

563; Cornsilk, Emma; F; 11/7/11-21; N.C. Cherokee; F; S; Dau.; 562; Yes; Yes; Unallotted

564; Cornsilk, Jacob; M; 3/5/14-19; N.C. Cherokee; F; S; Son; 563; Yes; Yes; Unallotted

565; Craig, Elvira; F; 6/2/97-35; N.C. Cherokee; 1/8; Wd.; Head; 564; Yes; Yes; Unallotted

566; Craig, Robert Lee; M; 1/9/16-17; N.C. Cherokee; 1/8; S; Son; 565; Yes; Yes; Unallotted

567; Craig, Winona J.; F; 4/26/17-15; N.C. Cherokee; 1/8; S; Dau.; 566; Yes; Yes; Unallotted

568; Craig, Wm. T.; M; 3/2/19-14; N.C. Cherokee; 1/16; S; Son; 567; Yes; Yes; Unallotted

569; Craig, Charles E.; M; 8/31/21-11; N.C. Cherokee; 1/16; S; Son; 568; Yes; Yes; Unallotted

570; Craig, Naomi K.; F; 5/12/25-7; N.C. Cherokee; 1/16; S; Dau.; 569; Yes; Yes; Unallotted

571; Craig (Lambert, Georgia M.), Georgia M.; F; 12/28/04-28; N.C. Cherokee; 1/32; M; Wife; 570; Yes; Yes; Unallotted

572; Craig, Gladys; F; 9/4/20-12; N.C. Cherokee; 1/64; S; Dau.; 571; Yes; Yes; Unallotted

573; Craig, Garnalee; M; 2/9/23-10; N.C. Cherokee; 1/64; S; Son; 572; Yes; Yes; Unallotted

574; Craig, Robert Donley; M; 4/12/05-27; N.C. Cherokee; 1/16; M; Head; 573; Yes; Yes; Unallotted

575; Craig, Bertha A.B.; F; 1/1/10-23; N.C. Cherokee; 1/4; M; Wife; 574; Yes; Yes; Unallotted

576; Craig, Bettie Ann; F; 6/23/29-3; N.C. Cherokee; 3/16; S; Dau.; 575; Yes; Yes; Unallotted

577; Craig, Jean Donley; F; 5/12/31-1; N.C. Cherokee; 3/16; S; Dau.; 576; Yes; Yes; Unallotted

Census of the **Eastern Cherokee** reservation of the **Cherokee, N.C.** jurisdiction, as of **April 1** , **1933,** taken by **R. L. Spalsbury** , Superintendent.

Key: Number; Surname, Given; Sex; Date of Birth-Age at Last Birthday; Tribe; Degree of Blood; Marital Status; Relationship to Head of Family; Last C. Roll No.; At Jurisdiction Where Enrolled (Yes/No); (If no – Where); Ward (Yes/No); Allotment, Annuity and Identification Numbers (if given).

578;   Craig, William W.; M; 8/20/86-46; N.C. Cherokee; 1/8; M; Head; 577; Yes; Yes; Unallotted

579;   Craig, Lillie V.; F; 11/18/14-18; N.C. Cherokee; 1/16; S; Dau.; 578; Yes; Yes; Unallotted

580;   Crawford, Oma; F; 6/10/16-16; N.C. Cherokee; 1/64; S; Alone; 579; No; Isabella, Polk, Tenn.; Yes; Unallotted

581;   Crawford, Fred; M; 4/17/18-14; N.C. Cherokee; 1/64; S; Bro.; 580; No; Isabella, Polk, Tenn.; Yes; Unallotted

582;   Cromwell, Margaret P.; F; 7/12/44-88; N.C. Cherokee; 1/16; Wd.; Head; 581; Yes; Yes; Unallotted

583;   Crooks (Meroney, Bessie), Bessie M.; F; 3/4/81-52; N.C. Cherokee; 1/8; M; Wife; 582; Yes; Yes; Unallotted

584;   Crowe, Aquishoe; M; 12/18/88-44; N.C. Cherokee; 7/8; M; Head; 583; Yes; Yes; Unallotted

585;   Crowe, Nannie; F; 12/18/84-48; N.C. Cherokee; 7/8; M; Wife; 584; Yes; Yes; Unallotted

586;   Crowe, Enoch; M; 5/10/17-15; N.C. Cherokee; 7/8; S; Son; 585; Yes; Yes; Unallotted

587;   Crowe, Boyd; M; 2/7/93-36; N.C. Cherokee; 7/8; M; Head; 586; Yes; Yes; Unallotted

588;   Crowe, David; M; 6/26/84-48; N.C. Cherokee; 3/4; M; Head; 587; Yes; Yes; Unallotted

589;   Crowe, Sallie; F; 1/7/87-46; N.C. Cherokee; 4/4; M; Wife; 588; Yes; Yes; Unallotted

590;   Crowe, Rachel; F; 11/24/07-25; N.C. Cherokee; 7/8; S; Dau.; 589; Yes; Yes; Unallotted

591;   Crowe, Sevier; M; 9/17/14-18; N.C. Cherokee; 7/8; S; Son; 590; Yes; Yes; Unallotted

592;   Crowe, Elnora; F; 2/3/15-18; N.C. Cherokee; 7/8; S; Dau.; 591; Yes; Yes; Unallotted

593;   Crowe, Luzene; F; 1/13/17-16; N.C. Cherokee; 7/8; S; Dau.; 592; Yes; Yes; Unallotted

594;   Crowe, Nellie; F; 2/29/20-13; N.C. Cherokee; 7/8; S; Dau.; 593; Yes; Yes; Unallotted

595;   Crowe, John Henry; M; 8/17/22-10; N.C. Cherokee; 7/8; S; Son; 594; Yes; Yes; Unallotted

596;   Crowe, Dora Crow; F; 7/30/28-4; N.C. Cherokee; 7/8; S; Dau.; 595; Yes; Yes; Unallotted

Census of the **Eastern Cherokee** reservation of the **Cherokee, N.C.** jurisdiction, as of **April 1** , 19**33,** taken by **R. L. Spalsbury** , Superintendent.

Key: Number; Surname, Given; Sex; Date of Birth-Age at Last Birthday; Tribe; Degree of Blood; Marital Status; Relationship to Head of Family; Last C. Roll No.; At Jurisdiction Where Enrolled (Yes/No); (If no – Where); Ward (Yes/No); Allotment, Annuity and Identification Numbers (if given).

597;   Crowe, John; M; 12/18/82-50; N.C. Cherokee; 3/4; M; Head; 596; Yes; Yes; Unallotted

598;   Crowe, Mary; F; 12/24/84-48; N.C. Cherokee; 4/4; M; Wife; 597; Yes; Yes; Unallotted

599;   Crowe, Callie; F; 5/26/04-28; N.C. Cherokee; 7/8; S; Dau.; 598; No; Ft. Sill, Indian School, Lawton, Comanche, Okla.; Yes; Unallotted

600;   Crowe, Lucy; F; 4/18/11-21; N.C. Cherokee; 7/8; S; Dau.; 599; Yes; Yes; Unallotted

601;   Crowe, Iva; F; 6/26/13-19; N.C. Cherokee; 7/8; S; Dau.; 600; Yes; Yes; Unallotted

602;   Crowe, Leuna; F; 4/30/16-16; N.C. Cherokee; 7/8; S; Dau.; 601; Yes;   Yes; Unallotted

603;   Crowe, Betty; F; 6/23/18-14; N.C. Cherokee; 7/8; S; Dau.; 602; Yes; Yes; Unallotted

604;   Crowe, Charles E.; M; 7/10/25-7; N.C. Cherokee; 7/8; S; Son; 603; Yes; Yes; Unallotted

605;   Crowe, Albert; M; 6/28/06-26; N.C. Cherokee; 7/8; Wd.; Head; 604; Yes; Yes; Unallotted

606;   Crowe, Alberta; F; 5/16/26-6; N.C. Cherokee; 1/16; S; Dau. (Illeg.); 605; Yes; Yes; Unallotted

607;   Crowe, John Wesley; M; 2/8/89-44; N.C. Cherokee; 1/2; M; Head; 606; Yes; Yes; Unallotted

608;   Crowe, Mollie W.E.; F; 8/6/78-54; N.C. Cherokee; 3/4; M; Wife; 607; Yes; Yes; Unallotted

609;   Crowe, Joseph; M; 3/2/12-21; N.C. Cherokee; 5/8; S; Son; 608; Yes; Yes; Unallotted

610;   Crowe, James D.; M; 6/11/14-18; N.C. Cherokee; 5/8; S; Son; 609; Yes; Yes; Unallotted

611;   Crowe, John A.; M; 10/7/17-15; N.C. Cherokee; 5/8; S; Son; 610; Yes; Yes; Unallotted

612;   Crowe, E. Thelma; F; 10/7/17-15; N.C. Cherokee; 5/8; S; Dau.; 611; Yes; Yes; Unallotted

613;   Crowe, Warren H.; M; 11/8/20-12; N.C. Cherokee; 5/8; S; Son; 612; Yes; Yes; Unallotted

614;   Crowe, Joseph; M; 3/8/65-68; N.C. Cherokee; 3/4; Wd.; Head; 613; Yes; Yes; Unallotted

615;   Crowe, Luther; M; 4/18/98-34; N.C. Cherokee; 5/16; S; Head; 614; Yes; Yes; Unallotted

616;   Crowe, Ossie; M; 5/29/82-50; N.C. Cherokee; 7/8; M; Head; 615; Yes; Yes; Unallotted

Census of the **Eastern Cherokee** reservation of the **Cherokee, N.C.** jurisdiction, as of **April 1** , **1933,** taken by **R. L. Spalsbury** , Superintendent.

Key: Number; Surname, Given; Sex; Date of Birth-Age at Last Birthday; Tribe; Degree of Blood; Marital Status; Relationship to Head of Family; Last C. Roll No.; At Jurisdiction Where Enrolled (Yes/No); (If no – Where); Ward (Yes/No); Allotment, Annuity and Identification Numbers (if given).

617;   Crowe, Martha; F; 7/24/89-43; N.C. Cherokee; 4/4; M; Wife; 616; Yes; Yes; Unallotted

618;   Crowe, Dinah; F; 9/23/13-19; N.C. Cherokee; 15/16; S; Dau.; 617; Yes; Yes; Unallotted

619;   Crowe, Stacy; F; 1/2/16-17; N.C. Cherokee; 15/16; S; Dau.; 618; Yes; Yes; Unallotted

620;   Crowe, Katie; F; 10/12/20-12; N.C. Cherokee; 15/16; S; Dau.; 619; Yes; Yes; Unallotted

621;   Crowe, Guyon; M; 3/31/23-10; N.C. Cherokee; 15/16; S; Son; 620; Yes; Yes; Unallotted

622;   Crowe, John Dobson; M; 10/9/27-4; N.C. Cherokee; 15/16; S; Son; 621; Yes; Yes; Unallotted

623;   Crowe, Robert; M; 12/25/93-39; N.C. Cherokee; 15/16; M; Head; 622; Yes; Yes; Unallotted

624;   Crowe, Samuel; M; 9/26/05-27; N.C. Cherokee; 7/8; M; Head; 623; Yes; Yes; Unallotted

625;   Crowe, Josephine L.; F; 9/26/09-23; N.C. Cherokee; 3/32; M; Wife; 624; Yes; Yes; Unallotted

626;   Crowe, Alyne; F; 10/9/27-5; N.C. Cherokee; 31/64; S; Dau.; 625; Yes;   Yes; Unallotted

627;   Crowe, Ann Lee; F; 3/21/31-2; N.C. Cherokee; 17/32; S; Dau.; 626; Yes; Yes; Unallotted

628;   Crowe, Sevier; M; 12/18/60-72; N.C. Cherokee; 5/8; M; Head; 627; Yes; Yes; Unallotted

629;   Crowe, Nancy S.; F; 12/24/51-81; N.C. Cherokee; 4/4; M; Wife; 628; Yes; Yes; Unallotted

630;   Crowe, Ute; M; 6/18/87-45; N.C. Cherokee; 15/16; M; Head; 629; Yes; Yes; Unallotted

631;   Crowe, Sallie S.; F; 5/24/03-29; N.C. Cherokee; 4/4; M; Wife; 630; Yes; Yes; Unallotted

632;   Crowe, William; M; 4/24/21-11; N.C. Cherokee; 31/32; S; Son; 631; Yes; Yes; Unallotted

633;   Crowe, Robert Henry; M; 7/24/14-18; N.C. Cherokee; 15/32; S; Son; 632; Yes; Yes; Unallotted

634;   Crowe, Mandy; F; 7/16/22-10; N.C. Cherokee; 15/32; S; Dau.; 633; Yes; Yes; Unallotted

635;   Crowe, Nora; F; 8/25/24-9; N.C. Cherokee; 15/32; S; Dau.; 634; Yes; Yes; Unallotted

636;   Crowe, Richard; M; 7/7/27-5; N.C. Cherokee; 15/32; S; Son; 635; Yes; Yes; Unallotted

Census of the **Eastern Cherokee** reservation of the **Cherokee, N.C.** jurisdiction, as of **April 1** , 19**33,** taken by **R. L. Spalsbury** , Superintendent.

Key: Number; Surname, Given; Sex; Date of Birth-Age at Last Birthday; Tribe; Degree of Blood; Marital Status; Relationship to Head of Family; Last C. Roll No.; At Jurisdiction Where Enrolled (Yes/No); (If no – Where); Ward (Yes/No); Allotment, Annuity and Identification Numbers (if given).

637; Crowe, Lucinda; F; 11/19/29-3; N.C. Cherokee; 31/32; S; Dau.; 636; Yes; Yes; Unallotted

638; Crowe, Wesley; M; 10/18/75-57; N.C. Cherokee; 3/4; S; Head; 637; Yes; Yes; Unallotted

639; Crowe, Wesley; M; 5/12/02-30; N.C. Cherokee; 5/16; M; Head; 638; Yes; Yes; Unallotted

640; Crowe, Minnie A.; F; 12/5/04-28; N.C. Cherokee; 1/32; M; Wife; 639; Yes; Yes; Unallotted

641; Crowe, Forrest Smith; M; 1/4/22-11; N.C. Cherokee; 11/64; S; Son; 640; Yes; Yes; Unallotted

642; Crowe, Juanita; F; 3/28/24-9; N.C. Cherokee; 11/64; S; Dau.; 641; Yes; Yes; Unallotted

643; Crowe, Junior; M; 5/3/26-6; N.C. Cherokee; 11/64; S; Son; 642; Yes; Yes; Unallotted

644; Cucumber, Arch; M; 3/27/90-43; N.C. Cherokee; 4/4; M; Head; 643; Yes; Yes; Unallotted

645; Cucumber, Ollie Y.; F; 9/18/69-63; N.C. Cherokee; 4/4; M; Wife; 644; Yes; Yes; Unallotted

646; Cucumber, Arch; M; 3/21/07-26; N.C. Cherokee; 4/4; S; Head; 645; Yes; Yes; Unallotted

647; Cucumber, Katie; F; 5/2/82-53; N.C. Cherokee; 4/4; Wd.; Head; 646; Yes; Yes; Unallotted

648; Cucumber, Spencer; M; 5/10/10-22; N.C. Cherokee; 4/4; S; Son; 647; Yes; Yes; Unallotted

649; Cucumber, Jack; M; 3/7/12-21; N.C. Cherokee; 4/4; S; Son; 648; Yes; Yes; Unallotted

650; Cucumber, Delliske; M; 4/27/20-12; N.C. Cherokee; 4/4; S; Son; 649; Yes; Yes; Unallotted

651; Cucumber, James; M; 8/9/91-41; N.C. Cherokee; 4/4; M; Head; 650; Yes; Yes; Unallotted

652; Cucumber, Lizzie Reed; F; 3/10/93-40; N.C. Cherokee; 7/8; M; Wife; 651; Yes; Yes; Unallotted

653; Cucumber, Jennie; F; 8/11/11-21; N.C. Cherokee; 15/16; S; Dau.; 652; Yes; Yes; Unallotted

654; Cucumber, Mason; M; 1/18/13-20; N.C. Cherokee; 15/16; S; Son; 653; Yes; Yes; Unallotted

655; Cucumber, Amanda; F; 3/1/16-17; N.C. Cherokee; 15/16; S; Dau.; 654; Yes; Yes; Unallotted

Census of the **Eastern Cherokee** reservation of the **Cherokee, N.C.** jurisdiction, as of **April 1**, **1933,** taken by **R. L. Spalsbury**, Superintendent.

Key: Number; Surname, Given; Sex; Date of Birth-Age at Last Birthday; Tribe; Degree of Blood; Marital Status; Relationship to Head of Family; Last C. Roll No.; At Jurisdiction Where Enrolled (Yes/No); (If no – Where); Ward (Yes/No); Allotment, Annuity and Identification Numbers (if given).

656; Cucumber, David; M; 2/27/18-15; N.C. Cherokee; 15/16; S; Son; 655; Yes; Yes; Unallotted

657; Cucumber, Madeline; F; 6/15/24-8; N.C. Cherokee; 15/16; S; Dau.; 656; Yes; Yes; Unallotted

658; Cucumber, John D.; M; 3/2/08-27; N.C. Cherokee; 4/4; S; Head; 657; Yes; Yes; Unallotted

659; Cucumber, Noah; M; 4/2/08-27; N.C. Cherokee; 4/4; M; Head; 658; Yes; Yes; Unallotted

660; Cucumber, Emmaline L.; F; 10/10/09-23; N.C. Cherokee; 4/4; M; Wife; 659; Yes; Yes; Unallotted

661; Cucumber, Alfred G.; M; 2/18/29-4; N.C. Cherokee; 4/4; S; Son; 660; Yes; Yes; Unallotted

662; Culberson, Sarah J.; F; 7/30/90-42; N.C. Cherokee; 1/4; M; Wife; 661; No; Kingston, Bartow, Ga.; Yes; Unallotted

663; Culwell (Raper, Bertha), Bertha; F; 3/20/96-37; N.C. Cherokee; 1/16; M; Wife; 662; No; Drumright, Creek, Okla.; Yes; Unallotted

664; Dailey (Robinson, Guita I.), Guita I.; F; 8/1/91-41; N.C. Cherokee; 1/16; M; Wife; 663; Yes; Yes; Unallotted

665; Dailey, Mattie Jane; F; 1/15/13-20; N.C. Cherokee; 1/32; S; Dau.; 664; Yes; Yes; Unallotted

666; Dailey, Noah; M; 11/26/16-16; N.C. Cherokee; 1/32; S; Son; 665; Yes; Yes; Unallotted

667; Dailey, Leonard; M; 7/1/18-14; N.C. Cherokee; 1/32; S; Son; 666; Yes; Yes; Unallotted

668; Dailey, Wilma; F; 11/1/20-12; N.C. Cherokee; 1/32; S; Dau.; 667; Yes; Yes; Unallotted

669; Darlon, Mack; M; 12/10/92-40; N.C. Cherokee; 1/64; M; Head; 668; Yes; Yes; Unallotted

670; Darlon, Sherley; F; 9/20/15-17; N.C. Cherokee; 1/128; S; Dau.; 669; Yes; Yes; Unallotted

671; Darlon, Parlee; F; 4/6/19-13; N.C. Cherokee; 1/128; S; Dau.; 670; Yes; Yes; Unallotted

672; Darlon, Minnie; F; 8/22/21-11; N.C. Cherokee; 1/128; S; Dau.; 671; Yes; Yes; Unallotted

673; Darlon, Nettie; F; 12/27/23-9; N.C. Cherokee; 1/128; S; Dau.; 672; Yes; Yes; Unallotted

674; Davis, Anita; F; 4/15/97-35; N.C. Cherokee; 4/4; S; Head; 673; Yes; Yes; Unallotted

Census of the **Eastern Cherokee** reservation of the **Cherokee, N.C.** jurisdiction, as of **April 1** , 19**33,** taken by **R. L. Spalsbury** , Superintendent.

Key: Number; Surname, Given; Sex; Date of Birth-Age at Last Birthday; Tribe; Degree of Blood; Marital Status; Relationship to Head of Family; Last C. Roll No.; At Jurisdiction Where Enrolled (Yes/No); (If no – Where); Ward (Yes/No); Allotment, Annuity and Identification Numbers (if given).

675; Davis, David; M; 5/18/01-32; N.C. Cherokee; 4/4; S; Head; 674; Yes; Yes; Unallotted

676; Davis, George; M; 7/5/05-27; N.C. Cherokee; 4/4; S; Bro.; 675; Yes; Yes; Unallotted

677; Davis, Elizabeth; F; 2/19/01-32; N.C. Cherokee; 1/64; M; Wife; 676; Yes; Yes; Unallotted

678; Davis, Mary Delle; F; 6/5/21-11; N.C. Cherokee; 1/128; S; Dau.; 677; Yes; Yes; Unallotted

679; Davis, Martha Jane; F; 3/29/23-10; N.C. Cherokee; 1/128; S; Dau.; 678; Yes; Yes; Unallotted

680; Davis, Isaac; M; 9/27/99-33; N.C. Cherokee; 4/4; M; Head; 679; Yes; Yes; Unallotted

681; Davis, Lena Long; F; 2/10/08-25; N.C. Cherokee; 3/4; M; Wife; 680; Yes; Yes; Unallotted

682; Davis, Israel; M; 6/6/94-38; N.C. Cherokee; 4/4; M; Head; 681; Yes; Yes; Unallotted

683; Davis, Margaret B.; F; 4/24/00-32; N.C. Cherokee; 1/4; M; Wife; 682; Yes; Yes; Unallotted

684; Davis, Cornelius; M; 5/19/22-10; N.C. Cherokee; 5/8; S; Son; 683; Yes; Yes; Unallotted

685; Davis, Joe; M; 7/21/73-59; N.C. Cherokee; 4/4; Wd.; Head; 684; Yes; Yes; Unallotted

686; Davis (Payne, Lydia), Lydia M.; F; 3/7/06-27; N.C. Cherokee; 1/32; M; Wife; 685; Yes; Yes; Unallotted

687; Dean, Sybil D.; F; 4/18/07-25; N.C. Cherokee; 3/16; M; Wife; 686; Yes; Yes; Unallotted

688; Dean, Henry L.; M; 9/13/23-9; N.C. Cherokee; 3/32; S; Son; 687; Yes; Yes; Unallotted

689; Deaton, Calcina S.; F; 4/26/93-39; N.C. Cherokee; 1/8; M; Wife; 688; Yes; Yes; Unallotted

690; Deaton, Woodrow; M; 2/20/28-5; N.C. Cherokee; 1/16; S; Son; 689; Yes; Yes; Unallotted

691; Deaver (Robinson, Mary E.), Mary E.; F; 9/23/74-58; N.C. Cherokee; 1/16; M; Wife; 690; No; Culberson, Cherokee, N.C.; Yes; Unallotted

692; Deaver, John Robert; M; 10/18/08-24; N.C. Cherokee; 1/32; S; Son; 691; No; Culberson, Cherokee, N.C.; Yes, Unallotted

Census of the **Eastern Cherokee** reservation of the **Cherokee, N.C.** jurisdiction, as of **April 1** , 19**33,** taken by **R. L. Spalsbury** , Superintendent.

Key: Number; Surname, Given; Sex; Date of Birth-Age at Last Birthday; Tribe; Degree of Blood; Marital Status; Relationship to Head of Family; Last C. Roll No.; At Jurisdiction Where Enrolled (Yes/No); (If no – Where); Ward (Yes/No); Allotment, Annuity and Identification Numbers (if given).

693; Delegeskie or Taylor, John; M; 12/21/59-73; N.C. Cherokee; 4/4; Wd.; Head; 692; Yes; Yes; Unallotted

694; Denton (Smith, Bessie), Bessie; F; 3/20/04-29; N.C. Cherokee; 1/8; M; Wife; 693; Yes; Yes; Unallotted

695; Dillard (Adams, Nora), Nora; F; 5/24/04-28; N.C. Cherokee; 1/64; M; Wife; 694; Yes; Yes; Unallotted

696; Dillard, Windle; M; 8/13/22-10; N.C. Cherokee; 1/128; S; Son; 695; Yes; Yes; Unallotted

697; Dillingham (Wakefield, Bettie), Bettie; F; 12/23/69-63; N.C. Cherokee; 1/32; M; Head; 696; Yes; Yes; Unallotted

698; Dills (Rogers, Villa), Villa; F; 6/24/99-33; N.C. Cherokee; 1/8; M; Wife; 697; Yes; Yes; Unallotted

699; Dills, Ruby; F; 6/28/15-17; N.C. Cherokee; 1/16; S; Dau.; 698; Yes; Yes; Unallotted

700; Dills, Louise; F; 5/8/18-14; N.C. Cherokee; 1/16; S; Dau.; 699; Yes; Yes; Unallotted

701; Dills, Turner; M; 8/4/21-11; N.C. Cherokee; 1/16; S; Son; 700; Yes; Yes; Unallotted

702; Dills, Lyle; M; 1/22/24-9; N.C. Cherokee; 1/16; S; Son; 701; Yes; Yes; Unallotted

703; Dockery (Payne, Emma), Emma J.; F; 10/7/81-51; N.C. Cherokee; 1/16; M; Wife; 702; Yes; Yes; Unallotted

704; Dockery, Ralph B.; M; 6/8/07-25; N.C. Cherokee; 1/32; S; Son; 703; Yes; Yes; Unallotted

705; Dockery, Dora Lee; F; 5/2/13-19; N.C. Cherokee; 1/32; S; Dau.; 704; Yes; Yes; Unallotted

706; Dockery, Roscoe A.; M; 7/11/16-16; N.C. Cherokee; 1/32; S; Son; 705; Yes; Yes; Unallotted

707; Dockery, Josephine; F; 8/31/19-13; N.C. Cherokee; 1/32; S; Dau.; 706; Yes; Yes; Unallotted

708; Dockery, Grace A.; F; 5/4/22-10; N.C. Cherokee; 1/32; S; Dau.; 707; Yes; Yes; Unallotted

709; Donley, Robert L.; M; 3/23/73-60; N.C. Cherokee; 1/8; Wd.; Head; 708; Yes; Yes; Unallotted

710; Driver, Betty; F; 12/21/44-88; N.C. Cherokee; 4/4; Wd.; Head; 709; Yes; Yes; Unallotted

Census of the **Eastern Cherokee** reservation of the **Cherokee, N.C.** jurisdiction, as of **April 1** , 19**33,** taken by **R. L. Spalsbury** , Superintendent.

Key: Number; Surname, Given; Sex; Date of Birth-Age at Last Birthday; Tribe; Degree of Blood; Marital Status; Relationship to Head of Family; Last C. Roll No.; At Jurisdiction Where Enrolled (Yes/No); (If no – Where); Ward (Yes/No); Allotment, Annuity and Identification Numbers (if given).

711; Driver, Chekelelee; M; 9/15/81-51; N.C. Cherokee; 4/4; Wd.; Head; 710; Yes; Yes; Unallotted

712; Driver, Mason; M; 9/23/09-23; N.C. Cherokee; 4/4; S; Son; 711; Yes; Yes; Unallotted

713; Driver, Amanda; F; 3/3/16-17; N.C. Cherokee; 4/4; S; Dau.; 712; Yes; Yes; Unallotted

714; Driver, James; M; 7/24/21-11; N.C. Cherokee; 4/4; S; Son; 713; Yes; Yes; Unallotted

715; Driver, Dickey; M; 6/21/47-85; N.C. Cherokee; 4/4; Wd.; Head; 714; Yes; Yes; Unallotted

716; Driver, John; M; 12/26/13-20; N.C. Cherokee; 9/16; S; Son; 715; Yes; Yes; Unallotted

717; Driver, George; M; 3/23/03-30; N.C. Cherokee; 4/4; M; Head; 716; Yes; Yes; Unallotted

718; Driver, Annie Bird; F; 1/14/07-26; N.C. Cherokee; 4/4; M; Wife; 717; Yes; Yes; Unallotted

719; Driver, John; M; 3/29/27-6; N.C. Cherokee; 4/4; S; Son; 718; Yes; Yes; Unallotted

720; Driver, Waidsutte; F; 6/7/30-2; N.C. Cherokee; 4/4; S; Dau.; 719; Yes; Yes; Unallotted

721; Driver, Lydia; F; 1/4/33-2/12; N.C. Cherokee; 4/4; S; Dau.; ---; Yes; Yes; Unallotted

722; Driver, James G.; M; 4/25/77-55; N.C. Cherokee; 4/4; M; Head; 720; Yes; Yes; Unallotted

723; Driver, John; M; 12/15/98-34; N.C. Cherokee; 4/4; M; Head; 721; Yes; Yes; Unallotted

724; Driver, Nannie T.; F; 12/18/02-30; N.C. Cherokee; 4/4; M; Wife; 722; Yes; Yes; Unallotted

725; Driver, Nicodemus; M; 3/23/20-13; N.C. Cherokee; 4/4; S; Son; 723; Yes; Yes; Unallotted

726; Driver, Quincy; M; 2/26/22-11; N.C. Cherokee; 4/4; S; Son; 724; Yes; Yes; Unallotted

727; Driver, Watty; M; 3/11/29-4; N.C. Cherokee; 4/4; S; Son; 725; Yes; Yes; Unallotted

728; Driver, Tom; M; 3/11/29-4; N.C. Cherokee; 4/4; S; Son; 726; Yes; Yes; Unallotted

729; Driver, Judas; M; 8/1/66-66; N.C. Cherokee; 4/4; M; Head; 727; Yes; Yes; Unallotted

730; Driver, Eliza; F; 7/4/66-66; N.C. Cherokee; 4/4; M; Wife; 728; Yes; Yes; Unallotted

Census of the **Eastern Cherokee** reservation of the **Cherokee, N.C.** jurisdiction, as of **April 1** , 19**33,** taken by **R. L. Spalsbury** , Superintendent.

Key: Number; Surname, Given; Sex; Date of Birth-Age at Last Birthday; Tribe; Degree of Blood; Marital Status; Relationship to Head of Family; Last C. Roll No.; At Jurisdiction Where Enrolled (Yes/No); (If no – Where); Ward (Yes/No); Allotment, Annuity and Identification Numbers (if given).

731; Driver, Ned; M; 8/9/00-32; N.C. Cherokee; 7/8; M; Head; 729; Yes; Yes; Unallotted

732; Driver, Dovi Smith; F; 2/22/09-24; N.C. Cherokee; 7/16; M; 2nd Wife; 2435; Yes; Yes; Unallotted

733; Driver, Adam West; M; 5/17/17-15; N.C. Cherokee; 15/16; S; Son; 730; Yes; Yes; Unallotted

734; Driver, Richard T.; M; 8/11/18-14; N.C. Cherokee; 15/16; S; Son; 731; Yes; Yes; Unallotted

735; Driver, MacAdoo; M; 2/19/20-13; N.C. Cherokee; 15/16; S; Son; 732; Yes; Yes; Unallotted

736; Driver, Ruth; F; 12/15/22-10; N.C. Cherokee; 15/16; S; Dau.; 733; Yes; Yes; Unallotted

737; Driver, Russel B.; M; 2/15/74-59; N.C. Cherokee; 4/4; M; Head; 734; No; Newton, Bucks, Pa.; Yes; Unallotted

738; Driver, Wesley; M; 2/23/71-62; N.C. Cherokee; 4/4; M; Head; 735; Yes; Yes; Unallotted

739; Driver, Agnes; F; 12/21/70-62; N.C. Cherokee; 4/4; M; Wife; 736; Yes; Yes; Unallotted

740; Driver, William; M; 8/21/73-59; N.C. Cherokee; 4/4; Wd.; Head; 737; Yes; Yes; Unallotted

741; Dunlap (Wolfe, Delia Ann), Delia Ann; F; 2/10/91-42; N.C. Cherokee; 1/8; M; Wife; 738; Yes; Yes; Unallotted

742; Dunlap, David H.; M; 12/21/22-10; N.C. Cherokee; 1/16; S; Son; 739; Yes; Yes; Unallotted

743; Dunlap, Mary Matilda; F; 7/9/13-19; N.C. Cherokee; 1/16; S; Alone; 740; Yes; Yes; Unallotted

744; Dunlap, John Robert; M; 11/13/15-17; N.C. Cherokee; 1/16; S; Bro.; 741; Yes; Yes; Unallotted

745; Dunlap, Robert L.; M; 1/8/90-43; N.C. Cherokee; 1/8; M; Head; 742; Yes; Yes; Unallotted

746; Dunlap, Odell; M; 11/14/21-11; N.C. Cherokee; 1/16; S; Son; 743; Yes; Yes; Unallotted

747; Enloe, Fallen L.; F; 4/24/15-17; N.C. Cherokee; 1/16; M; Wife; 744; Yes; Yes; Unallotted

748; Eller (Patterson, Josie), Josie P.; F; 11/11/00-32; N.C. Cherokee; 1/32; M; Wife; 745; Yes; Yes; Unallotted

Census of the **Eastern Cherokee** reservation of the **Cherokee, N.C.** jurisdiction, as of **April 1** , 19**33,** taken by **R. L. Spalsbury** , Superintendent.

Key: Number; Surname, Given; Sex; Date of Birth-Age at Last Birthday; Tribe; Degree of Blood; Marital Status; Relationship to Head of Family; Last C. Roll No.; At Jurisdiction Where Enrolled (Yes/No); (If no – Where); Ward (Yes/No); Allotment, Annuity and Identification Numbers (if given).

749; Ellis (Hardin, Celia), Celia H.; F; 5/17/94-38; N.C. Cherokee; 1/16; M; Wife; 746; Yes; Yes; Unallotted

750; Ellis, Magdalene E.; F; 5/12/17-15; N.C. Cherokee; 1/32; S; Dau.; 747; Yes; Yes; Unallotted

751; Ellis, Thomas J.; M; 7/9/20-12; N.C. Cherokee; 1/32; S; Son; 749; Yes; Yes; Unallotted

752; Ellis, Wm. Samuel; M; 10/27/18-14; N.C. Cherokee; 1/32; S; Son; 748; Yes; Yes; Unallotted

753; Ellis (Tatham, Olive), Olive T.; F; 4/1/04-29; N.C. Cherokee; 1/16; M; Wife; 750; Yes; Yes; Unallotted

754; Endros, Edwin; M; 2/1/08-25; N.C. Cherokee; 3/8; S; Head; 751; Yes; Yes; Unallotted

755; Enloe (Lambert, Mintha), Mintha D.; F; 10/9/12-20; N.C. Cherokee; 1/32; M; Wife; 752; Yes; Yes; Unallotted

756; Ewart, Tiney L.; F; 10/4/05-27; N.C. Cherokee; 1/4; M; Wife; 753; Yes; Yes; Unallotted

757; Ewart, Samuel; M; 10/21/25-7; N.C. Cherokee; 1/8; S; Son; 754; Yes; Yes; Unallotted

758; Eubank, Lillie; F; 1888-46; N.C. Cherokee; 1/4; M; Wife; 755; Yes; Yes; Unallotted

759; Feather, William; M; 5/2/20-12; N.C. Cherokee; 4/4; S; Alone; 756; Yes; Yes; Unallotted

760; Feather, Hettie; F; 3/24/98-35; N.C. Cherokee; 4/4; S; Head; 757; No; Philadelphia, Philadelphia, Pa; Yes; Unallotted

761; Feather, Lawyer; M; 12/12/68-64; N.C. Cherokee; 4/4; M; Head; 758; Yes; Yes; Unallotted

762; Feather, Mary; F; 12/12/67-65; N.C. Cherokee; 4/4; M; Wife; 759; Yes; Yes; Unallotted

763; Feather, Jonah; M; 7/5/05-27; N.C. Cherokee; 4/4; S; Son; 760; Yes; Yes; Unallotted

764; Featherhead, Wilson; M; 12/21/72-60; N.C. Cherokee; 4/4; Wd.; Head; 761; Yes; Yes; Unallotted

765; Falls, Bettie B.; F; 1900-33; N.C. Cherokee; 1/4; M; Wife; 762; Yes; Yes; Unallotted

228

Census of the **Eastern Cherokee** reservation of the **Cherokee, N.C.** jurisdiction, as of **April 1** , 1933, taken by **R. L. Spalsbury** , Superintendent.

Key: Number; Surname, Given; Sex; Date of Birth-Age at Last Birthday; Tribe; Degree of Blood; Marital Status; Relationship to Head of Family; Last C. Roll No.; At Jurisdiction Where Enrolled (Yes/No); (If no – Where); Ward (Yes/No); Allotment, Annuity and Identification Numbers (if given).

766; Finger, Sophronia; F; 11/2/76-56; N.C. Cherokee; 1/4; M; Wife; 763; Yes; Yes; Unallotted

767; Finger, Samuel A.; M; 2/20/98-35; N.C. Cherokee; 1/8; S; Son; 764; Yes; Yes; Unallotted

768; Finger, Leonia; F; 7/5/05-27; N.C. Cherokee; 1/8; S; Dau.; 765; Yes; Yes; Unallotted

769; Finger, Elmer E.; M; 4/26/08-24; N.C. Cherokee; 1/8; S; Son; 766; Yes; Yes; Unallotted

770; Finger, Ruby Irene; F; 9/6/11-21; N.C. Cherokee; 1/8; S; Dau.; 767; Yes; Yes; Unallotted

771; Finger, Cora J.; F; 8/5/17-15; N.C. Cherokee; 1/8; S; Dau.; 768; Yes; Yes; Unallotted

772; Fisher (McLeymore, Elsie), Elsie McL.; F; 6/15/08-24; N.C. Cherokee; 5/16; M; Wife; 769; Yes; Yes; Unallotted

773; Fisher, Frankie C.; F; 10/3/96-36; N.C. Cherokee; 1/16; M; Wife; 770; Yes; Yes; Unallotted

774; Fisher, Stacey A.; F; 4/28/22-10; N.C. Cherokee; 1/32; S; Dau.; 771; Yes; Yes; Unallotted

775; Fortner (Raper, Delia), Delia; F; 5/14/99-33; N.C. Cherokee; 1/16; M; Wife; 772; Yes; Yes; Unallotted

776; Fortner, June; F; 6/5/18-14; N.C. Cherokee; 1/32; S; Dau.; 773; Yes; Yes; Unallotted

777; Fortner, Sis; F; 12/24/76-57; N.C. Cherokee; 1/4; M; Wife; 774; Yes; Yes; Unallotted

778; Foster (Raper, Alice), Alice; F; 5/29/74-58; N.C. Cherokee; 1/8; M; Wife; 775; Yes; Yes; Unallotted

779; Foster, Robert; M; 4/16/01-31; N.C. Cherokee; 1/16; S; Son; 776; Yes; Yes; Unallotted

780; Foster, Burton; M; 7/26/03-29; N.C. Cherokee; 1/16; S; Son; 777; Yes; Yes; Unallotted

781; Foster, Leroy; M; 2/4/06-27; N.C. Cherokee; 1/16; S; Son; 778; Yes; Yes; Unallotted

782; Foster, William E.; M; 10/17/13-19; N.C. Cherokee; 1/16; S; Son; 779; Yes; Yes; Unallotted

783; French, Meroney; M; 12/15/98-34; N.C. Cherokee; 4/4; M; Head; 780; Yes; Yes; Unallotted

784; French, Callie R.; F; 10/28/10-22; N.C. Cherokee; 4/4; M; Wife 2nd; 781; Yes; Yes; Unallotted

785; French, Roy Daniel; M; 8/19/22-10; N.C. Cherokee; 4/4; S; Son; 782; Yes; Yes; Unallotted

Census of the **Eastern Cherokee** reservation of the **Cherokee, N.C.** jurisdiction, as of **April 1** , 19**33,** taken by **R. L. Spalsbury** , Superintendent.

Key: Number; Surname, Given; Sex; Date of Birth-Age at Last Birthday; Tribe; Degree of Blood; Marital Status; Relationship to Head of Family; Last C. Roll No.; At Jurisdiction Where Enrolled (Yes/No); (If no – Where); Ward (Yes/No); Allotment, Annuity and Identification Numbers (if given).

786; French, John K.; M; 1/7/24-9; N.C. Cherokee; 4/4; S; Son; 783; Yes; Yes; Unallotted

787; French, Manuel M.; M; 4/23/28-4; N.C. Cherokee; 4/4; S; Son; 784; Yes; Yes; Unallotted

788; French, Morgan; M; 12/15/98-34; N.C. Cherokee; 4/4; M; Head; 785; Yes; Yes; Unallotted

789; French, Ned; M; 11/8/99-33; N.C. Cherokee; 4/4; S; Head; 786; Yes; Yes; Unallotted

790; French, Jesse; M; 3/17/05-28; N.C. Cherokee; 4/4; S; Bro.; 787; Yes; Yes; Unallotted

791; French, Samuel; M; 11/6/16-15; N.C. Cherokee; 4/4; S; Alone; 788; Yes; Yes; Unallotted

792; French, Gerry; M; 5/18/18-14; N.C. Cherokee; 4/4; S; Bro.; 789; Yes; Yes; Unallotted

793; French, Judy; F; 5/29/21-11; N.C. Cherokee; 4/4; S; Sis.; 790; Yes; Yes; Unallotted

794; French, Saughee; M; 3/28/00-33; N.C. Cherokee; 4/4; S; Head; 791; Yes; Yes; Unallotted

795; French, George; M; 5/25/02-30; N.C. Cherokee; 4/4; S; Bro.; 792; Yes; Yes; Unallotted

796; Frye (Bauer, Owenah), Owenah A.; F; 10/17/95-37; N.C. Cherokee; 3/8; M; Wife; 793; Yes; Yes; Unallotted

797; Garland, Jesse L.; M; 8/31/56-76; N.C. Cherokee; 1/8; M; Head; 794; Yes; Yes; Unallotted

798; Garland, Emory; M; 2/19/03-30; N.C. Cherokee; 1/16; S; Son; 795; Yes; Yes; Unallotted

799; Garland, Radia Elmer; F; 9/11/05-27; N.C. Cherokee; 1/16; S; Dau.; 796; Yes; Yes; Unallotted

800; Garland, John B.; M; 1/22/79-54; N.C. Cherokee; 1/16; M; Head; 797; Yes; Yes; Unallotted

801; Garland, Frank; M; 3/10/06-27; N.C. Cherokee; 1/32; S; Son; 798; Yes; Yes; Unallotted

802; Garland, Fred; M; 7/12/08-24; N.C. Cherokee; 1/32; S; Son; 799; Yes; Yes; Unallotted

803; Garland, Edgar; M; 8/11/11-21; N.C. Cherokee; 1/32; S; Son; 800; Yes; Yes; Unallotted

804; Garland, Aud; M; 5/6/19-13; N.C. Cherokee; 1/32; S; Son; 801; Yes; Yes; Unallotted

Census of the **Eastern Cherokee** reservation of the **Cherokee, N.C.** jurisdiction, as of **April 1** , **1933,** taken by **R. L. Spalsbury** , Superintendent.

Key: Number; Surname, Given; Sex; Date of Birth-Age at Last Birthday; Tribe; Degree of Blood; Marital Status; Relationship to Head of Family; Last C. Roll No.; At Jurisdiction Where Enrolled (Yes/No); (If no – Where); Ward (Yes/No); Allotment, Annuity and Identification Numbers (if given).

805;   Garland, Leonzo[sic]; M; 5/22/85-47; N.C. Cherokee; 1/16; M; Head; 802; No; Culberson, Cherokee, N.C.; Yes; Unallotted

806;   Garland, Homer; M; 1/14/10-23; N.C. Cherokee; 1/32; S; Son; 803; No; Culberson, Cherokee, N.C.; Yes; Unallotted

807;   Garland, Ruth; F; 10/17/13-19; N.C. Cherokee; 1/32; S; Dau.; 804; No; Culberson, Cherokee, N.C.; Yes; Unallotted

808;   Garland, Charlie; M; 1/14/15-18; N.C. Cherokee; 1/32; S; Son; 805; No; Culberson, Cherokee, N.C.; Yes; Unallotted

809;   Garland, Edith; F; 4/21/18-14; N.C. Cherokee; 1/32; S; Dau.; 806; No; Culberson, Cherokee, N.C.; Yes; Unallotted

810;   Garland, Nettie; F; 4/11/20-12; N.C. Cherokee; 1/32; S; Dau.; 807; No; Culberson, Cherokee, N.C.; Yes; Unallotted

811;   Garland, Dora; F; 7/4/22-10; N.C. Cherokee; 1/32; S; Dau.; 808; No; Culberson, Cherokee, N.C.; Yes; Unallotted

812;   Garland, Emma; F; 3/28/24-9; N.C. Cherokee; 1/32; S; Dau.; 809; No; Culberson, Cherokee, N.C.; Yes; Unallotted

813;   Garland, Roxanna; F; 3/12/59-75; N.C. Cherokee; 1/8; S; Head; 810; No; Culberson, Cherokee, N.C.; Yes; Unallotted

814;   Garland, William S.; M; 6/27/66-66; N.C. Cherokee; 1/8; S; Head; 811; No; Culberson, Cherokee, N.C.; Yes; Unallotted

815;   Garren (Cole, Ida), Ida C.; F; 6/13/91-41; N.C. Cherokee; 1/16; M; Wife; 812; Yes; Yes; Unallotted

816;   Garren, Elmer; M; 10/9/14-18; N.C. Cherokee; 1/32; S; Son; 813; Yes; Yes; Unallotted

817;   Garren, Rosa; F; 3/27/20-13; N.C. Cherokee; 1/32; S; Dau.; 814; Yes; Yes; Unallotted

818;   George, Bessie T.; F; 5/8/97-35; N.C. Cherokee; 3/4; Wd.; Head; 815; Yes; Yes; Unallotted

819;   George, Florence; F; 8/15/16-16; N.C. Cherokee; 3/8; S; Dau.; 816; Yes; Yes; Unallotted

820;   George, Rosie E.B.; F; 7/14/79-53; N.C. Cherokee; 1/8; Wd.; Head; 817; Yes; Yes; Unallotted

821;   Biddix (George), Margaret; F; 1/17/17-16; N.C. Cherokee; 9/16; M; Wife; 818; Yes; Yes; Unallotted

822;   Biddix, Boony Louise; F; 4/19/32-11/12; N.C. Cherokee; 9/32; S; Granddaughter; ---; Yes; Yes; Unallotted

823;   George, Dawson; M; 6/14/60-72; N.C. Cherokee; 4/4; M; Head; 819; Yes; Yes; Unallotted

Census of the **Eastern Cherokee** reservation of the **Cherokee, N.C.** jurisdiction, as of **April 1** , 19**33,** taken by **R. L. Spalsbury** , Superintendent.

Key: Number; Surname, Given; Sex; Date of Birth-Age at Last Birthday; Tribe; Degree of Blood; Marital Status; Relationship to Head of Family; Last C. Roll No.; At Jurisdiction Where Enrolled (Yes/No); (If no – Where); Ward (Yes/No); Allotment, Annuity and Identification Numbers (if given).

824; George, Mary; F; 6/24/60-72; N.C. Cherokee; 7/8; M; Wife; 820; Yes; Yes; Unallotted

825; George, Annie; F; 12/30/83-49; N.C. Cherokee; 15/16; S; Dau.; 821; No; Little Neck, Long Island, N.Y.; Yes; Unallotted

826; George, Elijah; M; 4/1/74-59; N.C. Cherokee; 4/4; M; Head; 822; Yes; Yes; Unallotted

827 George, Nicey Wilnoty; F; 4/13/89-43; N.C. Cherokee; 4/4; M; Wife; 823; Yes; Yes; Unallotted

828; George, Lewis; M; 8/28/05-27; N.C. Cherokee; 4/4; S; Son; 824; Yes; Yes; Unallotted

829; George, Cornelia; F; 1/28/08-25; N.C. Cherokee; 4/4; M; Wife; 826; Yes; Yes; Unallotted

830; George, Annie; F; 4/13/16-16; N.C. Cherokee; 4/4; S; Dau.; 827; Yes; Yes; Unallotted

831; George, Bessie; F; 6/19/17-15; N.C. Cherokee; 4/4; S; Dau.; 828; Yes; Yes; Unallotted

832; George, Joseph; M; 5/14/19-13; N.C. Cherokee; 4/4; S; Son; 829; Yes; Yes; Unallotted

833; George, Guy; M; 4/13/21-11; N.C. Cherokee; 4/4; S; Son; 830; Yes; Yes; Unallotted

834; George, Janie; F; 3/10/25-8; N.C. Cherokee; 4/4; S; Dau.; 831; Yes; Yes; Unallotted

835; George, Davis D.; M; 5/12/27-5; N.C. Cherokee; 4/4; S; Son; 832; Yes; Yes; Unallotted

836; George, Lucy; F; 5/12/27-5; N.C. Cherokee; 4/4; S; Dau.; 833; Yes; Yes; Unallotted

837; George, Ollie; F; 9/14/29-3; N.C. Cherokee; 4/4; S; Dau.; 834; Yes; Yes; Unallotted

838; George, Elijah; M; 4/1/78-55; N.C. Cherokee; 4/4; S; Head; 835; Yes; Yes; Unallotted

839; George, Elizabeth; F; 12/21/60-72; N.C. Cherokee; 4/4; Wd.; Head; 836; Yes; Yes; Unallotted

840; George, Elmo Don; M; 5/8/03-29; N.C. Cherokee; 15/16; S; Head; 837; Yes; Yes; Unallotted

841; George, Goliath; M; 9/20/01-31; N.C. Cherokee; 4/4; M; Head; 838; Yes; Yes; Unallotted

842; George, Bessie B.; F; 11/5/00-32; N.C. Cherokee; 15/16; M; Wife; 839; Yes; Yes; Unallotted

843; George, Paulina; F; 8/27/20-12; N.C. Cherokee; 31/32; S; Dau.; 840; Yes; Yes; Unallotted

Census of the **Eastern Cherokee** reservation of the **Cherokee, N.C.** jurisdiction, as of **April 1**, **1933,** taken by **R. L. Spalsbury**, Superintendent.

Key: Number; Surname, Given; Sex; Date of Birth-Age at Last Birthday; Tribe; Degree of Blood; Marital Status; Relationship to Head of Family; Last C. Roll No.; At Jurisdiction Where Enrolled (Yes/No); (If no – Where); Ward (Yes/No); Allotment, Annuity and Identification Numbers (if given).

844;   George, Green; M; 6/2/00-32; N.C. Cherokee; 4/4; S; Head; 841; Yes; Yes; Unallotted

845;   George, Jackson; M; 8/5/02-30; N.C. Cherokee; 4/4; S; Head; 842; Yes; Yes; Unallotted

846;   George, Jacob; M; 3/9/94-39; N.C. Cherokee; 4/4; M; Head; 843; Yes; Yes; Unallotted

847;   George, Nola S.; F; 11/17/97-35; N.C. Cherokee; 4/4; M; Wife; 844; Yes; Yes; Unallotted

848;   George, Ammons; M; 6/12/15-17; N.C. Cherokee; 4/4; S; Son; 845; Yes; Yes; Unallotted

849;   George, Sherman; M; 12/22/16-16; N.C. Cherokee; 4/4; S; Son; 846; Yes; Yes; Unallotted

850;   George, Jonah; M; 2/16/19-14; N.C. Cherokee; 4/4; S; Son; 847; Yes; Yes; Unallotted

851;   George, Callie; F; 2/1/23-10; N.C. Cherokee; 4/4; S; Dau.; 848; Yes; Yes; Unallotted

852;   George, Josie; F; 10/16/23-9; N.C. Cherokee; 4/4; S; Alone; 849; Yes; Yes; Unallotted

853;   George (Lee, Julia), Julia V.; F; 2/22/75-58; N.C. Cherokee; 1/16; M; Wife; 850; Yes; Yes; Unallotted

854;   George, Logan; M; 7/21/88-44; N.C. Cherokee; 4/4; S; Head; 851; Yes; Yes; Unallotted

855;   George, Maggie R.; F; 3/24/89-44; N.C. Cherokee; 7/8; M; Wife; 852; Yes; Yes; Unallotted

856;   George, Manley; M; 5/29/89-43; N.C. Cherokee; 15/16; M; Head; 853; Yes; Yes; Unallotted

857;   George, Savannah P.; F; 9/2/07-25; N.C. Cherokee; 4/4; M; Wife; 854; Yes; Yes; Unallotted

858;   George, Annie; F; 8/10/25-7; N.C. Cherokee; 31/32; S; Dau.; 855; Yes; Yes; Unallotted

859;   George, Columbus; M; 6/18/27-5; N.C. Cherokee; 31/32; S; Son; 856; Yes; Yes; Unallotted

860;   George, Hoover; M; 2/6/29-4; N.C. Cherokee; 31/32; S; Son; 857; Yes; Yes; Unallotted

861;   George, Sallie; F; 6/6/30-2; N.C. Cherokee; 31/32; S; Dau.; 858; Yes; Yes; Unallotted

862;   George, Abraham; M; 7/13/32-8/12; N.C. Cherokee; 31/32; S; Son; ---; Yes; Yes; Unallotted

Census of the **Eastern Cherokee** reservation of the **Cherokee, N.C.** jurisdiction, as of **April 1** , 1933, taken by **R. L. Spalsbury** , Superintendent.

Key: Number; Surname, Given; Sex; Date of Birth-Age at Last Birthday; Tribe; Degree of Blood; Marital Status; Relationship to Head of Family; Last C. Roll No.; At Jurisdiction Where Enrolled (Yes/No); (If no – Where); Ward (Yes/No); Allotment, Annuity and Identification Numbers (if given).

863; George, Martha; F; 11/4/91-41; N.C. Cherokee; 15/16; Div.; Head; 859; Yes; Yes; Unallotted

864; George, Ben; M; 10/21/13-19; N.C. Cherokee; 15/32; S; Son; 860; Yes; Yes; Unallotted

865; George, Tom; M; 3/21/18-15; N.C. Cherokee; 15/32; S; Son; 861; Yes; Yes; Unallotted

866; George, Sam; M; 8/5/20-12; N.C. Cherokee; 15/32; S; Son; 862; Yes; Yes; Unallotted

867; George, Shell; M; 3/21/60-73; N.C. Cherokee; 4/4; S; Head; 863; Yes; Yes; Unallotted

868; George, Shon; M; 9/18/72-60; N.C. Cherokee; 4/4; S; Head; 864; Yes; Yes; Unallotted

869; Gilbert (Robinson, Emmaline), Emmaline; F; 10/9/97-35; N.C. Cherokee; 1/16; M; Wife; 865; Yes; Yes; Unallotted

870; Gilbert, Paul A.; M; 12/24/22-10; N.C. Cherokee; 1/32; S; Son; 866; Yes; Yes; Unallotted

871; Gilreath (Raper, Georgia), Georgia; F; 1/28/91-42; N.C. Cherokee; 1/16; M; Wife; 867; Yes; Yes; Unallotted

872; Gilreath, Albert B.; M; 10/6/13-19; N.C. Cherokee; 1/32; S; Son; 868; Yes; Yes; Unallotted

873; Gilreath, Rubia; F; 8/25/15-17; N.C. Cherokee; 1/32; S; Dau.; 869; Yes; Yes; Unallotted

874; Gilreath, Roxie; F; 5/29/17-15; N.C. Cherokee; 1/32; S; Dau.; 870; Yes; Yes; Unallotted

875; Gilreath, Cecil; M; 11/17/21-11; N.C. Cherokee; 1/32; S; Son; 871; Yes; Yes; Unallotted

876; Gilreath, Rittie; F; 5/18/23-9; N.C. Cherokee; 1/32; S; Dau.; 872; Yes; Yes; Unallotted

877; Gloyne, Lula O.; F; 12/27/91-41; N.C. Cherokee; 1/2; Wd.; Head; 873; Yes; Yes; Unallotted

878; Gloyne, Roberta; F; 4/19/19-13; N.C. Cherokee; 1/4; S; Dau.; 874; Yes; Yes; Unallotted

879; Gloyne, John H.; M; 4/10/21-11; N.C. Cherokee; 1/4; S; Son; 875; Yes; Yes; Unallotted

880; Gloyne, Daniel D.; M; 5/17/23-9; N.C. Cherokee; 1/4; S; Son; 876; Yes; Yes; Unallotted

881; Gloyne, Mary T.; F; 8/30/28-5; N.C. Cherokee; 1/4; S; Dau.; 877; Yes; Yes; Unallotted

Census of the **Eastern Cherokee** reservation of the **Cherokee, N.C.** jurisdiction, as of **April 1** , **1933,** taken by **R. L. Spalsbury** , Superintendent.

Key: Number; Surname, Given; Sex; Date of Birth-Age at Last Birthday; Tribe; Degree of Blood; Marital Status; Relationship to Head of Family; Last C. Roll No.; At Jurisdiction Where Enrolled (Yes/No); (If no – Where); Ward (Yes/No); Allotment, Annuity and Identification Numbers (if given).

882;   Goforth, Arthur; M; 3/8/11-22; N.C. Cherokee; 3/32; M; Head; 878; Yes; Yes; Unallotted

883;   Goin, Sallie; F; 12/21/49-83; N.C. Cherokee; 3/4; S; Alone; 879; Yes; Yes; Unallotted

884;   Going, Birdchopper; M; 12/21/69-63; N.C. Cherokee; 4/4; M; Head; 880; Yes; Yes; Unallotted
885;   Going, Ollie; F; 8/21/72-60; N.C. Cherokee; 4/4; M; Wife; 881; Yes; Yes; Unallotted
886;   Going, Emmaline; F; 3/5/09-24; N.C. Cherokee; 4/4; S; Dau.; 882; Yes; Yes; Unallotted
887;   Going, Emerson J.; M; 5/15/28-4; N.C. Cherokee; 1/2; S; Gr.Son (Illeg.); 883; Yes; Yes; Unallotted

888;   Going, George; M; 9/12/21-11; N.C. Cherokee; 4/4; S; Alone; 884; Yes; Yes; Unallotted

889;   Graves (Murphy, Inez), Inez; F; 10/14/93-39; N.C. Cherokee; 1/8; M; Wife; 885; No; Unaka, Cherokee, N.C.; Yes; Unallotted
890;   Graves, Fred; M; 8/25/13-19; N.C. Cherokee; 1/16; S; Son; 886; No; Unaka, Cherokee, N.C.; Yes; Unallotted
891;   Graves, Myrtle; F; 4/2/16-16; N.C. Cherokee; 1/16; S; Dau.; 887; No; Unaka, Cherokee, N.C.; Yes; Unallotted
892;   Graves, Mary; F; 8/28/18-14; N.C. Cherokee; 1/16; S; Dau.; 888; No; Unaka, Cherokee, N.C.; Yes; Unallotted
893;   Graves, Eva; F; 11/15/20-12; N.C. Cherokee; 1/16; S; Dau.; 889; No; Unaka, Cherokee, N.C.; Yes; Unallotted
894;   Graves, Hoyt; M; 1/15/23-10; N.C. Cherokee; 1/16; S; Son; 890; No; Unaka, Cherokee, N.C.; Yes; Unallotted

895;   Green (Payne, Cora), Cora E.; F; 4/8/84-48; N.C. Cherokee; 1/16; M; Wife; 891; No; Letitia, Cherokee, N.C.; Yes; Unallotted
896;   Green, Lurlie B.; F; 12/22/06-26; N.C. Cherokee; 1/32; S; Dau.; 892; No; Letitia, Cherokee, N.C.; Yes; Unallotted
897;   Green, Bonnie Lee; F; 9/10/09-23; N.C. Cherokee; 1/32; S; Dau.; 893; No; Letitia, Cherokee, N.C.; Yes; Unallotted
898;   Green, Blanche; F; 8/2/12-20; N.C. Cherokee; 1/32; S; Dau.; 894; No; Letitia, Cherokee, N.C.; Yes; Unallotted
899;   Green, Millie; F; 12/27/14-18; N.C. Cherokee; 1/32; S; Dau.; 895; No; Letitia, Cherokee, N.C.; Yes; Unallotted
900;   Green, Alfred; M; 8/12/18-14; N.C. Cherokee; 1/32; S; Son; 896; No; Letitia, Cherokee, N.C.; Yes; Unallotted
901;   Green, Margaret H.; F; 2/25/24-9; N.C. Cherokee; 1/32; S; Dau.; 897; No; Letitia, Cherokee, N.C.; Yes; Unallotted

Census of the **Eastern Cherokee** reservation of the **Cherokee, N.C.** jurisdiction, as of **April 1**, 19**33,** taken by **R. L. Spalsbury**, Superintendent.

Key: Number; Surname, Given; Sex; Date of Birth-Age at Last Birthday; Tribe; Degree of Blood; Marital Status; Relationship to Head of Family; Last C. Roll No.; At Jurisdiction Where Enrolled (Yes/No); (If no – Where); Ward (Yes/No); Allotment, Annuity and Identification Numbers (if given).

902; Green, Lena B.; F; 1904-29; N.C. Cherokee; -1/4; M; Wife; 898; No; Ensley, Jefferson, Ala.; Yes; Unallotted

903; Green (Rogers, Martha C.), Martha; F; 2/12/78-55; N.C. Cherokee; 1/16; M; Wife; 899; Yes; Yes; Unallotted

904; Greene (Baker, Stella), Stella B.; F; 3/13/98-35; N.C. Cherokee; 1/16; M; Wife; 900; Yes; Yes; Unallotted

905; Greene, Samuel P.; M; 3/17/22-11; N.C. Cherokee; 1/32; S; Son; 901; Yes; Yes; Unallotted

906; Greybeard, Sallie ; F; 3/14/99-34; N.C. Cherokee; 1/2; S; Head; 902; No; Philadelphia, Philadelphia, Pa.; Yes; Unallotted

~~Griffin, Ima; F; 12/15/12-20; N.C. Cherokee; 1/32; S; Alone; 903; Yes; Yes; Unallotted~~

907; Griffin, Iowa; F; 4/14/18-14; N.C. Cherokee; 1/32; S; Sister; 904; Yes; Yes; Unallotted

908; Griffin, Frankie; F; 9/23/20-12; N.C. Cherokee; 1/32; S; Sister; 905; Yes; Yes; Unallotted

909; Griffin (Murphy, Jane), Jane M.; F; 4/16/77-55; N.C. Cherokee; 1/8; M; Wife; 906; Yes; Yes; Unallotted

910; Griffin, Minnie Goforth; F; 1/4/87-46; N.C. Cherokee; 3/16; M; Wife; 907; Yes; Yes; Unallotted

911; Hagood (Meroney, Mayes), Mayes M.; F; 11/7/96-36; N.C. Cherokee; 1/16; M; Wife; 908; Yes; Yes; Unallotted

912; Haigler, Cora McL.; F; 5/29/05-27; N.C. Cherokee; 5/16; M; Wife; 909; Yes; Yes; Unallotted

913; Haigler, Frank W.; M; 2/12/24-9; N.C. Cherokee; 5/32; S; Son; 910; Yes; Yes; Unallotted

914; Hamby (Raper, Edna), Edna R.; F; 11/19/09-23; N.C. Cherokee; 1/32; M; Wife; 911; No; Oak Park, Cherokee, N.C.; Yes; Unallotted

915; Hamilton, Leona Jordan; F; 1876-57; N.C. Cherokee; -1/4; M; Wife; 912; Yes; Yes; Unallotted

916; Hardin, Dillard; M; 10/20/01-31; N.C. Cherokee; 1/32; M; Head; 913; Yes; Yes; Unallotted

917; Hardin, Dorothy; F; 9/5/23-10; N.C. Cherokee; 1/64; S; Dau.; 914; Yes; Yes; Unallotted

Census of the **Eastern Cherokee** reservation of the **Cherokee, N.C.** jurisdiction, as of **April 1** , 19**33,** taken by **R. L. Spalsbury** , Superintendent.

Key: Number; Surname, Given; Sex; Date of Birth-Age at Last Birthday; Tribe; Degree of Blood; Marital Status; Relationship to Head of Family; Last C. Roll No.; At Jurisdiction Where Enrolled (Yes/No); (If no – Where); Ward (Yes/No); Allotment, Annuity and Identification Numbers (if given).

918; Hardin, Dock; M; 8/10/86-46; N.C. Cherokee; 1/16; M; Head; 915; Yes; Yes; Unallotted

919; Hardin, Cluria; F; 6/10/07-25; N.C. Cherokee; 1/32; S; Dau.; 916; Yes; Yes; Unallotted

920; Hardin, Essie; F; 7/24/09-23; N.C. Cherokee; 1/32; S; Dau.; 917; Yes; Yes; Unallotted

921; Hardin, Gay; M; 2/14/12-20; N.C. Cherokee; 1/32; S; Son; 918; Yes; Yes; Unallotted

922; Hardin, Lury; F; 4/14/15-17; N.C. Cherokee; 1/32; S; Dau.; 919; Yes; Yes; Unallotted

923; Hardin, Arlie; M; 4/26/18-13; N.C. Cherokee; 1/32; S; Son; 912; Yes; Yes; Unallotted

924; Hardin, James O.; M; 11/4/03-29; N.C. Cherokee; 1/32; S; Head; 921; Yes; Yes; Unallotted

925; Hardin, Glenson; M; 12/18/07-25; N.C. Cherokee; 1/32; S; Bro.; 922; Yes; Yes; Unallotted

926; Hardin, Garfield; M; 11/19/09-23; N.C. Cherokee; 1/32; S; Bro.; 923; Yes; Yes; Unallotted

927; Hardin, Giles; M; 3/28/12-21; N.C. Cherokee; 1/32; S; Bro.; 924; Yes; Yes; Unallotted

928; Hardin, Raymond; M; 1/31/15-18; N.C. Cherokee; 1/32; S; Bro.; 925; Yes; Yes; Unallotted

929; Hardin, Elizabeth; F; 6/25/46-86; N.C. Cherokee; 1/8; M; Wife; 926; Yes; Yes; Unallotted

930; Hardin, Frank J.; M; 4/5/77-55; N.C. Cherokee; 1/16; M; Head; 927; Yes; Yes; Unallotted

931; Hardin, Herbert; M; 4/30/06-26; N.C. Cherokee; 1/32; S; Son; 928; Yes; Yes; Unallotted

932; Hardin, Mae; F; 5/10/09-23; N.C. Cherokee; 1/32; S; Dau.; 929; Yes; Yes; Unallotted

933; Hardin, Vernon; M; 1/17/11-22; N.C. Cherokee; 1/32; S; Son; 930; Yes; Yes; Unallotted

934; Hardin, Geneva; F; 6/30/14-18; N.C. Cherokee; 1/32; S; Dau.; 931; Yes; Yes; Unallotted

935; Hardin, Marvin; M; 7/17/16-16; N.C. Cherokee; 1/32; S; Son; 932; Yes; Yes; Unallotted

936; Hardin, James W.; M; 6/11/91-41; N.C. Cherokee; 1/32; M; Head; 933; Yes; Yes; Unallotted

937; Hardin, Odis; M; 7/21/09-23; N.C. Cherokee; 1/64; S; Son; 934; Yes; Yes; Unallotted

Census of the **Eastern Cherokee** reservation of the **Cherokee, N.C.** jurisdiction, as of **April 1**, **1933**, taken by **R. L. Spalsbury**, Superintendent.

Key: Number; Surname, Given; Sex; Date of Birth-Age at Last Birthday; Tribe; Degree of Blood; Marital Status; Relationship to Head of Family; Last C. Roll No.; At Jurisdiction Where Enrolled (Yes/No); (If no – Where); Ward (Yes/No); Allotment, Annuity and Identification Numbers (if given).

938; Hardin, Luke; M; 7/25/12-20; N.C. Cherokee; 1/64; S; Son; 935; Yes; Yes; Unallotted

939; Hardin, Monie; F; 1/29/15-18; N.C. Cherokee; 1/64; S; Dau.; 936; Yes; Yes; Unallotted

940; Hardin, Arlecy; F; 10/3/17-15; N.C. Cherokee; 1/64; S; Dau.; 937; Yes; Yes; Unallotted

941; Hardin, Edward; M; 9/18/21-11; N.C. Cherokee; 1/64; S; Son; 938; Yes; Yes; Unallotted

942; Hardin, Lonaino; M; 2/28/96-37; N.C. Cherokee; 1/32; M; Head; 939; Yes; Yes; Unallotted

943; Hardin, Arnold E.; M; 3/1/24-9; N.C. Cherokee; 1/64; S; Son; 940; Yes; Yes; Unallotted

944; Hardin, Loyd; M; 5/10/83-49; N.C. Cherokee; 1/16; M; Head; 941; Yes; Yes; Unallotted

945; Hardin, Pearly; M; 6/20/03-29; N.C. Cherokee; 1/32; S; Son; 942; Yes; Yes; Unallotted

946; Hardin, Romelus; M; 10/26/05-27; N.C. Cherokee; 1/32; S; Son; 943; Yes; Yes; Unallotted

947; Hardin, Bertie; M; 4/22/11-21; N.C. Cherokee; 1/32; S; Son; 944; Yes; Yes; Unallotted

948; Hardin, Ernest; M; 3/4/14-19; N.C. Cherokee; 1/32; S; Son; 945; Yes; Yes; Unallotted

949; Hardin, Nellie Audry; F; 7/5/16-16; N.C. Cherokee; 1/32; S; Dau.; 946; Yes; Yes; Unallotted

950; Hardin, Edith; F; 9/13/18-14; N.C. Cherokee; 1/32; S; Dau.; 947; Yes; Yes; Unallotted

951; Hardin, Richard; M; 1/12/93-40; N.C. Cherokee; 1/32; S; Head; 948; Yes; Yes; Unallotted

952; Hardin, Beula; F; 5/29/08-24; N.C. Cherokee; 1/32; S; Sister; 949; Yes; Yes; Unallotted

953; Hardin, Guion; M; 5/5/11-21; N.C. Cherokee; 1/32; S; Bro.; 950; Yes; Yes; Unallotted

954; Hardin, Flora; F; 11/27/12-20; N.C. Cherokee; 1/32; S; Sis.; 951; Yes; Yes; Unallotted

955; Hardin, Willard; M; 4/29/15-17; N.C. Cherokee; 1/32; S; Bro.; 952; Yes; Yes; Unallotted

956; Creasman, Golman; M; 12/7/18-14; N.C. Cherokee; 1/64; S; Nephew; 953; Yes; Yes; Unallotted

957; Hardin, Thomas J.; M; 8/1/96-36; N.C. Cherokee; 1/32; M; Head; 954; Yes; Yes; Unallotted

Census of the **Eastern Cherokee** reservation of the **Cherokee, N.C.** jurisdiction, as of **April 1** , **1933,** taken by **R. L. Spalsbury** , Superintendent.

Key: Number; Surname, Given; Sex; Date of Birth-Age at Last Birthday; Tribe; Degree of Blood; Marital Status; Relationship to Head of Family; Last C. Roll No.; At Jurisdiction Where Enrolled (Yes/No); (If no – Where); Ward (Yes/No); Allotment, Annuity and Identification Numbers (if given).

958; Hardin, Wyley; M; 11/18/17-15; N.C. Cherokee; 1/64; S; Son; 955; Yes; Yes; Unallotted

959; Hardin, Pauline R.; F; 9/12/19-13; N.C. Cherokee; 1/64; S; Dau.; 956; Yes; Yes; Unallotted

960; Hardin, Ada; F; 6/16/21-11; N.C. Cherokee; 1/64; S; Dau.; 957; Yes; Yes; Unallotted

961; Hardin, Virgil; M; 3/13/98-35; N.C. Cherokee; 1/32; M; Head; 958; Yes; Yes; Unallotted

962; Hardin, Frances; F; 4/13/22-10; N.C. Cherokee; 1/64; S; Dau.; 959; Yes; Yes; Unallotted

963; Hardin, William; M; 8/19/04-28; N.C. Cherokee; 1/64; S; Head; 960; Yes; Yes; Unallotted

964; Hardin, Grant; M; 9/9/05-27; N.C. Cherokee; 1/64; S; Bro.; 961; Yes; Yes; Unallotted

965; Hardin, Ruby; F; 4/23/07-25; N.C. Cherokee; 1/64; S; Sis.; 962; Yes; Yes; Unallotted

966; Hardin, Noah; M; 3/25/11-22; N.C. Cherokee; 1/64; S; Bro.; 963; Yes; Yes; Unallotted

967; Hardin, Guy; M; 3/20/13-20; N.C. Cherokee; 1/64; S; Bro.; 964; Yes; Yes; Unallotted

968; Hardin, Fotch; M; 9/11/18-14; N.C. Cherokee; 1/64; S; Bro.; 965; Yes; Yes; Unallotted

969; Hardin, William J.; M; 1/5/72-61; N.C. Cherokee; 1/16; M; Head; 966; Yes; Yes; Unallotted

970; Hardin, Hardie; M; 5/4/00-32; N.C. Cherokee; 1/32; S; Son; 967; Yes; Yes; Unallotted

971; Hardin, Roy; M; 11/18/04-28; N.C. Cherokee; 1/32; S; Son; 968; Yes; Yes; Unallotted

972; Hardin, Paul; M; 3/6/11-22; N.C. Cherokee; 1/32; S; Son; 969; Yes; Yes; Unallotted

973; Hardin, Vincent; M; 11/9/13-19; N.C. Cherokee; 1/32; S; Son; 970; Yes; Yes; Unallotted

974; Hardin, Gurley; M; 11/9/13-19; N.C. Cherokee; 1/32; S; Son; 971; Yes; Yes; Unallotted

975; Harding, Mary J.C.; F; 6/18/77-55; N.C. Cherokee; 1/8; M; Wife; 972; Yes; Yes; Unallotted

976; Harding, Harold; M; 5/28/12-20; N.C. Cherokee; 1/16; S; Son; 973; Yes; Yes; Unallotted

977; Harding, Florence S.; F; 11/27/13-19; N.C. Cherokee; 1/16; S; Dau.; 974; Yes; Yes; Unallotted

Census of the **Eastern Cherokee** reservation of the **Cherokee, N.C.** jurisdiction, as of **April 1** , 19**33,** taken by **R. L. Spalsbury** , Superintendent.

Key: Number; Surname, Given; Sex; Date of Birth-Age at Last Birthday; Tribe; Degree of Blood; Marital Status; Relationship to Head of Family; Last C. Roll No.; At Jurisdiction Where Enrolled (Yes/No); (If no – Where); Ward (Yes/No); Allotment, Annuity and Identification Numbers (if given).

978;   Harding, Lewis E.; M; 10/22/15-17; N.C. Cherokee; 1/16; S; Son; 975; Yes; Yes; Unallotted

979;   Harris, Ollie V.; F; 2/27/73-60; N.C. Cherokee; 1/32; M; Wife; 976; Yes; Yes; Unallotted

980;   Harris, Maggie E.; F; 10/28/06-26; N.C. Cherokee; 1/64; S; Dau.; 977; Yes; Yes; Unallotted

981;   Harris, Mary Lou; F; 1/22/11-22; N.C. Cherokee; 1/64; S; Dau.; 978; Yes; Yes; Unallotted

982;   Harris, Joseph Ed.; M; 1/25/13-20; N.C. Cherokee; 1/64; S; Son; 979; Yes; Yes; Unallotted

983;   Harris, Winnie Mae; F; 2/6/16-17; N.C. Cherokee; 1/64; S; Dau.; 980; Yes; Yes; Unallotted

984;   Harris, Rachel; F; 4/2/82-50; N.C. Cherokee; 4/4; M; Wife; 981; Yes; Yes; Unallotted

985;   Harris, William; M; 6/24/14-18; N.C. Cherokee; 1/2; S; Son; 982; Yes; Yes; Unallotted

986;   Harris, Juanita; F; 12/21/16-16; N.C. Cherokee; 1/2; S; Dau.; 983; Yes; Yes; Unallotted

987;   Hartness, Harvey; M; 6/12/01-31; N.C. Cherokee; 1/64; S; Head; 984; Yes; Yes; Unallotted

988;   Hartness, Jack; M; 6/12/05-27; N.C. Cherokee; 1/64; S; Head; 985; Yes; Yes; Unallotted

989;   Hartness, Julia; F; 6/12/85-47; N.C. Cherokee; 1/32; M; Wife; 986; Yes; Yes; Unallotted

990;   Hartness, Girty L.; F; 8/3/06-26; N.C. Cherokee; 1/64; S; Dau.; 987; Yes; Yes; Unallotted

991;   Hartness, Icey; F; 1/30/08-25; N.C. Cherokee; 1/64; S; Dau.; 988; Yes; Yes; Unallotted

992;   Hawkins (Raper, Dora P.), Dora P.; F; 4/20/82-50; N.C. Cherokee; 1/8; M; Wife; 989; No; Copperhill, Polk, Tenn.; Yes; Unallotted

993;   Hawkins, Charles L.; M; 9/27/03-29; N.C. Cherokee; 1/16; S; Son; 990; No; Copperhill, Polk, Tenn.; Yes; Unallotted

994;   Hawkins, Luther; M; 1/29/09-24; N.C. Cherokee; 1/16; S; Son; 991; No; Copperhill, Polk, Tenn.; Yes; Unallotted

995;   Hawkins, Della May; F; 12/26/10-22; N.C. Cherokee; 1/16; S; Dau.; 992; No; Copperhill, Polk, Tenn.; Yes; Unallotted

996;   Hawkins, Hammond Lee; M; 12/26/12-20; N.C. Cherokee; 1/16; S; Son; 993; No; Copperhill, Polk, Tenn.; Yes; Unallotted

Census of the **Eastern Cherokee** reservation of the **Cherokee, N.C.** jurisdiction, as of **April 1**, 19**33,** taken by **R. L. Spalsbury**, Superintendent.

Key: Number; Surname, Given; Sex; Date of Birth-Age at Last Birthday; Tribe; Degree of Blood; Marital Status; Relationship to Head of Family; Last C. Roll No.; At Jurisdiction Where Enrolled (Yes/No); (If no – Where); Ward (Yes/No); Allotment, Annuity and Identification Numbers (if given).

997;   Hawkins, Ruth; F; 7/30/15-17; N.C. Cherokee; 1/16; S; Dau.; 994; No; Copperhill, Polk, Tenn.; Yes; Unallotted

998;   Hawkins, Maud; F; 6/17/18-14; N.C. Cherokee; 1/16; S; Dau.; 995; No; Copperhill, Polk, Tenn.; Yes; Unallotted

999;   Hawkins, James; M; 8/3/21-11; N.C. Cherokee; 1/16; S; Son; 996; No; Copperhill, Polk, Tenn.; Yes; Unallotted

1000;   Hayes (Mashburn, Mattie), Mattie M.; F; 1/21/03-30; N.C. Cherokee; 3/32; M; Wife; 997; Yes; Yes; Unallotted

1001;   Hayes (Mashburn, Nina), Nina M.; F; 8/22/07-25; N.C. Cherokee; 3/32; M; Wife; 998; Yes; Yes; Unallotted

1002;   Hayman, Bessie Burgess; F; 4/20/96-36; N.C. Cherokee; 1/8; M; Wife; 999; Yes; Yes; Unallotted

1003;   Hensley, Grace Smith; F; 4/21/05-28; N.C. Cherokee; 3/16; M; Wife; 1000; Yes; Yes; Unallotted

1004;   Hensley, Naomi M.; F; 5/25/25-7; N.C. Cherokee; 3/32; S; Dau.; 1001; Yes; Yes; Unallotted

1005;   Hensley (Smith, Louisa), Louisa S.; F; 11/5/81-51; N.C. Cherokee; 1/4; M; Wife; 1002; No; Maryville, Blount, Tenn.; Yes; Unallotted

1006;   Hensley (Lambert, Oney), Oney L.; F; 6/11/06-26; N.C. Cherokee; 1/16; M; Wife; 1003; Yes; Yes; Unallotted

1007;   Henson, Everett; M; 12/25/16-16; N.C. Cherokee; 1/64; S; Alone; 1004; No; Ducktown, Polk, Tenn.; Yes; Unallotted

1008;   Herron (Wolfe, Amanda), Amanda J.W.; F; 9/22/99-33; N.C. Cherokee; 1/8; M; Wife; 1005; Yes; Yes; Unallotted

1009;   Higgins (Smith, Emma), Emma; F; 9/26/88-44; N.C. Cherokee; 1/4; M; Wife; 1006; No; Maryville, Blount, Tenn.; Yes; Unallotted

1010;   Higgins, Rose; F; 12/7/09-23; N.C. Cherokee; 1/8; S; Dau.; 1007; No; Maryville, Blount, Tenn.; Yes; Unallotted

1011;   Higgins, Lillie; F; 3/6/10-23; N.C. Cherokee; 1/8; S; Dau.; 1008; No; Maryville, Blount, Tenn.; Yes; Unallotted

1012;   Higgins, Charles; M; 2/5/13-20; N.C. Cherokee; 1/8; S; Son; 1009; No; Maryville, Blount, Tenn.; Yes; Unallotted

1013;   Higgins, Thelma; F; 9/12/14-18; N.C. Cherokee; 1/8; S; Dau.; 1010; No; Maryville, Blount, Tenn.; Yes; Unallotted

1014;   Higgins, Henry; M; 12/23/18-14; N.C. Cherokee; 1/8; S; Son; 1011; No; Maryville, Blount, Tenn.; Yes; Unallotted

Census of the **Eastern Cherokee** reservation of the **Cherokee, N.C.** jurisdiction, as of **April 1** , 19**33,** taken by **R. L. Spalsbury** , Superintendent.

Key: Number; Surname, Given; Sex; Date of Birth-Age at Last Birthday; Tribe; Degree of Blood; Marital Status; Relationship to Head of Family; Last C. Roll No.; At Jurisdiction Where Enrolled (Yes/No); (If no – Where); Ward (Yes/No); Allotment, Annuity and Identification Numbers (if given).

1015; Higgins, Willie; M; 12/31/22-10; N.C. Cherokee; 1/8; S; Son; 1012; No; Maryville, Blount, Tenn.; Yes; Unallotted

1016; Hill, Abraham; M; 5/15/64-68; N.C. Cherokee; 4/4; M; Head; 1013; Yes; Yes; Unallotted

1017; Hill, Annie; F; 9/20/72-60; N.C. Cherokee; 4/4; M; Wife; 1014; Yes; Yes; Unallotted

1018; Hill, Blaine; M; 7/20/86-46; N.C. Cherokee; 15/16; M; Head; 1015; Yes; Yes; Unallotted

1019; Hill, Luzene; F; 6/12/80-52; N.C. Cherokee; 4/4; M; Wife; 1016; Yes; Yes; Unallotted

1020; Hill, Viola N.; F; 9/27/09-23; N.C. Cherokee; 31/32; S; Dau.; 1017; Yes; Yes; Unallotted

1021; Hill, Elizabeth; F; 12/23/13-19; N.C. Cherokee; 31/32; S; Dau; 1018; Yes; Yes; Unallotted

1022; Hill, Blaine Jr.; M; 10/7/15-17; N.C. Cherokee; 31/32; S; Son; 1019; Yes; Yes; Unallotted

1023; Hill, Lloyd; M; 8/23/17-15; N.C. Cherokee; 31/32; S; Son; 1020; Yes; Yes; Unallotted

1024; Hill (Mr. Viola N.), James R.; M; 13/14/27-6; N.C. Cherokee; 1/4+; S; Grandson; 1021; Yes; Yes; Unallotted

1025; Hill (Mr.[sic] Viola N,), Amelia; F; 8/31/28-4; N.C. Cherokee; 1/4+; S;   Grand Dau.; 1022; Yes; Yes; Unallotted

1026; Hill, John; M; 6/21/56-76; N.C. Cherokee; 4/4; Wd.; Head; 1023; Yes; Yes; Unallotted

1027; Hill, Laura J. Wolfe; F; 4/2/90-42; N.C. Cherokee; 4/4; Wd.; Head; 1024; Yes; Yes; Unallotted

1028; Hill, Ned; M; 9/18/13-19; N.C. Cherokee; 31/32; S; Son; 1025; Yes; Yes; Unallotted

1029; Hill, Rufus Scott; M; 10/4/15-17; N.C. Cherokee; 31/32; S; Son; 1026; Yes; Yes; Unallotted

1030; Hill, Jake; M; 7/7/25-7; N.C. Cherokee; 31/32; S; Son; 1027; Yes; Yes; Unallotted

1031; Hill, Jesse; M; 10/5/27-5; N.C. Cherokee; 31/32; S; Son; 1028; Yes; Yes; Unallotted

1032; Hill, Ned; M; 3/28/88-44; N.C. Cherokee; 15/16; S; Head; 1029; Yes; Yes; Unallotted

1033; Hill, Etta; F; 12/26/74-58; N.C. Cherokee; 4/4; Wd.; Head; 1030; Yes; Yes; Unallotted

Census of the **Eastern Cherokee** reservation of the **Cherokee, N.C.** jurisdiction, as of **April 1**, 19**33,** taken by **R. L. Spalsbury**, Superintendent.

Key: Number; Surname, Given; Sex; Date of Birth-Age at Last Birthday; Tribe; Degree of Blood; Marital Status; Relationship to Head of Family; Last C. Roll No.; At Jurisdiction Where Enrolled (Yes/No); (If no – Where); Ward (Yes/No); Allotment, Annuity and Identification Numbers (if given).

1034; Hipps (Lambert, Nannie), Nannie; F; 11/5/92-40; N.C. Cherokee; 1/16; M; Wife; 1031; Yes; Yes; Unallotted

1035; Hipps, Nina Marie; F; 3/22/13-20; N.C. Cherokee; 1/32; S; Dau.; 1032; Yes; Yes; Unallotted

1036; Hipps, James D.; M; 6/15/17-15; N.C. Cherokee; 1/32; S; Son; 1033; Yes; Yes; Unallotted

1037; Hipps, Emmaline; F; 5/15/20-12; N.C. Cherokee; 1/32; S; Dau.; 1034; Yes; Yes; Unallotted

1038; Hipps, Joshua B.; M; 9/26/23-9; N.C. Cherokee; 1/32; S; Son; 1035; Yes; Yes; Unallotted

1039; Hipps (Lambert, Verdie), Verdie L.; F; 4/28/94-38; N.C. Cherokee; 1/16; M; Wife; 1036; Yes; Yes; Unallotted

1040; Hipps, Bernice Lee; F; 2/24/22-11; N.C. Cherokee; 1/32; S; Dau.; 1037; Yes; Yes; Unallotted

1041; Hipps, Joseph F.; M; 12/3/23-9; N.C. Cherokee; 1/32; S; Son; 1038; Yes; Yes; Unallotted

1042; Hodges, Ollie Jane; F; 1876-57; N.C. Cherokee; 1/4-; M; Wife; 1039; Yes; Yes; Unallotted

1043; Hodges, Ollie; F; 1901-32; N.C. Cherokee; 1/4-; S; Dau.; 1040; Yes; Yes; Unallotted

1044; Hogan (Lee, Edith), Edith L.; F; 6/28/96-36; N.C. Cherokee; 1/16; M; Wife; 1041; Yes; Yes; Unallotted

1045; Hogan, Wayne; M; 12/6/16-16; N.C. Cherokee; 1/32; S; Son; 1042; Yes; Yes; Unallotted

1046; Hogan, Floyd; M; 8/11/18-14; N.C. Cherokee; 1/32; S; Son; 1043; Yes; Yes; Unallotted

1047; Hogan, Norma; F; 11/10/21-11; N.C. Cherokee; 1/32; S; Dau.; 1044; Yes; Yes; Unallotted

1048; Hogan, Faye; F; 5/18/23-9; N.C. Cherokee; 1/32; S; Dau.; 1045; Yes; Yes; Unallotted

1049; Holland, David; M; 11/7/08-24; N.C. Cherokee; 3/8; S; Head; 1046; Yes; Yes; Unallotted

1050; Holland, Jesse; M; 3/12/58-75; N.C. Cherokee; 1/8; M; Head; 1047; Yes; Yes; Unallotted

1051; Hornbuckle, Andy; M; 7/9/03-29; N.C. Cherokee; 3/4; S; Head; 1048; Yes; Yes; Unallotted

1052; Hornbuckle, Charles; M; 4/11/17-15; N.C. Cherokee; 3/32; S; Alone; 1049; Yes; Yes; Unallotted

Census of the **Eastern Cherokee** reservation of the **Cherokee, N.C.** jurisdiction, as of **April 1**, **1933**, taken by **R. L. Spalsbury**, Superintendent.

Key: Number; Surname, Given; Sex; Date of Birth-Age at Last Birthday; Tribe; Degree of Blood; Marital Status; Relationship to Head of Family; Last C. Roll No.; At Jurisdiction Where Enrolled (Yes/No); (If no – Where); Ward (Yes/No); Allotment, Annuity and Identification Numbers (if given).

1053; Hornbuckle, Lottie; F; 3/28/20-13; N.C. Cherokee; 3/32; S; Sis.; 1050; Yes; Yes; Unallotted

1054; Hornbuckle, Daniel; M; 7/7/96-36; N.C. Cherokee; 3/4; M; Head; 1051; Yes; Yes; Unallotted

1055; Hornbuckle, Nannie; F; 5/17/05-27; N.C. Cherokee; 9/16; M; Wife; 1052; Yes; Yes; Unallotted

1056; Hornbuckle, Fred; M; 7/11/97-35; N.C. Cherokee; 1/8; S; Head; 1053; Yes; Yes; Unallotted

1057; Hornbuckle, George; M; 5/4/77-55; N.C. Cherokee; 1/4; M; Head; 1054; Yes; Yes; Unallotted

1058; Hornbuckle, Hartman; M; 4/16/01-31; N.C. Cherokee; 1/8; S; Son; 1055; Yes; Yes; Unallotted

1059; Hornbuckle, Wm. Allen; M; 9/29/07-25; N.C. Cherokee; 1/8; S; Son; 1056; Yes; Yes; Unallotted

1060; Hornbuckle, Clifford; M; 7/1/10-22; N.C. Cherokee; 1/8; S; Son; 1057; Yes; Yes; Unallotted

1061; Hornbuckle, Thurman; M; 8/12/12-20; N.C. Cherokee; 1/8; S; Son; 1058; Yes; Yes; Unallotted

1062; Hornbuckle, Clyda May; F; 7/22/15-17; N.C. Cherokee; 1/8; S; Dau.; 1059; Yes; Yes; Unallotted

1063; Hornbuckle, Benjamin; M; 7/19/18-14; N.C. Cherokee; 1/8; S; Son; 1060; Yes; Yes; Unallotted

1064; Hornbuckle, Israel; M; 6/9/87-45; N.C. Cherokee; 7/8; M; Head; 1061; Yes; Yes; Unallotted

1065; Hornbuckle, Addie Queen; F; 2/5/02-31; N.C. Cherokee; 5/8; M; Wife; 1062; Yes; Yes; Unallotted

1066; Hornbuckle, Jeff D.; M; 5/4/64-68; N.C. Cherokee; 1/2; M; Head; 1063; Yes; Yes; Unallotted

1067; Hornbuckle, Aninih B.; F; 12/21/48-84; N.C. Cherokee; 4/4; M; Wife; 1064; Yes; Yes; Unallotted

1068; Hornbuckle, Jeff D. Jr.; M; 9/27/92-40; N.C. Cherokee; 3/4; M; Head; 1065; Yes; Yes; Unallotted

1069; Hornbuckle, Sallie Otter; F; 11/9/01-31; N.C. Cherokee; 4/4; M; Wife; 1066; Yes; Yes; Unallotted

1070; Hornbuckle, Callie; F; 1/2/22-11; N.C. Cherokee; 7/8; S; Dau.; 1067; Yes; Yes; Unallotted

1071; Hornbuckle, Mattie; F; 12/21/63-69; N.C. Cherokee; 4/4; Wd.; Head; 1068; Yes; Yes; Unallotted

Census of the **Eastern Cherokee** reservation of the **Cherokee, N.C.** jurisdiction, as of **April 1** , **1933,** taken by **R. L. Spalsbury** , Superintendent.

Key: Number; Surname, Given; Sex; Date of Birth-Age at Last Birthday; Tribe; Degree of Blood; Marital Status; Relationship to Head of Family; Last C. Roll No.; At Jurisdiction Where Enrolled (Yes/No); (If no – Where); Ward (Yes/No); Allotment, Annuity and Identification Numbers (if given).

1072; Hornbuckle, John R.; M; 9/16/05-27; N.C. Cherokee; 1/8; M; Head; 1069; Yes; Yes; Unallotted

1073; Hornbuckle, Stacy C.; F; 11/29/09-23; N.C. Cherokee; 7/8; M; Wife; 1070; Yes; Yes; Unallotted

1074; Hornbuckle, Larens; M; 2/13/28-5; N.C. Cherokee; 1/2; S; Son; 1071; Yes; Yes; Unallotted

1075; Hornbuckle, Jean E.; F; 10/23/29-3; N.C. Cherokee; 1/2; S; Dau.; 1072; Yes; Yes; Unallotted

1076; Hornbuckle, Johnson; M; 11/19/01-31; N.C. Cherokee; 1/2; S; Head; 1073; Yes; Yes; Unallotted

1077; Hornbuckle, Julius; M; 2/2/00-33; N.C. Cherokee; 1/4; S; Head; 1074; Yes; Yes; Unallotted

1078; Hornbuckle, Maggie; F; 5/1/80-52; N.C. Cherokee; 7/8; S; Head; 1075; Yes; Yes; Unallotted

1079; Hornbuckle, William; M; 1/20/69-64; N.C. Cherokee; 1/4; M; Head; 1076; Yes; Yes; Unallotted

1080; Hornbuckle, Mary Maney; F; 6/19/04-28; N.C. Cherokee; 1/2; M; Wife; 1077; Yes; Yes; Unallotted

1081; Hornbuckle, Jennie; F; 3/6/11-22; N.C. Cherokee; 1/8; S; Dau.; 1078; Yes; Yes; Unallotted

1082; Hornbuckle, Minnie May; F; 9/4/21-11; N.C. Cherokee; 3/8; S; Dau.; 1079; Yes; Yes; Unallotted

1083; Hornbuckle, John S.; M; 5/9/25-7; N.C. Cherokee; 3/8; S; Son; 1080; Yes; Yes; Unallotted

1084; Hornbuckle, Evelyn N.; F; 1/22/30-2; N.C. Cherokee; 3/8; S; Dau.; 1081; Yes; Yes; Unallotted

1085; Hornbuckle, William; M; 12/25/81-51; N.C. Cherokee; 7/8; M; Head; 1082; Yes; Yes; Unallotted

1086; Hornbuckle, Annie O.; F; 5/31/94-38; N.C. Cherokee; 15/16; M; Wife; 1083; Yes; Yes; Unallotted

1087; Hornbuckle, Polly B.; F; 11/28/06-24; N.C. Cherokee; 1/16; Wd.; Head; 1084; Yes; Yes; Unallotted

1088; Hunter (Patterson, Celia), Celia; F; 6/12/01-31; N.C. Cherokee; 1/32; M; Wife; 1085; Yes; Yes; Unallotted

1089; Hunter, Agnes; F; 1/21/24-9; N.C. Cherokee; 1/64; S; Dau.; 1086; Yes; Yes; Unallotted

1090; Huskey, Birdie C.H.; F; 4/12/11-21; N.C. Cherokee; 31/32; M; Wife; 1087; Yes; Yes; Unallotted

Census of the **Eastern Cherokee** reservation of the **Cherokee, N.C.** jurisdiction, as of **April 1** , 19**33**, taken by   **R. L. Spalsbury**   , Superintendent.

Key: Number; Surname, Given; Sex; Date of Birth-Age at Last Birthday; Tribe; Degree of Blood; Marital Status; Relationship to Head of Family; Last C. Roll No.; At Jurisdiction Where Enrolled (Yes/No); (If no – Where); Ward (Yes/No); Allotment, Annuity and Identification Numbers (if given).

1091;   Hyde (Rose, Carrie), Carrie R.; F; 4/10/04-28; N.C. Cherokee; 1/16; M; Wife; 1088; Yes; Yes; Unallotted

1092;   Jackson (Raper, Dovie), Dovie; F; 3/15/03-30; N.C. Cherokee; 1/16; M; Wife; 1089; Yes; Yes; Unallotted

1093;   Jackson, Thelma Lee; F; 10/29/22-10; N.C. Cherokee; 1/32; S; Dau.; 1090; Yes; Yes; Unallotted

1094;   Jackson, Carl; M; 5/19/24-8; N.C. Cherokee; 1/32; S; Son; 1091; Yes; Yes; Unallotted

1095;   Jackson, Eddie; M; 3/10/04-29; N.C. Cherokee; 4/4; M; Head; 1092; Yes; Yes; Unallotted

1096;   Jackson, Margaret A.; F; 6/15/06-26; N.C. Cherokee; 15/16; M; Wife; 1093; Yes; Yes; Unallotted

1097;   Jackson, Edward; M; 8/30/26-6; N.C. Cherokee; 31/32; S; Son; 1094; Yes; Yes; Unallotted

1098;   Jackson, Lula; F; 3/13/32-1; N.C. Cherokee; 31/32; S; Dau.; 1095; Yes; Yes; Unallotted

1099;   Jackson, Jack; M; 2/2/92-41; N.C. Cherokee; 7/16; M; Head; 1096; Yes; Yes; Unallotted

1100;   Jackson, Mary Queen; F; 3/15/03-30; N.C. Cherokee; 5/8; M; Wife; 1097; Yes; Yes; Unallotted

1101;   Jackson, Walter S.; M; 5/29/23-9; N.C. Cherokee; 17/32; S; Son; 1098; Yes; Yes; Unallotted

1102;   Jackson, John S.; M; 1/21/25-8; N.C. Cherokee; 17/32; S; Son; 1099; Yes; Yes; Unallotted

1103;   Jackson, Boyd S.; M; 3/7/27-6; N.C. Cherokee; 17/32; S; Son; 1100; Yes; Yes; Unallotted

1104;   Jackson, Neoma K.; F; 2/26/29-4; N.C. Cherokee; 17/32; S; Dau.; 1101; Yes; Yes; Unallotted

1105;   Jackson, Mary E.; F; 8/12/31-1; N.C. Cherokee; 17/32; S; Dau.; 1102; Yes; Yes; Unallotted

1106;   Jackson, Jacob; M; 12/22/00-32; N.C. Cherokee; 4/4; M; Head; 1103; Yes; Yes; Unallotted

1107;   Jackson, Olivan B.; F; 7/18/01-31; N.C. Cherokee; 4/4; M; Wife; 1104; Yes; Yes; Unallotted

1108;   Jackson, Elijah; M; 5/16/18-14; N.C. Cherokee; 4/4; S; Son; 1105; Yes; Yes; Unallotted

1109;   Jackson, Bessie; F; 6/22/24-8; N.C. Cherokee; 4/4; S; Dau.; 1106; Yes; Yes; Unallotted

1110;   Jackson, John; M; 2/1/29-4; N.C. Cherokee; 4/4; S; Son; 1107; Yes; Yes; Unallotted

Census of the **Eastern Cherokee** reservation of the **Cherokee, N.C.** jurisdiction, as of **April 1** , **1933,** taken by **R. L. Spalsbury** , Superintendent.

Key: Number; Surname, Given; Sex; Date of Birth-Age at Last Birthday; Tribe; Degree of Blood; Marital Status; Relationship to Head of Family; Last C. Roll No.; At Jurisdiction Where Enrolled (Yes/No); (If no – Where); Ward (Yes/No); Allotment, Annuity and Identification Numbers (if given).

1111; Jackson, Jennie A.H.; F; 5/25/86-46; N.C. Cherokee; 3/4; M; Wife; 1108; Yes; Yes; Unallotted

1112; Jackson, Lawyer; M; 5/9/72-60; N.C. Cherokee; 4/4; M; Head; 1109; Yes; Yes; Unallotted

1113; Jackson, Dekie; F; 10/5/71-61; N.C. Cherokee; 4/4; M; Wife; 1110; Yes; Yes; Unallotted

1114; Jackson, Florence; F; 5/19/02-30; N.C. Cherokee; 4/4; S; Dau.; 1111; Yes; Yes; Unallotted

1115; Jackson (Murphy, Margaret), Margaret M.; F; 4/17/89-43; N.C. Cherokee; 1/8; M; Wife; 1112; Yes; Yes; Unallotted

1116; Hipps, Willard; M; 3/3/07-26; N.C. Cherokee; 1/16; S; Son; 1113; Yes; Yes; Unallotted

1117; Jackson, Robert; M; 10/24/75-57; N.C. Cherokee; 4/4; M; Head; 1114; Yes; Yes; Unallotted

1118; Jackson, Caroline; F; 4/30/77-55; N.C. Cherokee; 4/4; M; Wife; 1115; Yes; Yes; Unallotted

1119; Jackson, Isaac; M; 8/30/08-24; N.C. Cherokee; 4/4; S; Son; 1116; Yes; Yes; Unallotted

1120; Jackson, Stacey; F; 1/18/60-73; N.C. Cherokee; 4/4; Wd.; Head; 1117; Yes; Yes; Unallotted

1121; Jackson, Wesley; M; 10/17/99-33; N.C. Cherokee; 4/4; Div.; Head; 1118; Yes; Yes; Unallotted

1122; Jacobs (Driver, Helen), Helen E.; F; 6/7/08-24; N.C. Cherokee; 1/2; M; Wife; 1119; No; Mechanicsburg, Cunberland, Pa.; Yes; Unallotted

1123; James, Allen; M; 3/29/98-35; N.C. Cherokee; 1/64; S; Head; 1120; Yes; Yes; Unallotted

1124; James, Asa; M; 6/25/87-45; N.C. Cherokee; 1/64; M; Head; 1121; Yes; Yes; Unallotted

1125; James, Annie; F; 1/21/09-24; N.C. Cherokee; 1/128; S; Dau.; 1122; Yes; Yes; Unallotted

1126; James, Frank; M; 12/8/11-21; N.C. Cherokee; 1/128; S; Son; 1123; Yes; Yes; Unallotted

1127; James, Geneva; F; 8/5/14-18; N.C. Cherokee; 1/128; S; Dau.; 1124; Yes; Yes; Unallotted

1128; James, Sheridan; M; 4/29/17-15; N.C. Cherokee; 1/128; S; Son; 1125; Yes; Yes; Unallotted

Census of the **Eastern Cherokee** reservation of the **Cherokee, N.C.** jurisdiction, as of **April 1** , 1933, taken by **R. L. Spalsbury** , Superintendent.

Key: Number; Surname, Given; Sex; Date of Birth-Age at Last Birthday; Tribe; Degree of Blood; Marital Status; Relationship to Head of Family; Last C. Roll No.; At Jurisdiction Where Enrolled (Yes/No); (If no – Where); Ward (Yes/No); Allotment, Annuity and Identification Numbers (if given).

1129;   James, Dorothy; F; 11/27/19-13; N.C. Cherokee; 1/128; S; Dau.; 1126; Yes; Yes; Unallotted

1130;   James, Roscoe; M; 3/11/22-11; N.C. Cherokee; 1/128; S; Son; 1127; Yes; Yes; Unallotted

1131;   Jenkins (Cooper, Myrtle), Myrtle; F; 10/6/02-30; N.C. Cherokee; 1/16; M; Wife; 1128; Yes; Yes; Unallotted

1132;   Jessan, Nellie W.; F; 6/2/96-36; N.C. Cherokee; 7/8; Wd.; Head; 1129; Yes; Yes; Unallotted

1133;   Jessan, Elnora; F; 6/16/08-24; N.C. Cherokee; 13/16; S; Step-dau.; 1130; Yes; Yes; Unallotted

1134;   Jessan, Lillian; F; 8/10/10-22; N.C. Cherokee; 13/16; S; Step-dau.; 1131; Yes; Yes; Unallotted

1135;   Jessan, John J.; M; 5/10/13-19; N.C. Cherokee; 13/16; S; Step-son; 1132; Yes; Yes; Unallotted

1136;   Jessan, Mary Holt; F; 9/10/18-14; N.C. Cherokee; 7/8; S; Dau.; 1133; Yes; Yes; Unallotted

1137;   Jessan, Sim DeHart; M; 1/3/03-30; N.C. Cherokee; 4/4; M; Head; 1134; Yes; Yes; Unallotted

1138;   Jessan, Agnes Long; F; 1/19/04-29; N.C. Cherokee; 4/4; M; Wife; 1135; Yes; Yes; Unallotted

1139;   Johnson, Addison; M; 6/28/86-46; N.C. Cherokee; 3/8; M; Head; 1136; Yes; Yes; Unallotted

1140;   Johnson, Isaac; M; 7/14/93-39; N.C. Cherokee; 1/4; S; Head; 1137; Yes; Yes; Unallotted

1141;   Johnson (Loudermilk, Rebecca), Rebecca; F; 8/23/99-33; N.C. Cherokee; 1/16; M; Wife; 1138; Yes; Yes; Unallotted

1142;   Johnson, Tom; M; 5/16/09-23; N.C. Cherokee; 4/4; S; Head; 1139; Yes; Yes; Unallotted

1143;   Johnson, Jonah; M; 6/27/11-21; N.C. Cherokee; 4/4; S; Bro.; 1140; Yes; Yes; Unallotted

1144;   Johnson, Tuskegie; M; 12/22/78-55; N.C. Cherokee; 4/4; M; Head; 1141; Yes; Yes; Unallotted

1145;   Johnson, Sally O.; F; 12/22/84-48; N.C. Cherokee; 4/4; M; Wife; 1142; Yes; Yes; Unallotted

1146;   Johnson, Charles; M; 11/17/14-18; N.C. Cherokee; 4/4; S; Son; 1143; Yes; Yes; Unallotted

Census of the **Eastern Cherokee** reservation of the **Cherokee, N.C.** jurisdiction, as of **April 1**, **1933,** taken by **R. L. Spalsbury**, Superintendent.

Key: Number; Surname, Given; Sex; Date of Birth-Age at Last Birthday; Tribe; Degree of Blood; Marital Status; Relationship to Head of Family; Last C. Roll No.; At Jurisdiction Where Enrolled (Yes/No); (If no – Where); Ward (Yes/No); Allotment, Annuity and Identification Numbers (if given).

1147;   Johnson, Yona; M; 12/25/79-53; N.C. Cherokee; 4/4; M; Head; 1144; Yes; Yes; Unallotted

1148;   Johnson, Margaret G.; F; 9/14/12-20; N.C. Cherokee; 15/16; S; Dau.; 1145; Yes; Yes; Unallotted

1149;   Johnson, Joseph L.; M; 11/16/16-16; N.C. Cherokee; 15/16; S; Son; 1146; Yes; Yes; Unallotted

1150;   Johnson, Lloyd H.; M; 11/5/19-13; N.C. Cherokee; 15/16; S; Son; 1147; Yes; Yes; Unallotted

1151;   Jones (Hardin, Verdia), Verdia; F; 2/18/04-29; N.C. Cherokee; 1/32; M; Wife; 1148; Yes; Yes; Unallotted

1152;   Jones, Lyle; M; 6/14/23-10; N.C. Cherokee; 1/64; S; Son; 1149; Yes; Yes; Unallotted

1153;   Jordan (Lambert, Julia), Julia; F; 4/22/01-31; N.C. Cherokee; 1/16; M; Wife; 1150; Yes; Yes; Unallotted

1154;   Jordan, Wm. Carson; M; 3/5/20-13; N.C. Cherokee; 1/32; S; Son; 1151; Yes; Yes; Unallotted

1155;   Jordan, Mary E.; F; 1/3/23-10; N.C. Cherokee; 1/32; S; Dau.; 1152; Yes; Yes; Unallotted

1156;   Jordan, Clyde; M; 1880-53; N.C. Cherokee; 1/4-; M; Head; 1153; Yes; Yes; Unallotted

1157;   Jordan, Jake A.; M; 1890-43; N.C. Cherokee; 1/4-; M; Husb.; 1154; Yes; Yes; Unallotted

1158;   Jordan, John J.; M; 1886-47; N.C. Cherokee; 1/4-; M; Husb.; 1155; Yes; Yes; Unallotted

1159;   Jordan, John M.; M; 1893-40; N.C. Cherokee; 1/4-; S; Sing.; 1156; Yes; Yes; Unallotted

1160;   Jordan, Mark; M; 1873-60; N.C. Cherokee; 1/4-; M; Husb.; 1157; Yes; Yes; Unallotted

1161;   Jordan, Della; F; 1915-18; N.C. Cherokee; 1/4-; S; Dau.; 1158; Yes; Yes; Unallotted

1162;   Jordan, Leona; F; 1920-13; N.C. Cherokee; 1/4-; S; Dau.; 1159; Yes; Yes; Unallotted

1163;   Jordan, Zora; F; 1921-12; N.C. Cherokee; 1/4-; S; Dau.; 1160; Yes; Yes; Unallotted

1164;   Jordan, Wm. A.; M; 1889-44; N.C. Cherokee; 1/4-; M; Husb.; 1161; Yes; Yes; Unallotted

1165;   Jumper, Edward; M; 12/25/00-32; N.C. Cherokee; 4/4; M; Head; 1162; Yes; Yes; Unallotted

1166;   Jumper, Nancy W.; F; 7/4/06-26; N.C. Cherokee; 4/4; M; Wife; 1163; Yes; Yes; Unallotted

Census of the **Eastern Cherokee** reservation of the **Cherokee, N.C.** jurisdiction, as of **April 1** , **1933,** taken by **R. L. Spalsbury** , Superintendent.

Key: Number; Surname, Given; Sex; Date of Birth-Age at Last Birthday; Tribe; Degree of Blood; Marital Status; Relationship to Head of Family; Last C. Roll No.; At Jurisdiction Where Enrolled (Yes/No); (If no – Where); Ward (Yes/No); Allotment, Annuity and Identification Numbers (if given).

1167; Jumper, Ute; M; 7/21/23-9; N.C. Cherokee; 4/4; S; Son; 1164; Yes; Yes; Unallotted

1168; Jumper, Stancill; M; 10/24/99-33; N.C. Cherokee; 4/4; M; Head; 1165; Yes; Yes; Unallotted

1169; Jumper, Nola Long; F; 6/27/99-33; N.C. Cherokee; 4/4; M; Wife; 1166; Yes; Yes; Unallotted

1170; Jumper, Leona; F; 1/10/26-7; N.C. Cherokee; 4/4; S; Dau.; 1167; Yes; Yes; Unallotted

1171; Jumper, Nellie; F; 11/15/27-5; N.C. Cherokee; 4/4; S; Dau.; 1168; Yes; Yes; Unallotted

1172; Jumper, Stancill, Jr.; M; 2/15/30-3; N.C. Cherokee; 4/4; S; Son; 1169; Yes; Yes; Unallotted

1173; Jumper, Ute; M; 5/10/71-61; N.C. Cherokee; 4/4; M; Head; 1170; Yes; Yes; Unallotted

1174; Jumper, Betsy; F; 12/22/72-60; N.C. Cherokee; 4/4; M; Wife; 1171; Yes; Yes; Unallotted

1175; Jumper, James; M; 3/24/04-29; N.C. Cherokee; 4/4; S; Son; 1172; Yes; Yes; Unallotted

1176; Jumper, Thomas; M; 6/18/06-26; N.C. Cherokee; 4/4; S; Son; 1173; Yes; Yes; Unallotted

1177; Jumper, Henry; M; 6/21/08-24; N.C. Cherokee; 4/4; S; Son; 1174; Yes; Yes; Unallotted

1178; Jumper, Ella; F; 10/23/09-23; N.C. Cherokee; 4/4; S; Dau.; 1175; Yes; Yes; Unallotted

1179; Junaluskie, Emmaline; F; 11/8/98-34; N.C. Cherokee; 15/16; WD.; Head; 1176; Yes; Yes; Unallotted

1180; Junaluskie, Martha; F; 9/5/16-16; N.C. Cherokee; 31/32; S; Dau.; 1177; Yes; Yes; Unallotted

1181; Junaluskie, Mark; M; 9/19/17-15; N.C. Cherokee; 31/32; S; Son; 1178; Yes; Yes; Unallotted

1182; Junaluskie, Winnie; F; 5/5/19-13; N.C. Cherokee; 31/32; S; Dau.; 1179; Yes; Yes; Unallotted

1183; Junaluskie, Sallie Ann; F; 2/1/21-12; N.C. Cherokee; 31/32; S; Dau.; 1180; Yes; Yes; Unallotted

1184; Junaluskie, Arch; M; 2/19/23-10; N.C. Cherokee; 31/32; S; Son; 1181; Yes; Yes; Unallotted

1185; Junaluskie, Lillian; F; 1/25/32-1; N.C. Cherokee; 31/32; S; Dau.; 1182; Yes; Yes; Unallotted

1186; Kalonuheskie, Abraham; M; 8/1/84-48; N.C. Cherokee; 4/4; M; Head; 1183; Yes; Yes; Unallotted

Census of the **Eastern Cherokee** reservation of the **Cherokee, N.C.** jurisdiction, as of **April 1** , **1933,** taken by **R. L. Spalsbury** , Superintendent.

Key: Number; Surname, Given; Sex; Date of Birth-Age at Last Birthday; Tribe; Degree of Blood; Marital Status; Relationship to Head of Family; Last C. Roll No.; At Jurisdiction Where Enrolled (Yes/No); (If no – Where); Ward (Yes/No); Allotment, Annuity and Identification Numbers (if given).

1187; Kalonuheskie, Charles; M; 1/19/87-46; N.C. Cherokee; 1/2; M; Head; 1184; Yes; Yes; Unallotted

1188; Kalonuheskie, Sallie L.; F; 1/19/78-55; N.C. Cherokee; 1/2; M; Wife; 1185; Yes; Yes; Unallotted

1189; Kalonuheskie, Styles; M; 1/19/17-16; N.C. Cherokee; 1/2; S; Son; 1186; Yes; Yes; Unallotted

1190; Kalonuheskie, Edith; F; 8/16/08-21; N.C. Cherokee; 1/2; S; Alone; 1187; Yes; Yes; Unallotted

1191; Kalonuheskie, Esiah; M; 9/15/55-77; N.C. Cherokee; 4/4; Wd.; Head; 1188; Yes; Yes; Unallotted

1192; Kalonuheskie, Martha; F; 11/26/02-30; N.C. Cherokee; 1/2; S; Head; 1189; Yes; Yes; Unallotted

1193; Kalonuheskie, Nannie; F; 1/19/98-35; N.C. Cherokee; 4/4; S; Mother; 1190; Yes; Yes; Unallotted

1194; Kalonuheskie, Philip; M; 12/1/18-14; N.C. Cherokee; 13/16; S; Son; 1191; Yes; Yes; Unallotted

1195; Kalonuheskie, Tahow; M; 3/11/25-7; N.C. Cherokee; 1/2; S; Son; 1192; Yes; Yes; Unallotted

1196; Queen, Bascom; M; 1/18/32-1; N.C. Cherokee; 15/16; S; Son; 1193; Yes; Yes; Unallotted

1197; Kalonuheskie, Tom; M; 12/25/88-44; N.C. Cherokee; 1/2; M; Head; 1194; Yes; Yes; Unallotted

1198; Kalonuheskie, Awee S.; F; 11/13/98-34; N.C. Cherokee; 4/4; M; Wife; 1195; Yes; Yes; Unallotted

1199; Junaluskie, Leone; F; 11/17/16-16; N.C. Cherokee; 3/4; S; Dau.; 1196; Yes; Yes; Unallotted

1200; Kalonuheskie, Gwynn; M; 10/27/18-14; N.C. Cherokee; 3/4; S; Son; 1197; Yes; Yes; Unallotted

1201; Kalonuheskie, Simon; M; 11/27/22-10; N.C. Cherokee; 3/4; S; Son; 1198; Yes; Yes; Unallotted

1202; Keg, Matthews; M; 3/25/66-67; N.C. Cherokee; 3/4; M; Head; 1199; Yes; Yes; Unallotted

1203; Keg, Kiney Ben; F; 12/24/82-50; N.C. Cherokee; 4/4; M; Wife; 1200; Yes; Yes; Unallotted

1204; Quince, Jennie; F; 7/20/14-18; N.C. Cherokee; 4/4; S; St-Dau; 1201; Yes; Yes; Unallotted

1205; Kidd, David; M; 6/23/66-66; N.C. Cherokee; 1/32; M; Head; 1202; Yes; Yes; Unallotted

Census of the **Eastern Cherokee** reservation of the **Cherokee, N.C.** jurisdiction, as of **April 1** , 19**33,** taken by **R. L. Spalsbury** , Superintendent.

Key: Number; Surname, Given; Sex; Date of Birth-Age at Last Birthday; Tribe; Degree of Blood; Marital Status; Relationship to Head of Family; Last C. Roll No.; At Jurisdiction Where Enrolled (Yes/No); (If no – Where); Ward (Yes/No); Allotment, Annuity and Identification Numbers (if given).

1206; Kidd, Goffrey; M; 6/6/18-14; N.C. Cherokee; 1/64; S; Son; 1203; Yes; Yes; Unallotted

~~1207; Kidd, Luther; M;~~[sic]

1208; Kidd, Luther; M; 7/15/04-28; N.C. Cherokee; 1/64; S; Head; 1204; Yes; Yes; Unallotted

1209; Kidd, Walter; M; 2/8/89-44; N.C. Cherokee; 1/64; M; Head; 1205; Yes; Yes; Unallotted

1210; Kidd, Marcus; M; 5/22/14-18; N.C. Cherokee; 1/128; S; Son; 1206; Yes; Yes; Unallotted

1211; Kidd, Crawford; M; 5/16/16-16; N.C. Cherokee; 1/128; S; Son; 1207; Yes; Yes; Unallotted

1212; Kidd, Wm. H.; M; 5/26/97-35; N.C. Cherokee; 1/64; M; Head; 1208; Yes; Yes; Unallotted

1213; Killian (Raper, Viola), Viola E.; F; 12/19/03-29; N.C. Cherokee; 1/16; M; Wife; 1209; Yes; Yes; Unallotted

1214; Killingsworth (Thompson, Iris), Iris; F; 7/3/05-27; N.C. Cherokee; 1/16; M; Wife; 1210; Yes; Yes; Unallotted

1215; Killpatrick, Lydia; F; 3/19/00-33; N.C. Cherokee; 1/64; M; Wife; 1211; Yes; Yes; Unallotted

1216; King, (Tommy) Frederick; M; 11/18/18-14; N.C. Cherokee; 1/32; S; Alone; 1212; Yes; Yes; Unallotted

1217; Kunteeskih, Sahwahohi; F; 12/22/47-85; N.C. Cherokee; 4/4; Wd.; Head; 1213; Yes; Yes; Unallotted

1218; Kurry, Mandy Axe; F; 1/13/99-34; N.C. Cherokee; 4/4; M; Wife; 1214; Yes; Yes; Unallotted

1219; Kyker (Anderson, Bessie), Bessie; F; 8/11/02-30; N.C. Cherokee; 1/16; M; Wife; 1215; Yes; Yes; Unallotted

1220; Ladd (Rogers, Bonnie), Bonnie; F; 1/13/92-41; N.C. Cherokee; 1/8; M; Wife; 1216; Yes; Yes; Unallotted

1221; Ladd, Max; M; 3/9/11-22; N.C. Cherokee; 1/16; S; Son; 1217; Yes; Yes; Unallotted

1222; Ladd, Fay; F; 11/17/13-19; N.C. Cherokee; 1/16; S; Dau.; 1218; Yes; Yes; Unallotted

Census of the **Eastern Cherokee** reservation of the **Cherokee, N.C.** jurisdiction, as of **April 1** , 19**33**, taken by **R. L. Spalsbury** , Superintendent.

Key: Number; Surname, Given; Sex; Date of Birth-Age at Last Birthday; Tribe; Degree of Blood; Marital Status; Relationship to Head of Family; Last C. Roll No.; At Jurisdiction Where Enrolled (Yes/No); (If no – Where); Ward (Yes/No); Allotment, Annuity and Identification Numbers (if given).

1223; Ladd, Fern; F; 1/1/16-17; N.C. Cherokee; 1/16; S; Dau.; 1219; Yes; Yes; Unallotted

1224; Ladd, Glen; M; 3/30/33-1 day; N.C. Cherokee; 1/16; S; Son; ---; Yes; Yes; Unallotted

1225; Lambert, Andrew J.; M; 1/20/01-32; N.C. Cherokee; 1/32; M; Head; 1220; Yes; Yes; Unallotted

1226; Lambert, Nola Griffin; F; 9/27/10-22; N.C. Cherokee; 1/32; M; Wife; 1221; Yes; Yes; Unallotted

1227; Lambert, Charley; M; 11/14/85-47; N.C. Cherokee; 9/16; Wd.; Head; 1222; Yes; Yes; Unallotted

1228; Lambert, Jackson; M; 1/10/06-27; N.C. Cherokee; 21/32; S; Son; 1223; Yes; Yes; Unallotted

1229; Lambert, John Adam; M; 2/28/11-22; N.C. Cherokee; 21/32; S; Son; 1224; Yes; Yes; Unallotted

1230; Lambert, Luvenia; F; 5/20/15-17; N.C. Cherokee; 21/32; S; Dau.; 1225; Yes; Yes; Unallotted

1231; Lambert, Guy; M; 10/20/17-15; N.C. Cherokee; 21/32; S; Son; 1226; Yes; Yes; Unallotted

1232; Lambert, Mianna; F; 12/27/19-13; N.C. Cherokee; 25/32; S; Dau.; 1227; Yes; Yes; Unallotted

1233; Lambert, Lucinda; F; 4/13/22-10; N.C. Cherokee; 25/32; S; Dau.; 1228; Yes; Yes; Unallotted

1234; Lambert, Charlie; M; 3/20/89-44; N.C. Cherokee; 1/16; M; Head; 1229; Yes; Yes; Unallotted

1235; Lambert, Maggie W.; F; 9/9/00-32; N.C. Cherokee; 3/4; M; Wife; 1230; Yes; Yes; Unallotted

1236; Lambert, Joseph R.; M; 11/27/25-7; N.C. Cherokee; 13/32; S; Son; 1231; Yes; Yes; Unallotted

1237; Lambert, William N.; M; 3/18/28-5; N.C. Cherokee; 13/32; S; Son; 1232; Yes; Yes; Unallotted

1238; Lambert, Herbert A.; M; 6/7/31-1; N.C. Cherokee; 13/32; S; Son; 1233; Yes; Yes; Unallotted

1239; Lambert, Claude; M; 1/2/91-42; N.C. Cherokee; 1/16; M; Head; 1234; Yes; Yes; Unallotted

1240; Lambert, Ibeuria; F; 2/16/13-20; N.C. Cherokee; 1/32; S; Dau.; 1235; Yes; Yes; Unallotted

1241; Lambert, Georgia; F; 7/8/17-15; N.C. Cherokee; 1/32; S; Dau.; 1236; Yes; Yes; Unallotted

1242; Lambert, Jack Wm.; M; 2/11/20-13; N.C. Cherokee; 1/32; S; Son; 1237; Yes; Yes; Unallotted

Census of the **Eastern Cherokee** reservation of the **Cherokee, N.C.** jurisdiction, as of **April 1** , 19**33**, taken by **R. L. Spalsbury** , Superintendent.

Key: Number; Surname, Given; Sex; Date of Birth-Age at Last Birthday; Tribe; Degree of Blood; Marital Status; Relationship to Head of Family; Last C. Roll No.; At Jurisdiction Where Enrolled (Yes/No); (If no – Where); Ward (Yes/No); Allotment, Annuity and Identification Numbers (if given).

1243; Lambert, Samuel D.; M; 11/11/22-10; N.C. Cherokee; 1/32; S; Son; 1238; Yes; Yes; Unallotted

1244; Lambert, Columbus; M; 12/25/71-61; N.C. Cherokee; 1/16; M; Head; 1239; Yes; Yes; Unallotted

1245; Howard (Lambert, Cora), Cora P.; F; 2/21/06-28; N.C. Cherokee; 1/32; M; Wife; 1240; Yes; Yes; Unallotted

1246; Lambert, Leonard C.; M; 1/25/08-25; N.C. Cherokee; 1/32; S; Head; 1241; Yes; Yes; Unallotted

1247; Lambert, Willard; M; 7/6/10-22; N.C. Cherokee; 1/32; S; Bro.; 1242; Yes; Yes; Unallotted

1248; Lambert, Gillian; M; 7/4/12-20; N.C. Cherokee; 1/32; S; Bro.; 1243; Yes; Yes; Unallotted

1249; Lambert, Leona; F; 2/19/15-18; N.C. Cherokee; 1/32; S; Sis.; 1244; Yes; Yes; Unallotted

1250; Lambert, Philip; M; 1/31/18-15; N.C. Cherokee; 1/32; S; Bro.; 1245; Yes; Yes; Unallotted

1251; Lambert, Corbett; M; 3/12/97-36; N.C. Cherokee; 1/16; M; Head; 1246; Yes; Yes; Unallotted

1252; Lambert, Robert; M; 10/3/20-12; N.C. Cherokee; 1/32; S; Son; 1247; Yes; Yes; Unallotted

1253; Lambert, Samuel C.; M; 1/19/23-10; N.C. Cherokee; 1/32; S; Son; 1248; Yes; Yes; Unallotted

1254; Lambert, Edward; M; 3/21/85-46; N.C. Cherokee; 1/16; M; Head; 1249; Yes; Yes; Unallotted

1255; Lambert, Edward Monroe; M; 11/15/08-24; N.C. Cherokee; 1/32; S; Head; 1250; Yes; Yes; Unallotted

1256; Lambert, Fitzsimmons; M; 5/19/96-36; N.C. Cherokee; 1/16; M; Head; 1251; Yes; Yes; Unallotted

1257; Lambert, Fred G.; M; 8/1/91-42; N.C. Cherokee; 1/16; M; Head; 1252; Yes; Yes; Unallotted

1258; Lambert, Wymer Holt; M; 12/18/15-17; N.C. Cherokee; 1/32; S; Son; 1253; Yes; Yes; Unallotted

1259; Lambert, Venoia; F; 5/17/17-15; N.C. Cherokee; 1/32; S; Dau.; 1254; Yes; Yes; Unallotted

1260; Lambert, Joyce; F; 9/13/23-9; N.C. Cherokee; 1/32; S; Dau.; 1255; Yes; Yes; Unallotted

Census of the **Eastern Cherokee** reservation of the **Cherokee, N.C.** jurisdiction, as of **April 1** , **1933**, taken by **R. L. Spalsbury** , Superintendent.

Key: Number; Surname, Given; Sex; Date of Birth-Age at Last Birthday; Tribe; Degree of Blood; Marital Status; Relationship to Head of Family; Last C. Roll No.; At Jurisdiction Where Enrolled (Yes/No); (If no – Where); Ward (Yes/No); Allotment, Annuity and Identification Numbers (if given).

1261; Lambert, Henry H.; M; 1/11/04-29; N.C. Cherokee; 1/32; M; Head; 1256; Yes; Yes; Unallotted

1262; Lambert, Amanda G.; F; 5/29/11-21; N.C. Cherokee; 7/8; M; Wife; 1257; Yes; Yes; Unallotted

1263; Lambert, Tom H.; M; 8/20/28-4; N.C. Cherokee; 29/64; S; Son; 1258; Yes; Yes; Unallotted

1264; Lambert, David; M; 11/22/30-2; N.C. Cherokee; 29/64; S; Son; 1259; Yes; Yes; Unallotted

1265; Lambert, Hugh H.; M; 1/10/02-31; N.C. Cherokee; 1/32; M; Head; 1260; Yes; Yes; Unallotted

1266; Lambert, Hugh J.; M; 4/19/74-58; N.C. Cherokee; 1/16; M; Head; 1261; Yes; Yes; Unallotted

1267; Lambert, Isaac; M; 4/20/04-28; N.C. Cherokee; 1/32; S; Son; 1262; Yes; Yes; Unallotted

1268; Lambert, George; M; 10/15/09-23; N.C. Cherokee; 1/32; S; Son; 1263; Yes; Yes; Unallotted

1269; Lambert, Ethel; F; 8/1/13-19; N.C. Cherokee; 1/32; S; Dau.; 1264; Yes; Yes; Unallotted

1270; Lambert, Cato; M; 2/6/16-17; N.C. Cherokee; 1/32; S; Son; 1265; Yes; Yes; Unallotted

1271; Lambert, Vaniela; F; 4/10/18-14; N.C. Cherokee; 1/32; S; Dau.; 1266; Yes; Yes; Unallotted

1272; Lambert, Hugh N.; M; 12/26/80-52; N.C. Cherokee; 1/16; M; Head; 1267; Yes; Yes; Unallotted

1273; Lambert, Paul Leroy; M; 5/25/09-23; N.C. Cherokee; 7/32; S; Son; 1268; Yes; Yes; Unallotted

1274; Lambert, Arthur; M; 7/15/11-21; N.C. Cherokee; 7/32; S; Son; 1269; Yes; Yes; Unallotted

1275; Lambert, Albert S.; M; 1/24/14-19; N.C. Cherokee; 7/32; S; Son; 1270; Yes; Yes; Unallotted

1276; Lambert, Mary Ann; F; 2/15/16-17; N.C. Cherokee; 7/32; S; Dau.; 1271; Yes; Yes; Unallotted

1277; Lambert, Virginia C.; F; 7/21/18-14; N.C. Cherokee; 7/32; S; Dau.; 1272; Yes; Yes; Unallotted

1278; Lambert, Hugh N.; M; 4/14/21-11; N.C. Cherokee; 7/32; S; Son; 1273; Yes; Yes; Unallotted

1279; Lambert, Jesse L.; M; 1/7/24-9; N.C. Cherokee; 7/32; S; Son; 1274; Yes; Yes; Unallotted

1280; Lambert, James W.; M; 5/25/75-57; N.C. Cherokee; 1/16; M; Head; 1275; Yes; Yes; Unallotted

Census of the **Eastern Cherokee** reservation of the **Cherokee, N.C.** jurisdiction, as of **April 1**, **1933**, taken by **R. L. Spalsbury**, Superintendent.

Key: Number; Surname, Given; Sex; Date of Birth-Age at Last Birthday; Tribe; Degree of Blood; Marital Status; Relationship to Head of Family; Last C. Roll No.; At Jurisdiction Where Enrolled (Yes/No); (If no – Where); Ward (Yes/No); Allotment, Annuity and Identification Numbers (if given).

---; ~~Enloe (Lambert), Mintha; F; 10/9/12-20; N.C. Cherokee; 1/32; M; Dau.; 1276; Yes; Yes; Unallotted~~

1281; Lambert, Felix; M; 5/25/17-15; N.C. Cherokee; 1/32; S; Son; 1277; Yes; Yes; Unallotted

1282; Lambert, Mary N.[sic]; F; 9/26/19-13; N.C. Cherokee; 1/32; S; Dau.; 1278; Yes; Yes; Unallotted

1283; Lambert, Jesse; M; 3/8/93-40; N.C. Cherokee; 1/16; M; Head; 1279; Yes; Yes; Unallotted

1284; Lambert, Lelia L.; F; 4/20/19-13; N.C. Cherokee; 1/32; S; Dau.; 1280; Yes; Yes; Unallotted

1285; Lambert, Cleo.; F; 3/30/21-12; N.C. Cherokee; 1/32; S; Dau.; 1281; Yes; Yes; Unallotted

1286; Lambert, Floy Lilly; F; 4/24/23-9; N.C. Cherokee; 1/32; S; Dau.; 1282; Yes; Yes; Unallotted

1287; Lambert, Jesse B.; M; 1/13/77-56; N.C. Cherokee; 1/16; M; Head; 1283; Yes; Yes; Unallotted

1288; Lambert, Minnie E.S.; F; 11/5/90-42; N.C. Cherokee; 1/32; M; Wife; 1284; Yes; Yes; Unallotted

1289; Lambert, Jesse E.; F; 2/28/14-19; N.C. Cherokee; 3/64; S; Dau.; 1286; Yes; Yes; Unallotted

1290; Lambert, Ralph P.; M; 1/20/18-15; N.C. Cherokee; 3/64; S; Son; 1287; Yes; Yes; Unallotted

1291; Lambert, Carl G.; M; 6/11/11-21; N.C. Cherokee; 3/64; M; Son; 1285; Yes; Yes; Unallotted

1292; Lambert (Swayney, Laura), Laura; F; 9/17/12-20; N.C. Cherokee; 1/16; M; Dau.-in-law; 2631; Yes; Yes; Unallotted

1293; Lambert, John H.; M; 2/14/97-36; N.C. Cherokee; 1/32; M; Head; 1288; Yes; Yes; Unallotted

1294; Lambert, Joseph G.; M; 10/20/02-30; N.C. Cherokee; 1/32; M; Head; 1289; Yes; Yes; Unallotted

1295; Lambert, Louisa G.; F; 5/3/08-24; N.C. Cherokee; 3/32; M; Wife; 1290; Yes; Yes; Unallotted

1296; Lambert, Dorothy P.; F; 9/23/27-5; N.C. Cherokee; 4/64; S; Dau.; 1291; Yes; Yes; Unallotted

1297; Lambert, Lloyd; M; 8/28/82-50; N.C. Cherokee; 9/16; M; Head; 1292; Yes; Yes; Unallotted

1298; Lambert, Sallie; F; 4/4/77-55; N.C. Cherokee; 3/4; M; Wife; 1293; Yes; Yes; Unallotted

1299; Lambert, Nellie; F; 1/7/07-25; N.C. Cherokee; 21/32; S; Dau.; 1295; Yes; Yes; Unallotted

Census of the **Eastern Cherokee** reservation of the **Cherokee, N.C.** jurisdiction, as of **April 1** , **1933,** taken by **R. L. Spalsbury** , Superintendent.

Key: Number; Surname, Given; Sex; Date of Birth-Age at Last Birthday; Tribe; Degree of Blood; Marital Status; Relationship to Head of Family; Last C. Roll No.; At Jurisdiction Where Enrolled (Yes/No); (If no – Where); Ward (Yes/No); Allotment, Annuity and Identification Numbers (if given).

1300; Lambert, Jesse; M; 1/7/09-24; N.C. Cherokee; 21/32; S; Son; 1296; Yes; Yes; Unallotted

1301; Lambert, Ruth; F; 6/28/13-19; N.C. Cherokee; 21/32; S; Dau.; 1297; Yes; Yes; Unallotted

1302; Lambert, Freeman; M; 10/19/18-14; N.C. Cherokee; 21/32; S; Son; 1298; Yes; Yes; Unallotted

1303; Lambert, Edna; F; 5/2/24-8; N.C. Cherokee; 21/32; S; Dau.; 1299; Yes; Yes; Unallotted

1304; Cline (Lambert, Luzene), Luzene; F; 7/18/01-32; N.C. Cherokee; 3/8; M; Wife; 1294; Yes; Yes; Unallotted

1305; Lambert, Gwendolyn; F; 10/31/29-4; N.C. Cherokee; --; S; Dau. (Illeg.); 1300; Yes; Yes; Unallotted

1306; Cline, Marcell; M; 1/31/33-2/12; N.C. Cherokee; 3/16; S; Son; ---; Yes; Yes; Unallotted

1307; Lambert, Lucy; F; 3/25/23-10; N.C. Cherokee; 7/8; S; Alone; 1301; Yes; Yes; Unallotted

1308; Lambert, Samuel D.; M; 4/15/25-7; N.C. Cherokee; 3/8; S; Bro.; 1302; Yes; Yes; Unallotted

1309; Lambert, Ollie; F; 5/12/04-28; N.C. Cherokee; 21/32; S; Head; 1303; Yes; Yes; Unallotted

1310; Lambert, Winford; M; 3/11/22-11; N.C. Cherokee; 21/64; S; Son; 1304; Yes; Yes; Unallotted

1311; Lambert, Pearson; M; 7/4/00-32; N.C. Cherokee; 1/32; M; Head; 1305; Yes; Yes; Unallotted

1312; Lambert, Fannie M.; F; 12/24/18-14; N.C. Cherokee; 1/64; S; Dau.; 1306; Yes; Yes; Unallotted

1313; Lambert, Wm. Russel; M; 1/6/21-12; N.C. Cherokee; 1/64; S; Son; 1307; Yes; Yes; Unallotted

1314; Lambert, Josephine; F; 4/24/23-9; N.C. Cherokee; 1/64; S; Dau.; 1308; Yes; Yes; Unallotted

1315; Lambert, Samuel C.; M; 11/27/59-73; N.C. Cherokee; 1/8; M; Head; 1309; Yes; Yes; Unallotted

1316; Lambert, Theodore; M; 5/9/03-29; N.C. Cherokee; 1/16; S; Son; 1310; Yes; Yes; Unallotted

1317; Lambert, Gaylord; M; 12/31/09-23; N.C. Cherokee; 1/16; S; Son; 1311; Yes; Yes; Unallotted

1318; Lambert, Lillian; F; 3/13/13-20; N.C. Cherokee; 1/16; S; Dau.; 1312; Yes; Yes; Unallotted

1319; Lambert, Russell; M; 2/25/16-17; N.C. Cherokee; 1/16; S; Son; 1313; Yes; Yes; Unallotted

Census of the **Eastern Cherokee** reservation of the **Cherokee, N.C.** jurisdiction, as of **April 1** , 19**33,** taken by **R. L. Spalsbury** , Superintendent.

Key: Number; Surname, Given; Sex; Date of Birth-Age at Last Birthday; Tribe; Degree of Blood; Marital Status; Relationship to Head of Family; Last C. Roll No.; At Jurisdiction Where Enrolled (Yes/No); (If no – Where); Ward (Yes/No); Allotment, Annuity and Identification Numbers (if given).

1320; Lambert (McCoy, Stella), Stella; F; 11/25/05-28; N.C. Cherokee; 1/16; Div.; Head; 1314; Yes; Yes; Unallotted

1321; Lambert, Thomas O.; M; 2/12/79-54; N.C. Cherokee; 1/16; M; Head; 1315; Yes; Yes; Unallotted

1322; Lambert, John A.; M; 6/5/05-27; N.C. Cherokee; 1/32; S; Son; 1316; Yes; Yes; Unallotted

1323; Lambert, Cora H.; F; 6/30/13-19; N.C. Cherokee; 1/32; S; Dau.; 1317; Yes; Yes; Unallotted

1324; Lambert, Gracie N.; F; 6/15/15-17; N.C. Cherokee; 1/32; S; Dau.; 1318; Yes; Yes; Unallotted

1325; Lambert, Julia E.; F; 3/12/20-13; N.C. Cherokee; 1/32; S; Dau.; 1319; Yes; Yes; Unallotted

1326; Lambert, Thomas R.; M; 1/1/83-50; N.C. Cherokee; 1/16; M; Head; 1320; Yes; Yes; Unallotted

1327; Lambert, Nannie Y.; F; 7/18/90-42; N.C. Cherokee; 1/16; M; Wife; 1321; Yes; Yes; Unallotted

1328; Lambert, Seymour; M; 8/9/09-23; N.C. Cherokee; 1/16; S; Son; 1322; Yes; Yes; Unallotted

1329; Lambert, Amos; M; 12/23/17-15; N.C. Cherokee; 1/16; S; Son; 1323; Yes; Yes; Unallotted

1330; Lambert, Mary; F; 5/10/20-12; N.C. Cherokee; 1/16; S; Dau.; 1324; Yes; Yes; Unallotted

1331; Lambert, Willard; M; 5/27/24-8; N.C. Cherokee; 1/16; S; Son; 1325; Yes; Yes; Unallotted

1332; Larch, David; M; 4/24/81-51; N.C. Cherokee; 4/4; M; Head; 1326; Yes; Yes; Unallotted

1333; Larch, Winnie O.; F; 12/22/78-54; N.C. Cherokee; 4/4; M; Wife; 1327; Yes; Yes; Unallotted

1334; Larch, William D.; M; 8/11/74-58; N.C. Cherokee; 4/4; M; Head; 1328; Yes; Yes; Unallotted

1335; Larch, Anita Davis; F; 1897-36; N.C. Cherokee; 4/4; M; Wife; 1329; Yes; Yes; Unallotted

1336; Larch, Wm. Jr.; M; 10/25/29-3; N.C. Cherokee; 4/4; S; Son; 1330; Yes; Yes; Unallotted

1337; Larch, Florence; F; 5/25/31-1; N.C. Cherokee; 4/4; S; Dau.; 1331; Yes; Yes; Unallotted

1338; Ledford, Allen; M; 6/24/04-28; N.C. Cherokee; 4/4; S; Head; 1332; Yes; Yes; Unallotted

Census of the **Eastern Cherokee** reservation of the **Cherokee, N.C.** jurisdiction, as of **April 1**, **1933,** taken by **R. L. Spalsbury**, Superintendent.

Key: Number; Surname, Given; Sex; Date of Birth-Age at Last Birthday; Tribe; Degree of Blood; Marital Status; Relationship to Head of Family; Last C. Roll No.; At Jurisdiction Where Enrolled (Yes/No); (If no – Where); Ward (Yes/No); Allotment, Annuity and Identification Numbers (if given).

1339; Ledford (Rogers, Catherine), Catherine; F; 7/12/74-58; N.C. Cherokee; 1/16; M; Wife; 1333; No; Culberson, Cherokee, N.C.; Yes; Unallotted

1340; Ledford, Cora; F; 7/22/02-30; N.C. Cherokee; 1/32; S; Dau.; 1334; No; Culberson, Cherokee, N.C.; Yes; Unallotted

1341; Ledford, Adkins; M; 7/19/05-27; N.C. Cherokee; 1/32; S; Son; 1335; No; Culberson, Cherokee, N.C.; Yes; Unallotted

1342; Ledford, Charles A.; M; 1/31/08-25; N.C. Cherokee; 1/32; S; Son; 1336; No; Culberson, Cherokee, N.C.; Yes; Unallotted

1343; Ledford, Bonnie M.; F; 5/21/10-22; N.C. Cherokee; 1/32; S; Dau.; 1337; No; Culberson, Cherokee, N.C.; Yes; Unallotted

1344; Ledford, Cyrus Atlas; M; 6/18/12-20; N.C. Cherokee; 1/32; S; Son; 1338; No; Culberson, Cherokee, N.C.; Yes; Unallotted

1345; Ledford, Dorothy; F; 9/17/16-16; N.C. Cherokee; 1/32; S; Dau.; 1339; No; Culberson, Cherokee, N.C.; Yes; Unallotted

1346; Ledford, Charley; M; 5/5/83-49; N.C. Cherokee; 4/4; M; Head; 1340; Yes; Yes; Unallotted

1347; Ledford, Maggie W.; F; 9/16/92-40; N.C. Cherokee; 4/4; M; Wife; 1341; Yes; Yes; Unallotted

1348; Ledford, Jake; M; 3/25/77-56; N.C. Cherokee; 4/4; M; Head; 1342; Yes; Yes; Unallotted

1349; Ledford, Mary; F; 5/5/75-57; N.C. Cherokee; 4/4; M; Wife; 1343; Yes; Yes; Unallotted

1350; Ledford, Amy; F; 3/29/08-25; N.C. Cherokee; 4/4; S; Dau.; 1344; Yes; Yes; Unallotted

1351; Ledford (Patterson, Lura), Lura; F; 3/20/04-29; N.C. Cherokee; 1/32; M; Wife; 1345; No; Shooting Creek, Clay, N.C.; Yes; Unallotted

1352; Ledford, Helen; F; 2/22/23-10; N.C. Cherokee; 1/64; S; Dau.; 1346; No; Shooting Creek, Clay, N.C.; Yes; Unallotted

1353; Ledford (McDonald, Mae), Mae; F; 12/13/99-33; N.C. Cherokee; 1/64; M; Wife; 1347; Yes; Yes; Unallotted

1354; Ledford, Jodie; M; 12/5/22-10; N.C. Cherokee; 1/128; S; Son; 1348; Yes; Yes; Unallotted

1355; Ledford, Riley; M; 3/25/77-56; N.C. Cherokee; 4/4; Wd.; Head; 1349; Yes; Yes; Unallotted

1356; Ledford, Caroline; F; 1/25/07-26; N.C. Cherokee; 4/4; S; Dau.; 1350; Yes; Yes; Unallotted

1357; Ledford, Moses; M; 6/8/12-20; N.C. Cherokee; 4/4; S; Son; 1351; Yes; Yes; Unallotted

1358; Ledford, Nancy; F; 3/27/14-19; N.C. Cherokee; 4/4; S; Dau.; 1352; Yes; Yes; Unallotted

Census of the **Eastern Cherokee** reservation of the **Cherokee, N.C.** jurisdiction, as of **April 1** , 19**33,** taken by **R. L. Spalsbury** , Superintendent.

Key: Number; Surname, Given; Sex; Date of Birth-Age at Last Birthday; Tribe; Degree of Blood; Marital Status; Relationship to Head of Family; Last C. Roll No.; At Jurisdiction Where Enrolled (Yes/No); (If no – Where); Ward (Yes/No); Allotment, Annuity and Identification Numbers (if given).

1359; Ledford, James; M; 4/3/17-15; N.C. Cherokee; 4/4; S; Son; 1353; Yes; Yes; Unallotted

1360; Ledford, Elnora; F; 4/27/19-13; N.C. Cherokee; 4/4; S; Dau.; 1354; Yes; Yes; Unallotted

1361; Ledford, Noah; M; 5/9/21-11; N.C. Cherokee; 4/4; S; Son; 1355; Yes; Yes; Unallotted

1362; Ledford, Billy J.; M; 6/19/31-1; N.C. Cherokee; 1/2; S; Gr-Son (Illeg.); 1357; Yes; Yes; Unallotted

1363; Ledford, Glenn; M; 8/30/32-7/12; N.C. Cherokee; 1/2; S; Gr-Son; ---; Yes; Yes; Unallotted

1364; Ledford, Ruby; F; 9/17/18-14; N.C. Cherokee; 1/32; S; Alone; 1358; No; Culberson, Cherokee, N.C.; Yes; Unallotted

1365; Ledford, Jewel; F; 12/29/21-11; N.C. Cherokee; 1/32; S; Sis.; 1359; No; Culberson, Cherokee, N.C.; Yes; Unallotted

1366; Ledford, Sampson; M; 6/8/85-47; N.C. Cherokee; 4/4; M; Head; 1360; Yes; Yes; Unallotted

1367; Ledford, Nancy W.; F; 11/15/93-39; N.C. Cherokee; 4/4; M; Wife; 1361; Yes; Yes; Unallotted

1368; Ledford, Nicey; F; 1/24/16-17; N.C. Cherokee; 4/4; S; Dau.; 1362; Yes; Yes; Unallotted

1369; Ledford, Mason; M; 9/9/17-15; N.C. Cherokee; 4/4; S; Son; 1363; Yes; Yes; Unallotted

1370; Ledford, Wilson; M; 12/8/19-13; N.C. Cherokee; 4/4; S; Son; 1364; Yes; Yes; Unallotted

1371; Lee, Alonzo; M; 1/9/74-59; N.C. Cherokee; 1/16; M; Head; 1365; No; Silver Lake, Wyoming, N.Y.; Yes; Unallotted

1372; Lee, Ramona F.; F; 3/18/96-37; N.C. Cherokee; 1/8; M; Wife; 1366; Yes; Yes; Unallotted

1373; Lee, Ruby I.; F; 10/3/12-20; N.C. Cherokee; 1/16; S; Dau.; 1367; Yes; Yes; Unallotted

1374; Lee, Pearl A.; F; 7/1/15-17; N.C. Cherokee; 1/16; S; Dau.; 1368; Yes; Yes; Unallotted

1375; Lee, Ruth C.; F; 8/22/17-15; N.C. Cherokee; 1/16; S; Dau.; 1369; Yes; Yes; Unallotted

1376; Lee, Naomi M.; F; 10/24/19-13; N.C. Cherokee; 1/16; S; Dau; 1370; Yes; Yes; Unallotted

1377; Lee, William C.; M; 6/14/13-19; N.C. Cherokee; 1/32; S; Alone; 1371; Yes; Yes; Unallotted

1378; Lee, James F.; M; 6/3/15-17; N.C. Cherokee; 1/32; S; Bro.; 1372; Yes; Yes; Unallotted

Census of the **Eastern Cherokee** reservation of the **Cherokee, N.C.** jurisdiction, as of **April 1** , **1933,** taken by **R. L. Spalsbury** , Superintendent.

Key: Number; Surname, Given; Sex; Date of Birth-Age at Last Birthday; Tribe; Degree of Blood; Marital Status; Relationship to Head of Family; Last C. Roll No.; At Jurisdiction Where Enrolled (Yes/No); (If no – Where); Ward (Yes/No); Allotment, Annuity and Identification Numbers (if given).

1379; Le Fevers (Garland, Tamoxzena), Tamoxzena; F; 3/10/81-52; N.C. Cherokee; 1/16; M; Wife; 1373; Yes; Yes; Unallotted
1380; Le Fevers, Linnie; F; 11/14/99-33; N.C. Cherokee; 1/32; S; Dau.; 1374; Yes; Yes; Unallotted
1381; Le Fevers, William; M; 6/15/01-31; N.C. Cherokee; 1/32; S; Son; 1375; Yes; Yes; Unallotted

1382; Lillard (Crowe, Dora), Dora C.; F; 7/6/95-37; N.C. Cherokee; 3/16; M; Wife; 1376; Yes; Yes; Unallotted

1383; Littlejohn, Edison; M; 8/3/14-18; N.C. Cherokee; 15/16; S; Alone; 1377; Yes; Yes; Unallotted

1384; Littlejohn, Elowih; M; 2/15/76-57; N.C. Cherokee; 4/4; M; Head; 1378; Yes; Yes; Unallotted
1385; Littlejohn, Annie; F; 9/15/81-51; N.C. Cherokee; 4/4; M; Wife; 1379; Yes; Yes; Unallotted
1386; Littlejohn, Sherman; M; 4/12/04-28; N.C. Cherokee; 4/4; S; Son; 1380; Yes; Yes; Unallotted
1387; Littlejohn, Jefferson; M; 7/7/07-25; N.C. Cherokee; 4/4; S; Son; 1381; Yes; Yes; Unallotted
1388; Littlejohn, Lizzie; F; 3/5/13-20; N.C. Cherokee; 4/4; S; Dau.; 1382; Yes; Yes; Unallotted
1389; Littlejohn, George; M; 3/16/14-19; N.C. Cherokee; 4/4; S; Son; 1383; Yes; Yes; Unallotted
1390; Littlejohn, Ned; M; 1/2/19-13; N.C. Cherokee; 4/4; S; Son; 1384; Yes; Yes; Unallotted
1391; Littlejohn, Richard; M; 4/14/21-11; N.C. Cherokee; 4/4; S; Son; 1385; Yes; Yes; Unallotted

1392; Littlejohn, Guy; M; 5/11/96-36; N.C. Cherokee; 7/8; S; Head; 1386; Yes; Yes; Unallotted
1393; Littlejohn, Garret; M; 5/11/06-26; N.C. Cherokee; 7/8; S; Bro.; 1387; Yes; Yes; Unallotted

1394; Littlejohn, Henson; M; 5/27/98-34; N.C. Cherokee; 4/4; M; Head; 1388; Yes; Yes; Unallotted
1395; Littlejohn, Lewee Long; F; 7/1/98-34; N.C. Cherokee; 4/4; M; Wife; 1389; Yes; Yes; Unallotted
1396; Littlejohn, Alice; F; 9/15/20-12; N.C. Cherokee; 4/4; S; St-Da.; 1390; Yes; Yes; Unallotted
1397; Littlejohn, Boyd; M; 4/12/22-10; N.C. Cherokee; 4/4; S; St-S; 1391; Yes; Yes; Unallotted
1398; Littlejohn, Amanda; F; 1/18/24-9; N.C. Cherokee; 4/4; S; St-D; 1392; Yes; Yes; Unallotted

Census of the **Eastern Cherokee** reservation of the **Cherokee, N.C.** jurisdiction, as of **April 1** , 19**33,** taken by **R. L. Spalsbury** , Superintendent.

Key: Number; Surname, Given; Sex; Date of Birth-Age at Last Birthday; Tribe; Degree of Blood; Marital Status; Relationship to Head of Family; Last C. Roll No.; At Jurisdiction Where Enrolled (Yes/No); (If no – Where); Ward (Yes/No); Allotment, Annuity and Identification Numbers (if given).

1399; Littlejohn, Thomas; M; 7/5/20-13; N.C. Cherokee; 4/4; S; Son; 1393; Yes; Yes; Unallotted

1400; Littlejohn, Salina; F; 4/4/26-6; N.C. Cherokee; 4/4; S; Dau.; 1394; Yes; Yes; Unallotted

1401; Littlejohn, Isaac; M; 5/28/00-32; N.C. Cherokee; 7/8; M; Head; 1395; Yes; Yes; Unallotted

1402; Littlejohn, Eliza C.; F; 5/28/03-29; N.C. Cherokee; 15/16; M; Wife; 1396; Yes; Yes; Unallotted

1403; Littlejohn, Johnson; M; 3/23/22-10; N.C. Cherokee; 29/32; S; Son; 1397; Yes; Yes; Unallotted

1404; Littlejohn, Maggie D.; F; 12/6/25-7; N.C. Cherokee; 29/32; S; Dau.; 1398; Yes; Yes; Unallotted

1405; Littlejohn, John; M; 6/1/01-31; N.C. Cherokee; 4/4; M; Head; 1399; Yes; Yes; Unallotted

1406; Littlejohn, Nancy Blackfox; F; 3/1/12-21; N.C. Cherokee; 15/16; M; Wife; 219; Yes; Yes; Unallotted

1407; Littlejohn, Luke; M; 7/1/32-9/12; N.C. Cherokee; 31/32; S; Son; ---; Yes; Yes; Unallotted

1408; Littlejohn, Owen; M; 3/19/05-28; N.C. Cherokee; 4/4; S; Head; 1400; Yes; Yes; Unallotted

1409; Littlejohn, Ropetwister; M; 3/15/67-66; N.C. Cherokee; 3/4; M; Head; 1401; Yes; Yes; Unallotted

1410; Littlejohn, Annie; F; 10/5/77-55; N.C. Cherokee; 3/4; M; Wife; 1402; Yes; Yes; Unallotted

1411; Littlejohn, Sallie; F; 4/5/03-29; N.C. Cherokee; 3/4; S; Dau.; 1403; Yes; Yes; Unallotted

1412; Littlejohn, Isaac; M; 12/29/05-27; N.C. Cherokee; 3/4; S; Son; 1404; Yes; Yes; Unallotted

1413; Littlejohn, Eugene; M; 2/25/12-21; N.C. Cherokee; 3/4; S; Son; 1405; Yes; Yes; Unallotted

1414; Littlejohn, Bessie; F; 1/29/14-19; N.C. Cherokee; 3/4; S; Dau.; 1406; Yes; Yes; Unallotted

1415; Littlejohn, Thomas; M; 5/19/30-2; N.C. Cherokee; 13/16; S; Gr-Sn; ---; Yes; Yes; Unallotted

1416; Littlejohn, Saunooke; M; 12/16/62-70; N.C. Cherokee; 4/4; M; Head; 1407; Yes; Yes; Unallotted

1417; Littlejohn, Anna E.; F; 3/27/68-65; N.C. Cherokee; 4/4; M; Wife; 1408; Yes; Yes; Unallotted

1418; Littlejohn, Addie; F; 8/9/07-25; N.C. Cherokee; 4/4; S; Dau.; 1409; Yes; Yes; Unallotted

Census of the **Eastern Cherokee** reservation of the **Cherokee, N.C.** jurisdiction, as of **April 1** , **1933,** taken by **R. L. Spalsbury** , Superintendent.

Key: Number; Surname, Given; Sex; Date of Birth-Age at Last Birthday; Tribe; Degree of Blood; Marital Status; Relationship to Head of Family; Last C. Roll No.; At Jurisdiction Where Enrolled (Yes/No); (If no – Where); Ward (Yes/No); Allotment, Annuity and Identification Numbers (if given).

1419; Locust, Lewis; M; 8/5/01-31; N.C. Cherokee; 1/4; M; Head; 1410; Yes; Yes; Unallotted

1420; Locust, Jennie B.; F; 7/21/02-30; N.C. Cherokee; 1/16; M; Wife; 1411; Yes; Yes; Unallotted

1421; Locust, Harding; M; 2/6/21-12; N.C. Cherokee; 5/32; S; Son; 1412; Yes; Yes; Unallotted

1422; Locust, Alzino May; F; 11/20/25-7; N.C. Cherokee; 5/32; S; Dau.; 1413; Yes; Yes; Unallotted

1423; Locust, Noah; M; 7/8/83-49; N.C. Cherokee; 1/2; M; Head; 1414; Yes; Yes; Unallotted

1424; Locust, Homer; M; 3/22/11-22; N.C. Cherokee; 1/4; S; Son; 1415; Yes; Yes; Unallotted

1425; Locust, Wm. Arthur; M; 6/5/15-17; N.C. Cherokee; 1/4; S; Son; 1417; Yes; Yes; Unallotted

1426; Locust, Wm. Russel; M; 6/4/17-15; N.C. Cherokee; 1/4; S; Son; 1418; Yes; Yes; Unallotted

1427; Locust, Noah A.; M; 11/3/22-10; N.C. Cherokee; 1/4; S; Son; 1419; Yes; Yes; Unallotted

1428; Locust, Herbert F.; M; 4/17/28-4; N.C. Cherokee; 1/4; S; Son; 1420; Yes; Yes; Unallotted

1429; Loma, Dinah S.; F; 9/20/01-31; N.C. Cherokee; 4/4; M; Wife; 1421; Yes; Yes; Unallotted

1430; Long, Adam; M; 12/22/57-75; N.C. Cherokee; 4/4; M; Head; 1422; Yes; Yes; Unallotted

1431; Long, Polly; F; 12/22/56-76; N.C. Cherokee; 4/4; M; Wife; 1423; Yes; Yes; Unallotted

1432; Long, Charles B.; M; 12/22/89-43; N.C. Cherokee; 4/4; M; Head; 1424; Yes; Yes; Unallotted

1433; Long, Rosa D.; F; 11/22/03-29; N.C. Cherokee; 4/4; M; Wife; 1425; Yes; Yes; Unallotted

1434; Long, Fred; M; 5/21/20-12; N.C. Cherokee; 4/4; S; Son; 1426; Yes; Yes; Unallotted

1435; Long, Agnes; F; 8/23/22-10; N.C. Cherokee; 4/4; S; Dau.; 1427; Yes; Yes; Unallotted

1436; Long, Jackson; M; 11/8/27-5; N.C. Cherokee; 4/4; S; Son; 1428; Yes; Yes; Unallotted

1437; Long, Dobson; M; 1/22/62-71; N.C. Cherokee; 4/4; M; Head; 1429; Yes; Yes; Unallotted

1438; Long, Sallie; F; 12/22/65-67; N.C. Cherokee; 4/4; M; Wife; 1430; Yes; Yes; Unallotted

Census of the **Eastern Cherokee** reservation of the **Cherokee, N.C.** jurisdiction, as of **April 1** , 19**33,** taken by **R. L. Spalsbury** , Superintendent.

Key: Number; Surname, Given; Sex; Date of Birth-Age at Last Birthday; Tribe; Degree of Blood; Marital Status; Relationship to Head of Family; Last C. Roll No.; At Jurisdiction Where Enrolled (Yes/No); (If no – Where); Ward (Yes/No); Allotment, Annuity and Identification Numbers (if given).

1439; Long, Elizabeth; F; 12/7/01-31; N.C. Cherokee; 4/4; S; Dau.; 1431; Yes; Yes; Unallotted

1440; Long, Edna M.; F; 8/15/16-16; N.C. Cherokee; 7/8; S; Alone; 1432; Yes; Yes; Unallotted

1441; Long, Isaac; M; 12/22/06-26; N.C. Cherokee; 3/4; S; Head; 1433; Yes; Yes; Unallotted

1442; Long, Martha; F; 12/22/12-20; N.C. Cherokee; 3/4; S; Sis.; 1434; Yes; Yes; Unallotted

1443; Long, Joe; M; 12/22/65-67; N.C. Cherokee; 4/4; M; Head; 1435; Yes; Yes; Unallotted

1444; Long, Nancy G.; F; 12/22/41-91; N.C. Cherokee; 4/4; M; Wife; 1436; Yes; Yes; Unallotted

1445; Long, Charley; M; 5/10/94-38; N.C. Cherokee; 4/4; S; Son; 1437; No; Address unknown, Fla.; Yes; Unallotted

1446; Long, John; M; 12/22/74-58; N.C. Cherokee; 4/4; M; Head; 1438; Yes; Yes; Unallotted

1447; Long, Eve; F; 12/22/65-67; N.C. Cherokee; 4/4; M; Wife; 1439; Yes; Yes; Unallotted

1448; Long, Johnson; M; 12/22/63-69; N.C. Cherokee; 4/4; M; Head; 1440; Yes; Yes; Unallotted

1449; Long, Maggie; F; 4/18/76-56; N.C. Cherokee; 4/4; M; Wife; 1441; Yes; Yes; Unallotted

1450; Long, Annie; F; 4/10/07-25; N.C. Cherokee; 4/4; S; Dau.; 1442; Yes; Yes; Unallotted

1451; Long, Martha; F; 4/10/15-17; N.C. Cherokee; 4/4; S; Dau.; 1443; Yes; Yes; Unallotted

1452; Long, Joseph B.; M; 4/7/71-61; N.C. Cherokee; 4/4; M; Head; 1444; Yes; Yes; Unallotted

1453; Long, Sallie; F; 4/24/76-55; N.C. Cherokee; 13/16; M; Wife; 1445; Yes; Yes; Unallotted

1454; Long, Lucy; F; 7/13/05-27; N.C. Cherokee; 29/32; S; Dau.; 1446; Yes; Yes; Unallotted

1455; Long, Edna; F; 4/3/07-25; N.C. Cherokee; 29/32; S; Dau.; 1447; Yes; Yes; Unallotted

1456; Long, Lloyd; M; 4/19/09-23; N.C. Cherokee; 29/32; S; Son; 1448; Yes; Yes; Unallotted

1457; Long, Peter; M; 8/3/79-53; N.C. Cherokee; 4/4; M; Head; 1449; Yes; Yes; Unallotted

Census of the **Eastern Cherokee** reservation of the **Cherokee, N.C.** jurisdiction, as of **April 1** , **1933,** taken by **R. L. Spalsbury** , Superintendent.

Key: Number; Surname, Given; Sex; Date of Birth-Age at Last Birthday; Tribe; Degree of Blood; Marital Status; Relationship to Head of Family; Last C. Roll No.; At Jurisdiction Where Enrolled (Yes/No); (If no – Where); Ward (Yes/No); Allotment, Annuity and Identification Numbers (if given).

1458; Long, Anona C.; F; 10/31/91-41; N.C. Cherokee; 9/16; M; Wife; 1450; Yes; Yes; Unallotted

1459; Long, Joseph G.; M; 12/5/12-20; N.C. Cherokee; 9/32; S; St-S; 1451; Yes; Yes; Unallotted

1460; Long, Temotzema; F; 4/15/14-18; N.C. Cherokee; 25/32; S; Dau.; 1452; Yes; Yes; Unallotted

1461; Long, Stephen G.; M; 11/28/15-17; N.C. Cherokee; 25/32; S; Son; 1453; Yes; Yes; Unallotted

1462; Long, Wilbur; M; 4/16/18-14; N.C. Cherokee; 25/32; S; Son; 1454; Yes; Yes; Unallotted

1463; Long, William; M; 1/8/21-12; N.C. Cherokee; 25/32; S; Son; 1455; Yes; Yes; Unallotted

1464; Long, Rachel; F; 1/8/21-12; N.C. Cherokee; 25/32; S; Dau.; 1456; Yes; Yes; Unallotted

1465; Long, Laura; F; 8/30/23-9; N.C. Cherokee; 25/32; S; Dau.; 1457; Yes; Yes; Unallotted

1466; Long, Johnnie; M; 5/25/27-5; N.C. Cherokee; 25/32; S; Son; 1458; Yes; Yes; Unallotted

1467; Long, Robert E.; M; 4/8/30-3; N.C. Cherokee; 25/32; S; Son; 1459; Yes; Yes; Unallotted

1468; Long, Rachel; F; 12/22/74-58; N.C. Cherokee; 4/4; S; Head; 1460; Yes; Yes; Unallotted

1469; Long, Will West; M; 1/25/70-63; N.C. Cherokee; 4/4; M; Head; 1461; Yes; Yes; Unallotted

1470; Long, Mary W.; F; 12/7/70-62; N.C. Cherokee; 4/4; M; Wife; 1462; Yes; Yes; Unallotted

1471; Long, Allen W.; M; 6/2/17-15; N.C. Cherokee; 4/4; S; Son; 1463; Yes; Yes; Unallotted

1472; Long, William G.; M; 5/15/97-35; N.C. Cherokee; 4/4; M; Head; 1464; Yes; Yes; Unallotted

1473; Long, Susie W.; F; 9/15/96-36; N.C. Cherokee; 4/4; M; Wife; 1465; Yes; Yes; Unallotted

1474; Long, Ella; F; 11/1/19-13; N.C. Cherokee; 4/4; S; Dau.; 1466; Yes; Yes; Unallotted

1475; Long, Mary; F; 3/31/21-11; N.C. Cherokee; 4/4; S; Dau.; 1467; Yes; Yes; Unallotted

1476; Long, Adam; M; 3/9/23-9; N.C. Cherokee; 4/4; S; Son; 1468; Yes; Yes; Unallotted

1477; Lossie, Candy; M; 3/10/98-34; N.C. Cherokee; 4/4; S; Head; 1469; Yes; Yes; Unallotted

Census of the **Eastern Cherokee** reservation of the **Cherokee, N.C.** jurisdiction, as of **April 1** , 19**33,** taken by **R. L. Spalsbury** , Superintendent.

Key: Number; Surname, Given; Sex; Date of Birth-Age at Last Birthday; Tribe; Degree of Blood; Marital Status; Relationship to Head of Family; Last C. Roll No.; At Jurisdiction Where Enrolled (Yes/No); (If no – Where); Ward (Yes/No); Allotment, Annuity and Identification Numbers (if given).

1478; Lossie, John R.; M; 2/25/03-30; N.C. Cherokee; 4/4; S; Bro.; 1470; Yes; Yes; Unallotted

1479; Lossie, Hayes; M; 3/22/05-28; N.C. Cherokee; 4/4; S; Bro.; 1471; Yes; Yes; Unallotted

1480; Lossie, David; M; 6/16/93-39; N.C. Cherokee; 4/4; M; Head; 1472; Yes; Yes; Unallotted

1481; Lossie, Lydia W.; F; 4/21/13-19; N.C. Cherokee; 4/4; M; Wife; 1473; Yes; Yes; Unallotted

1482; Lossie, Sampson; M; 4/7/26-6; N.C. Cherokee; 4/4; S; Son; 1474; Yes; Yes; Unallotted

1483; Lossie, Charlie; M; 2/19/29-4; N.C. Cherokee; 4/4; S; Son; 1475; Yes; Yes; Unallotted

1484; Lossie, Annie; F; 11/2/31-1; N.C. Cherokee; 4/4; S; Dau.; 1476; Yes; Yes; Unallotted

1485; Lossie, Leander; M; 1/5/82-51; N.C. Cherokee; 4/4; M; Head; ---; Yes; Yes; Unallotted

1486; Lossie, Katy L.; F; 12/28/98-34; N.C. Cherokee; 7/8; M; Wife; 1477; Yes; Yes; Unallotted

1487; Lossie, Solomon; M; 9/4/99-33; N.C. Cherokee; 4/4; S; Head; 1478; Yes; Yes; Unallotted

1488; Lossih, Dom Thomas; M; 3/12/96-37; N.C. Cherokee; 4/4; M; Head; 1479; Yes; Yes; Unallotted

1489; Lossih, Bettie G.; F; 2/15/03-30; N.C. Cherokee; 3/4; M; Wife; 1480; Yes; Yes; Unallotted

1490; George, Judas; M; 10/29/20-12; N.C. Cherokee; 7/8; S; St-S; 1481; Yes; Yes; Unallotted

1491; Lossih, Henry; M; 8/15/70-60; N.C. Cherokee; 4/4; M; Head; 1482; Yes; Yes; Unallotted

1492; Lossih, Aggie; F; 4/8/80-52; N.C. Cherokee; 4/4; M; Wife; 1483; Yes; Yes; Unallotted

1493; Lossih, Rosy; F; 6/26/07-25; N.C. Cherokee; 4/4; S; Dau.; 1484; Yes; Yes; Unallotted

1494; Lossih, Calvin S.; M; 6/30/09-23; N.C. Cherokee; 4/4; S; Son; 1485; Yes; Yes; Unallotted

1495; Lossih, Abel; M; 6/10/11-21; N.C. Cherokee; 4/4; S; Son; 1486; Yes; Yes; Unallotted

1496; Lossih, Mary; F; 9/25/13-19; N.C. Cherokee; 4/4; S; Dau.; 1487; Yes; Yes; Unallotted

1497; Lossih, Adam Ross; M; 5/27/21-11; N.C. Cherokee; 4/4; S; Son; 1488; Yes; Yes; Unallotted

Census of the **Eastern Cherokee** reservation of the **Cherokee, N.C.** jurisdiction, as of **April 1**, **1933,** taken by **R. L. Spalsbury**, Superintendent.

Key: Number; Surname, Given; Sex; Date of Birth-Age at Last Birthday; Tribe; Degree of Blood; Marital Status; Relationship to Head of Family; Last C. Roll No.; At Jurisdiction Where Enrolled (Yes/No); (If no – Where); Ward (Yes/No); Allotment, Annuity and Identification Numbers (if given).

1498; Lossih (Mr. Rosy), Jonas Eli; M; 3/21/29-4; N.C. Cherokee; 31/32; S; Grandson; 1489; Yes; Yes; Unallotted

1499; Lossih, John D.; M; 6/14/70-62; N.C. Cherokee; 4/4; M; Head; 1490; Yes; Yes; Unallotted

1500; Lossih, Laura; F; 5/2/69-63; N.C. Cherokee; 7/8; M; Wife; 1491; Yes; Yes; Unallotted

1501; Lossih, John Jr.; M; 4/8/98-34; N.C. Cherokee; 15/16; S; Son; 1492; Yes; Yes; Unallotted

1502; Lossih, Jesse J.; M; 4/1/07-26; N.C. Cherokee; 15/16; S; Son; 1493; Yes; Yes; Unallotted

1503; Lossih, Jonas; M; 3/26/73-60; N.C. Cherokee; 4/4; M; Head; 1494; Yes; Yes; Unallotted

1504; Lossih, Nicey W.; F; 10/8/80-52; N.C. Cherokee; 4/4; M; Wife; 1495; Yes; Yes; Unallotted

1505; Lossih, Sarah; F; 4/18/23-9; N.C. Cherokee; 4/4; S; Alone; 1496; Yes; Yes; Unallotted

1506; Loudermilk (Raper, Cynthia), Cynthia A.; F; 7/31/62-70; N.C. Cherokee; 1/8; M; Wife; 1497; No; Culberson, Cherokee, N.C.; Yes; Unallotted

1507; Loudermilk, Elmer; M; 5/22/04-28; N.C. Cherokee; 1/32; M; Head; 1498; No; Ducktown, Polk, Tenn.; Yes; Unallotted

1508; Loudermilk, John R.; M; 7/7/79-53; N.C. Cherokee; 1/16; M; Head; 1499; Yes; Yes; Unallotted

1509; Loudermilk, Leroy; M; 9/13/09-23; N.C. Cherokee; 1/32; S; Son; 1500; Yes; Yes; Unallotted

1510; Loudermilk , Wilford T.; M; 1/5/13-20; N.C. Cherokee; 1/32; S; Son; 1501; Yes; Yes; Unallotted

1511; Loudermilk (Garland, Josephine), Josephine; F; 11/11/76-56; N.C. Cherokee; 1/16; M; Wife; 1502; No; Ducktown, Polk, Tenn.; Yes; Unallotted

1512; Loudermilk, Clinton; M; 6/12/08-24; N.C. Cherokee; 1/32; S; Son; 1503; No; Ducktown, Polk, Tenn.; Yes; Unallotted

1513; Loudermilk, Luther; M; 11/7/10-22; N.C. Cherokee; 1/32; S; Son; 1504; No; Ducktown, Polk, Tenn.; Yes; Unallotted

1514; Loudermilk, Willard L.; M; 6/12/15-17; N.C. Cherokee; 1/32; S; Son; 1505; No; Ducktown, Polk, Tenn.; Yes; Unallotted

1515; Loudermilk, Thomas L.; M; 7/31/00-32; N.C. Cherokee; 1/32; M; Head; 1506; No; Copperhill, Polk, Tenn.; Yes; Unallotted

Census of the **Eastern Cherokee** reservation of the **Cherokee, N.C.** jurisdiction, as of **April 1** , 19**33**, taken by **R. L. Spalsbury** , Superintendent.

Key: Number; Surname, Given; Sex; Date of Birth-Age at Last Birthday; Tribe; Degree of Blood; Marital Status; Relationship to Head of Family; Last C. Roll No.; At Jurisdiction Where Enrolled (Yes/No); (If no – Where); Ward (Yes/No); Allotment, Annuity and Identification Numbers (if given).

1516; Loudermilk, Cecil S.; M; 11/14/22-10; N.C. Cherokee; 1/64; S; Son; 1507; No; Copperhill, Polk, Tenn.; Yes; Unallotted

1517; Lovingood (Dockery, Elsie), Elsie A.; F; 1/20/05-28; N.C. Cherokee; 1/32; M; Wife; 1508; Yes; Yes; Unallotted

1518; Lowen, John; M; 12/22/60-72; N.C. Cherokee; 4/4; Wd.; Head; 1509; Yes; Yes; Unallotted

1519; Lowen, John B.; M; 5/22/60-72; N.C. Cherokee; 4/4; S; Head; 1510; Yes; Yes; Unallotted

1520; Ludwig, Bessie N.; F; 5/1/87-45; N.C. Cherokee; 1/4; M; Wife; 1511; Yes; Yes; Unallotted

1521; Lunsford, Inez Rogers; F; 4/22/07-25; N.C. Cherokee; 1/8; M; Wife; 1512; Yes; Yes; Unallotted

1522; Lunsford, Ted; M; 6/23/07-25; N.C. Cherokee; 1/64; S; Head; 1513; Yes; Yes; Unallotted
1523; Lunsford, Dee; M; 6/23/09-23; N.C. Cherokee; 1/64; S; Broth.; 1514; Yes; Yes; Unallotted
1524; Lunsford, Woodrow; M; 6/23/11-21; N.C. Cherokee; 1/64; S; Broth.; 1515; Yes; Yes; Unallotted
1525; Lunsford, Ausloo; M; 6/23/13-19; N.C. Cherokee; 1/64; S; Broth.; 1516; Yes; Yes; Unallotted
1526; Lunsford, Jane; F; 6/23/15-17; N.C. Cherokee; 1/64; S; Sis.; 1517; Yes; Yes; Unallotted
1527; Lunsford, May; F; 6/23/20-12; N.C. Cherokee; 1/64; S; Sis.; 1518; Yes; Yes; Unallotted
1528; Lunsford, Vernon; M; 6/23/21-11; N.C. Cherokee; 1/64; S; Broth.; 1519; Yes; Yes; Unallotted

1529; McAllister (Garland, Harriet), Harriet A.; F; 6/27/66-66; N.C. Cherokee; 1/8; M; Wife; 1520; Yes; Yes; Unallotted

1530; McCoy, David; M; 7/13/73-59; N.C. Cherokee; 1/8; M; Head; 1521; Yes; Yes; Unallotted
1531; McCoy, Bessie; F; 9/12/11-21; N.C. Cherokee; 1/16; S; Dau.; 1522; Yes; Yes; Unallotted
1532; McCoy (Owl), Eva; F; 8/22/13-20; N.C. Cherokee; 1/16; M; Dau.; 1523; Yes; Yes; Unallotted
1533; McCoy, Edna; F; 1/8/16-17; N.C. Cherokee; 1/16; S; Dau.; 1524; Yes; Yes; Unallotted

Census of the **Eastern Cherokee** reservation of the **Cherokee, N.C.** jurisdiction, as of **April 1** , **1933,** taken by **R. L. Spalsbury** , Superintendent.

Key: Number; Surname, Given; Sex; Date of Birth-Age at Last Birthday; Tribe; Degree of Blood; Marital Status; Relationship to Head of Family; Last C. Roll No.; At Jurisdiction Where Enrolled (Yes/No); (If no – Where); Ward (Yes/No); Allotment, Annuity and Identification Numbers (if given).

1534; McCoy, James; M; 12/1/81-51; N.C. Cherokee; 1/8; M; Head; 1525; Yes; Yes; Unallotted

1535; McCoy, William T.; M; 3/6/06-27; N.C. Cherokee; 1/16; S; Son; 1526; Yes; Yes; Unallotted

1536; McCoy, Joseph H.; M; 11/24/07-25; N.C. Cherokee; 1/16; S; Son; 1527; Yes; Yes; Unallotted

1537; McCoy, Frank; M; 12/28/12-20; N.C. Cherokee; 1/16; S; Son; 1528; Yes; Yes; Unallotted

1538; McCoy, Edith; F; 4/22/14-18; N.C. Cherokee; 1/16; S; Dau.; 1529; Yes; Yes; Unallotted

1539; McCoy, Olive; F; 8/26/16-16; N.C. Cherokee; 1/16; S; Dau.; 1530; Yes; Yes; Unallotted

1540; McCoy, Lola A.; F; 4/27/19-13; N.C. Cherokee; 1/16; S; Dau.; 1531; Yes; Yes; Unallotted

1541; McCoy, Russell D.; M; 8/4/22-10; N.C. Cherokee; 1/16; S; Son; 1532; Yes; Yes; Unallotted

1542; McCoy, Helen; F; 12/5/24-8; N.C. Cherokee; 1/16; S; Dau.; 1533; Yes; Yes; Unallotted

1543; McCoy, James; M; 10/6/04-28; N.C. Cherokee; 1/16; S; Head; 1534; Yes; Yes; Unallotted

1544; McCoy, James W.R.; M; 8/7/01-31; N.C. Cherokee; 1/16; M; Head; 1535; Yes; Yes; Unallotted

1545; McCoy, Eunice M.; F; 12/28/21-11; N.C. Cherokee; 1/32; S; Dau.; 1536; Yes; Yes; Unallotted

1546; McCoy, Margaret J.; F; 2/1/23-10; N.C. Cherokee; 1/32; S; Dau.; 1537; Yes; Yes; Unallotted

1547; McCoy, Jesse; M; 12/22/09-23; N.C. Cherokee; 1/16; M; Head; 1538; Yes; Yes; Unallotted

1548; McCoy (Owl, Ethel), Ethel; F; 10/19/04-28; N.C. Cherokee; 1/4; M; Wife; 1804; Yes; Yes; Unallotted

1549; McCoy, Edwin; M; 10/15/31-1; N.C. Cherokee; 5/32; S; Son; 3233; Yes; Yes; Unallotted

1550; McCoy, John C.; M; 2/3/77-56; N.C. Cherokee; 1/8; M; Head; 1539; Yes; Yes; Unallotted

1551; McCoy, Walter; M; 5/20/09-23; N.C. Cherokee; 1/16; S; Son; 1540; Yes; Yes; Unallotted

1552; McCoy, Pearson; M; 4/19/98-34; N.C. Cherokee; 1/16; M; Head; 1541; Yes; Yes; Unallotted

1553; McCoy, Sallie L.; F; 7/7/09-23; N.C. Cherokee; 1/32; M; Wife; 1542; Yes; Yes; Unallotted

Census of the **Eastern Cherokee** reservation of the **Cherokee, N.C.** jurisdiction, as of **April 1** , 19**33,** taken by **R. L. Spalsbury** , Superintendent.

Key: Number; Surname, Given; Sex; Date of Birth-Age at Last Birthday; Tribe; Degree of Blood; Marital Status; Relationship to Head of Family; Last C. Roll No.; At Jurisdiction Where Enrolled (Yes/No); (If no – Where); Ward (Yes/No); Allotment, Annuity and Identification Numbers (if given).

1554; McDaniel, Andy; M; 11/10/79-53; N.C. Cherokee; 1/32; M; Head; 1543; Yes; Yes; Unallotted

1555; McDaniel, Bob; M; 2/13/06-27; N.C. Cherokee; 1/64; S; Son; 1544; Yes; Yes; Unallotted

1556; McDaniel, Onie; F; 9/30/08-24; N.C. Cherokee; 1/64; S; Dau.; 1545; Yes; Yes; Unallotted

1557; McDaniel, Burgan; M; 2/23/11-22; N.C. Cherokee; 1/64; S; Son; 1546; Yes; Yes; Unallotted

1558; McDaniel, Dottie; F; 2/14/13-20; N.C. Cherokee; 1/64; S; Dau.; 1547; Yes; Yes; Unallotted

1559; McDaniel, Nina; F; 1/16/18-15; N.C. Cherokee; 1/64; S; Dau.; 1548; Yes; Yes; Unallotted

1560; McDaniel, Mary Lou; F; 12/2/21-11; N.C. Cherokee; 1/64; S; Dau.; 1549; Yes; Yes; Unallotted

1561; McDaniel, Belva; M; 11/15/88-44; N.C. Cherokee; 1/32; M; Head; 1550; Yes; Yes; Unallotted

1562; McDaniel, Fannie; F; 4/25/08-24; N.C. Cherokee; 1/64; S; Dau.; 1551; Yes; Yes; Unallotted

1563; McDaniel, Hobart; M; 3/5/05-28; N.C. Cherokee; 1/64; S; Head; 1552; Yes; Yes; Unallotted

1564; McDaniel, Dee; M; 6/23/07-25; N.C. Cherokee; 1/64; S; Bro.; 1553; Yes; Yes; Unallotted

1565; McDaniel, Pearl; F; 12/8/09-23; N.C. Cherokee; 1/64; S; Sis.; 1554; Yes; Yes; Unallotted

1566; McDaniel, Behaden; M; 6/10/11-21; N.C. Cherokee; 1/64; S; Bro.; 1555; Yes; Yes; Unallotted

1567; McDaniel, Louisel; F M; 12/23/13-19; N.C. Cherokee; 1/64; S; Bro[sic]; 1556; Yes; Should be female letter April 12, 1934; Yes; Unallotted

1568; McDaniel, Glin; M; 5/15/15-17; N.C. Cherokee; 1/64; S; Bro.; 1557; Yes; Yes; Unallotted

1569; McDonald, Addie; F; 12/3/01-31; N.C. Cherokee; 1/64; M; Wife; 1558; Yes; Yes; Unallotted

1570; McDonald, Eva Mae; F; 11/10/21-11; N.C. Cherokee; 1/128; S; Dau.; 1559; Yes; Yes; Unallotted

1571; McDonald, Harrison H.; M; 12/17/89-43; N.C. Cherokee; 1/32; M; Head; 1560; Yes; Yes; Unallotted

1572; McDonald, Bonnie; F; 6/20/11-21; N.C. Cherokee; 1/64; S; Dau.; 1561; Yes; Yes; Unallotted

1573; McDonald, Vesta; F; 8/27/13-19; N.C. Cherokee; 1/64; S; Dau.; 1562; Yes; Yes; Unallotted

Census of the **Eastern Cherokee** reservation of the **Cherokee, N.C.** jurisdiction, as of **April 1** , **1933,** taken by **R. L. Spalsbury** , Superintendent.

Key: Number; Surname, Given; Sex; Date of Birth-Age at Last Birthday; Tribe; Degree of Blood; Marital Status; Relationship to Head of Family; Last C. Roll No.; At Jurisdiction Where Enrolled (Yes/No); (If no – Where); Ward (Yes/No); Allotment, Annuity and Identification Numbers (if given).

1574; McDonald, Lawton; M; 12/21/15-17; N.C. Cherokee; 1/64; S; Son; 1563; Yes; Yes; Unallotted

1575; McDonald, Irene; F; 8/8/18-14; N.C. Cherokee; 1/64; S; Dau.; 1564; Yes; Yes; Unallotted

1576; McDonald, Lillian; F; 1/14/21-12; N.C. Cherokee; 1/64; S; Dau.; 1565; Yes; Yes; Unallotted

1577; McDonald, James; M; 12/30/76-56; N.C. Cherokee; 1/32; M; Head; 1566; Yes; Yes; Unallotted

1578; McDonald, May; F; 4/2/07-24; N.C. Cherokee; 1/64; S; Dau.; 1567; Yes; Yes; Unallotted

1579; McDonald, Tommie; M; 1/1/13-20; N.C. Cherokee; 1/64; S; Son; 1568; Yes; Yes; Unallotted

1580; McDonald, John; M; 6/12/73-60; N.C. Cherokee; 1/32; M; Head; 1569; Yes; Yes; Unallotted

1581; McDonald, Charlie; M; 1/23/08-25; N.C. Cherokee; 1/64; S; Son; 1570; Yes; Yes; Unallotted

1582; McDonald, Boyd; M; 5/28/12-20; N.C. Cherokee; 1/64; S; Son; 1571; Yes; Yes; Unallotted

1583; McDonald, Leonard; M; 11/10/14-18; N.C. Cherokee; 1/64; S; Son; 1572; Yes; Yes; Unallotted

1584; McGillis, Nellie F.; F; 9/2/01-31; N.C. Cherokee; 4/4; M; Wife; 1573; Yes; Yes; Unallotted

1585; McLeymore, Morrell; M; 9/9/00-32; N.C. Cherokee; 5/16; S; Head; 1574; Yes; Yes; Unallotted

1586; McLeymore, Samuel R.; M; 3/6/06-27; N.C. Cherokee; 5/16; S; Bro.; 1575; Yes; Yes; Unallotted

1587; McLeymore, Wm. Glen; M; 11/10/10-22; N.C. Cherokee; 5/16; S; Bro.; 1576; Yes; Yes; Unallotted

1588; McLeymore, Kermit C.; M; 1/13/13-20; N.C. Cherokee; 5/16; S; Bro.; 1577; Yes; Yes; Unallotted

1589; Madrano, Agnes Owl; F; 10/19/97-35; N.C. Cherokee; 1/2; M; Wife; 1578; Yes; Yes; Unallotted

1590; Maney, Bruce; M; 8/27/08-24; N.C. Cherokee; 1/32; S; Head; 1579; Yes; Yes; Unallotted

1591; Maney (Matthews, Eva), Eva A.; F; 11/13/04-28; N.C. Cherokee; 1/32; M; Wife; 1580; Yes; Yes; Unallotted

1592; Maney, Lillian R.; F; 8/20/20-12; N.C. Cherokee; 1/64; S; Dau.; 1581; Yes; Yes; Unallotted

Census of the **Eastern Cherokee** reservation of the **Cherokee, N.C.** jurisdiction, as of **April 1**, 19**33**, taken by **R. L. Spalsbury**, Superintendent.

Key: Number; Surname, Given; Sex; Date of Birth-Age at Last Birthday; Tribe; Degree of Blood; Marital Status; Relationship to Head of Family; Last C. Roll No.; At Jurisdiction Where Enrolled (Yes/No); (If no – Where); Ward (Yes/No); Allotment, Annuity and Identification Numbers (if given).

1593; Maney, Cecil; M; 12/26/22-10; N.C. Cherokee; 1/64; S; Son; 1582; Yes; Yes; Unallotted

1594; Maney, John; M; 5/10/06-26; N.C. Cherokee; 1/2; M; Head; 1583; Yes; Yes; Unallotted

1595; Maney (Bradley. Arnessa), Arnessa; F; 8/5/07-25; N.C. Cherokee; 29/32; M; Wife; 261; Yes; Yes; Unallotted

1596; Maney, John Wm. Jr.; M; 2/2/31-2; N.C. Cherokee; 45/64; S; Son; 1584; Yes; Yes; Unallotted

1597; Maney, Jacob; M; 5/26/08-24; N.C. Cherokee; 1/2; M; Head; 1585; Yes; Yes; Unallotted

1598; Maney (Powell, Emma), Emma; F; 5/1/15-18; N.C. Cherokee; 7/8; M; Wife; 1944; Yes; Yes; Unallotted

1599; Maney, Dorothy; F; 2/6/33-1/12; N.C. Cherokee; 11/16; S; Dau.; ---; Yes; Yes; Unallotted

1600; Maney, Caroline; F; 11/6/13-19; N.C. Cherokee; 1/2; S; Alone; 1586; Yes; Yes; Unallotted

1601; Maney, Simon P.; M; 3/11/14-19; N.C. Cherokee; 1/2; S; Bro.; 1587; Yes; Yes; Unallotted

1602; Maney, Jesse J.; M; 6/7/16-16; N.C. Cherokee; 1/2; S; Bro.; 1588; Yes; Yes; Unallotted

1603; Maney, Rachel A.; F; 11/30/01-31; N.C. Cherokee; 4/4; M; Wife; 1589; Yes; Yes; Unallotted

1604; Maney, Richard; M; 3/5/12-21; N.C. Cherokee; 1/4; S; Son (Fr. white); 1590; Yes; Yes; Unallotted

1605; Maney, James O.; M; 10/26/13-19; N.C. Cherokee; 1/4; S; Son; 1591; Yes; Yes; Unallotted

1606; Maney, Shufford; M; 2/29/16-17; N.C. Cherokee; 1/4; S; Son; 1592; Yes; Yes; Unallotted

1607; Maney, Frank D.; M; 6/30/17-15; N.C. Cherokee; 1/4; S; Son; 1593; Yes; Yes; Unallotted

1608; Martin, Lucy; F; 8/15/72-60; N.C. Cherokee; 4/4; Wd.; Head; 1594; Yes; Yes; Unallotted

1609; Martin, Charles; M; 12/19/08-24; N.C. Cherokee; 4/4; S; Son; 1595; Yes; Yes; Unallotted

1610; Martin (Lambert, Ida), Ida; F; 12/25/08-24; N.C. Cherokee; 1/32; M; Wife; 1596; Yes; Yes; Unallotted

Census of the **Eastern Cherokee** reservation of the **Cherokee, N.C.** jurisdiction, as of **April 1** , 19**33**, taken by **R. L. Spalsbury** , Superintendent.

Key: Number; Surname, Given; Sex; Date of Birth-Age at Last Birthday; Tribe; Degree of Blood; Marital Status; Relationship to Head of Family; Last C. Roll No.; At Jurisdiction Where Enrolled (Yes/No); (If no – Where); Ward (Yes/No); Allotment, Annuity and Identification Numbers (if given).

1611;   Martin, Thomas; M; 12/25/87-45; N.C. Cherokee; 4/4; Wd.; Head; 1597; Yes; Yes; Unallotted

1612;   Martin, Sarah; F; 3/31/22-11; N.C. Cherokee; 4/4; S; Dau.; 1598; Yes; Yes; Unallotted

1613;   Martin, Andy; M; 2/8/24-9; N.C. Cherokee; 4/4; S; Son; 1599; Yes; Yes; Unallotted

1614;   Martin, Jesse T.; M; 12/15/28-4; N.C. Cherokee; 4/4; S; Son; 1600; Yes; Yes; Unallotted

1615;   Martin, Wesley; M; 7/10/96-36; N.C. Cherokee; 4/4; M; Head; 1601; Yes; Yes; Unallotted

1616;   Martin, Louisa M.; F; 1/21/86-47; N.C. Cherokee; 1/8; M; Wife; 1602; Yes; Yes; Unallotted

1617;   Mashburn (Stiles, Alma), Alma; F; 3/23/02-31; N.C. Cherokee; 1/32; M; Wife; 1603; No; Birch, Cherokee, N.C.; Yes; Unallotted

1618;   Mashburn, Pearl N.; F; 3/26/23-10; N.C. Cherokee; 1/64; S; Dau.; 1604; No; Birch, Cherokee, N.C.; Yes; Unallotted

1619;   Mashburn, Frank; M; 1/21/00-33; N.C. Cherokee; 3/32; M; Head; 1605; Yes; Yes; Unallotted

1620;   Mashburn, Fred; M; 10/27/20-12; N.C. Cherokee; 3/64; S; Son; 1606; Yes; Yes; Unallotted

1621;   Mashburn, Claude; M; 12/9/22-10; N.C. Cherokee; 3/64; S; Son; 1607; Yes; Yes; Unallotted

1622;   Mashburn (Timpson, Harriett), Harriett A.; F; 9/23/78-55; N.C. Cherokee; 3/16; M; Wife; 1608; Yes; Yes; Unallotted

1623;   Mashburn, Bessie; F; 7/23/01-31; N.C. Cherokee; 3/32; S; Dau.; 1595; Yes; Yes; Unallotted

1624;   Mashburn, James L.; M; 10/17/03-29; N.C. Cherokee; 3/32; S; Son; 1610; Yes; Yes; Unallotted

1625;   Mashburn, Sarah A.; F; 1/25/06-27; N.C. Cherokee; 3/32; S; Dau.; 1611; Yes; Yes; Unallotted

1626;   Mashburn, Thomas R.; M; 6/26/11-21; N.C. Cherokee; 3/32; S; Son; 1612; Yes; Yes; Unallotted

1627;   Mashburn, Lorraine; F; 8/22/15-17; N.C. Cherokee; 3/32; S; Dau.; 1613; Yes; Yes; Unallotted

1628;   Mashburn, Lydia M.; F; 7/23/19-13; N.C. Cherokee; 3/32; S; Dau.; 1614; Yes; Yes; Unallotted

1629;   Mashburn, Cynthia N.; F; 5/9/23-10; N.C. Cherokee; 3/32; S; Dau.; 1615; Yes; Yes; Unallotted

1630;   Mashburn (Timpson, Leora), Leora; F; 5/10/83-49; N.C. Cherokee; 3/16; M; Wife; 1616; Yes; Yes; Unallotted

Census of the **Eastern Cherokee** reservation of the **Cherokee, N.C.** jurisdiction, as of **April 1** , **1933,** taken by **R. L. Spalsbury** , Superintendent.

Key: Number; Surname, Given; Sex; Date of Birth-Age at Last Birthday; Tribe; Degree of Blood; Marital Status; Relationship to Head of Family; Last C. Roll No.; At Jurisdiction Where Enrolled (Yes/No); (If no – Where); Ward (Yes/No); Allotment, Annuity and Identification Numbers (if given).

1631; Mashburn, Bertha; F; 8/17/05-27; N.C. Cherokee; 3/32; S; Dau.; 1617; Yes; Yes; Unallotted

1632; Mashburn, Myrtle; F; 10/21/09-23; N.C. Cherokee; 3/32; S; Dau.; 1618; Yes; Yes; Unallotted

1633; Matheson (Hardin, Odin), Odin; F; 12/2/03-29; N.C. Cherokee; 1/32; M; Wife; 1619; Yes; Yes; Unallotted

1634; Matthews (Lambert, Lillian), Lillian I.; F; 10/3/81-51; N.C. Cherokee; 1/16; M; Wife; 1620; Yes; Yes; Unallotted

1635; Matthews, Marshall; M; 12/22/13-19; N.C. Cherokee; 1/32; S; Son; 1621; Yes; Yes; Unallotted

1636; Matthews, Seaborne; M; 11/9/16-16; N.C. Cherokee; 1/32; S; Son; 1622; Yes; Yes; Unallotted

1637; Matthews, Ollie; F; 9/14/17-15; N.C. Cherokee; 1/64; S; Alone; 1623; Yes; Yes; Unallotted

1638; Meroney, Bailey B.; M; 10/21/66-66; N.C. Cherokee; 1/8; M; Head; 1624; Yes; Yes; Unallotted

1639; Meroney, Bailey B.; M; 8/18/01-31; N.C. Cherokee; 1/16; M; Head; 1625; Yes; Yes; Unallotted

1640; Meroney, Della; F; 5/6/06-26; N.C. Cherokee; 1/16; S; Alone; 1626; Yes; Yes; Unallotted

1641; Meroney, Felix P.; M; 3/27/05-28; N.C. Cherokee; 1/16; M; Head; 1627; Yes; Yes; Unallotted

1642; Meroney, Richard B.; M; 7/21/01-31; N.C. Cherokee; 1/16; M; Head; 1628; Yes; Yes; Unallotted

1643; Meroney, Barbara; F; 4/28/23-9; N.C. Cherokee; 1/32; S; Dau.; 1629; Yes; Yes; Unallotted

1644; Meroney, Wm. H.; M; 2/10/77-56; N.C. Cherokee; 1/8; M; Head; 1630; Yes; Yes; Unallotted

1645; Meroney, Raymond; M; 5/27/13-19; N.C. Cherokee; 1/16; S; Son; 1631; Yes; Yes; Unallotted

1646; Meroney, Martha D.; F; 7/25/14-18; N.C. Cherokee; 1/16; S; Dau.; 1632; Yes; Yes; Unallotted

1647; Meroney, David W.; M; 1/15/16-17; N.C. Cherokee; 1/16; S; Son; 1633; Yes; Yes; Unallotted

1648; Meroney, Wm. H.; M; 12/27/17-15; N.C. Cherokee; 1/16; S; Son; 1634; Yes; Yes; Unallotted

Census of the **Eastern Cherokee** reservation of the **Cherokee, N.C.** jurisdiction, as of **April 1** , **1933,** taken by **R. L. Spalsbury** , Superintendent.

Key: Number; Surname, Given; Sex; Date of Birth-Age at Last Birthday; Tribe; Degree of Blood; Marital Status; Relationship to Head of Family; Last C. Roll No.; At Jurisdiction Where Enrolled (Yes/No); (If no – Where); Ward (Yes/No); Allotment, Annuity and Identification Numbers (if given).

1649; Meroney, Louise M.; F; 5/29/20-12; N.C. Cherokee; 1/16; S; Dau.; 1635; Yes; Yes; Unallotted

1650; Miller (Rogers, Flonnie), Flonnie; F; 4/15/89-43; N.C. Cherokee; 1/8; M; Wife; 1636; Yes; Yes; Unallotted
1651; Miller, Lissie; F; 8/2/08-24; N.C. Cherokee; 1/16; S; Dau.; 1637; Yes; Yes; Unallotted
1652; Miller, Bessie; F; 1/21/10-23; N.C. Cherokee; 1/16; S; Dau.; 1638; Yes; Yes; Unallotted
1653; Miller, Vertie; F; 9/11/11-21; N.C. Cherokee; 1/16; S; Dau.; 1639; Yes; Yes; Unallotted
1654; Miller, Vernon; M; 2/3/13-20; N.C. Cherokee; 1/16; S; Son; 1640; Yes; Yes; Unallotted
1655; Miller, Adella; F; 8/3/14-18; N.C. Cherokee; 1/16; S; Dau.; 1641; Yes; Yes; Unallotted
1656; Miller, Baskey; M; 1/7/16-17; N.C. Cherokee; 1/16; S; Son; 1642; Yes; Yes; Unallotted
1657; Miller, Arnold; M; 10/27/19-13; N.C. Cherokee; 1/16; S; Son; 1644; Yes; Yes; Unallotted
1658; Miller, Alanerd; F; 3/7/23-10; N.C. Cherokee; 1/16; S; Dau.; 1645; Yes; Yes; Unallotted
1659; Miller, Bedonard; F; 3/7/23-10; N.C. Cherokee; 1/16; S; Dau.; 1646; Yes; Yes; Unallotted

1660; Miller (Porter, Iris), Iris P.; F; 8/1/92-40; N.C. Cherokee; 1/16; M; Wife; 1647; Yes; Yes; Unallotted

1661; Monroe (Lee, Nora), Nora A.; F; 7/12/80-52; N.C. Cherokee; 1/16; M; Wife; 1648; Yes; Yes; Unallotted

1662; Moody, Callie O.; F; 9/30/87-45; N.C. Cherokee; 1/4; M; Wife; 1649; Yes; Yes; Unallotted
1663; Moody, Harlin; M; 7/2/14-18; N.C. Cherokee; 1/8; S; Son; 1650; Yes; Yes; Unallotted
1664; Moody, Garland; M; 12/24/15-17; N.C. Cherokee; 1/8; S; Son; 1651; Yes; Yes; Unallotted
1665; Moody, Russell P.; M; 3/26/18-15; N.C. Cherokee; 1/8; S; Son; 1652; Yes; Yes; Unallotted
1666; Moody, Solomon; M; 12/31/19-13; N.C. Cherokee; 1/8; S; Son; 1653; Yes; Yes; Unallotted
1667; Moody, Bonnie Lee; F; 2/8/22-11; N.C. Cherokee; 1/8; S; Dau.; 1654; Yes; Yes; Unallotted
1668; Moody, Ruth P.; F; 5/6/24-8; N.C. Cherokee; 1/8; S; Dau.; 1655; Yes; Yes; Unallotted

Census of the **Eastern Cherokee** reservation of the **Cherokee, N.C.** jurisdiction, as of **April 1** , 19**33,** taken by **R. L. Spalsbury** , Superintendent.

Key: Number; Surname, Given; Sex; Date of Birth-Age at Last Birthday; Tribe; Degree of Blood; Marital Status; Relationship to Head of Family; Last C. Roll No.; At Jurisdiction Where Enrolled (Yes/No); (If no – Where); Ward (Yes/No); Allotment, Annuity and Identification Numbers (if given).

1669; Moore, Georgia C.; F; 10/28/82-50; N.C. Cherokee; 1/8; M; Wife; 1656; Yes; Yes; Unallotted

1670; Moore (Tallent, Luretta), Luretta C.; F; 7/4/89-43; N.C. Cherokee; 1/64; M; Wife; 1657; Yes; Yes; Unallotted

1671; Morgan, Mary A.; F; 5/2/12-20; N.C. Cherokee; 1/32; S; Dau. (Fr. white); 1658; Yes; Yes; Unallotted
1672; Morgan, Rena C.; F; 5/27/14-18; N.C. Cherokee; 1/32; S; Dau.; 1659; Yes; Yes; Unallotted
1673; Morgan, Wm. Albert; M; 10/27/16-16; N.C. Cherokee; 1/32; S; Son; 1660; Yes; Yes; Unallotted
1674; Morgan, Stella G.; F; 1/30/18-15; N.C. Cherokee; 1/32; S; Dau.; 1661; Yes; Yes; Unallotted
1675; Morgan, Carroll V.; F; 8/27/21-11; N.C. Cherokee; 1/32; S; Dau.; 1662; Yes; Yes; Unallotted

1676; Morrison, Fred; M; 2/22/02-33; N.C. Cherokee; 1/64; M; Head; 1663; Yes; Yes; Unallotted

1677; Morrison, Bruce; M; 1909-24; N.C. Cherokee; 1/4-; M; Head; 1664; Yes; Yes; Unallotted

1678; Morrison, Ollie; F; 2/20/81-52; N.C. Cherokee; 1/32; M; Wife; 1665; Yes; Yes; Unallotted
1679; Morrison, Blanche; F; 6/11/05-27; N.C. Cherokee; 1/64; S; Dau.; 1666; Yes; Yes; Unallotted
1680; Morrison, Beulah; F; 6/11/05-27; N.C. Cherokee; 1/64; S; Dau.; 1667; Yes; Yes; Unallotted
1681; Morrison, Marie; F; 2/20/12-23; N.C. Cherokee; 1/64; S; Dau.; 1668; Yes; Yes; Unallotted

1682; Morrow (Baker, Dona), Dona; F; 3/12/95-38; N.C. Cherokee; 1/16; M; Wife; 1669; No; Culberson, Cherokee, N.C,; Yes; Unallotted
1683; Morrow, Harford; M; 3/27/16-17; N.C. Cherokee; 1/32; S; Son; 1670; No; Culberson, Cherokee, N.C,; Yes; Unallotted

1684; Mull (Raper, Effie), Effie; F; 3/28/94-39; N.C. Cherokee; 1/16; M; Wife; 1671; No; Kannapolis, Caburrus, N.C,; Yes; Unallotted
1685; Mull, Bertha M.; F; 12/16/11-21; N.C. Cherokee; 1/32; S; Dau.; 1672; No; Kannapolis, Caburrus, N.C,; Yes; Unallotted
1686; Mull, Wm. Roy; M; 3/26/14-19; N.C. Cherokee; 1/32; S; Son; 1673; No; Kannapolis, Caburrus, N.C,; Yes; Unallotted
1687; Mull, John R.; M; 6/26/20-12; N.C. Cherokee; 1/32; S; Son; 1674; No; Kannapolis, Caburrus, N.C,; Yes; Unallotted

276

Census of the **Eastern Cherokee** reservation of the **Cherokee, N.C.** jurisdiction, as of **April 1** , **1933,** taken by **R. L. Spalsbury** , Superintendent.

Key: Number; Surname, Given; Sex; Date of Birth-Age at Last Birthday; Tribe; Degree of Blood; Marital Status; Relationship to Head of Family; Last C. Roll No.; At Jurisdiction Where Enrolled (Yes/No); (If no – Where); Ward (Yes/No); Allotment, Annuity and Identification Numbers (if given).

1688; Mull, Ruth E.; F; 12/4/21-11; N.C. Cherokee; 1/32; S; Dau.; 1675; No; Kannapolis, Caburrus, N.C,; Yes; Unallotted

1689; Mumblehead, James W.; M; 10/5/88-44; N.C. Cherokee; 4/4; M; Head; 1676; Yes; Yes; Unallotted

1690; Mumblehead, Lorena S.; F; 10/6/64-66; N.C. Cherokee; 1/4; Wd.; Head; 1677; Yes; Yes; Unallotted
1691; Murphy, Fred; M; 4/16/07-25; N.C. Cherokee; 1/4; S; Head; 1678; Yes; Yes; Unallotted

1692; Murphy, Gay; M; 1/29/06-27; N.C. Cherokee; 1/8; M; Head; 1679; No; Violet, Cherokee, N.C.; Yes; Unallotted

1693; Murphy, Greeley; M; 1/29/06-27; N.C. Cherokee; 1/8; S; Head; 1680; No; Violet, Cherokee, N.C.; Yes; Unallotted

1694; Murphy, Howard; M; 1/7/95-38; N.C. Cherokee; 1/8; M; Head; 1681; Yes; Yes; Unallotted
1695; Murphy, Jesse; M; 12/23/63-69; N.C. Cherokee; 1/4; M; Head; 1682; Yes; Yes; Unallotted
1696; Murphy, Mary M.; F; 6/25/69-63; N.C. Cherokee; 1/8; M; Wife; 1683; Yes; Yes; Unallotted

1697; Murphy, Joseph L.; M; 4/16/93-39; N.C. Cherokee; 1/8; M; Head; 1684; No; Struthers, Mahoning, Ohio; Yes; Unallotted
1698; Murphy, Sadie; F; 10/24/16-16; N.C. Cherokee; 1/16; S; Dau.; 1685; No; Struthers, Mahoning, Ohio; Yes; Unallotted

1699; Murphy, Joseph M.; M; 3/25/65-68; N.C. Cherokee; 1/4; M; Head; 1686; Yes; Yes; Unallotted
1700; Murphy, Ella; F; 8/8/12-20; N.C. Cherokee; 1/8; S; Alone; 1687; Yes; Yes; Unallotted
1701; Murphy, Cordelia; F; 1/26/15-18; N.C. Cherokee; 1/8; S; Sis.; 1688; Yes; Yes; Unallotted
1702; Murphy, Ralph; M; 10/26/29-3; N.C. Cherokee; --; S; nephew; 1689; Yes; Yes; Unallotted

1703; Murphy, Leander, Jr.; M; 7/19/95-37; N.C. Cherokee; 1/8; M; Head; 1690; Yes; Yes; Unallotted
1704; Murphy, Hollis; F; 3/1/21-12; N.C. Cherokee; 1/16; S; Dau.; 1691; Yes; Yes; Unallotted
1705; Murphy, Dale; F; 12/28/22-10; N.C. Cherokee; 1/16; S; Dau.; 1692; Yes; Yes; Unallotted

Census of the **Eastern Cherokee** reservation of the **Cherokee, N.C.** jurisdiction, as of **April 1**, 1933, taken by **R. L. Spalsbury**, Superintendent.

Key: Number; Surname, Given; Sex; Date of Birth-Age at Last Birthday; Tribe; Degree of Blood; Marital Status; Relationship to Head of Family; Last C. Roll No.; At Jurisdiction Where Enrolled (Yes/No); (If no – Where); Ward (Yes/No); Allotment, Annuity and Identification Numbers (if given).

1706; Murphy, Manco, Jr.; M; 3/29/93-40; N.C. Cherokee; 1/8; M; Head; 1693; Yes; Yes; Unallotted

1707; Murphy, Walter; M; 4/16/00-32; N.C. Cherokee; 1/16; M; Head; 1694; Yes; Yes; Unallotted

1708; Murphy, Marinda M.; F; 1/28/00-33; N.C. Cherokee; 1/16; M; Wife; 1695; Yes; Yes; Unallotted

1709; Murphy, Ethel; F; 4/18/16-16; N.C. Cherokee; 1/16; S; Dau.; 1696; Yes; Yes; Unallotted

1710; Murphy, Alice; F; 4/17/17-15; N.C. Cherokee; 1/16; S; Dau.; 1697; Yes; Yes; Unallotted

1711; Murphy, William; M; 1/6/90-43; N.C. Cherokee; 3/16; M; Head; 1698; Yes; Yes; Unallotted

1712; Murphy, Manco L.; M; 4/9/10-22; N.C. Cherokee; 3/32; S; Son; 1699; Yes; Yes; Unallotted

1713; Murphy, Robert; M; 1/28/12-21; N.C. Cherokee; 3/32; S; Son; 1700; Yes; Yes; Unallotted

1714; Murphy, Luther; M; 6/15/15-17; N.C. Cherokee; 3/32; S; Son; 1701; Yes; Yes; Unallotted

1715; Murphy, Lawrence; M; 6/14/18-14; N.C. Cherokee; 3/32; S; Son; 1702; Yes; Yes; Unallotted

1716; Murphy, Clarence; M; 6/14/18-14; N.C. Cherokee; 3/32; S; Son; 1703; Yes; Yes; Unallotted

1717; Murphy, Mary Etta; F; 3/28/21-12; N.C. Cherokee; 3/32; S; Dau.; 1704; Yes; Yes; Unallotted

1718; Ned, Ezekiel; M; 8/15/64-68; N.C. Cherokee; 4/4; M; Head; 1705; Yes; Yes; Unallotted

1719; Ned, Susan; F; 3/1/63-70; N.C. Cherokee; 4/4; M; Wife; 1706; Yes; Yes; Unallotted

1720; Newton, James D.; M; 8/1/72-60; N.C. Cherokee; 1/16; M; Head; 1707; Yes; Yes; Unallotted

1721; Nick, Chiltoskey; M; 1/6/83-50; N.C. Cherokee; 1/4; S; Head; 1708; No; Ohio; Yes; Unallotted

1722; Nottytom, Peter; M; 6/20/69-63; N.C. Cherokee; 4/4; Wd.; Head; 1709; Yes; Yes; Unallotted

1723; Okwataga, Elizabeth; F; 12/23/42-90; N.C. Cherokee; 4/4; Wd.; Head; 1710; Yes; Yes; Unallotted

Census of the **Eastern Cherokee** reservation of the **Cherokee, N.C.** jurisdiction, as of **April 1** , 19**33**, taken by **R. L. Spalsbury** , Superintendent.

Key: Number; Surname, Given; Sex; Date of Birth-Age at Last Birthday; Tribe; Degree of Blood; Marital Status; Relationship to Head of Family; Last C. Roll No.; At Jurisdiction Where Enrolled (Yes/No); (If no – Where); Ward (Yes/No); Allotment, Annuity and Identification Numbers (if given).

1724; Oocumma, Alex; M; 12/23/66-66; N.C. Cherokee; 7/8; M; Head; 1711; Yes; Yes; Unallotted

1725; Oocumma, Annie; F; 12/23/86-46; N.C. Cherokee; 4/4; M; Wife; 1712; Yes; Yes; Unallotted

1726; Oocumma, John; M; 1/20/12-21; N.C. Cherokee; 15/16; S; Son; 1713; Yes; Yes; Unallotted

1727; Oocumma, Joseph; M; 6/19/21-11; N.C. Cherokee; 15/16; S; Son; 1715; Yes; Yes; Unallotted

1728; Oocumma, Andy; M; 4/24/24-8; N.C. Cherokee; 15/16; S; Son; 1716; Yes; Yes; Unallotted

1729; Oocumma, Enoch; M; 12/1/90-42; N.C. Cherokee; 15/16; M; Head; 1717; Yes; Yes; Unallotted

1730; Oocumma, Malinda Q.; F; 6/20/04-28; N.C. Cherokee; 5/8; M; Wife; 1718; Yes; Yes; Unallotted

1731; Oocumma, Wilson; M; 5/30/24-8; N.C. Cherokee; 25/32; S; Son; 1719; Yes; Yes; Unallotted

1732; Oocumma, Wilson; M; 9/12/77-55; N.C. Cherokee; 15/16; M; Head; 1720; Yes; Yes; Unallotted

1733; Oocumma, Rachel W.R.; F; 1/23/85-48; N.C. Cherokee; 4/4; M; Wife; 1721; Yes; Yes; Unallotted

1734; Oosowee, David S.; M; 5/7/72-60; N.C. Cherokee; 4/4; M; Head; 1722; Yes; Yes; Unallotted

1735; Oosowee, Susie; F; 6/20/76-56; N.C. Cherokee; 4/4; M; Wife; 1723; Yes; Yes; Unallotted

1736; Oosowee, Tahquette; M; 6/27/99-33; N.C. Cherokee; 4/4; M; Head; 1724; Yes; Yes; Unallotted

1737; Oosowee, Nancy S.; F; 12/23/83-49; N.C. Cherokee; 4/4; M; Wife; 1725; Yes; Yes; Unallotted

1738; Otter, Andrew; M; 10/11/67-65; N.C. Cherokee; 4/4; Wd.; Head; 1726; Yes; Yes; Unallotted

1739; Otter, Jackson; M; 11/23/97-35; N.C. Cherokee; 4/4; M; Head; 1727; Yes; Yes; Unallotted

1740; Otter, Mary S.; F; 4/10/03-29; N.C. Cherokee; 4/4; M; Wife; 1728; Yes; Yes; Unallotted

1741; Otter, Sallie T.; F; 12/18/20-12; N.C. Cherokee; 4/4; S; Dau.; 1729; Yes;Yes; Unallotted

1742; Otter, Samuel Wm.; M; 12/13/22-10; N.C. Cherokee; 4/4; S; Son; 1730; Yes; Yes; Unallotted

Census of the **Eastern Cherokee** reservation of the **Cherokee, N.C.** jurisdiction, as of **April 1** , 19**33,** taken by **R. L. Spalsbury** , Superintendent.

Key: Number; Surname, Given; Sex; Date of Birth-Age at Last Birthday; Tribe; Degree of Blood; Marital Status; Relationship to Head of Family; Last C. Roll No.; At Jurisdiction Where Enrolled (Yes/No); (If no – Where); Ward (Yes/No); Allotment, Annuity and Identification Numbers (if given).

1743; Otter, Henry D.; M; 5/21/25-8; N.C. Cherokee; 4/4; S; Son; 1731; Yes; Yes; Unallotted

1744; Otter, Oliver; M; 8/3/29-3; N.C. Cherokee; 4/4; S; Son; 1732; Yes; Yes; Unallotted

1745; Owenby (Wakefield, Kate), Kate; F; 5/7/08-24; N.C. Cherokee; 1/64; M; Wife; 1733; Yes; Yes; Unallotted

1746; Owenby, Ruth; F; 9/6/23-9; N.C. Cherokee; 1/128; S; Dau.; 1734; Yes; Yes; Unallotted

1747; Owl, Adam; M; 1/27/60-73; N.C. Cherokee; 1/2; M; Head; 1735; Yes; Yes; Unallotted

1748; Owl, Cornelia; F; 12/23/63-69; N.C. Cherokee; 4/4; M; Wife; 1736; Yes; Yes; Unallotted

1749; Owl, Quincy; M; 12/1/04-28; N.C. Cherokee; 3/4; S; Son; 1737; Yes; Yes; Unallotted

1750; Owl, Allen; M; 2/26/90-43; N.C. Cherokee; 4/4; M; Head; 1738; Yes; Yes; Unallotted

1751; Owl, Martha; F; 2/8/14-19; N.C. Cherokee; 1/2; S; Dau.; 1739; Yes; Yes; Unallotted

1752; Owl, Noah; M; 3/31/16-16; N.C. Cherokee; 1/2; S; Son; 1740; Yes; Yes; Unallotted

1753; Owl, Ammons; M; 2/24/90-43; N.C. Cherokee; 4/4; M; Head; 1741; Yes; Yes; Unallotted

1754; Owl, Elizabeth; F; 6/22/86-46; N.C. Cherokee; 4/4; M; Wife; 1742; Yes; Yes; Unallotted

1755; Owl, Gertrude E.; F; 9/7/14-18; N.C. Cherokee; 4/4; S; Dau.; 1743; Yes; Yes; Unallotted

1756; Owl, Raymond; M; 1/5/18-15; N.C. Cherokee; 4/4; S; Son; 1744; Yes; Yes; Unallotted

1757; Owl, Alice C.; F; 4/6/24-8; N.C. Cherokee; 4/4; S; Dau.; 1745; Yes; Yes; Unallotted

1758; Owl, Charlotte; F; 3/8/09-24; N.C. Cherokee; 1/2; S; Head; 1746; Yes; Yes; Unallotted

1759; Owl, Dahney; F; 9/30/81-51; N.C. Cherokee; 15/16; Div.; Head; 1747; Yes; Yes; Unallotted

1760; Owl, David; M; 7/11/93-40; N.C. Cherokee; 1/2; M; Head; 1748; Yes; Yes; Unallotted

Census of the **Eastern Cherokee** reservation of the **Cherokee, N.C.** jurisdiction, as of **April 1** , **1933,** taken by **R. L. Spalsbury** , Superintendent.

Key: Number; Surname, Given; Sex; Date of Birth-Age at Last Birthday; Tribe; Degree of Blood; Marital Status; Relationship to Head of Family; Last C. Roll No.; At Jurisdiction Where Enrolled (Yes/No); (If no – Where); Ward (Yes/No); Allotment, Annuity and Identification Numbers (if given).

1761; Owl, David; M; 10/17/97-35; N.C. Cherokee; 3/4; M; Head; 1749; Yes; Yes; Unallotted

1762; Owl, Elizabeth; F; 2/17/02-31; N.C. Cherokee; 7/16; M; Wife; 1750; Yes; Yes; Unallotted

1763; Owl, Caledonia; F; 6/11/18-14; N.C. Cherokee; 19/32; S; Dau.; 1751; Yes; Yes; Unallotted

1764; Owl, Lloyd J.; M; 6/9/20-12; N.C. Cherokee; 19/32; S; Son; 1752; Yes; Yes; Unallotted

1765; Owl, Dinah; F; 12/22/58-74; N.C. Cherokee; 4/4; Wd.; Head; 1753; Yes; Yes; Unallotted

1766; Owl, William; M; 2/16/92-41; N.C. Cherokee; 4/4; S; Son; 1754; Yes; Yes; Unallotted

1767; Owl, Enoch; M; 3/9/99-34; N.C. Cherokee; 4/4; M; Head; 1755; Yes; Yes; Unallotted

1768; Owl, Ollie Q.; F; 2/28/99-34; N.C. Cherokee; 5/8; M; Wife; 1756; Yes; Yes; Unallotted

1769; Owl, Frell; M; 3/1/99-34; N.C. Cherokee; 1/2; M; Head; 1757; Yes; Yes; Unallotted

1770; Owl, George; M; 12/26/95-37; N.C. Cherokee; 1/2; M; Head; 1758; No; Seymour, New Haven, Conn.; Yes; Unallotted

1771; Owl, George Jr.; M; 8/1/20-12; N.C. Cherokee; 1/4; S; Son; 1759; No; Seymour, New Haven, Conn.; Yes; Unallotted

1772; Owl, Rebecca; F; 4/27/23-9; N.C. Cherokee; 1/4; S; Dau.; 1760; No; Seymour, New Haven, Conn.; Yes; Unallotted

1773; Owl, Hilary S.; M; 4/5/26-6; N.C. Cherokee; 1/4; S; Son; 1761; No; Seymour, New Haven, Conn.; Yes; Unallotted

1774; Owl, Henry; M; 8/1/97-35; N.C. Cherokee; 1/2; S; Head; 1762; Yes; Yes; Unallotted

1775; Owl, James; M; 10/20/86-46; N.C. Cherokee; 4/4; M; Head; 1763; Yes; Yes; Unallotted

1776; Owl, Charlotte; F; 8/13/94-38; N.C. Cherokee; 4/4; M; Wife; 1764; Yes; Yes; Unallotted

1777; Owl, Lloyd; M; 11/21/09-23; N.C. Cherokee; 4/4; S; Son; 1765; Yes; Yes; Unallotted

1778; Owl, Jefferson; M; 10/30/14-18; N.C. Cherokee; 4/4; S; Son; 1766; Yes; Yes; Unallotted

1779; Owl, Charles; M; 2/2/20-13; N.C. Cherokee; 4/4; S; Son; 1767; Yes; Yes; Unallotted

Census of the **Eastern Cherokee** reservation of the **Cherokee, N.C.** jurisdiction, as of **April 1**, 1933, taken by **R. L. Spalsbury**, Superintendent.

Key: Number; Surname, Given; Sex; Date of Birth-Age at Last Birthday; Tribe; Degree of Blood; Marital Status; Relationship to Head of Family; Last C. Roll No.; At Jurisdiction Where Enrolled (Yes/No); (If no – Where); Ward (Yes/No); Allotment, Annuity and Identification Numbers (if given).

1780; Owl, Harriett N.; F; 7/15/30-2; N.C. Cherokee; 4/4; S; Dau.; 1768; Yes; Yes; Unallotted

1781; Owl, Johnson; M; 5/27/79-53; N.C. Cherokee; 4/4; M; Head; 1769; Yes; Yes; Unallotted

1782; Owl, Stacey; F; 3/29/80-53; N.C. Cherokee; 4/4; M; Wife; 1770; Yes; Yes; Unallotted

1783; Owl, Joseph; M; 8/10/13-19; N.C. Cherokee; 4/4; S; Son; 1771; Yes; Yes; Unallotted

1784; Owl, Sallie S.; F; 12/15/88-44; N.C. Cherokee; 4/4; Wd.; Wife; 1773; Yes; Yes; Unallotted

1785; Owl (Mr. Julia Sanders), Philip; M; 6/29/09-23; N.C. Cherokee; 11/16; S; Son; 1774; Yes; Yes; Unallotted

1786; Owl, Ellis; M; 11/13/13-19; N.C. Cherokee; 11/16; S; Son; 1775; Yes; Yes; Unallotted

1787; Owl, Lloyd; M; 8/22/99-33; N.C. Cherokee; 1/4; M; Head; 1776; Yes; Yes; Unallotted

1788; Owl, Jessie E.; F; 6/16/22-10; N.C. Cherokee; 5/8; S; Dau.; 1777; Yes; Yes; Unallotted

1789; Owl, Robert E.; M; 4/27/24-8; N.C. Cherokee; 5/8; S; Son; 1778; Yes; Yes; Unallotted

1790; Owl, Louis; M; 2/28/08-25; N.C. Cherokee; 4/4; S; Head; 1779; Yes; Yes; Unallotted

1791; Owl, Mark; M; 6/2/92-40; N.C. Cherokee; 1/4; M; Head; 1780; Yes; Yes; Unallotted

1792; Owl, Belva S.; F; 2/28/92-41; N.C. Cherokee; 1/4; M; Wife; 1781; Yes; Yes; Unallotted

1793; Owl, Jarrett; M; 6/28/11-21; N.C. Cherokee; 1/4; S; Son; 1782; Yes; Yes; Unallotted

1794; Owl, Oscar; M; 11/5/12-20; N.C. Cherokee; 1/4; S; Son; 1783; Yes; Yes; Unallotted

1795; Owl, Ralph; M; 3/19/15-18; N.C. Cherokee; 1/4; S; Son; 1784; Yes; Yes; Unallotted

1796; Owl, Eugene; M; 8/22/17-15; N.C. Cherokee; 1/4; S; Son; 1785; Yes; Yes; Unallotted

1797; Owl, Clifton; M; 3/20/20-13; N.C. Cherokee; 1/4; S; Son; 1786; Yes; Yes; Unallotted

1798; Owl, Clifford; M; 3/20/20-13; N.C. Cherokee; 1/4; S; Son; 1787; Yes; Yes; Unallotted

1799; Owl, Edna; F; 8/25/21-11; N.C. Cherokee; 1/4; S; Dau.; 1788; Yes; Yes; Unallotted

Census of the **Eastern Cherokee** reservation of the **Cherokee, N.C.** jurisdiction, as of **April 1** , **1933,** taken by **R. L. Spalsbury** , Superintendent.

Key: Number; Surname, Given; Sex; Date of Birth-Age at Last Birthday; Tribe; Degree of Blood; Marital Status; Relationship to Head of Family; Last C. Roll No.; At Jurisdiction Where Enrolled (Yes/No); (If no – Where); Ward (Yes/No); Allotment, Annuity and Identification Numbers (if given).

1800; Owl, Viola; F; 5/8/26-6; N.C. Cherokee; 1/4; S; Dau.; 1789; Yes; Yes; Unallotted
1801; Owl, Rosie E.; F; 1/10/28-5; N.C. Cherokee; 1/4; S; Dau.; 1790; Yes; Yes; Unallotted
1802; Owl, Nettie E.; F; 5/14/31-1; N.C. Cherokee; 1/4; S; Dau.; 1791; Yes; Yes; Unallotted

1803; Owl, Moses; M; 3/26/89-44; N.C. Cherokee; 3/4; M; Head; 1792; Yes; Yes; Unallotted

1804; Owl, Sampson; M; 11/17/54-78; N.C. Cherokee; 4/4; M; Head; 1793; Yes; Yes; Unallotted

1805; Owl, Samuel; M; 10/28/97-35; N.C. Cherokee; 3/4; M; Head; 1794; Yes; Yes; Unallotted
1806; Owl, Callie S.; F; 3/23/01-32; N.C. Cherokee; 3/16; M; Wife; 1795; Yes; Yes; Unallotted
1807; Owl, Samuel F.; M; 9/2/18-14; N.C. Cherokee; 15/32; S; Son; 1796; Yes; Yes; Unallotted
1808; Owl, Ethlyn R.; F; 4/10/20-12; N.C. Cherokee; 15/32; S; Dau.; 1797; Yes; Yes; Unallotted
1809; Owl, John L.; M; 6/22/22-10; N.C. Cherokee; 15/32; S; Son; 1798; Yes; Yes; Unallotted
1810; Owl, Dora; F; 10/23/24-8; N.C. Cherokee; 15/32; S; Dau.; 1799; Yes; Yes; Unallotted
1811; Owl, Bennie L.; M; 7/18/30-2; N.C. Cherokee; 15/32; S; Son; 1800; Yes; Yes; Unallotted
1812; Owl, Betty Jane; F; 8/7/32-7/12; N.C. Cherokee; 15/32; S; Dau.; ---; Yes; Yes; Unallotted

1813; Owl, Solomon; M; 8/22/63-69; N.C. Cherokee; 1/2; M; Head; 1801; Yes; Yes; Unallotted
1814; Owl, Alfred B.; M; 4/18/97-35; N.C. Cherokee; 1/4; S; Son; 1802; Yes; Yes; Unallotted
1815; Owl, Cornelius; M; 3/24/02-31; N.C. Cherokee; 1/4; S; Son; 1803; Yes; Yes; Unallotted
1816; Owl, William D.; M; 2/18/07-26; N.C. Cherokee; 1/4; S; Son; 1805; Yes; Yes; Unallotted
1817; Owl, DeWitt; M; 6/7/08-24; N.C. Cherokee; 1/4; S; Son; 1806; Yes; Yes; Unallotted
1818; Owl, Edward; M; 3/27/10-23; N.C. Cherokee; 1/4; S; Son; 1807; Yes; Yes; Unallotted
1819; Owl (Mr[sic] Evy McCoy), Bessie E.; F; 10/11/30-2; N.C. Cherokee; 5/32; S; Granddau.; 1808; Yes; Yes; Unallotted

Census of the **Eastern Cherokee** reservation of the **Cherokee, N.C.** jurisdiction, as of **April 1** , 19**33,** taken by **R. L. Spalsbury** , Superintendent.

Key: Number; Surname, Given; Sex; Date of Birth-Age at Last Birthday; Tribe; Degree of Blood; Marital Status; Relationship to Head of Family; Last C. Roll No.; At Jurisdiction Where Enrolled (Yes/No); (If no – Where); Ward (Yes/No); Allotment, Annuity and Identification Numbers (if given).

1820; Owl, Thomas; M; 3/19/87-46; N.C. Cherokee; 3/4; M; Head; 1809; Yes; Yes; Unallotted

1821; Owl, W. Thomas; M; 1/25/05-28; N.C. Cherokee; 1/2; S; Head; 1810; Yes; Yes; Unallotted

1822; Owl, William; M; 4/20/84-48; N.C. Cherokee; 3/4; M; Head; 1811; Yes; Yes; Unallotted

1823; Palmer, Dora Owl; F; 1/23/90-43; N.C. Cherokee; 1/4; M; Wife; 1812; Yes; Yes; Unallotted

1824; Palmer, Ledford; M; 1/17/12-21; N.C. Cherokee; 1/8; S; Son; 1813; Yes; Yes; Unallotted

1825; Palmer, Haddington; M; 10/1/13-19; N.C. Cherokee; 1/8; S; Son; 1814; Yes; Yes; Unallotted

1826; Palmer, Nettie M.; F; 10/16/15-17; N.C. Cherokee; 1/8; S; Dau.; 1815; Yes; Yes; Unallotted

1827; Palmer, Holt; M; 9/17/17-15; N.C. Cherokee; 1/8; S; Son; 1816; Yes; Yes; Unallotted

1828; Palmer, Theodore; M; 5/31/19-13; N.C. Cherokee; 1/8; S; Son; 1817; Yes; Yes; Unallotted

1829; Palmer, Irene; F; 4/1/21-11; N.C. Cherokee; 1/8; S; Dau.; 1818; Yes; Yes; Unallotted

1830; Palmer, Martin L.; M; 4/16/23-9; N.C. Cherokee; 1/8; S; Son; 1819; Yes; Yes; Unallotted

1831; Palmer, James; M; 5/22/25-7; N.C. Cherokee; 1/8; S; Son; 1820; Yes; Yes; Unallotted

1832; Palmer, Edward; M; 4/24/27-5; N.C. Cherokee; 1/8; S; Son; 1821; Yes; Yes; Unallotted

1833; Palmer, Lewis; M; 9/19/29-3; N.C. Cherokee; 1/8; S; Son; 1822; Yes; Yes; Unallotted

1834; Panther, Mark; M; 11/22/75-57; N.C. Cherokee; 4/4; M; Head; 1823; Yes; Yes; Unallotted

1835; Panther, Windy L.; F; 8/1/88-44; N.C. Cherokee; 4/4; M; Wife; 1824; Yes; Yes; Unallotted

1836; Panther, Samuel; M; 4/4/13-19; N.C. Cherokee; 4/4; S; Son; 1825; Yes; Yes; Unallotted

1837; Panther, Juanita; F; 1/17/17-16; N.C. Cherokee; 4/4; S; Dau.; 1826; Yes; Yes; Unallotted

1838; Panther, Olivan; F; 4/30/22-10; N.C. Cherokee; 4/4; S; Dau.; 1827; Yes; Yes; Unallotted

1839; Parker (Lambert, Cora), Cora L.; F; 4/23/99-33; N.C. Cherokee; 1/16; M; Wife; 1828; Yes; Yes; Unallotted

284

Census of the **Eastern Cherokee** reservation of the **Cherokee, N.C.** jurisdiction, as of **April 1** , **1933,** taken by **R. L. Spalsbury** , Superintendent.

Key: Number; Surname, Given; Sex; Date of Birth-Age at Last Birthday; Tribe; Degree of Blood; Marital Status; Relationship to Head of Family; Last C. Roll No.; At Jurisdiction Where Enrolled (Yes/No); (If no – Where); Ward (Yes/No); Allotment, Annuity and Identification Numbers (if given).

1840; Parker, John W.; M; 1/10/24-9; N.C. Cherokee; 1/32; S; Son; 1829; Yes; Yes; Unallotted

1841; Parker (Lambert, Flora), Flora L.; F; 9/9/02-30; N.C. Cherokee; 1/4; M; Wife; 1830; Yes; Yes; Unallotted

1842; Parker, Helen K[sic]; F; 9/2/21-11; N.C. Cherokee; 1/8; S; Dau.; 1831; Yes; Yes; Unallotted

1843; Parker, Mary K.; F; 12/3/22-10; N.C. Cherokee; 1/8; S; Dau.; 1832; Yes; Yes; Unallotted

1844; Parker, Edgar K.; M; 9/2/24-8; N.C. Cherokee; 1/8; S; Son; 1833; Yes; Yes; Unallotted

1845; Parker, Jerome; M; 8/26/28-4; N.C. Cherokee; 1/8; S; Son; 1834; Yes; Yes; Unallotted

1846; Parker (Voiles, Josie), Josie; F; 11/24/77-55; N.C. Cherokee; 1/16; M; Wife; 1835; Yes; Yes; Unallotted

1847; Parris, Lola (Lula); F; 2/4/12-19; N.C. Cherokee; 1/16; S; Alone; 1836; No; 441 W. 37th St., Chattanooga, Hamilton, Tenn.; Yes; Unallotted

1848; Parton (Baker, Crickett), Crickett; F; 3/13/02-30; N.C. Cherokee; 1/16; M; Wife; 1837; No; Culberson, Cherokee, N. C.; Yes; Unallotted

1849; Parton, Thelma; F; 7/23/23-10; N.C. Cherokee; 1/32; S; Dau.; 1838; No; Culberson, Cherokee, N. C.; Yes; Unallotted

1850; Partridge, Bessie; F; 7/20/10-22; N.C. Cherokee; 4/4; S; Head; 1839; Yes; Yes; Unallotted

1851; Partridge, Bird; M; 8/4/79-53; N.C. Cherokee; 4/4; M; Head; 1840; Yes; Yes; Unallotted

1852; Partridge, Elsie G.; F; 10/11/84-48; N.C. Cherokee; 7/8; M; Wife; 1841; Yes; Yes; Unallotted

1853; Partridge, John; M; 6/17/11-21; N.C. Cherokee; 15/16; S; Son; 1842; Yes; Yes; Unallotted

1854; Partridge, Dahney; F; 12/14/13-19; N.C. Cherokee; 15/16; S; Dau.; 1843; Yes; Yes; Unallotted

1855; Partridge, Sallie; F; 12/13/17-15; N.C. Cherokee; 15/16; S; Dau.; 1844; Yes; Yes; Unallotted

1856; Partridge, Nora; F; 4/12/19-13; N.C. Cherokee; 15/16; S; Dau.; 1845; Yes; Yes; Unallotted

1857; Partridge, Mollie; F; 3/10/22-11; N.C. Cherokee; 15/16; S; Dau.; 1846; Yes; Yes; Unallotted

1858; Patterson, Alonzo; M; 12/29/96-36; N.C. Cherokee; 1/32; M; Head; 1847; No; Loving, Fannin, Ga.; Yes; Unallotted

Census of the **Eastern Cherokee** reservation of the **Cherokee, N.C.** jurisdiction, as of **April 1** , **1933,** taken by **R. L. Spalsbury** , Superintendent.

Key: Number; Surname, Given; Sex; Date of Birth-Age at Last Birthday; Tribe; Degree of Blood; Marital Status; Relationship to Head of Family; Last C. Roll No.; At Jurisdiction Where Enrolled (Yes/No); (If no – Where); Ward (Yes/No); Allotment, Annuity and Identification Numbers (if given).

1859; Patterson, Leonard; M; 9/4/16-16; N.C. Cherokee; 1/64; S; Son; 1848; No; Loving, Fannin, Ga.; Yes; Unallotted

1860; Patterson, Zell; F; 5/23/18-14; N.C. Cherokee; 1/64; S; Dau.; 1849; No; Loving, Fannin, Ga.; Yes; Unallotted

1861; Patterson, Alyne; F; 12/23/19-13; N.C. Cherokee; 1/64; S; Dau.; 1850; No; Loving, Fannin, Ga.; Yes; Unallotted

1862; Patterson, Clyta; F; 8/31/21-11; N.C. Cherokee; 1/64; S; Dau.; 1851; No; Loving, Fannin, Ga.; Yes; Unallotted

1863; Patterson, L.C.; M; 3/12/23-10; N.C. Cherokee; 1/64; S; Son; 1852; No; Loving, Fannin, Ga.; Yes; Unallotted

1864; Patterson (Cole, Ella), Ella C.; F; 5/22/77-55; N.C. Cherokee; 1/16; M; Wife; 1853; No; Lewner, Union, Ga.; Yes; Unallotted

1865; Patterson, Arvil; M; 3/12/06-27; N.C. Cherokee; 1/32; S; Son; 1854; No; Lewner, Union, Ga.; Yes; Unallotted

1866; Patterson, Beadie; F; 12/30/08-24; N.C. Cherokee; 1/32; S; Dau.; 1855; No; Lewner, Union, Ga.; Yes; Unallotted

1867; Patterson, Zida; F; 11/11/10-22; N.C. Cherokee; 1/32; S; Dau.; 1856; No; Lewner, Union, Ga.; Yes; Unallotted

1868; Patterson, Redie; F; 8/21/12-20; N.C. Cherokee; 1/32; S; Dau.; 1857; No; Lewner, Union, Ga.; Yes; Unallotted

1869; Patterson, Clifton; M; 4/22/14-18; N.C. Cherokee; 1/32; S; Son; 1858; No; Lewner, Union, Ga.; Yes; Unallotted

1870; Patterson, Ruby; F; 3/26/16-17; N.C. Cherokee; 1/32; S; Dau.; 1859; No; Lewner, Union, Ga.; Yes; Unallotted

1871; Patterson, L.J.; M; 11/12/18-14; N.C. Cherokee; 1/32; S; Son; 1860; No; Lewner, Union, Ga.; Yes; Unallotted

1872; Patterson, Hobart; M; 11/11/03-29; N.C. Cherokee; 1/32; M; Head; 1861; No; Hayesville, Clay, N.C.; Yes; Unallotted

1873; Patterson, Delmer; M; 8/20/23-9; N.C. Cherokee; 1/64; S; Son; 1862; No; Hayesville, Clay, N.C.; Yes; Unallotted

1874; Patterson (Raper, Iowa), Iowa; F; 3/6/81-52; N.C. Cherokee; 1/16; M; Wife; 1863; No; Hayesville, Clay, N.C.; Yes; Unallotted

1875; Patterson , Eunice; F; 2/14/07-26; N.C. Cherokee; 1/32; S; Dau.; 1864; No; Hayesville, Clay, N.C.; Yes; Unallotted

1876; Patterson , Eula; F; 1/3/10-23; N.C. Cherokee; 1/32; S; Dau.; 1865; No; Hayesville, Clay, N.C.; Yes; Unallotted

1877; Patterson, Ray; M; 11/29/12-20; N.C. Cherokee; 1/32; S; Son; 1866; No; Hayesville, Clay, N.C.; Yes; Unallotted

1878; Patterson, Lyle; M; 7/11/15-17; N.C. Cherokee; 1/32; S; Son; 1867; No; Hayesville, Clay, N.C.; Yes; Unallotted

1879; Patterson, John; M; 3/13/18-15; N.C. Cherokee; 1/32; S; Son; 1868; No; Hayesville, Clay, N.C.; Yes; Unallotted

Census of the **Eastern Cherokee** reservation of the **Cherokee, N.C.** jurisdiction, as of **April 1** , **1933,** taken by **R. L. Spalsbury** , Superintendent.

Key: Number; Surname, Given; Sex; Date of Birth-Age at Last Birthday; Tribe; Degree of Blood; Marital Status; Relationship to Head of Family; Last C. Roll No.; At Jurisdiction Where Enrolled (Yes/No); (If no – Where); Ward (Yes/No); Allotment, Annuity and Identification Numbers (if given).

1880; Patterson , Mary Joe; F; 2/29/24-9; N.C. Cherokee; 1/32; S; Dau.; 1869; No; Hayesville, Clay, N.C.; Yes; Unallotted

1881; Patterson, Oldham; M; 7/5/01-31; N.C. Cherokee; 1/16; S; Head; 1870; No; Gastonia, Gaston, N.C.; Yes; Unallotted

1882; Patterson, Almer; M; 4/12/06-26; N.C. Cherokee; 1/16; S; Bro.; 1871; No; Gastonia, Gaston, N.C.; Yes; Unallotted

1883; Patterson, Alwain; M; 5/16/10-22; N.C. Cherokee; 1/16; S; Bro.; 1872; No; Gastonia, Gaston, N.C.; Yes; Unallotted

1884; Passmore (Lee, Nancy), Nancy J.; F; 9/8/77-55; N.C. Cherokee; 1/16; M; Wife; 1873; Yes; Yes; Unallotted

1885; Passmore, Thomas N.; M; 4/12/02-30; N.C. Cherokee; 1/32; S; Son; 1874; Yes; Yes; Unallotted

1886; Passmore, Charles A.; M; 6/16/03-29; N.C. Cherokee; 1/32; S; Son; 1875; Yes; Yes; Unallotted

1887; Passmore, Rose C.; F; 5/28/05-27; N.C. Cherokee; 1/32; S; Dau.; 1876; Yes; Yes; Unallotted

1888; Passmore, Oscar; M; 9/22/07-25; N.C. Cherokee; 1/32; S; Son; 1877; Yes; Yes; Unallotted

1889; Passmore, David; M; 3/26/12-21; N.C. Cherokee; 1/32; S; Son; 1878; Yes; Yes; Unallotted

1890; Passmore, Mary; F; 9/26/13-19; N.C. Cherokee; 1/32; S; Dau.; 1879; Yes; Yes; Unallotted

1891; Passmore, Sarah; F; 8/11/15-17; N.C. Cherokee; 1/32; S; Dau.; 1880; Yes; Yes; Unallotted

1892; Passmore, Palace; F; 7/26/18-14; N.C. Cherokee; 1/32; S; Dau.; 1881; Yes; Yes; Unallotted

1893; Passmore, Alice; F; 7/26/18-14; N.C. Cherokee; 1/32; S; Dau.; 1882; Yes; Yes; Unallotted

1894; Passmore, Belvia; F; 5/3/21-11; N.C. Cherokee; 1/32; S; Dau.; 1883; Yes; Yes; Unallotted

1895; Payne, Albert F.; M; 8/1/99-33; N.C. Cherokee; 1/32; M; Head; 1884; Yes; Yes; Unallotted

1896; Payne, David L.; M; 12/12/74-58; N.C. Cherokee; 1/32; M; Head; 1885; Yes; Yes; Unallotted

1897; Payne, Clarence; M; 9/25/14-18; N.C. Cherokee; 1/64; S; Son; 1886; Yes; Yes; Unallotted

1898; Payne, Rosa Mae; F; 5/31/16-16; N.C. Cherokee; 1/64; S; Dau.; 1887; Yes; Yes; Unallotted

1899; Payne, Desser L.; M; 5/28/18-14; N.C. Cherokee; 1/64; S; Son; 1888; Yes; Yes; Unallotted

Census of the **Eastern Cherokee** reservation of the **Cherokee, N.C.** jurisdiction, as of **April 1** , 1933, taken by **R. L. Spalsbury** , Superintendent.

Key: Number; Surname, Given; Sex; Date of Birth-Age at Last Birthday; Tribe; Degree of Blood; Marital Status; Relationship to Head of Family; Last C. Roll No.; At Jurisdiction Where Enrolled (Yes/No); (If no – Where); Ward (Yes/No); Allotment, Annuity and Identification Numbers (if given).

1900; Payne, Georgia; F; 5/10/20-12; N.C. Cherokee; 1/64; S; Dau.; 1889; Yes; Yes; Unallotted

1901; Payne, Oveliva; F; 3/18/22-11; N.C. Cherokee; 1/64; S; Dau.; 1890; Yes; Yes; Unallotted

1902; Payne, Elisha; M; 2/6/85-48; N.C. Cherokee; 1/32; M; Head; 1891; No; Hiawassee, Cherokee, N.C.; Yes; Unallotted

1903; Payne, Buster; M; 6/14/08-24; N.C. Cherokee; 1/64; S; Son; 1892; No; Hiawassee, Cherokee, N.C.; Yes; Unallotted

1904; Payne, Lou Belle; F; 3/2/12-21; N.C. Cherokee; 1/64; S; Dau.; 1893; No; Hiawassee, Cherokee, N.C.; Yes; Unallotted

1905; Payne, Cuba; F; 11/14/14-18; N.C. Cherokee; 1/64; S; Dau.; 1894; No; Hiawassee, Cherokee, N.C.; Yes; Unallotted

1906; Payne, Manda; F; 9/7/16-16; N.C. Cherokee; 1/64; S; Dau.; 1895; No; Hiawassee, Cherokee, N.C.; Yes; Unallotted

1907; Payne (Taylor, Estie), Estie T.; F; 10/9/00-32; N.C. Cherokee; 1/32; M; Wife; 1896; No; Hiawassee, Cherokee, N.C.; Yes; Unallotted

1908; Payne, Walter; M; 5/28/21-11; N.C. Cherokee; 1/64; S; Son; 1897; No; Hiawassee, Cherokee, N.C.; Yes; Unallotted

1909; Payne, Earl; M; 4/1/23-10; N.C. Cherokee; 1/64; S; Son; 1898; No; Hiawassee, Cherokee, N.C.; Yes; Unallotted

1910; Payne, James M.; M; 2/25/76-57; N.C. Cherokee; 1/16; M; Head; 1899; No; Ranger, Cherokee, N.C.; Yes; Unallotted

1911; Payne, Carrie; F; 6/4/10-22; N.C. Cherokee; 1/32; S; Dau.; 1900; No; Ranger, Cherokee, N.C.; Yes; Unallotted

1912; Payne, Margie E.; F; 9/19/13-19; N.C. Cherokee; 1/32; S; Dau.; 1901; No; Ranger, Cherokee, N.C.; Yes; Unallotted

1913; Payne, Jim; M; 12/20/88-44; N.C. Cherokee; 1/32; M; Head; 1902; Yes; Yes; Unallotted

1914; Payne, Clifford; M; 6/14/10-22; N.C. Cherokee; 1/64; S; Son; 1903; Yes; Yes; Unallotted

1915; Payne, Junaita[sic]; F; 7/16/14-18; N.C. Cherokee; 1/64; S; Dau.; 1904; Yes; Yes; Unallotted

1916; Payne, Thelma; F; 10/8/16-16; N.C. Cherokee; 1/64; S; Dau.; 1905; Yes; Yes; Unallotted

1917; Payne, James; M; 12/11/18-14; N.C. Cherokee; 1/64; S; Son; 1906; Yes; Yes; Unallotted

1918; Payne, Calvin; M; 12/2/20-12; N.C. Cherokee; 1/64; S; Son; 1907; Yes; Yes; Unallotted

1919; Payne, Pauline; F; 5/15/23-9; N.C. Cherokee; 1/64; S; Dau.; 1908; Yes; Yes; Unallotted

Census of the **Eastern Cherokee** reservation of the **Cherokee, N.C.** jurisdiction, as of **April 1** , **1933,** taken by **R. L. Spalsbury** , Superintendent.

Key: Number; Surname, Given; Sex; Date of Birth-Age at Last Birthday; Tribe; Degree of Blood; Marital Status; Relationship to Head of Family; Last C. Roll No.; At Jurisdiction Where Enrolled (Yes/No); (If no – Where); Ward (Yes/No); Allotment, Annuity and Identification Numbers (if given).

1920; Payne, Oliver C.; M; 1/1/92-41; N.C. Cherokee; 1/16; M; Head; 1909; No; Birch, Cherokee, N.C.; Yes; Unallotted

1921; Payne, Mabel J.; F; 2/16/14-19; N.C. Cherokee; 1/32; S; Dau.; 1910; No; Birch, Cherokee, N.C.; Yes; Unallotted

1922; Payne, Claude H.; M; 12/4/15-17; N.C. Cherokee; 1/32; S; Son; 1911; No; Birch, Cherokee, N.C.; Yes; Unallotted

1923; Payne, Lois E.; F; 12/30/17-15; N.C. Cherokee; 1/32; S; Dau.; 1912; No; Birch, Cherokee, N.C.; Yes; Unallotted

1924; Payne, Ralph G.; M; 2/7/22-11; N.C. Cherokee; 1/32; S; Son; 1913; No; Birch, Cherokee, N.C.; Yes; Unallotted

1925; Payne, Ohlen; M; 7/19/23-9; N.C. Cherokee; 1/32; S; Son; 1914; No; Birch, Cherokee, N.C.; Yes; Unallotted

1926; Payne, Poley E.; M; 6/23/96-36; N.C. Cherokee; 1/32; M; Head; 1915; No; Kinsey, Cherokee, N.C.; Yes; Unallotted

1927; Payne, Neil; M; 8/8/20-12; N.C. Cherokee; 1/64; S; Son; 1916; No; Kinsey, Cherokee, N.C.; Yes; Unallotted

1928; Payne, Lucy; F; 3/27/22-11; N.C. Cherokee; 1/64; S; Dau.; 1917; No; Kinsey, Cherokee, N.C.; Yes; Unallotted

1929; Payne, Rollin T.; M; 1/28/97-35; N.C. Cherokee; 1/32; M; Head; 1918; No; Etowah, McMinn, Tenn.; Yes; Unallotted

1930; Payne, William E.; M; 4/10/72-60; N.C. Cherokee; 1/16; M; Head; 1919; No; Gastonia, Gaston, N.C.; Yes; Unallotted

1931; Payne, William A.; M; 11/11/03-29; N.C. Cherokee; 1/32; S; Son; 1920; No; Gastonia, Gaston, N.C.; Yes; Unallotted

1932; Payne, Cynthia; F; 12/29/07-25; N.C. Cherokee; 1/32; S; Dau.; 1921; No; Gastonia, Gaston, N.C.; Yes; Unallotted

1933; Payne, Gertrude; F; 3/19/10-23; N.C. Cherokee; 1/32; S; Dau.; 1922; No; Gastonia, Gaston, N.C.; Yes; Unallotted

1934; Payne, Annie Lee; F; 12/31/16-16; N.C. Cherokee; 1/32; S; Dau.; 1923; No; Gastonia, Gaston, N.C.; Yes; Unallotted

1935; Peckerwood, McKinley; M; 10/6/02-31; N.C. Cherokee; 4/4; M; Head; 1924; Yes; Yes; Unallotted

1936; Peckerwood, Mary A.; F; 3/27/88-45; N.C. Cherokee; 3/4; M; Wife; 1925; Yes; Yes; Unallotted

1937; Peckerwood, Tom Ross; M; 3/19/31-2; N.C. Cherokee; 7/8; S; Son; 1926; Yes; Yes; Unallotted

1938; Pheasant, William; M; 4/25/80-52; N.C. Cherokee; 4/4; M; Head; 1927; Yes; Yes; Unallotted

1939; Pheasant, Rachel W.; F; 3/15/92-41; N.C. Cherokee; 4/4; M; Wife; 1928; Yes; Yes; Unallotted

Census of the **Eastern Cherokee** reservation of the **Cherokee, N.C.** jurisdiction, as of **April 1**, 19**33**, taken by **R. L. Spalsbury**, Superintendent.

Key: Number; Surname, Given; Sex; Date of Birth-Age at Last Birthday; Tribe; Degree of Blood; Marital Status; Relationship to Head of Family; Last C. Roll No.; At Jurisdiction Where Enrolled (Yes/No); (If no – Where); Ward (Yes/No); Allotment, Annuity and Identification Numbers (if given).

1940; Pheasant, Wallie; M[sic]; 12/26/17-15; N.C. Cherokee; 4/4; S; Son[sic]; 1929; Yes; Yes; Unallotted

1941; Pheasant, Driver; M; 3/11/20-12; N.C. Cherokee; 4/4; S; Son; 1930; Yes; Yes; Unallotted

1942; Pheasant, Ellie; F; 11/4/22-10; N.C. Cherokee; 4/4; S; Dau.; 1931; Yes; Yes; Unallotted

1943; Pheasant, Irene; F; 6/3/26-6; N.C. Cherokee; 4/4; S; Dau.; 1932; Yes; Yes; Unallotted

1944; Pike, Lillie A.; F; 2/8/70-63; N.C. Cherokee; 3/32; Wd.; Head; 1933; Yes; Yes; Unallotted

1945; Pope (Patterson, Elizabeth), Elizabeth; F; 4/20/00-32; N.C. Cherokee; 1/32; M; Wife; 1934; Yes; Yes; Unallotted

1946; Porter (Meroney, Florence), Florence; F; 3/16/63-70; N.C. Cherokee; 1/8; M; Wife; 1935; Yes; Yes; Unallotted

1947; Porter, James D.; M; 4/30/89-43; N.C. Cherokee; 1/16; M; Head; 1936; Yes; Yes; Unallotted

1948; Potter, Thomas R.; M; 11/5/95-37; N.C. Cherokee; 3/16; M; Head; 1937; Yes; Yes; Unallotted

1949; Potts (Smith, Rosanna), Rosanna; F; 3/22/00-33; N.C. Cherokee; 1/8; M; Wife; 1938; Yes; Yes; Unallotted

1950; Powell, Doogah; F; 12/23/71-61; N.C. Cherokee; 4/4; Wd.; Head; 1939; Yes; Yes; Unallotted

1951; Powell, Holmes; M; 2/9/02-31; N.C. Cherokee; 3/4; S; Son; 1940; Yes; Yes; Unallotted

1952; Powell, Noah; M; 3/10/08-25; N.C. Cherokee; 3/4; S; Son; 1941; Yes; Yes; Unallotted

1953; Powell, Moses; M; 6/7/88-44; N.C. Cherokee; 3/4; Wd.; Head; 1942; Yes; Yes; Unallotted

1954; Powell, Catherine; F; 8/27/25-8; N.C. Cherokee; 7/8; S; Dau.; 1945; Yes; Yes; Unallotted

1955; Powell, Beulah L.; F; 12/8/27-5; N.C. Cherokee; 7/8; S; Dau.; 1946; Yes; Yes; Unallotted

1956; Powell, Berdina A.; F; 4/21/30-3; N.C. Cherokee; 7/8; S; Dau.; 1947; Yes; Yes; Unallotted

1957; Powell, Stancill; M; 12/17/91-41; N.C. Cherokee; 3/4; M; Head; 1948; Yes; Yes; Unallotted

Census of the **Eastern Cherokee** reservation of the **Cherokee, N.C.** jurisdiction, as of **April 1** , **1933,** taken by **R. L. Spalsbury** , Superintendent.

Key: Number; Surname, Given; Sex; Date of Birth-Age at Last Birthday; Tribe; Degree of Blood; Marital Status; Relationship to Head of Family; Last C. Roll No.; At Jurisdiction Where Enrolled (Yes/No); (If no – Where); Ward (Yes/No); Allotment, Annuity and Identification Numbers (if given).

1958; Powell, Kina S.; F; 2/11/99-34; N.C. Cherokee; 4/4; M; Wife; 1949;Yes; Yes; Unallotted

1959; Powell, Dorothy H.; F; 9/22/29-3; N.C. Cherokee; 7/8; S; Dau.; 1950; Yes; Yes; Unallotted

1960; Price, Grace H.; F; 1/3/07-26; N.C. Cherokee; 3/8; M; Wife; 1951;Yes; Yes; Unallotted

1961; Pullium, Carolina; F; 6/29/80-52; N.C. Cherokee; 1/32; M; Wife; 1952;Yes; Yes; Unallotted

1962; Pullium, John; M; 9/26/06-26; N.C. Cherokee; 1/64; S; Son; 1953; Yes; Yes; Unallotted

1963; Pullium, Decatur; M; 11/22/03-29; N.C. Cherokee; 1/64; S; Head; 1954; Yes; Yes; Unallotted

1964; Pullium, Galusha; M; 5/21/99-33; N.C. Cherokee; 1/64; S; Head; 1955; Yes; Yes; Unallotted

1965; Pittman, Ella B.; F; 1909-24; N.C. Cherokee; 1/4-; S; Head; 1956; Yes; Yes; Unallotted

1966; Queen, Jasper; M; 2/23/94-39; N.C. Cherokee; 5/8; M; Head; 1957; Yes; Yes; Unallotted

1967; Queen, Luzene R.; F; 2/28/99-34; N.C. Cherokee; 15/16; M; Wife; 1958; Yes; Yes; Unallotted

1968; Queen, Kina; F; 2/22/20-13; N.C. Cherokee; 25/32; S; Dau.; 1959; Yes; Yes; Unallotted

1969; Queen, Blaine; M; 1/29/21-12; N.C. Cherokee; 25/32; S; Son; 1960; Yes; Yes; Unallotted

1970; Queen, Awee; F; 7/24/22-10; N.C. Cherokee; 25/32; S; Dau.; 1961; Yes; Yes; Unallotted

1971; Queen, Minnie; F; 6/26/26-6; N.C. Cherokee; 25/32; S; Dau.; 1962; Yes; Yes; Unallotted

1972; Queen, Louis; M; 7/30/28-4; N.C. Cherokee; 25/32; S; Son; 1963; Yes; Yes; Unallotted

1973; Queen, Jessie; F; 7/9/30-2; N.C. Cherokee; 25/32; S; Dau.; 1964; Yes; Yes; Unallotted

1974; Queen, Annie; F; 7/22/32-8/12; N.C. Cherokee; 25/32; S; Dau.; ---; Yes; Yes; Unallotted

1975; Queen (Lambert, Lora), Lora; F; 10/18/07-25; N.C. Cherokee; 1/32; M; Wife; 1965; Yes; Yes; Unallotted

Census of the **Eastern Cherokee** reservation of the **Cherokee, N.C.** jurisdiction, as of **April 1** , 19**33,** taken by **R. L. Spalsbury** , Superintendent.

Key: Number; Surname, Given; Sex; Date of Birth-Age at Last Birthday; Tribe; Degree of Blood; Marital Status; Relationship to Head of Family; Last C. Roll No.; At Jurisdiction Where Enrolled (Yes/No); (If no – Where); Ward (Yes/No); Allotment, Annuity and Identification Numbers (if given).

1976; Queen, Lelia C.; F; 8/25/98-34; N.C. Cherokee; 1/16; M; Wife; 1966; Yes; Yes; Unallotted

1977; Queen, Lois R.; F; 1/5/23-10; N.C. Cherokee; 1/32; S; Dau.; 1967; Yes; Yes; Unallotted

1978; Queen, Levi; M; 6/7/70-62; N.C. Cherokee; 1/4; M; Head; 1968; Yes; Yes; Unallotted

1979; Queen, Mary; F; 2/10/80-53; N.C. Cherokee; 4/4; M; Wife; 1969; Yes; Yes; Unallotted

1980; Queen, Abraham; M; 7/11/99-33; N.C. Cherokee; 5/8; S; Son; 1970; Yes; Yes; Unallotted

1981; Queen, Lillian; F; 12/11/12-20; N.C. Cherokee; 5/8; S; Dau.; 1971; Yes; Yes; Unallotted

1982; Queen, Martha; F; 5/30/14-18; N.C. Cherokee; 5/8; S; Dau.; 1972; Yes; Yes; Unallotted

1983; Queen, Stacey; F; 10/31/16-16; N.C. Cherokee; 5/8; S; Dau.; 1973; Yes; Yes; Unallotted

1984; Queen, Cowan; M; 7/23/19-13; N.C. Cherokee; 5/8; S; Son; 1974; Yes; Yes; Unallotted

1985; Queen, Simpson; M; 9/15/73-59; N.C. Cherokee; 1/4; Wd.; Head; 1975; Yes; Yes; Unallotted

1986; Queen, John; M; 5/15/07-25; N.C. Cherokee; 5/8; S; Son; 1976; Yes; Yes; Unallotted

1987; Queen, Rachel; F; 8/19/09-23; N.C. Cherokee; 5/8; S; Dau.; 1977; Yes; Yes; Unallotted

1988; Queen, Lucy; F; 3/24/12-21; N.C. Cherokee; 5/8; S; Dau.; 1978; Yes; Yes; Unallotted

1989; Queen, Solomon; M; 11/17/15-17; N.C. Cherokee; 5/8; S; Son; 1979; Yes; Yes; Unallotted

1990; Queen, Nolan; M; 1/27/01-32; N.C. Cherokee; 5/8; M; Head; 1980; Yes; Yes; Unallotted

1991; Queen, Golinda A.; F; 4/10/07-25; N.C. Cherokee; 4/4; M; Wife; 1981; Yes; Yes; Unallotted

1992; Queen, Sam; M; 5/2/27-5; N.C. Cherokee; 13/16; S; Son; 1982; Yes; Yes; Unallotted

1993; Quinlan, Mary C.; F; 1899-34; N.C. Cherokee; 1/4-; M; Wife; 1983; Yes; Yes; Unallotted

1994; Rakestraw, Lena B.; F; 2/25/05-28; N.C. Cherokee; 1/64; M; Wife; 1984; Yes; Yes; Unallotted

Census of the **Eastern Cherokee** reservation of the **Cherokee, N.C.** jurisdiction, as of **April 1**, **1933,** taken by **R. L. Spalsbury**, Superintendent.

Key: Number; Surname, Given; Sex; Date of Birth-Age at Last Birthday; Tribe; Degree of Blood; Marital Status; Relationship to Head of Family; Last C. Roll No.; At Jurisdiction Where Enrolled (Yes/No); (If no – Where); Ward (Yes/No); Allotment, Annuity and Identification Numbers (if given).

1995; Ramsey, Roxey W.; F; 2/11/09-24; N.C. Cherokee; 1/16; S; Head; 1985; Yes; Yes; Unallotted

1996; Raper, Alexander; M; 2/27/44-89; N.C. Cherokee; 1/4; M; Head; 1986; Yes; Yes; Unallotted

1997; Raper, Alonzo; M; 5/2/95-35; N.C. Cherokee; 1/16; M; Head; 1987; Yes; Yes; Unallotted
1998; Raper, Bonetta; F; 2/25/19-14; N.C. Cherokee; 1/32; S; Dau.; 1988; Yes; Yes; Unallotted
1999; Raper, Jeanette; F; 2/6/21-12; N.C. Cherokee; 1/32; S; Dau.; 1989; Yes; Yes; Unallotted
2000; Raper, Opal; F; 3/1/23-10; N.C. Cherokee; 1/32; S; Dau.; 1990; Yes; Yes; Unallotted
2001; Raper, Myrtle; F; 5/28/24-8; N.C. Cherokee; 1/32; S; Dau.; 1991; Yes; Yes; Unallotted

2002; Raper, Alvin; M; 4/9/92-40; N.C. Cherokee; 1/16; M; Head; 1992; Yes; Yes; Unallotted
2003; Raper, Clifton; M; 7/31/16-16; N.C. Cherokee; 1/32; S; Son; 1993; Yes; Yes; Unallotted
2004; Raper, Carmen; F; 12/11/18-14; N.C. Cherokee; 1/32; S; Dau.; 1994; Yes; Yes; Unallotted
2005; Raper, Pearl; F; 4/12/20-12; N.C. Cherokee; 1/32; S; Dau.; 1995; Yes; Yes; Unallotted
2006; Raper, Clarence; M; 7/1/23-9; N.C. Cherokee; 1/32; S; Son; 1996; Yes; Yes; Unallotted

2007; Raper (children Marshall Raper), Amos Lloyd; M; 12/3/14-18; N.C. Cherokee; 1/16; S; Son; 1997; Yes; Yes; Unallotted
2008; Raper, Atha G.; F; 1/1/17-16; N.C. Cherokee; 1/16; S; Dau.; 1998; Yes; Yes; Unallotted
2009; Raper, Howard H.; M; 4/16/19-14; N.C. Cherokee; 1/16; S; Son; 1999; Yes; Yes; Unallotted
2010; Raper, Verdie H.; F; 3/27/21-12; N.C. Cherokee; 1/16; S; Dau.; 2000; Yes; Yes; Unallotted
2011; Raper, James H.; M; 3/31/23-10; N.C. Cherokee; 1/16; S; Son; 2001; Yes; Yes; Unallotted

2012; Raper, Asa; M; 3/1/86-46; N.C. Cherokee; 1/16; M; Head; 2002; Yes; Yes; Unallotted

2013; Raper, Augustus; M; 5/27/02-30; N.C. Cherokee; 1/16; M; Head; 2003; Yes; Yes; Unallotted

Census of the **Eastern Cherokee** reservation of the **Cherokee, N.C.** jurisdiction, as of **April 1**, 19**33**, taken by **R. L. Spalsbury**, Superintendent.

Key: Number; Surname, Given; Sex; Date of Birth-Age at Last Birthday; Tribe; Degree of Blood; Marital Status; Relationship to Head of Family; Last C. Roll No.; At Jurisdiction Where Enrolled (Yes/No); (If no – Where); Ward (Yes/No); Allotment, Annuity and Identification Numbers (if given).

2014; Raper, Norma W.; F; 12/27/02-30; N.C. Cherokee; 1/16; M; Wife; 2004; Yes; Yes; Unallotted

2015; Raper, Berry B.B.; M; 3/20/59-74; N.C. Cherokee; 1/8; M; Head; 2005; Yes; Yes; Unallotted

2016; Raper, Charles B.; M; 9/17/75-57; N.C. Cherokee; 1/8; M; Head; 2006; No; Culberson, Cherokee, N.C.; Yes; Unallotted
2017; Raper, Homer W.; M; 1/10/11-22; N.C. Cherokee; 1/16; S; Son; 2007; No; Culberson, Cherokee, N.C.; Yes; Unallotted
2018; Raper, Lela; F; 2/16/13-20; N.C. Cherokee; 1/16; S; Dau.; 2008; No; Culberson, Cherokee, N.C.; Yes; Unallotted
2019; Raper, Cleaston; M; 5/17/18-14; N.C. Cherokee; 1/16; S; Son; 2009; No; Culberson, Cherokee, N.C.; Yes; Unallotted
2020; Raper, Austin; M; 1/25/23-10; N.C. Cherokee; 1/16; S; Son; 2010; No; Culberson, Cherokee, N.C.; Yes; Unallotted

2021; Raper, Clarence A.; M; 1/4/00-33; N.C. Cherokee; 1/16; M; Head; 2011; Yes; Yes; Unallotted
2022; Raper, Juanita; F; 12/15/23-9; N.C. Cherokee; 1/32; S; Dau.; 2012; Yes; Yes; Unallotted

2023; Raper, Cly Victor; M; 10/3/97-35; N.C. Cherokee; 1/16; M; Head; 2013; No; Culberson, Cherokee, N.C.; Yes; Unallotted
2024; Raper, James V.; M; 3/3/18-15; N.C. Cherokee; 1/32; S; Son; 2014; No; Culberson, Cherokee, N.C.; Yes; Unallotted
2025; Raper, Dewey E.; M; 9/18/20-12; N.C. Cherokee; 1/32; S; Son; 2015; No; Culberson, Cherokee, N.C.; Yes; Unallotted

2026; Raper, Delta C.; M; 5/30/00-32; N.C. Cherokee; 1/16; M; Head; 2016; No; Culberson, Cherokee, N.C.; Yes; Unallotted
2027; Raper, Claude; M; 12/28/18-14; N.C. Cherokee; 1/32; S; Son; 2017; No; Culberson, Cherokee, N.C.; Yes; Unallotted
2028; Raper, Clifford; M; 12/16/20-12; N.C. Cherokee; 1/32; S; Son; 2018; No; Culberson, Cherokee, N.C.; Yes; Unallotted

2099; Raper, Denver Lee; M; 6/19/98-34; N.C. Cherokee; 1/16; M; Head; 2019; No; Culberson, Cherokee, N.C.; Yes; Unallotted
2030; Raper, Marie; F; 12/12/14-18; N.C. Cherokee; 1/32; S; Dau.; 2020; No; Culberson, Cherokee, N.C.; Yes; Unallotted
2031; Raper, Dewey; M; 7/14/22-10; N.C. Cherokee; 1/32; S; Son; 2021; No; Culberson, Cherokee, N.C.; Yes; Unallotted

2032; Raper, Edgar; M; 5/2/94-38; N.C. Cherokee; 1/16; M; Head; 2022; Yes; Yes; Unallotted

Census of the **Eastern Cherokee** reservation of the **Cherokee, N.C.** jurisdiction, as of **April 1** , **1933,** taken by **R. L. Spalsbury** , Superintendent.

Key: Number; Surname, Given; Sex; Date of Birth-Age at Last Birthday; Tribe; Degree of Blood; Marital Status; Relationship to Head of Family; Last C. Roll No.; At Jurisdiction Where Enrolled (Yes/No); (If no – Where); Ward (Yes/No); Allotment, Annuity and Identification Numbers (if given).

2033; Raper, Carrie W.; F; 3/3/00-33; N.C. Cherokee; 1/16; M; Wife; 2023; Yes; Yes; Unallotted

2034; Raper, Wm. Roy; M; 11/4/21-11; N.C. Cherokee; 1/16; S; Son; 2024; Yes; Yes; Unallotted

2035; Raper, Robert L.; M; 1/18/24-9; N.C. Cherokee; 1/16; S; Son; 2025; Yes; Yes; Unallotted

2036; Raper, Fred; M; 3/20/03-30; N.C. Cherokee; 1/16; S; Head; 2026; No; Wichita Falls, Wichita, Tex.; Yes; Unallotted

2037; Raper, Gano; M; 5/15/83-49; N.C. Cherokee; 1/16; M; Head; 2027; No; Douglas, Coffee, Ga.; Yes; Unallotted

2038; Raper, Harley; M; 3/20/86-47; N.C. Cherokee; 1/16; M; Head; 2028; No; Hale Center, Hale, Tex.; Yes; Unallotted

2039; Raper, Henry J.; M; 12/23/86-46; N.C. Cherokee; 1/8; M; Head; 2029; No; Clover, York, S.C.; Yes; Unallotted

2040; Raper, Ivan; M; 4/27/05-27; N.C. Cherokee; 1/16; S; Son; 2030; No; Clover, York, S.C.; Yes; Unallotted

2041; Raper, Delia; F; 1/22/08-25; N.C. Cherokee; 1/16; S; Dau.; 2031; No; Clover, York, S.C.; Yes; Unallotted

2042; Raper, Ira; M; 12/21/10-22; N.C. Cherokee; 1/16; S; Son; 2032; No; Clover, York, S.C.; Yes; Unallotted

2043; Raper, Clyde; M; 12/29/16-16; N.C. Cherokee; 1/16; S; Son; 2033; No; Clover, York, S.C.; Yes; Unallotted

2044; Raper, Dewey; M; 2/5/20-13; N.C. Cherokee; 1/16; S; Son; 2034; No; Clover, York, S.C.; Yes; Unallotted

2045; Raper, Harford; M; 10/11/22-10; N.C. Cherokee; 1/16; S; Son; 2035; No; Clover, York, S.C.; Yes; Unallotted

2046; Raper, James; M; 3/31/95-38; N.C. Cherokee; 1/16; M; Head; 2036; No; Oak Park, Cherokee, N.C.; Yes; Unallotted

2047; Raper, Marcus; M; 5/3/16-16; N.C. Cherokee; 1/32; S; Son; 2037; No; Oak Park, Cherokee, N.C.; Yes; Unallotted

2048; Raper, Lillian; F; 11/15/17-15; N.C. Cherokee; 1/32; S; Dau.; 2038; No; Yes; Oak Park, Cherokee, N.C.; Yes; Unallotted

2049; Raper, Thomas; M; 11/14/19-13; N.C. Cherokee; 1/32; S; Son; 2039; No; Oak Park, Cherokee, N.C.; Yes; Unallotted

2050; Raper, Windell; M; 11/9/21-11; N.C. Cherokee; 1/32; S; Son; 2040; No; Oak Park, Cherokee, N.C.; Yes; Unallotted

2051; Raper, James W.; M; 11/9/63-69; N.C. Cherokee; 1/8; M; Head; 2041; No; R.R. #2 Clever, Christian, No.[sic]; Yes; Unallotted

Census of the **Eastern Cherokee** reservation of the **Cherokee, N.C.** jurisdiction, as of **April 1** , 19**33,** taken by **R. L. Spalsbury** , Superintendent.

Key: Number; Surname, Given; Sex; Date of Birth-Age at Last Birthday; Tribe; Degree of Blood; Marital Status; Relationship to Head of Family; Last C. Roll No.; At Jurisdiction Where Enrolled (Yes/No); (If no – Where); Ward (Yes/No); Allotment, Annuity and Identification Numbers (if given).

2052; Raper, Jesse L.; M; 8/21/70-62; N.C. Cherokee; 1/8; M; Head; 2042; Yes; Yes; Unallotted

2053; Raper, Claude E.; M; 6/15/99-33; N.C. Cherokee; 1/16; S; Son; 2043; Yes; Yes; Unallotted

2054; Raper, Curley C.; M; 6/3/01-31; N.C. Cherokee; 1/16; S; Son; 2044; Yes; Yes; Unallotted

2055; Raper, Minnie C.; F; 7/5/07-25; N.C. Cherokee; 1/16; S; Dau.; 2045; Yes; Yes; Unallotted

2056; Raper, William C.; M; 6/4/12-20; N.C. Cherokee; 1/16; S; Son; 2046; Yes; Yes; Unallotted

2057; Raper, John H.; M; 4/30/83-49; N.C. Cherokee; 1/16; M; Head; 2047; No; Bradenton, Manatee, Fla.; Yes; Unallotted

2058; Raper, Lillie M.; F; 4/30/07-25; N.C. Cherokee; 1/32; S; Dau.; 2048; No; Bradenton, Manatee, Fla.; Yes; Unallotted

2059; Raper, Herman E.; M; 4/30/09-23; N.C. Cherokee; 1/32; S; Son; 2049; No; Bradenton, Manatee, Fla.; Yes; Unallotted

2060; Raper, Ralph J.; M; 4/30/17-15; N.C. Cherokee; 1/32; S; Son; 2050; No; Bradenton, Manatee, Fla.; Yes; Unallotted

2061; Raper, Nellie A.; F; 4/30/20-12; N.C. Cherokee; 1/32; S; Dau.; 2051; No; Bradenton, Manatee, Fla.; Yes; Unallotted

2062; Raper, Lich; M; 5/3/89-43; N.C. Cherokee; 1/16; M; Head; 2052; Yes; Yes; Unallotted

2063; Raper, Lon; M; 3/30/81-52; N.C. Cherokee; 1/16; M; Head; 2053; No; Oak Park, Cherokee, N.C.; Yes; Unallotted

2064; Raper, Marseilla; F; 10/28/12-20; N.C. Cherokee; 1/32; S; Dau.; 2054; No; Oak Park, Cherokee, N.C.; Yes; Unallotted

2065; Raper, Vivian; F; 12/20/14-18; N.C. Cherokee; 1/32; S; Dau.; 2055; No; Oak Park, Cherokee, N.C.; Yes; Unallotted

2066; Raper, Merideth; M; 11/15/16-16; N.C. Cherokee; 1/32; S; Son; 2056; No; Oak Park, Cherokee, N.C.; Yes; Unallotted

2067; Raper, Thelma; F; 1/4/19-14; N.C. Cherokee; 1/32; S; Dau.; 2057; No; Oak Park, Cherokee, N.C.; Yes; Unallotted

2068; Raper, Jesse Willard; M; 5/30/22-10; N.C. Cherokee; 1/32; S; Son; 2058; No; Oak Park, Cherokee, N.C.; Yes; Unallotted

2069; Raper, Marshall; M; 1/4/73-60; N.C. Cherokee; 1/8; M; Head; 2059; No; Culberson, Cherokee, N.C.; Yes; Unallotted

2070; Raper, Clinton; M; 1/6/02-31; N.C. Cherokee; 1/16; S; Son; 2060; No; Culberson, Cherokee, N.C.; Yes; Unallotted

2071; Raper, Bonnie B.; F; 1/14/07-26; N.C. Cherokee; 1/16; S; Dau.; 2061; No; Culberson, Cherokee, N.C.; Yes; Unallotted

Census of the **Eastern Cherokee** reservation of the **Cherokee, N.C.** jurisdiction, as of **April 1**, **1933**, taken by **R. L. Spalsbury**, Superintendent.

Key: Number; Surname, Given; Sex; Date of Birth-Age at Last Birthday; Tribe; Degree of Blood; Marital Status; Relationship to Head of Family; Last C. Roll No.; At Jurisdiction Where Enrolled (Yes/No); (If no – Where); Ward (Yes/No); Allotment, Annuity and Identification Numbers (if given).

2072; Raper, Wm. Taft; M; 2/9/09-24; N.C. Cherokee; 1/16; S; Son; 2062; No; Culberson, Cherokee, N.C.; Yes; Unallotted

2073; Raper, Rose Ella; F; 9/9/11-21; N.C. Cherokee; 1/16; S; Dau.; 2063; No; Culberson, Cherokee, N.C.; Yes; Unallotted

2074; Raper, Martin; M; 5/23/89-43; N.C. Cherokee; 1/16; M; Head; 2064; No; Patrick, Cherokee, N.C.; Yes; Unallotted

2075; Raper, Glenn; M; 11/14/14-18; N.C. Cherokee; 1/32; S; Son; 2065; No; Patrick, Cherokee, N.C.; Yes; Unallotted

2076; Raper, Lois; F; 12/31/17-15; N.C. Cherokee; 1/32; S; Dau.; 2066; No; Patrick, Cherokee, N.C.; Yes; Unallotted

2077; Raper, Blanche; F; 3/5/20-13; N.C. Cherokee; 1/32; S; Dau.; 2067; No; Patrick, Cherokee, N.C.; Yes; Unallotted

2078; Raper, Charley; M; 3/4/22-11; N.C. Cherokee; 1/32; S; Son; 2068; No; Patrick, Cherokee, N.C.; Yes; Unallotted

2079; Raper, Marty A.; M; 10/2/92-40; N.C. Cherokee; 1/16; M; Head; 2069; Yes; Yes; Unallotted

2080; Raper, Everett G.; M; 5/8/18-14; N.C. Cherokee; 1/32; S; Son; 2070; Yes; Yes; Unallotted

2081; Raper, Edna D.; F; 1/22/20-13; N.C. Cherokee; 1/32; S; Dau.; 2071; Yes; Yes; Unallotted

2082; Raper, Clarence W.; M; 7/24/22-10; N.C. Cherokee; 1/32; S; Son; 2072; Yes; Yes; Unallotted

2083; Raper, Oscar; M; 3/20/86-47; N.C. Cherokee; 1/16; M; Head; 2073; Yes; Yes; Unallotted

2084; Raper, Robert; M; 3/20/99-34; N.C. Cherokee; 1/16; M; Head; 2074; Yes; Yes; Unallotted

2085; Raper, Rosa May; F; 3/20/01-32; N.C. Cherokee; 1/16; S; Head; 2075; No; Marietta, Cobb, Ga.; Yes; Unallotted

2086; Raper, Thomas; M; 12/23/58-74; N.C. Cherokee; 1/8; M; Head; 2076; No; Oak Park, Cherokee, N.C.; Yes; Unallotted

2087; Raper, Clifton; M; 4/15/06-26; N.C. Cherokee; 1/16; S; Son; 2077; No; Oak Park, Cherokee, N.C.; Yes; Unallotted

2088; Raper, Earnest; M; 9/13/12-20; N.C. Cherokee; 1/16; S; Son; 2078; No; Oak Park, Cherokee, N.C.; Yes; Unallotted

2089; Raper, Whoola B.; M; 3/23/88-45; N.C. Cherokee; 1/16; M; Head; 2079; No; Birch, Cherokee, N.C.; Yes; Unallotted

2090; Raper, Jefferson; M; 8/16/20-12; N.C. Cherokee; 1/32; S; Son; 2080; No; Birch, Cherokee, N.C.; Yes; Unallotted

Census of the **Eastern Cherokee** reservation of the **Cherokee, N.C.** jurisdiction, as of **April 1**, 19**33,** taken by **R. L. Spalsbury**, Superintendent.

Key: Number; Surname, Given; Sex; Date of Birth-Age at Last Birthday; Tribe; Degree of Blood; Marital Status; Relationship to Head of Family; Last C. Roll No.; At Jurisdiction Where Enrolled (Yes/No); (If no – Where); Ward (Yes/No); Allotment, Annuity and Identification Numbers (if given).

2091; Raper, William A.; M; 6/15/84-48; N.C. Cherokee; 1/16; M; Head; 2081; No; Clever, Christian, Mo.; Yes; Unallotted

2092; Raper, William; M; 2/21/08-25; N.C. Cherokee; 1/16; S; Head; 2082; No; Culberson, Cherokee, N.C.; Yes; Unallotted

2093; Raper, William B.; M; 1/3/79-54; N.C. Cherokee; 1/16; M; Head; 2083; No; Brasstown, Clay, N.C.; Yes; Unallotted

2094; Raper, William P.; M; 11/18/11-21; N.C. Cherokee; 1/32; S; Son; 2084; No; Brasstown, Clay, N.C.; Yes; Unallotted

2095; Raper, William T.; M; 4/7/68-64; N.C. Cherokee; 1/8; M; Head; 2085; No; Culberson, Cherokee, N.C.; Yes; Unallotted

2096; Raper, James G.; M; 1/24/04-29; N.C. Cherokee; 1/16; S; Son; 2086; No; Culberson, Cherokee, N.C.; Yes; Unallotted

2097; Raper, William A.; M; 4/27/08-24; N.C. Cherokee; 1/16; S; Son; 2087; No; Culberson, Cherokee, N.C.; Yes; Unallotted

2098; Raper, Bertha M.; F; 1/11/10-23; N.C. Cherokee; 1/16; S; Dau.; 2088; No; Culberson, Cherokee, N.C.; Yes; Unallotted

2099; Raper, Melba L.; F; 8/18/21-11; N.C. Cherokee; 1/16; S; Dau.; 2089; No; Culberson, Cherokee, N.C.; Yes; Unallotted

2100; Raper, Ruby L.; F; 6/15/23-9; N.C. Cherokee; 1/16; S; Dau.; 2090; No; Culberson, Cherokee, N.C.; Yes; Unallotted

2101; Rattler, George W.; M; 3/15/73-60; N.C. Cherokee; 4/4; M; Head; 2091; Yes; Yes; Unallotted

2102; Rattler, Hettie S.; F; 12/25/98-34; N.C. Cherokee; 4/4; M; Wife; 2092; Yes; Yes; Unallotted

2103; Rattler, Ammons; M; 5/30/11-21; N.C. Cherokee; 4/4; S; Son; 2093; Yes; Yes; Unallotted

2104; Rattler, Iva R.; F; 1/3/30-3; N.C. Cherokee; 4/4; S; Dau.; 2094; Yes; Yes; Unallotted

2105; Rattler, Henson; M; 12/7/02-30; N.C. Cherokee; 4/4; M; Head; 2095; Yes; Yes; Unallotted

2106; Rattler, Fanny O.; F; 3/6/09-24; N.C. Cherokee; 4/4; M; Wife; 2096; Yes; Yes; Unallotted

2107; Rattler, John; M; 12/14/84-48; N.C. Cherokee; 4/4; M; Head; 2097; Yes; Yes; Unallotted

2108; Rattler, Emmaline; F; 3/29/87-46; N.C. Cherokee; 4/4; M; Wife; 2098; Yes; Yes; Unallotted

2109; Rattler, John W.; M; 12/20/06-26; N.C. Cherokee; 1/2; S; Son; 2099; Yes; Yes; Unallotted

Census of the **Eastern Cherokee** reservation of the **Cherokee, N.C.** jurisdiction, as of **April 1** , **1933,** taken by **R. L. Spalsbury** , Superintendent.

Key: Number; Surname, Given; Sex; Date of Birth-Age at Last Birthday; Tribe; Degree of Blood; Marital Status; Relationship to Head of Family; Last C. Roll No.; At Jurisdiction Where Enrolled (Yes/No); (If no – Where); Ward (Yes/No); Allotment, Annuity and Identification Numbers (if given).

2110; Rattler, Lucy; F; 6/3/09-23; N.C. Cherokee; 4/4; S; Dau.; 2100; Yes; Yes; Unallotted

2111; Rattler, Willie; M; 8/7/11-21; N.C. Cherokee; 4/4; S; Son; 2101; Yes; Yes; Unallotted

2112; Rattler, Joseph; M; 5/11/14-18; N.C. Cherokee; 4/4; S; Son; 2102; Yes; Yes; Unallotted

2113; Rattler, Wilson; M; 11/16/16-16; N.C. Cherokee; 4/4; S; Son; 2103; Yes; Yes; Unallotted

2114; Rattler, Mike; M; 7/21/19-13; N.C. Cherokee; 4/4; S; Son; 2104; Yes; Yes; Unallotted

2115; Rattler, Roxie; F; 6/19/21-11; N.C. Cherokee; 4/4; S; Dau.; 2105; Yes; Yes; Unallotted

2116; Rattler, Morgan; M; 1/5/05-28; N.C. Cherokee; 4/4; WD; Head; 2106; Yes; Yes; Unallotted

2117; Rattler, Nancy; F; 12/31/46-86; N.C. Cherokee; 4/4; Wd.; Head; 2107; Yes; Yes; Unallotted

2118; Rattler, Jonah; M; 3/15/89-44; N.C. Cherokee; 4/4; S; Son; 2108; Yes; Yes; Unallotted

2119; Rattler, Walter; M; 4/9/04-28; N.C. Cherokee; 1/2; M; Head; 2109; Yes; Yes; Unallotted

2120; Rattler, Charles; M; 10/18/22-10; N.C. Cherokee; 1/4; S; Son; 2110; Yes; Yes; Unallotted

2121; Ratliff, Lawyer; M; 3/15/75-58; N.C. Cherokee; 1/8; Wd.; Head; 2111; No; Andrews, Cherokee, N.C.; Yes; Unallotted

2122; Ratliff, Emma; F; 4/15/29-3; N.C. Cherokee; 1/16; S; Dau.; 2112; No; Andrews, Cherokee, N.C.; Yes; Unallotted

2123; Ratliff, William B.; M; 6/1/73-59; N.C. Cherokee; 1/8; M; Head; 2113; Yes; Yes; Unallotted

2124; Ratliff, Elizabeth; F; 5/1/76-56; N.C. Cherokee; 4/4; M; Wife; 2114; Yes; Yes; Unallotted

2125; Ratliff, Emma C.; F; 5/26/01-31; N.C. Cherokee; 9/16; S; Dau.; 2115; Yes, Yes; Unallotted

2126; Ratliff, Jacob R.; M; 1/23/04-29; N.C. Cherokee; 9/16; S; Son; 2116; Yes, Yes; Unallotted

2127; Ratliff, Ella Mae; F; 11/15/06-26; N.C. Cherokee; 9/16; S; Dau.; 2117; Yes, Yes; Unallotted

2128; Rattliff, Jonah A.; M; 7/6/10-22; N.C. Cherokee; 9/16; S; Son; 2118; Yes, Yes; Unallotted

2129; Ratliff, Myrtle M.; F; 2/6/12-21; N.C. Cherokee; 9/16; S; Dau.; 2119; Yes, Yes; Unallotted

Census of the **Eastern Cherokee** reservation of the **Cherokee, N.C.** jurisdiction, as of **April 1**, 19**33**, taken by **R. L. Spalsbury**, Superintendent.

Key: Number; Surname, Given; Sex; Date of Birth-Age at Last Birthday; Tribe; Degree of Blood; Marital Status; Relationship to Head of Family; Last C. Roll No.; At Jurisdiction Where Enrolled (Yes/No); (If no – Where); Ward (Yes/No); Allotment, Annuity and Identification Numbers (if given).

2130; Ratliff, Isaac W.; M; 9/6/15-17; N.C. Cherokee; 9/16; S; Son; 2120; Yes, Yes; Unallotted

2131; Rave, Martha C.; F; 3/7/85-48; N.C. Cherokee; 4/4; M; Wife; 2121; Yes; Yes; Unallotted

2132; Rave, Maurice W.; M; 2/22/13-20; N.C. Cherokee; 1/2; S; Son; 2122; Yes, Yes; Unallotted

2133; Rave, Wilma[sic] A.; M; 3/3/15-18; N.C. Cherokee; 1/2; S; Son; 2123; Yes, Yes; Unallotted

2134; Reagan (Lambert, Hester), Hester L.; F; 4/15/87-45; N.C. Cherokee; 1/16; M; Wife; 2124; Yes; Yes; Unallotted

2135; Reagan, Emmet; M; 2/19/08-25; N.C. Cherokee; 1/32; S; Son; 2125; Yes, Yes; Unallotted

2136; (Knight), Paulina; F; 1/21/10-23; N.C. Cherokee; 1/32; M; Dau.; 2126; Yes, Yes; Unallotted

2137; Reagan, Pollard; M; 3/11/12-21; N.C. Cherokee; 1/32; S; Son; 2127; Yes, Yes; Unallotted

2138; Reagan, Mary E.; F; 10/8/14-18; N.C. Cherokee; 1/32; S; Dau.; 2128;Yes, Yes; Unallotted

2139; Reagan, Stella S.; F; 2/21/16-17; N.C. Cherokee; 1/32; S; Dau.; 2129;Yes, Yes; Unallotted

2140; Reagan, John P.; M; 7/4/18-14; N.C. Cherokee; 1/32; S; Son; 2130; Yes, Yes; Unallotted

2141; Reagan, Hubert; M; 3/22/20-13; N.C. Cherokee; 1/32; S; Son; 2131; Yes, Yes; Unallotted

2142; Reagan, Daniel; M; 4/13/24-8; N.C. Cherokee; 1/32; S; Son; 2132; Yes, Yes; Unallotted

2143; Reed, Adam; M; 11/11/75-47; N.C. Cherokee; 7/8; M; Head; 2133; Yes; Yes; Unallotted

2144; Reed, Margaret; F; 4/20/91-42; N.C. Cherokee; 4/4; M; Wife; 2134; Yes; Yes; Unallotted

2145; Reed, Moody; M; 12/22/14-18; N.C. Cherokee; 7/8; S; Son; 2135; Yes, Yes; Unallotted

2146; Reed, Gladys M.; F; 2/3/20-13; N.C. Cherokee; 15/16; S; Dau.; 2136; Yes; Yes; Unallotted

2147; Reed, Sallie S.; F; 11/11/22-10; N.C. Cherokee; 15/16; S; Dau.; 2137; Yes; Yes; Unallotted

2148; Reed, Nellie A.; F; 3/17/25-9; N.C. Cherokee; 15/16; S; Dau.; 2138; Yes; Yes; Unallotted

2149; Reed, Charlotte; F; 3/30/29-4; N.C. Cherokee; 15/16; S; Dau.; 2139; Yes; Yes; Unallotted

Census of the **Eastern Cherokee** reservation of the **Cherokee, N.C.** jurisdiction, as of **April 1** , **1933,** taken by **R. L. Spalsbury** , Superintendent.

Key: Number; Surname, Given; Sex; Date of Birth-Age at Last Birthday; Tribe; Degree of Blood; Marital Status; Relationship to Head of Family; Last C. Roll No.; At Jurisdiction Where Enrolled (Yes/No); (If no – Where); Ward (Yes/No); Allotment, Annuity and Identification Numbers (if given).

2150; Reed, David; M; 3/15/61-72; N.C. Cherokee; 3/4; S; Head; 2140; Yes; Yes; Unallotted

2151; Reed, Deweese; M; 5/31/79-53; N.C. Cherokee; 7/8; M; Head; 2141; Yes; Yes; Unallotted

2152; Reed, Minda Q.; F; 10/27/95-37; N.C. Cherokee; 5/8; M; Wife; 2142; Yes; Yes; Unallotted

2153; Reed, Robert; M; 7/4/19-13; N.C. Cherokee; 12/16; S; Son; 2143; Yes, Yes; Unallotted

2154; Reed (Raper, Elizabeth), Elizabeth; F; 7/9/98-34; N.C. Cherokee; 1/16; M; Wife; 2144; No; Firestone Park Sta., Akron, Summit, Ohio; Yes; Unallotted

2155; Reed, Frances H.; M; 10/12/21-11; N.C. Cherokee; 1/32; S; Son; 2145; No; Firestone Park Sta., Akron, Summit, Ohio; Yes; Unallotted

2156; Reed, Fidele; M; 9/12/69-63; N.C. Cherokee; 3/4; M; Head; 2146; Yes; Yes; Unallotted

2157; Reed, Addie H.; F; 1/17/92-41; N.C. Cherokee; 1/8; M; Dau.[sic]; 2147; Yes; Yes; Unallotted

2158; Reed, Rachel; F; 3/25/14-19; N.C. Cherokee; 7/16; S; Dau.; 2148; Yes; Yes; Unallotted

2159; Reed, Cinda; F; 2/2/16-17; N.C. Cherokee; 7/16; S; Dau.; 2149; Yes; Yes; Unallotted

2160; Reed, Lula; F; 3/21/19-14; N.C. Cherokee; 7/16; S; Dau.; 2150; Yes; Yes; Unallotted

2161; Reed, Wilson; M; 3/21/21-12; N.C. Cherokee; 7/16; S; Son; 2151; Yes, Yes; Unallotted

2162; Reed, Anna M.; F; 9/6/23-9; N.C. Cherokee; 7/16; S; Dau.; 2152; Yes; Yes; Unallotted

2163; Reed, Maggie M.; F; 1/12/26-7; N.C. Cherokee; 7/16; S; Dau.; 2153; Yes; Yes; Unallotted

2164; Reed, Henry J.; M; 2/2/28-5; N.C. Cherokee; 7/16; S; Son; 2154; Yes, Yes; Unallotted

2165; Reed, Glen Gilbert; M; 1/21/33-2/12; N.C. Cherokee; 7/16; S; Son; ---; Yes, Yes; Unallotted

2166; Reed, James; M; 5/2/90-42; N.C. Cherokee; 7/8; M; Head; 2155; Yes; Yes; Unallotted

2167; Reed, Minda L.; F; 5/30/93-39; N.C. Cherokee; 4/4; M; Wife; 2156; Yes; Yes; Unallotted

2168; Reed, Margaret; F; 8/30/17-15; N.C. Cherokee; 15/16; S; Dau.; 2157; Yes; Yes; Unallotted

2169; Reed, Martha; F; 7/29/19-13; N.C. Cherokee; 15/16; S; Dau.; 2158; Yes; Yes; Unallotted

Census of the **Eastern Cherokee** reservation of the **Cherokee, N.C.** jurisdiction, as of **April 1** , 19**33,** taken by **R. L. Spalsbury** , Superintendent.

Key: Number; Surname, Given; Sex; Date of Birth-Age at Last Birthday; Tribe; Degree of Blood; Marital Status; Relationship to Head of Family; Last C. Roll No.; At Jurisdiction Where Enrolled (Yes/No); (If no – Where); Ward (Yes/No); Allotment, Annuity and Identification Numbers (if given).

2170; Reed, Ollie; F; 4/10/22-10; N.C. Cherokee; 15/16; S; Dau.; 2159; Yes; Yes; Unallotted

2171; Reed, Malone; M; 7/11/25-7; N.C. Cherokee; 15/16; S; Son; 2160; Yes; Yes; Unallotted

2172; Reed, James; M; 12/23/52-80; N.C. Cherokee; 3/4; S; Head; 2161; Yes; Yes; Unallotted

2173; Reed, James W.; M; 4/30/67-65; N.C. Cherokee; 3/4; M; Head; 2162; No; Salisbury, Rowan, N.C.; Yes; Unallotted

2174; Reed, Johnson; M; 3/5/05-28; N.C. Cherokee; 15/16; M; Head; 2163; Yes; Yes; Unallotted

2175; Reed, Dinah; F; 10/20/05-27; N.C. Cherokee; 4/4; M; Wife; 2164; Yes; Yes; Unallotted

2176; Reed, Peter; M; 5/17/25-7; N.C. Cherokee; 31/32; S; Son; 2165; Yes; Yes; Unallotted

2177; Reed, Helen; F; 4/2/27-5; N.C. Cherokee; 31/32; S; Dau.; 2166; Yes; Yes; Unallotted

2178; Reed, Lloyd; M; 4/15/89-43; N.C. Cherokee; 7/8; M; Head; 2167; Yes; Yes; Unallotted

2179; Reed, Rachel; F; 12/23/51-81; N.C. Cherokee; 3/4; Wd.; Head; 2168; Yes; Yes; Unallotted

2180; Reed, Samuel; M; 3/7/11-22; N.C. Cherokee; 7/8; S; Head; 2169; Yes; Yes; Unallotted

2181; Reed, Matilda; F; 2/6/16-17; N.C. Cherokee; 7/8; S; Sis.; 2170; Yes; Yes; Unallotted

2182; Reed, Mark; M; 4/11/20-12; N.C. Cherokee; 7/8; S; Bro.; 2171; Yes; Yes; Unallotted

2183; Reed, Sarah; F; 6/19/12-20; N.C. Cherokee; 7/8; S; Alone; 2172; Yes; Yes; Unallotted

2184; Reed, Sarah J.; F; 5/8/15-17; N.C. Cherokee; 7/16; S; Alone; 2173; Yes; Yes; Unallotted

2185; Reed, Theodore; M; 8/29/85-47; N.C. Cherokee; 1/4; M; Head; 2174; Yes; Yes; Unallotted

2186; Reed, Theodore E.; M; 6/29/16-16; N.C. Cherokee; 1/8; S; Son; 2175; Yes; Yes; Unallotted

Census of the **Eastern Cherokee** reservation of the **Cherokee, N.C.** jurisdiction, as of **April 1**, **1933,** taken by **R. L. Spalsbury**, Superintendent.

Key: Number; Surname, Given; Sex; Date of Birth-Age at Last Birthday; Tribe; Degree of Blood; Marital Status; Relationship to Head of Family; Last C. Roll No.; At Jurisdiction Where Enrolled (Yes/No); (If no – Where); Ward (Yes/No); Allotment, Annuity and Identification Numbers (if given).

2187; Reed, William; M; 4/15/82-50; N.C. Cherokee; 7/8; M; Head; 2176; Yes; Yes; Unallotted

2188; Reed, Katie K.; F; 12/23/90-42; N.C. Cherokee; 1/2; M; Wife; 2177; Yes; Yes; Unallotted

2189; Reed, Jackson; M; 1/4/09-24; N.C. Cherokee; 11/16; S; Son; 2178; Yes; Yes; Unallotted

2190; Reed, Cornelia; F; 11/13/11-21; N.C. Cherokee; 11/16; S; Dau.; 2179; Yes; Yes; Unallotted

2191; Reed, Esther; F; 4/30/13-19; N.C. Cherokee; 11/16; S; Dau.; 2180;Yes; Yes; Unallotted

2192; Reed, Noah; M; 1/26/18-15; N.C. Cherokee; 11/16; S; Son; 2181; Yes; Yes; Unallotted

2193; Reed, David; M; 7/26/20-12; N.C. Cherokee; 11/16; S; Son; 2182; Yes; Yes; Unallotted

2194; Reed, McKinley; M; 7/3/23-9; N.C. Cherokee; 11/16; S; Son; 2183; Yes; Yes; Unallotted

2195; Reed, Susie; F; 2/18/29-4; N.C. Cherokee; 11/16; S; Dau.; 2184; Yes; Yes; Unallotted

2196; Reed, Alexander; M; 4/28/31-1; N.C. Cherokee; 11/16; S; Son; 2185; Yes; Yes; Unallotted

2197; Reynolds (Raper, Eva), Eva R.; F; 2/12/04-29; N.C. Cherokee; 1/16; M; Wife; 2186; No; Akron, Summit, Ohio; Yes; Unallotted

2198; Reynolds, Artie G.; M; 1/22/23-10; N.C. Cherokee; 1/32; S; Son; 2187; No; Akron, Summit, Ohio; Yes; Unallotted

2199; Reynolds, Geneva; F; 5/10/24-8; N.C. Cherokee; 1/32; S; Dau.; 2188; No; Akron, Summit, Ohio; Yes; Unallotted

2200; Richards, Mamie P.; F; 1/27/87-46; N.C. Cherokee; 1/16; M; Wife; 2189; Yes; Yes; Unallotted

2201; Richards, Ruby K.; F; 9/11/06-26; N.C. Cherokee; 1/32; S; Dau.; 2190; Yes; Yes; Unallotted

2202; Richards (Cole, Orney), Orney; F; 11/7/93-39; N.C. Cherokee; 1/16; M; Wife; 2191; Yes; Yes; Unallotted

2203; Richards, Doyle; M; 8/24/15-17; N.C. Cherokee; 1/32; S; Son; 2192; Yes; Yes; Unallotted

2204; Richards, Zelzie; M; 8/13/17-15; N.C. Cherokee; 1/32; S; Son; 2193; Yes; Yes; Unallotted

2205; Richards, Edward; M; 8/10/19-13; N.C. Cherokee; 1/32; S; Son; 2194; Yes; Yes; Unallotted

2206; Riffey (Wolfe, Eliza), Eliza P.; F; 9/30/02-30; N.C. Cherokee; 1/8; M; Wife; 2195; Yes; Yes; Unallotted

Census of the **Eastern Cherokee** reservation of the **Cherokee, N.C.** jurisdiction, as of **April 1** , 19**33,** taken by **R. L. Spalsbury** , Superintendent.

Key: Number; Surname, Given; Sex; Date of Birth-Age at Last Birthday; Tribe; Degree of Blood; Marital Status; Relationship to Head of Family; Last C. Roll No.; At Jurisdiction Where Enrolled (Yes/No); (If no – Where); Ward (Yes/No); Allotment, Annuity and Identification Numbers (if given).

2207; Riley, James; M; 5/3/01-31; N.C. Cherokee; 1/4; S; Head; 2196; Yes; Yes; Unallotted

2208; Roberts (Smith, Josephine), Josephine; F; 9/30/95-37; N.C. Cherokee; 1/8; M; Wife; 2197; Yes; Yes; Unallotted

2209; Roberts, Pauline; F; 7/15/14-18; N.C. Cherokee; 1/16; S; Dau.; 2198; Yes; Yes; Unallotted

2210; Roberts, Leroy; M; 1/5/17-16; N.C. Cherokee; 1/16; S; Son; 2199; Yes; Yes; Unallotted

2211; Roberts, Wane; M; 11/2/19-13; N.C. Cherokee; 1/16; S; Son; 2200; Yes; Yes; Unallotted

2212; Roberts, Glenn; M; 2/27/21-12; N.C. Cherokee; 1/16; S; Son; 2201; Yes; Yes; Unallotted

2213; Roberts (Smith, Lottie), Lottie; F; 9/26/83-49; N.C. Cherokee; 3/8; M; Wife; 2202; No; Sweetwater, Monroe, Tenn.; Yes; Unallotted

2214; Roberts, Walter; M; 6/20/03-29; N.C. Cherokee; 3/16; S; Son; 2203; No; Sweetwater, Monroe, Tenn.; Yes; Unallotted

2215; Roberts, Fred; M; 5/12/05-27; N.C. Cherokee; 3/16; S; Son; 2204; No; Sweetwater, Monroe, Tenn.; Yes; Unallotted

2216; Roberts, Lula; F; 5/6/07-25; N.C. Cherokee; 3/16; S; Dau.; 2205; No; Sweetwater, Monroe, Tenn.; Yes; Unallotted

2217; Roberts, G.W.; M; 8/15/13-19; N.C. Cherokee; 3/16; S; Son; 2206; No; Sweetwater, Monroe, Tenn.; Yes; Unallotted

2218; Roberts, Emma; F; 1/7/18-15; N.C. Cherokee; 3/16; S; Dau.; 2207; No; Sweetwater, Monroe, Tenn.; Yes; Unallotted

2219; Roberts, Leona; F; 8/5/21-11; N.C. Cherokee; 3/16; S; Dau.; 2208; No; Sweetwater, Monroe, Tenn.; Yes; Unallotted

2220; Roberson (Raper, Iowa), Iowa; F; 12/2/88-44; N.C. Cherokee; 1/8; M; Wife; 2209; No; Culberson, Cherokee, N.C.; Yes; Unallotted

2221; Roberson, A.J.; M; 8/12/12-20; N.C. Cherokee; 1/16; S; Son; 2210; No; Culberson, Cherokee, N.C.; Yes; Unallotted

2222; Roberson, Walter A.; M; 9/5/14-18; N.C. Cherokee; 1/16; S; Son; 2211; No; Culberson, Cherokee, N.C.; Yes; Unallotted

2223; Roberson, Wayne C.; M; 7/5/17-15; N.C. Cherokee; 1/16; S; Son; 2212; No; Culberson, Cherokee, N.C.; Yes; Unallotted

2224; Roberson, Nona D.; F; 2/25/23-10; N.C. Cherokee; 1/16; S; Dau.; 2213; No; Culberson, Cherokee, N.C.; Yes; Unallotted

2225; Robinson, Birgie; F; 1883-50; N.C. Cherokee; 1/4-; M; Wife; 2214; No; Rossville, Walker, Ga.; Yes; Unallotted

2226; Robinson, Charles H.; M; 1/13/05-28; N.C. Cherokee; 1/32; S; Head; 2215; No; Schoolfield, Pitsylvania, Pa.; Yes; Unallotted

Census of the **Eastern Cherokee** reservation of the **Cherokee, N.C.** jurisdiction, as of **April 1**, **1933,** taken by **R. L. Spalsbury**, Superintendent.

Key: Number; Surname, Given; Sex; Date of Birth-Age at Last Birthday; Tribe; Degree of Blood; Marital Status; Relationship to Head of Family; Last C. Roll No.; At Jurisdiction Where Enrolled (Yes/No); (If no – Where); Ward (Yes/No); Allotment, Annuity and Identification Numbers (if given).

2227; Robinson, Howard G.; M; 5/5/07-25; N.C. Cherokee; 1/32; S; Bro.; 2216; No; Schoolfield, Pitsylvania, Pa.; Yes; Unallotted

2228; Robinson, Henry H.; M; 5/30/10-22; N.C. Cherokee; 1/32; S; Bro.; 2217; No; Schoolfield, Pitsylvania, Pa.; Yes; Unallotted

2229; Robinson, Alvin W.; M; 4/6/12-20; N.C. Cherokee; 1/32; S; Bro.; 2218; No; Schoolfield, Pitsylvania, Pa.; Yes; Unallotted

2230; Robinson, Malvin O.; M; 3/14/14-19; N.C. Cherokee; 1/32; S; Bro.; 2219; No; Schoolfield, Pitsylvania, Pa.; Yes; Unallotted

2231; Robinson, Bessie I.; F; 11/28/16-16; N.C. Cherokee; 1/32; S; Sis.; 2220; No; Schoolfield, Pitsylvania, Pa.; Yes; Unallotted

2232; Robinson (Raper, Ellen), Ellen; F; 2/4/66-67; N.C. Cherokee; 1/8; M; Wife; 2221; No; Murphy, Cherokee, N.C.; Yes; Unallotted

2233; Robinson, Hadley; M; 2/26/99-34; N.C. Cherokee; 1/16; S; Son; 2222; No; Murphy, Cherokee, N.C.; Yes; Unallotted

2234; Robinson, Thomas L.; M; 7/15/83-49; N.C. Cherokee; 1/16; M; Head; 2223; No; Murphy, Cherokee, N.C.; Yes; Unallotted

2235; Robinson, William R.; M; 11/19/05-27; N.C. Cherokee; 1/32; S; Son; 2224; No; Murphy, Cherokee, N.C.; Yes; Unallotted

2236; Robinson, Harley T.; M; 12/30/08-24; N.C. Cherokee; 1/32; S; Son; 2225; No; Murphy, Cherokee, N.C.; Yes; Unallotted

2237; Robinson, Sarah E.; F; 4/18/12-20; N.C. Cherokee; 1/32; S; Dau.; 2226; No; Murphy, Cherokee, N.C.; Yes; Unallotted

2238; Robinson, Luther; M; 4/14/14-18; N.C. Cherokee; 1/32; S; Son; 2227; No; Murphy, Cherokee, N.C.; Yes; Unallotted

2239; Robinson, Clara N.; F; 1/2/17-16; N.C. Cherokee; 1/32; S; Dau.; 2228; No; Murphy, Cherokee, N.C.; Yes; Unallotted

2240; Robinson, Edward; M; 2/2/19-14; N.C. Cherokee; 1/32; S; Son; 2229; No; Murphy, Cherokee, N.C.; Yes; Unallotted

2241; Robinson, Susie M.; F; 7/15/22-10; N.C. Cherokee; 1/32; S; Dau.; 2230; No; Murphy, Cherokee, N.C.; Yes; Unallotted

2242; Robinson, Rose Bell; F; 6/2/24-8; N.C. Cherokee; 1/32; S; Dau.; 2231; No; Murphy, Cherokee, N.C.; Yes; Unallotted

2243; Robinson, Willis O.; M; 10/3/80-52; N.C. Cherokee; 1/16; M; Head; 2232; No; Murphy, Cherokee, N.C.; Yes; Unallotted

2244; Robinson, Fred A.; M; 1/16/19-14; N.C. Cherokee; 1/32; S; Son; 2233; No; Murphy, Cherokee, N.C.; Yes; Unallotted

2245; Rogers, Astor; M; 5/23/05-27; N.C. Cherokee; 1/8; S; Head; 2234; Yes; Yes; Unallotted

2246; Rogers, Junior C.; M; 4/7/26-9[sic]; N.C. Cherokee; 1/16; S; Son; 2235; Yes; Yes; Unallotted

Census of the **Eastern Cherokee** reservation of the **Cherokee, N.C.** jurisdiction, as of **April 1** , 19**33**, taken by **R. L. Spalsbury** , Superintendent.

Key: Number; Surname, Given; Sex; Date of Birth-Age at Last Birthday; Tribe; Degree of Blood; Marital Status; Relationship to Head of Family; Last C. Roll No.; At Jurisdiction Where Enrolled (Yes/No); (If no – Where); Ward (Yes/No); Allotment, Annuity and Identification Numbers (if given).

2247; Rogers, Floyd; M; 4/4/02-30; N.C. Cherokee; 1/8; M; Head; 2236; Yes; Yes; Unallotted

2248; Rogers, Maud S.; F; 11/11/98-34; N.C. Cherokee; 1/8; M; Wife; 2237; Yes; Yes; Unallotted

2249; Rogers, Samuel R.; M; 1/27/22-11; N.C. Cherokee; 1/8; S; Son; 2238; Yes; Yes; Unallotted

2250; Rogers, Irwin; M; 7/21/90-42; N.C. Cherokee; 1/16; M; Head; 2239; No; Adairsville, Bartow, Ga. Yes; Unallotted

2251; Rogers (Cole, Lula), Lula; F; 1/17/07-26; N.C. Cherokee; 1/16; M; Wife; 2240; Yes; Yes; Unallotted

2252; Rogers, Oscar; M; 8/7/96-36; N.C. Cherokee; 1/8; M; Head; 2241; Yes; Yes; Unallotted

2253; Rogers, Clarence; M; 5/5/15-17; N.C. Cherokee; 1/16; S; Son; 2242; Yes; Yes; Unallotted

2254; Rogers, Elsie; F; 7/24/17-15; N.C. Cherokee; 1/16; S; Dau.; 2243; Yes; Yes; Unallotted

2255; Rogers, Shirley; M[sic]; 11/12/19-13; N.C. Cherokee; 1/16; S; Son[sic]; 2244; Yes; Yes; Unallotted

2256; Rogers, Ruth M.; F; 3/24/24-9; N.C. Cherokee; 1/16; S; Dau.; 2245; Yes; Yes; Unallotted

2257; Rogers, Charles F.; M; 3/31/31-2; N.C. Cherokee; 1/16; S; Son; 2246; Yes; Yes; Unallotted

2258; Rollins, Dovie; F; 4/17/62-70; N.C. Cherokee; 1/8; M; Wife; 2247; No; Rossville, Walker, Ga.; Yes; Unallotted

2259; Rose (Sneed, Florence), Florence; F; 11/20/69-63; N.C. Cherokee; 1/8; M; Wife; 2248; Yes; Yes; Unallotted

2260; Rose, Benjamin T.; M; 6/30/07-25; N.C. Cherokee; 1/16; S; Son; 2249; Yes; Yes; Unallotted

2261; Rose, Thurman; M; 3/16/10-23; N.C. Cherokee; 1/16; S; Son; 2250; Yes; Yes; Unallotted

2262; Rose, Wayne; M; 1/17/13-20; N.C. Cherokee; 1/16; S; Son; 2251; Yes; Yes; Unallotted

2263; Rose, Jake; M; 4/8/95-37; N.C. Cherokee; 1/16; M; Head; 2252; Yes; Yes; Unallotted

2264; Rose, Velma; F; 6/8/19-13; N.C. Cherokee; 1/32; S; Dau.; 2253; Yes; Yes; Unallotted

2265; Rose, Thelma; F; 2/22/22-11; N.C. Cherokee; 1/32; S; Dau.; 2254; Yes; Yes; Unallotted

Census of the **Eastern Cherokee** reservation of the **Cherokee, N.C.** jurisdiction, as of **April 1** , 19**33,** taken by **R. L. Spalsbury** , Superintendent.

Key: Number; Surname, Given; Sex; Date of Birth-Age at Last Birthday; Tribe; Degree of Blood; Marital Status; Relationship to Head of Family; Last C. Roll No.; At Jurisdiction Where Enrolled (Yes/No); (If no – Where); Ward (Yes/No); Allotment, Annuity and Identification Numbers (if given).

2266; Rose, William; M; 8/31/92-39; N.C. Cherokee; 1/16; M; Head; 2255; Yes; Yes; Unallotted

2267; Rose, Horace J.; M; 2/8/22-11; N.C. Cherokee; 1/32; S; Son; 2256; Yes; Yes; Unallotted

2268; Rose, Nora Lee; F; 6/1/24-8; N.C. Cherokee; 1/32; S; Dau.; 2257; Yes; Yes; Unallotted

2269; Ross, Katie; F; 1/6/13-20; N.C. Cherokee; 7/8; S; ~~Dau.~~ Sister; 2259; Yes; Yes; Unallotted

2270; Ross, Olive E.; F; 3/9/18-15; N.C. Cherokee; 7/8; S; Sis.; 2260; Yes; Yes; Unallotted

2271; Ross, Leroy; M; 7/14/20-12; N.C. Cherokee; 7/8; S; Bro.; 2261; Yes; Yes; Unallotted

2272; Ross, Kane T.; M; 2/28/88-45; N.C. Cherokee; 4/4; M; Head; 2262; Yes; Yes; Unallotted

2273; Ross, Josie T.; F; 2/3/08-25; N.C. Cherokee; 4/4; M; Wife; 2263; Yes; Yes; Unallotted

2274; Ross, William; M; 4/8/90-42; N.C. Cherokee; 4/4; Wd; Head; 2264; Yes; Yes; Unallotted

2275; Ross, Isaac; M; 2/2/17-16; N.C. Cherokee; 4/4; S; Son; 2266; Yes; Yes; Unallotted

2276; Ross, Minnie; F; 3/7/20-13; N.C. Cherokee; 4/4; S; Son[sic]; 2267; Yes; Yes; Unallotted

2277; Ross, Russell; M; 3/19/23-10; N.C. Cherokee; 4/4; S; Son; 2268; Yes; Yes; Unallotted

2278; Ross, Wilson M.; M; 2/16/28-5; N.C. Cherokee; 4/4; S; Son; 2269; Yes; Yes; Unallotted

2279; Ross, Deedanuskie; M; 2/19/32-1; N.C. Cherokee; 4/4; S; Son; 2270; Yes; Yes; Unallotted

2280; Ross, McKinley; M; 12/25/99-33; N.C. Cherokee; 1/2; M; Head; 2271; Yes; Yes; Unallotted

2281; Ross, Robert; M; 2/8/33-1/12; N.C. Cherokee; 1/4; S; Son; ---; Yes; Yes; Unallotted

2282; Runion (Raper, Julia), Julia R.; F; 12/23/00-32; N.C. Cherokee; 1/16; M; Wife; 2272; No; Farner, Polk, Tenn.; Yes; Unallotted

2283; Runion, Charlie; M; 8/14/17-15; N.C. Cherokee; 1/32; S; Son; 2273; No; Farner, Polk, Tenn.; Yes; Unallotted

2284; Runion, Pauline; F; 9/26/19-13; N.C. Cherokee; 1/32; S; Dau.; 2274; No; Farner, Polk, Tenn.; Yes; Unallotted

2285; Runion, Lake; M; 9/14/22-10; N.C. Cherokee; 1/32; S; Son; 2275; No; Farner, Polk, Tenn.; Yes; Unallotted

Census of the **Eastern Cherokee** reservation of the **Cherokee, N.C.** jurisdiction, as of **April 1** , 19**33,** taken by **R. L. Spalsbury** , Superintendent.

Key: Number; Surname, Given; Sex; Date of Birth-Age at Last Birthday; Tribe; Degree of Blood; Marital Status; Relationship to Head of Family; Last C. Roll No.; At Jurisdiction Where Enrolled (Yes/No); (If no – Where); Ward (Yes/No); Allotment, Annuity and Identification Numbers (if given).

2286; Salerno, Lucinda W.; F; 12/23/83-49; N.C. Cherokee; 4/4; M; Wife; 2276; Yes; Yes; Unallotted

2287; Sampson, James; M; 1/18/53-80; N.C. Cherokee; 4/4; M; Head; 2277; Yes; Yes; Unallotted

2288; Sampson, Sallie; F; 1/10/63-70; N.C. Cherokee; 4/4; M; Wife; 2278; Yes; Yes; Unallotted

2289; Sanders, Cudge; M; 6/10/61-71; N.C. Cherokee; 1/4; Wd; Head; 2279; Yes; Yes; Unallotted

2290; Sanders, Moses; M; 10/4/96-36; N.C. Cherokee; 3/8; M; Head; 2281; Yes; Yes; Unallotted

2291; Sanders, Jennie M.; F; 6/11/15-17; N.C. Cherokee; 3/16; S; Dau.; 2282; Yes; Yes; Unallotted

2292; Sanders, Wm. Adron; M; 11/24/18-14; N.C. Cherokee; 3/16; S; Son; 2283; Yes; Yes; Unallotted

2293; Sanders, Theodore; M; 4/27/22-10; N.C. Cherokee; 3/16; S; Son; 2284; Yes; Yes; Unallotted

2294; Sanders, Vernon; M; 4/26/24-8; N.C. Cherokee; 3/16; S; Son; 2285; Yes; Yes; Unallotted

2295; Satterfield (Loudermilk, Julia), Julia L.; F; 6/6/06-26; N.C. Cherokee; 1/32; M; Wife; 2286; No; Culberson, Cherokee, N.C.; Yes; Unallotted

2296; Satterfield, Lottie; F; 2/3/24-9; N.C. Cherokee; 1/64; S; Dau.; 2287; No; Culberson, Cherokee, N.C.; Yes; Unallotted

2297; Saunooke, Amoneeta; M; 1/17/94-39; N.C. Cherokee; 4/4; M; Head; 2288; Yes; Yes; Unallotted

2298; Saunooke, Nancy T.; F; 8/10/01-31; N.C. Cherokee; 4/4; M; Wife; 2289; Yes; Yes; Unallotted

2299; Saunooke, Lydia T.; F; 4/18/31-1; N.C. Cherokee; 4/4; S; Dau.; 2290; Yes; Yes; Unallotted

2300; Saunooke, Margaret; F; 11/24/32-4/12; N.C. Cherokee; 4/4; S; Dau.; ---; Yes; Yes; Unallotted

2301; Saunooke, Anderson; M; 1/1/04-29; N.C. Cherokee; 1/2; M; Head; 2291; Yes; Yes; Unallotted

2302; Saunooke, Stacy E.P.; F; 10/28/29-23; N.C. Cherokee; 7/8; M; Wife; 2292; Yes; Yes; Unallotted

2303; Saunooke, Edna V.; F; 7/18/29-3; N.C. Cherokee; 11/16; S; Dau.; 2293; Yes; Yes; Unallotted

2304; Saunooke, Robert G.; M; 8/5/31-1; N.C. Cherokee; 11/16; S; Son; 2294; Yes; Yes; Unallotted

Census of the **Eastern Cherokee** reservation of the **Cherokee, N.C.** jurisdiction, as of **April 1** , **1933,** taken by **R. L. Spalsbury** , Superintendent.

Key: Number; Surname, Given; Sex; Date of Birth-Age at Last Birthday; Tribe; Degree of Blood; Marital Status; Relationship to Head of Family; Last C. Roll No.; At Jurisdiction Where Enrolled (Yes/No); (If no – Where); Ward (Yes/No); Allotment, Annuity and Identification Numbers (if given).

2305; Saunooke, Cain; M; 12/2/07-26; N.C. Cherokee; 4/4; M; Head; 2295; Yes; Yes; Unallotted

2306; Saunooke, Margaret Smith; F; 6/12/11-21; N.C. Cherokee; 1/8; M; Wife; 2296; Yes; Yes; Unallotted

2307; Saunooke, Golinda; F; 10/17/31-1; N.C. Cherokee; 5/8; S; Dau.; 2297; Yes; Yes; Unallotted

2308; Saunooke, Edward; M; 9/2/00-32; N.C. Cherokee; 1/2; M; Head; 2298; Yes; Yes; Unallotted

2309; Saunooke, Jackson; M; 3/30/83-53; N.C. Cherokee; 4/4; S; Head; 2299; No; Preston, Richardson, Neb.; Yes; Unallotted

2310; Saunooke, James; M; 6/18/87-45; N.C. Cherokee; 4/4; M; Head; 2300; Yes; Yes; Unallotted

2311; Saunooke, Rachel T.; F; 9/21/95-37; N.C. Cherokee; 4/4; M; Wife; 2301; Yes; Yes; Unallotted

2312; Saunooke, Nicodemus; M; 8/11/18-14; N.C. Cherokee; 4/4; S; Son; 2302; Yes; Yes; Unallotted

2313; Saunooke, Jackson; M; 3/8/28-5; N.C. Cherokee; 4/4; S; Son; 2303; Yes; Yes; Unallotted

2314; Saunooke, Joseph; M; 9/4/72-60; N.C. Cherokee; 4/4; Wd.; Head; 2304; Yes; Yes; Unallotted

2315; Saunooke, Richard; M; 8/6/15-17; N.C. Cherokee; 31/32; S; Son; 2286; Yes; Yes; Unallotted

2316; Saunooke, Edison J.; M; 9/22/18-14; N.C. Cherokee; 31/32; S; Son; 2307; Yes; Yes; Unallotted

2317; Saunooke, Welch Lee; M; 3/31/20-13; N.C. Cherokee; 31/32; S; Son; 2308; Yes; Yes; Unallotted

2318; Saunooke, Thelma M.; F; 1/25/24-9; N.C. Cherokee; 31/32; S; Dau.; 2309; Yes; Yes; Unallotted

2319; Saunooke, Malinda; F; 2/18/86-47; N.C. Cherokee; 4/4; S; Head; 2310; Yes; Yes; Unallotted

2320; Saunooke, Stephen; M; 12/25/97-35; N.C. Cherokee; 4/4; M; Head; 2311; Yes; Yes; Unallotted

2321; Saunooke, Callie D.; F; 7/5/08-24; N.C. Cherokee; 4/4; M; Wife; 2312; Yes; Yes; Unallotted

2322; Saunooke, Samuel; M; 12/15/78-54; N.C. Cherokee; 7/8; M; Head; 2313; Yes; Yes; Unallotted

2323; Saunooke, Harvey S.; M; 7/30/20-12; N.C. Cherokee; 7/16; S; Son; 2314; Yes; Yes; Unallotted

Census of the **Eastern Cherokee** reservation of the **Cherokee, N.C.** jurisdiction, as of **April 1** , 19**33,** taken by **R. L. Spalsbury** , Superintendent.

Key: Number; Surname, Given; Sex; Date of Birth-Age at Last Birthday; Tribe; Degree of Blood; Marital Status; Relationship to Head of Family; Last C. Roll No.; At Jurisdiction Where Enrolled (Yes/No); (If no – Where); Ward (Yes/No); Allotment, Annuity and Identification Numbers (if given).

2324; Saunooke, Stillwell; M; 9/1/91-41; N.C. Cherokee; 7/8; M; Head; 2315; Yes; Yes; Unallotted

2325; Saunooke, William; M; 7/4/70-61; N.C. Cherokee; 4/4; M; Head; 2316; Yes; Yes; Unallotted

2326; Saunooke, Osler; M; 7/19/06-26; N.C. Cherokee; 1/2; S; Son; 2317; Yes; Yes; Unallotted

2327; Saunooke, Cowanah; M; 4/6/09-23; N.C. Cherokee; 1/2; S; Son; 2318; Yes; Yes; Unallotted

2328; Saunooke, Freeman; M; 2/8/11-22; N.C. Cherokee; 1/2; S; Son; 2319; Yes; Yes; Unallotted

2329; Saunooke, Nettie; F; 7/11/13-19; N.C. Cherokee; 1/2; S; Dau.; 2320; Yes; Yes; Unallotted

2330; Saunooke, Cora; F; 2/22/15-18; N.C. Cherokee; 1/2; S; Dau.; 2321; Yes; Yes; Unallotted

2331; Saunooke, Matilda; F; 1/2/18-15; N.C. Cherokee; 1/2; S; Dau.; 2322; Yes; Yes; Unallotted

2332; Saunooke (Standingdeer), William; M; 4/13/14-18; N.C. Cherokee; 31/32; M; Head; 2323; Yes; Yes; Unallotted

2333; Saunooke (Locust, Josephine), Josephine; F; 12/17/14-18; N.C. Cherokee; 1/4; M; Wife; 1416; Yes; Yes; Unallotted

2334; Sauve, Minnie E.; F; 5/4/81-51; N.C. Cherokee; 1/4; M; Wife; 2324; Yes; Yes; Unallotted

2335; Sawyer, Allen; M; 5/3/77-55; N.C. Cherokee; 4/4; M; Head; 2325; Yes; Yes; Unallotted

2336; Sawyer, Kiney; F; 5/17/84-48; N.C. Cherokee; 4/4; M; Wife; 2326; Yes; Yes; Unallotted

2337; Sawyer, Thomas; M; 6/25/05-27; N.C. Cherokee; 4/4; S; Son; 2327; Yes; Yes; Unallotted

2338; Sawyer (Hardin, Inez), Inez E.; F; 7/8/05-27; N.C. Cherokee; 1/32; M; Wife; 2328; Yes; Yes; Unallotted

2339; Nichols, Thelma; F; 3/16/20-13; N.C. Cherokee; 1/64; S; Dau.; 2329; Yes; Yes; Unallotted

2340; Screamer, Cornelia; F; 5/13/22-10; N.C. Cherokee; 4/4; S; Orphan; 2330; Yes; Yes; Unallotted

2341; Screamer, Nellie; F; 2/13/24-9; N.C. Cherokee; 4/4; S; Orphan; 2331; Yes; Yes; Unallotted

2342; Screamer, James; M; 12/23/59-73; N.C. Cherokee; 4/4; M; Head; 2332; Yes; Yes; Unallotted

Census of the **Eastern Cherokee** reservation of the **Cherokee, N.C.** jurisdiction, as of **April 1**, **1933,** taken by **R. L. Spalsbury**, Superintendent.

Key: Number; Surname, Given; Sex; Date of Birth-Age at Last Birthday; Tribe; Degree of Blood; Marital Status; Relationship to Head of Family; Last C. Roll No.; At Jurisdiction Where Enrolled (Yes/No); (If no – Where); Ward (Yes/No); Allotment, Annuity and Identification Numbers (if given).

2343; Screamer, Cinda; F; 10/15/71-61; N.C. Cherokee; 4/4; M; Wife; 2333; Yes; Yes; Unallotted

2344; Screamer, Soggie; M; 7/31/93-39; N.C. Cherokee; 4/4; S; Son; 2334; No; Okla.; Yes; Unallotted

2345; Screamer, Kane; M; 9/19/91-41; N.C. Cherokee; 4/4; M; Head; 2335; Yes; Yes; Unallotted

2346; Screamer, Polly S.; F; 12/26/06-26; N.C. Cherokee; 15/16; M; Wife; 2336; Yes; Yes; Unallotted

2347; Screamer, Annie R.; F; 8/14/25-8; N.C. Cherokee; 31/32; S; Dau.; 2337; Yes; Yes; Unallotted

2348; Screamer, James; M; 1/28/29-4; N.C. Cherokee; 31/32; S; Son; 2338; Yes; Yes; Unallotted

2349; Screamer, Jennie L.; F; 3/2/32-1; N.C. Cherokee; 31/32; S; Dau.; 2339; Yes; Yes; Unallotted

2350; Screamer, Manus; M; 9/19/82-50; N.C. Cherokee; 4/4; M; Head; 2340; Yes; Yes; Unallotted

2351; Screamer, Nannie; F; 5/18/77-55; N.C. Cherokee; 4/4; M; Wife; 2341; Yes; Yes; Unallotted

2352; Screamer, Mianna; F; 11/3/12-20; N.C. Cherokee; 4/4; S; Dau.; 2342;Yes; Yes; Unallotted

2353; Screamer, Manus, Jr.; M; 9/12/14-18; N.C. Cherokee; 4/4; S; Son; 2343; Yes; Yes; Unallotted

2354; Scruggs (Keg, Rebecca), Rebecca; F; 2/10/10-23; N.C. Cherokee; 7/8; M; Wife; 2344; Yes; Yes; Unallotted

2355; Sequoyah (Runningwolf), Ammons; M; 8/23/02-30; N.C. Cherokee; 4/4; M; Separated; 2345; No; In Navy.; Yes; Unallotted

2356; Sequoyah, Ollick O.; F; 6/17/03-29; N.C. Cherokee; 4/4; M; Separated; 2346; Yes; Yes; Unallotted

2357; Sequoyah, Mable; F; 1/6/22-11; N.C. Cherokee; 4/4; S; Dau.; 2347;Yes; Yes; Unallotted

2358; Sequoyah, Ammons; M; 4/3/05-27; N.C. Cherokee; 7/8; M; Head; 2348; Yes; Yes; Unallotted

2359; Sequoyah, Kina L.L.; F; 12/4/02-30; N.C. Cherokee; 4/4; M; Wife; 2349; Yes; Yes; Unallotted

2360; Sequoyah, Willie L.; F; 2/9/30-3; N.C. Cherokee; 15/16; S; Dau.; 2350; Yes; Yes; Unallotted

2361; Sequoyah, Lloyd; M; 6/30/99-33; N.C. Cherokee; 4/4; M; Head; 2351; Yes; Yes; Unallotted

Census of the **Eastern Cherokee** reservation of the **Cherokee, N.C.** jurisdiction, as of **April 1** , 19**33,** taken by **R. L. Spalsbury** , Superintendent.

Key: Number; Surname, Given; Sex; Date of Birth-Age at Last Birthday; Tribe; Degree of Blood; Marital Status; Relationship to Head of Family; Last C. Roll No.; At Jurisdiction Where Enrolled (Yes/No); (If no – Where); Ward (Yes/No); Allotment, Annuity and Identification Numbers (if given).

2362; Sequoyah, Lizzy W.; F; 7/6/01-31; N.C. Cherokee; 4/4; M; Wife; 2352; Yes; Yes; Unallotted

2363; Sequoyah, Edward; M; 6/16/19-13; N.C. Cherokee; 4/4; S; Son; 2353; Yes; Yes; Unallotted

2364; Sequoyah, Lucy; F; 12/23/22-10; N.C. Cherokee; 4/4; S; Dau.; 2354; Yes; Yes; Unallotted

2365; Sequoyah, Mildred; F; 1/6/33-2/12; N.C. Cherokee; 4/4; S; Dau.; ---; Yes; Yes; Unallotted

2366; Sequoyah (Runningwolf) Sequoia; M; 5/15/78-54; N.C. Cherokee; 4/4; M; Head; Separated, 2355; Yes; Yes; Unallotted

2367; Sequoyah, Mollie; F; 6/11/82-50; N.C. Cherokee; 4/4; M; Wife; 2356; Yes; Yes; Unallotted

2368; Sequoyah, Minda E.; F; 6/21/18-14; N.C. Cherokee; 4/4; SM; Dau.; 2357; Yes; Yes; Unallotted

2369; Sequoyah, Amanda; F; 10/27/21-11; N.C. Cherokee; 4/4; S; Dau.; 2358;Yes; Yes; Unallotted

2370; Sequoyah, Wilma; F; 1/24/33-2/12; N.C. Cherokee; 4/4; S; Grand-dau.; ---; Yes; Yes; Unallotted

2371; Sequoyah, Louise H.; F; 6/8/59-73; N.C. Cherokee; 7/8; Wd.; Head; 2359; Yes; Yes; Unallotted

2372; Shake-ear (Skitty), Fidella; M; 12/23/71-61; N.C. Cherokee; 4/4; M; Head; 2360; Yes; Yes; Unallotted

2373; Sequoyah, Lizzie; F; 12/23/64-68; N.C. Cherokee; 4/4; M; Wife; 2361; Yes; Yes; Unallotted

2374; Shell, John; M; 12/23/58-74; N.C. Cherokee; 4/4; Wd.; Head; 2362; Yes; Yes; Unallotted

2375; Shell, Ute; M; 6/18/77-55; N.C. Cherokee; 4/4; Wd.; Head; 2363; Yes; Yes; Unallotted

2376; Shell, Joseph; M; 9/5/01-31; N.C. Cherokee; 4/4; S; Son; 2364; Yes; Yes; Unallotted

2377; Shell, Joshua; M; 8/23/08-24; N.C. Cherokee; 4/4; S; Son; 2365; Yes; Yes; Unallotted

2378; Shell, Boyd; M; 3/23/11-22; N.C. Cherokee; 4/4; S; Son; 2366; Yes; Yes; Unallotted

2379; Shell, Nancy; F; 7/20/15-17; N.C. Cherokee; 4/4; S; Dau.; 2367; Yes; Yes; Unallotted

2380; Shell, Lilly; F; 3/7/16-17; N.C. Cherokee; 4/4; S; Dau.; 2368; Yes; Yes; Unallotted

2381; Shell, Celia; F; 12/18/18-14; N.C. Cherokee; 4/4; S; Dau.; 2369; Yes; Yes; Unallotted

Census of the **Eastern Cherokee** reservation of the **Cherokee, N.C.** jurisdiction, as of **April 1** , **1933,** taken by **R. L. Spalsbury** , Superintendent.

Key: Number; Surname, Given; Sex; Date of Birth-Age at Last Birthday; Tribe; Degree of Blood; Marital Status; Relationship to Head of Family; Last C. Roll No.; At Jurisdiction Where Enrolled (Yes/No); (If no – Where); Ward (Yes/No); Allotment, Annuity and Identification Numbers (if given).

2382; Shell, Couney; M; 5/3/26-6; N.C. Cherokee; 4/4; S; Son; 2370; Yes; Yes; Unallotted

2383; Sherrill, John; M; 11/10/73-60; N.C. Cherokee; 3/4; M; Head; 2371; Yes; Yes; Unallotted

2384; Sherrill, Mollie; F; 12/11/80-52; N.C. Cherokee; 4/4; M; Wife; 2372; Yes; Yes; Unallotted

2385; Sherrill, Julia; F; 5/27/06-26; N.C. Cherokee; 7/8; S; Dau.; 2373; Yes; Yes; Unallotted

2386; Sherrill, Samuel; M; 8/29/08-24; N.C. Cherokee; 7/8; S; Son; 2374; Yes; Yes; Unallotted

2387; Sherrill, Alice; F; 12/29/11-21; N.C. Cherokee; 7/8; S; Dau.; 2375; Yes; Yes; Unallotted

2388; Sherrill, Andy; M; 4/5/13-19; N.C. Cherokee; 7/8; S; Son; 2376; Yes; Yes; Unallotted

2389; Sherrill, Dinah; F; 7/5/15-17; N.C. Cherokee; 7/8; S; Dau.; 2377; Yes; Yes; Unallotted

2390; Sherrill (Maney, Ruth), Ruth; F; 12/6/06-26; N.C. Cherokee; 1/32; M; Wife; 2378; No; 412 N. Green St., Winston-Salem, Forsyth, N.C.; Yes; Unallotted

2391; Shook, Ollie May; F; 3/29/09-24; N.C. Cherokee; 1/16; S; Dau. (Fr. white); 2379; Yes; Yes; Unallotted

2392; Shook, Ethel; F; 5/16/11-21; N.C. Cherokee; 1/16; SM; Dau.; 2380; Yes; Yes; Unallotted

2393; Shook, Clifford; M; 10/21/15-17; N.C. Cherokee; 1/16; S; Son; 2381; Yes; Yes; Unallotted

2394; Shook, Clarence; M; 3/22/19-14; N.C. Cherokee; 1/16; S; Son; 2382; Yes; Yes; Unallotted

2395; Shook, Boyd; M; 10/26/23-9; N.C. Cherokee; 1/16; S; Son; 2383; Yes; Yes; Unallotted

2396; Simpson, Martha O.; F; 1/21/76-57; N.C. Cherokee; 4/4; M; Wife; 2384; No; 1057 Ramona St., Palo Alto, Santa Clara, Cal.; Yes; Unallotted

2397; Skaggs, Nora; F; 2/15/88-45; N.C. Cherokee; 1/16; M; Wife; 2385; No; Ozark, Christian, Mo.; Yes; Unallotted

2398; Skitty, Sevier; M; 12/23/48-84; N.C. Cherokee; 4/4; S; Head; 2386; Yes; Yes; Unallotted

2399; Smith, Annie; F; 7/17/11-21; N.C. Cherokee; 5/8; S; Alone; 2387; Yes; Yes; Unallotted

2400; Smith, Rosie; F; 7/3/13-19; N.C. Cherokee; 5/8; S; Sis.; 2388; Yes; Yes; Unallotted

Census of the **Eastern Cherokee** reservation of the **Cherokee, N.C.** jurisdiction, as of **April 1**, **1933,** taken by **R. L. Spalsbury**, Superintendent.

Key: Number; Surname, Given; Sex; Date of Birth-Age at Last Birthday; Tribe; Degree of Blood; Marital Status; Relationship to Head of Family; Last C. Roll No.; At Jurisdiction Where Enrolled (Yes/No); (If no – Where); Ward (Yes/No); Allotment, Annuity and Identification Numbers (if given).

2401; Smith, Mary; F; 2/3/15-18; N.C. Cherokee; 5/8; S; Sis.; 2389; Yes; Yes; Unallotted

2402; Shone, Mary; F; 1876-57; N.C. Cherokee; 1/4-; M; Wife; 2390; No; Ensley, Jefferson, Ala.; Yes; Unallotted

2403; Smith, Arthur; M; 4/4/85-47; N.C. Cherokee; 1/4; M; Head; 2391; No; Knoxville, Knox, Tenn.; Yes; Unallotted

2404; Smith, Oveda; F; 11/15/20-12; N.C. Cherokee; 1/8; S; Dau.; 2392; No; Knoxville, Knox, Tenn.; Yes; Unallotted

2405; Smith, Louise; F; 6/15/23-9; N.C. Cherokee; 1/8; S; Dau.; 2393; No; Knoxville, Knox, Tenn.; Yes; Unallotted

2406; Smith, David M.; M; 1/20/00-33; N.C. Cherokee; 1/4; M; Head; 2394; No; In Army,; Yes; Unallotted

2407; Smith, Duffy; M; 11/26/80-52; N.C. Cherokee; 1/2; S; Head; 2395; Yes; Yes; Unallotted

2408; Smith, Frances E.; M; 3/23/86-47; N.C. Cherokee; 1/2; M; Head; 2396; Yes; Yes; Unallotted

2409; Smith, Betty W.; F; 4/1/81-51; N.C. Cherokee; 7/8; M; Wife; 2397; Yes; Yes; Unallotted

2410; Smith, Victor C.; M; 4/11/11-21; N.C. Cherokee; 11/16; S; Son; 2398; Yes; Yes; Unallotted

2411; Smith, Edgar A.; M; 9/18/12-20; N.C. Cherokee; 11/16; S; Son; 2399; Yes; Yes; Unallotted

2412; Smith, Clifford; M; 4/12/14-18; N.C. Cherokee; 11/16; S; Son; 2400; Yes; Yes; Unallotted

2413; Smith, Alvin E.; M; 6/5/16-16; N.C. Cherokee; 11/16; S; Son; 2401; Yes; Yes; Unallotted

2414; Smith, Sheridan; M; 11/24/17-15; N.C. Cherokee; 11/16; S; Son; 2402; Yes; Yes; Unallotted

2415; Smith, Frances; F; 8/6/20-12; N.C. Cherokee; 11/16; S; Dau.; 2403; Yes; Yes; Unallotted

2416; Smith, Leta B.; F; 11/27/24-8; N.C. Cherokee; 11/16; S; Dau.; 2404; Yes; Yes; Unallotted

2417; Smith, George L.; M; 12/25/80-52; N.C. Cherokee; 3/8; M; Head; 2405; No; Bristol, Bucks, Pa.;; Yes; Unallotted

2418; Smith, Harley; M; 3/26/13-20; N.C. Cherokee; 1/8; S; Alone; 2406; Yes; Yes; Unallotted

Census of the **Eastern Cherokee** reservation of the **Cherokee, N.C.** jurisdiction, as of **April 1** , 1933, taken by **R. L. Spalsbury** , Superintendent.

Key: Number; Surname, Given; Sex; Date of Birth-Age at Last Birthday; Tribe; Degree of Blood; Marital Status; Relationship to Head of Family; Last C. Roll No.; At Jurisdiction Where Enrolled (Yes/No); (If no – Where); Ward (Yes/No); Allotment, Annuity and Identification Numbers (if given).

2419; Smith, Hartman; M; 10/15/97-35; N.C. Cherokee; 3/16; M; Head; 2407; Yes; Yes; Unallotted

2420; Smith; Russel; M; 8/2/04-28; N.C. Cherokee; 3/8; S; Head; 2408; Yes; Yes; Unallotted

2421; Smith, Elizabeth Welch; F; 5/25/09-23; N.C. Cherokee; 1/2; M; Wife; 3062; Yes; Yes; Unallotted

2422; Smith, Maxine; F; 6/19/31-1; N.C. Cherokee; 7/16; S; Dau.; ---; Yes; Yes; Unallotted

2423; Smith, Samuel E.; M; 3/28/33-3 days; N.C. Cherokee; 7/16; S; Son; ---; Yes; Yes; Unallotted

2424; Smith, Myrtle; F; 12/13/08-24; N.C. Cherokee; 3/8; S; Sis.; 2409; Yes; Yes; Unallotted

2425; Smith, Bessie; F; 9/29/13-19; N.C. Cherokee; 3/8; S; Sis.; 2410; Yes; Yes; Unallotted

2426; Smith, Henry; M; 9/12/91-41; N.C. Cherokee; 1/4; M; Head; 2411; No; Maryville, Blount, Tenn.; Yes; Unallotted

2427; Smith, Juanetta; F; 2/28/21-12; N.C. Cherokee; 1/8; S; Dau.; 2412; No; Maryville, Blount, Tenn.; Yes; Unallotted

2428; Smith, Henry H. Jr.; M; 5/16/24-9; N.C. Cherokee; 1/8; S; Son; 2413; No; Maryville, Blount, Tenn.; Yes; Unallotted

2429; Smith, Jacob L.; M; 12/23/79-53; N.C. Cherokee; 5/8; M; Head; 2414; Yes; Yes; Unallotted

2430; Smith, Ollie; F; 8/12/76-56; N.C. Cherokee; 4/4; M; Wife; 2415; Yes; Yes; Unallotted

2431; Smith, Lawrence; M; 3/20/07-26; N.C. Cherokee; 13/16; S; Son; 2416; Yes; Yes; Unallotted

2432; Smith, Charles H.; M; 1/11/11-22; N.C. Cherokee; 13/16; S; Son; 2417; Yes; Yes; Unallotted

2433; Smith, Arthur; M; 11/30/12-20; N.C. Cherokee; 13/16; S; Son; 2418; Yes; Yes; Unallotted

2434; Smith, Bernice; F; 4/26/16-16; N.C. Cherokee; 13/16; S; Dau.; 2419; Yes; Yes; Unallotted

2435; Smith, David; M; 10/7/32-6/12; N.C. Cherokee/Creek; 3/8-1/2; S; Gr-Son; ---; Yes; Yes; Unallotted

2436; Smith, James D.; M; 4/25/78-54; N.C. Cherokee; 1/2; M; Head; 2420; Yes; Yes; Unallotted

2437; Smith, Bertha; F; 1/23/14-19; N.C. Cherokee; 1/4; S; Dau.; 2421; Yes; Yes; Unallotted

2438; Smith, John Ross; M; 4/25/16-16; N.C. Cherokee; 1/4; S; Son; 2422; Yes; Yes; Unallotted

Census of the **Eastern Cherokee** reservation of the **Cherokee, N.C.** jurisdiction, as of **April 1** , 19**33,** taken by **R. L. Spalsbury** , Superintendent.

Key: Number; Surname, Given; Sex; Date of Birth-Age at Last Birthday; Tribe; Degree of Blood; Marital Status; Relationship to Head of Family; Last C. Roll No.; At Jurisdiction Where Enrolled (Yes/No); (If no – Where); Ward (Yes/No); Allotment, Annuity and Identification Numbers (if given).

2439; Smith, Ethel L.; F; 11/25/31-1; N.C. Cherokee; 1/4; S; Dau.; 2423; Yes; Yes; Unallotted

2440; Smith, James G.W.; M; 3/26/94-39; N.C. Cherokee; 1/8; M; Head; 2424; Yes; Yes; Unallotted

2441; Smith, Zelma R.; F; 11/25/14-18; N.C. Cherokee; 1/16; S; Dau.; 2425; Yes; Yes; Unallotted

2442; Smith, Gladys; F; 6/18/17-15; N.C. Cherokee; 1/16; S; Dau.; 2426; Yes; Yes; Unallotted

2443; Smith, John D.; M; 11/17/06-26; N.C. Cherokee; 7/16; M; Head; 2427; Yes; Yes; Unallotted

2444; Smith, Mary M.; F; 2/10/30-3; N.C. Cherokee; 7/32; S; Dau.; 2428; Yes; Yes; Unallotted

2445; Smith, John Q.A.; M; 8/12/70-62; N.C. Cherokee; 1/4; M; Head; 2429; Yes; Yes; Unallotted

2446; Smith, Robert S.; M; 4/1/04-28; N.C. Cherokee; 1/8; S; Son; 2430; Yes; Yes; Unallotted

2447; Smith, Ross B.; M; 12/25/07-25; N.C. Cherokee; 1/8; S; Son; 2431; Yes; Yes; Unallotted

2448; Smith, (Bates, Lizzie), Lizzie; F; 7/28/02-30; N.C. Cherokee; 1/16; S; Head; 2432; Yes; Yes; Unallotted

2449; Smith, Oscar G.; M; 6/21/21-11; N.C. Cherokee; 1/32; S; Son; 2433; Yes; Yes; Unallotted

2450; Smith, Lloyd H.; M; 2/25/73-60; N.C. Cherokee; 7/8; M; Head; 2434; Yes; Yes; Unallotted

2451; Smith, Nancy; F; 12/23/51-81; N.C. Cherokee; 4/4; Wd.; Head; 2436; Yes; Yes; Unallotted

2452; Smith, Margaret; F; 2/9/12-21; N.C. Cherokee; 1/64; S; Dau.; 2437; Yes; Yes; Unallotted

2453; Smith, Earlie; M; 5/6/14-18; N.C. Cherokee; 1/64; S; Son; 2438; Yes; Yes; Unallotted

2454; Smith, Marshall; M; 9/12/97-35; N.C. Cherokee; 1/16; S; Head; 2439; Yes; Yes; Unallotted

2455; Smith, (Raper, Mary), Mary; F; 4/30/01-31; N.C. Cherokee; 1/16; M; Wife; 2440; Yes; Yes; Unallotted

2456; Smith, Edna; F; 8/30/20-12; N.C. Cherokee; 1/32; S; Dau.; 2441; Yes; Yes; Unallotted

Census of the **Eastern Cherokee** reservation of the **Cherokee, N.C.** jurisdiction, as of **April 1** , **1933,** taken by **R. L. Spalsbury** , Superintendent.

Key: Number; Surname, Given; Sex; Date of Birth-Age at Last Birthday; Tribe; Degree of Blood; Marital Status; Relationship to Head of Family; Last C. Roll No.; At Jurisdiction Where Enrolled (Yes/No); (If no – Where); Ward (Yes/No); Allotment, Annuity and Identification Numbers (if given).

2457; Smith, Mary M.; F; 6/18/52-80; N.C. Cherokee; 1/4; Wd.; Head; 2442; Yes; Yes; Unallotted

2458; Smith, Minnie; F; 12/3/17-15; N.C. Cherokee; 1/8; S; Alone; 2443; Yes; Yes; Unallotted

2459; Smith, Noah; M; 9/5/03-29; N.C. Cherokee; 7/16; M; Head; 2444; Yes; Yes; Unallotted
2460; Smith, Stella A.; F; 11/7/07-25; N.C. Cherokee; 1/16; M; Wife; 2445; Yes; Yes; Unallotted
2461; Smith, Philip H.; M; 6/24/29-3; N.C. Cherokee; 1/4; S; Son; 2446; Yes; Yes; Unallotted

2462; Smith, Noah Ed.; M; 3/27/83-50; N.C. Cherokee; 1/2; M; Head; 2447; No; Wis.; Yes; Unallotted

2463; Smith, Oliver; M; 10/31/96-36; N.C. Cherokee; 1/2; M; Head; 2448; Yes; Yes; Unallotted
2464; Smith, Nan S.; F; 8/7/90-42; N.C. Cherokee; 4/4; M; Wife; 2449; Yes; Yes; Unallotted
2465; Smith, Charlotte; F; 8/28/16-16; N.C. Cherokee; 3/4; S; Dau.; 2450; Yes; Yes; Unallotted
2466; Smith, Milton P.; M; 4/27/19-13; N.C. Cherokee; 3/4; S; Son; 2451; Yes; Yes; Unallotted

2467; Smith, Roberson; M; 5/2/00-32; N.C. Cherokee; 7/16; M; Head; 2452; Yes; Yes; Unallotted
2468; Smith, Jarret J.; M; 6/3/23-9; N.C. Cherokee; 7/32; S; Son; 2453; Yes; Yes; Unallotted
2469; Smith, Joseph A.; M; 5/31/25-7; N.C. Cherokee; 7/32; S; Son; 2454; Yes; Yes; Unallotted

2470; Smith, Samuel A.; M; 2/25/64-69; N.C. Cherokee; 1/4; M; Head; 2455; Yes; Yes; Unallotted
2471; Smith, Goldman; M; 12/24/98-34; N.C. Cherokee; 1/4; S; Son; 2456; Yes; Yes; Unallotted
2472; Smith, Jesse H.; M; 4/14/03-29; N.C. Cherokee; 1/4; Wd.; Son; 2457; No; Duncan, Stephens, Okla.; Yes; Unallotted
2473; Smith, Martin; M; 11/7/12-20; N.C. Cherokee; 1/8; S; Son; 2458; Yes; Yes; Unallotted
2474; Smith, Sallie; F; 3/7/14-19; N.C. Cherokee; 1/8; S; Dau.; 2459; Yes; Yes; Unallotted
2475; Smith, Franklin; M; 1/11/16-17; N.C. Cherokee; 1/8; S; Son; 2460; Yes; Yes; Unallotted

Census of the **Eastern Cherokee** reservation of the **Cherokee, N.C.** jurisdiction, as of **April 1** , 19**33**, taken by **R. L. Spalsbury** , Superintendent.

Key: Number; Surname, Given; Sex; Date of Birth-Age at Last Birthday; Tribe; Degree of Blood; Marital Status; Relationship to Head of Family; Last C. Roll No.; At Jurisdiction Where Enrolled (Yes/No); (If no – Where); Ward (Yes/No); Allotment, Annuity and Identification Numbers (if given).

2476; Smith, James; M; 9/8/17-15; N.C. Cherokee; 1/8; S; Son; 2461; Yes; Yes; Unallotted

2477; Smith, Toddie; F; 4/3/20-12; N.C. Cherokee; 1/8; S; Dau.; 2462; Yes; Yes; Unallotted

2478; Smith, Tiney Mae; F; 5/20/22-10; N.C. Cherokee; 1/8; S; Dau.; 2463; Yes; Yes; Unallotted

2479; Smith, Henry; M; 4/7/24-8; N.C. Cherokee; 1/8; S; Son; 2464; Yes; Yes; Unallotted

2480; Smith, Levi; M; 7/4/28-4; N.C. Cherokee; 1/8; S; Son; 2465; Yes; Yes; Unallotted

2481; Smith, T. Sibbald; M; 8/13/78-54; N.C. Cherokee; 3/8; M; Head; 2466; No; Patrick, Cherokee, N.C.; Yes; Unallotted

2482; Smith, Muriel; F; 12/31/09-23; N.C. Cherokee; 3/16; S; Dau.; 2467; No; Patrick, Cherokee, N.C.; Yes; Unallotted

2483; Smith, Helen; F; 11/3/12-20; N.C. Cherokee; 3/16; S; Dau.; 2468; No; Patrick, Cherokee, N.C.; Yes; Unallotted

2484; Smith, Carrie E.; F; 2/19/15-18; N.C. Cherokee; 3/16; S; Dau.; 2469; No; Patrick, Cherokee, N.C.; Yes; Unallotted

2485; Smith, R. Madge; F; 4/12/18-14; N.C. Cherokee; 3/16; S; Dau.; 2470; No; Patrick, Cherokee, N.C.; Yes; Unallotted

2486; Smith, Phoebe E.; F; 9/27/21-11; N.C. Cherokee; 3/16; S; Dau.; 2471; No; Patrick, Cherokee, N.C.; Yes; Unallotted

2487; Smith, Sibbald; M; 2/3/29-4; N.C. Cherokee; 3/16; S; Son; 2472; No; Patrick, Cherokee, N.C.; Yes; Unallotted

2488; Smith, Zona F.; F; 2/5/31-2; N.C. Cherokee; 3/16; S; Dau.; 2473; No; Patrick, Cherokee, N.C.; Yes; Unallotted

2489; Smith, Thomas; M; 4/15/83-49; N.C. Cherokee; 7/8; M; Head; 2474; Yes; Yes; Unallotted

2490; Smith, Leuna; F; 4/10/11-21; N.C. Cherokee; 7/16; S; Dau.; 2476; Yes; Yes; Unallotted

2491; Smith, Hosea G.; M; 4/15/13-19; N.C. Cherokee; 7/16; S; Son; 2477; Yes; Yes; Unallotted

2492; Smith, Gertrude; F; 11/6/16-16; N.C. Cherokee; 7/16; S; Dau.; 2478; Yes; Yes; Unallotted

2493; Smith, Rachel; F; 6/13/20-12; N.C. Cherokee; 7/16; S; Dau.; 2479; Yes; Yes; Unallotted

2494; Smith, James E.; M; 4/13/23-9; N.C. Cherokee; 7/16; S; Son; 2480; Yes; Yes; Unallotted

2495; Smith, Buford; M; 7/10/09-23; N.C. Cherokee; 7/16; S; Son; 2475; Yes; Yes; Unallotted

2496; Smith, Alyne; F; 12/28/30-2; N.C. Cherokee; 1/4; S; Gr-son[sic].; 2481; Yes; Yes; Unallotted

Census of the **Eastern Cherokee** reservation of the **Cherokee, N.C.** jurisdiction, as of **April 1** , **1933,** taken by **R. L. Spalsbury** , Superintendent.

Key: Number; Surname, Given; Sex; Date of Birth-Age at Last Birthday; Tribe; Degree of Blood; Marital Status; Relationship to Head of Family; Last C. Roll No.; At Jurisdiction Where Enrolled (Yes/No); (If no – Where); Ward (Yes/No); Allotment, Annuity and Identification Numbers (if given).

2497; Smoker, Charles; M; 1/5/04-29; N.C. Cherokee; 4/4; S; Head; 2482; Yes; Yes; Unallotted

2498; Smoker (Mr.[sic] Hettie Smoker Rattler), Dinah; F; 3/19/21-12; N.C. Cherokee; 4/4; S; Dau.; 2483; Yes; Yes; Unallotted

2499; Smoker, Davidson; M; 12/13/11-21; N.C. Cherokee; 4/4; S; Son; 2484; Yes; Yes; Unallotted

2500; Smoker, Owen; M; 2/24/14-19; N.C. Cherokee; 4/4; S; Son; 2485; Yes; Yes; Unallotted

2501; Smoker, Lloyd; M; 1/18/71-62; N.C. Cherokee; 4/4; Wd.; Head; 2486; Yes; Yes; Unallotted

2502; Smoker, Moses (Ross); M; 11/27/97-35; N.C. Cherokee; 4/4; Wd.; Head; 2487; Yes; Yes; Unallotted

2503; Smoker, Will S.; M; 1/5/71-62; N.C. Cherokee; 4/4; M; Head; 2488; Yes; Yes; Unallotted

2504; Smoker, Alkinney; F; 1/5/78-55; N.C. Cherokee; 4/4; M; Wife; 2489; Yes; Yes; Unallotted

2505; Smoker, Lucy; F; 1/7/07-26; N.C. Cherokee; 4/4; S; Dau.; 2490; Yes; Yes; Unallotted

2506; Smoker, Martha B.; F; 6/9/09-23; N.C. Cherokee; 4/4; S; Dau.; 2491; Yes; Yes; Unallotted

2507; Smoker, Ute; M; 3/20/12-21; N.C. Cherokee; 4/4; S; Son; 2492; Yes; Yes; Unallotted

2508; Smoker, Bessie; F; 5/30/14-18; N.C. Cherokee; 4/4; S; Dau.; 2493; Yes; Yes; Unallotted

2509; Smoker, Amanda; F; 12/13/16-16; N.C. Cherokee; 4/4; S; Dau.; 2494; Yes; Yes; Unallotted

2510; Smoker, Jack C.; M; 8/28/19-13; N.C. Cherokee; 4/4; S; Son; 2495; Yes; Yes; Unallotted

2511; Sneed, Annie L.; F; 11/30/97-35; N.C. Cherokee; 1/8; S; Head; 2496; Yes; Yes; Unallotted

2512; Sneed, Gladys E.; F; 4/29/23-9; N.C. Cherokee; 1/16; S; Dau.; 2497; Yes; Yes; Unallotted

2513; Sneed, Blakely; M; 11/1/04-28; N.C. Cherokee; 1/16; M; Head; 2498; Yes; Yes; Unallotted

2514; Sneed, Campbell; M; 11/20/87-45; N.C. Cherokee; 1/8; M; Head; 2499; Yes; Yes; Unallotted

2515; Sneed, Minda B.; F; 11/28/89-43; N.C. Cherokee; 1/2; M; Wife; 2500; Yes; Yes; Unallotted

Census of the **Eastern Cherokee** reservation of the **Cherokee, N.C.** jurisdiction, as of **April 1** , 19**33,** taken by **R. L. Spalsbury** , Superintendent.

Key: Number; Surname, Given; Sex; Date of Birth-Age at Last Birthday; Tribe; Degree of Blood; Marital Status; Relationship to Head of Family; Last C. Roll No.; At Jurisdiction Where Enrolled (Yes/No); (If no – Where); Ward (Yes/No); Allotment, Annuity and Identification Numbers (if given).

2516; Sneed, Carrie; F; 7/18/08-24; N.C. Cherokee; 5/16; S; Dau.; 2501; Yes; Yes; Unallotted

2517; Sneed, Ernest; M; 4/20/10-22; N.C. Cherokee; 5/16; S; Son; 2502; Yes; Yes; Unallotted

2518; Sneed, Pocahontas; F; 11/12/11-21; N.C. Cherokee; 5/16; S; Dau.; 2503; Yes; Yes; Unallotted

2519; Sneed, Patrick; M; 4/25/13-19; N.C. Cherokee; 5/16; S; Son; 2504; Yes; Yes; Unallotted

2520; Sneed, Claudia M.; F; 4/20/15-17; N.C. Cherokee; 5/16; S; Dau.; 2505; Yes; Yes; Unallotted

2521; Sneed, Marie; F; 10/18/17-15; N.C. Cherokee; 5/16; S; Dau.; 2506; Yes; Yes; Unallotted

2522; Sneed, Virginia; F; 12/29/20-12; N.C. Cherokee; 5/16; S; Dau.; 2507; Yes; Yes; Unallotted

2523; Sneed, Vernon; M; 1/7/22-11; N.C. Cherokee; 5/16; S; Son; 2508; Yes; Yes; Unallotted

2524; Sneed, Winifred; F; 3/25/24-8; N.C. Cherokee; 5/16; S; Dau.; 2509; Yes; Yes; Unallotted

2525; Sneed, Priscilla; F; 10/8/28-4; N.C. Cherokee; 5/16; S; Dau.; 2510; Yes; Yes; Unallotted

2526; Sneed, Gertha; F; 3/13/32-1; N.C. Cherokee; 5/16; S; Grand-dau.; 2511; Yes; Yes; Unallotted

2527; Sneed, James P.; M; 9/7/61-71; N.C. Cherokee; 1/4; M; Head; 2512; Yes; Yes; Unallotted

2528; Sneed, Manco; M; 2/18/85-48; N.C. Cherokee; 1/8; M; Head; 2513; Yes; Yes; Unallotted

2529; Sneed, Rosebud; F; 3/29/91-42; N.C. Cherokee; 1/8; M; Wife; 2514; Yes; Yes; Unallotted

2530; Sneed, Lawrence; M; 6/13/12-20; N.C. Cherokee; 1/8; S; Son; 2515; Yes; Yes; Unallotted

2531; Sneed, Dakota; F; 9/22/15-17; N.C. Cherokee; 1/8; S; Dau.; 2516; Yes; Yes; Unallotted

2532; Sneed, Mary; F; 8/29/17-15; N.C. Cherokee; 1/8; S; Dau.; 2517; Yes; Yes; Unallotted

2533; Sneed, Martha; F; 8/29/17-15; N.C. Cherokee; 1/8; S; Dau.; 2518; Yes; Yes; Unallotted

2534; Sneed, Ella; F; 7/10/20-12; N.C. Cherokee; 1/8; S; Dau.; 2519; Yes; Yes; Unallotted

2535; Sneed, Russell; M; 10/2/24-8; N.C. Cherokee; 1/8; S; Son; 2520; Yes; Yes; Unallotted

2536; Sneed, Irene; F; 4/6/27-5; N.C. Cherokee; 1/8; S; Dau.; 2521; Yes; Yes; Unallotted

Census of the **Eastern Cherokee** reservation of the **Cherokee, N.C.** jurisdiction, as of **April 1**, **1933**, taken by **R. L. Spalsbury**, Superintendent.

Key: Number; Surname, Given; Sex; Date of Birth-Age at Last Birthday; Tribe; Degree of Blood; Marital Status; Relationship to Head of Family; Last C. Roll No.; At Jurisdiction Where Enrolled (Yes/No); (If no – Where); Ward (Yes/No); Allotment, Annuity and Identification Numbers (if given).

2537; Sneed, Osco; M; 3/10/79-54; N.C. Cherokee; 1/8; M; Head; 2522; Yes; Yes; Unallotted

2538; Sneed, Thomas M.; M; 2/20/07-26; N.C. Cherokee; 1/16; S; Son; 2523; Yes; Yes; Unallotted

2539; Sneed, John G.; M; 5/29/14-18; N.C. Cherokee; 1/16; S; Son; 2524; Yes; Yes; Unallotted

2540; Sneed, Charlotte; F; 2/28/17-16; N.C. Cherokee; 1/16; S; Dau.; 2525; Yes; Yes; Unallotted

2541; Sneed, Elba; F; 2/15/19-14; N.C. Cherokee; 1/16; S; Dau.; 2526; Yes; Yes; Unallotted

2542; Sneed, Kenneth O.; M; 3/21/22-11; N.C. Cherokee; 1/16; S; Son; 2527; Yes; Yes; Unallotted

2543; Sneed, Peco; M; 9/25/75-57; N.C. Cherokee; 1/8; M; Head; 2528; Yes; Yes; Unallotted

2544; Arkansas, (Sneed, Kate), L. Kate; F; 4/12/10-22; N.C. Cherokee; 1/16; M; Dau.; 2529; Yes; Yes; Unallotted

2545; Sneed, Woodrow; M; 2/10/13-20; N.C. Cherokee; 1/16; S; Son; 2530; Yes; Yes; Unallotted

2546; Sneed, M. Ruth; F; 3/28/16-17; N.C. Cherokee; 1/16; S; Dau.; 2531; Yes; Yes; Unallotted

2547; Sneed, Savannah; F; 4/13/19-13; N.C. Cherokee; 1/16; S; Dau.; 2532; Yes; Yes; Unallotted

2548; Sneed, John B.; M; 12/5/22-10; N.C. Cherokee; 1/16; S; Son; 2533; Yes; Yes; Unallotted

2549; Sneed, William S.; M; 3/28/62-71; N.C. Cherokee; 1/4; M; Head; 2534; Yes; Yes; Unallotted

2550; Souther, Dora Cole; F; 6/15/88-44; N.C. Cherokee; 1/8; M; Wife; 2535; No; Blairsville, Union, Ga.; Yes; Unallotted

2551; Souther, Delpha; F; 9/19/08-24; N.C. Cherokee; 1/16; S; Dau.; 2536; No; Blairsville, Union, Ga.; Yes; Unallotted

2552; Souther, Hartford; M; 9/7/10-22; N.C. Cherokee; 1/16; S; Son; 2537; No; Blairsville, Union, Ga.; Yes; Unallotted

2553; Souther, Myrtle; F; 1/23/13-20; N.C. Cherokee; 1/16; S; Dau.; 2538; No; Blairsville, Union, Ga.; Yes; Unallotted

2554; Souther, Deva; F; 7/2/15-17; N.C. Cherokee; 1/16; S; Dau.; 2539; No; Blairsville, Union, Ga.; Yes; Unallotted

2555; Souther, Vaughn; M; 7/11/17-15; N.C. Cherokee; 1/16; S; Son; 2540; No; Blairsville, Union, Ga.; Yes; Unallotted

2556; Souther, Ina; F; 3/30/20-13; N.C. Cherokee; 1/16; S; Dau.; 2541; No; Blairsville, Union, Ga.; Yes; Unallotted

Census of the **Eastern Cherokee** reservation of the **Cherokee, N.C.** jurisdiction, as of **April 1** , 19**33,** taken by **R. L. Spalsbury** , Superintendent.

Key: Number; Surname, Given; Sex; Date of Birth-Age at Last Birthday; Tribe; Degree of Blood; Marital Status; Relationship to Head of Family; Last C. Roll No.; At Jurisdiction Where Enrolled (Yes/No); (If no – Where); Ward (Yes/No); Allotment, Annuity and Identification Numbers (if given).

2557;   Spencer, Roxie S.; F; 5/5/87-45; N.C. Cherokee; 7/8; M; Wife; 2542; Yes; Yes; Unallotted

2558;   Spray, Gertrude S.; F; 6/17/94-38; N.C. Cherokee; 7/8; S; Head; 2543; Yes; Yes; Unallotted

2559;   Squirrel, Daniel; M; 2/4/04-29; N.C. Cherokee; 4/4; S; Head; 2544; Yes; Yes; Unallotted

2560;   Squirrel, Ollie; F; 3/22/06-27; N.C. Cherokee; 4/4; S; Sis.; 2545; Yes; Yes; Unallotted

2561;   Squirrel, Shepherd; M; 4/28/08-24; N.C. Cherokee; 4/4; S; Bro.; 2546; Yes; Yes; Unallotted

2562;   Squirrel, Abel; M; 5/20/10-22; N.C. Cherokee; 4/4; S; Bro.; 2547; Yes; Yes; Unallotted

2563;   Squirrel, David; M; 7/6/14-18; N.C. Cherokee; 4/4; S; Bro.; 2548; Yes; Yes; Unallotted

2564;   Squirrel, George; M; 4/15/68-64; N.C. Cherokee; 4/4; M; Head; 2549; Yes; Yes; Unallotted

2565;   Squirrel, Rebecca; F; 5/17/72-60; N.C. Cherokee; 4/4; M; Wife; 2550; Yes; Yes; Unallotted

2566;   Squirrel, Sequechee; M; 5/8/00-32; N.C. Cherokee; 4/4; S; Son; 2551; Yes; Yes; Unallotted

2567;   Squirrel, Kinsey; M; 4/8/96-36; N.C. Cherokee; 4/4; M; Head; 2552; Yes; Yes; Unallotted

2568;   Squirrel, Lydia T.W.; F; 1/20/91-42; N.C. Cherokee; 13/16; M; Wife; 2553; Yes; Yes; Unallotted

2569;   Squirrel, Emma; F; 7/4/20-12; N.C. Cherokee; 29/32; S; Dau.; 2554; Yes; Yes; Unallotted

2570;   Squirrel, Adam; M; 8/10/24-7; N.C. Cherokee; 1/4+; S; Son; 2555; Yes; Yes; Unallotted

2571;   Squirrel, Abel; M; 8/15/27-5; N.C. Cherokee; 1/4+; S; Son; 2556; Yes; Yes; Unallotted

2572;   Squirrel, Gene T.; M; 3/26/30-3; N.C. Cherokee; 29/32; S; Son; 2557; Yes; Yes; Unallotted

2573;   Stalcup (Thompson, Atha), Atha W.; F; 12/19/02-30; N.C. Cherokee; 1/16; M; Wife; 2558; No; Taft, Kern, Cal.; Yes; Unallotted

2574;   Standingdeer, Margaret; F; 11/15/54-78; N.C. Cherokee; 4/4; Wd.; Head; 2559; Yes; Yes; Unallotted

2575;   Standingdeer, Carl; M; 12/12/81-51; N.C. Cherokee; 4/4; M; Head; 2560; Yes; Yes; Unallotted

Census of the **Eastern Cherokee** reservation of the **Cherokee, N.C.** jurisdiction, as of **April 1** , **1933,** taken by **R. L. Spalsbury** , Superintendent.

Key: Number; Surname, Given; Sex; Date of Birth-Age at Last Birthday; Tribe; Degree of Blood; Marital Status; Relationship to Head of Family; Last C. Roll No.; At Jurisdiction Where Enrolled (Yes/No); (If no – Where); Ward (Yes/No); Allotment, Annuity and Identification Numbers (if given).

2576; Standingdeer, Anna Tooni; F; 11/14/76-56; N.C. Cherokee; 4/4; M; Wife; 2561; Yes; Yes; Unallotted

2577; Standingdeer, Roxanna; F; 10/9/11-21; N.C. Cherokee; 13/16; S; Dau.; 2562; Yes; Yes; Unallotted

2578; Standingdeer, Virginia; F; 4/14/08-24; N.C. Cherokee; 13/16; S; Dau.; 2563; Yes; Yes; Unallotted

2579; Standingdeer, Mary Janet; F; 9/26/13-19; N.C. Cherokee; 13/16; S; Dau.; 2564; Yes; Yes; Unallotted

2580; Standingdeer, Carl, Jr.; M; 1/11/15-18; N.C. Cherokee; 13/16; S; Son; 2565; Yes; Yes; Unallotted

2581; Standingdeer, Junaluska; M; 12/12/81-51; N.C. Cherokee; 4/4; M; Head; 2566; No; Minneapolis, Hennepin, Minn.; Yes; Unallotted

2582; Standingdeer, Lowen; M; 11/14/82-50; N.C. Cherokee; 4/4; M; Head; 2567; Yes; Yes; Unallotted

2583; Standingdeer, Nannie S.; F; 4/18/94-38; N.C. Cherokee; 15/16; M; Wife; 2568; Yes; Yes; Unallotted

2584; Standingdeer, Simon; M; 7/14/21-11; N.C. Cherokee; 31/32; S; Son; 2569; Yes; Yes; Unallotted

2585; Standingdeer, Alex; M; 12/24/58-74; N.C. Cherokee; 4/4; Wd.; Head; 2570; Yes; Yes; Unallotted

2586; Standingdeer (Lambert), Sallie Ann; F; 4/28/09-23; N.C. Cherokee; 1/2; M; Wife; 2571; Yes; Yes; Unallotted

2587; Standingdeer, Caroline S.; F; 9/17/28-4; N.C. Cherokee; 1/4; S; Dau.; 2572; Yes; Yes; Unallotted

2588; Lambert, Dorothy; F; 9/19/30-2; N.C. Cherokee; 17/64; S; Dau.; 2573; Yes; Yes; Unallotted

2589; Standingdeer, Clyde; M; 10/29/32-5/12; N.C. Cherokee; 17/64; S; Son; ---; Yes; Yes; Unallotted

2590; Stamper, Ned; M; 7/12/68-64; N.C. Cherokee; 3/4; M; Head; 2574; Yes; Yes; Unallotted

2591; Stamper, Sallie Ann; F; 5/15/75-57; N.C. Cherokee; 3/4; M; Wife; 2575; Yes; Yes; Unallotted

2592; Stamper, Sarah; F; 10/15/07-25; N.C. Cherokee; 3/4; S; Dau.; 2576; Yes; Yes; Unallotted

2593; Stamper, Robertson; M; 2/13/12-21; N.C. Cherokee; 3/4; S; Son; 2577; Yes; Yes; Unallotted

2594; Stamper, Margaret; F; 7/8/14-18; N.C. Cherokee; 3/4; S; Dau.; 2578; Yes; Yes; Unallotted

Census of the **Eastern Cherokee** reservation of the **Cherokee, N.C.** jurisdiction, as of **April 1**, 1933, taken by **R. L. Spalsbury**, Superintendent.

Key: Number; Surname, Given; Sex; Date of Birth-Age at Last Birthday; Tribe; Degree of Blood; Marital Status; Relationship to Head of Family; Last C. Roll No.; At Jurisdiction Where Enrolled (Yes/No); (If no – Where); Ward (Yes/No); Allotment, Annuity and Identification Numbers (if given).

2595; Stamper, William; M; 2/14/01-31; N.C. Cherokee; 3/4; M; Head; 2579; Yes; Yes; Unallotted

2596; Stamper, Lottie Q.; F; 1/4/07-26; N.C. Cherokee; 5/8; M; Wife; 2580; Yes; Yes; Unallotted

2597; Stepp, Ida M.A.; F; 6/27/08-24; N.C. Cherokee; 1/32; M; Wife; 2581; Yes; Yes; Unallotted

2598; Stiles, Gilbert; M; 6/6/93-39; N.C. Cherokee; 1/32; M; Head; 2582; No; Marble, Cherokee, N.C.; Yes; Unallotted

2599; Stiles, Annie P.; F; 8/30/18-14; N.C. Cherokee; 1/64; S; Dau.; 2583; No; Marble, Cherokee, N.C.; Yes; Unallotted

2600; Stiles, Forrest J.; M; 10/19/19-13; N.C. Cherokee; 1/64; S; Son; 2584; No; Marble, Cherokee, N.C.; Yes; Unallotted

2601; Stiles, Jessie E.; F; 5/1/21-11; N.C. Cherokee; 1/64; S; Dau.; 2585; No; Marble, Cherokee, N.C.; Yes; Unallotted

2602; Stiles (Loudermilk, Hollie), Hollie L.; F; 9/24/88-44; N.C. Cherokee; 1/16; M; Wife; 2586; No; Culberson, Cherokee, N.C.; Yes; Unallotted

2603; Stiles, Floyd; M; 9/10/10-22; N.C. Cherokee; 1/32; S; Son; 2587; No; Culberson, Cherokee, N.C.; Yes; Unallotted

2604; Stiles, Sadie Lee; F; 8/10/12-20; N.C. Cherokee; 1/32; S; Dau.; 2588; No; Culberson, Cherokee, N.C.; Yes; Unallotted

2605; Stiles, Wm. S.; M; 8/26/15-17; N.C. Cherokee; 1/32; S; Son; 2589; No; Culberson, Cherokee, N.C.; Yes; Unallotted

2606; Stiles, Elsie V.; F; 12/4/17-15; N.C. Cherokee; 1/32; S; Dau.; 2590; No; Culberson, Cherokee, N.C.; Yes; Unallotted

2607; Stiles, Beulah R.; F; 2/22/20-13; N.C. Cherokee; 1/32; S; Dau.; 2591; No; Culberson, Cherokee, N.C.; Yes; Unallotted

2608; Stiles, Hazel; F; 9/15/22-10; N.C. Cherokee; 1/32; S; Dau.; 2592; No; Culberson, Cherokee, N.C.; Yes; Unallotted

2609; Stiles, Floyd; M; 3/16/05-28; N.C. Cherokee; 1/32; M; Head; 2593; Yes; Yes; Unallotted

2610; Stiles, Lester T.; M; 10/7/98-34; N.C. Cherokee; 1/32; M; Head; 2594; No; Gastonia, Gaston, N.C.; Yes; Unallotted

2611; Stiles, Evelyn E.; F; 2/24/21-12; N.C. Cherokee; 1/64; S; Dau.; 2595; No; Gastonia, Gaston, N.C.; Yes; Unallotted

2612; Stiles, Mary C.; F; 2/31/23-10; N.C. Cherokee; 1/64; S; Dau.; 2596; No; Gastonia, Gaston, N.C.; Yes; Unallotted

2613; Stiles (Raper, Lula), Lula; F; 12/8/08-24; N.C. Cherokee; 1/16; M; Wife; 2597; No; Oak Park, Cherokee, N.C.; Yes; Unallotted

Census of the **Eastern Cherokee** reservation of the **Cherokee, N.C.** jurisdiction, as of **April 1** , **1933,** taken by **R. L. Spalsbury** , Superintendent.

Key: Number; Surname, Given; Sex; Date of Birth-Age at Last Birthday; Tribe; Degree of Blood; Marital Status; Relationship to Head of Family; Last C. Roll No.; At Jurisdiction Where Enrolled (Yes/No); (If no – Where); Ward (Yes/No); Allotment, Annuity and Identification Numbers (if given).

2614; Stiles (Payne, Mary), Mary; F; 12/22/69-63; N.C. Cherokee; 1/16; M; Wife; 2598; Yes; Yes; Unallotted
2615; Stiles, Clem O.; M; 9/6/03-29; N.C. Cherokee; 1/32; S; Son; 2599; Yes; Yes; Unallotted
2616; Stiles, Hal V.; M; 3/5/06-27; N.C. Cherokee; 1/32; S; Son; 2600; Yes; Yes; Unallotted

2617; Stiles, Oliver; M; 2/22/98-35; N.C. Cherokee; 1/32; M; Head; 2601; No; Marble, Cherokee, N.C.; Yes; Unallotted
2618; Stiles, Herman; M; 10/20/19-13; N.C. Cherokee; 1/64; S; Son; 2602; No; Marble, Cherokee, N.C.; Yes; Unallotted
2619; Stiles, Kenneth; M; 6/20/21-11; N.C. Cherokee; 1/64; S; Son; 2603; No; Marble, Cherokee, N.C.; Yes; Unallotted
2620; Stiles, Homer; M; 8/8/23-8; N.C. Cherokee; 1/64; S; Son; 2604; No; Marble, Cherokee, N.C.; Yes; Unallotted

2621; Stiles (Payne, Theodosia), Theodosia; F; 6/22/78-54; N.C. Cherokee; 1/16; M; Wife; 2605; Yes; Yes; Unallotted
2622; Stiles, Ella; F; 5/16/07-25; N.C. Cherokee; 1/32; S; Dau.; 2606; Yes; Yes; Unallotted
2623; Stiles, Wilfred; M; 9/20/09-23; N.C. Cherokee; 1/32; S; Son; 2607; Yes; Yes; Unallotted
2624; Stiles, Noah Neil; M; 12/2/12-20; N.C. Cherokee; 1/32; S; Son; 2608; Yes; Yes; Unallotted

2625; Stiles, Virgil R.; M; 12/25/00-32; N.C. Cherokee; 1/32; M; Head; 2609; No; Box 491, Etowah, McMinn, Tenn.; Yes; Unallotted
2626; Stiles, Fay E.; F; 11/21/20-12; N.C. Cherokee; 1/64; S; Dau.; 2610; No; Box 491, Etowah, McMinn, Tenn.; Yes; Unallotted
2627; Stiles, Blanche; F; 11/13/22-10; N.C. Cherokee; 1/64; S; Dau.; 2611; No; Box 491, Etowah, McMinn, Tenn.; Yes; Unallotted

2628; St. Jermain, Nicie; F; 3/4/70-63; N.C. Cherokee; 1/4; M; Wife; 2612; Yes; Yes; Unallotted

2629; Sutaga, Mary; F; 1/19/61-72; N.C. Cherokee; 4/4; Wd.; Head; 2613; Yes; Yes; Unallotted

2630; Swafford (Lee, Debrader), Debrader; F; 2/21/97-36; N.C. Cherokee; 1/16; M; Wife; 2614; Yes; Yes; Unallotted
2631; Swafford, Wm. Tray; M; 2/19/14-19; N.C. Cherokee; 1/32; S; Son; 2615; Yes; Yes; Unallotted
2632; Swafford, Ruby E.; F; 12/18/15-17; N.C. Cherokee; 1/32; S; Dau.; 2616; Yes; Yes; Unallotted

Census of the **Eastern Cherokee** reservation of the **Cherokee, N.C.** jurisdiction, as of **April 1** , 19**33,** taken by **R. L. Spalsbury** , Superintendent.

Key: Number; Surname, Given; Sex; Date of Birth-Age at Last Birthday; Tribe; Degree of Blood; Marital Status; Relationship to Head of Family; Last C. Roll No.; At Jurisdiction Where Enrolled (Yes/No); (If no – Where); Ward (Yes/No); Allotment, Annuity and Identification Numbers (if given).

2633; Swafford, James R.; M; 10/2/17-15; N.C. Cherokee; 1/32; S; Son; 2617; Yes; Yes; Unallotted

2634; Swafford, Edwin Lee; M; 7/8/19-13; N.C. Cherokee; 1/32; S; Son; 2618; Yes; Yes; Unallotted

2635; Swafford, Rachel L.; F; 7/1/21-11; N.C. Cherokee; 1/32; S; Dau.; 2619; Yes; Yes; Unallotted

2636; Swafford, John R.; M; 11/1/22-10; N.C. Cherokee; 1/32; S; Son; 2620; Yes; Yes; Unallotted

2637; Swafford (Thompson, Verdie), Verdie T.; F; 9/16/02-30; N.C. Cherokee; 1/16; M; Wife; 2621; Yes; Yes; Unallotted

2638; Swanson (Loudermilk, Cora), Cora; F; 5/18/06-26; N.C. Cherokee; 1/32; M; Wife; 2622; Yes; Yes; Unallotted

2639; Swayney, Jesse W.; M; 8/2/88-44; N.C. Cherokee; 1/8; M; Head; 2623; Yes; Yes; Unallotted

2640; Swayney, Laura J.; F; 2/28/16-17; N.C. Cherokee; 1/16; S; Dau.; 2624; Yes; Yes; Unallotted

2641; Swayney, Jesse L.; M; 7/22/17-15; N.C. Cherokee; 1/16; S; Son; 2625; Yes; Yes; Unallotted

2642; Swayney, Leonard; M; 10/24/21-11; N.C. Cherokee; 1/16; S; Son; 2626; Yes; Yes; Unallotted

2643; Swayney, David W.; M; 6/14/28-4; N.C. Cherokee; 1/16; S; Son; 2627; Yes; Yes; Unallotted

2644; Swayney, Edith B.; F; 9/26/30-2; N.C. Cherokee; 1/16; S; Dau.; 2628; Yes; Yes; Unallotted

2645; Swayney, John W.; M; 1/9/83-50; N.C. Cherokee; 1/8; M; Head; 2629; Yes; Yes; Unallotted

2646; Swayney, Alvin W.; M; 11/5/10-22; N.C. Cherokee; 1/16; S; Son; 2630; Yes; Yes; Unallotted

2647; Swayney, Winona L.; F; 6/8/15-17; N.C. Cherokee; 1/16; S; Dau.; 2632; Yes; Yes; Unallotted

2648; Swayney, James H.; M; 3/4/18-15; N.C. Cherokee; 1/16; S; Son; 2633; Yes; Yes; Unallotted

2649; Swayney, Roxana A.; F; 3/17/21-12; N.C. Cherokee; 1/16; S; Dau.; 2634; Yes; Yes; Unallotted

2650; Swayney, Allegra L.; F; 10/3/23-9; N.C. Cherokee; 1/16; S; Dau.; 2635; Yes; Yes; Unallotted

2651; Swayney, Laura J.; F; 12/6/57-75; N.C. Cherokee; 1/4; Wd.; Head; 2636; Yes; Yes; Unallotted

Census of the **Eastern Cherokee** reservation of the **Cherokee, N.C.** jurisdiction, as of **April 1** , 19**33**, taken by   **R. L. Spalsbury**   , Superintendent.

Key: Number; Surname, Given; Sex; Date of Birth-Age at Last Birthday; Tribe; Degree of Blood; Marital Status; Relationship to Head of Family; Last C. Roll No.; At Jurisdiction Where Enrolled (Yes/No); (If no – Where); Ward (Yes/No); Allotment, Annuity and Identification Numbers (if given).

2652; Swayney, Lorenzo D.; M; 10/5/78-54; N.C. Cherokee; 1/8; M; Head; 2637; No; Cramerton, Gaston, N.C.; Yes; Unallotted

2653; Swayney, Frank D.; M; 2/14/05-28; N.C. Cherokee; 1/16; S; Son; 2638; No; Cramerton, Gaston, N.C.; Yes; Unallotted

2654; Swayney, Grace; F; 2/1/10-23; N.C. Cherokee; 1/16; S; Dau.; 2639; No; Cramerton, Gaston, N.C.; Yes; Unallotted

2655; Swayney, Dora E.; F; 5/6/12-20; N.C. Cherokee; 1/16; S; Dau.; 2640; No; Cramerton, Gaston, N.C.; Yes; Unallotted

2656; Swayney, Chiltoskey; M; 5/2/15-17; N.C. Cherokee; 1/16; S; Son; 2641; No; Cramerton, Gaston, N.C.; Yes; Unallotted

2657; Swayney, Nathaniel; M; 3/28/17-16; N.C. Cherokee; 1/16; S; Son; 2642; No; Cramerton, Gaston, N.C.; Yes; Unallotted

2658; Swayney, Thurman; M; 10/14/07-25; N.C. Cherokee; 1/16; M; Head; 2643; No; Cramerton, Gaston, N.C.; Yes; Unallotted

2659; Swayney, Walter D.; M; 4/13/17-15; N.C. Cherokee; 1/16; S; Alone; 2644; Yes; Yes; Unallotted

2660; Swimmer, Lucy; F; 6/18/86-46; N.C. Cherokee; 4/4; Wd.; Head; 2645; Yes; Yes; Unallotted

2661; Swimmer, Grace; F; 6/15/07-25; N.C. Cherokee; 4/4; S; Dau.; 2646; Yes; Yes; Unallotted

2662; Swimmer, Luke; M; 3/17/10-23; N.C. Cherokee; 4/4; S; Son; 2647; Yes; Yes; Unallotted

2663; Swimmer, Thomas; M; 4/2/14-18; N.C. Cherokee; 4/4; S; Son; 2648; Yes; Yes; Unallotted

2664; Swimmer (Mr. Grace), David; M; 7/31/25-7; N.C. Cherokee; 4/4; S; Gr-S; 2649; Yes; Yes; Unallotted

2665; Swimmer, Sarah J.; F; 4/19/12-20; N.C. Cherokee; 4/4; Wd.; Head; 2650; Yes; Yes; Unallotted

2666; Swimmer, Lucy Ann; F; 9/12/28-4; N.C. Cherokee; 4/4; S; Dau.; 2651; Yes; Yes; Unallotted

2667; Swimmer, Runaway; M; 8/7/77-55; N.C. Cherokee; 4/4; M; Head; 2652; Yes; Yes; Unallotted

2668; Swimmer, Anna; F; 5/15/80-52; N.C. Cherokee; 4/4; M; Wife; 2653; Yes; Yes; Unallotted

2669; Swimmer, Anna; F; 2/1/62-70; N.C. Cherokee; 4/4;Wd.; Head; 2655; Yes; Yes; Unallotted

2670; Tahlala, Homer W.; M; 6/5/17-15; N.C. Cherokee; 1/2; S; Son; 2656; Yes; Yes; Unallotted

Census of the **Eastern Cherokee** reservation of the **Cherokee, N.C.** jurisdiction, as of **April 1**, **1933**, taken by **R. L. Spalsbury**, Superintendent.

Key: Number; Surname, Given; Sex; Date of Birth-Age at Last Birthday; Tribe; Degree of Blood; Marital Status; Relationship to Head of Family; Last C. Roll No.; At Jurisdiction Where Enrolled (Yes/No); (If no – Where); Ward (Yes/No); Allotment, Annuity and Identification Numbers (if given).

2671; Tahquette, John; M; 12/4/54-78; N.C. Cherokee; 4/4; M; Head; 2657; No; Hulbert, Cherokee, Okla.; Yes; Unallotted

2672; Tahquette, John A.; M; 4/27/70-62; N.C. Cherokee; 1/2; Wd.; Head; 2658; Yes; Yes; Unallotted

2673; Tahquette, Frank G.; M; 1/3/07-26; N.C. Cherokee; 3/4; S; Son; 2659; Yes; Yes; Unallotted

2674; Tahquette, Howard W.; M; 11/13/09-23; N.C. Cherokee; 3/4; S; Son; 2660; Yes; Yes; Unallotted

2675; Tahquette, Amy E.; F; 1/9/11-21; N.C. Cherokee; 3/4; S; Dau.; 2661; Yes; Yes; Unallotted

2676; Tahquette, Marion P.; F; 1/9/11-21; N.C. Cherokee; 3/4; S; Dau.; 2662; Yes; Yes; Unallotted

2677; Tahquette, Ernest D.; M; 5/7/16-16; N.C. Cherokee; 3/4; S; Son; 2663; Yes; Yes; Unallotted

2678; Tahquette, Martha; F; 12/24/63-69; N.C. Cherokee; 4/4; S; Head; 2664; Yes; Yes; Unallotted

2679; Tatham, Mary; F; 11/18/06-26; N.C. Cherokee; 1/16; S; Head; 2665; Yes; Yes; Unallotted

2680; Tatham, Leunia; F; 4/11/11-21; N.C. Cherokee; 1/16; S; Sis.; 2666; Yes; Yes; Unallotted

2681; Taylor, Eliza; F; 12/4/56-76; N.C. Cherokee; 1/4; Wd.; Head; 2667; Yes; Yes; Unallotted

2682; Taylor, David; M; 6/29/03-29; N.C. Cherokee; 5/8; S; Son; 2668; Yes; Yes; Unallotted

2683; Taylor (Mr.[sic] Mary Sneed Adkins), Inez C.; F; 5/24/14-18; N.C. Cherokee; 1/16; S; Dau.; 2669; Yes; Yes; Unallotted

2684; Taylor, Gerald F.; M; 7/23/21-11; N.C. Cherokee; 1/16; S; Son; 2670; Yes; Yes; Unallotted

2685; Taylor, Jack; M; 6/8/88-44; N.C. Cherokee; 5/8; M; Head; 2671; Yes; Yes; Unallotted

2686; Taylor, Rebecca; F; 5/28/97-35; N.C. Cherokee; 4/4; M; Wife; 2672; Yes; Yes; Unallotted

2687; Taylor, Bettie J.; F; 10/2/17-15; N.C. Cherokee; 13/16; S; Dau.; 2673; Yes; Yes; Unallotted

2688; Taylor, Celia; F; 5/15/20-12; N.C. Cherokee; 13/16; S; Dau.; 2674; Yes; Yes; Unallotted

2689; Taylor, Annie; F; 3/28/22-11; N.C. Cherokee; 13/16; S; Dau.; 2675; Yes; Yes; Unallotted

2690; Taylor, Philip; M; 5/6/24-8; N.C. Cherokee; 13/16; S; Son; 2676; Yes; Yes; Unallotted

Census of the **Eastern Cherokee** reservation of the **Cherokee, N.C.** jurisdiction, as of **April 1** , **1933,** taken by **R. L. Spalsbury** , Superintendent.

Key: Number; Surname, Given; Sex; Date of Birth-Age at Last Birthday; Tribe; Degree of Blood; Marital Status; Relationship to Head of Family; Last C. Roll No.; At Jurisdiction Where Enrolled (Yes/No); (If no – Where); Ward (Yes/No); Allotment, Annuity and Identification Numbers (if given).

2691;   Taylor, James; M; 6/15/04-28; N.C. Cherokee; 13/16; S; Head; 2677; Yes; Yes; Unallotted

2692;   Taylor, John; M; 12/4/90-42; N.C. Cherokee; 5/8; M; Head; 2678; Yes; Yes; Unallotted

2693;   Taylor, Nora S.; F; 9/14/98-34; N.C. Cherokee; 4/4; M; Wife; 2679; Yes; Yes; Unallotted

2694;   Taylor, George; M; 12/14/16-16; N.C. Cherokee; 13/16; S; Son; 2680; Yes; Yes; Unallotted

2695;   Taylor, Jesse; M; 6/6/25-7; N.C. Cherokee; 13/16; S; Son; 2681; Yes; Yes; Unallotted

2696;   Taylor, Herbert; M; 9/19/29-3; N.C. Cherokee; 13/16; S; Son; 2682; Yes; Yes; Unallotted

2697;   Taylor, Julius; M; 1/3/78-55; N.C. Cherokee; 3/4; M; Head; 2683; Yes; Yes; Unallotted

2698;   Taylor, Stacey; F; 6/6/76-56; N.C. Cherokee; 7/8; M; Wife; 2684; Yes; Yes; Unallotted

2699;   Taylor, Julius; M; 12/20/98-34; N.C. Cherokee; 5/8; M; Head; 2685; Yes; Yes; Unallotted

2700;   Taylor, Julia Ned; F; 9/17/02-30; N.C. Cherokee; 4/4; M; Wife; 2686; Yes; Yes; Unallotted

2701;   Taylor, Rachel; F; 2/12/22-10; N.C. Cherokee; 13/16; S; Dau.; 2687; Yes; Yes; Unallotted

2702;   Taylor, Sallie; F; 10/21/24-8; N.C. Cherokee; 13/16; S; Dau.; 2688; Yes; Yes; Unallotted

2703;   Taylor, Mary; F; 2/17/27-6; N.C. Cherokee; 13/16; S; Dau.; 2689; Yes; Yes; Unallotted

2704;   Taylor, Jarrett; M; 10/23/31-1; N.C. Cherokee; 13/16; S; Son; 2690; Yes; Yes; Unallotted

2705;   Taylor, John; M; 3/16/09-24; N.C. Cherokee; 5/8; S; Head; 2691; Yes; Yes; Unallotted

2706;   Taylor (Meroney, Lula), Lula M.; F; 9/9/91-41; N.C. Cherokee; 1/16; M; Wife; 2692; Yes; Yes; Unallotted

2707;   Taylor, Fred, Jr.; M; 1/1/06-27; N.C. Cherokee; 1/32; S; Son; 2693; Yes; Yes; Unallotted

2708;   Taylor, James A.; M; 3/15/16-17; N.C. Cherokee; 1/32; S; Son; 2694; Yes; Yes; Unallotted

2709;   Taylor, Gertrude A.; F; 7/24/18-14; N.C. Cherokee; 1/32; S; Dau.; 2695; Yes; Yes; Unallotted

Census of the **Eastern Cherokee** reservation of the **Cherokee, N.C.** jurisdiction, as of **April 1** , 19**33,** taken by **R. L. Spalsbury** , Superintendent.

Key: Number; Surname, Given; Sex; Date of Birth-Age at Last Birthday; Tribe; Degree of Blood; Marital Status; Relationship to Head of Family; Last C. Roll No.; At Jurisdiction Where Enrolled (Yes/No); (If no – Where); Ward (Yes/No); Allotment, Annuity and Identification Numbers (if given).

2710; Taylor, Nancy W.; F; 6/17/94-38; N.C. Cherokee; 4/4; Div.; Head; 2696; Yes; Yes; Unallotted

2711; Taylor, Eva K.; F; 4/2/11-21; N.C. Cherokee; 13/16; S; Dau.; 2697; Yes; Yes; Unallotted

2712; Taylor, Simeon; M; 12/20/14-18; N.C. Cherokee; 13/16; S; Son; 2698; Yes; Yes; Unallotted

2713; Taylor, Sally Ann; F; 6/16/22-10; N.C. Cherokee; 29/32; S; Dau.; 2699; Yes; Yes; Unallotted

2714; Taylor, Sherman; M; 7/6/82-50; N.C. Cherokee; 3/4; Wd.; Head; 2700; Yes; Yes; Unallotted

2715; Taylor (Saunooke), Eva; F; 4/22/11-21; N.C. Cherokee; 7/8; S; Dau.; 2701; Yes; Yes; Unallotted

2716; Taylor, Larch; M; 11/6/14-18; N.C. Cherokee; 7/8; S; Son; 2702; Yes; Yes; Unallotted

2717; Taylor, Hettie; F; 4/23/16-16; N.C. Cherokee; 7/8; S; Dau.; 2703; Yes; Yes; Unallotted

2718; Taylor, Cindy; F; 3/17/19-13; N.C. Cherokee; 7/8; S; Dau.; 2704; Yes; Yes; Unallotted

2719; Taylor, Julius; M; 7/9/21-11; N.C. Cherokee; 7/8; S; Son; 2705; Yes; Yes; Unallotted

2720; Taylor, Stacy; F; 6/8/27-5; N.C. Cherokee; 7/8; S; Dau.; 2706; Yes; Yes; Unallotted

2721; Taylor, Stacey; F; 12/4/60-72; N.C. Cherokee; 4/4; Wd.; Head; 2707; Yes; Yes; Unallotted

2722; Taylor, Thomas E.; M; 3/30/77-56; N.C. Cherokee; 1/16; M; Head; 2708; No; Hiawassee, Cherokee, N.C.; Yes; Unallotted

2723; Taylor, Oliver; M; 8/2/06-26; N.C. Cherokee; 1/32; S; Son; 2709; No; Hiawassee, Cherokee, N.C.; Yes; Unallotted

2724; Taylor, Alvin; M; 3/24/08-25; N.C. Cherokee; 1/32; S; Son; 2710; No; Hiawassee, Cherokee, N.C.; Yes; Unallotted

2725; Taylor, Howard; M; 10/12/11-21; N.C. Cherokee; 1/32; S; Son; 2711; No; Hiawassee, Cherokee, N.C.; Yes; Unallotted

2726; Taylor, Molt; M; 1/19/13-20; N.C. Cherokee; 1/32; S; Son; 2712; No; Hiawassee, Cherokee, N.C.; Yes; Unallotted

2727; Taylor, Elmer; M; 6/30/15-17; N.C. Cherokee; 1/32; S; Son; 2713; No; Hiawassee, Cherokee, N.C.; Yes; Unallotted

2728; Taylor, Timpson; M; 1/15/00-33; N.C. Cherokee; 5/8; M; Head; 2714; Yes; Yes; Unallotted

2729; Taylor, Cinda R.; F; 4/17/97-35; N.C. Cherokee; 7/8; M; Wife; 2715; Yes; Yes; Unallotted

Census of the **Eastern Cherokee** reservation of the **Cherokee, N.C.** jurisdiction, as of **April 1** , **1933,** taken by **R. L. Spalsbury** , Superintendent.

Key: Number; Surname, Given; Sex; Date of Birth-Age at Last Birthday; Tribe; Degree of Blood; Marital Status; Relationship to Head of Family; Last C. Roll No.; At Jurisdiction Where Enrolled (Yes/No); (If no – Where); Ward (Yes/No); Allotment, Annuity and Identification Numbers (if given).

2730; Taylor, Richard; M; 4/13/21-11; N.C. Cherokee; 3/4; S; Son; 2716; Yes; Yes; Unallotted

2731; Taylor, Reuben E.; M; 11/7/25-7; N.C. Cherokee; 3/4; S; Son; 2717; Yes; Yes; Unallotted

2732; Taylor, Remus E.; M; 4/11/29-3; N.C. Cherokee; 3/4; S; Son; 2718; Yes; Yes; Unallotted

2733; Taylor, Helen E.; F; 7/31/31-1; N.C. Cherokee; 3/4; S; Dau.; 2719; Yes; Yes; Unallotted

2734; Taylor, William; M; 11/8/06-26; N.C. Cherokee; 5/8; M; Head; 2720; Yes; Yes; Unallotted

2735; Taylor, Cecelia; F; 10/28/06-26; N.C. Cherokee; 13/16; M; Wife; 2721; Yes; Yes; Unallotted

2736; Taylor, William Jr.; M; 1/11/26-7; N.C. Cherokee; 13/32; S; Son; 2722; Yes; Yes; Unallotted

2737; Taylor, Wilmer; M; 11/30/28-4; N.C. Cherokee; 13/32; S; Son; 2723; Yes; Yes; Unallotted

2738; Taylor, Lucy F.; F; 8/30/30-2; N.C. Cherokee; 13/32; S; Dau.; 2724; Yes; Yes; Unallotted

2739; Teague, Mable; F; 9/12/14-18; N.C. Cherokee; 1/32; S; Alone; 2725; No; Ducktown, Polk, Tenn.; Yes; Unallotted

2740; Teague, Wade; M; 2/17/16-17; N.C. Cherokee; 1/32; S; Bro.; 2726; No; Ducktown, Polk, Tenn.; Yes; Unallotted

2741; Teesateskie, Jesse; M; 5/14/86-46; N.C. Cherokee; 4/4; M; Head; 2727; Yes; Yes; Unallotted

2742; Teesateskie, Polly Bird; F; 1/5/84-49; N.C. Cherokee; 4/4; M; Wife; 2728; Yes; Yes; Unallotted

2743; Teesateskie, Sarah; F; 5/25/12-20; N.C. Cherokee; 4/4; S; Dau.; 2729; Yes; Yes; Unallotted

2744; Teesateskie, Joseph; M; 7/10/14-18; N.C. Cherokee; 4/4; S; Son; 2730; Yes; Yes; Unallotted

2745; Teesateskie, Lee; M; 9/29/18-14; N.C. Cherokee; 4/4; S; Son; 2731; Yes; Yes; Unallotted

2746; Teesateskie, Lilly; F; 3/26/20-13; N.C. Cherokee; 4/4; S; Dau.; 2732; Yes; Yes; Unallotted

2747; Teesateskie, Susie; F; 6/29/22-10; N.C. Cherokee; 4/4; S; Dau.; 2733; Yes; Yes; Unallotted

2748; Teesateskie, Dinah; F; 4/27/24-8; N.C. Cherokee; 4/4; S; Dau.; 2734; Yes; Yes; Unallotted

2749; Teesateskie, John; M; 1/5/50-83; N.C. Cherokee; 4/4; M; Head; 2735; Yes; Yes; Unallotted

331

Census of the **Eastern Cherokee** reservation of the **Cherokee, N.C.** jurisdiction, as of **April 1**, 19**33**, taken by **R. L. Spalsbury**, Superintendent.

Key: Number; Surname, Given; Sex; Date of Birth-Age at Last Birthday; Tribe; Degree of Blood; Marital Status; Relationship to Head of Family; Last C. Roll No.; At Jurisdiction Where Enrolled (Yes/No); (If no – Where); Ward (Yes/No); Allotment, Annuity and Identification Numbers (if given).

2750; Teesateskie, Betty B.; F; 2/26/00-33; N.C. Cherokee; 4/4; M; Wife; 2736; Yes; Yes; Unallotted

2751; Teesateskie, Chicoah; F; 5/3/21-11; N.C. Cherokee; 4/4; S; Dau.; 2737; Yes; Yes; Unallotted

2752; Teesateskie, Ida; F; 8/3/23-9; N.C. Cherokee; 4/4; S; Dau.; 2738; Yes; Yes; Unallotted

2753; Teesateskie, Rogers; M; 8/3/23-9; N.C. Cherokee; 4/4; S; Son; 2739; Yes; Yes; Unallotted

2754; Teesateskie, Jonah; M; 1/20/04-29; N.C. Cherokee; 4/4; M; Head; 2740; Yes; Yes; Unallotted

2755; Teesateskie, Josiah E.; M; 8/2/30-2; N.C. Cherokee; 4/4; S; Son; 2741; Yes; Yes; Unallotted

2756; Teesateskie, Noah; M; 1/5/85-47; N.C. Cherokee; 4/4; M; Head; 2742; Yes; Yes; Unallotted

2757; Teesateskie, Winnie W.; F; 8/15/07-25; N.C. Cherokee; 4/4; M; Wife; 2743; Yes; Yes; Unallotted

2758; Teesateskie, George; M; 5/9/11-21; N.C. Cherokee; 4/4; S; Son; 2744; Yes; Yes; Unallotted

2759; Teesateskie, Mary; F; 2/9/14-19; N.C. Cherokee; 4/4; S; Dau.; 2745; Yes; Yes; Unallotted

2760; Teesateskie, Matthew; M; 12/17/15-17; N.C. Cherokee; 4/4; S; Son; 2746; Yes; Yes; Unallotted

2761; Teesateskie, Sampson; M; 10/15/91-41; N.C. Cherokee; 4/4; M; Head; 2747; Yes; Yes; Unallotted

2762; Teesateskie, Nessie W.; F; 2/15/82-51; N.C. Cherokee; 4/4; M; Wife; 2748; Yes; Yes; Unallotted

2763; Teesateskie, Welch; M; 1/18/99-34; N.C. Cherokee; 3/4; M; Head; 2749; Yes; Yes; Unallotted

2764; Teesateskie, Tommie; M; 7/10/23-9; N.C. Cherokee; 7/8; S; Son; 2750; Yes; Yes; Unallotted

2765; Teesateskie, Nessih; F; 4/17/55-77; N.C. Cherokee; 4/4; Wd.; Head; 2751; Yes; Yes; Unallotted

2766; Teesateskie, Willie; M; 7/14/07-25; N.C. Cherokee; 4/4; M; Head; 2752; Yes; Yes; Unallotted

2767; Teesateskie, Lillian S.; F; 7/8/07-25; N.C. Cherokee; 4/4; M; Wife; 2753; Yes; Yes; Unallotted

2768; Teleskie, Jesse; M; 12/4/90-42; N.C. Cherokee; 4/4; M; Head; 2754; Yes; Yes; Unallotted

Census of the **Eastern Cherokee** reservation of the **Cherokee, N.C.** jurisdiction, as of **April 1** , 19**33,** taken by **R. L. Spalsbury** , Superintendent.

Key: Number; Surname, Given; Sex; Date of Birth-Age at Last Birthday; Tribe; Degree of Blood; Marital Status; Relationship to Head of Family; Last C. Roll No.; At Jurisdiction Where Enrolled (Yes/No); (If no – Where); Ward (Yes/No); Allotment, Annuity and Identification Numbers (if given).

2769; Teleskie, Sallie L.; F; 4/17/80-52; N.C. Cherokee; 4/4; M; Wife; 2755; Yes; Yes; Unallotted

2770; Thompson, Ahsinnah; M; 9/5/83-49; N.C. Cherokee; 4/4; M; Head; 2756; Yes; Yes; Unallotted

2771; Thompson, Mary E.; F; 1/1/83-50; N.C. Cherokee; 1/2; M; Wife; 2757; Yes; Yes; Unallotted

2772; Thompson, Jefferson; M; 2/12/17-16; N.C. Cherokee; 3/4; S; Son; 2758; Yes; Yes; Unallotted

2773; Thompson, Allene; F; 10/7/18-14; N.C. Cherokee; 3/4; S; Dau.; 2759; Yes; Yes; Unallotted

2774; Thompson, Pearl C.; F; 8/11/20-12; N.C. Cherokee; 3/4; S; Dau.; 2760; Yes; Yes; Unallotted

2775; Thompson, Reginald R.; M; 3/12/23-10; N.C. Cherokee; 3/4; S; Son; 2761; Yes; Yes; Unallotted

2776; Thompson, Annie; F; 3/30/06-27; N.C. Cherokee; 4/4; S; Head; 2762; Yes; Yes; Unallotted

2777; Thompson (Loudermilk, Daffney Raper), Daffney; F; 3/29/98-35; N.C. Cherokee; 1/16; M; Wife; 2763; Yes; Yes; Unallotted

2778; Thompson, Sanford D.; M; 5/24/20-12; N.C. Cherokee; 1/32; S; Son; 2764; Yes; Yes; Unallotted

2779; Thompson, Greeley; M; 4/11/99-33; N.C. Cherokee; 1/16; M; Head; 2765; Yes; Yes; Unallotted

2780; Thompson, Jackson; M; 1/7/03-30; N.C. Cherokee; 4/4; M; Head; 2766; Yes; Yes; Unallotted

2781; Thompson, Alice W.; F; 3/12/06-27; N.C. Cherokee; 4/4; M; Wife; 2767; Yes; Yes; Unallotted

2782; Thompson, Joseph W.; M; 6/9/27-5; N.C. Cherokee; 4/4; S; Son; 2768; Yes; Yes; Unallotted

2783; Thompson, McKinley; M; 6/25/31-1; N.C. Cherokee; 4/4; S; Son; 2769; Yes; Yes; Unallotted

2784; Thompson, Johnson; M; 4/12/68-64; N.C. Cherokee; 4/4; M; Head; 2770; Yes; Yes; Unallotted

2785; Thompson, Nancy; F; 12/7/69-63; N.C. Cherokee; 4/4; M; Wife; 2771; Yes; Yes; Unallotted

2786; Thompson, Simon; M; 6/1/94-38; N.C. Cherokee; 4/4; S; Son; 2772; Yes; Yes; Unallotted

2787; Thompson, David; M; 12/21/96-36; N.C. Cherokee; 4/4; S; Son; 2773; Yes; Yes; Unallotted

Census of the **Eastern Cherokee** reservation of the **Cherokee, N.C.** jurisdiction, as of **April 1**, 19**33,** taken by **R. L. Spalsbury**, Superintendent.

Key: Number; Surname, Given; Sex; Date of Birth-Age at Last Birthday; Tribe; Degree of Blood; Marital Status; Relationship to Head of Family; Last C. Roll No.; At Jurisdiction Where Enrolled (Yes/No); (If no – Where); Ward (Yes/No); Allotment, Annuity and Identification Numbers (if given).

2788; Thompson, Jonah; M; 10/17/00-32; N.C. Cherokee; 4/4; M; Head; 2774; Yes; Yes; Unallotted

2789; Thompson, Lucinda; F; 2/10/10-22; N.C. Cherokee; 4/4; M; Wife; 2775; Yes; Yes; Unallotted

2790; Thompson, Abe; M; 9/12/30-2; N.C. Cherokee; 4/4; S; Son; 2776; Yes; Yes; Unallotted

2791; Thompson, Nellie Ann; F; 8/14/32-7/12; N.C. Cherokee; 4/4; S; Dau.; ---; Yes; Yes; Unallotted

2792; Thompson (Webster, Marhta[sic]), Martha; F; 2/11/74-58; N.C. Cherokee; 1/8; M; Wife; 2777; No; Culberson, Cherokee, N.C.; Yes; Unallotted

2793; Thompson, William; M; 12/4/94-38; N.C. Cherokee; 1/16; S; Son; 2778; No; Culberson, Cherokee, N.C.; Yes; Unallotted

2794; Thompson, Minnie; F; 5/22/98-34; N.C. Cherokee; 1/16; S; Dau.; 2779; No; Culberson, Cherokee, N.C.; Yes; Unallotted

2795; Thompson, Elbert; M; 12/1/99-33; N.C. Cherokee; 1/16; S; Son; 2780; No; Culberson, Cherokee, N.C.; Yes; Unallotted

2796; Thompson, Jewel; M; 1/23/05-28; N.C. Cherokee; 1/16; S; Son; 2781; No; Culberson, Cherokee, N.C.; Yes; Unallotted

2797; Thompson, Marvin; M; 4/25/06-26; N.C. Cherokee; 1/16; S; Son; 2782; No; Culberson, Cherokee, N.C.; Yes; Unallotted

2798; Thompson, Walter; M; 1/22/08-25; N.C. Cherokee; 1/16; S; Son; 2783; No; Culberson, Cherokee, N.C.; Yes; Unallotted

2799; Thompson (Webster, Mary), Mary W.; F; 10/22/76-56; N.C. Cherokee; 1/8; M; Wife; 2784; No; Alton Park, Hamilton, Tenn.; Yes; Unallotted

2800; Thompson, Lawrence; M; 12/3/08-24; N.C. Cherokee; 1/16; S; Son; 2785; No; Alton Park, Hamilton, Tenn.; Yes; Unallotted

2801; Thompson, Willard; M; 10/31/11-21; N.C. Cherokee; 1/16; S; Son; 2786; No; Alton Park, Hamilton, Tenn.; Yes; Unallotted

2802; Thompson, Rosa; F; 10/9/17-15; N.C. Cherokee; 1/16; S; Dau.; 2787; No; Alton Park, Hamilton, Tenn.; Yes; Unallotted

2803; Thompson, Claude; M; 5/10/20-12; N.C. Cherokee; 1/16; S; Son; 2788; No; Alton Park, Hamilton, Tenn.; Yes; Unallotted

2804; Thompson, Olin; M; 2/26/97-36; N.C. Cherokee; 1/16; M; Head; 2789; Yes; Yes; Unallotted

2805; Thompson, Peter; M; 7/18/86-46; N.C. Cherokee; 13/16; S; Head; 2790; Yes; Yes; Unallotted

2806; Thompson, Goliath; M; 8/17/98-34; N.C. Cherokee; 13/16; S; Bro.; 2791; Yes; Yes; Unallotted

2807; Thompson, Ruth V.; F; 2/8/83-50; N.C. Cherokee; 3/16; M; Wife; 2792; Yes; Yes; Unallotted

Census of the **Eastern Cherokee** reservation of the **Cherokee, N.C.** jurisdiction, as of **April 1** , **1933,** taken by **R. L. Spalsbury** , Superintendent.

Key: Number; Surname, Given; Sex; Date of Birth-Age at Last Birthday; Tribe; Degree of Blood; Marital Status; Relationship to Head of Family; Last C. Roll No.; At Jurisdiction Where Enrolled (Yes/No); (If no – Where); Ward (Yes/No); Allotment, Annuity and Identification Numbers (if given).

2808; Thompson (Wolf, Sophronia I.), Sophronia; F; 7/16/96-36; N.C. Cherokee; 1/8; M; Wife; 2793; Yes; Yes; Unallotted

2809; Thompson, Paul L.; M; 4/17/15-17; N.C. Cherokee; 1/16; S; Son; 2794; Yes; Yes; Unallotted

2810; Thompson, Nola B.; F; 4/11/17-15; N.C. Cherokee; 1/16; S; Dau.; 2795; Yes; Yes; Unallotted

2811; Thompson, Charles B.; M; 3/27/19-13; N.C. Cherokee; 1/16; S; Son; 2796; Yes; Yes; Unallotted

2812; Thompson, Wilson; M; 8/13/92-40; N.C. Cherokee; 13/16; M; Head; 2797; Yes; Yes; Unallotted

2813; Thompson, Martha Owl; F; 7/11/99-33; N.C. Cherokee; 3/4; M; Wife; 2798; Yes; Yes; Unallotted

2814; Thompson, Enos; M; 11/8/24-8; N.C. Cherokee; 25/32; S; Son; 2799; Yes; Yes; Unallotted

2815; Thompson, Adam; M; 9/5/27-5; N.C. Cherokee; 25/32; S; Son; 2800; Yes; Yes; Unallotted

2816; Thompson, Lawrence; M; 4/2/31-1; N.C. Cherokee; 25/32; S; Son; 2801; Yes; Yes; Unallotted

2817; Timpson, Bertha; F; 12/28/96-36; N.C. Cherokee; 1/64; M; Wife; 2802; Yes; Yes; Unallotted

2818; Timpson, Humphrey P.; M; 12/26/58-74; N.C. Cherokee; 3/8; S; Head; 2803; Yes; Yes; Unallotted

2819; Timpson, James; M; 12/1/52-80; N.C. Cherokee; 3/8; S; Head; 2804; Yes; Yes; Unallotted

2820; Timpson, James A.; M; 12/1/80-52; N.C. Cherokee; 3/16; M; Head; 2805; Yes; Yes; Unallotted

2821; Timpson, Lawrence A.; M; 8/9/09-23; N.C. Cherokee; 3/32; S; Son; 2806; Yes; Yes; Unallotted

2822; Timpson, Lexie; F; 2/27/12-20; N.C. Cherokee; 3/32; S; Dau.; 2807; Yes; Yes; Unallotted

2823; Timpson, Glenn; M; 3/23/14-19; N.C. Cherokee; 3/32; S; Son; 2808; Yes; Yes; Unallotted

2824; Timpson, Flora; F; 7/25/16-16; N.C. Cherokee; 3/32; S; Dau.; 2809; Yes; Yes; Unallotted

2825; Timpson, Cecil; M; 5/15/18-14; N.C. Cherokee; 3/32; S; Son; 2810; Yes; Yes; Unallotted

2826; Timpson, Coy; M; 9/20/20-12; N.C. Cherokee; 3/32; S; Son; 2811; Yes; Yes; Unallotted

Census of the **Eastern Cherokee** reservation of the **Cherokee, N.C.** jurisdiction, as of **April 1**, 19**33**, taken by **R. L. Spalsbury**, Superintendent.

Key: Number; Surname, Given; Sex; Date of Birth-Age at Last Birthday; Tribe; Degree of Blood; Marital Status; Relationship to Head of Family; Last C. Roll No.; At Jurisdiction Where Enrolled (Yes/No); (If no – Where); Ward (Yes/No); Allotment, Annuity and Identification Numbers (if given).

2827; Timpson, John S.; M; 8/8/85-47; N.C. Cherokee; 3/16; M; Head; 2812; Yes; Yes; Unallotted

2828; Timpson, Vestraex; F; 9/10/13-19; N.C. Cherokee; 13/128; S; Dau.; 2813; Yes; Yes; Unallotted

2829; Timpson, Elsie; F; 8/29/15-17; N.C. Cherokee; 13/128; S; Dau.; 2814; Yes; Yes; Unallotted

2830; Timpson, Wilma; F; 5/29/20-12; N.C. Cherokee; 13/128; S; Dau.; 2815; Yes; Yes; Unallotted

2831; Tincher (Sneed, Lula), Lula S.; F; 12/14/87-45; N.C. Cherokee; 1/8; M; Wife; 2816; Yes; Yes; Unallotted

2832; Toineeta, Arneach; M; 7/3/93-39; N.C. Cherokee; 4/4; M; Head; 2818; Yes; Yes; Unallotted

2833; Toineeta, Martha Y.; F; 5/15/92-40; N.C. Cherokee; 4/4; M; Wife; 2819; Yes; Yes; Unallotted

2834; Toineeta, Jefferson; M; 2/27/17-16; N.C. Cherokee; 4/4; S; Son; 2820; Yes; Yes; Unallotted

2835; Toineeta, Jeremiah; M; 2/14/21-12; N.C. Cherokee; 4/4; S; Son; 2821; Yes; Yes; Unallotted

2836; Toineeta, Alice; F; 4/3/23-9; N.C. Cherokee; 4/4; S; Dau.; 2822; Yes; Yes; Unallotted

2837; Toineeta, Joseph; M; 2/14/27-5; N.C. Cherokee; 4/4; S; Son; 2823; Yes; Yes; Unallotted

2838; Toineeta, Joshua; M; 10/15/28-4; N.C. Cherokee; 4/4; S; Son; 2824; Yes; Yes; Unallotted

2839; Toineeta, Geneva; F; 9/7/30-2; N.C. Cherokee; 4/4; S; Dau.; 2825; Yes; Yes; Unallotted

2840; Toineeta, Edwin T.; M; 9/10/08-24; N.C. Cherokee; 3/16; S; Head; 2826; Yes; Yes; Unallotted

2841; Toineeta, George; M; 1/18/83-50; N.C. Cherokee; 4/4; M; Head; 2827; Yes; Yes; Unallotted

2842; Toineeta, Pearl W.; F; 12/22/88-44; N.C. Cherokee; 1/2; M; Wife; 2828; Yes; Yes; Unallotted

2843; Toineeta, F. Geneva; F; 6/17/10-22; N.C. Cherokee; 11/16; S; Dau.; 2829; Yes; Yes; Unallotted

2844; Toineeta, Loney; M; 6/1/13-19; N.C. Cherokee; 11/16; S; Son; 2830; Yes; Yes; Unallotted

2845; Toineeta, George H.; M; 8/2/17-15; N.C. Cherokee; 3/4; S; Son; 2831; Yes; Yes; Unallotted

2846; Toineeta, Margaret; F; 10/3/19-13; N.C. Cherokee; 3/4; S; Dau.; 2832; Yes; Yes; Unallotted

Census of the **Eastern Cherokee** reservation of the **Cherokee, N.C.** jurisdiction, as of **April 1**, **1933**, taken by **R. L. Spalsbury**, Superintendent.

Key: Number; Surname, Given; Sex; Date of Birth-Age at Last Birthday; Tribe; Degree of Blood; Marital Status; Relationship to Head of Family; Last C. Roll No.; At Jurisdiction Where Enrolled (Yes/No); (If no – Where); Ward (Yes/No); Allotment, Annuity and Identification Numbers (if given).

2847; Toineeta, Dorothy; F; 11/2/27-6; N.C. Cherokee; 3/4; S; Dau.; 2833; Yes; Yes; Unallotted

2848; Toineeta, Sally; F; 12/24/60-72; N.C. Cherokee; 4/4; Wd.; Head; 2834; Yes; Yes; Unallotted

2849; Toineeta, West; M; 12/10/81-51; N.C. Cherokee; 4/4; S; Son; 2835; Yes; Yes; Unallotted

2850; Toineeta, Nick; M; 4/22/67-65; N.C. Cherokee; 4/4; M; Head; 2836; Yes; Yes; Unallotted

2851; Toineeta, Betty; F; 12/24/62-70; N.C. Cherokee; 4/4; M; Wife; 2837; Yes; Yes; Unallotted

2852; Toineeta, Suagiah; M; 3/21/69[sic]-44; N.C. Cherokee; 4/4; S; Son; 2838; Yes; Yes; Unallotted

2853; Tollie (Bradley, Lizzie), Lizzie; F; 6/13/87-45; N.C. Cherokee; 1/2; M; Wife; 2839; Yes; Yes; Unallotted

2854; Tooni, Elijah; M; 12/27/99-33; N.C. Cherokee; 4/4; M; Head; 2840; Yes; Yes; Unallotted

2855; Tooni, Aggie G.; F; 6/8/04-28; N.C. Cherokee; 4/4; M; Wife; 2841; Yes; Yes; Unallotted

2856; George, Dinah; F; 8/1/22-10; N.C. Cherokee; 4/4; S; Step-Dau.; 2842; Yes; Yes; Unallotted

2857; Tooni, Ike; M; 2/8/26-7; N.C. Cherokee; 4/4; S; Son; 2843; Yes; Yes; Unallotted

2858; Tooni, Annie; F; 4/5/30-2; N.C. Cherokee; 4/4; S; Dau.; 2844; Yes; Yes; Unallotted

2859; Tooni, Stan; M; 1/26/32-1; N.C. Cherokee; 4/4; S; Son; 2845; Yes; Yes; Unallotted

2860; Tooni, Lizzie D.; F; 1/30/82-50; N.C. Cherokee; 4/4; Wd.; Head; 2846; Yes; Yes; Unallotted

2861; Tooni, Rachel; F; 9/28/08-24; N.C. Cherokee; 4/4; S; Dau.; 2847; Yes; Yes; Unallotted

2862; Tooni, Russel; M; 10/30/11-21; N.C. Cherokee; 4/4; S; Son; 2848; Yes; Yes; Unallotted

2863; Tooni, Michael; M; 12/17/13-19; N.C. Cherokee; 4/4; S; Son; 2849; Yes; Yes; Unallotted

2864; Tooni, Rebecca; F; 11/1/18-14; N.C. Cherokee; 4/4; S; Dau.; 2850; Yes; Yes; Unallotted

2865; Tooni, Mary; F; 4/13/21-11; N.C. Cherokee; 4/4; S; Dau.; 2851; Yes; Yes; Unallotted

Key: Number; Surname, Given; Sex; Date of Birth-Age at Last Birthday; Tribe; Degree of Blood; Marital Status; Relationship to Head of Family; Last C. Roll No.; At Jurisdiction Where Enrolled (Yes/No); (If no – Where); Ward (Yes/No); Allotment, Annuity and Identification Numbers (if given).

2866; Tooni (Mr. Annie Standingdeer), Tom; M; 10/20/13-19; N.C. Cherokee; 4/4; S; Son; 2852; Yes; Yes; Unallotted

2867; Tooni, Ollie Ann; F; 10/5/16-16; N.C. Cherokee; 4/4; S; Dau.; 2853; Yes; Yes; Unallotted

2868; Tramper, Amineeta; M; 6/12/86-46; N.C. Cherokee; 4/4; M; Head; 2854; Yes; Yes; Unallotted

2869; Tramper, Lucinda; F; 8/4/93-39; N.C. Cherokee; 9/16; M; Wife; 2855; Yes; Yes; Unallotted

2870; Tramper, Elziney; F; 9/30/17-15; N.C. Cherokee; 25/32; S; Dau.; 2856; Yes; Yes; Unallotted

2871; Tramper, Sallie; F; 8/11/23-9; N.C. Cherokee; 25/32; S; Dau.; 2857; Yes; Yes; Unallotted

2872; Tramper, John A.; M; 8/26/28-4; N.C. Cherokee; 25/32; S; Son; 2858; Yes; Yes; Unallotted

2873; Tramper, Dorothy Marie; F; 12/12/32-3/12; N.C. Cherokee; 25/32; S; Dau.; ---; Yes; Yes; Unallotted

2874; Tramper, Chiltoskey; M; 4/10/82-50; N.C. Cherokee; 4/4; M; Head; 2859; Yes; Yes; Unallotted

2875; Tramper, Emma Axe; F; 8/20/97-35; N.C. Cherokee; 4/4; M; Wife; 2860; Yes; Yes; Unallotted

2876; Tramper, Welch; M; 11/2/18-14; N.C. Cherokee; 4/4; S; Son; 2861; Yes; Yes; Unallotted

2877; Tramper, Lillian; F; 1/8/23-10; N.C. Cherokee; 4/4; S; Dau.; 2862; Yes; Yes; Unallotted

2878; Tramper, Tonie; M; 5/20/28-4; N.C. Cherokee; 4/4; S; Son; 2863; Yes; Yes; Unallotted

2879; Tramper, Kahlie; F; 4/17/30-2; N.C. Cherokee; 4/4; S; Dau.; 2864; Yes; Yes; Unallotted

2880; Tramper, Alyne; F; 3/1/33-1/12; N.C. Cherokee; 4/4; S; Dau.; ---; Yes; Yes; Unallotted

2881; Treadway, Mary L.; F; 9/26/10-22; N.C. Cherokee; 1/32; M; Wife; 2865; Yes; Yes; Unallotted

2882; Treadway(Griffin, Ima), Ima; F; 12/15/12-20; N.C. Cherokee; 1/32; M; Wife; 903; Yes; Yes; Unallotted

2883; Truett, Reuben; M; 8/16/10-22; N.C. Cherokee; 1/32; S; Head; 2866; Yes; Yes; Unallotted

2884; Truett, Vinson; M; 3/9/13-20; N.C. Cherokee; 1/32; S; Bro.; 2867; Yes; Yes; Unallotted

2885; Truett, Edward; M; 3/14/17-16; N.C. Cherokee; 1/32; S; Bro.; 2868; Yes; Yes; Unallotted

Census of the **Eastern Cherokee** reservation of the **Cherokee, N.C.** jurisdiction, as of **April 1** , 19**33,** taken by **R. L. Spalsbury** , Superintendent.

Key: Number; Surname, Given; Sex; Date of Birth-Age at Last Birthday; Tribe; Degree of Blood; Marital Status; Relationship to Head of Family; Last C. Roll No.; At Jurisdiction Where Enrolled (Yes/No); (If no – Where); Ward (Yes/No); Allotment, Annuity and Identification Numbers (if given).

2886; Truett, Clara B.; F; 9/27/20-12; N.C. Cherokee; 1/32; S; Sis.; 2869; Yes; Yes; Unallotted

2887; Twin, Viola; F; 3/10/10-23; N.C. Cherokee; 3/8; S; Alone; 2870; Yes; Yes; Unallotted

2888; Lindsey, Jackie; M; 5/27/31-1; N.C. Cherokee; 3/16; S; Son; 2871; Yes; Yes; Unallotted

2889; Voiles, Jane; F; 5/10/57-75; N.C. Cherokee; 1/8; M; Wife; 2872; No; Rossville, Walker, Ga.; Yes; Unallotted

2890; Voiles, Vinson; M; 4/10/79-53; N.C. Cherokee; 1/16; M; Head; 2873; No; Lookout Mtn., Hamilton, Tenn.; Yes; Unallotted

2891; Voiles, William; M; 6/10/81-51; N.C. Cherokee; 1/16; M; Head; 2874; No; Rossville, Walker, Ga.; Yes; Unallotted

2892; Wachacha, Charles; M; 4/30/90-42; N.C. Cherokee; 4/4; Wd.; Head; 2875; Yes; Yes; Unallotted

2893; Wachacha, Moses; M; 12/22/21-11; N.C. Cherokee; 4/4; S; Son; 2876; Yes; Yes; Unallotted

2894; Wachacha, Jack; M; 11/15/93-39; N.C. Cherokee; 4/4; M; Head; 2877; Yes; Yes; Unallotted

2895; Wachacha, Dinah C.; F; 8/10/96-36; N.C. Cherokee; 4/4; M; Wife; 2878; Yes; Yes; Unallotted

2896; Wachacha, Claude; M; 1/17/23-10; N.C. Cherokee; 4/4; S; Son; 2879; Yes; Yes; Unallotted

2897; Wachacha, James; M; 12/25/83-49; N.C. Cherokee; 4/4; M; Head; 2880; Yes; Yes; Unallotted

2898; Wachacha, Sarah Axe; F; 9/12/97-35; N.C. Cherokee; 4/4; M; Wife; 2881; Yes; Yes; Unallotted

2899; Wachacha, Carrie; F; 6/10/21-11; N.C. Cherokee; 4/4; S; Dau.; 2882; Yes; Yes; Unallotted

2900; Wachacha, Henry; M; 3/25/23-10; N.C. Cherokee; 4/4; S; Son; 2883; Yes; Yes; Unallotted

2901; Wachacha, Jarret; M; 12/15/84-48; N.C. Cherokee; 4/4; M; Head; 2884; Yes; Yes; Unallotted

2902; Wachacha, Amanda T.; F; 9/28/94-38; N.C. Cherokee; 4/4; M; Wife; 2885; Yes; Yes; Unallotted

2903; Wachacha, Linda; F; 2/10/13-20; N.C. Cherokee; 4/4; S; Dau.; 2886; Yes; Yes; Unallotted

Census of the **Eastern Cherokee** reservation of the **Cherokee, N.C.** jurisdiction, as of **April 1** , 19**33,** taken by **R. L. Spalsbury** , Superintendent.

Key: Number; Surname, Given; Sex; Date of Birth-Age at Last Birthday; Tribe; Degree of Blood; Marital Status; Relationship to Head of Family; Last C. Roll No.; At Jurisdiction Where Enrolled (Yes/No); (If no – Where); Ward (Yes/No); Allotment, Annuity and Identification Numbers (if given).

2904; Wachacha, Raleigh; M; 8/21/15-17; N.C. Cherokee; 4/4; S; Son; 2887; Yes; Yes; Unallotted

2905; Wachacha, Mollie; F; 5/22/18-14; N.C. Cherokee; 4/4; S; Dau.; 2888; Yes; Yes; Unallotted

2906; Wachacha, John W.; M; 10/15/98-34; N.C. Cherokee; 4/4; M; Head; 2889; Yes; Yes; Unallotted

2907; Wachacha, Martha W.; F; 4/26/10-22; N.C. Cherokee; 4/4; M; Wife; 2890; Yes; Yes; Unallotted

2908; Wachacha, Posey; M; 3/15/94-41; N.C. Cherokee; 4/4; Wd.; Head; 2891; Yes; Yes; Unallotted

2909; Wachacha, Sarah; M; 4/15/89-43; N.C. Cherokee; 4/4; S; Head; 2892; Yes; Yes; Unallotted

2910; Wachacha, Oney; F; 5/15/04-28; N.C. Cherokee; 4/4; S; Sis.; 2893; Yes; Yes; Unallotted

2911; Wahyahneetah, Allen; M; 5/5/73-43; N.C. Cherokee; 4/4; M; Head; 2894; Yes; Yes; Unallotted

2912; Wahyahneetah, Sallie; F; 7/10/69-63; N.C. Cherokee; 4/4; M; Wife; 2895; Yes; Yes; Unallotted

2913; Wahyahneetah, Awee; F; 12/24/53-79; N.C. Cherokee; 4/4; Wd.; Head; 2896; Yes; Yes; Unallotted

2914; Wahyahneetah, Posey; M; 12/4/00-32; N.C. Cherokee; 4/4; Wd.; Head; 2897; Yes; Yes; Unallotted

2915; Wahyahneetah, William; M; 8/13/70-62; N.C. Cherokee; 4/4; M; Head; 2898; Yes; Yes; Unallotted

2916; Wahyahneetah, Kamie; F; 9/28/77-55; N.C. Cherokee; 1/2; M; Wife; 2899; Yes; Yes; Unallotted

2917; Wahyahneetah, Leroy; M; 7/22/06-26; N.C. Cherokee; 3/4; S; Son; 2901; Yes; Yes; Unallotted

2918; Wahyahneetah, Robert; M; 11/10/13-19; N.C. Cherokee; 3/4; S; Son; 2903; Yes; Yes; Unallotted

2919; Wahyahneetah, John; M; 4/5/19-13; N.C. Cherokee; 3/4; S; Son; 2904; Yes; Yes; Unallotted

2920; Wahyahneetah, Samuel; M; 7/5/03-29; N.C. Cherokee; 3/4; M; Head; 2900; Yes; Yes; Unallotted

2921; Wahyahneetah (Arch, Cora), Cora; F; 9/2/07-26; N.C. Cherokee; 5/8; M; Wife; 65; Yes; Yes; Unallotted

Census of the **Eastern Cherokee** reservation of the **Cherokee, N.C.** jurisdiction, as of **April 1** , **1933,** taken by **R. L. Spalsbury** , Superintendent.

Key: Number; Surname, Given; Sex; Date of Birth-Age at Last Birthday; Tribe; Degree of Blood; Marital Status; Relationship to Head of Family; Last C. Roll No.; At Jurisdiction Where Enrolled (Yes/No); (If no – Where); Ward (Yes/No); Allotment, Annuity and Identification Numbers (if given).

2922; Waidsutte, Bird; M; 12/14/77-55; N.C. Cherokee; 4/4; M; Head; 2905; Yes; Yes; Unallotted

2923; Waidsutte, Mary; F; 12/14/70-62; N.C. Cherokee; 4/4; M; Wife; 2906; Yes; Yes; Unallotted

2924; Waidsutte, Lee; M; 1/7/03-30; N.C. Cherokee; 4/4; S; Son; 2907; Yes; Yes; Unallotted

2925; Waidsutte, Davis; M; 12/21/67-65; N.C. Cherokee; 4/4; M; Head; 2908; Yes; Yes; Unallotted

2926; Waidsutte, Nancy; F; 5/5/71-61; N.C. Cherokee; 4/4; M; Wife; 2909; Yes; Yes; Unallotted

2927; Waidsutte, Bird; M; 6/10/01-31; N.C. Cherokee; 4/4; S; Son; 2910; Yes; Yes; Unallotted

2928; Waidsutte, Addison; M; 10/15/10-22; N.C. Cherokee; 4/4; S; Son; 2911; Yes; Yes; Unallotted

2929; Waidsutte, Margaret; F; 2/4/12-21; N.C. Cherokee; 4/4; S; Alone; 2912; Yes; Yes; Unallotted

2930; Wakefield, Albert; M; 4/7/79-53; N.C. Cherokee; 1/32; M; Head; 2913; Yes; Yes; Unallotted

2931; Wakefield, Charlie; M; 6/6/74-58; N.C. Cherokee; 1/32; M; Head; 2914; Yes; Yes; Unallotted

2932; Wakefield, Ruth; F; 4/12/10-22; N.C. Cherokee; 1/64; S; Dau.; 2915; Yes; Yes; Unallotted

2933; Wakefield, Elizabeth; F; 7/29/13-19; N.C. Cherokee; 1/64; S; Dau.; 2916; Yes; Yes; Unallotted

2934; Wakefield, Charles Jr.; M; 11/23/15-17; N.C. Cherokee; 1/64; S; Dau.[sic]; 2917; Yes; Yes; Unallotted

2935; Wakefield, Annie; F; 4/24/17-15; N.C. Cherokee; 1/64; S; Dau.; 2918; Yes; Yes; Unallotted

2936; Wakefield, Luther; M; 4/24/20-12; N.C. Cherokee; 1/64; S; Son; 2919; Yes; Yes; Unallotted

2937; Wakefield, Ralph; M; 8/1/23-9; N.C. Cherokee; 1/64; S; Son; 2920; Yes; Yes; Unallotted

2938; Wakefield, David Lee; M; 3/4/14-19; N.C. Cherokee; 1/64; S; Son (Mr. White); 2921; Yes; Yes; Unallotted

2939; Wakefield, Marie; F; 1/13/16-17; N.C. Cherokee; 1/64; S; Dau.; 2922; Yes; Yes; Unallotted

2940; Wakefield, Kathleen; F; 11/12/17-15; N.C. Cherokee; 1/64; S; Dau.; 2923; Yes; Yes; Unallotted

2941; Wakefield, Maxine; F; 11/23/19-13; N.C. Cherokee; 1/64; S; Dau.; 2924; Yes; Yes; Unallotted

Census of the **Eastern Cherokee** reservation of the **Cherokee, N.C.** jurisdiction, as of **April 1** , 19**33**, taken by **R. L. Spalsbury** , Superintendent.

Key: Number; Surname, Given; Sex; Date of Birth-Age at Last Birthday; Tribe; Degree of Blood; Marital Status; Relationship to Head of Family; Last C. Roll No.; At Jurisdiction Where Enrolled (Yes/No); (If no – Where); Ward (Yes/No); Allotment, Annuity and Identification Numbers (if given).

2942;   Wakefield, Kenneth; M; 3/17/22-11; N.C. Cherokee; 1/64; S; Son; 2925; Yes; Yes; Unallotted

2943;   Wakefield, Edmond S.; M; 2/22/77-56; N.C. Cherokee; 1/32; S; Head; 2926; Yes; Yes; Unallotted

2944;   Wakefield, Esco; M; 10/16/66-66; N.C. Cherokee; 1/32; M; Head; 2927; Yes; Yes; Unallotted

2945;   Wakefield, Thomas; M; 12/9/05-27; N.C. Cherokee; 1/64; S; Son; 2928; Yes; Yes; Unallotted

2946;   Wakefield, Wiley E.; M; 12/4/09-23; N.C. Cherokee; 1/64; S; Son; 2929; Yes; Yes; Unallotted

2947;   Wakefield, Lycurgus; M; 5/13/81-51; N.C. Cherokee; 1/32; S; Head; 2930; Yes; Yes; Unallotted

2948;   Wakefield, Lucy; F; 5/11/95-37; N.C. Cherokee; 1/64; S; Head; 2931; Yes; Yes; Unallotted

2949;   Wakefield, Virginia; F; 5/13/81-51; N.C. Cherokee; 1/32; S; Head; 2932; Yes; Yes; Unallotted

2950;   Walker, Amanda C.; F; 12/7/98-34; N.C. Cherokee; 4/4; M; Wife; 2933; Yes; Yes; Unallotted

2951;   Walker, Lucile; F; 12/31/21-11; N.C. Cherokee; 1/2; S; Dau.; 2934; Yes; Yes; Unallotted

2952;   Walker, George Wm.; M; 5/11/23-9; N.C. Cherokee; 1/2; S; Son; 2935; Yes; Yes; Unallotted

2953;   Walker, Eugene; M; 6/2/28-4; N.C. Cherokee; 1/2; S; Son; 2936; Yes; Yes; Unallotted

2954;   Walker, Pauline; F; 7/3/30-2; N.C. Cherokee; 1/2; S; Dau.; 2937; Yes; Yes; Unallotted

2955;   Walker (Taylor, Edith), Edith; F; 5/5/04-28; N.C. Cherokee; 1/32; M; Wife; 2938; No; Hiwassee, Cherokee, N.C.; Yes; Unallotted

2956;   Walker, D.O.; M; 10/12/23-9; N.C. Cherokee; 1/64; M; Son; 2939; No; Hiwassee, Cherokee, N.C.; Yes; Unallotted

2957;   Walkingstick, Bascomb; M; 8/13/88-44; N.C. Cherokee; 4/4; M; Head; 2940; Yes; Yes; Unallotted

2958;   Walkingstick, Alice S.; F; 4/1/03-30; N.C. Cherokee; 15/16; M; Wife; 2941; Yes; Yes; Unallotted

2959;   Walkingstick, William; M; 8/28/14-18; N.C. Cherokee; 4/4; S; Son; 2942; Yes; Yes; Unallotted

Census of the **Eastern Cherokee** reservation of the **Cherokee, N.C.** jurisdiction, as of **April 1** , 19**33,** taken by   **R. L. Spalsbury**   , Superintendent.

Key: Number; Surname, Given; Sex; Date of Birth-Age at Last Birthday; Tribe; Degree of Blood; Marital Status; Relationship to Head of Family; Last C. Roll No.; At Jurisdiction Where Enrolled (Yes/No); (If no – Where); Ward (Yes/No); Allotment, Annuity and Identification Numbers (if given).

2960;   Walkingstick, Henry; M; 8/10/16-16; N.C. Cherokee; 4/4; S; Son; 2943; Yes; Yes; Unallotted

2961;   Walkingstick, Wayne; M; 4/20/21-11; N.C. Cherokee; 4/4; S; Son; 2944; Yes; Yes; Unallotted

2962;   Walkingstick, Virgil; M; 11/7/31-1; N.C. Cherokee; 4/4; S; Son; 2945; Yes; Yes; Unallotted

2963;   Walkingstick, James; M; 12/28/85-47; N.C. Cherokee; 4/4; M; Head; 2946; Yes; Yes; Unallotted

2964;   Walkingstick, Mandy T.; F; 11/12/90-42; N.C. Cherokee; 4/4; M; Wife; 2947; Yes; Yes; Unallotted

2965;   Walkingstick, Jasper; M; 10/14/72-60; N.C. Cherokee; 4/4; Wd.; Head; 2948; Yes; Yes; Unallotted

2966;   Walkingstick, Willie; M; 10/1/06-26; N.C. Cherokee; 4/4; S; Son; 2949; Yes; Yes; Unallotted

2967;   Walkingstick, John; M; 8/13/11-21; N.C. Cherokee; 4/4; S; Son; 2950; Yes; Yes; Unallotted

2968;   Walkingstick, Samuel; M; 11/13/13-19; N.C. Cherokee; 4/4; S; Son; 2951; Yes; Yes; Unallotted

2969;   Walkingstick, John; M; 12/23/52-80; N.C. Cherokee; 4/4; Wd; Head; 2952; Yes; Yes; Unallotted

2970;   Walkingstick, Enoch; M; 7/2/09-23; N.C. Cherokee; 4/4; S; Son; 2953; Yes; Yes; Unallotted

2971;   Walkingstick, Maggie Axe; F; 9/12/94-38; N.C. Cherokee; 4/4; Div.; Head; 2954; Yes; Yes; Unallotted

2972;   Walkingstick, Mason; M; 1/6/03-30; N.C. Cherokee; 4/4; M; Head; 2955; Yes; Yes; Unallotted

2973;   Walkingstick, Lucy Bird; F; 4/6/08-24; N.C. Cherokee; 4/4; M; Wife; 2956; Yes; Yes; Unallotted

2974;   Walkingstick, Samuel Edward; M; 12/31/32-3/12; N.C. Cherokee; 4/4; S; Son; ---; Yes; Yes; Unallotted

2975;   Walkingstick, Mike; M; 2/20/02-31; N.C. Cherokee; 4/4; M; Head; 2957; Yes; Yes; Unallotted

2976;   Walkingstick, Emily T.; F; 9/24/05-27; N.C. Cherokee; 3/4; M; Wife; 2958; Yes; Yes; Unallotted

2977;   Walkingstick, Alfred K.; M; 5/3/27-5; N.C. Cherokee; 7/8; S; Son; 2959; Yes; Yes; Unallotted

2978;   Walkingstick, Moses; M; 3/25/96-37; N.C. Cherokee; 4/4; M; Head; 2960; Yes; Yes; Unallotted

Census of the **Eastern Cherokee** reservation of the **Cherokee, N.C.** jurisdiction, as of **April 1** , 19**33**, taken by **R. L. Spalsbury** , Superintendent.

Key: Number; Surname, Given; Sex; Date of Birth-Age at Last Birthday; Tribe; Degree of Blood; Marital Status; Relationship to Head of Family; Last C. Roll No.; At Jurisdiction Where Enrolled (Yes/No); (If no – Where); Ward (Yes/No); Allotment, Annuity and Identification Numbers (if given).

2979; Walkingstick, Jennie W.; F; 12/24/90-42; N.C. Cherokee; 4/4; M; Wife; 2961; Yes; Yes; Unallotted

2980; Walkingstick, Ancy; F; 3/20/20-13; N.C. Cherokee; 4/4; S; Dau.; 2962; Yes; Yes; Unallotted

2981; Walkingstick, Emmaline; F; 2/5/24-9; N.C. Cherokee; 4/4; S; Dau.; 2963; Yes; Yes; Unallotted

2982; Walkingstick, Linda G.; F; 3/5/85-48; N.C. Cherokee; 4/4; Wd.; Head; 2964; Yes; Yes; Unallotted

2983; Walkingstick, Lydia; F; 6/10/13-19; N.C. Cherokee; 4/4; S; Dau.; 2965; Yes; Yes; Unallotted

2984; Walkingstick, Minda; F; 9/10/19-13; N.C. Cherokee; 4/4; S; Dau.; 2966; Yes; Yes; Unallotted

2985; Walkingstick, Edward; M; 3/14/21-11; N.C. Cherokee; 4/4; S; Son; 2967; Yes; Yes; Unallotted

2986; Walkingstick, Abraham; M; 8/30/24-8; N.C. Cherokee; 4/4; S; Son; 2968; Yes; Yes; Unallotted

2987; Walkingstick, Tom; M; 1/17/08-25; N.C. Cherokee; 4/4; S; Head; 2969; Yes; Yes; Unallotted

2988; Wallace, James; M; 1/15/78-56; N.C. Cherokee; 4/4; M; Head; 2970; Yes; Yes; Unallotted

2989; Wallace, Sallie L.; F; 12/10/64-68; N.C. Cherokee; 4/4; M; Wife; 2971; Yes; Yes; Unallotted

2990; Wallace, Tahquette; M; 10/14/03-29; N.C. Cherokee; 15/16; M; Head; 2972; Yes; Yes; Unallotted

2991; Wallace, Margarind; F; 10/10/12-20; N.C. Cherokee; 4/4; M; Wife; 2973; Yes; Yes; Unallotted

2992; Wallace, Stacy; F; 10/14/21-11; N.C. Cherokee; 31/32; S; Dau.; 2974; Yes; Yes; Unallotted

2993; Wallace, Marjorie; F; 8/10/22-10; N.C. Cherokee; 31/32; S; Dau.; 2975; Yes; Yes; Unallotted

2994; Wallace, Ollie; F; 10/8/29-3; N.C. Cherokee; 31/32; S; Dau.; 2976; Yes; Yes; Unallotted

2995; Warrick, Selma C.; F; 2/22/08-25; N.C. Cherokee; 1/16; M; Wife; 2977; Yes; Yes; Unallotted

2996; Washington, Jesse; M; 3/5/73-60; N.C. Cherokee; 4/4; M; Head; 2978; Yes; Yes; Unallotted

2997; Washington, Ollie; F; 12/26/76-56; N.C. Cherokee; 7/8; M; Wife; 2979; Yes; Yes; Unallotted

Census of the **Eastern Cherokee** reservation of the **Cherokee, N.C.** jurisdiction, as of **April 1**, 19**33,** taken by **R. L. Spalsbury**, Superintendent.

Key: Number; Surname, Given; Sex; Date of Birth-Age at Last Birthday; Tribe; Degree of Blood; Marital Status; Relationship to Head of Family; Last C. Roll No.; At Jurisdiction Where Enrolled (Yes/No); (If no – Where); Ward (Yes/No); Allotment, Annuity and Identification Numbers (if given).

2998; Washington, Emma; F; 8/16/04-28; N.C. Cherokee; 15/16; S; Dau.; 2980; Yes; Yes; Unallotted

2999; Washington, George; M; 7/6/06-26; N.C. Cherokee; 15/16; S; Son; 2981; Yes; Yes; Unallotted

3000; Washington, Jonas; M; 3/9/09-24; N.C. Cherokee; 15/16; S; Son; 2982; Yes; Yes; Unallotted

3001; Washington, Joseph; M; 2/20/82-51; N.C. Cherokee; 4/4; M; Head; 2983; Yes; Yes; Unallotted

3002; Washington, Stella B.; F; 3/17/84-49; N.C. Cherokee; 1/2; M; Wife; 2984; Yes; Yes; Unallotted

3003; Washington, Richard; M; 9/27/10-22; N.C. Cherokee; 3/4; S; Son; 2985; Yes; Yes; Unallotted

3004; Washington, Josephine; F; 4/29/13-19; N.C. Cherokee; 3/4; S; Dau.; 2986; Yes; Yes; Unallotted

3005; Washington, Erma L.; F; 2/5/16-17; N.C. Cherokee; 3/4; S; Dau.; 2987; Yes; Yes; Unallotted

3006; Watson (Foster, Elsie), Elsie; F; 6/17/99-33; N.C. Cherokee; 1/16; M; Wife; 2988; No; Culberson, Cherokee, N.C.; Yes; Unallotted

3007; Watson, Virginia; F; 8/13/21-11; N.C. Cherokee; 1/32; S; Dau.; 2989; No; Culberson, Cherokee, N.C.; Yes; Unallotted

3008; Watson, James H.; M; 2/13/22-11; N.C. Cherokee; 1/32; S; Son; 2990; No; Culberson, Cherokee, N.C.; Yes; Unallotted

3009; Watty, Goolarche; M; 12/20/76-56; N.C. Cherokee; 4/4; M; Head; 2991; Yes; Yes; Unallotted

3010; Watty, Nessih; F; 12/15/76-56; N.C. Cherokee; 4/4; M; Wife; 2992; Yes; Yes; Unallotted

3011; Watty, Stephen; M; 1/25/98-35; N.C. Cherokee; 4/4; S; Son; 2993; Yes; Yes; Unallotted

3012; Watty, Jessan; M; 3/17/16-17; N.C. Cherokee; 4/4; S; Son; 2994; Yes; Yes; Unallotted

3013; Watty, Ollie; F; 12/23/09-23; N.C. Cherokee; 4/4; S; Dau.; 2995; Yes; Yes; Unallotted

3014; Wayne, Will; M; 12/26/75-57; N.C. Cherokee; 4/4; Wd.; Head; 2996; Yes; Yes; Unallotted

3015; Wayne, Agnes; F; 8/20/11-21; N.C. Cherokee; 4/4; S; Dau.; 2997; Yes; Yes; Unallotted

3016; Wayne, Sara; F; 8/22/30-2; N.C. Cherokee; 4/4; S; Grand-dau.; 2998; Yes; Yes; Unallotted

3017; Webb, Fannie C.; F; 9/17/00-32; N.C. Cherokee; 1/16; M; Wife; 2999; Yes; Yes; Unallotted

Census of the **Eastern Cherokee** reservation of the **Cherokee, N.C.** jurisdiction, as of **April 1** , 19**33**, taken by **R. L. Spalsbury** , Superintendent.

Key: Number; Surname, Given; Sex; Date of Birth-Age at Last Birthday; Tribe; Degree of Blood; Marital Status; Relationship to Head of Family; Last C. Roll No.; At Jurisdiction Where Enrolled (Yes/No); (If no – Where); Ward (Yes/No); Allotment, Annuity and Identification Numbers (if given).

3018; Webb, Winifred C.; F; 10/25/22-10; N.C. Cherokee; 1/32; S; Dau.; 3000; Yes; Yes; Unallotted

3019; Webster, Galer B.; M; 4/2/71-61; N.C. Cherokee; 1/8; M; Head; 3001; No; Choteau, Mayes, Okla.; Yes; Unallotted

3020; Webster, Harry T.; M; 4/2/98-34; N.C. Cherokee; 1/16; S; Head; 3002; No; Choteau, Mayes, Okla.; Yes; Unallotted

3021; Webster, Rachel A.; F; 2/16/41-92; N.C. Cherokee; 1/4; Wd.; Head; 3003; Yes; Yes; Unallotted

3022; Webster, Ralph W.; M; 4/2/96-36; N.C. Cherokee; 1/16; M; Head; 3004; No; Wetumka, Hughes, Okla.; Yes; Unallotted

3023; Webster, William; M; 10/10/69-63; N.C. Cherokee; 1/8; M; Head; 3005; No; Culberson, Cherokee, N.C.; Yes; Unallotted
3024; Webster, Jetter C.; M; 2/19/97-36; N.C. Cherokee; 1/16; S; Son; 3006; No; Culberson, Cherokee, N.C.; Yes; Unallotted
3025; Webster, William R.; M; 2/22/06-27; N.C. Cherokee; 1/16; S; Son; 3007; No; Culberson, Cherokee, N.C.; Yes; Unallotted
3026; Webster, William L.; M; 7/2/12-20; N.C. Cherokee; 1/16; S; Son; 3008; No; Culberson, Cherokee, N.C.; Yes; Unallotted
3027; Webster, Thomas D.; M; 11/14/14-18; N.C. Cherokee; 1/16; S; Son; 3009; No; Culberson, Cherokee, N.C.; Yes; Unallotted

3028; Welch, Adam; M; 12/4/84-48; N.C. Cherokee; 4/4; M; Head; 3010; Yes; Yes; Unallotted
3029; Welch, Anna P.; F; 12/25/93-39; N.C. Cherokee; 13/16; M; Wife; 3011; Yes; Yes; Unallotted
3030; Welch, Charlotte; F; 10/9/13-19; N.C. Cherokee; 29/32; S; Dau.; 3012; Yes; Yes; Unallotted
3031; Welch, Wilson; M; 10/14/14-18; N.C. Cherokee; 29/32; S; Son; 3013; Yes; Yes; Unallotted
3032; Welch, Elijah; M; 12/27/17-15; N.C. Cherokee; 29/32; S; Son; 3014; Yes; Yes; Unallotted
3033; Welch, Simpson; M; 7/14/21-11; N.C. Cherokee; 29/32; S; Son; 3015; Yes; Yes; Unallotted
3034; Welch, John; M; 4/11/30-2; N.C. Cherokee; 29/32; S; Son; 3016; Yes; Yes; Unallotted
3035; Welch, Akin; M; 4/11/27-5; N.C. Cherokee; 29/32; S; Son; 3017; Yes; Yes; Unallotted

3036; Welch, Cornetta; M; 10/15/80-52; N.C. Cherokee; 4/4; M; Head; 3018; Yes; Yes; Unallotted

Census of the **Eastern Cherokee** reservation of the **Cherokee, N.C.** jurisdiction, as of **April 1** , **1933,** taken by **R. L. Spalsbury** , Superintendent.

Key: Number; Surname, Given; Sex; Date of Birth-Age at Last Birthday; Tribe; Degree of Blood; Marital Status; Relationship to Head of Family; Last C. Roll No.; At Jurisdiction Where Enrolled (Yes/No); (If no – Where); Ward (Yes/No); Allotment, Annuity and Identification Numbers (if given).

3037;   Welch, Nicey T.; F; 2/16/73-57; N.C. Cherokee; 4/4; M; Wife; 3019; Yes; Yes; Unallotted

3038;   Welch (Mr. Liddy Squirrell), David; M; 11/16/11-21; N.C. Cherokee; 29/32; S; Son; 3020; Yes; Yes; Unallotted
3039;   Welch, Lucinda; F; 5/4/14-18; N.C. Cherokee; 29/32; S; Dau.; 3021; Yes; Yes; Unallotted

3040;   Welch, Awee; F; 5/15/80-52; N.C. Cherokee; 4/4; Wd.; Head; 3022; Yes; Yes; Unallotted
3041;   Welch, James B.; M; 4/25/91-41; N.C. Cherokee; 4/4; S; Son; 3023; Yes; Yes; Unallotted

3042;   Welch, Jane; F; 7/16/08-24; N.C. Cherokee; 4/4; S; Dau.; 3024; Yes; Yes; Unallotted

3043;   Welch, Edward; M; 10/14/02-30; N.C. Cherokee; 7/8; S; Head; 3025; Yes; Yes; Unallotted

3044;   Welch, Ephesus; M; 10/19/83-49; N.C. Cherokee; 4/4; M; Head; 3027; Yes; Yes; Unallotted
3045;   Welch, Stacy; F; 2/26/90-43; N.C. Cherokee; 4/4; M; Wife; 3028; Yes; Yes; Unallotted
3046;   Welch, Juna; M; 10/19/07-25; N.C. Cherokee; 4/4; S; Son; 3029; Yes; Yes; Unallotted
3047;   Welch, Isaac; M; 10/6/19-13; N.C. Cherokee; 4/4; S; Son; 3030; Yes; Yes; Unallotted
3048;   Welch, Mike; M; 2/4/23-10; N.C. Cherokee; 4/4; S; Son; 3031; Yes; Yes; Unallotted
3049;   Welch, Nannie; F; 1/29/26-7; N.C. Cherokee; 4/4; S; Dau.; 3032; Yes; Yes; Unallotted
3050;   Welch, James Blue; M; 7/19/29-3; N.C. Cherokee; 4/4; S; Son; 3033; Yes; Yes; Unallotted

3051;   Welch, Frank C.; M; 4/17/09-23; N.C. Cherokee; 29/32; M; Head; 3034; Yes; Yes; Unallotted
3052;   Welch, Dinah C.; F; 4/24/10-22; N.C. Cherokee; 4/4; M; Wife; 3035; Yes; Yes; Unallotted
3053;   Welch, Henderson; M; 4/20/29-3; N.C. Cherokee; 61/64; S; Son; 3036; Yes; Yes; Unallotted

3054;   Welch, James B.; M; 5/12/75-57; N.C. Cherokee; 1/4; M; Head; 3037; Yes; Yes; Unallotted

Census of the **Eastern Cherokee** reservation of the **Cherokee, N.C.** jurisdiction, as of **April 1** , 19**33,** taken by **R. L. Spalsbury** , Superintendent.

Key: Number; Surname, Given; Sex; Date of Birth-Age at Last Birthday; Tribe; Degree of Blood; Marital Status; Relationship to Head of Family; Last C. Roll No.; At Jurisdiction Where Enrolled (Yes/No); (If no – Where); Ward (Yes/No); Allotment, Annuity and Identification Numbers (if given).

3055; Welch, Yihginneh; F; 3/27/00-33; N.C. Cherokee; 4/4; Wd.; Head; 3038; Yes; Yes; Unallotted

3056; Welch, Adam; M; 5/22/25-7; N.C. Cherokee; 4/4; S; Son; 3039; Yes; Yes; Unallotted

3057; Welch, Daniel; M; 10/7/27-5; N.C. Cherokee; 4/4; S; Son; 3040; Yes; Yes; Unallotted

3058; Welch, Mary Bell; F; 12/15/29-3; N.C. Cherokee; 4/4; S; Dau.; 3041; Yes; Yes; Unallotted

3059; Welch, James G.; M; 5/23/91-41; N.C. Cherokee; 9/16; M; Head; 3042; Yes; Yes; Unallotted

3060; Welch, Lottie T.; F; 10/28/90-42; N.C. Cherokee; 4/4; M; Wife; 3043; Yes; Yes; Unallotted

3061; Welch, Elizabeth; F; 7/5/13-20; N.C. Cherokee; 25/32; S; Dau.; 3044; Yes; Yes; Unallotted

3062; Welch, Amy; F; 10/28/15-17; N.C. Cherokee; 25/32; S; Dau.; 3045; Yes; Yes; Unallotted

3063; Welch, Irving; M; 3/19/18-15; N.C. Cherokee; 25/32; S; Son; 3046; Yes; Yes; Unallotted

3064; Welch, Oscar; M; 5/24/21-11; N.C. Cherokee; 25/32; S; Son; 3047; Yes; Yes; Unallotted

3065; Welch, Myrtle; F; 4/2/24-8; N.C. Cherokee; 25/32; S; Dau.; 3048; Yes; Yes; Unallotted

3066; Welch, Mary Jane; F; 5/3/27-5; N.C. Cherokee; 25/32; S; Dau.; 3049; Yes; Yes; Unallotted

3067; Welch, Charlotte; F; 11/10/29-3; N.C. Cherokee; 25/32; S; Dau.; 3050; Yes; Yes; Unallotted

3068; Welch, John; M; 9/26/93-39; N.C. Cherokee; 7/8; M; Head; 3051; Yes; Yes; Unallotted

3069; Welch, Mary; F; 6/12/91-41; N.C. Cherokee; 7/8; M; Wife; 3052; Yes; Yes; Unallotted

3070; Welch, Lloyd; M; 8/18/95-37; N.C. Cherokee; 5/16; M; Head; 3053; Yes; Yes; Unallotted

3071; Welch, Mark; M; 5/21/00-32; N.C. Cherokee; 4/4; M; Head; 3054; Yes; Yes; Unallotted

3072; Welch, Polly C.; F; 3/19/94-39; N.C. Cherokee; 4/4; M; Wife; 3055; Yes; Yes; Unallotted

3073; Welch, Sally; F; 5/29/21-11; N.C. Cherokee; 4/4; S; Dau.; 3056; Yes; Yes; Unallotted

3074; Welch, Mark G.; M; 4/21/77-55; N.C. Cherokee; 3/4; S; Head; 3057; Yes; Yes; Unallotted

Census of the **Eastern Cherokee** reservation of the **Cherokee, N.C.** jurisdiction, as of **April 1** , **1933,** taken by **R. L. Spalsbury** , Superintendent.

Key: Number; Surname, Given; Sex; Date of Birth-Age at Last Birthday; Tribe; Degree of Blood; Marital Status; Relationship to Head of Family; Last C. Roll No.; At Jurisdiction Where Enrolled (Yes/No); (If no – Where); Ward (Yes/No); Allotment, Annuity and Identification Numbers (if given).

3075; Welch, Moses; M; 3/1/86-47; N.C. Cherokee; 4/4; M; Head; 3058; Yes; Yes; Unallotted

3076; Welch, Cindy; F; 6/15/98-34; N.C. Cherokee; 4/4; M; Wife; 3059; Yes; Yes; Unallotted

3077; Welch, Nancy; F; 12/25/65-67; N.C. Cherokee; 4/4; Wd.; Head; 3060; Yes; Yes; Unallotted

3078; Welch, Ned; M; 4/16/03-29; N.C. Cherokee; 4/4; D̶i̶v̶. M; Head; 3061; Yes; Yes; Unallotted

3079; Welch, Ethel Wahnetah; F; 3/12/11-22; N.C. Cherokee; 3/4; M; Wife; 2902; Yes; Yes; Unallotted

3080; Welch, Richard; M; 6/30/03-29; N.C. Cherokee; 11/16; S; Head; 3063; Yes; Yes; Unallotted

3081; Welch, Sampson; M; 8/4/61-71; N.C. Cherokee; 4/4; M; Head; 3064; Yes; Yes; Unallotted

3082; Welch, Lizzie; F; 12/4/62-70; N.C. Cherokee; 4/4; M; Wife; 3065; Yes; Yes; Unallotted

3083; Welch, Tempe J.; F; 1/22/88-45; N.C. Cherokee; 1/4; M; Wife; 3066; Yes; Yes; Unallotted

3084; Welch, Theodore; M; 7/1/97-35; N.C. Cherokee; 5/16; M; Head; 3067; Yes; Yes; Unallotted

3085; Welch, Willie; M; 7/14/89-43; N.C. Cherokee; 9/16; M; Head; 3068; Yes; Yes; Unallotted

3086; Welch, Maude F.; F; 5/24/94-38; N.C. Cherokee; 4/4; M; Wife; 3069; Yes; Yes; Unallotted

3087; Welch, Elliott; M; 3/29/15-18; N.C. Cherokee; 25/32; S; Son; 3070; Yes; Yes; Unallotted

3088; Welch, Edna; F; 9/25/16-16; N.C. Cherokee; 25/32; S; Dau.; 3071; Yes; Yes; Unallotted

3089; Welch, Edith; F; 9/30/18-14; N.C. Cherokee; 25/32; S; Dau.; 3072; Yes; Yes; Unallotted

3090; Wesley, Judas; M; 12/16/78-54; N.C. Cherokee; 7/8; M; Head; 3073; Yes; Yes; Unallotted

3091; Wesley, Jennie; F; 12/20/55-77; N.C. Cherokee; 4/4; M; Wife; 3074; Yes; Yes; Unallotted

3092; West, Buck; M; 4/11/98-34; N.C. Cherokee; 7/8; M; Head; 3075; Yes; Yes; Unallotted

Census of the **Eastern Cherokee** reservation of the **Cherokee, N.C.** jurisdiction, as of **April 1** , 19**33**, taken by **R. L. Spalsbury** , Superintendent.

Key: Number; Surname, Given; Sex; Date of Birth-Age at Last Birthday; Tribe; Degree of Blood; Marital Status; Relationship to Head of Family; Last C. Roll No.; At Jurisdiction Where Enrolled (Yes/No); (If no – Where); Ward (Yes/No); Allotment, Annuity and Identification Numbers (if given).

3093; West, Susan B.; F; 7/6/01-31; N.C. Cherokee; 15/16; M; Wife; 3076; Yes; Yes; Unallotted

3094; West, Alfred; M; 4/24/21-11; N.C. Cherokee; 29/32; S; Son; 3077; Yes; Yes; Unallotted

3095; West, Cecil; M; 4/20/23-9; N.C. Cherokee; 29/32; S; Son; 3078; Yes; Yes; Unallotted

3096; West, Doris; F; 6/1/25-7; N.C. Cherokee; 29/32; S; Dau.; 3079; Yes; Yes; Unallotted

3097; West, James; M; 11/2/94-38; N.C. Cherokee; 7/8; S; Head; 3080; Yes; Yes; Unallotted

3098; Whip-poor-will, Manley; M; 6/15/84-48; N.C. Cherokee; 4/4; S; Head; 3081; Yes; Yes; Unallotted

3099; Whitaker, James M.; M; 8/23/46-86; N.C. Cherokee; 1/16; S; Head; 3082; Yes; Yes; Unallotted

3100; Whitaker, Jud; M; 5/19/00-32; N.C. Cherokee; 1/32; M; Head; 3083; Yes; Yes; Unallotted

3101; Whitaker, Willard; M; 4/27/21-11; N.C. Cherokee; 1/64; S; Son; 3084; Yes; Yes; Unallotted

3102; Whitaker, Herman; M; 11/19/22-10; N.C. Cherokee; 1/64; S; Son; 3085; Yes; Yes; Unallotted

3103; Whitaker (Harden, Rutha), Rutha; F; 3/4/79-54; N.C. Cherokee; 1/16; M; Wife; 3086; Yes; Yes; Unallotted

3104; Whitaker, Ross; M; 2/8/11-22; N.C. Cherokee; 1/32; S; Son; 3087; Yes; Yes; Unallotted

3105; Whitaker, Stephen; M; 8/12/55-77; N.C. Cherokee; 1/16; M; Head; 3088; Yes; Yes; Unallotted

3106; White (Harden, Bettie), Bettie; F; 3/4/89-43; N.C. Cherokee; 1/16; M; Wife; 3089; No; Lorey Mills Station, Gastonia, Gaston, N.C.; Yes; Unallotted

3107; White, Mary; F; 6/14/09-23; N.C. Cherokee; 1/32; S; Dau.; 3090; No; Lorey Mills Station, Gastonia, Gaston, N.C.; Yes; Unallotted

3108; White, Robert; M; 3/26/13-20; N.C. Cherokee; 1/32; S; Son; 3091; No; Lorey Mills Station, Gastonia, Gaston, N.C.; Yes; Unallotted

3109; White, John; M; 5/20/17-15; N.C. Cherokee; 1/32; S; Son; 3092; No; Lorey Mills Station, Gastonia, Gaston, N.C.; Yes; Unallotted

3110; White, Inez; F; 12/19/19-13; N.C. Cherokee; 1/32; S; Dau.; 3093; No; Lorey Mills Station, Gastonia, Gaston, N.C.; Yes; Unallotted

3111; White, Pink; M; 8/13/22-10; N.C. Cherokee; 1/32; S; Son; 3094; No; Lorey Mills Station, Gastonia, Gaston, N.C.; Yes; Unallotted

Census of the **Eastern Cherokee** reservation of the **Cherokee, N.C.** jurisdiction, as of **April 1**, **1933,** taken by **R. L. Spalsbury**, Superintendent.

Key: Number; Surname, Given; Sex; Date of Birth-Age at Last Birthday; Tribe; Degree of Blood; Marital Status; Relationship to Head of Family; Last C. Roll No.; At Jurisdiction Where Enrolled (Yes/No); (If no – Where); Ward (Yes/No); Allotment, Annuity and Identification Numbers (if given).

3112; White, Dee; M; 4/17/06-26; N.C. Cherokee; 1/32; M; Head; 3095; Yes; Yes; Unallotted

3113; White, Dillard; M; 6/17/04-28; N.C. Cherokee; 1/32; M; Head; 3096; Yes; Yes; Unallotted

3114; White-tree, Floy B.; F; 7/1/99-33; N.C. Cherokee; 1/8; M; Wife; 3097; Yes; Yes; Unallotted

3115; White-tree, F. Wenonah; F; 7/11/16-16; N.C. Cherokee; 1/16; S; Dau.; 3098; Yes; Yes; Unallotted

3116; White-tree, John; M; 8/3/20-12; N.C. Cherokee; 1/16; S; Son; 3099; Yes; Yes; Unallotted

3117; White-tree, Alva E.; M; 10/29/22-10; N.C. Cherokee; 1/16; S; Son; 3100; Yes; Yes; Unallotted

3118; Wildcat, Dahola; M; 1/8/81-51; N.C. Cherokee; 4/4; M; Head; 3101; Yes; Yes; Unallotted

3119; Wildcat, Sallie; F; 2/16/81-52; N.C. Cherokee; 4/4; M; Wife; 3102; Yes; Yes; Unallotted

3120; Wildcat, Addison; M; 2/21/20-13; N.C. Cherokee; 4/4; S; Son; 3103; Yes; Yes; Unallotted

3121; Wildcat, Boyman; M; 2/21/20-13; N.C. Cherokee; 4/4; S; Son; 3004; Yes; Yes; Unallotted

3122; Will, John; M; 12/26/62-70; N.C. Cherokee; 4/4; M; Head; 3105; Yes; Yes; Unallotted

3123; Will, Jane; F; 12/20/73-59; N.C. Cherokee; 4/4; M; Wife; 3106; Yes; Yes; Unallotted

3124; Will, James; M; 2/2/01-32; N.C. Cherokee; 4/4; S; Son; 3107; Yes; Yes; Unallotted

3125; Will, David; M; 10/29/06-26; N.C. Cherokee; 4/4; S; Son; 3108; Yes; Yes; Unallotted

3126; Will (Thompson), Luzene; F; 1/7/09-24; N.C. Cherokee; 4/4; S; Dau.; 3109; Yes; Yes; Unallotted

3127; Will, Nellie; F; 10/15/11-21; N.C. Cherokee; 4/4; S; Dau.; 3110; Yes; Yes; Unallotted

3128; Wilnoty, Joseph; M; 5/5/94-38; N.C. Cherokee; 3/4; M; Head; 3111; Yes; Yes; Unallotted

3129; Wilnoty, Ned; M; 9/9/96-36; N.C. Cherokee; 3/4; S; Bro.; 3112; Yes; Yes; Unallotted

3130; Wilnoty, Tidmarsh; M; 8/11/31-1; N.C. Cherokee; 7/16; S; Son; 3113; Yes; Yes; Unallotted

Census of the **Eastern Cherokee** reservation of the **Cherokee, N.C.** jurisdiction, as of **April 1** , 19**33,** taken by   **R. L. Spalsbury**   , Superintendent.

Key: Number; Surname, Given; Sex; Date of Birth-Age at Last Birthday; Tribe; Degree of Blood; Marital Status; Relationship to Head of Family; Last C. Roll No.; At Jurisdiction Where Enrolled (Yes/No); (If no – Where); Ward (Yes/No); Allotment, Annuity and Identification Numbers (if given).

3131;   Wilnoty, Moses; M; 8/23/83-49; N.C. Cherokee; 4/4; M; Head; 3114; Yes; Yes; Unallotted

3132;   Wilnoty, Alice M.; F; 6/1/98-34; N.C. Cherokee; 1/8; M; Wife; 3115; Yes; Yes; Unallotted

3133;   Wilnoty, Julius; M; 12/18/09-23; N.C. Cherokee; 9/16; S; Son; 3116; Yes; Yes; Unallotted

3134;   Wilnoty, Elizabeth; F; 2/23/14-19; N.C. Cherokee; 9/16; S; Dau.; 3117; Yes; Yes; Unallotted

3135;   Wilnoty, Fred; M; 8/8/28-4; N.C. Cherokee; 9/16; S; Son; 3118; Yes; Yes; Unallotted

3136;   Wilnoty, Zenobia Verna; F; 2/14/33-1/12; N.C. Cherokee; 5/8; S; Grand-dau.; ---; Yes; Yes; Unallotted

3137;   Wilnoty, Sallie; F; 12/26/50-82; N.C. Cherokee; 4/4; Wd.; Head; 3119; Yes; Yes; Unallotted

3138;   Wilnoty, Simon; M; 6/19/92-40; N.C. Cherokee; 4/4; M; Head; 3120; Yes; Yes; Unallotted

3139;   Wilnoty, Josephine; F; 6/5/06-26; N.C. Cherokee; 1/2; M; Wife; 3121; Yes; Yes; Unallotted

3140;   Wilnoty, Bettie Lou; F; 8/28/28-4; N.C. Cherokee; 3/4; S; Dau.; 3122; Yes; Yes; Unallotted

3141;   Wilnoty, Paul R.; M; 4/18/31-1; N.C. Cherokee; 3/4; S; Son; 3123; Yes; Yes; Unallotted

3142;   Winkler, Maybelle; F; 5/12/13-19; N.C. Cherokee; 1/32; S; Dau., (Mr. White); 3124; Yes; Yes; Unallotted

3143;   Winkler, Dennis; M; 1/9/16-17; N.C. Cherokee; 1/32; S; Son; 3125; Yes; Yes; Unallotted

3144;   Winkler, Hazel; F; 8/28/18-14; N.C. Cherokee; 1/32; S; Dau.; 3126; Yes; Yes; Unallotted

3145;   Winkler, Lois; F; 11/15/20-12; N.C. Cherokee; 1/32; S; Dau.; 3127; Yes; Yes; Unallotted

3146;   Winkler, Harrell; M; 1/4/23-10; N.C. Cherokee; 1/32; S; Son; 3128; Yes; Yes; Unallotted

3147;   Wolfe, Callie; F; 7/4/77-55; N.C. Cherokee; 4/4; Wd.; Head; 3129; Yes; Yes; Unallotted

3148;   Wolfe, Charles; M; 8/22/92-40; N.C. Cherokee; 1/2; S; Head; 3130; Yes; Yes; Unallotted

3149;   Wolfe, David; M; 1/2/40-93; N.C. Cherokee; 1/2; M; Head; 3131; Yes; Yes; Unallotted

Census of the **Eastern Cherokee** reservation of the **Cherokee, N.C.** jurisdiction, as of **April 1** , **1933,** taken by **R. L. Spalsbury** , Superintendent.

Key: Number; Surname, Given; Sex; Date of Birth-Age at Last Birthday; Tribe; Degree of Blood; Marital Status; Relationship to Head of Family; Last C. Roll No.; At Jurisdiction Where Enrolled (Yes/No); (If no – Where); Ward (Yes/No); Allotment, Annuity and Identification Numbers (if given).

3150; Wolfe, Dawson; M; 8/15/87-45; N.C. Cherokee; 4/4; M; Head; 3132; Yes; Yes; Unallotted

3151; Wolfe, Polly W.; F; 9/1/04-28; N.C. Cherokee; 4/4; M; Wife; 3133; Yes; Yes; Unallotted

3152; Wolfe, Dinah; F; 3/15/14-19; N.C. Cherokee; 4/4; S; Dau.; 3134; Yes; Yes; Unallotted

3153; Wolfe, James; M; 3/16/15-18; N.C. Cherokee; 4/4; S; Son; 3135; Yes; Yes; Unallotted

3154; Wolfe, Ina; F; 7/3/23-9; N.C. Cherokee; 4/4; S; Dau.; 3136; Yes; Yes; Unallotted

3155; Wolfe, Edward; M; 11/8/91-41; N.C. Cherokee; 7/8; M; Head; 3137; Yes; Yes; Unallotted

3156; Wolfe, George L.; M; 5/10/67-65; N.C. Cherokee; 1/4; M; Head; 3138; Yes; Yes; Unallotted

3157; Wolfe, Jacob; M; 4/2/71-61; N.C. Cherokee; 4/4; M; Head; 3139; No; Decatur, Benyon[sic], Ark.; Yes; Unallotted

3158; Wolfe, Jesse; M; 7/21/00-32; N.C. Cherokee; 4/4; S; Son; 3140; Yes; Yes; Unallotted

3159; Wolfe, Jacob; M; 3/15/13-20; N.C. Cherokee; 4/4; S; Son; 3141; Yes; Yes; Unallotted

3160; Wolfe, James T.; M; 8/5/85-47; N.C. Cherokee; 1/2; M; Head; 3142; Yes; Yes; Unallotted

3161; Wolfe, Bettie S.; F; 10/15/96-36; N.C. Cherokee; 1/2; M; Wife; 3143; Yes; Yes; Unallotted

3162; Wolfe, Wm. Wallace; M; 2/18/12-21; N.C. Cherokee; 1/2; S; Son; 3144; Yes; Yes; Unallotted

3163; Wolfe, Edwin W.; M; 4/18/14-18; N.C. Cherokee; 1/2; S; Son; 3145; Yes; Yes; Unallotted

3164; Wolfe, Donald G.; M; 9/6/16-16; N.C. Cherokee; 1/2; S; Son; 3146; Yes; Yes; Unallotted

3165; Wolfe, Robert W.; M; 2/13/19-14; N.C. Cherokee; 1/2; S; Son; 3147; Yes; Yes; Unallotted

3166; Wolfe, Wade H.; M; 3/11/21-12; N.C. Cherokee; 1/2; S; Son; 3148; Yes; Yes; Unallotted

3167; Wolfe, Mary Iva; F; 12/29/23-9; N.C. Cherokee; 1/2; S; Dau.; 3149; Yes; Yes; Unallotted

3168; Wolfe, Bettie W.; F; 6/17/26-6; N.C. Cherokee; 1/2; S; Dau.; 3150; Yes; Yes; Unallotted

3169; Wolfe, James T.; M; 5/14/30-2; N.C. Cherokee; 1/2; S; Son; 3151; Yes; Yes; Unallotted

Census of the **Eastern Cherokee** reservation of the **Cherokee, N.C.** jurisdiction, as of **April 1**, 19**33,** taken by **R. L. Spalsbury**, Superintendent.

Key: Number; Surname, Given; Sex; Date of Birth-Age at Last Birthday; Tribe; Degree of Blood; Marital Status; Relationship to Head of Family; Last C. Roll No.; At Jurisdiction Where Enrolled (Yes/No); (If no – Where); Ward (Yes/No); Allotment, Annuity and Identification Numbers (if given).

3170; Wolfe, John; M; 9/12/71-61; N.C. Cherokee; 4/4; M; Head; 3152; Yes; Yes; Unallotted

3171; Wolfe, Linda; F; 6/10/78-54; N.C. Cherokee; 4/4; M; Wife; 3153; Yes; Yes; Unallotted

3172; Wolfe, Walker; M; 4/21/05-27; N.C. Cherokee; 4/4; S; Son; 3154; Yes; Yes; Unallotted

3173; Wolfe, Salkinney; F; 7/16/11-21; N.C. Cherokee; 4/4; S; Dau.; 3155; Yes; Yes; Unallotted

3174; Wolfe, Josephine; F; 2/22/13-20; N.C. Cherokee; 4/4; S; Dau.; 3156; Yes; Yes; Unallotted

3175; Wolfe, Rebecca; F; 3/17/15-18; N.C. Cherokee; 4/4; S; Dau.; 3157; Yes; Yes; Unallotted

3176; Wolfe, John R.; M; 5/3/03-29; N.C. Cherokee; 1/8; M; Head; 3158; No; Hulmeville, Bucks, Pa.; Yes; Unallotted

3177; Wolfe (Bradley, Sarah), Sarah; F; 3/26/02-31; N.C. Cherokee; 1/2; M; Wife; 315; No; Hulmeville, Bucks, Pa.; Yes; Unallotted

3178; Wolfe, William H.; M; 3/23/05-28; N.C. Cherokee; 1/8; S; Head; 3159; Yes; Yes; Unallotted

3179; Wolfe, Charles; M; 9/5/10-22; N.C. Cherokee; 1/8; S; Head; 3160; Yes; Yes; Unallotted

3180; Wolfe, Jessie M.; M; 7/15/09-23; N.C. Cherokee; 1/8; S; Head; 3161; Yes; Yes; Unallotted

3181; Wolfe, Marian E.; F; 4/22/29-3; N.C. Cherokee; 1/16; S; Dau.; 3162; Yes; Yes; Unallotted

3182; Wolfe, Jonah; M; 9/16/93-39; N.C. Cherokee; 4/4; M; Head; 3163; Yes; Yes; Unallotted

3183; Wolfe, Minda H.; F; 10/6/98-34; N.C. Cherokee; 15/16; M; Wife; 3164; Yes; Yes; Unallotted

3184; Wolfe, Ned W.; M; 4/4/20-12; N.C. Cherokee; 31/32; S; Son; 3165; Yes; Yes; Unallotted

3185; Wolfe, Katherine; F; 12/26/23-9; N.C. Cherokee; 31/32; S; Dau.; 3166; Yes; Yes; Unallotted

3186; Wolfe, Ollie; F; 6/4/26-7; N.C. Cherokee; 31/32; S; Dau.; 3167; Yes; Yes; Unallotted

3187; Wolfe, Maggie; F; 4/8/29-3; N.C. Cherokee; 31/32; S; Dau.; 3168; Yes; Yes; Unallotted

3188; Wolfe, Lillian; F; 11/15/31-1; N.C. Cherokee; 31/32; S; Dau.; 3169; Yes; Yes; Unallotted

Census of the **Eastern Cherokee** reservation of the **Cherokee, N.C.** jurisdiction, as of **April 1** , **1933,** taken by **R. L. Spalsbury** , Superintendent.

Key: Number; Surname, Given; Sex; Date of Birth-Age at Last Birthday; Tribe; Degree of Blood; Marital Status; Relationship to Head of Family; Last C. Roll No.; At Jurisdiction Where Enrolled (Yes/No); (If no – Where); Ward (Yes/No); Allotment, Annuity and Identification Numbers (if given).

3189; Wolfe, Joseph H.; M; 2/23/71-62; N.C. Cherokee; 4/4; M; Head; 3170; Yes; Yes; Unallotted

3190; Wolfe, Jennie; F; 2/16/69-64; N.C. Cherokee; 4/4; M; Wife; 3171; Yes; Yes; Unallotted

3191; Wolfe, Joseph J.; M; 11/15/97-35; N.C. Cherokee; 4/4; M; Head; 3172; Yes; Yes; Unallotted

3192; Wolfe, Lizzie W.; F; 6/8/05-27; N.C. Cherokee; 4/4; M; Wife; 3173; Yes; Yes; Unallotted

3193; Wolfe, Amble S.; M; 6/8/21-11; N.C. Cherokee; 4/4; S; Son; 3174; Yes; Yes; Unallotted

3194; Wolfe, Richard; M; 6/22/23-9; N.C. Cherokee; 4/4; S; Son; 3175; Yes; Yes; Unallotted

3195; Wolfe, Morgan C.; M; 7/29/26-7; N.C. Cherokee; 4/4; S; Son; 3176; Yes; Yes; Unallotted

3196; Wolfe, Lula M.; F; 6/20/30-2; N.C. Cherokee; 4/4; S; Dau.; 3177; Yes; Yes; Unallotted

3197; Wolfe, Junaluska; M; 3/15/86-47; N.C. Cherokee; 4/4; M; Head; 3178; Yes; Yes; Unallotted

3198; Wolfe, Bird; M; 4/24/18-14; N.C. Cherokee; 4/4; S; Son; 3180; Yes; Yes; Unallotted

3199; Wolfe, Nancy; F; 4/24/25-7; N.C. Cherokee; 4/4; S; Dau.; 3181; Yes; Yes; Unallotted

3200; Wolfe, Lewis D.; M; 9/22/93-39; N.C. Cherokee; 1/8; M; Head; 3182; Yes; Yes; Unallotted

3201; Wolfe, Lewis H.; M; 12/24/71-61; N.C. Cherokee; 1/4; M; Head; 3183; Yes; Yes; Unallotted

3202; Wolfe, James W.; M; 3/25/06-27; N.C. Cherokee; 1/8; S; Son; 3184; Yes; Yes; Unallotted

3203; Wolfe, Frederick; M; 7/8/09-23; N.C. Cherokee; 1/8; S; Son; 3185; Yes; Yes; Unallotted

3204; Wolfe, Dessie C.; F; 6/19/13-19; N.C. Cherokee; 1/8; S; Dau.; 3186; Yes; Yes; Unallotted

3205; Wolfe, Jane; F; 3/4/58-74; N.C. Cherokee; 4/4; Wd.; Head; 3187; Yes; Yes; Unallotted

3206; Wolfe, Owen; M; 12/18/84-48; N.C. Cherokee; 4/4; M; Head; 3188; Yes; Yes; Unallotted

3207; Wolfe, Lucy A.D.; F; 12/1/90-42; N.C. Cherokee; 4/4; M; Wife; 3189; Yes; Yes; Unallotted

Census of the **Eastern Cherokee** reservation of the **Cherokee, N.C.** jurisdiction, as of **April 1**, 19**33,** taken by **R. L. Spalsbury**, Superintendent.

Key: Number; Surname, Given; Sex; Date of Birth-Age at Last Birthday; Tribe; Degree of Blood; Marital Status; Relationship to Head of Family; Last C. Roll No.; At Jurisdiction Where Enrolled (Yes/No); (If no – Where); Ward (Yes/No); Allotment, Annuity and Identification Numbers (if given).

3208; Wolfe, Jeremiah; M; 8/28/24-8; N.C. Cherokee; 4/4; S; Son; 3190; Yes; Yes; Unallotted

3209; Wolfe, Ward; M; 9/26/90-42; N.C. Cherokee; 4/4; M; Head; 3191; Yes; Yes; Unallotted

3210; Wolfe, Carolina; F; 11/1/98-34; N.C. Cherokee; 4/4; M; Wife; 3192; Yes; Yes; Unallotted

3211; Wolfe, Elnora; F; 7/12/16-16; N.C. Cherokee; 4/4; S; Dau.; 3193; Yes; Yes; Unallotted

3212; Wolfe, William; M; 3/2/20-13; N.C. Cherokee; 4/4; S; Son; 3194; Yes; Yes; Unallotted

3213; Wolfe, Daniel; M; 8/28/22-10; N.C. Cherokee; 4/4; S; Son; 3195; Yes; Yes; Unallotted

3214; Wolfe, William J.; M; 12/30/77-55; N.C. Cherokee; 4/4; Wd.; Head; 3196; Yes; Yes; Unallotted

3215; Wolfe, Joe; M; 7/29/02-30; N.C. Cherokee; 4/4; S; Son; 3197; No; Canton Asylum, Canton, Lincoln, S.D.; Yes; Unallotted

3216; Wolfe, Addison; M; 12/25/06-26; N.C. Cherokee; 4/4; S; Son; 3198; Yes; Yes; Unallotted

3217; Wolfe, Lilly; F; 7/25/09-23; N.C. Cherokee; 4/4; S; Dau.; 3199; Yes; Yes; Unallotted

3218; Wolfe, Eli; M; 12/25/12-20; N.C. Cherokee; 4/4; S; Son; 3200; Yes; Yes; Unallotted

3219; Wright (Parris, Laura), Laura M.; F; 5/15/06-26; N.C. Cherokee; 1/16; M; Wife; 3201; No; Culberson, Cherokee, N.C.; Yes; Unallotted

3220; Yonce (Lambert, Nancy), Nancy; F; 3/18/52-81; N.C. Cherokee; 1/8; M; Wife; 3202; Yes; Yes; Unallotted

3221; Young, Catherine; F; 8/13/86-46; N.C. Cherokee; 7/8; M; Wife; 3203; Yes; Yes; Unallotted

3222; Young, Willie B.; F; 9/14/02-30; N.C. Cherokee; 1/8; M; Wife; 3204; Yes; Yes; Unallotted

3223; Young, William E.; M; 9/3/27-5; N.C. Cherokee; 1/16; S; Son; 3205; Yes; Yes; Unallotted

3224; Young, Robert; M; 10/8/30-2; N.C. Cherokee; 1/16; S; Son; 3206; Yes; Yes; Unallotted

3225; Youngbird, Rufus; M; 4/8/87-45; N.C. Cherokee; 7/8; M; Head; 3207; Yes; Yes; Unallotted

3226; Youngbird, Amanda W.; F; 8/15/90-42; N.C. Cherokee; 1/2; M; Wife; 3208; Yes; Yes; Unallotted

Census of the **Eastern Cherokee** reservation of the **Cherokee, N.C.** jurisdiction, as of **April 1** , 19**33,** taken by **R. L. Spalsbury** , Superintendent.

Key: Number; Surname, Given; Sex; Date of Birth-Age at Last Birthday; Tribe; Degree of Blood; Marital Status; Relationship to Head of Family; Last C. Roll No.; At Jurisdiction Where Enrolled (Yes/No); (If no – Where); Ward (Yes/No); Allotment, Annuity and Identification Numbers (if given).

3227; Youngbird, Carol; F; 7/23/16-16; N.C. Cherokee; 11/16; S; Dau.; 3209; Yes; Yes; Unallotted

3228; Youngbird, Myrtle E.; F; 10/18/19-13; N.C. Cherokee; 11/16; S; Dau.; 3210; Yes; Yes; Unallotted

3229; Youngbird, Ruth; F; 12/12/22-10; N.C. Cherokee; 11/16; S; Dau.; 3211; Yes; Yes; Unallotted

3230; Youngbird, Saughee; M; 8/20/91-41; N.C. Cherokee; 7/8; M; Head; 3212; Yes; Yes; Unallotted

3231; Youngbird, Lizzie; F; 4/8/03-29; N.C. Cherokee; 7/8; M; Wife; 3213; Yes; Yes; Unallotted

3232; Youngbird, Edmond; M; 2/26/22-11; N.C. Cherokee; 7/8; S; Son; 3214; Yes; Yes; Unallotted

3233; Youngbird, John A.; M; 8/13/24-8; N.C. Cherokee; 7/8; S; Son; 3215; Yes; Yes; Unallotted

3234; Youngbird, James; M; 1/21/26-7; N.C. Cherokee; 7/8; S; Son; 3216; Yes; Yes; Unallotted

3235; Youngbird, David; M; 10/26/27-5; N.C. Cherokee; 7/8; S; Son; 3217; Yes; Yes; Unallotted

3236; Youngbird, Ned; M; 11/24/29-3; N.C. Cherokee; 7/8; S; Son; 3218; Yes; Yes; Unallotted

3237; Youngbird, Yohnih; M; 5/30/92-40; N.C. Cherokee; 7/8; S; Head; 3219; Yes; Yes; Unallotted

3238; Youngbird, Wesley; M; 3/25/94-39; N.C. Cherokee; 7/8; S; Bro.; 3220; Yes; Yes; Unallotted

3239; Youngbird, Wah-kin-nih; F; 3/4/04-29; N.C. Cherokee; 7/8; S; Sis.; 3221; Yes; Yes; Unallotted

3240; Youngdeer, Jacob; M; 7/20/72-60; N.C. Cherokee; 4/4; Wd.; Head; 3222; Yes; Yes; Unallotted

3241; Youngdeer, Jesse; M; 5/7/84-48; N.C. Cherokee; 4/4; M; Head; 3223; Yes; Yes; Unallotted

3242; Youngdeer, Martha; F; 8/12/94-38; N.C. Cherokee; 1/4; M; Wife; 3224; Yes; Yes; Unallotted

3243; Youngdeer, Jesse H.; M; 10/2/17-15; N.C. Cherokee; 5/8; S; Son; 3225; Yes; Yes; Unallotted

3244; Youngdeer, Robert S.; M; 4/13/22-11; N.C. Cherokee; 5/8; S; Son; 3226; Yes; Yes; Unallotted

3245; Youngdeer, Betsy; F; 7/7/49-83; N.C. Cherokee; 4/4; Wd.; Head; 3227; Yes; Yes; Unallotted

3246; Youngdeer, Eli; M; 7/20/81-51; N.C. Cherokee; 4/4; S; Son; 3228; Yes; Yes; Unallotted

Census of the **Eastern Cherokee** reservation of the **Cherokee, N.C.** jurisdiction, as of **April 1** , **1933,** taken by **R. L. Spalsbury** , Superintendent.

Key: Number; Surname, Given; Sex; Date of Birth-Age at Last Birthday; Tribe; Degree of Blood; Marital Status; Relationship to Head of Family; Last C. Roll No.; At Jurisdiction Where Enrolled (Yes/No); (If no – Where); Ward (Yes/No); Allotment, Annuity and Identification Numbers (if given).

3247; Youngdeer, Jonah; M; 6/29/83-49; N.C. Cherokee; 4/4; S; Son; 3229; Yes; Yes; Unallotted

3248; Youngdeer, Moody; M; 6/30/99-33; N.C. Cherokee; 4/4; S; Son; 3230; Yes; Yes; Unallotted

3249; Zimmerman, Norma; F; 2/1/03-30; N.C. Cherokee; 1/64; M; Wife; 3231; Yes; Yes; Unallotted

3247; Correct Census as of April 1, 1933.

        Note: 1933 Census #308, Rachel Bradley, stricken out, duplicated by #242, page 19.
1933 Census #1207, page 95, stricken out, duplicated by #1208, same page.

1933
Census

    (1) ADDITIONS made to 1933 Census over 1932 Census and reasons.

1485; Lossie, Leander; M; 1/5/82-51; N.C. Cherokee; 4/4; M; Head Husband; ---; Yes; Omitted on 1932 Census; Yes; Yes; Unallotted

    (1) SUBTRACTIONS made to 1933 Census from 1932 Census and reasons.

308; Bradley, Rachel; F; 7/15/06-26; N.C. Cherokee; 1/4; S; Head; ---; Yes; Duplication – also shown on 1932 Census as #308; Yes; Unallotted

358

Census of the Cherokee Tribe
Eastern Cherokee Agency, N.C.
BIRTHS -
Unreported on 1931 Census (Births)

April 1,1930 – March 31, 1931 (1932 Births)

April 1,1931 – March 31, 1932 (Live Births)

April 1, 1931 and March 31, 1932 (1932 Births)

Census of the **Eastern Cherokee** reservation of the **Cherokee, N.C.** jurisdiction, as of **April 1** , **1932,** taken by **R. L. Spalsbury** , Superintendent.

Key: Census Number; Surname, Given; Sex; Date of Birth-Age at Last Birthday; Tribe; Degree of Blood; Marital Status; Relationship to Head of Family; At Jurisdiction Where Enrolled (Yes/No); (If no – Where); Ward (Yes/No); Allotment, Annuity and Identification Numbers (if given).

1932   BIRTHS   unreported on 1931 Census

1. 458;   Chekelelee, Ed;   M; 5/21/29-2; N.C. Cherokee; F; S; Son; Yes; Yes; Unallotted

2. 575;   Craig, Bettie Ann;   F; 6/23/29-2; N.C. Cherokee; 3/16; S; Daughter; Yes; Yes; Unallotted

3. 2976;   Wallace, Ollie;   F; 10/8/29-2; N.C. Cherokee; 31/32; S; Daughter; Yes; Yes; Unallotted

4. 3017;   Welch, Akin;   M; 4/11/27-4; N.C. Cherokee; 29/32; S; Son; Yes; Yes; Unallotted

5. ---;   Sequoyah, Frances;   F; 10/1/27-4; N.C. Cherokee; 15/16; S; Daughter; Yes; (#8 on 1931 census death report) (Never shown on census and died 4/7/30)

Census of the **Eastern Cherokee** reservation of the **Cherokee, N.C.** jurisdiction, as of **April 1** , 19**32,** taken by   **R. L. Spalsbury**   , Superintendent.

Key: Census Number; Surname, Given; Sex; Date of Birth - Age; Tribe; Degree of Blood; Marital Status; Relationship to Head of Family; Where Enrolled (Yes/No); (If no – Where); Ward (Yes/No); Allotment, Annuity and Identification Numbers (if given).

<u>1932</u>   (2) <u>BIRTHS</u> April 1,1930 – March 31, 1931

1 93;   Armachain, Stacy; F; 3/6/31-1; N.C. Cherokee; 7/8; S; Daughter; Yes; Yes; Unallotted

2 106;   Armachain, Wayne Lewis; M; 6/28/30-1; N.C. Cherokee; 9/16; S; Son; Yes; Yes; Unallotted

3 117;   Ashe, Margie L.; F; 10/14/30-1; N.C. Cherokee; 1/8; S; Daughter; Yes; Yes; Unallotted

4 321;   Bradley, Constance; F; 2/17/31-1; N.C. Cherokee; 1/2; S; Daughter; Yes; Yes; Unallotted

5 360;   Burgess, Mary C.; F; 1/5/31-1; N.C. Cherokee; 3/16; S; Daughter; Yes; Yes; Unallotted

6 515;   Conley, Selma; F; 4/21/30-1; N.C. Cherokee; 15/16; S; Daughter; Yes; Yes; Unallotted

7 519;   Conseen, Mark; M; 4/23/30-1; N.C. Cherokee; 1/2; S; Son; Yes; Yes; Unallotted

8 520;   Conseen, George; M; 4/23/30-1; N.C. Cherokee; 1/2; S; Son; Yes; Yes; Unallotted

9 626;   Crowe, Ann Lee; F; 3/21/31-1; N.C. Cherokee; 17/32; S; Daughter; Yes; Yes; Unallotted

10 719;   Driver, Waidsutte; F; 6/7/30-1; N.C. Cherokee; 4/4; S; Daughter; Yes; Yes; Unallotted

11 858;   George, Sallie; F; 6/6/30-1; N.C. Cherokee; 31/32; S; Daughter; Yes; Yes; Unallotted

12 ---;   Jackson, Jefferson R.; M; 6/6/30-7/12; N.C. Cherokee; 29/32; S; Son; Yes; (#4 on 1932 census death record); Yes; Unallotted

13 1259;   Lambert, David H.; M; 11/22/30-1; N.C. Cherokee; 29/64; S; Son; Yes; Yes; Unallotted

14 2573;   Lambert, Dorothy; F; 9/19/30-1; N.C. Cherokee; 17/64; S; Daughter; Yes; Yes; Unallotted

15 1459;   Long, Robert E.; M; 4/8/30-2; N.C. Cherokee; 25/32; S; Son; Yes; Yes; Unallotted

16 1584;   Maney, John Wm. Jr.; M; 2/2/31-1; N.C. Cherokee; 3/4; S; Son; Yes; Yes; Unallotted

17 ----;   Maney, Baby Boy; M; 11/24/30-; N.C. Cherokee; 1/2; S; Son; Yes; (#5 on census 1931 death report) Yes; Unallotted

18 1768;   Owl, Harriet N.; F; 7/15/30-1; N.C. Cherokee; 4/4; S; Daughter; Yes; Yes; Unallotted

19 1800;   Owl, Bennie L.; M; 7/18/30-1; N.C. Cherokee; 15/32; S; Son; Yes; Yes; Unallotted

20 1808;   Owl, Bessie E.; F; 10/11/30-1; N.C. Cherokee; 1/4; S; Daughter; Yes; Yes; Unallotted

21 1926;   Peckerwood, Tom Ross; M; 3/19/31-1; N.C. Cherokee; 7/8; S; Son; Yes; Yes; Unallotted

Census of the **Eastern Cherokee** reservation of the **Cherokee, N.C.** jurisdiction, as of **April 1** , 19**32**, taken by **R. L. Spalsbury** , Superintendent.

Key: Census Number; Surname, Given; Sex; Date of Birth - Age; Tribe; Degree of Blood; Marital Status; Relationship to Head of Family; Where Enrolled (Yes/No); (If no – Where); Ward (Yes/No); Allotment, Annuity and Identification Numbers (if given).

22 1947; Powell, Berdina; F; 4/21/30-2; N.C. Cherokee; 7/8; S; Daughter; Yes; Yes; Unallotted

23 1964; Queen, Jessie; F; 7/9/30-1; N.C. Cherokee; 25/32; S; Daughter; Yes; Yes; Unallotted

24 ----; Reed, Wm. H.; M; 6/26/30-1; N.C. Cherokee; 7/16; S; Son; Yes; (#8 on 1932 census death record) Yes; Unallotted

25 2246; Rogers, Charles F.; M; 3/31/31-1; N.C. Cherokee; 1/16; S; Son; Yes; Yes; Unallotted

26 2473; Smith, Zona F.; F; 2/5/31-1; N.C. Cherokee; 3/16; S; Daughter; Yes; Yes; Unallotted

27 2481; Smith, Alyne; F; 12/28/30-1; N.C. Cherokee; 1/4; S; Daughter; Yes; Yes Unallotted

28 2628; Swayney, Edith B.; F; 9/26/30-1; N.C. Cherokee; 1/16; S; Daughter; Yes; Yes; Unallotted

29 2724; Taylor, Lucy F.; F; 8/30/30-1; N.C. Cherokee; 13/32; S; Daughter; Yes; Yes; Unallotted

30 2741; Teesateskie, Josiah E.; M; 8/2/30-1; N.C. Cherokee; 4/4; S; Son; Yes; Yes; Unallotted

31 2776; Thompson, Abe; M; 9/12/30-1; N.C. Cherokee; 4/4; S; Son; Yes; Yes; Unallotted

32 2825; Toineeta, Geneva; F; 9/7/30-1; N.C. Cherokee; 4/4; S; Daughter; Yes; Yes; Unallotted

33 ----; Tolley, Baby Boy; M; 9/10/30-; N.C. Cherokee; 1/4; S; Son; Yes; (#11 on census 1931 death report) Yes; Unallotted

34 2844; Tooni, Annie; F; 4/5/30-1; N.C. Cherokee; 4/4; S; Daughter; Yes; Yes; Unallotted

35 2864; Tramper, Kahlie; F; 4/17/30-1; N.C. Cherokee; 4/4; S; Daughter; Yes; Yes; Unallotted

36 2937; Walker, Pauline; F; 7/3/30-1; N.C. Cherokee; 1/2; S; Daughter; Yes; Yes; Unallotted

37 2998; Wayne, Sara; F; 8/22/30-1; N.C. Cherokee; 4/4; S; Daughter; Yes; Yes; Unallotted

38 3016; Welch, John; M; 4/11/30-1; N.C. Cherokee; 29/32; S; Son; Yes; Yes; Unallotted

39 3177; Wolfe, Lula M.; F; 6/20/30-1; N.C. Cherokee; 4/4; S; Daughter; Yes; Yes; Unallotted

40 3151; Wolfe, James T.; M; 5/14/30-1; N.C. Cherokee; 1/2; S; Son; Yes; Yes; Unallotted

41 3206; Young, Robert; M; 10/8/30-1; N.C. Cherokee; 1/16; S; Son; Yes; Yes; Unallotted

State **North Carolina,** Reservation **Eastern Cherokee,** Agency or jurisdiction,
Cherokee, N.C. Office of Indian Affairs
Live Births Occuring Between the Dates of April 1, 1931 and March 31, 1932 to Parents Enrolled at Jurisdiction

Key: 1932 Census Roll Number; Surname, Given; Date of Birth (Year-Month-Day); Live Births (Yes unless otherwise given); Still Births (blank unless otherwise given); Sex; Tribe (N.C. Cherokee unless given otherwise); Ward (Yes/No); Degree of Blood (Father; Mother; Child); At Jurisdiction Where Enrolled (Yes/No); (If no – Where)

3232;	Arch, William Howard; 1931-Nov.-2; M; N.C. Cherokee; Yes; 5/8; 7/8; 6/8; yes
330;	Brady, Baby Male; 1931-June-26; M; N.C. Cherokee; Yes; 1/2; 1/4; 3/8; yes
459;	Chekelelee, Boyd; 1931-July-16; M; N.C. Cherokee; Yes; F; F; F; yes
516;	Conley, Richard; 1932-Feb.-28; M; N.C. Cherokee; Yes; F; 7/8; 15/16;
--	Conseen, Baby Female; 1931-June-24; F; N.C. Cherokee; Yes; F; 29/32; 61/64; yes
531;	Conseen, Erwin; 1931-Sept.-6; M; N.C. Cherokee; Yes; F; F; F; yes
576;	Craig, Jean Donley; 1931-May-12; F; N.C. Cherokee; Yes; 1/16; 1/4; 3/16; yes
1095;	Jackson, Lula; 1932-March-13; F; N.C. Cherokee; Yes; F; 15/16; 29/32; yes
1102;	Jackson, Mary Edith; 1931-Aug.-12; F; N.C. Cherokee; Yes; 7/16; 5/8; 17/32; yes
243;	Johnson (Blythe), Alta Maine; 1931-Oct.-22; F; N.C. Cherokee; Yes; 5/16; 1/4; 1/2; yes
1182;	Junaluskie, Lillian; 1932-Jan.-25; F; N.C. Cherokee; Yes; Ille.; 15/16; 1/2; yes
1233;	Lambert, Herbert Allen; 1931-June-7; M; N.C. Cherokee; Yes; 1/16; 3/4; 13/32; yes
1331;	Larch, Florence; 1931-May-25; F; N.C. Cherokee; Yes; F; F; F; yes
1357;	Ledford, Billy J.; 1931-June-19; M; N.C. Cherokee; Yes; Ille.; F; 1/2; yes
1356;	Ledford, Nellie; 1932-March-21; F; N.C. Cherokee; Yes; Ille.; F; 1/2; yes
2871;	Lindsey (Mother Twin, Viola), Jackie; 1931-May-27; M; N.C. Cherokee; Yes; -; 3/8; 3/16; yes
--	Littlejohn John[sic], John; 1931-May-5; M; N.C. Cherokee; Yes; N.C. Cherokee; -; F; 1/2; yes
1476;	Lossie, Annie; 1931-Nov.-2; F; N.C. Cherokee; Yes; F; F; F; yes
3233;	McCoy, Edwin; 1931-Oct.-15; M; N.C. Cherokee; Yes; 1/16; 1/4; 3/16; yes
301;	Moles, Racheal Maxine; 1931-June-23; F; N.C. Cherokee; Yes; -; 1/4; 1/8; yes
1791;	Owl, Nettie E.; 1931-May-14; F; N.C. Cherokee; Yes; 1/4; 1/4; 1/4; yes
1193;	Queen (Kalonuheskie), Bascom; 1932-Jan.-18; M; N.C. Cherokee; Yes; 5/8; 4/4; 15/16; yes
2185;	Reed, Alexander; 1931-April-28; M; N.C. Cherokee; Yes; 7/8; 1/2; 11/16; yes
2270;	Ross, Deedanuskie E.; 1932-Feb.-19; M; N.C. Cherokee; Yes; F; F; F; yes

State **North Carolina,** Reservation **Eastern Cherokee,** Agency or jurisdiction, **Cherokee, N.C.** Office of Indian Affairs

Live Births Occuring Between the Dates of April 1, 1931 and March 31, 1932 to Parents Enrolled at Jurisdiction

Key: 1932 Census Roll Number; Surname, Given; Date of Birth (Year-Month-Day); Live Births (Yes unless otherwise given); Still Births (blank unless otherwise given); Sex; Tribe (N.C. Cherokee unless given otherwise); Ward (Yes/No); Degree of Blood (Father; Mother; Child); At Jurisdiction Where Enrolled (Yes/No); (If no – Where)

--	Sanders, Stillborn; 1931-May-24; N.C. Cherokee; F; N.C. Cherokee; Yes; 3/8; 3/8; 3/8; yes
2290;	Saunooke, Lydia; 1931-April-18; F; N.C. Cherokee; Yes; F; F; F; yes
2294;	Saunooke, Robert Gloyne; 1931-Aug.-5; M; N.C. Cherokee; Yes; 1/2; 7/8; 11/16; yes
2297;	Saunooke, Golinda; 1931-Oct.-17; F; N.C. Cherokee; Yes; F; 1/8; 5/8; yes
2339;	Screamer, Jennie Lee; 1932-Mar.-2; F; N.C. Cherokee; Yes; F; 15/16; 31/32; yes
2423;	Smith, Ethel Louise; 1931-Nov.-25; F; N.C. Cherokee; Yes; 1/2; -; 1/4; yes
2511;	Sneed, Gertha; 1932-Mar.-13; F; N.C. Cherokee; Yes; 5/16; 5/16; 5/16; yes
2690;	Taylor, Jarrett; 1931-Oct.-23; M; N.C. Cherokee; Yes; 5/8; 4/4; 13/16; yes
2719;	Taylor, Helen E.; 1931-July-31; F; N.C. Cherokee; Yes; 5/8; 7/8; 3/4; yes
2769;	Thompson, McKinley; 1931-June-25; M; N.C. Cherokee; Yes; F; F; F; yes
2801;	Thompson, Lawrence; 1931-Apr.-2; M; N.C. Cherokee; Yes; 13/16; 3/4; 25/32; yes
2845;	Tooni, Stan; 1932-Jan.-26; M; N.C. Cherokee; Yes; F; F; F; yes
2945;	Walkingstick, Virgil; 1931-Nov.-7; M; N.C. Cherokee; Yes; 4/4; 4/4; 4/4; yes
3113;	Wilnoty, Tidmarsh; 1931-Aug.-11; M; N.C. Cherokee; Yes; 3/4; -; 7/16; yes
3123;	Wilnoty, Paul R.; 1931-Apr.-18; M; N.C. Cherokee; Yes; 4/4; 1/2; 3/4; yes
3169;	Wolfe, Lillian; 1931-Nov.-15; F; N.C. Cherokee; Yes; 4/4; 15/16; 31/32; yes
--	Saunooke, Catherine; 1931-June-16; F; N.C. Cherokee; Yes; Authority letter agt.; 4/4; 4/4; 4/4; yes

Census of the **Eastern Cherokee** reservation of the **Cherokee, N.C.** jurisdiction, as of **April 1** , 19**32**, taken by **R. L. Spalsbury** , Superintendent.

Key: Census Number; Surname, Given; Sex; Date of Birth - Age; Tribe; Degree of Blood; Marital Status; Relationship to Head of Family; Where Enrolled (Yes/No); (If no - Where); Ward (Yes/No); Allotment, Annuity and Identification Numbers (if given).

1932   (2) BIRTHS   April 1,1931 – March 31st, 1932

1 3232;   Arch, Wm. Howard; M; 11/2/31-4/12; N.C. Cherokee; 6/8; S; Son; Yes; Yes; Unallotted

2 330;   Brady, Baby Male; M; 6/26/31-9/12; N.C. Cherokee; 3/8; S; Son; Yes; Yes; Unallotted

3 459;   Chekelelee, Boyd; M; 7/16/31-8/12; N.C. Cherokee; 4/4; S; Son; Yes; Yes; Unallotted

4 516;   Conley, Richard; M; 2/28/32-1/12; N.C. Cherokee; 15/16; S; Son; Yes; Yes; Unallotted

5 ---;   Conseen, Baby Female; F; 6/24/31-; N.C. Cherokee; 61/64; S; Daughter; Yes; (#1, 1932 census death report); Yes; Unallotted

6 531;   Conseen, Erwin; M; 9/6/31-6/12; N.C. Cherokee; 4/4; S; Son; Yes; Yes; Unallotted

7 576;   Craig, Jean Donley; F; 5/12/31-10/12; N.C. Cherokee; 3/16; S; Daughter; Yes; Yes; Unallotted

8 1095;   Jackson, Lula; F; 3/13/32-18 days; N.C. Cherokee; 29/32; S; Daughter; Yes; Yes; Unallotted

9 1102;   Jackson, Mary Edith.; F; 8/12/31-7/12; N.C. Cherokee; 17/32; S; Daughter; Yes; Yes; Unallotted

10 243;   Johnson (Blythe), Alta Maine.; F; 10/22/31-5/12; N.C. Cherokee; 1/2; S; Daughter; Yes; Yes; Unallotted

11 1182;   Junaluskie, Lillian; F; 1/25/32-2/12; N.C. Cherokee; 1/2; S; Daughter; Yes; Yes; Unallotted

12 1233;   Lambert, Herbert A.; M; 6/7/31-9/12; N.C. Cherokee; 13/32; S; Son; Yes; Yes; Unallotted

13 1331;   Larch, Florence; F; 5/25/31-10/12; N.C. Cherokee; 4/4; S; Daughter; Yes; Yes; Unallotted

14 1357;   Ledford, Billy J.; M; 6/19/31-9/12; N.C. Cherokee; 1/2; S; Son; Yes; Yes; Unallotted

15 1356;   Ledford, Nellie; F; 3/21/32-10 days; N.C. Cherokee; 1/2; S; Daughter; Yes; Yes; Unallotted

16 2871;   Lindsay (Mr. Viola Twin), Jackie; M; 5/27/31-10/12; N.C. Cherokee; 3/16; S; Son; Yes; Yes; Unallotted

17 --;   Littlejohn, John; M; 5/5/31-10/12; N.C. Cherokee; 1/2; S; Son; Yes; (#6 on 1932 census death report); Yes; Unallotted

18 1476;   Lossie, Annie; F; 11/2/31-4/12; N.C. Cherokee; 4/4; S; Daughter; Yes; Yes; Unallotted

19 3233;   McCoy, Edwin; M; 10/15/31-5/12; N.C. Cherokee; 3/16; S; Son; Yes; Yes; Unallotted

20 301;   Moles, Racheal M.; F; 6/23/31-9/12; N.C. Cherokee; 1/8; S; Daughter; Yes; Yes; Unallotted

21 1791;   Owl, Nettie E.; F; 5/14/31-10/12; N.C. Cherokee; 1/4; S; Daughter; Yes; Yes; Unallotted

Census of the **Eastern Cherokee** reservation of the **Cherokee, N.C.** jurisdiction, as of **April 1** , 19**32**, taken by **R. L. Spalsbury** , Superintendent.

Key: Census Number; Surname, Given; Sex; Date of Birth - Age; Tribe; Degree of Blood; Marital Status; Relationship to Head of Family; Where Enrolled (Yes/No); (If no – Where); Ward (Yes/No); Allotment, Annuity and Identification Numbers (if given).

22 1193;   Queen (Kalonuheskie), Bascom; M; 1/18/32-2/12; N.C. Cherokee; 15/16; S; Son; Yes; Unallotted

23 2185;   Reed, Alexander; M; 4/28/31-11/12; N.C. Cherokee; 11/16; S; Son; Yes; Yes; Unallotted

24 2270;   Ross, Deedanuskie; M; 2/19/32-1/12; N.C. Cherokee; 4/4; S; Son; Yes; Yes; Unallotted

25 ----;   Sanders, Stillborn; F; 5/24/31-; N.C. Cherokee; 3/8; S; Daughter; Yes; (#10 on 1932 census death report) Yes; Unallotted

26 2290;   Saunooke, Lydia; F; 4/18/31-11/12; N.C. Cherokee; 4/4; S; Daughter; Yes; Yes; Unallotted

27 2294;   Saunooke, Robert G.; M; 8/5/31-7/12; N.C. Cherokee; 11/16; S; Son; Yes; Yes; Unallotted

28 2297;   Saunooke, Golinda; F; 10/17/31-5/12; N.C. Cherokee; 5/8; S; Daughter; Yes; Yes; Unallotted

29 2339;   Screamer, Jennie Lee; F; 3/2/32-29 days; N.C. Cherokee; 31/32; S; Daughter; Yes; Yes; Unallotted

30 2423;   Smith, Ethel L.; F; 11/25/31-4/12; N.C. Cherokee; 1/4; S; Daughter; Yes; Yes; Unallotted

31 2511;   Sneed, Gertha; F; 3/13/32-18 days; N.C. Cherokee; 5/16; S; Daughter; Yes; Yes; Unallotted

32 2690;   Taylor, Jarrett; M; 10/23/31-5/12; N.C. Cherokee; 13/16; S; Son; Yes; Yes; Unallotted

33 2719;   Taylor, Helen E.; F; 7/31/31-8/12; N.C. Cherokee; 3/4; S; Daughter; Yes; Yes; Unallotted

34 2769;   Thompson, McKinley; M; 6/25/31-9/12; N.C. Cherokee; 4/4; S; Son; Yes; Yes; Unallotted

35 2801;   Thompson, Lawrence; M; 4/2/31-11/12; N.C. Cherokee; 25/32; S; Son; Yes; Yes; Unallotted

36 2845;   Tooni, Stan; M; 1/26/32-2/12; N.C. Cherokee; 4/4; S; Son; Yes; Yes; Unallotted

37 2945;   Walkingstick, Virgil; M; 11/7/31-4/12; N.C. Cherokee; 4/4; S; Son; Yes; Yes; Unallotted

38 3113;   Wilnoty, Tidmarsh; M; 8/11/31-7/12; N.C. Cherokee; 7/16; S; Son; Yes; Yes; Unallotted

39 3123;   Wilnoty, Paul R.; M; 4/18/31-11/12; N.C. Cherokee; 3/4; S; Son; Yes; Yes; Unallotted

40 3169;   Wolfe, Lillian; F; 11/15/31-4/12; N.C. Cherokee; 31/32; S; Daughter; Yes; Yes; Unallotted

Census of the Cherokee Tribe

Eastern Cherokee Agency, N.C.

DEATHS -

Unreported on 1931 Census (Deaths)

Apr. 1, 1930 – Mar. 31, 1931 (1930 Deaths)

April 1, 1931 and March 31, 1932 (Deaths Occurring Between)

Apr. 1, 1931 – Mar. 31, 1932 (1931 Deaths)

Census of the **Eastern Cherokee** reservation of the **Cherokee, N.C.** jurisdiction, as of **April 1** , 19**32,** taken by **R. L. Spalsbury** , Superintendent.

Key: Census Number; Surname, Given; Sex; Date of Death; Tribe; Degree of Blood; Marital Status; Relationship to Head of Family; At Jurisdiction Where Enrolled (Yes/No); (If no – Where); Ward (Yes/No); Allotment, Annuity and Identification Numbers (if given).

1930   DEATHS   unreported on 1931 Census

Died
1. 597;   Crowe, Maggie H.E.;   11/4/28; N.C. Cherokee; 1/4; M; Wife; Yes;
                                        Yes; Unallotted
2. 1971;   Queen, Sallie;   7/25/25; N.C. Cherokee; 4/4; M; Wife; Yes;
                                        Yes; Unallotted
3. 2803;   Toineeta, Johnny;   7/1/25; N.C. Cherokee; 4/4; S; Son; Yes; Yes;
                                        Unallotted
4. 2936;   Walkingstick, Owen;   11/20/29; N.C. Cherokee; 4/4; M; Husband;
                                        Yes; Yes; Unallotted

Census of the **Eastern Cherokee** reservation of the **Cherokee, N.C.** jurisdiction, as of **April 1**, 19**32,** taken by **R. L. Spalsbury**, Superintendent.

Key: Number; Surname, Given; Sex; Age at Last Birthday; Tribe; Degree of Blood; Marital Status; Relationship to Head of Family; At Jurisdiction Where Enrolled (Yes/No); (If no – Where); Ward (Yes/No); Allotment, Annuity and Identification Numbers (if given).

<u>1930</u>   (3) <u>DEATHS</u>   Apr. 1, 1930 – Mar. 31, 1931

1 189;   Bird, David A.; M; 37; N.C. Cherokee; 15/16; M; Husband; Yes; Yes; Unallotted

2 782;   French, Jonah; M; 26; N.C. Cherokee; 4/4; S; Son; Yes; Yes; Unallotted

3 1347;   Ledford, Mary M.; F; 6; N.C. Cherokee; 4/4; S; Daughter; Yes; Yes; Unallotted

4 1577;   Maney, Alice; F; 20; N.C. Cherokee; 1/2; S; Daughter; Yes; Yes; Unallotted

5 ----;   Maney, Baby Boy; M; Stillborn; N.C. Cherokee; 1/4; S; Son; Yes; (#17 on 1931 census birth record); Yes; Unallotted

6 1591;   Martin, Emmaline; F; 30; N.C. Cherokee; 4/4; M; Wife; Yes; Yes; Unallotted

7 2304;   Saunooke, Lorena; F; 1; N.C. Cherokee; 4/4; S; Daughter; Yes; Yes; Unallotted

8 ----;   Sequoyah, Frances; F; 4; N.C. Cherokee; 15/16; S; Daughter; Yes; (#5 on reported births as of Apr. 1, 1932); Yes; Unallotted

9 2510;   Sneed, Wilburn; M; 22; N.C. Cherokee; 1/16; S; Son; Yes; Yes; Unallotted

10 2614;   Swayney, Ethel; F; 10; N.C. Cherokee; 1/16; S; Daughter; Yes; Yes; Unallotted

11 ----;   Tolley, Baby Boy; M; Stillborn; N.C. Cherokee; 1/4; S; Son; Yes; (#33 on 1931 census birth record); Yes; Unallotted

<u>1931</u>

12 3154;   Wolfe, Lloyd L.; M; 38; N.C. Cherokee; 4/4; S; Son; Yes; Yes; Unallotted

[Note: Several of the parties on this short list had discrepancies in age, roll number, blood quantum, etc., compared to the Subtractions list April 1, 1932.]

State **North Carolina** Reservation **Eastern Cherokee** Agency or jurisdiction,
Cherokee, N.C. Office of Indian Affairs
Exclusive of Stillbirths
Deaths Ocurring Between the Dates of April 1, 1931 and March 31, 1932 of Indians Enrolled at Jurisdiction

Key: Year and Number Last Census Roll; Surname, Given; Date of Birth (Year-Month-Day); Age at Death; Sex; Tribe (N.C. Cherokee unless stated otherwise); Ward (Yes/No); Degree of Blood; Cause of Death (if given); At Jurisdiction Where Enrolled (Yes/No); (If no – Where)

---- - ---- ; Conseen, Baby Female; 1931-June-24; --; F; N.C. Cherokee; Yes; 61/64; Stillbirth; yes

1931 - 753; Featherhead, Ella J.; 1932-Feb.-24; 72; F; N.C. Carolina; yes; F; Carcinoma of Uterus; yes

1931-1076; Hornbuckle, Wilson; 1931-July-14; 30; M; N.C. Carolina; yes; 1/8; Peritonitis; yes

1931-1088; Jackson, Robert Jef.; 1932-Feb.-4; 1; M; N.C. Carolina; yes; 29/32; T.B. Meningitis; yes

1931-1136; Johnson, Jessie (Gussie); 1932-Jan.-19; 13; F; N.C. Carolina; yes; F; Unknown; yes

---- - ---- ; Littlejohn, John; 1931-May-7; 2 days; M; N.C. Cherokee; Yes; 1/2; Deformed Head; yes

1931-1700; Oocumma, Sam; 1932-Feb.-29; 14; M; N.C. Carolina; yes; 15/16; Burns & Pneumonia; yes

1931-2140; Reed, Billy Hardy; 1931-Dec.-14; 1-1/2; M; N.C. Carolina; yes; 7/16; Pneumonia, etc.; yes

1931-2243; Ross, Adam; 1931-Nov.-9; 49; M; N.C. Carolina; yes; 4/4; Uremic Poisoning; yes

---- - ---- ; Sanders, Baby Female; 1931-May-24; --; F; N.C. Cherokee; Yes; 3/8; Stillbirth; yes

1931-2927; Walkingstick, Rufus; 1931-June-25; 2; M; N.C. Carolina; yes; 4/4; Dysentery; yes

1931-3107; Wolfe, Able; 1931-Oct.-4; 28; M; N.C. Carolina; yes; 4/4; Drowning; yes

Census of the **Eastern Cherokee** reservation of the **Cherokee, N.C.** jurisdiction, as of **April 1** , 19**32,** taken by **R. L. Spalsbury** , Superintendent.

Key: Number; Surname, Given; Sex; Date of Death-Age; Tribe; Degree of Blood; Marital Status; Relationship to Head of Family; At Jurisdiction Where Enrolled (Yes/No); (If no – Where); Ward (Yes/No); Allotment, Annuity and Identification Numbers (if given).

1931   (3) DEATHS   Apr. 1, 1931 – Mar. 31, 1932

1   ---; Conseen, Baby Female; F; 6/24/31-; N.C. Cherokee; 61/64; S; Daughter; Yes; (#5 on 1932 census birth record); Yes; Unallotted

2   753; Featherhead, Ella J.; F; 72; N.C. Cherokee; 4/4; M; Wife; Yes; Yes; Unallotted

3   1076; Hornbuckle, Wilson; M; 7/14/31-30; N.C. Cherokee; 1/8; M; Husband; Yes; Yes; Unallotted

4   1088; Jackson, Robert J.; M; 2/4/32-1; N.C. Cherokee; 29/32; S; Son; Yes; (#12 on 1931census birth record) Yes; Unallotted

5   1136; Johnson, Jessie (Gussie); F; 1/19/32-13; N.C. Cherokee; 4/4; S; Daughter; Yes; Yes; Unallotted

6   ----; Littlejohn, John; M; 5/7/31-2 days; N.C. Cherokee; 1/2; S; Son; Yes; (#17 on 1932 census birth record) Yes; Unallotted

7   1700; Oocumma, Sam; M; 2/29/32-14; N.C. Cherokee; 15/16; S; Son; Yes; Yes; Unallotted

8   2140; Reed, Billy H.; M; 12/14/31-1 1/2; N.C. Cherokee; 7/16; S; Son; Yes; (#24 on 1931census birth record) Yes; Unallotted

9   2243; Ross, Adam; M; 11/9/31-49; N.C. Cherokee; 4/4; M; Husband; Yes; Yes; Unallotted

10   ---- ; Sanders, Baby Female; F; 5/24/31-; N.C. Cherokee; 3/8; S; Daughter; Yes; (#25 on 1932 census birth record) Yes; Unallotted

11 2927; Walkingstick, Rufus; M; 6/25/31-2; N.C. Cherokee; 4/4; S; Son; Yes; Yes; Unallotted

12 3107; Wolfe, Able; M; 10/4/31-28; N.C. Cherokee; 4/4; S; Son; Yes; Yes; Unallotted

[Note: Several of the parties on this short list had discrepancies in, age, roll number, blood quantum, etc., compared to the Subtractions list April 1, 1932.]

ADAMS
  Daisy.................................12,198
  Emma Lee...............................173
  Ethel.................................28,214
  Martha E...........................21,207
  Nora.................................39,225
ADKINS, Mr Mary Sneed.....141,328
ALLEN, Lorena...........................181
ANDERSON
  Bessie................................66,252
  Cora..................................20,206
ARCH
  Cora....................................340
  Horace..................................170
  William Howard.....................364
  Wm Howard....................178,366
ARKANSAS, L Kate...................320
ARMACHAIN
  Jesse...................................173
  Jesse James...........................173
  Lucy Long.............................173
  Stacy...............................173,362
  Stella E.................................173
  Wayne L................................173
  Wayne Lewis..........................362
ASHE, Margie L....................173,362
AUSTIN
  Howard.................................173
  Jack....................................173
  James...................................173
  Lelia...................................173
BAKER
  Crickett.............................98,285
  Dona.................................89,276
  Stella................................50,236
BATES
  Lizzie..............................129,316
  Willard................................181
BAUER, Owenah....................44,230
BECK, Gady E..........................181
BIDDIX
  Boony Louise..........................231
  Margaret...............................231
BIRD
  David...................................181
  David A................................372
BISHOP
  Hattie B...............................173

  Lillie....................................173
BLYTHE
  Alta M..................................173
  Alta Maine.......................364,366
BOWMAN
  Harold..............................16,202
  Jacob T.................................181
  Paul....................................202
  Willie..................................181
BRADLEY
  Constance........................173,362
  Doris...................................181
  Estella.................................181
  Etta L..................................207
  John....................................181
  Lizzie..............................150,336
  Pauline.................................181
  Rache..................................358
  Racheal M.................173,204,366
  Rachel.............................173,357
  Sarah...................................353
  Virginia................................181
  Vivian..................................181
BRADY, Baby Male.......173,364,366
BRASLEY, Arnessa....................271
BREWSTER, Linnie L J..............174
BRYSON
  Clifford.................................181
  Robert..................................181
BURGESS, Mary C..............174,362
BURRELL
  Ernest...................................181
  Hugh...................................181
CHEKELELEE
  Boyd.........................174,364,366
  Ed..............................174,361
CHURCHILL, Ella McCoy.....10,196
CLINE
  Luzene..................................256
  Marcell.................................257
COLE
  Elizabeth............................9,195
  Ella..................................99,285
  Elmira..............................10,196
  Ida..................................45,231
  Lula.................................119,305
  Orney...............................116,303
CONCEEN, Job............................30

CONLEY
Richard...................... 174,364,366
Selma 174,362
CONSEEN
Baby Female 364,366,373,374
Erwin......................... 174,364,366
George............................. 174,362
Mark................................ 174,362
COOPER
Curtis, Jr.................................. 181
Harry 182
Helen...................................... 181
James....................................... 181
Myrtle 61,248
Thomas K............................... 181
Wilma 181
CRAIG
Bettie Ann 174,361
Jean Donley................ 174,364,366
CREASMAN, Golman.................. 52
CREASMEN, Golman 238
CROW, Henrietta.................... 10,196
CROWE
Ann Lee............................ 174,362
Dora 74,259
Maggie H E 182,371
DAVIS
David.................................... 174
George.................................... 174
Henry L 38
Woodrow 38
DOCKERY, Elsie 81,267
DRIVER
Helen................................ 61,247
Waidsutte 174,362
DUNLAP, Wm H.......................... 182
ENLOE
Alberta H................................. 182
Edith....................................... 183
Minta...................................... 170
Mintha.............................. 69,255
EUBANK, Lillie 174
FALLS, Bettie B 174
FEATHERHEAD, Ella J....... 182,373,
.... 374
FORTNER, Sis 174
FOSTER, Elsie..................... 157,344
FRENCH, Jonah 182,372

GARLAND
Addie L................................ 5,191
Elizabeth........................... 20,207
Harriet............................... 81,268
Josephine 80,267
Tamoxzena 74,259
GEORGE
Judas................................. 79,266
Sallie 174,362
GRACE, Mr............................... 140
GREEN, Lena B 174
GRIFFIN, Ima 338
HAMILTON, Leona J 174
HARDEN
Rutha 163,350
Willie Pearl...................... 12,199
HARDIN
Celia 41,228
Inez................................. 123,310
Odin 86,273
Verdia 62,249
HIPPS
Nellie Sue 182
Willard.............................. 60,247
HODGES
Ollie.................................... 175
Ollie J 174
HORNBUCKLE
Alberta................................. 34
Wilson 182,373,374
HOWARD
Cora P............................... 66,253
David 182
Katie 182
Mary 182
HUNTER, Celia 245
JACKSON
Jefferson R............................. 362
Lula.......................... 175,364,366
Mary E................................... 175
Mary Edith....................... 364,366
Robert J 374
Robert Jef 373
JAMES, Mary Holt................. 61,248
JENKINS, Lucile........................ 182
JOHNSON
Alta M 173
Alta Maine....................... 364,366

Guessie..............................373,374
Gussie 182
Jesseie 374
Jessie.................................373
JONES
  Alice A...............................173
  Alice Austin 9,195
JORDAN
  Clyde.................................175
  Della.................................175
  Jake A 175
  John J 175
  John M 175
  Leona 175
  Mark.................................175
  Wm A................................175
  Zora..................................175
JUMPER, Sarah 182
JUNALUSKIE
  Leone 65,251
  Lillian.....................175,364,366
KALONUHESKIE, Bascom..175,364
KEG, Rebecca........................124,311
KEY
  Clarance 182
  Nola May 182
  Wm H.................................182
KING, Tommy........................65,252
KNIGHT
  James.................................184
  Paulina 113,299
LAMBERT
  Alice..................................182
  Cape..................................182
  Cora..................................97,284
  Daniel.................................183
  David.............................175,182
  David H..............................362
  Dorothy 136,177,323,362
  Edith..................................183
  Eugene 182
  Eula..................................183
  Flora..................................98,284
  Florence 16,202
  Frederick..............................183
  Georgia M.........................32,218
  Herbert A 175,366
  Herbert Allen 364

Hester 113,299
Hoover....................................182
Hugh......................................182
Ida...................................85,272
James 183
Julia 62,249
Lillian 87,273
Lora 104,291
Lula...................................26,213
Miles.....................................182
Minta 170
Mintha 42,228
Nancy 169,356
Nannie 56,242
Nannie I................................5
Oney 54,241
Pearl...................................18,204
Sallie Ann 136,323
Stella...................................175
Verdie 56,243
LARCH, Florence...........175,364,366
LEDFORD
  Billy J 175,364,366
  Mary 183
  Mary M..............................372
  Nellie 364
  Nellie M............................175,366
LEE
  Debrader.........................138,325
  Edith 56,243
  Julia 47,233
  Nancy 100,286
  Nora..................................88,275
  Virginia...............................183
LINDSEY
  Jackie................177,338,364,366
  Viola..............................364,366
LITTLEJOHN, John.............364,366,
 373,374
LOCUST
  Bessie 8,194
  Josephine 309
  Martha 8,194
LONG
  Robert E..............................362
  Robt E.................................175
LOSSIE
  Annie 176,364,366

Charlie...176
Leander 358
Sampson.......................................175
LOUDERMILK
Cora.....................................138,325
Daffney Raper.....................146,333
Hollie 137,323
Julia....................................121,308
Rebeca..248
Rebecca..62
LUNSFORD, Callie.................23,209
MANEY
Alice....................................183,372
Baby Boy 362,372
John Wm, Jr 362
John, Jr.......................................176
Olive 183
Ralph..183
Ruth.....................................126,313
MARTIN
Emmaline 183,372
Roxie..183
MASHBURN
Annie L 183
David...183
Ed T 183
Fred H 184
Jesse, Jr 183
Kate.......................................10,196
Mary W 183
Mattie....................................54,241
Milton B 183
Minnie...................................20,206
Ned T 183
Nina.......................................54,241
MATTHEWS
Eva..84,271
Gady......................................11,197
MCCOY
Edwin.......................178,364,366
Eleanor..183
James...183
Jesse 170
Jessie 183
Julia.......................................17,203
Mary.....................................18,204
Mr Evy 96,283
Stella 71,175,257

MCDONALD, Mae.........................72
MCLEMORE, Elsie 229
MCLEYMORE, Elsie....................43
MERONEY
Bessie 32,219
Florence............................103,290
Lula....................................142,329
Margaret 4,190
Mayes 50,236
Sallie Belle 1,189
MILLER
Agnes R 184
Charles....................................184
MOLES
Dorothy Elaine........................204
Racheal M............18,173,204,366
Racheal Maxine......................364
Vera Bradley.............................18
Vera W 18
MORRISON, Bruce 176
MR GRACE 327
MR TWIN 366
MR VIOLA N 242
MULLINS
Maggie A.................................173
Maggie Austin 9,195
MURPHY
Inez....................................49,235
Isabella 23,209
Jane....................................50,236
Lillie B..................................4,190
Margaret 60,247
NICHOLS, Thelma.............123,310
OCCUMMA, Samuel...................170
OOCUMMA
Sam....................................373,374
Samuel......................................184
OWL
Bennie L 176,362
Bessie E 176,362
Ethel 269
Eva..268
Harriet.......................................176
Harriet N...................................362
Nettie E....................176,364,366
PARKER, Harold Lee 184
PARRIS
Laura................................169,356

Lula 98,285
PATTERSON
   Celia 59,245
   Elizabeth 103,289
   Ethel 21,207
   Josie 41,227
   Lura 72,259
PAYNE
   Clara 22,208
   Cora 49,235
   Emma 39,225
   Erma 191
   Grace Lee 10,196
   Lydia 224
   Mary 137,324
   Stella 23,209
   Theodocia 138
   Theodosia 324
PECKERWOOD, Tom Ross..176,362
PITMAN, Ella B 176
PORTER, Iris 88,275
POWELL
   Berdina 176,363
   Emma 272
QUEEN
   Bascom 64,175,251,364,367
   Jessie 176,363
   Sallie 184,371
QUINCE, Jennie 65,251
QUINLAN, Mary C 176
RAPER
   Alice 43,229
   Bertha 37,223
   Cynthia 80,267
   Delia 43,229
   Dessie 10,196
   Dona 5,191
   Dora P 54
   Dovie 59,246
   Edna 50,236
   Effie 89,276
   Elizabeth 114,300
   Ellen 118,304
   Elzie 20,207
   Eva 116,303
   Georgia 48,234
   Hattie 24,210
   Iowa 99,117,286,304

Ivy Ann 27,213
Jessie L 31,217
Julia 120,307
Lucy 25,212
Lula 137,324
Marshall 106,293
Mary 129,316
Pearl 6,192
Viola 65,252
RATTLER, Mr Hettie Smoker 131,
....318
REAGAN, James 184
REED
   Alexander 176,364,367
   Billy H 374
   Billy Hardy 373
   James 176
   Meekerson 184
   Wm Elmer 184
   Wm H 363
ROBERS, Villa 39
ROBINSON
   Birgie 176
   Emmaline 48,234
   Fannie 11,197
   Guita I 37,223
   Martha 26,212
   Mary E 38,224
ROGERS
   Bonnie 66,252
   Catherine 72,258
   Charles F 363
   Chas 176
   Flonnie 87,274
   Inez 81
   Martha C 49,236
   Villa 225
ROSE
   Carrie 59,245
   Glenn 184
   Wm P 184
ROSS
   Adam 170,184,373,374
   Deedamisloe E 364
   Deedanuskie 176,367
ROSY, Mr 80
RUNNINGWOLF
   Ammons 124,311

Sequoia 125,311
SANDERS
    Baby Female 373,374
    Mr Julia 95,282
    Stillborn 364,367
SAUNOOKE
    Anderson 184
    Catherine 365
    Eva 143,329
    Golinda 176,364,367
    Harvey 177
    Larseen 184
    Lorena 184,372
    Lydia 176,364,367
    Robert G 367
    Robert Gloyne 364
    Robt. 176
    Samuel 176
SCREAMER
    Jennie L 177,367
    Jennie Lee 364
SEQUOYAH, Frances 361,372
SHAKE-EAR, Fidella 312
SHONE, Mary 177
SKITTY, Fidella 312
SMITH
    Alyne 177,363
    Bessie 38,225
    Emma 55,241
    Ethel L 177,367
    Ethel Louise 364
    Josephine 117,303
    Lottie 117,303
    Louisa 54,241
    Margaret 122
    Rosanna 103,290
    Zona F 177,363
SMOKED, Ross 318
SMOKER, Ross 132
SNEED
    Florence 119,306
    Georgia 184
    Gertha 177,364,367
    Lula 147,335
    Wilburn 184,372
SQUIRRELL, Mr Liddy 159,346
STANDINGDEER
    Dorothy 177

    Mr Annie 150,336
    William 123,309
STEPP, Luther 184
STILES
    Alma 86,273
    Emma 22,208
SWAYNEY
    Edith 177
    Edith B 363
    Ethel 184,372
    Laura 256
TAHLALA, Homer W 140
TALLENT, Luretta 88,275
TATHAM, Olive 42,228
TAYLOR
    Edith 155,342
    Estie 101,288
    Helen E 177,364,367
    Jarrett 177,364,367
    Lucy 177,363
TEESATESKIE
    Josiah 177
    Josiah E 363
THOMPSON
    Abe 177,363
    Atha 135,322
    Iowa 16,202
    Iris 65,252
    Lawrence 177,364,367
    Luzene 164,351
    McKinley 364,367
    Mckinley 177
    Verdie 138,325
TIMPSON
    Caldonia 15,201
    Harriett 86,273
    Leora 86,273
TOINEETA
    Geneva 177,363
    Johnny 184,371
TOLLEY, Baby Boy 363,372
TOONI
    Annie 177,363
    Stan 177,364,367
TRAMPER, Kahlie 177,363
TWIN
    Mr 177
    Mr Viola 151

Viola 177
VOILES, Josie 98,285
WACHACHA
    Mollie.......................................178
    Raleigh....................................177
WAKEFIELD
    Bettie.................................39,225
    Kate...................................93,279
WALKER, Pauline.................178,363
WALKINGSTICK
    Owen..............................184,371
    Rufus........................184,373,374
    Virgil........................178,365,367
WALLACE, Ollie 178,361
WAYNE, Sara........................178,363
WEBSTER
    Bonnie F...............................9,195
    Marhta.....................................333
    Martha.....................................146
    Mary...................................147,334
WELCH
    Akin 178,361
    John.....................................178,363
WHITAKER, Ada....................23,210
WHITE
    Mr 128,154,341,352
    Ollie May 126
WILNOTY
    Paul R........................178,365,367
    Tidmarsh 178,365,367
WOLF, Sophronia I...............147,334
WOLFE
    Able............................184,373,374
    Amanda..............................54,241
    Delia Ann............................41,227
    Eliza.................................116,303
    James T 178,363
    Lillian........................178,365,367
    Lloyd L 185,372
    Lula M 178,363
YOUNG, Robert 178,363

Other Books and Series by Jeff Bowen

Compilation of History of the Cherokee Indians and Early History of the Cherokees by Emmet Starr with Combined Full Name Index
(Hardbound & Softbound)

1901-1907 Native American Census Seneca, Eastern Shawnee, Miami, Modoc, Ottawa, Peoria, Quapaw, and Wyandotte Indians (Under Seneca School, Indian Territory)

1932 Census of The Standing Rock Sioux Reservation with Births And Deaths 1924-1932

Census of The Blackfeet, Montana, 1897- 1901 Expanded Edition

Eastern Cherokee by Blood, 1906-1910, Volumes I thru XIII

Choctaw of Mississippi Indian Census 1929-1932 with Births and Deaths 1924-1931   Volume I
Choctaw of Mississippi Indian Census 1933, 1934 & 1937, Supplemental Rolls to 1934 & 1935 with Births and Deaths 1932-1938, and Marriages 1936-1938 Volume II

Eastern Cherokee Census Cherokee, North Carolina 1930-1939
Census 1930-1931 with Births And Deaths 1924-1931 Taken By Agent L. W. Page Volume I
Eastern Cherokee Census Cherokee, North Carolina 1930-1939
Census 1932-1933 with Births And Deaths 1930-1932 Taken By Agent R. L. Spalsbury   Volume II
Eastern Cherokee Census Cherokee, North Carolina 1930-1939
Census 1934-1937 with Births and Deaths 1925-1938 and Marriages 1936 & 1938 Taken by Agents R. L. Spalsbury And Harold W. Foght Volume III

Seminole of Florida Indian Census, 1930-1940 with Birth and Death Records, 1930-1938

Texas Cherokees 1820-1839 A Document For Litigation 1921

Starr Roll 1894 (Cherokee Payment Rolls) Districts: Canadian, Cooweescoowee, and Delaware Volume One
Starr Roll 1894 (Cherokee Payment Rolls) Districts: Flint, Going Snake, and Illinois   Volume Two
Starr Roll 1894 (Cherokee Payment Rolls) Districts: Saline, Sequoyah, and Tahlequah; Including Orphan Roll   Volume Three

Cherokee Intruder Cases Dockets of Hearings 1901-1909 Volumes I & II

Indian Wills, 1911-1921 Records of the Bureau of Indian Affairs
Books One thru Seven

Other Books and Series by Jeff Bowen

Native American Wills & Probate Records 1911-1921

Turtle Mountain Reservation Chippewa Indians 1932 Census with Births & Deaths, 1924-1932

Chickasaw By Blood Enrollment Cards 1898-1914 Volume I thru V

Cherokee Descendants East An Index to the Guion Miller Applications Volume I
Cherokee Descendants West An Index to the Guion Miller Applications Volume II (A-M)
Cherokee Descendants West An Index to the Guion Miller Applications Volume III (N-Z)

Applications for Enrollment of Seminole Newborn Freedmen, Act of 1905

Eastern Cherokee Census, Cherokee, North Carolina, 1915-1922, Taken by Agent James E. Henderson   *Volume I (1915-1916)*
    Volume II (1917-1918)
    Volume III (1919-1920)
    Volume IV (1921-1922)

Complete Delaware Roll of 1898

Eastern Cherokee Census, Cherokee, North Carolina, 1923-1929, Taken by Agent James E. Henderson   *Volume I (1923-1924)*
    Volume II (1925-1926)
    Volume III (1927-1929)

Applications for Enrollment of Seminole Newborn Act of 1905 Volumes I & II

North Carolina Eastern Cherokee Indian Census 1898-1899, 1904, 1906, 1909-1912, 1914   Revised and Expanded Edition

1932 Hopi and Navajo Native American Census with Birth & Death Rolls (1925-1931) Volume 1 - Hopi
1932 Hopi and Navajo Native American Census with Birth & Death Rolls (1930-1932) Volume 2 - Navajo

Western Navajo Reservation Navajo, Hopi and Paiute 1933 Census with Birth & Death Rolls 1925-1933

Cherokee Citizenship Commission Dockets 1880-1884 and 1887-1889 Volumes I thru V

Applications for Enrollment of Chickasaw Newborn Act of 1905 Volumes I thru VII

Other Books and Series by Jeff Bowen

Cherokee Intermarried White 1906 Volume I thru X

Applications for Enrollment of Creek Newborn Act of 1905 Volumes I thru XIV

Applications for Enrollment of Choctaw Newborn Act of 1905 Volumes I thru XX

Choctaw By Blood Enrollment Cards 1898-1914 Volumes I thru XX

Oglala Sioux Indians Pine Ridge Reservation 1932 Census Book I
Oglala Sioux Indians Pine Ridge Reservation Birth and Death Rolls 1924-1932 Book II

Census of the Sioux and Cheyenne Indians of Pine Ridge Agency 1896 - 1897 Book I
Census of the Sioux and Cheyenne Indians of Pine Ridge Agency 1898 - 1899 Book II

Northern Cheyenne Tongue River, Montana 1904 - 1932 Census 1904-1916 Volume I

Northern Cheyenne Tongue River, Montana 1904 - 1932 Census 1917-1926 Volume II

Identified Mississippi Choctaw Enrollment Cards 1902-1909 Volumes I, II & III

Sac & Fox - Shawnee Estates 1885-1910 (Under Sac & Fox Agency) Volumes I-VIII
Sac & Fox - Shawnee Estates 1920-1924 (Under The Sac & Fox Agency, Oklahoma) & Wills 1889-1924 Volume IX
Sac & Fox - Shawnee Deaths, Cemetery, Births, & Marriage Cards (Under The Sac & Fox Agency, Oklahoma) 1853-1933 Volume X
Sac & Fox - Shawnee Marriages, Divorces, Estates Log Books Volumes 1 & 2, Log Book Births & Deaths (Under Sac & Fox Agency, Oklahoma)1846-1924 Volume XI
Sac & Fox - Shawnee Guardianships Part 1 (Under Sac & Fox Agency, Oklahoma) 1892-1909 Volume XII
Sac & Fox - Shawnee Guardianships, Part 2 (Under The Sac & Fox Agency, Oklahoma) 1902-1910 Volume XIII
Sac & Fox - Shawnee Guardianships, Part 3 (Under The Sac & Fox Agency, Oklahoma) 1906-1914 Volume XIV

Visit our website at **www.nativestudy.com** to learn more about these
and other books and series by Jeff Bowen

Willie and Maude Welch
Qualla Boundary
Cherokee, North Carolina